FrontPage 2000:
The Complete Reference

About the Authors . . .

Martin S. Matthews is the best-selling author of over 50 books, including *FrontPage 98: The Complete Reference, Windows 98 Answers: Certified Tech Support, Office 97 Answers: Certified Tech Support*, and *Outlook 98 Made Easy*. Martin, who has more than 30 years of computer experience, also does consulting and training on a wide variety of computer topics with a number of firms nationwide.

Erik B. Poulsen is the principal web developer for Arcadia Web Services. Erik has more than 12 years of computer experience and has worked with Marty on a number of book projects, including *FrontPage 98: The Complete Reference*.

FrontPage 2000:
The Complete Reference

Martin S. Matthews
Erik B. Poulsen

Osborne/**McGraw-Hill**

Berkeley   New York   St. Louis   San Francisco
Auckland   Bogotá   Hamburg   London   Madrid
Mexico City   Milan   Montreal   New Delhi   Panama City
Paris   São Paulo   Singapore   Sydney
Tokyo   Toronto

Osborne/**McGraw-Hill**
2600 Tenth Street
Berkeley, California 94710
U.S.A.

For information on translations or book distributors outside the U.S.A., or to arrange bulk purchase discounts for sales promotions, premiums, or fund-raisers, please contact Osborne/**McGraw-Hill** at the above address.

FrontPage 2000: The Complete Reference

1234567890 AGM AGM 90198765432109

ISBN 0-07-211939-X

Publisher
Brandon A. Nordin

Associate Publisher and Editor in Chief
Scott Rogers

Acquisitions Editor
Wendy Rinaldi

Project Editor
Ron Hull

Editorial Assistant
Monika Faltiss

Technical Editor
John Cronan

Copy Editor
Gary Morris

Proofreader
Rhonda Holmes

Indexer
James Minkin

Computer Designer
Ann Sellers
Mickey Galicia
Jani Beckwith

Illustrator
Robert Hansen
Beth Young

Series Design
Peter Hancik

For Daniel G. Gestaut.
Of all my friends,
only a very few have been such
for the better part of my life.
Dan Gestaut is one.
Quite simply, he is always there.

Martin Matthews

For my Father, Werner B. Poulsen,
who taught me how to see and how to think,
and my Mother, Ida B. Poulsen,
who understands me.
For my siblings: Peter, Allen, and Annette;
and Scoey Garlinghouse, friend and son.
For Linda Lou Marshall and Jeff Sherman,
friends who transcend the meaning of the word.

Erik Poulsen

Contents

Part II

Creating Web Sites

Part III
Working Behind the Scenes

Acknowledgments

Gordon Coale "The WebGuy," who wrote Chapters 20 and 22 and added much to Chapter 1, brought a lot of web crafting experience to the book and was fun to work with. Thanks, Gordy!

Wendy Rinaldi, acquisitions editor extraordinaire, works in partnership with her authors, but does so without ever taking over the authorship. She is always there with whatever support, encouragement, and gentle direction is needed. Wendy has put a lot of herself in this book and it is a much better book as a result. Thanks, Wendy!

John Cronan, technical editor, corrected many errors, added many tips and notes, and otherwise significantly improved the book. Thanks, John!

Greg Sherman, database programmer and musician extraordinaire provided much needed advice for Chapter 18. Greg's understanding of the hidden nature of data and how to reveal its secrets constantly expands my horizons. His music accompanied much of the writing of this book, and has enriched my life beyond words. It is art, Greg, and always will be. Thanks, Greg!

Monika Faltiss, editorial assistant, kept us on schedule and kept the book moving through the editorial process, handling all the little things that often get overlooked. And as important, she did this with a friendly and gracious nature that made working with her fun. Thanks, Monika!

George Henny, **Jeff Wallace**, and **Julie O'Brien** of WhidbeyNet, Marty's Internet service provider, have been helpful in trying to set up the FrontPage Server Extensions and in answering his questions. Thanks, George, Jeff, and Julie!

Carole Boggs Matthews, Marty's life partner, sharer of their parenting thrills and spills, and an author in her own right, provided him with the necessary support without which no project like this could ever get done. In addition, Carole had the daunting task of contacting a myriad of software publishers, determining what should be included on the companion CD, and then making that happen. Thanks, Carole!

Introduction

As the interest in the Internet and its World Wide Web has skyrocketed, so has the desire of both organizations and individuals to have a presence there, to put up their own web sites and be a part of the Internet phenomenon. At the same time, organizations are using the same technology to install intranets at a geometric rate, and therefore they have the need to create their own web sites to use internally. The problem has been that the tools to create both Internet and intranet web sites have been very crude and anything but easy to use. FrontPage has changed all of that. FrontPage provides a very easy-to-use, full-featured set of tools for the full-featured creation, delivery, and maintenance of web sites. And FrontPage does this in a WYSIWYG environment where you can see what you are doing as you are doing it.

Unfortunately, FrontPage comes with a slim manual that gives only the briefest of instructions. *FrontPage 2000: The Complete Reference* fills this void by giving you a clear, concise, hands-on guide to this extremely powerful product.

About This Book

FrontPage 2000: The Complete Reference leads you through the planning, creation, testing, deployment, and maintenance of both intranet and Internet web sites with FrontPage. It does this using substantial real-world examples and clear, step-by-step instructions. All of the major features of FrontPage are explained and demonstrated in such a way that you can follow along and see for yourself how each is used, including database connectivity, the addition of multimedia, the creation of an e-commerce site, and the incorporation of Java, ActiveX, JavaScript, and Visual Basic Script. In addition, this book takes you beyond basic FrontPage web site creation and introduces you to HTML, VRML, and XML and how to use them with FrontPage, as well as how to set up an intranet site, how to manage Internet and intranet security, and how to publish and promote your web site. *FrontPage 2000: The Complete Reference* provides the one complete reference on how to make the most of FrontPage. If you are going to purchase FrontPage, or if you already use it, you need this book!

How This Book Is Organized

FrontPage 2000: The Complete Reference is written the way most people learn. It starts by reviewing the basic concepts and then uses a learn-by-doing method to demonstrate the major features of the product. Throughout, the book uses detailed examples and clear explanations to give you the insight needed to make the fullest use of FrontPage.

Part I, "Getting Started," introduces you to web sites and FrontPage; it includes Chapters 1 through 5.

- Chapter 1, "Designing and Creating Quality Web Applications," explores the world of the Internet and intranets and looks at what makes good web pages.
- Chapter 2, "Exploring FrontPage," takes you on a tour of the major FrontPage features, giving you a taste of the power inherent in this product.
- Chapter 3, "Using Wizards and Themes," shows you how to create webs and web pages with these powerful tools.
- Chapter 4, "Using Templates," not only demonstrates the use of templates in creating both webs and web pages, but also how to create templates themselves.
- Chapter 5, "Creating Graphics with Image Composer and PhotoDraw," shows you how to create and edit graphics that can be used in webs.

Part II, "Creating Web Sites," demonstrates each of the major features of FrontPage by leading you through examples of their implementation; it includes Chapters 6 through 12.

- Chapter 6, "Creating and Formatting a Web Page from Scratch," sets aside the wizards and templates and looks at the steps necessary to create a full-featured web on your own.
- Chapter 7, "Adding and Managing Hyperlinks and Hotspots," explores how to add interactivity and interconnectedness to your web.
- Chapter 8, "Using Tables and Frames," describes two completely different methods of segmenting a page and shows how you can make the best use of these tools.

- Chapter 9, "Working with Forms," explains ways to let the web user communicate back to you, the web creator.

- Chapter 10, "Using FrontPage Components," describes how to automate some of the web creation process and extend a web's interactive features.

- Chapter 11, "Advanced Formatting Techniques," covers customizing themes, creating and using style sheets, positioning and wrapping text, adding Dynamic HTML animation effects, and choosing web-safe colors.

- Chapter 12, "Importing and Integrating Office and Other Files," shows you how to use existing (or *legacy*) files in your intranet and Internet webs.

Part III, "Working Behind the Scenes," delves into the inner workings of a web site by exploring the languages behind and ways of activating a web; it includes Chapters 13 through 19.

- Chapter 13, "Working with HTML," provides an extensive introduction to the HTML language and how to use it with FrontPage.

- Chapter 14, "Advanced Markup Languages (DHTML, VRML, and XML)," looks into the expanding frontiers of web applications with the latest additions to the programmer's toolbox.

- Chapter 15, "Web Scripting Languages," describes and shows you how to use JavaScript and Visual Basic Script with your FrontPage webs.

- Chapter 16, "Active Server Pages," explores how to create and use JavaScript and VBScript to control and run tasks on the web server to greatly expand the capability of a web.

- Chapter 17, "Advanced Active Server Pages," takes a deeper look at the functionality Active Server Pages brings to web applications.

- Chapter 18, "Working with Databases," introduces you to interactive databases and shows you how to incorporate them in your own FrontPage webs to dynamically change the webs' contents.

- Chapter 19, "Activating Your Webs," describes how Java and ActiveX can be used to activate web sites and then shows you how to incorporate them in your own webs.

Part IV, "Extending Your Web Site," covers ways of extending and enhancing what you can do with FrontPage; it includes Chapters 20 through 24.

- Chapter 20, "Adding Multimedia to Your Web Site," shows you how to add regular and streaming audio files, both prerecorded and live, to your web site.

- Chapter 21, "Security on the Web," looks at what the Internet and intranet security issues are and explains what you can do to minimize the risks.

- Chapter 22, "Doing E-Commerce," explores the issues behind doing business on the Web and then explains how to build a web store.

■ Chapter 23, "Setting Up an Intranet Web Site," leads you through the steps to create an intranet in your organization and describes a case study of doing it in an intermediate sized firm.

■ Chapter 24, "Publishing and Promoting Webs on the Internet," looks at how to locate an Internet service provider, how to transfer your completed webs to their servers, and then how to promote your webs once they're online.

Part V, "Appendixes," concludes *FrontPage 2000: The Complete Reference*.

■ Appendix A, "Installing FrontPage 2000," provides a detailed set of instructions on how to install the FrontPage related components in the Microsoft Office 2000 Premium Edition or stand-alone FrontPage 2000 packages.

> **Note**   *It is strongly recommended that you choose the Typical installation and that you let the Setup program create the default directories where FrontPage will be installed.*

■ Appendix B, "Creating Web Templates," shows you a thorough example of how to create a web template.

■ Appendix C, "Using the Companion CD," describes the many pieces of software that are included on the CD that is packaged with the book, as well as the files that were used or created in this book.

Conventions Used in This Book

FrontPage 2000: The Complete Reference uses several conventions designed to make the book easier for you to follow. Among these are

■ **Bold type** is used for text that you are to type from the keyboard.

■ *Italic type* is used for a word or phrase that is being defined or otherwise deserves special emphasis.

■ The Courier typeface is used for the HTML code that is either produced by FrontPage or entered by the user.

■ SMALL CAPITAL LETTERS are used for keys on the keyboard such as ENTER and SHIFT.

■ When you are expected to enter a command, you are told to press the key(s). If you are to enter text or numbers, you are told to type them.

The word "Windows" in this book refers to either Windows 95 or Windows 98, whereas Windows NT 4 and Windows 2000 are always called out by name.

The Complete Reference

FrontPage 2000

Part I

Getting Started

Chapter 1

Designing Quality Web Applications

Communication, whether it be within a small group, throughout a large organization, or among many organizations, can almost always be improved—made faster, easier to receive, and easier to respond to. The *web application*, a multimedia form of communication including text, graphics, audio, video, and scripts transmitted by computers, is the latest improvement. While computers sit on the sending and receiving ends of web communication, it is what links the computers that gives web applications one of their most important features. The link means that senders and receivers can operate independently—senders can put the web content up according to their schedule, and receivers can get it anytime thereafter. The link used for the transmission of web content is one of two forms of networking, either the public *Internet*, which uses public and private networks, including phone lines; or a private *intranet*, which uses a *local area network* (LAN), generally within an organization.

The Internet is at the foundation of a global communications revolution that has changed the way people communicate, work, and conduct business. The Internet makes it easier and cheaper to exchange information, ideas, and products around the globe. Accessing a web site in Australia is as easy as accessing one across the street.

In this book you will learn how you can be part of this revolution. You will learn how to use FrontPage to create and maintain a presence on the Web for your business, your organization, or for yourself. This book will take you through all the steps necessary to create your own web application—from initial design to placing your content on a web server where it can be accessed by anyone on the Web.

The Internet

The Internet is a network infrastructure of computers, communications lines, and switches (really other computers) that use a set of computer hardware and software standards, or *protocols*, that allow computers to exchange data with other computers. The computers can be in the same room, or they can be located around the world from each other. They can use the same operating system software, such as Windows 98, or each can use a different computer operating system, such as Macintosh System 8.0 or UNIX. The standards that make up the Internet have become a modern *lingua franca*—a language enabling any computer connected to the Internet to exchange information with any other computer also connected to the Internet, regardless of the operating systems the computers use.

The birth of the Internet can be traced back to the late 1960s when the use of computers by Advanced Research Projects Agency (ARPA) and other government agencies had expanded so much that a way for the computer systems to share data was needed. ARPANET, the predecessor to what we now know as the Internet, was created to meet this need.

Another milestone in the history of the Internet came in the mid-1980s, when the National Science Foundation (NSF) added its five supercomputing centers (NSFNET) to the Internet. This gave educational centers, the military, and other NSF grantees access to the power of these supercomputers and, more importantly, created the backbone of today's information superhighway. This backbone is made up of all the high-capacity (or wide-bandwidth) phone lines and data links needed to effectively transfer all the information now on the Internet. Until this wide-bandwidth infrastructure existed, the potential of ARPANET, NSFNET, and now the Internet couldn't be realized. By the end of the 1980s almost all the pieces were in place for a global telecommunications revolution.

The World Wide Web

By 1990 the Internet had grown to be a highway linking computers across the United States and around the world, but it was still a character-based system. That is, what appeared on computer screens connected to the Internet was simply text. There were no graphics or hyperlinks. A *graphical user interface* (GUI) to the Internet needed to be developed. Tim Berners-Lee, a scientist working at the European Laboratory for Particle Physics (CERN) in Geneva, Switzerland, proposed a set of protocols for the transfer of graphical information over the Internet in 1989. Berners-Lee's proposals were adopted by other groups, and the World Wide Web was born.

The Internet is a *wide area network* (WAN), as compared with a local area network (LAN) among computers in proximity. For computers to share information over a WAN, there must be a physical connection (the communications infrastructure created by ARPA and the NSF and now maintained by private industry) and a common software standard that the computers use to transfer data. The physical connection depends on whether you use a modem to dial up to the Internet, or whether your computer is part of a LAN with an Internet connection. The physical layer includes the modem or network interface card in your computer. You also need a phone or dedicated network line that connects you to the Internet backbone. In either case, your computer, connected to the Internet either with a dialup or network connection, is capable of sharing information with any other computer connected to the Internet anywhere in the world.

Note *The term "modem" as used here includes DSL and ISDN "adapters." Such devices provide the means to dial up an Internet connection over ordinary phone lines.*

LANs and an Intranet

As important as the Internet has become to society, local area networks have become even more important to the exchange of information and communication within organizations. LANs started out as a way to share programs and data files among several people in an organization. This was then augmented by electronic mail (e-mail) for sending and receiving messages over the LAN. Recently, intranets have been added to LANs to provide a miniature version of the World Wide Web within an organization—a place for people to post and read text and graphics documents whenever they choose.

A good example of how an intranet can be put to use is a project report. Instead of e-mailing a weekly update to a long list of potentially uninterested people (and filling up everybody's inbox in the process), you could post a web page on the intranet that would give not only the current status, but also other, more static information, such as the people working on the project, its goals, and its funding. In this way, those people who are truly interested can get the information.

With Active Server Pages (included with Microsoft's Internet Information Services) and Microsoft Office, even more intranet interactivity is possible. Users can send commands to the web application and then receive customized responses. Any Microsoft Office document can be included in a web page. Databases can be queried, and custom web pages can automatically be generated to display query results. Integrating Office and other files with your FrontPage web sites is covered in Chapter 12, Active Server Pages is covered in Chapter 16, and working with databases is covered in Chapter 18.

Note   *Internet Information Services (IIS) is included with Microsoft's Windows NT Server. IIS and FrontPage provide all the software tools you need to set up a full-scale intranet or World Wide Web site. FrontPage along with the Microsoft Personal Web Server can host limited web sites by themselves.*

Except for possibly the content, there is no difference between a web site on the World Wide Web and a web site on an intranet. They are created the same way and can have the same features and components. The discussion and instructions throughout this book are aimed equally at the World Wide Web and an intranet, and there are examples of each. So in learning to create a web application, you can apply that knowledge to either form of dissemination.

Tip   *Think of the Internet and a LAN as equivalent means of information transmission, one public and the other private. And think of the World Wide Web and an intranet as equivalent means of posting and reading information being transmitted over the Internet or a LAN, respectively. The World Wide Web and an intranet are just advanced electronic bulletin boards, and a web page is an electronic document posted on that bulletin board.*

Note   *In a unique blending of two concepts, intranets can be extended to outside users, creating an extranet. For example, a corporation may provide other businesses, such as vendors or customers, access to a select subset of corporate data and a way to exchange the information.*

Internet Protocols

The Internet and the Web are built upon several protocols:

- **Transmission Control Protocol/Internet Protocol (TCP/IP)** controls how information is packaged to be transferred between computers connected through the Internet.

- **Hypertext Transfer Protocol (HTTP)** is the language the computers use to exchange information on the Web.

- **Hypertext Markup Language (HTML)** is the programming language used to create the documents that are distributed on the Web and displayed on your monitor.

TCP/IP

To transfer information over the Internet or within a LAN, several requirements must be met. These include a way to assign each computer or site on the network a unique address (just like having a unique postal address) and "packaging" the information for transmission. These functions are handled by the Transmission Control Protocol and the Internet Protocol.

Internet Protocol

The foundation of the system is the Internet Protocol (IP). The IP converts data into packets and provides an address for each site on the Internet. *Packets* are like the pages of a book. An entire book contains too much information to be printed on one page, so it is divided into multiple pages. This makes the information in the book much more manageable. The Internet Protocol does the same thing with the information in a file that is to be transmitted over the Internet or a LAN. It divides the information into packets that can be handled more easily by the network.

The other primary function of the IP is to provide addresses for the computers connected to the Internet. Each computer needs its own *IP address,* a group of four decimal numbers that provides a unique address for the computer. Examples of IP addresses are 198.68.191.10 and 204.250.144.70. These IP addresses are actually decimal representations of single 32-bit binary numbers. While a computer may be comfortable with 11000110 01000100 10111111 00001010 or 11001100 11111010 10010000 01000110 as an address, most people find decimal numbers easier to work with. This system of numbering allows for about 4.3 billion (2^{32}) possible combinations. If you are setting up a web server, you will need to get an IP address. You may also need a domain name. A *domain name* is a unique name that identifies a computer or network, much like the name of a city in a postal address, and is matched to a unique IP address. Examples of domain names are "microsoft.com" and "netscape.com." The .COM extension identifies the domain as commercial. Other domain extensions include .ORG for nonprofit organizations and .GOV for government agencies. These are assigned by the Internet Network Information Center (InterNIC, **http://www.internic.net**). Your

Internet service provider (ISP) can help you get an IP address and domain name. You can also have your web site located as part of an existing domain. If you will be using an existing web server, the network administrator or webmaster will be able to tell you what the IP addresses are.

Transmission Control Protocol

While the Internet Protocol provides the basics for sharing information over the Internet, it leaves some things to be desired. The two most important are ensuring that all the packets reach their destination and that they arrive in the proper order. This is where the Transmission Control Protocol (TCP) steps in. To understand how it works, assume you want to send a book to someone and you have to mail it one page (or packet) at a time. Also assume that there are no page numbers in the book.

How will recipients know that they have received all the pages, and how will they know the proper order of the pages? TCP solves these problems by creating an "envelope" for each packet generated by the IP. Each envelope has a serialized number that identifies the packet inside it. As each packet is sent, the TCP assigns it a number that increases by 1 for each packet sent. When the packets are received, the numbers are checked for continuity and sequence. If any numbers are missing, the receiving computer requests that the missing packet be re-sent. If the packets are out of sequence, the receiving computer puts them back in order. TCP also makes sure the information arrives in the same condition it was sent (that the data was not corrupted in transit).

TCP/IP provides the basic tools for transferring information over the Internet. The next layer up the ladder is the Hypertext Transfer Protocol, the traffic director for the Web.

 To set up an intranet on a LAN, you must add the TCP/IP protocols to the existing networking protocols—possibly either IPX/SPX (Integrated Packet Exchange/ Sequenced Packet Exchange) or NetBEUI (NetBIOS Extended User Interface)— on both the server and all clients. Chapter 23 tells you how to do this.

Hypertext Transfer Protocol

The Hypertext Transfer Protocol (HTTP) is the heart of the World Wide Web and is also used with an intranet. HTTP composes the messages and handles the information that is sent between computers on the Internet using TCP/IP. To understand how HTTP works, you first need to understand the nature of client/server relationships.

Client/Server Relationships

The basic function of the Internet or a LAN is to provide a means for transferring information between computers. To do this, one computer (the *server*) will contain information and another (the *client*) will request it. The server will process a client's request and transfer the information. The server may be required to process the request before it can be filled. For example, if the request is for information contained in a database, such as a request submitted to the AltaVista web search engine, the server would first have to extract the information from the database before it could be sent to the client.

The passing of information between a client and a server has four basic steps:

1. A connection is made between the client and the server. This is handled by TCP/IP.
2. The client sends a request to the server in the form of an HTTP message.
3. The server processes the request and responds to the client, again in the form of an HTTP message.
4. The connection between the client and the server is terminated.

TCP/IP creates the connection between the client and the server, and HTTP composes the request for information. The response from the server is composed as an HTTP response. This is how HTTP is used to transfer information over a TCP/IP connection.

To access information on the Web or an intranet, you need an application that can send requests to a server and that can process and display the server's response. This is the function of web browsers. The two most common web browsers are Microsoft's Internet Explorer and Netscape's Navigator/Communicator.

Note *With the release of versions 4.0, both Microsoft's browser, Internet Explorer, and Netscape's browser, Navigator, have grown into integrated suites of applications. Microsoft has kept the name Internet Explorer for their browser suite while Netscape renamed theirs Communicator. Netscape Navigator is available both as a stand-alone browser and as part of Communicator. The term Netscape Navigator is used to refer both to the stand-alone Navigator and the browser component of Communicator.*

Hypertext Markup Language

The parts of the Web or an intranet covered so far, TCP/IP and HTTP, control how information is transferred over the network. Hypertext Markup Language (HTML) is the component that controls how the information is displayed. The information sent from a web server is an HTML document. Here's what a simple HTML document looks like:

```
<HTML>
<HEAD>
<TITLE>A Simple HTML Document</TITLE>
</HEAD>
<BODY>
<H1>A Simple HTML Document</H1>
<P><B>This text is bold</B> and <I>this text is italic</I>.</P>
</BODY>
</HTML>
```

Figure 1-1 shows how a web browser displays this HTML document. Web browsers interpret the HTML document and display the results on your monitor. HTML files are simple ASCII text files that contain formatting tags that control how information (text and graphics) is displayed and how other file types are executed (audio and video files, for example).

HTML tags are usually used in pairs. An HTML document must begin with the <HTML> opening tag and end with the </HTML> closing tag. The <HEAD></HEAD> tags enclose information about the web page, such as the title, which is defined by the <TITLE></TITLE> tags and displayed in the title bar of the web browser. The body of the web page is enclosed by the <BODY></BODY> tags. The <H1></H1> tags define the enclosed text as a level-1 heading. The <B></B> and <I></I> tags, respectively, define text as bold or italic, as you saw in the listing above. Each paragraph is usually enclosed in the <P></P> tags.

Note *HTML tags are not case sensitive. They can be upper- or lowercase, or mixed case, such as <Body>.*

In the early days of the Web, these tags were typed in by use of a simple text editor to create web pages. This was time-consuming and not much fun. Today you can use

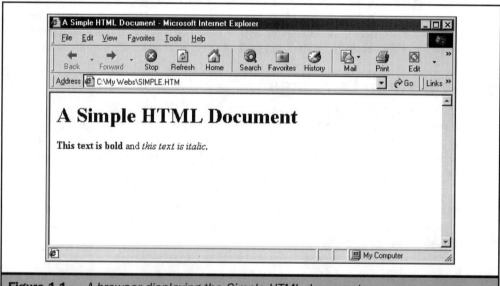

Figure 1-1.   *A browser displaying the Simple HTML document*

FrontPage, a true WYSIWYG (what you see is what you get) HTML editor, to create your web pages. Gone are the days when you had to learn all the HTML tags and proper syntax. With FrontPage you design a page, and the proper HTML is created automatically. It's never been easier to create your own web site.

What Is a Web Page?

A web application consists of one or more web pages that are interconnected. Since the focus of this book is how to create web applications that are collections of web pages, here's a more detailed definition of what a web page is. A good starting place is that a *web page* is a text file containing Hypertext Markup Language (HTML) formatting tags, and links to graphics files and other web pages. The text file is stored on a *web server* and can be accessed by other computers connected to the server, via the Internet or a LAN. The file can be accessed by the use of *web browsers*—programs that download the file to your computer, interpret the HTML tags and links, and display the results on your monitor. Another definition is that a web page is an interactive form of communication that uses a computer network.

There are two properties of web pages that make them unique: they are interactive and they can use multimedia. The term *multimedia* is used to describe text, audio, animation, and video files that are combined to present information—for example, in an interactive encyclopedia or a game. When those same types of files are distributed over the Internet or a LAN, you can use the term *hypermedia* to describe them. With the World Wide Web it is now possible to have true multimedia over the Internet. However, unless your clients have a high-speed service, such as the Integrated Services Digital Network's (ISDN) 128-Kbps service or Digital Subscriber Line (DSL) from 56 Kbps to over 1 Mbps, downloading the large hypermedia files can take too long to routinely use them. On most LANs, which are considerably faster, this is much more feasible, but there are still limitations and a potential need to keep the LAN open for high-volume data traffic.

Web pages are interactive to allow the reader or user to send information or commands back to the web site that hosts the application web. For example, Figure 1-2 shows the home page of the AltaVista web search engine. The AltaVista home page gives you access to an application that searches the AltaVista database of web sites. You can use this and other search engines to locate sites on the Web. From this web page you can select which part of the Internet to search, how the results of the search will be displayed, and the keywords that the search will be based on. When you click on the Search button, the information you've entered is sent to the AltaVista web server. The database is then searched, and the results are used to create a new web

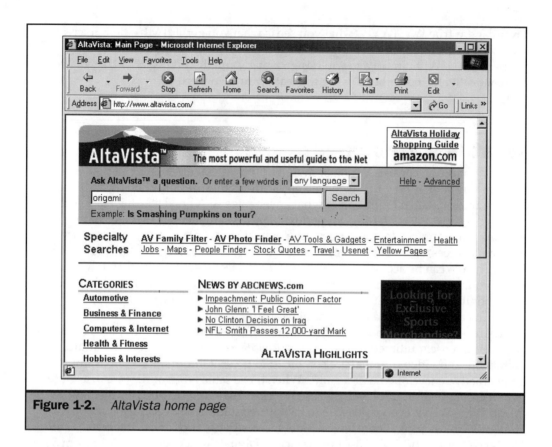

Figure 1-2.   *AltaVista home page*

page, which is displayed by your web browser. Figure 1-3 shows the results of a search using the keyword "origami."

Each web page has an address called the *uniform resource locator* (URL). The URL for the AltaVista home page is **http://www.altavista.com**. The URL is displayed in the Address combo box (a combination of a text box and a drop-down list) at the top of the screen (below the toolbar). A URL is the path on the Internet to a specific web page. It is used in the same way you use a path name to locate files on your computer. In this case, the URL tells you that the web page is located on a web server with the domain name *altavista.com* connected to the World Wide Web ("www"). A *domain* is one or more networked computers; the domain name provides a single address to access the network from the Internet. The network's domain server routes the request to the correct place within the network. The actual filename of the *home page* (the top-level page of the web, which usually serves as a table of contents for the web) is usually either Default.htm or Index.htm; it is implied by being unstated. The default web page filename is set on the web server. This is the page that will be displayed if no web page

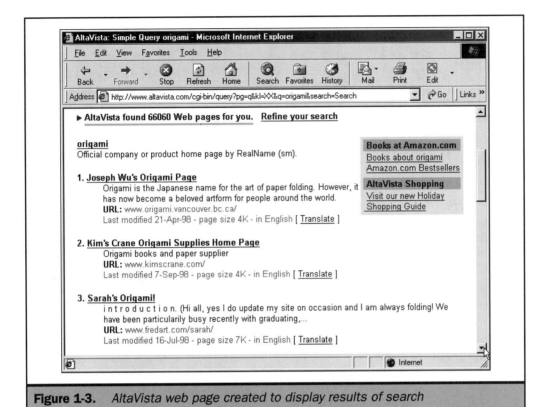

Figure 1-3.   *AltaVista web page created to display results of search*

filename is specified. On a LAN the URL is similar; it uses the server name in a format like http://*servername*/*folder*/*homepage filename*. The server name is the functional equivalent of the domain name in this case. The home page filename can also be left off if it is the default filename.

Note   *Web pages located on web servers using the UNIX operating system generally have an .HTML extension, while web pages located on Windows NT web servers generally have an .HTM extension. Active Server web pages have an .ASP extension. Also, not all URLs include the "www." This is determined by how the URL is programmed into the network routers. Routers perform the task of matching IP (Internet protocol) addresses to domain names. It's a good idea to have your Internet service provider (ISP) program your domain name both with and without the "www" in their routers. IP addresses and domain names are covered in the "TCP/IP" section later in this chapter.*

AltaVista found about 66,060 web pages containing the keyword "origami." The web page created by the AltaVista server displays the title of each web page, an excerpt from the text on the page, and the URL for the page. The title of the page is displayed in a different color than the other text and is underlined. This indicates it is a *hyperlink*. Clicking on a hyperlink will cause your browser to load the location (web page) specified in the hyperlink. The hyperlink may take you to an actual location, or *bookmark,* within the same document, the way a bookmark works in a word processor file, or it may link you to a web site anywhere in the world. In fact, if a web page doesn't have an obvious identifier to its location, you may not even be aware of what country the web server you are connected to is in. You may start "surfing" the Web by clicking on hyperlinks on various pages to follow a train of thought and end up "traveling" around the world.

Tip   *With the Microsoft Internet Explorer (3.0 or later) and Netscape Navigator (3.0 or later) browsers, it is not necessary to enter **http://** in the Address box. With Microsoft's Internet Explorer 3.0 or later you can also access the Yahoo search engine by typing **go** followed by the keywords in the Address box—for example, **go origami** (without the "http://" prefix). You can also type **go origami** in Netscape Navigator 4.0 or later and you will access the Excite search engine and see sites that relate to the word "origami."*

Note   *Hyperlinks do not have to be underlined, although they should be displayed in a different color than the body text. With Netscape Navigator (and Communicator) 4.03 and later, you can use the Preferences option in the Edit menu; with Microsoft Internet Explorer, you can use the Internet Options option in the View menu (IE 4.0) or Tools menu (IE 5.0) to control whether hyperlinks will be underlined, and you can also set the color they will be displayed in.*

When you submit keywords or other information to a web site, such as AltaVista, you are actually running an application on the web server. Web servers can also download applications—for example, a Java applet or an ActiveX control—to your computer. *Java* is a programming language that extends the flexibility and functions of the Web. *Applets* are small programs that are downloaded to your computer and then executed. *ActiveX controls* are similar in use and function to Java applets, but are written in programming languages such as Visual Basic. Java applets and ActiveX controls are used to add games, chat, menus, and other interactive components to web pages. You do not have to know how to program in Java or Visual Basic to use a Java applet or ActiveX control—a growing library of applets and controls is already available on the Web. A good place to start looking for Java applets is the Java home page, **http://www.java.sun.com**, or the Gamelan home page, **http://www.gamelan.com**. For ActiveX controls, Microsoft's web site, **http://www.microsoft.com**, is the place to start. Java and ActiveX are described in Chapter 19; Visual Basic Scripting Edition (VBScript) and JavaScript are described in Chapter 15.

> **Tip** *You can turn support for Java applets on or off in Internet Explorer by opening the Internet Options dialog box from the View menu (IE 4.0) or Tools menu (IE 5.0), selecting the Advanced tab, and clicking the Java JIT Compiler Enabled check box. In Netscape Navigator 4.5 you can turn support for Java applets and JavaScript on or off by opening the Network Preferences dialog box from the Options menu, selecting the Languages tab, and then clicking on the Enable Java and Enable JavaScript check boxes. In Netscape Communicator and Navigator 4.0 or later, Java and JavaScript support are turned on or off by opening the Preferences dialog box from the Edit menu, selecting Advanced in the Category list box, and then clicking on the Enable Java and Enable JavaScript check boxes.*

As you can see, the World Wide Web is a flexible and powerful means of communication. Next look at how you can design and create a web application to use this powerful medium.

Designing Quality Web Applications

To many, web application design is limited to what is often called the look and feel of the web pages—things like where do you put the navigation bar or buttons, or what kind of graphics do you use and how are they arranged on the web page. Good web design, though, also means having a clear understanding of the goals of the web application and good organization of the information in the web application.

A lot of decisions about the design of the page are based on general design practices seen in the print media. The Web is its own medium with its own peculiarities. How it is different is partially based on the nature of the Internet and the World Wide Web. The differences are also caused by the medium with which you view the Web: the computer and its monitor. Understanding these differences is important because some things that work in print just do not translate well to the web. But the Web can also do things that print cannot do. On the Web, you can read about and see a performer, hear the performer live, and then interact with that performer in real time. Try that in a magazine!

Designing for a web application is also a process. You just don't decide that you are going to design a web application and start laying out a web page and expect to end up with a useable product without a lot of going back and filling in the details. Good design, in addition to knowing your media and tools, has four major components:

- Gathering requirements
- Organizing information
- Structuring the web application
- Developing a navigation scheme

This chapter will give you a process that takes you from the initial idea of doing a web application to a completed web application that you, your customer, and most important, the end user of the web application, can all be happy with.

So where do you start? Begin at the beginning. Why are you doing a web application?

Gathering Requirements

Start out by asking yourself these questions:

- What is the purpose of this web application?
- What is it supposed to do?
- What are the goals of the web application?
- Is it to amuse, amaze, educate, or sell a product?
- Is it to show off your web development skills, record a family event, or cybercast a live event?

It could be one or several of these, but the basic reason is to communicate, and you need to be clear on what it is you are communicating.

Most often you are doing the web application for up to three groups of people. The first, although often considered last, is the end user. This is the person who will use the web application and is your audience. You are also doing it for the person or group that wants the web application built—your customer, someone you, the web designer, are working for. And last, and usually least, you are doing it for yourself, to create something that will be a good example of what you can do. What do all three of these groups want? What do all three need? The answers to these questions will provide the requirements for the web application. The answers can also produce three different sets of requirements, and they often can be conflicting.

The web developer needs to integrate these requirements and satisfy as many of them as possible. The web developer then needs to communicate well with the customer so that both have the same understanding of what the web application is supposed to do and where it is going. Everything that comes after this needs to be bounced back against these requirements. If it supports the requirements, it is the right thing to do. If it doesn't, it shouldn't be done unless you want to go back and revise the requirements.

The requirements stage will determine what the content and functionality will be. With this understanding of why you are doing the web application, you can start gathering and organizing the contents.

Organizing Information

Once you have defined the requirements, you then have the job of collecting and organizing the contents. This means locating a big pile of stuff and sorting it out into logical buckets of information. This stage, and the previous one of figuring out why you are doing the web application, are not glamorous and often are not as fun as making impressive graphics, but your customer and audience will certainly appreciate it when they try to use your web application. It is here that you set the stage for the structure of your web application. Every web application presents a different problem, but there are some general approaches. Keep the end user in mind when organizing information. Does it make sense? Will it enable the user to develop a mental map of the web application? And most important, can the user easily find and use what they want?

The following are some common ways of organizing information. They are meant to get you thinking about different ways of organizing your material and are not the only ways to do so. One of the following may not work for your project. If it doesn't, see if you can come up with another scheme. Again, keep the end user in mind.

There are two general classes of schemes. The first are those that rely on an obvious order such as the alphabetical order of the phone book's white pages where it is clear what the order is and how to search. The second class are those schemes that are arranged in an order that is not so obvious—such as the phone book's yellow pages, which uses topics that may or may not be well understood.

Obvious Order

Schemes with an obvious order are the easy ones to use. Once you decide to use one of them, organizing the material becomes a no-brainer. But they have their limitations, since they require the user to know what they are looking for. Three obvious orders are the alphabetical, the chronological, and the geographical.

ALPHABETICAL   The white pages of the phone book are a good example of alphabetical organization. The names are arranged in the order of letters of the alphabet. It is easy to find a person if you know the name of the person.

The drawback is that a person can be difficult to find if you don't know how to spell the name, or if you are not sure of the name, or if all you know about the person is that he or she is a web developer. Alphabetical organization can be used for organizing any list of things from departments of a company to a list of recipes.

CHRONOLOGICAL   Events, or anything that is associated with a date, lend themselves to a chronological organization. A list of concert dates is often arranged chronologically. Press releases are dated and can be organized by that date. Chronological organization is useful, as long there is a clear date or time or years attached to what you are organizing. Figure 1-4 shows how a list of performances is arranged in chronological order.

You also need to ask if your user would want to look for it by date. A list like this puts the priority on when rather than whom. People may find the date more important when they are looking for a specific performance, but some may prefer to search by whom rather than by when. Then an alphabetical listing would be more appropriate.

GEOGRAPHICAL   Some things are tied to a geographic location. A business may want to organize the information on its different sites by their location. Weather is also

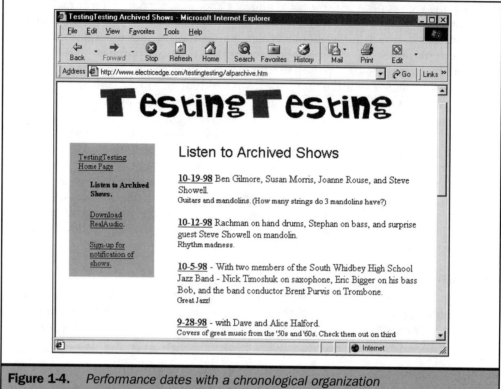

Figure 1-4. *Performance dates with a chronological organization*

tied to geographic locations. When you look at a weather report, you want to check a specific location. It could be at different geographical scales, such as a city like Duluth or a continent like Asia, but it is still a geographical place. Figure 1-5 shows how a coffee company presents information on its stores by geographic location.

Not-So-Obvious Order

These schemes are more difficult to set up and more open to interpretation, but people often don't know exactly what they are looking for when they begin searching. Because of that these schemes are often very useful. Four less obvious orders are topical, task, priority, and metaphor.

TOPICAL   Music stores arrange their music by topics such as *Folk*, *Rock*, *Jazz*, *Alternative*, etc. You may be looking for a specific artist and know that they play jazz, so you look in the jazz section. Or you may just be looking for a jazz album without a clear preference for an artist. A topical arrangement could look like this:

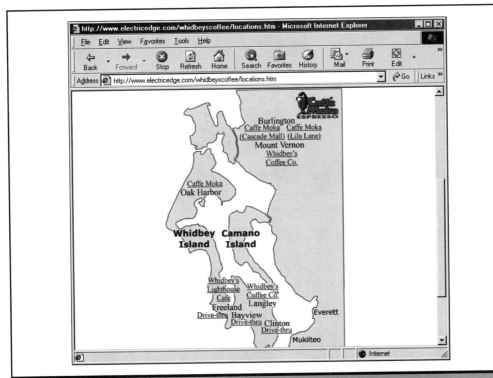

Figure 1-5.   *Company information with a geographical organization*

But are the topics clear? Is there a definite understanding of what constitutes a Folk group or a Rock group? What is the difference between Rock, Folk and Folk-Rock? And just what is Adult Contemporary Rock? There isn't always a clear definition, but it is still useful to categorize them this way even though you may run into a lot of gray areas. It is important to organize the topics in a sensible way that makes things easy to find. Try to keep the gray areas to a minimum. Keep it simple!

TASK   Task schemes are organized around things that you do. The web browser is set up that way with selections for *File*, *Edit*, and *View*. Task-oriented schemes are useful if the web application is dealing with processes, tasks, or actions that you want the user to do. Here is a task organization with the tasks *Listen*, *Download*, and *Sign-up*.

PRIORITY   Sometimes things need to be arranged around their importance or priority. If you are organizing the departments of a corporation alphabetically, you would put *Accounting* in front of the *Office of the President*. But if you are organizing by importance, or priority, the *Office of the President* will be first. Figure 1-6 shows information ordered by priority.

This type of organizing scheme can be full of political implications from within an organization. And everyone outside the organization would have his or her own perception of what may be more important.

METAPHOR   *Metaphor* is the use of one object's meaning transferred to another to make a new idea easier to understand. One of the great metaphors on the computer desktop is Apple's use of the trashcan as a metaphor for deleting files. Figure 1-7 shows a site organized around metaphors.

Metaphorical organization must be used carefully because not all metaphors have the clear connection of the Macintosh trashcan. The associations people make may be unexpected, or there may be no association at all. For example, what is the *Lounge* in Figure 1-7. It also may not be clear what the *Mailroom* and the *Reception* areas are.

Mixing Organizational Schemes

One of the greatest causes of confusion to the user is the mixing of organizing schemes. The organizing scheme is what helps the user create a mental map of the web

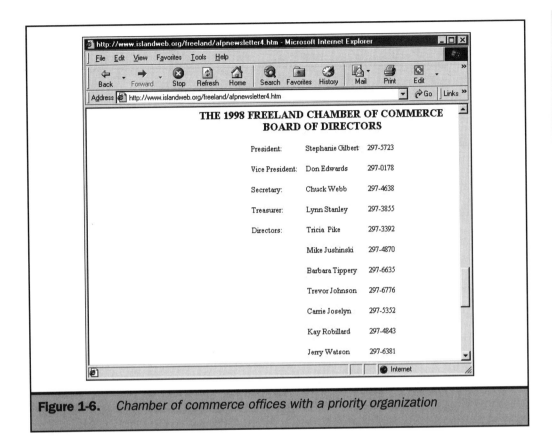

Figure 1-6.   *Chamber of commerce offices with a priority organization*

application. When you mix schemes, it becomes very difficult to develop a mental map of the web application, and this causes confusion. It is the old apples-and-oranges comparison. While apples and oranges share the status of fruit, they are also dissimilar enough to be called different. So it is with organizing schemes. The mind tries to make patterns out of what it sees, and when things the mind expects to be the same are actually far apart, there is a mental grinding of gears trying to reconcile them.

This is not the last word on organizing schemes. Above all, put yourself in the mind of the user. How will the user look at and use the information? It requires looking at organizing material with fresh eyes. That is always hard to do with something you are very close to. Better yet, get a user to look at what you have done and see if it makes sense to someone who is not familiar with the material but wants to use it. If that user doesn't understand your organizing scheme, don't assume it's his or her fault.

With the material organized, you can begin laying out the structure of the web application.

Structuring the Web Application

How you have organized your material is going to determine how you structure your web application. Three major ways to structure a web application are hierarchical,

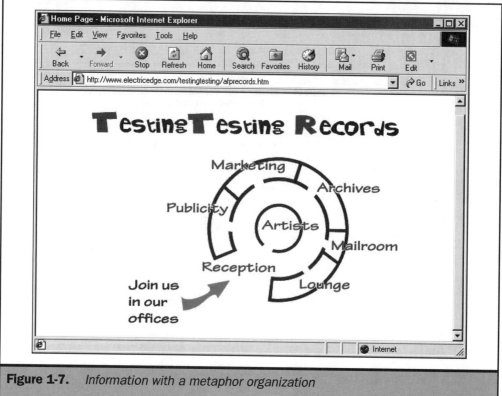

Figure 1-7.   *Information with a metaphor organization*

hypertext, and database. These methods can be used alone or in different combinations, as the material requires.

Hierarchical Structure

Hierarchical structure is the traditional top-down approach. It is creating high-level categories and then arranging material underneath in logical subcategories. You can divide music into:

- Types (Rock, Classical, etc.)
- Periods of the music type (Baroque, Classical, etc.)
- Composers of the period (Bach, Mozart, etc.)
- Forms of music the composer wrote (symphonies, sonatas, etc.)
- Specific pieces the composer wrote (*Symphony No. 41, Eine Kleine Nachtmusik*, etc.)

Each of these is a level in a hierarchical structure, like this:

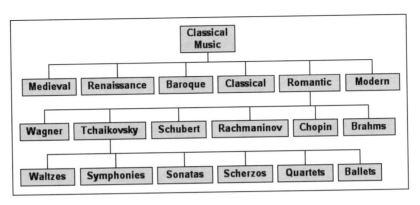

This is a classification scheme most people are familiar with, and it helps users create a mental map of the structure of the site. This in turn helps them in moving around the site without getting confused or lost.

In designing a hierarchical structure, you want to keep a balance between the width and depth of the hierarchy. The extremes are the *narrow and deep hierarchy* and the *broad and shallow hierarchy*.

NARROW AND DEEP HIERARCHY   A narrow and deep hierarchy is organized so that there are just a few classifications at the top and the user is forced to move down through many levels to get the information desired. This becomes extra work for the user, making it difficult to keep track of where he or she is in the web application. In this example, there are seven clicks to get from *Page A* to *Page B*.

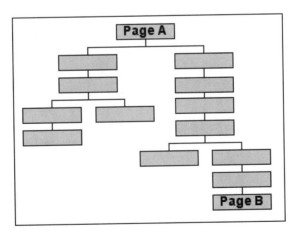

A good rule of thumb for depth is to structure the web application so that users will be able to get the information they want in three levels. Once they go to four or five levels without getting what they want, confusion and frustration set in.

BROAD AND SHALLOW HIERARCHY   The opposite problem is when there are many classifications at the top level and very few levels underneath. This can present the user with too many choices to keep track of, as illustrated here:

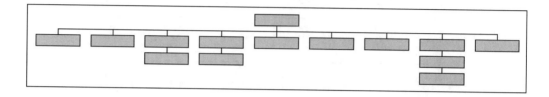

The human short-term memory is limited to around seven items. When they get to the eight or ninth item, users start forgetting the early ones. As the items become more complex, the ability to remember them decreases. You can go up to nine items, if they are simple, or keep it down to five items if the material is more complex.

It is useful to draw a diagram of your site hierarchy that shows the pages and their relationships. You can refer to this diagram, or storyboard, when you create your web pages.

Hypertext Structure

Hypertext is text or images that are linked to other text, images, or audio or video pieces. These links can be located throughout the page and provide a way to move quickly to related data. This is a very nonlinear approach to structure, as you can see here:

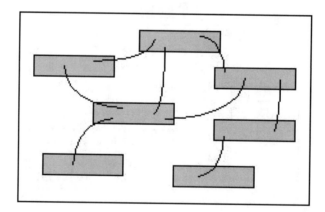

Using hypertext can be very confusing and should be employed carefully. It works best as a secondary, or supporting, structure. Because of its nonlinearity, the user can get lost quickly and will find it difficult to make a mental map of the web application. Using hypertext works best if the link is to data that is at a dead end. The user would then move back to the main hierarchical structure and not have other choices that would move him or her further away.

Database Structure

A database can be used for structuring a site by building pages of information out of a database as the information is requested. This works well for large sites with related information. Using a database can also give a lot of flexibility in presenting only the information requested. Chapter 18 describes using databases with FrontPage.

With a structure for your web application, you will next develop the tools for the user to navigate through this structure.

Developing a Navigation Scheme

The navigation scheme of your web application is highly dependent on the structure you have developed, and directly affects how the user will move around your site and access the material you present.

There are a lot of ways to provide navigation. If you have been on the Web for a while, you have seen many of them and probably gotten lost using some. There is a natural tendency for web developers to come up with new ways to dazzle their audience. But it is often best to keep navigation simple, or your audience will be dazzled and confused.

The next several sections discuss the major issues that need to be considered in setting up navigation schemes, including browser navigation, maintaining the hierarchy and structure of your design, providing flexibility in navigation, and the use of navigation bars, frames, and menus. This will be followed by an example of a navigation scheme.

Browser Navigation

Because your web application will run inside a web browser, it has navigation tools before you even start building it. Most modern web browsers provide the following variety of tools independent of your web application:

- Forward and backward arrows, which let the user move forward and backward through web pages
- *Bookmark* or *Favorites* lists, which allow the user to save the URL of a page and return directly there without going through the front door of the web application
- Page URLs, which allow the user to go directly to any page desired.
- Status bar display of a link's URL, which gives users a sense of where they are going if you have carefully labeled your folders and files.

However, one of the most useful navigation features that the browser provides is one that web developers try to subvert most often—the use of blue underlined type to indicate an unvisited text link, and purple underlined type to indicate a visited link. It is a navigation scheme common to all browsers and one that every beginning web user learns very early. It makes it easy to scan a page and see where the links are and to know whether you have used a particular link. No other navigation scheme provides that much information or is as universally understood. To use any other scheme is to force your user to stop and learn your scheme before being able to proceed.

Maintaining the Design Hierarchy and Structure

Your navigation scheme will be the primary way for the user to get a sense of the structure of your web application. The user is not using the navigation scheme to just find places to go, but also to see where they are and how they are related to the rest of the web application.

When using a hierarchical structure, it is useful for the navigation scheme to reflect that. But many such schemes do not differentiate between pages that are at different levels of the hierarchy. They treat them as if they are equal, as you can see here:

| **Music Home Page** | **Alternative** | **Blues** | **Classical** | **Folk** | **Jazz** | **Rock** |

One of the most recognized ways of showing hierarchy and structure is the outline form. The top levels of the hierarchy are flush left and each level down is indented to the right an equal amount, as here:

I. Classical Music
 A. *Modern*
 B. *Romantic*
  1. Brahms
  2. Chopin
  3. Rachmaninov
  4. Schubert
  5. Tchaikovsky
   a) **Ballets**
   b) **Quartets**
   c) **Scherzos**
   d) **Sonatas**
   e) **Symphonies**
   f) **Waltzes**
  6. Wagner
 C. *Classical*
 D. *Baroque*
 E. *Renaissance*
 F. *Medieval*

This outline structure visually shows where each section is and how it relates to the hierarchy. Your navigation scheme should provide this kind of information.

Providing Flexibility in Navigation

Providing flexibility in navigation is a balancing act. The web developer is acting as *Director of Traffic* when designing the navigation scheme. How do you get the users to their destination quickly without getting them lost? Look at the extremes in order to see the middle.

The least flexibility is to provide links that only go down or up the hierarchy tree one level at a time with no lateral links, as you can see here:

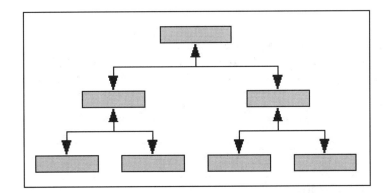

This forces the user to travel back up, one page at a time, and then back down the tree, one page at a time, to go from one part of the web application to another. This may keep users from getting lost, but they are not going to be able to get around the web application quickly.

The most flexibility, the other extreme, is when everything is linked to everything else, as here:

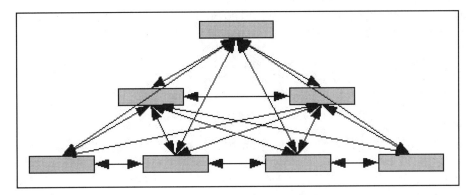

The user has maximum flexibility to move around the web application and, as you can see, maximum opportunity for confusion. You have presented the user with too much information. The trick is to balance the amount of information to maximize flexibility without confusing the user.

As you move down the hierarchy tree, it is recommended that you provide links back up the tree to the home page so that the user can quickly return there. It is also useful to provide lateral links to pages on the same level since these pages should all be related information if the hierarchy tree is set up correctly. Lateral links to pages one level above may be useful, but be careful that you don't offer so many choices that the user may become confused.

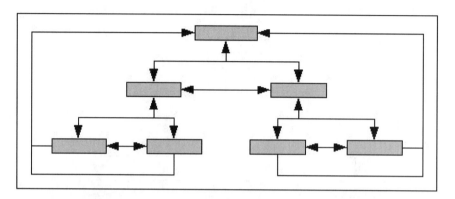

Consistent Labeling

The labels used for navigation links need to reflect the material they represent. This isn't the place to get fancy. Users need to be able to scan your navigation links and have a clear understanding of where they are going.

If you have organized your material well, your labels should fall into place. If the material is arranged by task, the labels should identify those tasks. If it is arranged by topic, the labels should identify the topics.

The wording for the labels should be consistent. The words should use the same verb tense, punctuation, capitalization, and so on. Put yourself in the place of a user new to your material. Keep your labels concise and clear. Avoid abbreviations and acronyms, because the confusion they cause is always greater then the space they save.

Once you have labels that are consistent and clear, be sure to use the same ones on the navigation link and in the heading of the page to which it is linked. If they are different, users will think they have clicked the wrong link and gone to the wrong page.

Navigation Bars

When you have come up with a navigation scheme and identified all the labels for the links, you need to determine where to put the links. The simplest answer is to gather all the navigation links on a *navigation bar,* which is a set of buttons or text links that allow you to jump to another place in your web application. Navigation bars can be on the top, the bottom, the left side, or the right side of a web page. The major concern is that the location is consistent. Every page must use the same scheme for navigation. The home page defines where it is and what it looks like. All the other pages of the web application should follow that lead.

There are certain limitations with navigation bars on top of the page. The horizontal layout makes it difficult to show hierarchy, and the width of the page limits the entries in the navigation bar unless you go to a smaller font. The top navigation bar is also in the way of the object of the page, which is its content.

Navigation bars on the bottom of the page are only there if there is also one on the top. It has the same limitations as to content and becomes another element to maintain. And there may be a bit of confusion here. When you look at the navigation bar, are you at the top or the bottom of the page? When the navigation bar is in one place, it acts like an anchor to the page. It becomes a consistent visual point of reference as to where you are on the page. When it is in two places, it doesn't.

The left side of the page has become the standard place to put navigation bars. It is not so limiting as to the length of the labels and gives more room to show hierarchy without getting in the way of the content. The vertical navigation bar should be placed high so that when the users are at the top of the page, they will also see the top of the navigation bar.

Putting the navigation bar on the right side is not a common approach, but is useful in certain limited conditions. Often in a large web application, the home page becomes more of an index of links to the rest of the web application. In such cases it makes sense to use a right navigation bar to important pages within the web application, as long as it's set up so a user with a small display will not have to scroll horizontally.

TEXT VS. ICONS   They say a picture is worth a thousand words, but it took words to say that. Try saying it in a picture. Try saying it in a very little picture. Icons have a very limited use unless it is for a very common function, such as returning to the home page. Whenever you see an icon, there is usually a text link along with it. So what is the purpose of the icon? Typically it is no more than eye candy. At most, an icon can supplement a text link. It can provide some additional visual information that supports the text link, but the text link is still the primary link that users will focus on. Icons also take additional time to create, maintain, and download, so use them carefully. Seldom can they stand on their own.

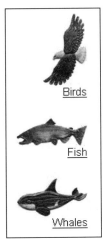

TEXT LINKS VS. NAVIGATION BUTTONS   In a navigation bar you can use either text links (text with a link associated with it) or navigation buttons (small graphics with a text label and an associated link). Navigation buttons allow the web developer to use a variety of fonts and backgrounds for the link. This is usually done for aesthetic reasons to better integrate the text of the links into the design of the other graphics used on the page. The following example shows navigation buttons and text links.

However, whenever you use something other than the default text links, you slow users down because they have to decipher what are links and what are not. The default text link has the advantage of already being familiar to many users. Using alternatives also forfeits the ability to tell if you have used that link or not. With the default text link, the color changes when it has been used. It is also very easy to modify a navigation bar of text links, but much more difficult and time-consuming if you have to create a new graphic every time you want to edit or create a new link.

Frames

Frames divide a web page into independently scrollable panes and should only be used with caution as a navigation tool. They present a very different navigation model than the normal page-based system. Frames display two or more different pages in different panes. This adversely affects several navigation features of the browser such as bookmarking, and visited and unvisited links. Figure 1-8 shows a frames-based web page. Frames are discussed briefly in Chapter 2 and in depth in Chapter 8.

Frames are much more difficult to incorporate in a design, and different browsers display frames differently. If you are not careful with your links, you can have frames within frames.

Printing is also a problem. Only one frame will print, not all of what you see on the screen, which is made of several frames (although newer browsers let you choose "entire page" or "selected frame"). And it is not always clear which frame will print.

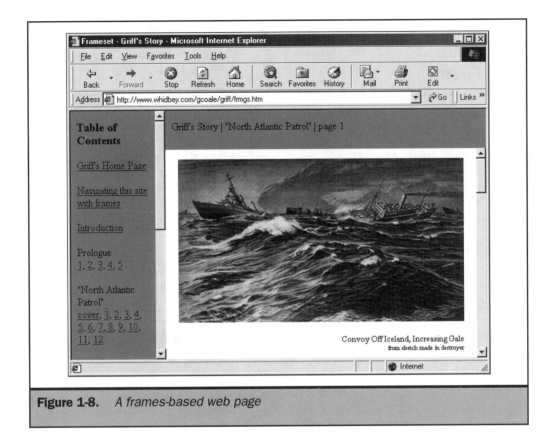

Figure 1-8. *A frames-based web page*

Drop-Down List Boxes

Drop-down list boxes can put a lot of selections in a small space. The pull-down menu only takes up one line until it is selected, and then it will display its contents for selection. The user, though, cannot see what is in the pull-down menu until it is selected. If there are several drop-down list boxes, users will not be able to remember what is in each one and will be clicking back and forth to find what they want. The following example shows how a pull-down menu will show its information when selected.

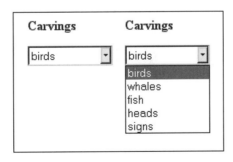

It is better to have everything the user needs clearly visible. Navigation is not a treasure hunt. Make it easy.

Image Maps

Image maps, which are graphics with "hotspots" that are links the user can click, can be especially useful if your information is organized around geographical locations. It is often not clear that an image can be used to select links. Any navigation system should be usable without instructions on how to use it. To force users to wave their cursor over an image to see if there are any links is to put them on another treasure hunt, which they don't often have the patience for. Even when it is clear that there are hotspots on the image for selection, care must be taken to make it obvious where those hotspots are. Figure 1-9 shows an image map in FrontPage with boxes defining the hotspots. Image maps and hotspots are discussed further in Chapters 2 and 7.

Additional Navigation Aids

Sometimes a site map, an index, and/or a table of contents are used to supplement the primary navigation scheme. Generally speaking, these are admissions of defeat. They

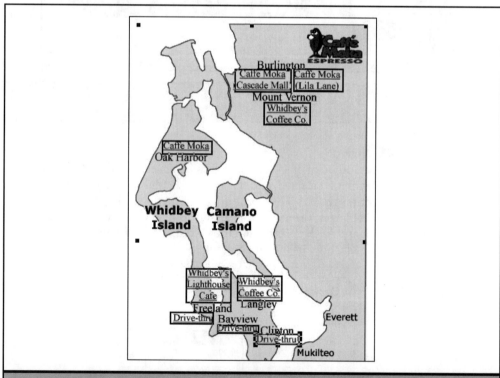

Figure 1-9. *An image map showing hotspots*

are mostly used as an alternative to good organization and a well-designed navigation scheme. They have possibilities as a supplement to the primary navigation scheme, but usually the time spent on these aids would be better spent on improving the organization and primary navigation.

Subsites

After all the emphasis on consistency of navigation devices throughout your web application, there is a situation for which it makes sense to change the navigation: in large sites, particularly large corporate intranets. As you move down the tree to lower levels, you come to sections where the content is very different and needs to be organized differently. Sites for different organizations in a large corporation are a good example of this. These become subsites, and there is often a lot of latitude in how they are presented as long as they are consistent within themselves and still provide navigation links back up to the primary site.

An Example Navigation Scheme

What does a navigation scheme that meets the above requirements look like? The following is an example of one way to do it. Users have found it easy to use this scheme, but that does not mean this is the only way. If you can find a better way that is easier for the user, then do it. But always keep your focus on the needs of the user when designing a navigation scheme.

The following navigation scheme is for classical music. It will start at the top level and break down into individual types of music by a composer. You will look at the navigation concepts along the way. Figure 1-10, example a, shows the top level.

The home page is at the top. Since this is the page you are on, there is no link. It is frustrating to users to have the page they are on have a link to itself. The unlinked text is bold to distinguish it from the linked text. The links are all text links in the default colors, and they are all indented evenly like an outline. This shows they are all on the same level and one level below the home page in the web application hierarchy. Users will thus know where they are and what the structure is for one level.

This example is built with a table within a table to align and indent the links. The link labels are for the different standard genres of classical music. The genres are date related and are organized by those dates, with the most recent on top. The dates could have been included in labels. This is also a good illustration of how not to do labels. The label *Classical* appears in both levels. Since this is common usage, it is used here, but it always causes confusion.

Next, go down one level by selecting the link *Romantic*. Figure 1-10, example b, shows what this would look like.

Another level opens up that has composers from the Romantic period. It is indented to the right, indicating another level down in the web application hierarchy. Since the page you are on is *Romantic*, it is bold and not linked. You can see where you are. You can also see the pages one level below, as well as those at the same level and the page one level up. This allows you to move down, laterally, and up.

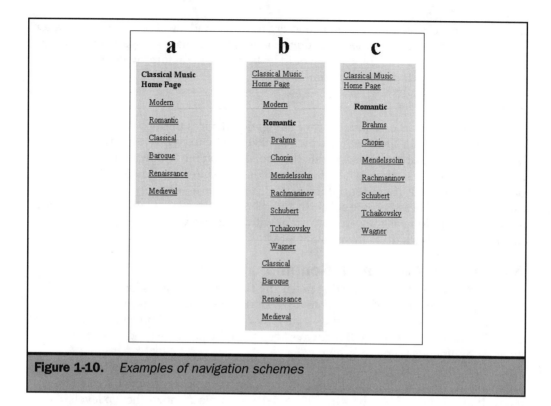

Figure 1-10.   *Examples of navigation schemes*

Figure 1-10, example c, shows another way this might be displayed.

Here the lateral moves have been eliminated but you can still move up and down from this point. Whether you want to collapse the structure like this depends on the material and the number of links shown.

Go down one more level by selecting Tchaikovsky. Figure 1-11, example a, shows what the navigation bar might now look like.

Now Tchaikovsky is unlinked and bold since that is where the user is. The pages one level below are shown, along with those on the same level. But the pages on the level above have been collapsed. To add all the pages at that level would start overloading the navigation bar. From here you can go down, laterally, or up to either level above.

If it starts to get confusing you might want to collapse the lateral links as in Figure 1-11, example b.

Using this scheme will tell you where you are and what is around you in the web application. You can collapse the levels, depending on the material and number of links, so that the resulting navigation bar provides the most flexibility in moving up, down, and laterally without becoming too confusing.

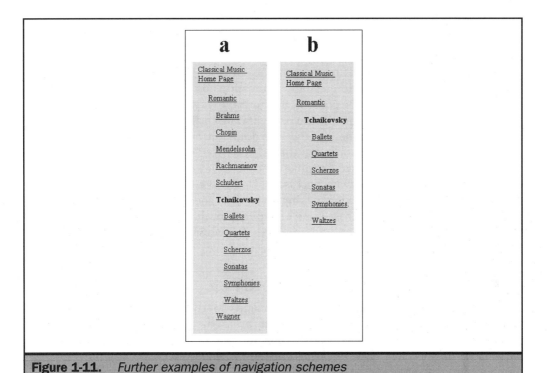

Figure 1-11. *Further examples of navigation schemes*

With the navigation bar designed for the site you are building, look at how to handle the graphics.

Working with Graphics

The work you have done on organizing, structuring, and developing the navigation of your web application results in a site that is easy to use. All the graphics in the world are not going to make a poorly organized site any easier to use. Graphics can, however, make your site attractive and fun to use. This section will give some highlights on graphics for the web and encourage you to learn more.

What Are Graphics For?

What are graphics anyway? Most people think the term indicates pictures, icons, and illustrations. And, for the purpose of this section, that is what it will mean (in FrontPage they are all "pictures"). But the term really includes much more. Graphics include not only picture elements but also typography. And typography isn't just about the shapes of letters and typefaces, but also about white spaces: the spaces between letters, and lines, and paragraphs. Graphics covers how all the visual elements on a page are put together.

What are graphics for? In a broad sense, they are there to support the content. They are there to make the information visually interesting and understandable. As such, they play a supporting role. The content, the message, is what is primary. If the graphics help that message jump off the page, and be easily understood, they are good graphics. If they become dominant, if they are done for their own sake, if they get in the way of the message, they are bad graphics.

Do you really need graphics? Graphics, and here we shift back to meaning picture elements, are useful but not always necessary. Using pictures and illustrations is often a case of less is more. A lone red rose lying on a white sheet becomes a much more powerful image that the same rose lying on a pile of multicolored rags. There are many beautiful pages with only text and white spaces. It is how the graphics are arranged and how they serve the content that are important.

What Kinds of Graphics Are There?

There are many different formats for digital images. Many are unique to the graphics program they are created in, and many formats are created to be universal formats that can be read by many programs. Another consideration in digital formats is file size, particularly for the Web, because of the time they take to download. So some digital formats have been created that compress file size as well as being universal.

The Web uses two of these compression formats: GIF and JPEG. There are some new formats that are being developed, but these two are the most widely supported and used today.

GIF

The *Graphic Interchange Format* (GIF) was originally developed by CompuServe and is a *lossless* compression scheme. Lossless compression compresses and decompresses a file, returning it exactly as it started without losing any pieces.

GIF files contain only 256 colors or less. This is compatible with many computers, which have 8-bit, or 256-color, displays. The user can define the 256 colors.

The way a GIF file is compressed gives us some clues on how it is best used. The GIF compression is based on horizontal pixel transitions. It creates a number that defines the color and how long the run of that color is. So, if you have a solid color or solid horizontal lines, there is a much higher compression than if you had a lot of changes in color horizontally. For example, if you took the graphic shown next with horizontal lines and compressed it as a GIF, the GIF file size would be 3K. If you rotate the graphic and compress it as a GIF, the file size jumps up 19K.

One of the best ways to keep file size down when using GIF compression is to create illustrations that use large areas of solid colors. When you have continuous tone images, like a photograph where the colors change every pixel, the file size will be much larger.

Tip   *Create your web graphics at 72 pixels per inch since the GIF compression scheme converts your graphic to 72 pixels per inch.*

There are two types of GIF compressions: GIF87a and GIF89a. GIF89a builds on the older GIF87a by adding interlacing, transparency, and animation.

INTERLACING   When an image is *interlaced*, it is loaded and displayed at full size, but not all the information is used. The image appears "out of focus" and gets sharper in a series of passes. It takes four passes to display an interlaced GIF in its final form. Interlaced GIFs are only used for larger graphics that will take a while to download. They can be annoying. *Noninterlaced* GIFs are displayed one stripe at a time, and each stripe is displayed at the final resolution. FrontPage has an option that allows you to make a GIF file interlaced.

TRANSPARENCY   *Transparent backgrounds* are created when one color in the GIF is replaced by the color of the background it is displayed on. This is a very useful feature for creating irregular-shaped images, such as text that you want to have floating over the background rather than in a rectangular box. You would also have to change the background color in the GIF if you changed the web page background. The fish on the left, shown next, is the full graphic where you can see the rectangular shape, while the fish on the right has the transparent background.

ANIMATION *Animated GIFs* are a series of static GIF images that are displayed in succession to create the illusion of movement. These static GIFs, along with the timing information, are saved as a single animated GIF image file. An example of this is the Microsoft Internet Explorer logo button. Animated GIFs are supported by Netscape Navigator 2.0 and later, and by Internet Explorer 3.0 and later. To create animated GIFs, you need a program such as the GIF Construction Set for Windows (available at **http://www.mindworkshop.com/alchemy/alchemy1.html#software**).

Care must be taken to keep the file size down since there is no compression between animated GIF frames. If you create an animated GIF file with ten 4K files, you will have a 40K file.

Animated GIFs should be used with extreme caution. Any motion, particularly repetitive motion, is very distracting. It draws the eye every time it moves. It affects that reptilian part of the brain that sees no motion as safe, and motion as danger or something tasty. Animated GIFs are discussed further and their construction is demonstrated in Chapter 5.

JPEG

The *Joint Photographic Exchange Group* (JPEG) format is a *lossy* format. Image data is lost whenever the file is compressed. Compression can be as much as 100:1. The amount of compression is variable depending on the graphic program.

Low compression will change the picture little, while high compression will cause noticeable change. Run some tests to see how much you can compress and still get an image you like.

Create your graphics at 72 pixels per inch. Unlike GIF compression, JPEG compression will retain the resolution of the original graphic. The screen resolution on a Macintosh computer is 72 pixels per inch. Windows monitors have a slightly higher resolution but use 72 pixels per inch. If you exceed 72 pixels per inch, you will create detail that will not be seen, and you will have a large file because of the extra detail.

The JPEG format is a 24-bit format, which gives it over 16.7 million colors. However, if the viewer's computer only has an 8-bit display, it will only display 256 colors. JPEG compression works best on continuous tone images like photographs.

Where Do Graphics Come From?

Graphics for your web application can be purchased as clip art, created in graphics programs, scanned from existing images, or taken with a digital camera.

Clip Art

Clip art are images that are already created and usable as they are. Clip art used to mean little line drawings, but that has changed. Now the term includes all manner of images including large collections of photographs on CDs.

A good place to get clip art is on the Web. Go to Yahoo and search for *clip art*. You will find sites with collections of clip art that is free or for sale over the Web. Always be aware of copyright infringement when using clip art. When people give away free clip art, it may not be theirs to give away.

 Make sure you have the right to display an image before using it in your web application.

There are many collections of clip art CDs available at computer and other stores. There are also many stock photo houses that are putting their photo collections on CD. The reputable CDs of photos are not inexpensive, but you do get the legal right to use high-quality images.

The big disadvantage of clip art is that you aren't the only one using these images. They show up all over the place. You've probably seen print ads from different companies that used the same image. Clip art also often has a sameness about it that screams *clip art*. Originality does count.

Graphics Programs

When you decide you want to be original and create your own graphics, you can use any one of a number of different graphics programs. The problem is that using them isn't simple. There are paint programs, draw programs, and combinations of the two.

PAINT PROGRAMS   Paint programs are the mainstay of web graphics. A paint program is a pixel-based, or bitmap, program. Whether you bring in a photograph, put in some type, or create some shapes, the program only recognizes the pixels it has created. It doesn't know what the pixels represent. It only knows that they are pixels and what the hue and values are. This is also called *raster graphics*. But a paint program has a lot of flexibility in color control for creating web graphics. It is the best program for dealing with photographic images.

Adobe PhotoShop is the most popular paint program used for web graphics. Fractal Paint offers a lot of artistic flexibility in making more painterly graphics and is a good supplement to PhotoShop. CorelPhoto-Paint is used by many. And there are some good shareware programs if PhotoShop is too expensive for you. Paint Shop Pro is very popular. Microsoft PhotoDraw in the Office 2000 Premium Edition or Microsoft Image Composer in the FrontPage 2000 stand-alone edition are also good choices and are described in Chapter 5.

DRAW PROGRAMS   Draw programs use vector graphics. They are not pixel based. The shapes are defined mathematically and are always editable. For example, text always remains editable (it doesn't become mere pixels when you leave the text function), and you can change the font, colors, or any other characteristic at any time. When you zoom in on a graphic created by a paint program, you see the individual pixels. There are no pixels in a draw program. You can zoom in all you want and you still have sharp edges and clean colors.

However, paint programs like Adobe PhotoShop are better for final preparation of web graphics since GIFs and JPEGs are pixel based. It often works well to use the draw program for the elements, such as text, that it does well and then export the file to the paint program. You can see the difference between paint and draw programs (or between raster and vector graphics) here, where the draw program with vector graphics is on the left and the paint program with bitmap or raster graphics is on the right:

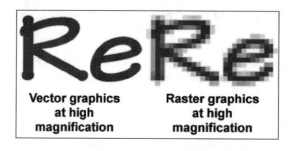

Adobe Illustrator is one of the main draw programs, and it provides much better control of text than paint programs do. CorelDRAW is another popular draw program.

Scanners

A scanner can be a powerful tool to use with a paint program. You can convert any image on a flat surface into a digital image. These images are scanned into a paint program where they can be manipulated and integrated into your web graphics. Scanners often come with a low-end paint program not really suitable for serious web graphics.

While high-end flatbed scanners go for up to $1,500, you can get a very good scanner in the $300 range.

Note   *Scanners can be used for more than copying images. They also come with optical character recognition (OCR) programs. These programs scan text documents, turn them into bitmap images, compare the shapes of the text to the shapes of letters in its memory, and create a text file that can be loaded into a word processing document.*

Digital Cameras

One of the new ways to get images is with a digital camera. Although they are more expensive than a film-based camera, you eliminate all the film and developing costs. A reasonable camera for web application use can be purchased in the $500 range. For $1,000 you get a camera with more pixels that can make high-quality photographic prints with a good ink jet printer.

The images are downloaded into your computer and manipulated with a paint program. The digital cameras come with paint programs, but they are pretty simple programs and are not a substitute for a higher-end paint program when it comes to doing web graphics.

Monitor Color Settings

On a PC, the number of colors a monitor can display can be 16 or 256 or 64,000 (16-bit High Color) or 16 million (24-bit True Color). Again, you have no control over how many colors will be displayed when your work goes onto the Web; some monitors still display only 16 colors.

You can expect the number of colors available to continue increasing; you may even have 32-bit True Color on your system. Regardless, you can count on your work being displayed at minimum on a 16-color system.

The decision you have as a web page designer is whether to limit yourself to the lowest common denominator (16-color, 640×480 resolution) or to work at a higher standard. If you are designing a simple page with minimal graphics, limiting your design to 16 colors may make sense. It ensures compatibility with virtually all the systems your work will be displayed on. (If someone is using a monochrome monitor to view your work, the point is moot, of course.)

However, if you limit yourself to 16 colors, you will not be able to effectively use scanned photographs or graphics with subtle shadings. In that case it would be better to use at least 256 colors. You cannot limit yourself to the lowest common denominator in every case. You simply have to accept that your work will not look its best on lower-end systems. (The people with these systems hopefully will upgrade them as they discover that other people's systems look a lot better!)

Another point to remember about color is that every monitor will display colors a little differently. There are many factors at play here, ranging from the age of the monitor to the light in the room. If you've worked with programs like Adobe PhotoShop and have output to color printers, you know how difficult it can be to get the printed output to exactly match the colors you see on the monitor. If it's important that a particular color appear exactly the correct shade on a web page—when it's part of a logo, for example—you're simply out of luck. You can calibrate your own monitor and ensure the color is correct on a calibrated system, but once you turn it loose on the Web, you have no control over how it will appear.

If you design your web pages to be displayed on a 256-color, 640×480-resolution monitor and remember it will look different at other video resolutions, you can count on most people seeing your work the way you intended. See "Monitor Display" later in this chapter for more information on how a monitor's resolution affects the way a web page appears to the user.

Some Tips for Professional Looking Graphics

Creating web graphics can fill up a whole book—actually, many books, judging from bookstore shelves. But the following three tips cover a lot of mistakes that beginners make.

Browser-Safe Palette

GIFs use up to 256 colors. But which 256 colors? Well, it can be any 256 colors. And this is not good. You painstakingly create a graphic with a nice solid color, and when you look at it on your monitor, it isn't solid anymore. What happened? If your monitor is set to display 256 colors, it is displaying a defined set of 256 colors. And they may not be the same colors you used in your graphic.

When the computer runs across a color outside of its 256-color palette, it approximates that color by combining two of its colors. This is called *dithering*. When you look closely, you can see that the dithered color has clumps of different-colored pixels while the nondithered example does not, as in the dithered example here on the left:

Fortunately, browsers use a common palette of colors, although it has been reduced to 216. If you use these 216 colors when creating your graphics, they will display as solid, nondithered, colors. You can find out what these colors are at two excellent web sites on web graphics: Lynda Weinman's site at **http://www.lynda.com** and David Siegal's *Creating Killer Web Sites* at **http://www.killersites.com/core.html**.

Lynda's site has two graphics that give the Red, Green, Blue (RGB) values for all 216 browser-safe colors. You can use these RGB values in FrontPage for defining the background colors, or in your graphics program to make sure your colors will not dither. Both Lynda's and David's site have a graphic with these colors that you can load into Adobe PhotoShop and turn into a palette which will allow you to select the colors directly.

Anti-aliasing

Why do some web graphics have little jagged edges and others do not? It is because the smooth-edged web graphics use *anti-aliasing*. GIFS are created at 72 pixels per inch. When you put a solid color, irregular-shaped image on top of a solid-color background, the edge is visibly jagged. Anti-aliasing creates a buffer zone of transition colors between the shape and the background. This tricks the eye into seeing the edge as smooth. Make sure your paint program has anti-aliasing turned on when you create text and shapes. Here's a comparison of aliased (on the right) and anti-aliased characters (on the left):

Halos

A possible problem with anti-aliasing is that halos appear around an image when the image has been anti-aliased, compressed as a GIF, and had the background made transparent. That process causes the white line or halo to appear around this fish head:

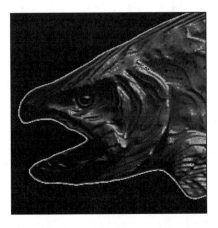

The buffer pixels between the image and background that anti-aliasing introduces are color keyed to the background color of the graphic and not the web page background. The solution is to not use the transparent function of GIF89a, but to create the graphic with the graphic background using the same browser-safe color as the web page background. Then the rectangular edges of the graphic blend in with the web page background.

This won't work with textured or tiled backgrounds since there is no way to control the registration of the background image with the graphic.

 It is not recommended to use images as a background since the background then starts to fight with the foreground for attention and it is the foreground that has your content.

Next, put all you have learned above together and make a set of web pages or a web application.

Laying out Web Pages

You are almost ready to start laying out a page. Look first at some of the restrictions you have to deal with in page layout, what elements will go into the page, and how you'll arrange those elements.

Layout Restrictions

Layout restrictions include the limitations of the language used to create a web page (HTML), the limitations of both a browser and the user's monitor, and the fact that everything on your page must be downloaded to users at the speed of their modem or LAN connection. All of these factors require serious consideration when laying out a page.

HTML Limitations

Your web application is created using the Hypertext Markup Language (HTML). As you read earlier in this chapter, HTML is a formatting language that consists of ASCII text and, since ASCII text contains extremely limited formatting information, a system of formatting tags is used to contain the formatting information.

There are tags that begin and end a web page, define the sections of the web page, tags that call for images, execute programs, and affect how the text is displayed. There are lots of tags and more of them on their way. In fact, there are way more tags than you probably want to deal with, and with a program like FrontPage, you really don't have to deal with tags at all. Just in case you do, Chapter 13 goes into some depth on HTML.

FrontPage is a WYSIWYG (what you see is what you get) HTML editor. FrontPage allows you to do the page layout much as you would using a word processor—but unfortunately—a pretty stupid word processor. This is not a shortcoming of FrontPage, but the limitations of HTML. Like everything on the Web, though, this is changing.

Although you don't need to know HTML to produce excellent web applications with FrontPage, there will come a time when you have to look at the HTML to troubleshoot something and it is real helpful to know what you are looking at. Chapter 13 will give you a good start on this, and the HTMLLIB (an HTML library) on the CD that accompanies this book provides all the detail you will need.

 As a historical aside, in the early 1980s, personal computer word processing programs were ASCII text editors with formatting tags that were interpreted when the document was printed, much like a web browser does today when it displays a web page.

Browser Display

When you want to view a web page on your browser, you are requesting an HTML document with its ASCII text and HTML tags. The browser analyzes the HTML tags to determine what formatting to use. When it comes to a tag that indicates an image, it sends another request to the server for that image. Each time it comes to an image, it sends another request. It goes through the entire document getting images and other secondary files, and then displays the page.

The HTML document leaves all the actual decisions of how the text is to be displayed up to the browser software. This wouldn't be a problem if there were just one browser. But there are different browser manufacturers, and each manufacturer has different versions of their browser. Each manufacturer displays the standards slightly differently, each version of a browser adheres to different standards, and each manufacturer has created their own nonstandard standards. This is why browsers display web pages differently.

If you keep to the industry-standard tags, everything works pretty well even though the display will look slightly different from one manufacturer's browser to the other. When you move into the more advanced browser capabilities, like cascading style sheets or Java scripts, you will run into major headaches, because what will work on one browser will not work on a competitor's browser. And they won't work at all on older browsers.

 Scripting languages like JavaScript and VBScript give the web developer a lot of capabilities, but there are so many problems if you use them on the client (browser) side that it is recommended you keep them on the server side.

There is no one good source that documents all the differences among browsers. The only way to deal with these is to keep your design and layout simple and look at your page in at least Netscape Navigator and Microsoft Internet Explorer. If you are working in an intranet environment where everyone has the same browser, you are blessed.

Monitor Display

Monitor resolution affects the width of the page displayed. It is measured by the width of the screen in pixels by the height of the screen in pixels. The three most common displays are 640×480 pixels, 800×600 pixels, and 1024×768 pixels.

When you lay out your page, you need to consider that it will be viewed in all three formats and that it should look good in all three. It certainly isn't going to look the same, however. Figures 1-12 through 1-14 show how a web page will look in all three formats.

The best way to tell how your design will appear is to test it on your monitor at each of the three different sizes.

Tip
You can set the dimensions of your web browsers using the FrontPage Preview In Browser command (located in the File menu). If you are using Windows 95 or 98, you can often change your resolution without rebooting by right-clicking the desktop, choosing Properties, selecting Settings, and changing the Desktop Area.

Note
If you design your pages to display full screen on an 800×600 display, you will force users viewing a 640×480 display to scroll horizontally as well as vertically. This makes it almost impossible for the viewer to look at your pages. It becomes very disorienting scrolling both directions.

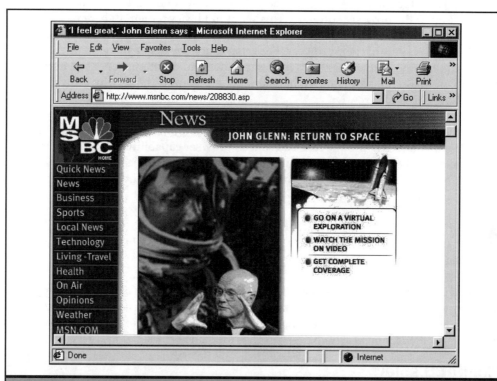

Figure 1-12.   *Web page at 640×480 resolution*

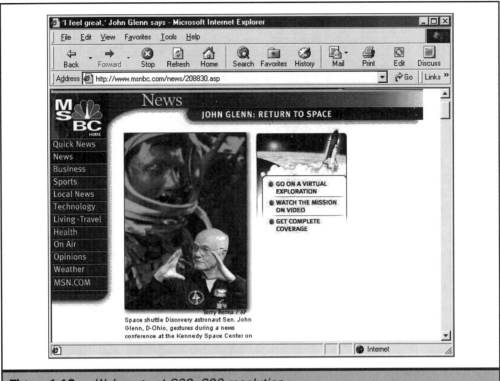

Figure 1-13.   *Web page at 800×600 resolution*

Data Transfer

Making people wait too long for your web page to download is a sure way to get your viewers to go elsewhere. Elsewhere is a simple click of the mouse. The two major factors in long downloads are the user's connection speed, usually a modem being the slowest, and the total file size of your HTML and any other files, such as images, that your web page uses. Some users are still on 14.4 Kbps modems, but these are becoming rarer. 28.8 Kbps is still very common. Try to keep your download times under 30 seconds for a 28.8 Kbps modem user.

FrontPage tells you in the lower-right corner of the Page view window the average download time of a page with a 28.8 modem.

You can't control the user's modem speed, but you can control the size of the files that make up your web page. Keep unnecessary graphics off your page. When you do have graphics, make their file size small. You can keep the user's attention longer if

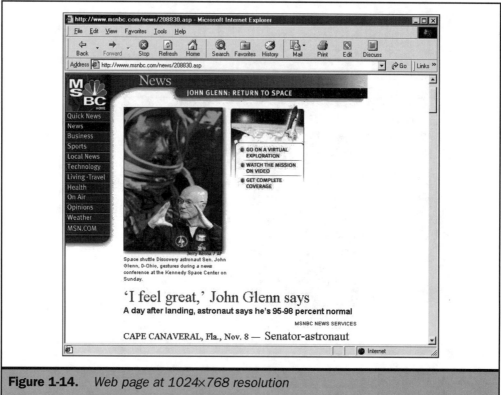

Figure 1-14.   *Web page at 1024×768 resolution*

there is text to read while images lower in the page are loading. You also can make the page shorter so that there is not as much on it. Users are not nearly as impressed with pages that have lots of fancy graphics and a long download as they are with quick-loading pages.

Page Elements

There are some page elements to consider adding to every web application, such as banner identification, a simple page background, short line length, and contact information. On the other hand, some page elements such as horizontal lines and bullets may be overused and so better left off.

Banner Identification

Using a banner at the top of the page is the best way to identify the web application from page to page. Using the same banner on all the pages provides an effective visual anchor. If the banner always stays the same, and the page underneath it changes, it is clear to the users that they are in the same web application.

It also helps to visually differentiate the banner on the home page from the following pages. Making the banners on the following pages smaller than the home page helps establish the position of the home page in the hierarchy of the web application.

Page Background

The default background for web pages is either white or, in older browsers, gray. This color can be changed to other solid colors, or an image can be tiled in the background. Always be careful about placing anything other than a solid color under text. If there is a textured background, the text will be hard to read, which will only get in the way of your message. If you use a dark color, you will have to use a lighter-colored text to make it readable. This is called *inverted text* and is more difficult to read. Using colored text on a colored background may be useful, as is inverted text, for setting off a piece of text, but for larger areas of text it is better to maximize contrast for readability. Black letters on a white background are the easiest to read. Ever read a book that was anything other than black letters on a white page?

Line Length

In the early days of web design, most web developers let their text run the width of the page. Some still do. This makes reading very difficult; when the eye gets to the end of the line it is reading, it must traverse back to the beginning of the line below. If it's a long line, the eye gets confused about which is the next line it is trying to pick up, and it is tiring to read. This concept is even more important for screen text than print text. It is ideal to have no more than 10-12 words on a line or no more than 60 to 80 characters. Putting your text in a table whose cells are 400 to 420 pixels wide will accomplish this

Contact Information

One of the beauties of the web is its interactivity. The user can speak back. Provide a way for this to happen with at least an e-mail address. Let the user of the site communicate directly with the owner of the site. This is normally done at the bottom of the home page with a copyright notice and the name, address, e-mail address, and sometimes the phone number of the owner of the web application.

Horizontal Rules

Horizontal rules are seen everywhere on the Web and are sometimes misused to separate elements of a page. Horizontal rules can separate too much. They don't cause the eye to pause; they cause it to come to a halt. It is often better to use well-organized white space for vertical separation. On the other hand, when you want the eye to make a clear break, such as between a banner and a navigation bar, or between a navigation bar and the body text, then a horizontal rule may make sense. When there is a need to provide a stronger break between two sections, there is also an alternative called a *printer's mark*. This is a small graphic such as a 10×10-pixel square or diamond, as shown here:

If you want to use a horizontal line, try something other than the 2-pixel-high, full-width horizontal rule. It is easy in FrontPage to make the horizontal rule thinner and shorter. Try a 1-pixel thick rule at 50% of your page width.

Bullets

Bullets on lists are also sometimes misused. They don't carry information and can be a distraction from the content. Bullets are often used in print since vertical space is expensive and the bullet helps the eye identify an individual element in a list. Vertical space is cheap on the Web. As an alternative, you can use white space and indenting to set off elements of a list.

Page Layout

Page layout is about placing all these elements along with the text, images, and navigation bars on the page, controlling where everything goes on the page. This can sometimes be a sporting proposition using HTML, but there are some tools—most importantly, tables—that let you put things down and have them stay there whether the display is 640 or 1024 pixels wide.

Tables vs. Frames

There are two basic approaches for controlling space on the web page: tables and frames. We have talked about the inadequacies of frames for navigation. They also present problems for page layout. They take up valuable real estate on the page and do not begin to offer the much finer control that tables offer. Tables do not offer all the control you might like from a proper page layout program such as a desktop publishing program, but they are the best tool you have for now.

FrontPage makes using tables much easier than doing it directly in HTML since the table structure is easy to see in FrontPage's Page view. Trying to use tables extensively in a text editor is almost impossible, but in FrontPage they can be constructed quickly and modified easily. This doesn't mean that they don't do weird things sometimes, so keep checking the page in a browser to see just how it is going to look. Tables and frames are discussed in depth in Chapter 8.

Invisible Tables

When you use tables, you normally want to turn off all borders since they often get in the way of the information they surround. Borders are a visual element meant to provide separation for the text they surround, but they often fight for the eye's attention. It is better to use vertical and horizontal white space to separate and accentuate a table's contents.

Nested Tables

A table within a table is a nested table. After establishing the table and cell structure for the overall page, it may be necessary to control page elements within individual cells. The indented links in the navigation bar are accomplished with nested tables. The following example has the table borders turned on so that you can see where the tables are and how nested tables are used within the cells. Nested tables are a very powerful tool in the layout of a web page.

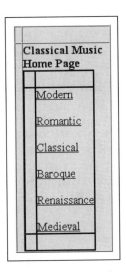

Absolute and Relative Cell Size

Table cells can be very elastic. They can move all over the place, so in order to control where elements are placed on the page, you need to control cell width. This is done in three different ways: by unconstrained width, relative width, or absolute width.

UNCONSTRAINED WIDTH If the width of the cell is not otherwise defined, the text and images that are in it will define its width. When you create a table with undefined sizes for both the table and the cells, put in text and images, and move the width of the browser in and out, you will see how the cells change their size to match the browser width. It is impossible to control how the page looks with this scheme. The top of Figure 1-15 shows how this looks in a 600×480-pixel display, while the bottom shows how it changes in a 1024×780-pixel display.

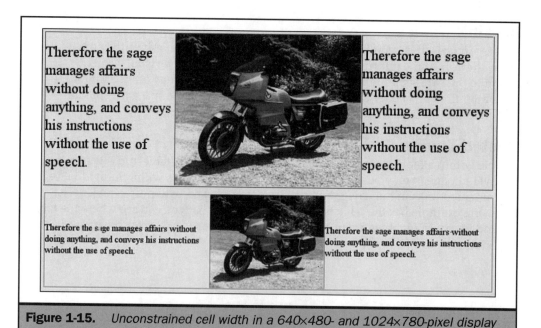

Figure 1-15.   *Unconstrained cell width in a 640×480- and 1024×780-pixel display*

RELATIVE SIZE   Tables and cells can be defined as a percentage of the browser width. This becomes an improvement over the undefined size, but it is still not enough to accurately control the page layout. When using relative size, the look of the page changes dramatically between a 640×480 display, shown at the top of Figure 1-16, and a 1024×768 display, shown in the bottom of that figure.

ABSOLUTE SIZE   Defining table and cell size by pixels is the only way to control the placement of the elements in your page. If you apply pixel values to a table's widths and move the browser width in and out, the page stays the same, independent of whether your display is 640×480, as shown in the top of Figure 1-17, or 1024×768, as shown in the bottom. The page and its elements are stable.

Table Weirdness

Even when using absolute-size tables, weird things can happen. When you stuff a big image in a smaller cell, the table will try to adjust the best it can. If you are using empty cells to control vertical space, they may not display and you will need to specify the height of the cell. Always look at the page in a browser to see how the table is going to display.

FrontPage makes it easier to work with tables, but when you start nesting tables, you do need to be careful that they don't start interacting with each other. Pay attention to the widths of the tables being nested and keep checking it in the browser.

Therefore the sage manages affairs without doing anything, and conveys his instructions without the use of speech.

Therefore the sage manages affairs without doing anything, and conveys his instructions without the use of speech.

Therefore the sage manages affairs without doing anything, and conveys his instructions without the use of speech.

Therefore the sage manages affairs without doing anything, and conveys his instructions without the use of speech.

Figure 1-16.   *Relative cell width in a 640×480- and 1024×780-pixel display*

Therefore the sage manages affairs without doing anything, and conveys his instructions without the use of speech.

Therefore the sage manages affairs without doing anything, and conveys his instructions without the use of speech.

Therefore the sage manages affairs without doing anything, and conveys his instructions without the use of speech.

Therefore the sage manages affairs without doing anything, and conveys his instructions without the use of speech.

Figure 1-17.   *Absolute cell width in a 640×480- and 1024×768-pixel display*

Two-Page Layout Examples

In the following two sections, we describe two layout examples that pull together all that has been discussed so far. While these examples incorporate many good techniques of page layout, there are probably ways that they can be improved. If you see such an improvement, note it down and try it out on your own pages.

There are two common approaches to page layout. Both use vertical navigation bars on the left side of the web page, and both use a color behind the navigation bar to separate it from the rest of the page. They are different in the way the color is applied. One uses a background image and the other uses cell color.

The background image layout was developed before cells could be colored, but it still has its uses. It gives a color bar that runs to the top of the page and all the way to the left of the page. Using a background image allows the web developer to use more than one color. However, it provides an unbalanced layout at the 800×600-pixel display and a very unbalanced layout at the 1024×768-pixel display. Figure 1-18 shows an example of this.

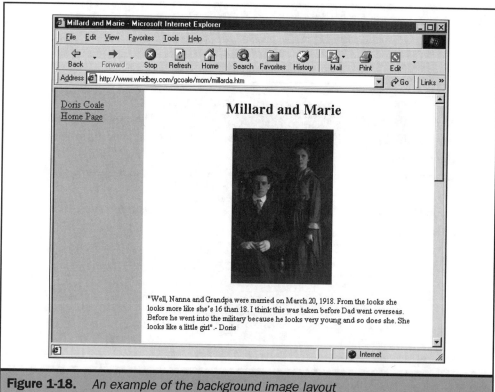

Figure 1-18.   *An example of the background image layout*

The cell-colored layout uses cell coloring for the navigation bar. Because of table offset, the color does not go to the edge or to the top of the screen. You are also limited to one color. Since there is not an image to download and tile, it will make it a little quicker to load. Since you don't have to place it over a background, you can center the layout, which looks much better at higher screen resolutions. Figure 1-19 is an example of the cell-colored layout.

Page layout is not an exercise to show off how many tricks you know but a platform for communicating your message. Be aware of your material, and its message will come through.

Background Image Layout

The background image layout should be set up so that it will fill the browser in a 640×480 display. In an 800×600 or 1024×768 display, the right side will have added

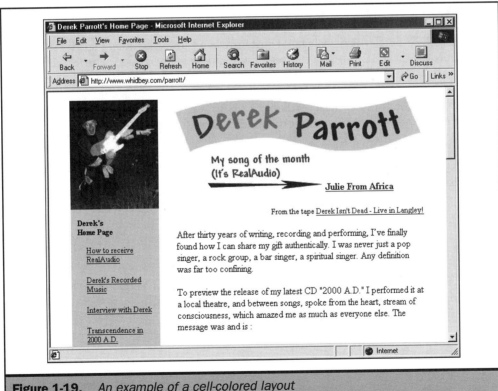

Figure 1-19.   *An example of a cell-colored layout*

white space. Other factors in this layout include putting a different color behind the navigation bar and using a three-cell table.

 The browser takes up screen width with the scroll bar, so make the table no more than 600 pixels wide to fit within a 640-pixel-wide window.

NAVIGATION BAR BACKGROUND   The vertical navigation bar on the left side of Figure 1-18 uses a vertical bar of a different color, or colors, to set off the navigation bar from the body of the page. This is done with a tiled image in the page background. When using this method, make sure the links are still readable over the color background.

The background image used here is 25 pixels high and 1200 pixels wide. This is a compromise that gives a small file size and will still tile quickly. It needs to be wide enough so that the navigation bar background does not appear on the right when it is viewed on a 1024-pixel display. The left side of the image will be the color under the navigation bar. The color should be wide enough for the navigation bar.

Be aware that the table is offset from the left browser edge, so that the left side of the image will not be the same as the left side of the table. To make it worse, the offset is different between Microsoft and Netscape browsers. All you can do is look at it in both browsers and adjust as necessary.

THREE-CELL TABLE   The basic table structure is a three-cell table. Figure 1-20 shows the cell borders turned on so you can see how the cells are arranged. The left cell holds the navigation bar, and the right cell holds the content of the page. The middle cell acts as a spacer between the right and left cells. The width of this cell is adjusted so that the navigation bar does not fall off its background and the content has enough white space between itself and navigation bar background. Use the necessary nested tables in the right cell to lay out the content.

Cell-Colored Layout

The cell-colored layout that you saw in Figure 1-19 has a fixed width and is centered in the browser. It is set up to fill the browser in a 640-pixel display. In an 800- or 1024-pixel display, there will be equal amounts of white space on the sides. Remember: The browser takes up screen width with the scroll bar, so make the table 600 pixels wide to fit within a 640-pixel-wide window.

NAVIGATION BAR BACKGROUND   Make the background a solid color and set the navigation bar off from the content by using cell coloring. Use a color that will not get in the way of the links.

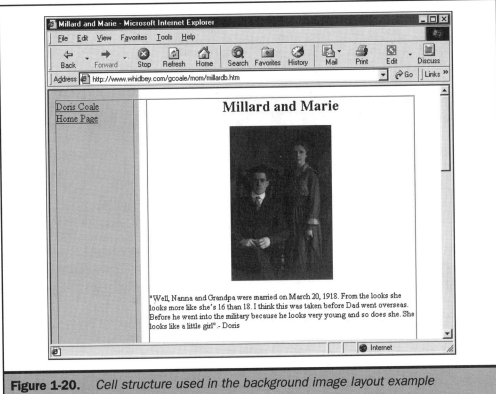

Figure 1-20.   *Cell structure used in the background image layout example*

THREE-CELL TABLE   The basic table structure is the three-cell table shown in Figure 1-21, where the cell borders are turned on so you can see how the cells are arranged.

The left cell holds the navigation bar, and the right cell holds the content of the page. The middle cell acts as a spacer between the right and left cells. Adjust the width of this cell so that the background and the content have enough white space between them.

The left cell could be colored but the color would run the entire height of the table and continue below the navigation bar. Or you could just color the nested cells that contain the navigation bar and put the rest of the left cell in a different color and use it for another purpose. Use the necessary nested tables in the right cell to layout the content.

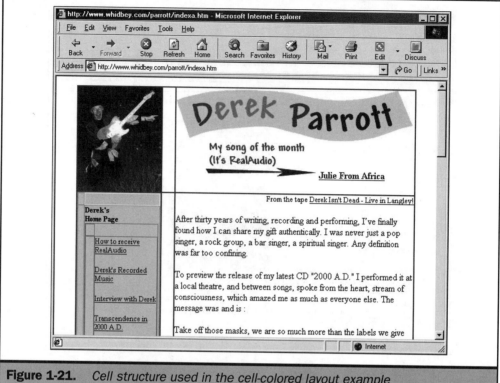

Figure 1-21. *Cell structure used in the cell-colored layout example*

Testing, Testing, Testing

When you finish laying out the pages of your web application, you have to test them to see if they actually work the way you want them to. This process is in two parts: functional testing and usability testing.

Functional Testing

Functional testing determines whether the web application works at the functional level. Do all the links work? Do all the forms work? Do all the images load? FrontPage offers a lot of checks to make sure everything is going to work well, but there is no substitute for clicking all the links and using all the functionality you have designed into the web application in a real-world situation. Surprises always happen. Use the web application under the same conditions the user will experience to see what really is going to happen.

Usability Testing

The hardest testing can be the usability testing. This is where you test the human element. And those pesky humans always seem to do things you didn't expect.

Large corporations organize focus groups to do this testing. All you need to do is invite some friends over and, without telling them anything, watch them use your web application. No coaching! Look at what they click on. Notice how they move through your web application. Watch when they pause. Are they confused? Are they getting the message? Again, no coaching!

They are giving you a lot of valuable information just by how they use your web application. And if they do something wrong, it is probably because your design is unclear and needs more work. Listen to them carefully. Afterwards, ask them for their comments. They may have your solutions for you.

Keep Them Coming Back

No matter what the subject of your web application, you should expect competition. So how do you keep people coming back to your web application? If it is a hobby, such as an application for a favorite pastime, encouraging return visits may not matter to you. However, if you want it to be profitable, you have basically three paths: advertising, subscriptions, or selling merchandise. In each case you need to build and maintain a high volume of users.

Good design for your web pages is only half the battle. You must also make them interesting—there has to be a reason for people to visit them. Keep the following guidelines in mind when creating your web pages: they have to be rich in content, they must stay fresh, and they must make the user feel part of a community.

Rich Content

First and foremost, your web application has to be rich in content, not hype. For example, if it was created for marketing your line of kayaks, include the history of the sport, stories (with photos) of trips your users have taken, information for people new to the sport, hyperlinks to related sites (not necessarily your competitors'), and anything else you can think of that might be interesting to kayakers. Don't just put up an online catalog and expect people to come back.

Stay Fresh

Keep your application fresh. Update as often as you can. People are not going to come back to see the same old stuff. In the kayaking example, consider updating the trips featured every month. In winter (in the Northern Hemisphere), feature trips in New Zealand. Compare your web application to a magazine—no one would subscribe to a magazine that was exactly the same every month; it would be boring. Your web application is no different.

Community

Design and content only go so far to keep people coming back. The final element for a successful web application is a sense of community. The Web is not a one-way environment. It allows the user to respond back to the owners of the web application and also to the other users.

There are three tools that can help you achieve this: guest books, message boards, and chat.

- **Guest books** are the simplest way for the user to interact with the owner of the web application and other users. The user enters their comments in a form, and these comments are added on top of a page with the other users' comments. These are usually CGI scripts. Check with your Internet Service Provider; they often have scripts available for customer use. Another source is Matt's Script Archive at **http://www.worldwidemart.com/scripts/**

- **Message boards** are simply the familiar electronic bulletin boards that have been a mainstay of electronic communication. By creating a place for your users to post their ideas and engage in conversation with other users, you give them an additional reason to come back to your site often. With FrontPage's Discussion Web (see Chapter 3), you can easily create your own message boards.

- **Chat** is a more immediate form of message boards. The conversation takes place in real time, with each user's comments appearing on the other users' screens shortly after they are typed in. Due to the inevitable delays, this can be similar to having a conversation at a party, with several conversation threads going at once. You must be careful with chat rooms to stay focused on the supporting of your application or it can get out of control. You need to monitor what is going on. There are two ways to do chat: *Internet Relay Chat* (IRC) and web-based chat.

To do IRC chat, you need an IRC server, which is simply a software application that can run on the same computer as your web server. The user needs a chat client such as Pirch (**http://www.pirch.com**). The disadvantage of Pirch (from the webmaster's point of view) is that it is a stand-alone application. In other words, the user does not need a web browser, nor does he or she need to log on to your web application to chat.

A better solution (again, from the webmaster's point of view) is a web-based application such as ConferenceRoom (**http://www.webmaster.com**), a Java-based chat server and client applet that is embedded into a web page. This allows you to make your chat an integral part of your web application. The downside to this is that, since you are downloading a client-side application, the download time is increased and it won't work on many browsers. There are also some server-side web-based chat programs such as the CGI chat script at Extropia.com (**http://www.extropia.com**).

The proper balance of design, content, and community is the foundation of a successful web application.

Do It!

Putting together a useful web application can be a lot of work. There's a lot to know, but the best way to learn it is to just do it. Build your web application, and see what works and what doesn't work. Change it and remember what to do for the next time. Not all web applications need to be high-powered business applications. You could just be putting up pictures of your daughter's wedding, or your child's first birthday, or pictures of your vacation.

You can communicate throughout the world using the Web. This book will show you how to do it with FrontPage.

FrontPage 2000

Chapter 2

Exploring FrontPage

Microsoft FrontPage is an authoring and publishing system for creating and delivering formatted content over the Internet or over a local area network (LAN). FrontPage provides the means to design, organize, and deliver an online application, called a *web*, which may be one or more pages on the Internet's World Wide Web (the *Web*) or on a LAN's intranet. To both create and deliver web content requires two or, for the best results, three major modules:

- **FrontPage** itself, which allows you to create, format, and lay out text; add pictures created outside of FrontPage; establish hyperlinks; and organize your webs and their links by using several views of the pages in a web in a drag-and-drop environment.

- **Microsoft Personal Web Server (MSPWS),** which allows you to directly deliver your webs to someone seeking them, as well as to provide file-management support for your webs.

- **FrontPage Server Extensions**, which are available for most popular Internet servers, add the functionality needed to implement the interactive parts of a FrontPage web.

Creating a Web

The FrontPage process of creating a web is unique. The following steps provide an overview:

1. Plan the web—what the goals are; what text, pictures, forms, and hyperlinks it will contain; how it will flow; how the user will get around; and roughly what the pages will look like.

2. If you followed the instructions on installing FrontPage in Appendix A, the Microsoft Personal Web Server should automatically start when you start your computer. If not, start your personal web server, and then start FrontPage.

3. In FrontPage, create the structure of the new web by using a wizard and/or template, or simply by starting with a blank page. If desired, you can also import existing webs into yours.

4. Open Tasks view, and create the items you want to include on the list of tasks to be completed before your web is ready to publish. If you used a wizard to create your structure, you will automatically have items in the Tasks list that you can edit.

5. Open Folders view, and double-click the first page you want to work on to open it in Page view.

6. In Page view, enter, format, and position the text you want to use. Insert the pictures, sound, video, hyperlinks, frames, tables, and forms.

7. As each page is completed, save it and mark the task as complete. From Folders view, select the next page you want to work on, and open it in Page view.

8. Periodically open a web browser such as Microsoft Internet Explorer or Netscape Navigator from Page view using the Preview In Browser toolbar button, and look at the web you are creating (better yet, use both browsers to see what your web will look like). This allows you to test the full functionality of your web with your personal web server. You will be able to see and interact with the web as the user will. You can then revise the web by changing or updating the content, adjusting the page layouts, and reordering the pages and sections using one or more of the FrontPage views.

9. In Reports view, look for errors and potential problems with the web in the reports that are available on files, links, tasks, and themes.

10. In Hyperlinks view, verify the hyperlinks that you have placed in your web.

11. When you are satisfied with your web, release it for use by publishing it on the server from which you want to make it available.

12. Using your browser, download, view, and manipulate the web as the user would. Note the load times and the impression you are getting of the web. Ask others to view and use your web and to give you their impressions and suggestions.

13. Revise and maintain the web as necessary, either by directly editing the copy on the server, or by editing your local copy and then replacing the server copy.

Tip *If someone other than yourself has permission to edit a web you are about to work on, you should copy the current version from the server and then edit it, rather than trusting the copy on your local machine. This avoids the "Twilight Zone Effect," where a web is edited by more than one person at one time. Also see Chapter 23 for information on Microsoft Visual SourceSafe, which prevents this effect on intranets.*

Creating a web with FrontPage gives you important advantages over using other authoring systems. You can

- Graphically visualize and organize a complex web with a number of pages, images, and other elements by using Folders view

- Create and edit a complex web page in a WYSIWYG environment by using Page view without having to use or know HTML, the language of the Web

- Easily manage the tasks that are required to build a web, who has responsibility for them, and their completion by using Tasks view

- Quickly create an entire web, a page, or an element on a page by using wizards or templates

■ Easily add interactive functions such as forms, text searches, and discussion forums without the use of programming, by using FrontPage Components (formerly WebBots)

■ Directly view and use a web on your hard disk by using your personal web server

FrontPage is a true client/server application that provides all of the pieces necessary to create and deliver formatted text and graphical information over both a LAN and the Internet. FrontPage is the client side, and a combination of MSPWS and the FrontPage Extensions is the server side.

FrontPage Views

FrontPage offers six different views you can use when creating or managing a web:

■ **Page view** allows you to create and edit a web page by adding and laying out formatted text, pictures, sounds, video, frames, tables, forms, hyperlinks, and other interactive elements. Page view provides a WYSIWYG (what you see is what you get) editing environment where you can edit new webs and existing webs, including those created elsewhere on the Web. In Page view you can use page wizards, templates, and themes; apply FrontPage Components for interactive functions; create forms and tables; add image maps with clickable hotspots; and convert popular image formats into GIF and JPEG formats used on the Web.

■ **Folders view** allows you to look at and manage an entire web from its files and folders level.

■ **Reports view** allows you to look for errors or potential problems with your web in any one of over ten reports on such subjects as Unlinked Files, Slow Pages, Broken Links, and Component Errors.

■ **Navigation view** allows you to check and change the way a user would get from one page to another and then back to the "Home" page.

■ **Hyperlinks view** allows you to check and organize the hyperlinks in a web in a drag-and-drop environment.

■ **Tasks view**, which displays the Tasks list, allows you to track the tasks required to produce a web, identifying who is responsible for them, their priority, and status.

Within the FrontPage package, you also have the Microsoft Image Composer and PhotoDraw to create and modify pictures for your webs (see Chapter 5).

In the next several sections of this chapter you will further explore the FrontPage views. While it is not mandatory, it will be beneficial if you are looking at these on your own computer. To do that, start FrontPage by opening the Windows Start menu, choosing Programs, and selecting Microsoft FrontPage.

The Microsoft Personal Web Server should be configured to start automatically upon startup of Windows. You can tell it's running by the icon that appears in the notification area on the right end of the taskbar, as shown here. If yours is not running, see Appendix A for more information on how the MSPWS is started and controlled.

Page View

When you first start FrontPage, Page view is normally the view that you will see. If you have chosen to use a template or a wizard to create a web, or you have imported a web, FrontPage may open in Folders view. In that case, double-click the page you want to work on to open it in Page view. You can also click the Page view icon in the Views bar or choose Page in the Views menu. In any case, when you are in Page view, you'll see a window that looks very much like most word processors—in particular, Microsoft Word—as you can see in Figure 2-1. This is where you can enter and edit text. It is also where you can add pictures, frames, tables, forms, sound, video, hyperlinks (including hotspots on pictures), and active FrontPage Components to your page, as you'll read about in a moment.

As you saw in Chapter 1, a web page is a lot of HTML (Hypertext Markup Language) and a little bit of text. If you use a normal word processor or text editor (without any optional HTML features added) to create a web page, you must learn and use HTML. With the FrontPage Page view, you don't need to know HTML. You simply enter the text you want, format it using normal word processing formatting tools, and add pictures, tables, forms, and other elements. When you are done, FrontPage will generate the HTML for you. It is no harder than creating and formatting any other document, and what you see on the screen is very close to what you would see in a web browser. Not only does Page view convert the text and formatting that you enter to HTML, but you can also import RTF, ASCII, and Microsoft Office files into Page view, and they will have the HTML added to them.

If you want to see the HTML behind a web page, select the HTML tab at the bottom of Page view. If you are comfortable with directly editing HTML, you can do so in this HTML window of Page view. If you're not familiar with editing HTML, directly changing the HTML could create a problem.

Formatting Text

The formatting that is available from Page view is quite extensive, but it is limited to the type of formatting that is available with HTML. For example, HTML predefines a number of formatting styles whose names and definitions are unique to the Web. Some

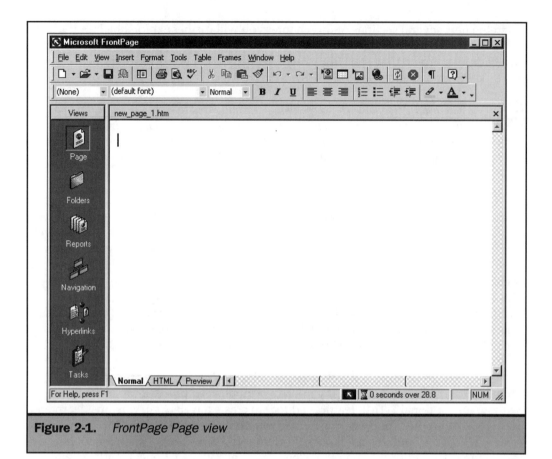

Figure 2-1. FrontPage Page view

formatting tags are dependent on the web browser being used to display your web page. For example, both Internet Explorer and Netscape Navigator accept a Font tag that allows you to change the font (for example, <FONT FACE="Arial">*text to be formatted*</FONT>), but other browsers may not. The paragraph styles supported in FrontPage are described in Table 2-1 and shown in Figure 2-2. They are applied from the Style drop-down list on the left of the toolbar.

*To have text displayed in a specified font, the browser must support the Font tag, and the specified font must be installed on the user's computer. More information about using fonts on the Web, as well as a selection of fonts that can be downloaded, can be found on Microsoft's web site, **http://www.microsoft.com/truetype/**.*

Paragraph Style	How It Looks
Normal	Displayed with the proportional font, normally Times New Roman.
Formatted	Displayed with the fixed-width font, normally Courier.
Address	Displayed with the proportional font in an italic style. Often used to display information on how to contact the owner of the web.
Heading 1-6	Displayed with the proportional font in a bold style in six sizes.

Table 2-1.   *Paragraph Styles*

 The Formatted paragraph style is the only tag that allows you to use multiple spaces in text. HTML throws out all but one space when it encounters multiple spaces, except when the Formatted style is used. This can be used for forms, to get labels to right-align and text boxes to left-align. You can also use tables to align labels and form fields (see Chapters 8 and 9).

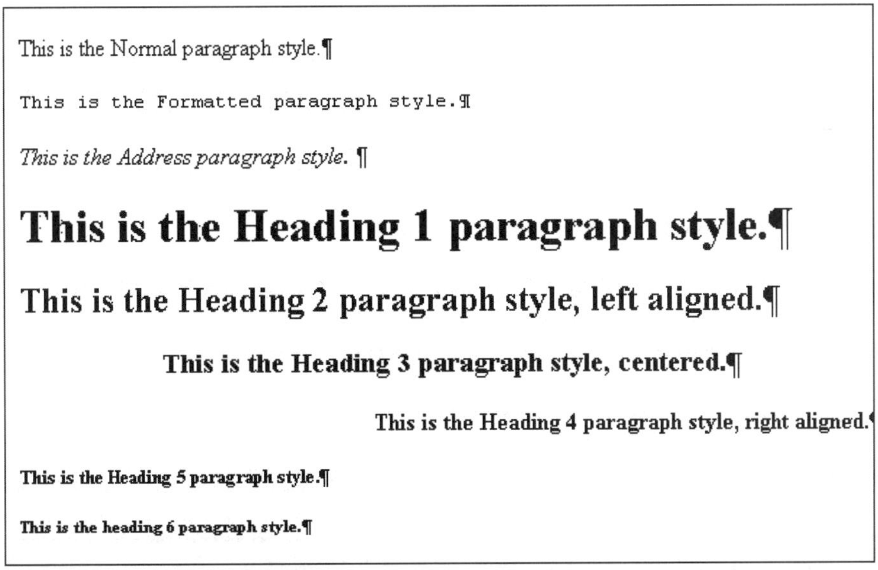

This is the Normal paragraph style.¶

This is the Formatted paragraph style.¶

This is the Address paragraph style. ¶

This is the Heading 1 paragraph style.¶

This is the Heading 2 paragraph style, left aligned.¶

This is the Heading 3 paragraph style, centered.¶

This is the Heading 4 paragraph style, right aligned.

This is the Heading 5 paragraph style.¶

This is the heading 6 paragraph style.¶

Figure 2-2.   *Examples of paragraph styles*

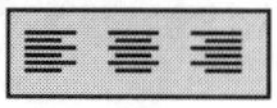

Any of the paragraph styles can use left, center, or right paragraph alignment applied either from the Paragraph dialog box (accessed by choosing Paragraph from the Format menu) or with the alignment buttons in the toolbar. You can also use Justify alignment available from the Paragraph dialog box to align both the left and right sides.

Standard font (or character) styles that are available are regular, bold, italic, and bold italic. These are applied using the formatting toolbar buttons for that purpose. In addition there are 18 font effects that are described in Table 2-2 and some samples are shown in Figure 2-3. The font effects are applied in the Font dialog box, which is opened with the Font option on the Format menu.

Strong, Emphasis, Sample, Definition, Citation, Variable, Keyboard, and Code effects are *logical* styles. The appearance of the text with these tags is determined by the browser. Older browsers allowed you to change the defaults for these tags, but this feature seems to have disappeared. Bold, Italic, Underline, Strikethrough, Overline, Blink, Superscript, Subscript, Small Caps, All Caps, Capitalize, and Hidden are *physical* styles that are not changeable by the browser.

Note   *Unlike earlier versions of FrontPage, FrontPage 2000 generates the <B> tag for bold and the <I> tag for italic. If you want the <STRONG> and <EM> tags, you must select Strong and Emphasis from the Font dialog box.*

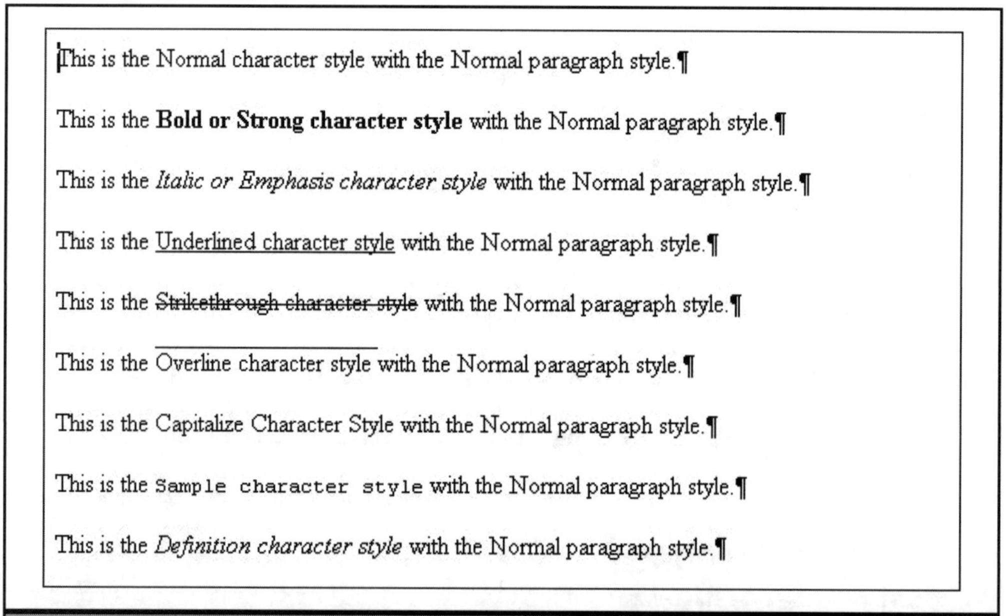

This is the Normal character style with the Normal paragraph style.¶

This is the **Bold or Strong character style** with the Normal paragraph style.¶

This is the *Italic or Emphasis character style* with the Normal paragraph style.¶

This is the Underlined character style with the Normal paragraph style.¶

This is the ~~Strikethrough character style~~ with the Normal paragraph style.¶

This is the Overline character style with the Normal paragraph style.¶

This is the Capitalize Character Style with the Normal paragraph style.¶

This is the Sample character style with the Normal paragraph style.¶

This is the *Definition character style* with the Normal paragraph style.¶

Figure 2-3.   *Examples of some of the available font effects*

Font Effect	What It Does
Underline	Makes text underlined.
Strikethrough	Puts a line through text.
Overline	Puts a line above the text.
Blink	Makes text blink (defined only in Netscape Navigator).
Superscript	Raises text above the baseline.
Subscript	Lowers text below the baseline.
Small Caps	Makes normally lowercase letters small capitals.
All Caps	Makes all letters capitals.
Capitalize	Makes the leading character of all words a capital.
Hidden	The affected text will not be displayed.
Strong	Usually makes text bold.
Emphasis	Usually makes text italic.
Sample	Formats text in the Sample style, normally in a fixed-width font.
Definition	Formats text in the Definition style, normally italic.
Citation	Formats text in the Citation style, normally italic.
Variable	Formats text in the Variable style, normally italic.
Keyboard	Formats text in the Keyboard style, normally the fixed-width font with a bold style.
Code	Formats text in the Code style, normally the fixed-width font.

Table 2-2.   *Font Effects*

Characters in any style can be one of seven preset sizes from 8 points to 36 points, as shown in Figure 2-4; one of 16 preset colors or a custom color; and either superscript or subscript position. Character size and color can be changed with the respective toolbar drop-down list or button, shown here, or through the Font dialog box.

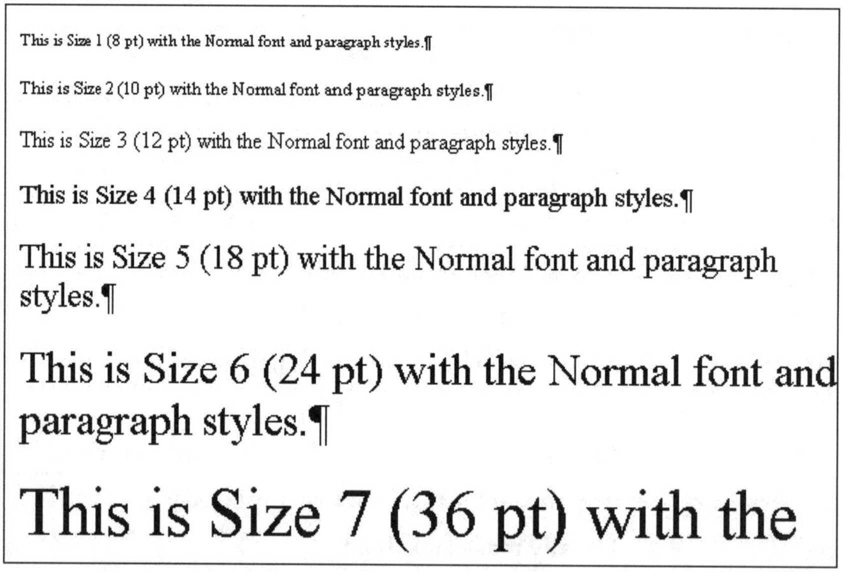

This is Size 1 (8 pt) with the Normal font and paragraph styles.¶

This is Size 2 (10 pt) with the Normal font and paragraph styles.¶

This is Size 3 (12 pt) with the Normal font and paragraph styles.¶

This is Size 4 (14 pt) with the Normal font and paragraph styles.¶

This is Size 5 (18 pt) with the Normal font and paragraph styles.¶

This is Size 6 (24 pt) with the Normal font and paragraph styles.¶

This is Size 7 (36 pt) with the

Figure 2-4.   *The seven preset font sizes*

In addition to the paragraph styles that you have already seen, HTML and FrontPage allow you to define several types of lists. Table 2-3 describes the available list styles, which are shown in Figure 2-5. Note that at this time there is no difference between bulleted, directory, and menu lists. It is possible that this will change in the future.

Tip   *You can end any list by pressing CTRL+ENTER.*

Not all web browsers treat the formatting in a web the same; they may even ignore some formatting. Blink, in particular, is a style that is ignored by all but Netscape Navigator. Also, several styles may produce exactly the same effect in many browsers. For example, in most instances, the Emphasis, Citation, Definition, and Italic styles often produce the same effect. If you are creating a web for a broad public audience, it is worthwhile to test it in recent versions of the two primary web browsers: Netscape Navigator and Microsoft Internet Explorer.

Tip   *Use only the physical styles that exclude Blink to be assured of the greatest consistency.*

The Font dialog box or the Font Color button on the toolbar allow you to set the color of selected text. You can also set the color of text for an entire page through the Background tab on the Page Properties dialog box, which is opened from the File menu

List Style	How It Looks
Numbered List	Series of paragraphs with a hanging indent and a number on the left
Bulleted List	Series of paragraphs with a hanging indent and a bullet on the left
Directory List	Series of short (normally less than 20 characters) paragraphs
Menu List	Series of paragraphs, one line or less in length, in a vertically compact format
Definition and Definition Term	Pairs of paragraphs as terms, which are left-aligned, and definitions, which are indented similarly to dictionary definitions

Table 2-3. *List Styles*

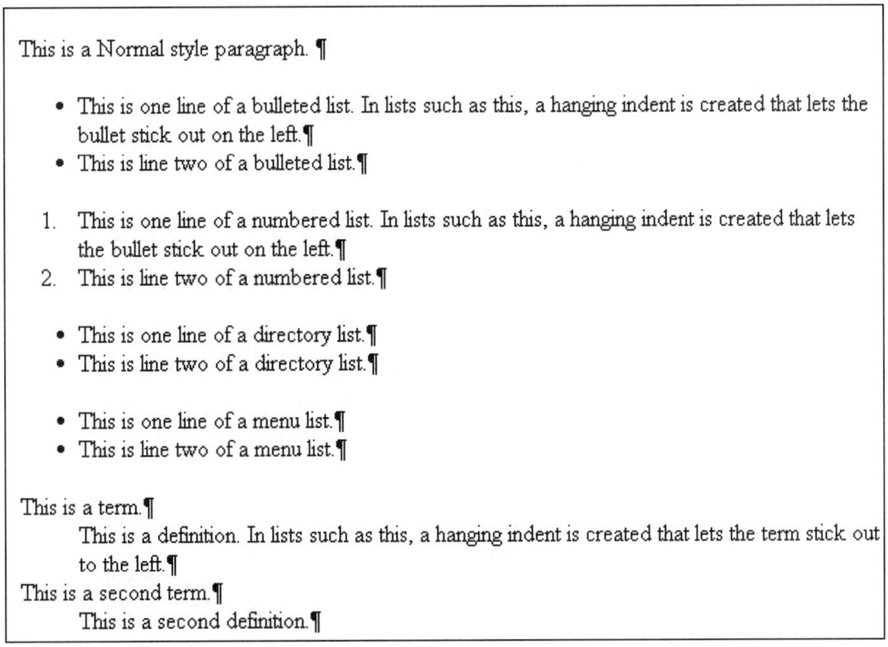

This is a Normal style paragraph. ¶

- This is one line of a bulleted list. In lists such as this, a hanging indent is created that lets the bullet stick out on the left.¶
- This is line two of a bulleted list.¶

1. This is one line of a numbered list. In lists such as this, a hanging indent is created that lets the bullet stick out on the left.¶
2. This is line two of a numbered list.¶

- This is one line of a directory list.¶
- This is line two of a directory list.¶

- This is one line of a menu list.¶
- This is line two of a menu list.¶

This is a term.¶
    This is a definition. In lists such as this, a hanging indent is created that lets the term stick out to the left.¶
This is a second term.¶
    This is a second definition.¶

Figure 2-5. *List style examples*

and shown in Figure 2-6. Colored text is useful on colored backgrounds to create an unusual look on a page.

You can open the Page Properties dialog box by right-clicking the page and selecting Page Properties from the context menu.

Inserting Pictures

FrontPage allows you to add pictures to a web page in two ways:

- You can add a background picture, which you can specify in the Page Properties dialog box (Figure 2-6), that fills a page. By placing a picture in the background, you can enter text on top of it.

A background picture will be tiled if it doesn't fill the screen. Even if it fills the screen at 640×480, it may be tiled at higher resolutions.

- You can add a stand-alone picture that you can specify in the Image dialog box opened from the Insert menu (Insert | Picture) or the Insert Picture button on the toolbar. You can size the picture either before you insert it (using a graphics

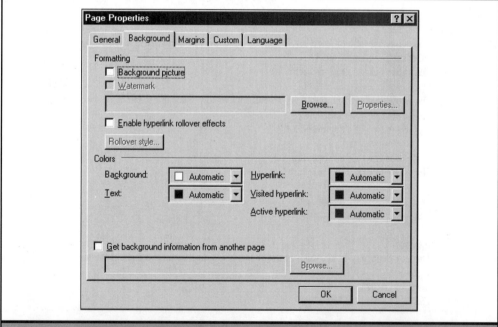

Figure 2-6.   *Setting background colors in the Page Properties dialog box*

program) or after using FrontPage. Once it is inserted and selected, the Picture toolbar automatically appears at the bottom of the FrontPage window as you can see in Figure 2-7. You also can right-click the picture and select Picture Properties to open the Picture Properties dialog box. Here you can enter the alignment; the amount of space to place above and to the left of a picture; the thickness of a border, if any; and, on the General tab, the alternative text to display if the picture is not displayed. You can also identify a hyperlink to follow if the user clicks on the picture.

Tip   *You can left-, center-, or right-align a picture by selecting it and clicking the Align Left, Center, or Align Right buttons in the toolbar normally used to align text.*

Pictures that are included in web pages must be GIF, JPEG, or PNG format. This has presented a problem in the past, because many clip-art and graphics programs use other formats. FrontPage has solved this problem by allowing you to import other file

Figure 2-7.   *Picture toolbar appears at the bottom of the FrontPage window when a picture is selected*

formats that FrontPage will convert to GIF, JPEG, or PNG. The file formats that
FrontPage can accept are

GIF (.GIF)
JPEG (.JPG or .JFF)
PNG (.PNG)
Kodak PhotoCD (.PCD)
PCX (.PCX)
Encapsulated PostScript (.EPS)
SUN Raster (.RAS)
Targa (.TGA)
TIFF (.TIF)
Windows Metafile (.WMF)
Windows or OS/2 bitmap (.BMP)

   *FrontPage converts pictures with up to 256 colors to GIF files and pictures with more
than 256 colors to JPEG files.*

Remember, pictures take a long time to download and therefore become frustrating
for the user who has to wait for them. Even though a picture may look really neat, if
users have to wait several minutes for it to download, they probably are not going to
appreciate it or stick around to look at it.

   *You can tell how long a page will take to download using a 28.8 Kbps modem (or some
other speed you choose) by the number of seconds on the right of the status bar, like this:*

> ⏳ 7 seconds over 28.8

Adding Forms

So far you have seen how to display text and pictures on a web page—how to deliver
information to the user. In Page view you can also add a form in which the user of your
web can send you information. You can create a form either field-by-field, or all at once
by using the Form Page Wizard. You'll see how the Form Page Wizard works in a later
section of this chapter ("Working with Wizards and Templates"). For now, let's look at
the field-by-field approach. You can use the form option on the Insert menu to create a
Forms toolbar with the forms option on it by "dragging off" the menu, as shown in
Figure 2-8. The Forms toolbar buttons are described in Table 2-4.

To use the Forms toolbar, simply place the insertion point where you want the
field, and then click the button for the field you want. A dialog box will open and ask
you to name the field and specify other aspects of it, such as the width of the box on the
form and the number of characters that can be entered. Figure 2-9 shows one way a

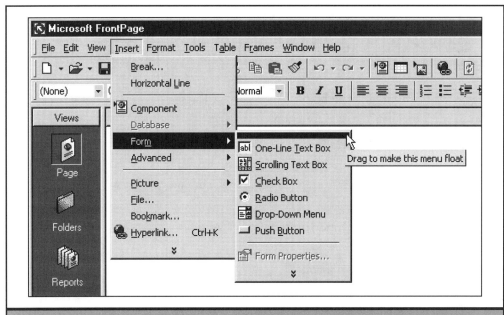

Figure 2-8.   *You can create a Forms toolbar by "dragging it off" the Insert menu*

form can be built. In Chapter 9 you'll go through the detailed steps of designing and building a form.

> **Tip**
>
> *If you put form fields in the same form block (area created by the Form button and enclosed by a dashed line) and use SHIFT+ENTER to create a new line, you can stack the fields closer together, and they will all have the same form properties.*

> **Tip**
>
> *If you format form fields with the Formatted paragraph style, you can align the labels and text boxes using multiple spaces as shown in Figure 2-9. However, it's not always possible to get all the form elements to line up exactly using Formatted text. This is because a space in a form text box is not the same width as a character space. As you will see in the section "Working with Wizards and Templates" later in this chapter, you can also use tables to align form elements, often with better results.*

When you create a form field by field, you need to provide a means of gathering the data that is entered on it. With FrontPage you can handle the form data in a number of ways:

Button	Description	Example(s) in Figure 2-9
	Form	Dashed outline of form
	One-line text box	Address
	Scrolling text box	Comments
	Check box	Using our products?
	Radio or Option button	Age
	Drop-down menu	Which products?
	Push button	Submit and Reset
	Image	Thanks
	Label separate from field	E-mail address
	Form Properties	Opens the Form Properties dialog box (not shown in Figure 2-9)

Table 2-4.   *Form Field Creation Buttons*

- You can save the information to a file as HTML, formatted text, or as a text database that can be imported into most database programs.
- You can also have the results sent as an e-mail or posted to a discussion group, or register the sender to access a password-protected area of a web.
- You can also have the form results sent to a custom script for processing.

To choose how your form results will be handled, right-click the form, and then choose Form Properties. This opens the Form Properties dialog box, shown in

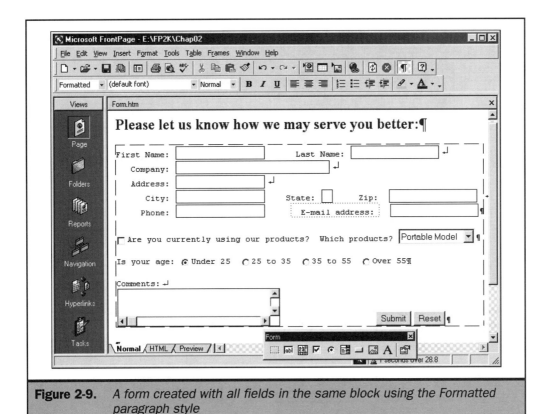

Figure 2-9. *A form created with all fields in the same block using the Formatted paragraph style*

Figure 2-10, where you can select or create a file to save the form information, specify an e-mail address to send it to, or select a custom script to process the information. Clicking the Options button opens the Options For Saving Results Of Form dialog box shown in Figure 2-11. Here you can set the options for each method of processing the form data. You may or may not want to include the field names in the output or in the additional information. You must repeat these steps for each field that is in a separate form block (the area enclosed with a dashed line) with the options under the Saved Fields tab of the Options For Saving Results Of Form dialog box.

When you create a form, you may have certain fields that must be filled in (such as first and last name) or fields that have to contain a certain type of information (such as numeric for a phone number). To force the user to enter the proper type of information where required, you can create validation rules for each form field. You do this by right-clicking the form field you want validated, then selecting Form Field Validation from the context menu to open a validation dialog box. The Text Box Validation dialog box is shown in Figure 2-12. (Different types of form fields will display different validation dialog boxes.)

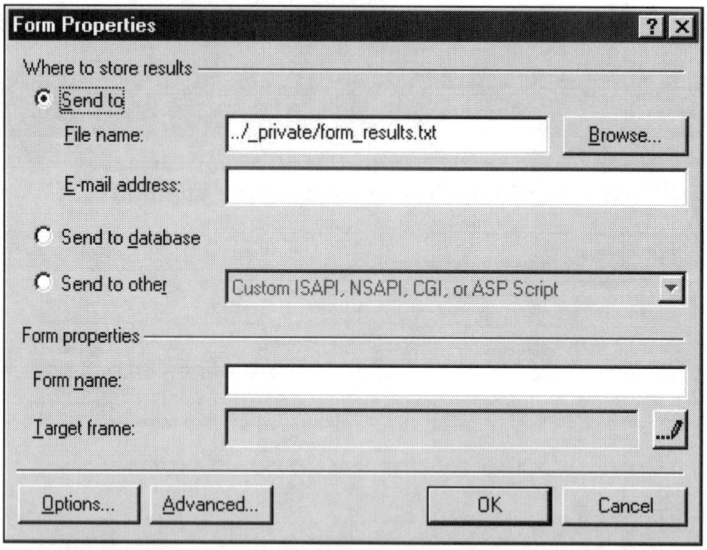

Figure 2-10. *Form Properties dialog box*

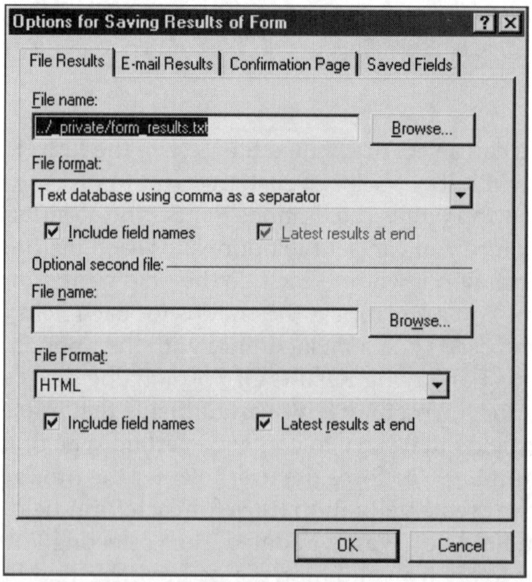

Figure 2-11. *Options for Savings Results of Form dialog box*

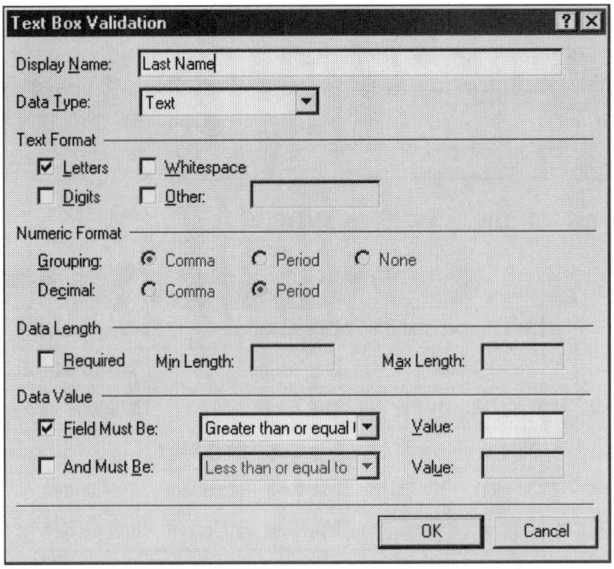

![Text Box Validation dialog box]

Figure 2-12. *Text Box Validation dialog box*

Using Tables

In webs, tables provide a means of dividing some or all of a page into rows and columns. Tables can be used to display tabular data as well as to simply position information on a page, perhaps with a border around it. FrontPage has an extensive capability for creating and working with tables such as the one shown in Figure 2-13.

Tables are created by use of either the Insert Table button in the toolbar (which allows you to set the number of rows and columns in the table) or the Insert option on the Table menu, which opens the Insert Table dialog box. This dialog box allows you to specify the size, layout, and width of the table you are creating. Once a table is created, you can modify it through the table's context menu, which appears when you can right-click the table. From the menu, you can choose Table Properties to change the overall properties of the table, or Cell Properties to change the properties of a single cell. Chapter 8 will go into tables in depth.

Working with Wizards and Templates

In Page view, wizards and templates allow you to automatically create a new page with many features on it. Wizards and templates differ only in the amount of interaction between you and the computer during the creation process. *Templates* create a ready-made page without interacting with you. *Wizards* use one or more dialog boxes

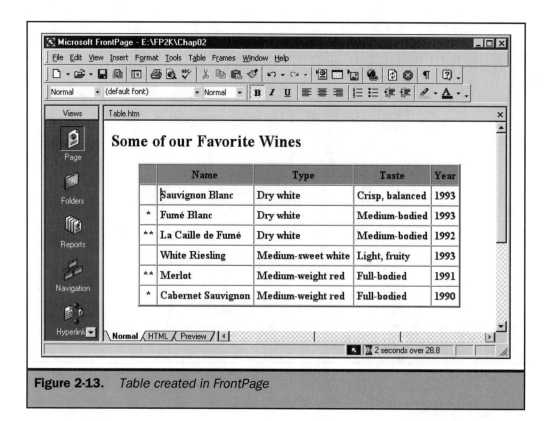

Figure 2-13.   *Table created in FrontPage*

to ask you a series of questions during creation. Based on your answers to these questions, a customized page is created. Whether you use a template or a wizard, you can customize the resultant web pages and elements in Page view. The General tab of the New dialog box (opened from the File menu or by pressing CTRL+N) in Page view provides a number of *page* wizards and templates (as distinct from the *web* wizards and templates available in Folders view) to help you create many specialized pages. These are shown in Figure 2-14.

The New Page button on the toolbar gives you a new page using the Normal Page template—it does not open the New dialog box, which provides access to the list of templates and wizards.

For example, to use a wizard to create a custom form similar to the one created earlier, you would select the Form Page Wizard. This opens a series of dialog boxes

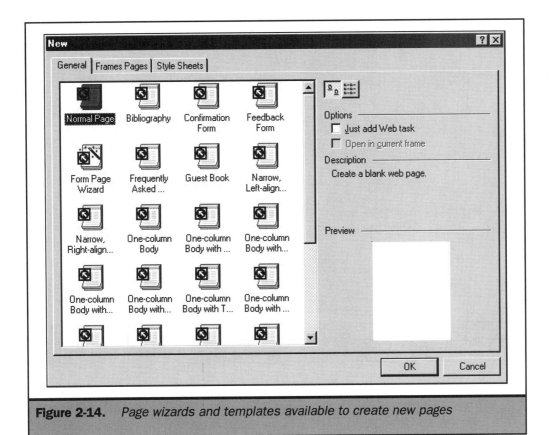

Figure 2-14.   *Page wizards and templates available to create new pages*

that ask you questions about what you want on the form you want to build, an example of which is shown in Figure 2-15. When you are done, a form is automatically created (Figure 2-16).

Note   *The form in Figure 2-16 was created by use of a table. The Form Wizard can also generate Formatted text for aligning labels and form fields.*

The page templates, like their web counterparts in Folders view, simply create a new formatted page for you without any input from you. With both wizards and templates, though, you can customize the resulting web page as you see fit. The wizards and templates provide an excellent way to get a quick start on a large variety of web pages, as described in Table 2-5.

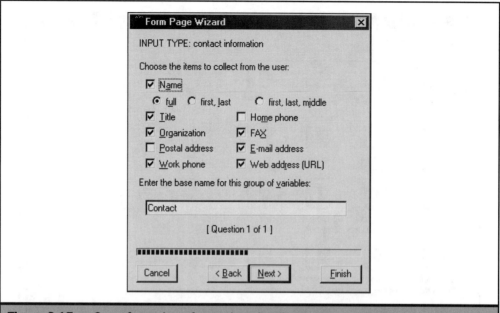

Figure 2-15.   *One of a series of questions leading to the creation of a form*

Tip   *Wizards and templates quickly get you over the "where do I start" hurdle and give you a "first cut" that you can customize.*

FRAMES   Frames are a way to organize a web page by combining several pages on one page, each in a tile or *frame*. You use the Frames Pages tab of the New dialog box to create the several pages necessary for a given layout. In the Frames Pages tab you can choose one of several templates, as shown in Table 2-6, or you can create a custom layout with the rows, columns, and dimensions that you want. After creating the layout you want, you are shown the layout and asked how you want to determine the page contents, as shown in Figure 2-17. Frames are discussed in-depth in Chapter 8.

Note   *Frames are another area of HTML programming that is not supported by all browsers, though Netscape Navigator has supported them since version 2.0, and Internet Explorer has supported them since version 3.0. As you will learn in Chapter 8, you can create alternate pages that will be loaded by browsers that do not support frames when a frame page is encountered. (A frame page defines and identifies the set of pages, each containing the contents of one frame, that go together to create the single frame page in a browser.)*

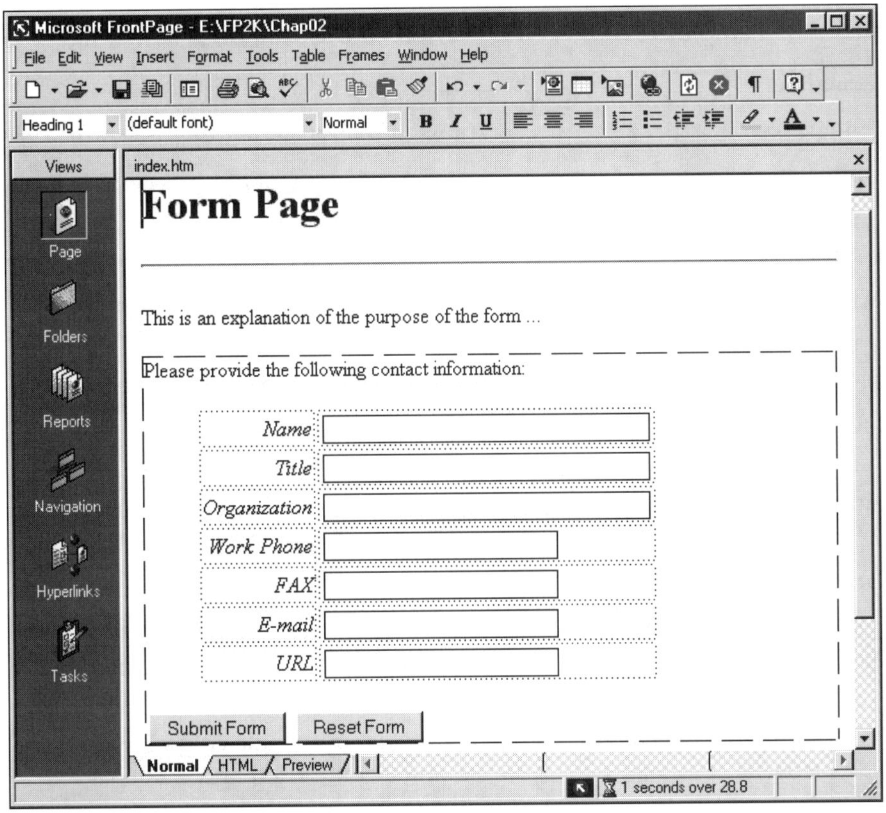

Figure 2-16. *A form created by the Form Page Wizard*

Using FrontPage Components

FrontPage Components (WebBots, in earlier versions of FrontPage) provide automation in a web—the ability to do more than just provide text and pictures on a page. For example, components return information to you that has been entered on a form, or enable users to participate in a discussion group. Most of FrontPage's Components, though, just make creating and maintaining a web easier. In other web-authoring packages, this same capability requires various levels of programming. In FrontPage you simply have to set up and enable a component.

The Discussion Component is automatically enabled when you create a new web from Folders view by using the Discussion Web Wizard. The Save Results Component is automatically enabled when you use the Form Page Wizard in Page view, or as you saw earlier, you can enable it manually in the Forms Properties dialog box. All other

Wizard or Template	What Is Created on a New Page
Normal Page	Blank page
Bibliography	List of references to other pages or works
Confirmation Form	Acknowledgment of the receipt of input from the user
Feedback Form	Form for a user to give you comments
Form Page Wizard	Custom form you have designed using this wizard
Frequently Asked Questions	List of questions and their answers
Guest Book	Form for users of your web to leave their identification and comments
Narrow, Left-aligned Body	Body text formatted in a narrow, left-aligned column on the left
Narrow, Right-aligned Body	Body text formatted in a narrow, right-aligned column on the right
One-column Body	Single-column body text centered on the page
One-column Body with Contents and Sidebar	Body text in a single column with the contents on the left and a sidebar on the right
One-column Body with Contents on Left	Contents in a narrow column on the left with body text on the right
One-column Body with Contents on Right	Contents in a narrow column on the right with body text on the left
One-column Body with Staggered Sidebar	Body text in one column on the right with two columns of staggered sidebar on the left
One-column Body with Two Sidebars	Body text in a center column with a two-column staggered sidebar on the left and a one-column sidebar on the right
One-column Body with Two-column Sidebar	Body text in a single column on the left with a two-column sidebar on the right

Table 2-5.   *Page Wizards and Templates Available in Page View*

Wizard or Template	What Is Created on a New Page
Search Page	Search engine for finding keywords within the pages of a web
Table of Contents	List, in outline format, of hyperlinks to the other pages in your web
Three-column Body	Body text in three columns
Two-column Body	Body text in two columns
Two-column Body with Contents and Sidebar	Body text in two columns with a sidebar-like contents column on the left and a sidebar on the right.
Two-column Body with Contents on Left	Body text in two right-aligned columns with contents in a left-aligned column
Two-column Staggered Body	Body text in two staggered columns
Two-column Staggered Body with Contents and Sidebar	Body text in two staggered columns in the center with a contents column on the left and a sidebar on the right
User Registration	Form for registering to use a secure web
Wide Body with headings	Body text in a single wide body with subheadings

Table 2-5.   *Page Wizards and Templates Available in Page View* (continued)

Template	What Is Created on a New Frame Page
Banner and Contents	Creates three frames: a banner across the top, a contents frame on the left, and a main frame.
Contents	Creates two frames: a contents frame on the left and a main frame.
Footer	Creates a main frame with a narrow footer frame across the bottom.

Table 2-6.   *Frame Templates Available in Page View*

Template	What Is Created on a New Frame Page
Footnotes	Creates a main frame with a footnote frame across the bottom.
Header	Creates a main frame with a narrow header frame across the top.
Header, Footer and Contents	Creates four frames: a header frame across the top, a contents frame on the left side, a main frame, and a footer frame across the bottom.
Horizontal Split	Creates two frames, split horizontally.
Nested Hierarchy	Creates a full-height contents frame on the left, a header frame, and a main frame.
Top-Down Hierarchy	Creates three frames, split horizontally.
Vertical Split	Creates two frames, split vertically.

Table 2-6. *Frame Templates Available in Page View* (continued)

components are enabled through the Insert Component menu (shown next) opened by choosing Component from the Insert menu. The components that you can place on a page are described in Table 2-7.

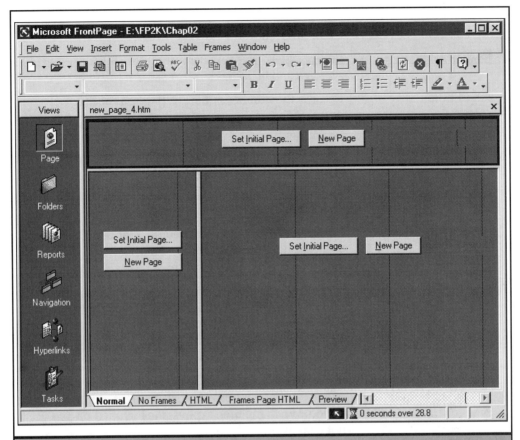

Figure 2-17.   *Frame page layout allowing you to choose each frame's content*

Component	Capability Added to a Web Page
Office Spreadsheet	Adds an interactive spreadsheet to a web page in which the web viewer can change the data and see the results.
Office PivotTable	Adds an interactive PivotTable to a web page in which the web viewer can change the data and see the results.
Office Chart	Adds an interactive chart to a web page for which the web viewer can change the data and see the results.

Table 2-7.   *Components That Can Be Inserted on a Page from the Insert Components Menu*

Component	Capability Added to a Web Page
Banner Ad Manager	Inserts a banner in a web page within which a series of pictures will be rotated.
Hit Counter	Records the number of times a page has been downloaded.
Hover Button	Inserts a button in a web page that will change color and execute a special effect (such as "Glow") when the mouse pointer is hovering over it.
Marquee	Inserts a marquee on a web page in which text is scrolled or slid across the marquee.
Confirmation Field	Echoes the information entered on a form by users, so you can show users what they entered.
Include Page	Allows you to include one web page on another. If you want to have a constant header on every page, you can put the header on a web page and then include that page on all others in the web.
Scheduled Image	Allows you to display an image in a web page for a given period. When the time expires, the image is not displayed.
Scheduled Include Page	Allows you to include one page on another for a given period. When the time expires, the included page is not displayed.
Substitution	Substitutes a value on a web page with a configuration variable when the page is viewed by the user.
Categories	Allows you to establish dynamic categories for grouping the pages in a web. Dynamic categories allow the addiing and removing of pages with the automatic updating of the category list.
Search Form	Inserts a Search For field with Start and Reset buttons to allow the user to search your web.
Table of Contents	Creates a table of contents that lists all of the pages in a web hierarchically.

Table 2-7. *Components That Can Be Inserted on a Page from the Insert Components Menu* (continued)

Adding Hyperlinks and Mapping Hotspots

In Page view you can add hyperlinks (or *links*), which allow the user of a web to quickly jump from one page to another, or to a particular element on the same or another page (called a *bookmark*), or to a different web or web site. You can make either text or a picture be the element the user clicks to make the link, and you can map certain areas of a picture to be different links (called *hotspots*). You create a link by first selecting the object that you want the user to click and then clicking the Hyperlink button in the toolbar, or by choosing Hyperlink from the Insert menu. In either case, the Create Hyperlink dialog box will open as shown in Figure 2-18.

Within the Create Hyperlink dialog box, you can select a bookmark on any open page or just an open page without a bookmark, any page in the current web with or without a bookmark, any URL or address on the World Wide Web, or a new page yet to be defined in the current web. The address on the Web can be another web or HTTP site, or an FTP, Gopher, Mail, News, Telnet, or Wais site, all of which are older

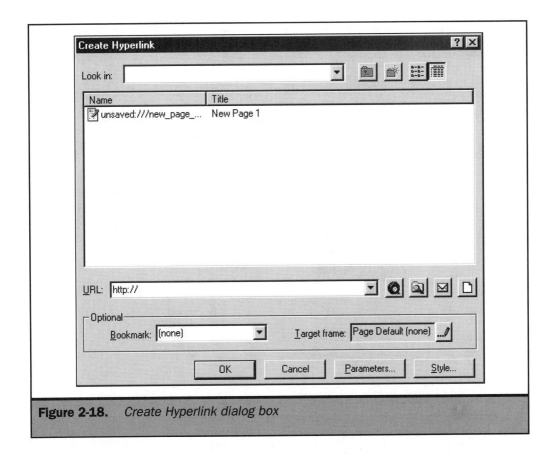

Figure 2-18.   *Create Hyperlink dialog box*

alternative Internet services to the World Wide Web, but, except for Mail, seldom used. When you have created a hyperlink, the object on which the user is to click changes to a different color and may become underlined.

A picture can have its entire area defined as a link, or you can identify specific areas in a picture as separate links, while any unidentified areas are assigned a default link. For example, you could provide a map that allows the user to quickly get to information about a particular area of the world by simply clicking that area, as you can see in Figure 2-19.

 The left end of the status bar informs you of the link under the mouse pointer.

You place hotspots on a picture by using the hotspot drawing tools (shown next) located on the right side of the Picture toolbar. The Picture toolbar will be displayed when you select the picture, if it isn't already displayed. (Working with pictures is covered in Chapter 5.)

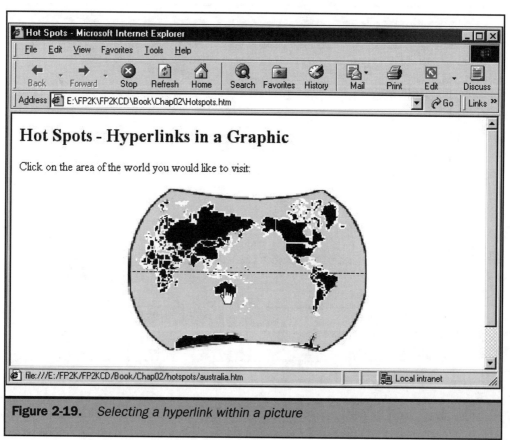

Figure 2-19.   *Selecting a hyperlink within a picture*

First select the picture, then select the rectangle, circle, or polygon tool. Use it to draw a border around the area of the picture you want to be the hotspot. When you complete a closed area, you'll be asked to enter the URL (bookmark, web site, or page reference) where the browser should transfer when that area is clicked. When you are done identifying all the hotspots, your picture will look something like this (although users won't see the lines in a browser):

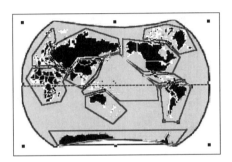

 Another useful tool on the Image toolbar is the Set Transparent Color tool. This tool lets you click any color in the picture and make it transparent, allowing the page background to show through.

 Transparent backgrounds only work with GIF 89a files. If you try using a transparent background with a JPEG, you'll get a dialog box that says the JPEG will be converted to a GIF.

Other FrontPage Views

While Page view is the place where you construct the individual pages that make up a web, FrontPage offers you five other views that let you look at the web at a higher level. You can look at the complete web and see all of it pages, files, and links, or you can look at a segment of the web and see the components of that segment. As you saw earlier in this chapter, the other views are Folders view, Reports view, Navigation view, Hyperlinks view, and Tasks view.

Folders View

 Folders view is similar in a number of ways to the Windows Explorer. In Folders view, for example, the left pane (or Folder List) displays a hierarchical structure of folders, while the right pane (or Contents pane) displays a list of the files supporting the web, as shown in Figure 2-20.

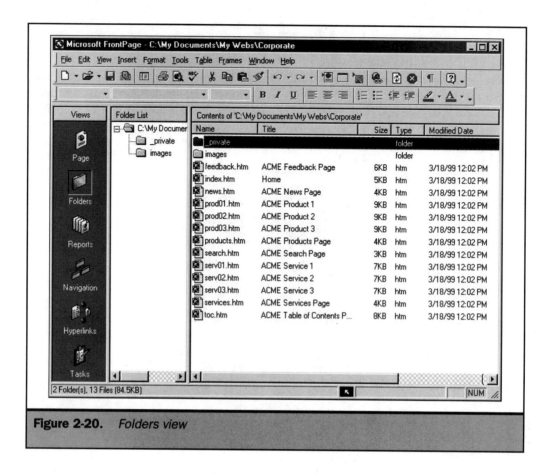

Figure 2-20. Folders view

By clicking the plus and minus icons in the left pane, you can expand or collapse the view of the hierarchy. If you right-click an object in either pane, its context menu will open, which, among other options, allows you to open the object's Properties dialog box. A final way that Folders view is like the Windows Explorer is that in Folders view, you can sort the list of files by clicking the column name immediately above the list.

In Folders view, you can use wizards and templates to automatically create entire webs including a full set of pages, links, and other elements. As in Page view, wizards and templates differ only in the amount of interaction between you and the computer during the creation process. Web templates create a ready-made web without interacting with you. Web wizards use one or more dialog boxes to ask you a series of questions during creation. Based on your answers to these questions, a customized web is created. You can customize the resultant web pages and elements with Page view. You can also create a web with a single blank page by double-clicking the One Page Web icon in the New FrontPage Web dialog box, or import an existing web by double-clicking the Import Web Wizard icon.

The web templates and wizards that are currently available in FrontPage are shown in Table 2-8. You can use these templates and wizards to create either new webs or additions to existing webs. Also, wizards and templates automatically create the tasks in Tasks view that support the pages that are created. As you'll see in Chapter 4, you can build your own templates to create a standard look—for example, across all departments in a corporate intranet.

Template or Wizard	Characteristics of Web Created
Templates	
One Page Web	Has a single blank page.
Customer Support Web	Tells customers how to contact you and provides a form where they can leave information so you can contact them. Includes an FTP download area, a frequently asked questions (FAQ) area, and a form for leaving suggestions and contact information.
Empty Web	Has no pages, so you can import pages from another web.
Personal Web	Has a single page with personal and professional information and ways to be contacted.
Project Web	Provides a way to communicate the status of a project including its schedule, who is working on it, and its accomplishments.
Wizards	
Corporate Presence Wizard	Provides information about a company, including what it does, what its products and services are, how to contact it, and a means to leave feedback for it.
Discussion Web Wizard	Is an electronic bulletin board where users can leave messages and others can reply to those messages.
Import Web Wizard	Provides assistance in collecting all of the components of a web and bringing them into FrontPage.

Table 2-8. *Web Templates and Wizards*

Reports View

Reports view provides a series of reports that tell you about your web, as you can see in Figure 2-21. To see the detail of any report, double-click it. You can then return to the Site Summary by opening the View menu and choosing Reports Site Summary. There is a great amount of valuable information in the reports that FrontPage provides. The best way to get familiar with it is to open each of the reports and study the contents.

Some of the reports do not open and only provide information at the summary level.

You can open a Reporting toolbar from the View menu Toolbars option; once open, it will automatically appear whenever you open the Reports view. The Reporting toolbar lets you select what is displayed in the Reports view. You can also edit and verify hyperlinks; and using the down arrow in the upper-left corner, you can add or remove (customize) the other toolbar contents.

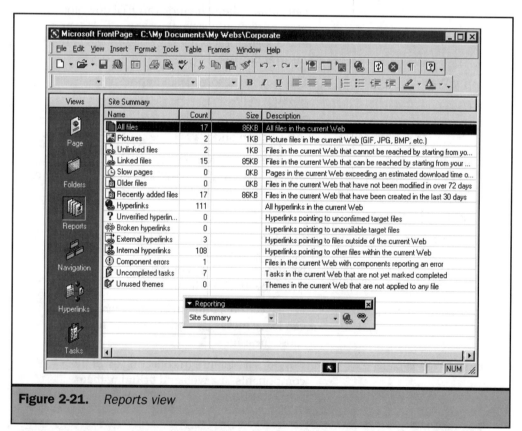

Figure 2-21. *Reports view*

Navigation View

Navigation view, shown in Figure 2-22, gives you a graphical overview of how the web is organized. A list of the files supporting the web is displayed in the left pane, and a graphical representation of the hyperlinks used to go from page to page is shown in the right pane. By clicking the plus and minus signs in the right pane, you can expand or collapse the hierarchy of links. You can also drag a page from one position to another and change its link by doing so.

Hyperlinks View

Hyperlinks view allows you to look at the links among the pages in a web, as well as the links to external sites. Web pages and their links create a hierarchical structure that is shown in the Folder List, which is the left pane of Hyperlinks view, as shown in Figure 2-23. You create this structure either by adding pages one at a time and then linking them, or by using one of the web wizards or templates to automatically create the desired pages and their links.

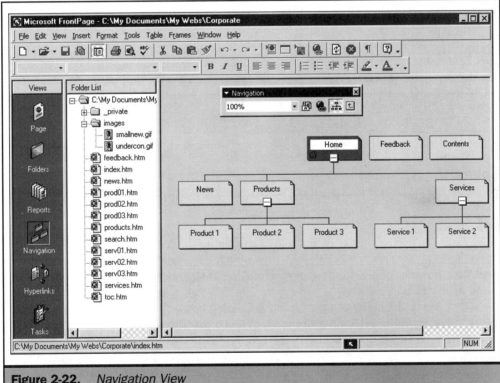

Figure 2-22. *Navigation View*

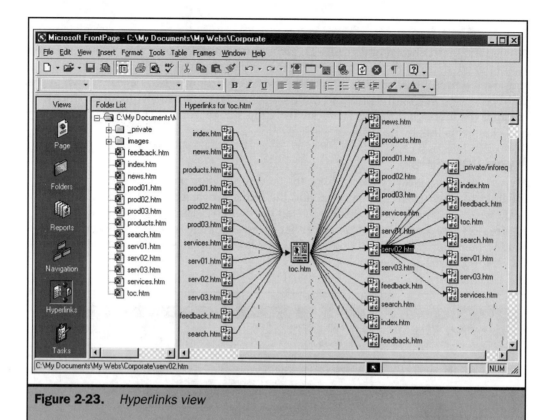

Figure 2-23. Hyperlinks view

Tasks View

Task view (Figure 2-24) lists the tasks that must be accomplished to complete the web application you are building. The items on the Tasks list are placed there either by a web wizard

or by you. You can add tasks in any view by opening the New button and choosing Tasks. You can also add tasks by right-clicking a file in another view and selecting Add Task from the context menu, or by choosing Task and Add Task from the Edit menu in any view.

When you add a new task, the New Task dialog box will appear. Here, give the task a name, assign it to an individual, give it a priority, and type in a description. Once you have a complete Tasks list, use it to go to the various sections of a web that still require work by right-clicking a task and selecting Start Task. This will open Page view and display the page that needs work. When you have completed the task, you can return to Tasks view, then right-click the task, and select Mark As Completed from the context menu, which will mark the task as completed and leave it in the list, or

GETTING STARTED

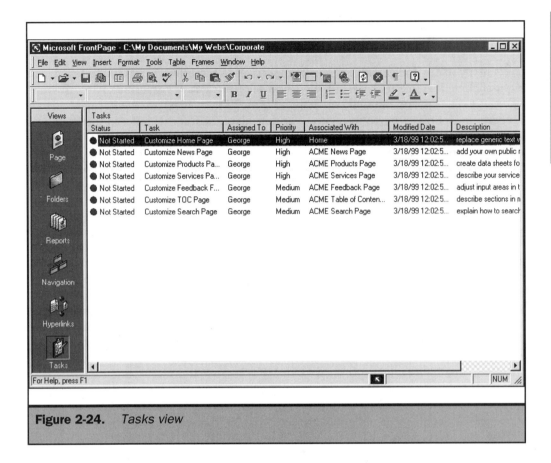

Figure 2-24. *Tasks view*

select Delete from the context menu to delete the task from the list. By right-clicking an uncompleted task and selecting Edit Task from the context menu, you can modify who the task is assigned to, its priority, its description, and the task name. For a completed task, you can only edit the description.

 You can sort the tasks in Tasks view on any column by clicking the column name at the top of the list.

Accessing Other Functions in FrontPage

As you are working on your web, you can open Page view in several ways:

- Using either the Page option in the View menu or the Page button in the Views bar

■ Double-clicking the page filename (or icon) you want to edit in one of several views of FrontPage

When you are done creating a web, you can test a hyperlink to external sites by right-clicking the link in Hyperlink view and selecting Verify Hyperlink. Also, if you have edited a web and removed or changed some of the pages, use the Recalculate Hyperlinks option in the Tools menu to update all of the internal links so there is no reference to a nonexistent page. Finally, when everything is the way you want it, you can copy your web to the server, provided you weren't already working on the server, by using the Publish Web option in the File menu (or by using the Publish Web button on the toolbar).

Personal Web Server

The Microsoft Personal Web Server (MSPWS) allows you to publish a web on your computer rather than on some other Internet server. MSPWS simply sits in the background as a task, is based on Microsoft's Internet Information Services (IIS), and is included in the Windows 98 package. (IIS is included with Windows NT 4.0 and Windows 2000 Server and is all the web server you need to run a full World Wide Web site.)

There is no default server for FrontPage, so you may use any for your web development, but MSPWS is the recommended choice, although it is not included in the FrontPage 2000 package. Release 4.0 of MPWS is in Windows 98, and Release 3.0 was included in the FrontPage 98 package. If you do not have either of those, you can download MPWS Release 4.0 from Microsoft (**http:www.microsoft.com/ie/pws/**). Appendix A details the installation and setup of MSPWS, and this book will assume that MSPWS is running.

Once MSPWS is running, you can double-click its icon on the right of the taskbar and the Personal Web Manager will open as shown in Figure 2-25. Here you can start and stop the MSPWS, see some statistics about the numbers of people visiting your web, publish a web, and learn more about MSPWS.

FrontPage Server Extensions

If you want to use all of the components of FrontPage, especially the interactive components, you need to have the FrontPage Server Extensions installed on both your Personal Web Server and the web server your web presence provider (WPP) is using. If your web presence provider is not using the FrontPage Server Extensions, you should suggest that they do so (see Chapter 23 for information on using the server extensions on a web server). The server extensions are available from Microsoft

GETTING STARTED

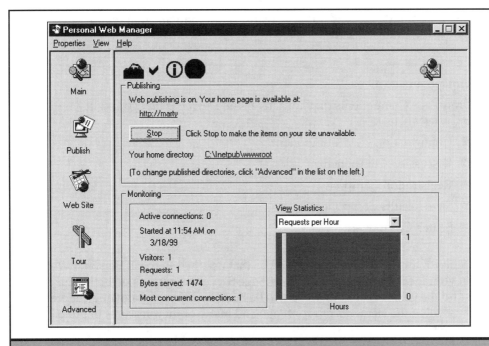

Figure 2-25. *Personal Web Manager for controlling the MSPWS*

(**http://www.microsoft.com/frontpage/wpp/**) for virtually every popular Windows NT- and UNIX-based server. If your WPP doesn't want to run the server extensions, then you might consider changing providers. Microsoft maintains a rapidly growing list of WPPs that do have the FrontPage Server Extensions installed (**http://microsoft.saltmine.com/frontpage/wpp/list/**), and from this list you should be able to locate a suitable provider. Also remember that, with the Web, it is not necessary to be physically close to your provider to have a successful working relationship. Quality of service and features are more important.

Note   *Though the terms Internet service provider (ISP) and web presence provider (WPP) are sometimes used interchangeably, there is a difference. An ISP provides access to the Internet, usually through a dialup (modem) connection. A WPP hosts web sites. That is, a WPP stores the web files on a server that is accessible over the Internet. Often your ISP and your WPP will be the same company. In this book the terms presence provider and web host refer to an WPP.*

Among the components and advance features in FrontPage that require the FrontPage Server Extensions are

- Forms
- Hotspot image maps
- FrontPage Components that are active while a web is being used in a browser, such as:
  - Confirmation Field Component
  - Discussion Component
  - Registration Component
  - Save Results Component
  - Search Component

The focus of this book is on creating webs that use the Microsoft Personal Web Server on your local machine and the FrontPage Server Extensions on both your MSPWS and the web server your webs will be hosted on. In the following chapters you will use all of the elements of FrontPage and many of their features to build your own webs.

Chapter 3

Using Wizards and Themes

A s you saw in Chapter 2, the easiest way to create a web with FrontPage is by using a wizard or a template. You'll remember that *wizards* ask you questions about the web you want to create and then build a web based on your answers. *Templates* create a particular kind of web without input from you. In this chapter you'll see how to use wizards to create webs, and the results that they produce. (Templates are covered in Chapter 4.) The purpose of this is twofold: to acquaint you with the wizards and to demonstrate many of FrontPage's features, which have been included in the wizard-produced webs.

 All but one of the wizards are web wizards, which create the folder structure and pages that make a complete web. The exception is the Form Page Wizard, which is a page wizard that creates only a single page. It was briefly demonstrated in Chapter 2 and will be covered further in Chapter 9.

Web Wizards

Begin looking at the FrontPage wizards by loading FrontPage as you did in Chapter 2. (For the remainder of this book, it is assumed that you are using the Microsoft Personal Web Server (MSPWS) with the FrontPage Server Extensions and have MSPWS set to start up automatically when you turn on your computer, as explained in Appendix A.)

After FrontPage has loaded, you can start a new web in three ways:

■ You can simply start creating the first web page and then add additional pages to it as necessary.

■ You can open the New toolbar button and choose Web, as shown left:

■ You can open the File menu, choose New, and then choose Web.

In the last two alternatives the New dialog box will be displayed, as shown in Figure 3-1. In this dialog box, icons for the following web wizards are displayed:

■ **Corporate Presence Wizard** allows you to create a complete web site to promote your company or business. With it you can

  ■ Create web pages that tell customers what's new with your company (for example, by using press releases)

  ■ Inform customers about your products and services

  ■ Create a table of contents to help visitors navigate your web site

  ■ Provide a feedback form so your customers can give you their opinions

  ■ Provide a search form that visitors to your web site can use to quickly find specific information on your site

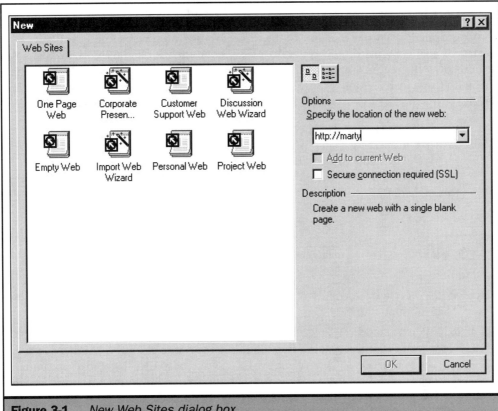

Figure 3-1.   *New Web Sites dialog box*

- **Discussion Web Wizard** creates web pages that allow the web user to submit comments to a discussion. It also provides a table of contents, a search form, a page to follow threaded replies, and a confirmation page so users know their comments have been received. *Threaded replies* link multiple comments on the same subject. This allows the reader to go directly from one comment to the next on a given subject.

- **Import Web Wizard** lets you quickly convert existing non-FrontPage web pages and content into a FrontPage web by collecting web pages from your local drive, or from an intranet or the Internet, and organize them into a FrontPage web. This is an important feature if you need to convert a number of existing webs into FrontPage, to update them, or to incorporate any of FrontPage's Active Elements, Components, or other dynamic FrontPage elements in them.

Using the Corporate Presence Wizard

The Corporate Presence web is one of the more sophisticated webs that FrontPage creates. By using a wizard, you get to do a lot of customizing as you build. In this section you will create a Corporate Presence web ("Corporate web," for short). Do that now with these instructions (FrontPage should be loaded and Page view open on your screen):

1. Open the File menu and choose New | Web. Click the Corporate Presence Wizard in the New dialog box Web Sites tab, and enter the URL or address for the new web (**Corporate** will work well for the name) in the Specify The Location Of The Web drop-down list. For example, on a server named "Marty," this is the URL:

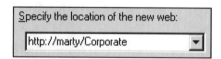

    Specify the location of the new web:

    http://marty/Corporate

   - If you will be normally working directly on your web server, this should be its domain name.

   - If you are working on your local computer and intend to publish your web on your web server later, this would be the name of your computer (as it was in the case of "Marty" above). (You may also use "localhost" for your web server. Localhost is a default network name for your computer—see the discussion of installing a personal web server in Appendix A.)

   - If you are creating a disk-based web, you would enter the path to the web on your hard drive.

   - If you do not have a server name entered, select or enter the domain name of the server or computer where your web will reside. The Secure Connection Required (SSL) check box should be unchecked. (See Chapter 21 for a discussion of using SSL.)

2. Click OK to close the New Web Sites dialog box. If your server requires it, you will be prompted to enter your name and password in the Name And Password Required dialog box. This is to verify that you are authorized to create webs on your server. Enter your name and password and click OK.

3. The first Corporate Presence Web Wizard dialog box will be displayed, telling you that you will be asked a series of questions. Click Next, opening the second wizard dialog box (shown in Figure 3-2), which displays the list of pages that can be included in the web.

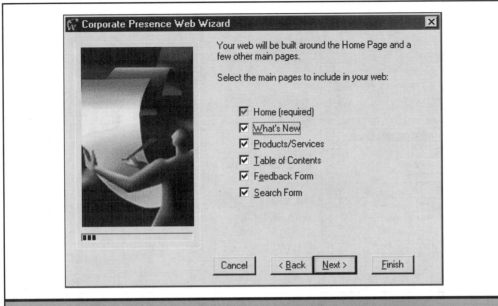

Figure 3-2.   *Choosing the web pages to be included in the Corporate web*

4. Select all of the options (to include all the possible pages) and click Next. This brings up a list of topics that can be included on the home page.

5. Choose all the check boxes and default options in this and the following wizard dialog boxes, and supply requested information about your company or organization. (One of the choices is whether you want to use the Under Construction icon on your pages. See the following Tip on this choice.) After you select web options and supply information about your site, you will reach the dialog box that gives you the option of choosing a web theme you want to use in your web. Click Choose Web Theme in this dialog box (you will explore Themes in detail later in this chapter).

Tip   *Using the Under Construction icon is generally not a good idea. If at all possible, finish the web before putting it on the server for public consumption. (The icon is shown on the screen shots later in this chapter so you can see what it looks like.)*

6. In the Choose Theme dialog box (see Figure 3-3) that appears, select the All Pages option (if it isn't already selected) and look at a number of the options.

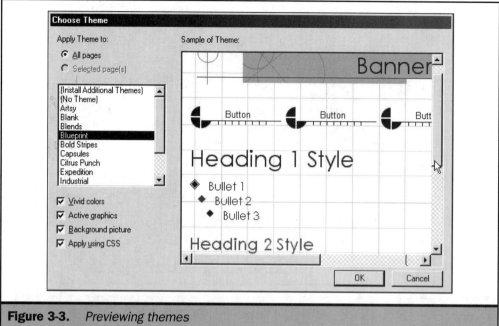

Figure 3-3.   *Previewing themes*

7. Choose the one you want (Blueprint is used in the figures later in this chapter). Make sure all four check boxes are selected in the Choose Theme dialog box so you can experience all the theme features.

"CSS," in the check box in the lower left of the Choose Theme dialog box stands for "cascading style sheets," which are used to apply consistent styles in a web site. CSS is discussed further in Chapters 11 and 13.

8. Click OK and then click Next. In the final dialog box of the Corporate Presence Web Wizard, make sure the Show Tasks View After Web Is Uploaded check box is checked and then click Finish. The web will be created and displayed in Tasks view. The Tasks view shows what you need to do to finish the web that was generated by the Corporate Presence Web Wizard, as you can see in Figure 3-4.

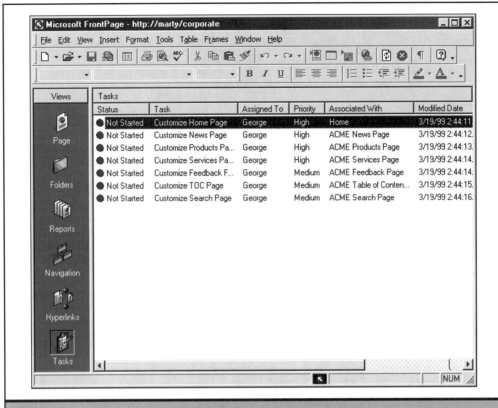

Figure 3-4.   *Corporate web in Tasks view*

9. Click the Navigation view icon in the Views bar on the left side of the FrontPage window to show the Corporate web in Navigation view, as in Figure 3-5. This shows all of the main web pages and their relationship to each other.

10. Select Hyperlinks view by clicking the Hyperlinks view icon in the Views bar. As you can see in Figure 3-6, the Corporate Presence Web Wizard has not only created all the pages you selected in the wizard, but it has also created the basic hyperlinks between the pages, represented by the arrows in the right pane of the FrontPage window.

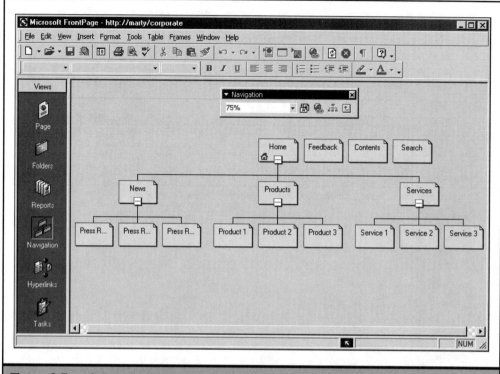

Figure 3-5.   *Corporate web in Navigation view*

11. Right-click the Home Page file, which is Default.htm, in either pane of Hyperlinks view, and choose Properties from the context menu that opens. The Properties dialog box for the home page, similar to the one shown in Figure 3-7, will open. Here you can see the filename, title, and URL that have been generated for the home page. In the Summary tab you can see when and by whom the page was created and modified. You can also add comments.

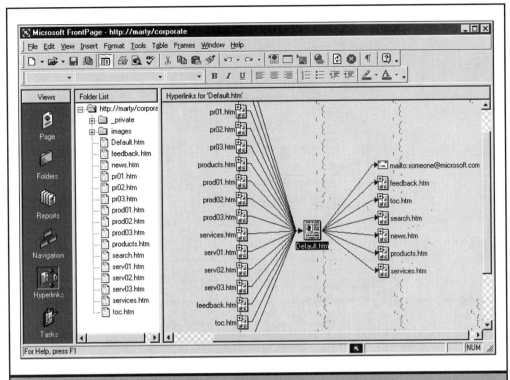

Figure 3-6.   *Links between web objects are shown in Hyperlinks view*

Note   *By default, if you have the MSPWS installed, FrontPage names the home page for a web Default.htm. Without MSPWS, the default home page name is Index.htm. The name of the home page for a web is important since this will determine whether your web server will display the home page when accessed without the home page filename (http://webname/) or whether the full URL will be required (http://webname/pagename.htm). Different web servers have different default settings for the home page name. Check with your web server administrator for the default home page name on your web server.*

12. Click OK. The Properties dialog box closes. Click the Tasks view icon in the Views bar to return to the Tasks list (shown previously in Figure 3-4).

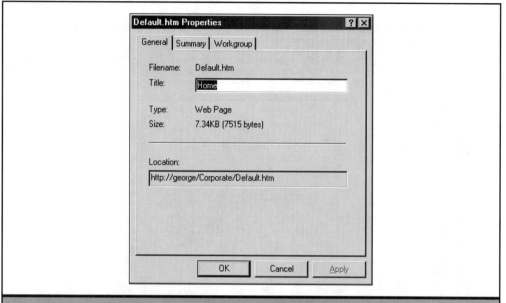

Figure 3-7.   *Examining properties for the home page*

13. Right-click the first task (Customize Home Page), and choose Start Task from the context menu. Page view will open with the home page displayed, as shown in Figure 3-8. On the home page you can see some of the features incorporated in this web (scroll through the page to make sure you see everything). Here are some of the features to note (see Figure 3-8 for the first four features):

Tip   *If your folder list is still open, click the Folder list icon in the toolbar (fifth icon from the left) to close it and gain more screen area to display the page.*

- Hyperlink buttons (like "Home," "Feedback," "Contents," and "Search") at the top of the page allow visitors to jump to other pages in your web site.

- The page title, "Home," and the page background are graphics. You can create such graphics in Microsoft PhotoDraw, Microsoft Image Composer, CorelDRAW, Adobe PhotoShop, Fractal Design Painter, or other graphics packages and then place them in FrontPage. (Chapter 5 will discuss using Microsoft Image Composer and Microsoft PhotoDraw.)

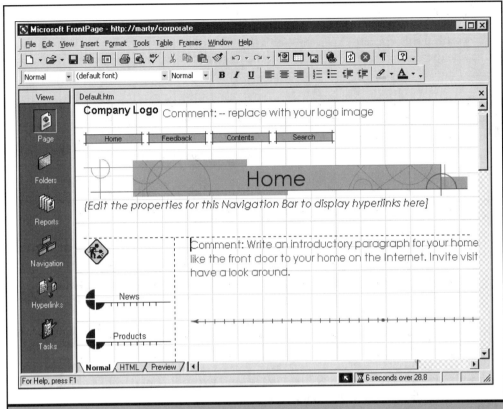

Figure 3-8. *Corporate web home page in Page view*

- The *navigation bar* (also called a *navbar*) is a series of graphics, one for each of the hyperlinks, and is included in a *shared border* that is used at the top of each regular web page. In Figure 3-8, there are three navbars: one under the company logo ("Home," "Feedback," "Contents," and "Search"; one under the Home banner (you mus edit it for the buttons to be visible); and one on the left (you can see only the first two links, "News" and "Products"). You will explore shared borders toward the end of this chapter.

- The line beneath the Comment is a graphic.

- The phone numbers, postal address, and e-mail addresses are entered and maintained through the Substitution FrontPage Component. (FrontPage Components are discussed in Chapter 10.)

14. Select Open from the File menu or click Open on the toolbar to display the Open dialog box.

15. Select News.htm and click Open. When the News.htm file is loaded in Page view, you can see the common elements that are included on each page created with the Corporate Presence Web Wizard. Notice that the "Home" banner below the company logo on the home page has been replaced by one that says "News." Each page in the Corporate web will have its own banner graphic to identify it.

Tip   *If you do not see file extensions, you can turn them on by opening the Windows Explorer and its View menu, choosing Folder Options, selecting the View tab, and clearing the Hide File Extensions For Known File Types check box.*

On any of the pages you can enter and format text, insert graphics, and add forms, tables, and other elements, as you saw in Chapter 2. In later chapters you will do all of these tasks. The purpose here is simply to see that the Corporate Presence Web Wizard does, in fact, create a complete web. It also creates all of the structure (shown in Figure 3-6) that is behind a web in FrontPage.

The web pages generated by the Corporate Presence Web Wizard include text and graphics, as well as content that is stored in shared borders. Those shared borders, on the top, bottom, and left of the page, will be explored later in this chapter, after you have examined the rest of the page contents.

Looking at the News Page

The News page of your Corporate web serves as a central location to list changes to your web site, press releases, media coverage, and to provide hyperlinks to the individual pages that describe the pages in more detail.

Each element on the page has its own properties you can view and change by right-clicking the object and selecting Properties from the context menu. In the following steps you will look at the Properties dialog boxes for the different types of objects on the News page.

1. Scroll down the News page and right-click the small "NEW" image on the left of "Acme Industries Inc." In the context menu, select Picture Properties to open the Picture Properties dialog box in Figure 3-9.

   ■ In the General tab of the Picture Properties dialog box you can select the image to be displayed, provide text to be displayed in browsers that do not display graphics (this text will also be displayed for a few seconds if you point on the graphic in a browser), and create a hyperlink for the graphic.

   ■ In the Appearance tab you can set the alignment of the graphic on the page, specify horizontal and vertical spacing around the graphic, create a border for it, and specify the size.

   ■ The Video tab is where you select a video file and modify how the video appears, how long it plays, and when it starts.

Figure 3-9. *Picture Properties dialog box*

2. Close the Picture Properties dialog box, and right-click any of the horizontal lines on the page. Select Horizontal Line Properties from the context menu. Many of the properties for the horizontal line on this page are defined by the web's theme, but you can edit these settings in the dialog box as shown next.

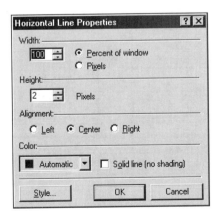

3. Close the Horizontal Line Properties dialog box and right-click the hyperlink Press Release in the line following the "NEW" image. Select Hyperlink Properties to display the Edit Hyperlink dialog box shown in Figure 3-10. You use this dialog box to set hyperlinks on either text or graphics in your web pages to other locations in your web, to other intranet webs, or to the Web. You can also set hyperlinks to bookmarks on the same page.

4. Click Cancel to close the Edit Hyperlink dialog box. Right-click the same Press Release hyperlink again, and select Follow Hyperlink in the context menu to open the Press Release 1 page (pr01.htm) in Page view, as shown in Figure 3-11. The Press Release 1 template includes space for the title of your announcement, the date of the release, and contact information for the press.

Tip

In Page view, you have to open the context menu and select Follow Hyperlink to open the target of a link. In a web browser or the Preview tab, you simply click the hyperlink itself.

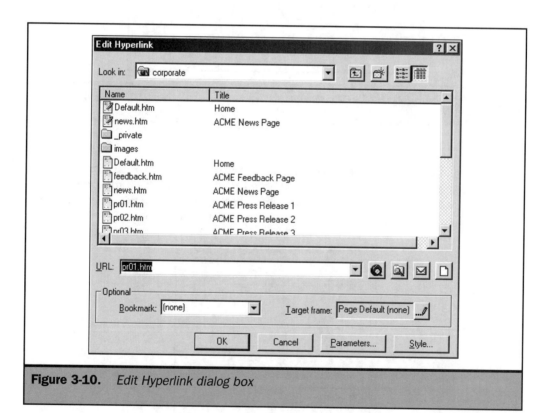

Figure 3-10. *Edit Hyperlink dialog box*

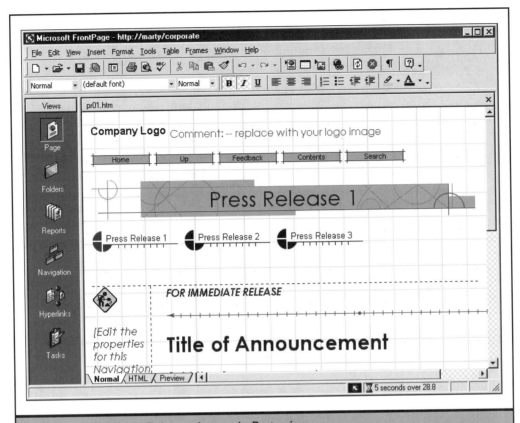

Figure 3-11.   *Press Release 1 page in Page view*

Note   *The Press Release pages, as well as the Product and Service pages, are all numbered 1 through 3. In the Corporate Presence Web Wizard, the default number of pages to be created for these three types of web pages was 3. The next time you create a web with this wizard, you can choose the number of Product and Service pages that best fits your needs.*

5. Close the Press Release 1 page by selecting Close from the File menu.

The Table of Contents Page

The Table of Contents page provides the user with a single location to open any page in a web.

1. Open the Table of Contents page in Page view by double-clicking Toc.htm in the Open File dialog box. (Recall that the Open File dialog box is accessed either by use of the Open toolbar button or by selecting Open in the File menu.) Figure 3-12 shows the page in Page view.

2. The pages listed in the Table of Contents are automatically generated, starting from the home page. In Page view this does not look like much, but in a browser this is automatically expanded to include references to each page and to each bookmark on each page.

3. Open the File menu and select Preview In Browser. (You may have to fully extend the menu.) In the Preview In Browser dialog box that is displayed, shown next, you can select a web browser to view your page, add a browser you have installed on your computer, and select the size at which the browser

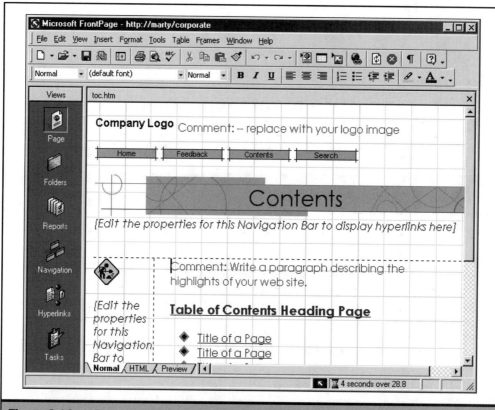

Figure 3-12.   *Table of Contents page in Page view*

will be opened. (If you click the Preview In Browser toolbar button, you do not get the choice of browsers; your default browser opens. Of course if you have only one browser installed, that is what you get in either case.) Depending on your server and network configuration, you may be prompted to log onto the Internet first.

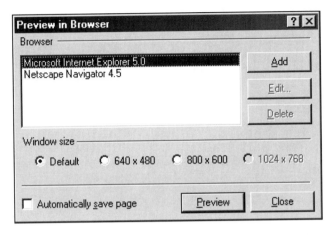

4. Click Preview to open the Table of Contents page in your selected browser. Figure 3-13 shows the Table of Contents page after the FrontPage Component has created the hyperlinks.

5. Close your browser, return to Page view, and close the Table of Contents page.

The Feedback Page

There are many reasons to get feedback from the people who visit your web site. If your site is designed to promote a product or service, you will want to know what visitors think of your products, and to give users a simple method to contact you with questions. The Feedback page in the Corporate web does exactly that, as you will see by following these instructions:

1. Open the Feedback page in Page view by selecting Feedback.htm in the Open File dialog box and clicking Open.

2. When the Feedback page is opened, scroll through it to see all the elements. The lower part of the page should look like Figure 3-14.

The body of the Feedback page is a form. As you saw in Chapter 2, a form is used to gather information on a web page and then transfer the information to a FrontPage Component or another application. This Feedback form includes a scrolling text box to enter the users' comments, a drop-down menu for users to select the subject of their

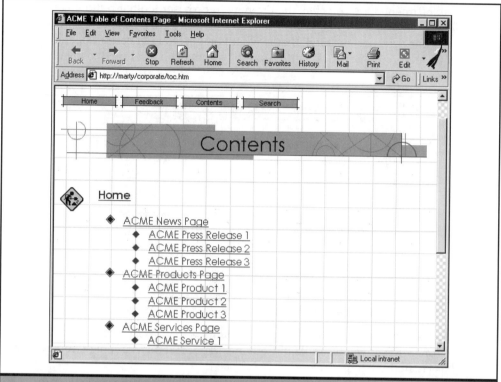

Figure 3-13. *Table of Contents page in web browser*

comments, seven one-line text boxes for users to enter information about themselves, and buttons to submit or clear the form.

To see the contents of a drop-down menu on a form field in Page view, double-click the drop-down menu. Click Cancel when you are done looking at this dialog box.

3. Right-click anywhere on the form except on one of the form fields, and select Form Properties from the context menu. The file in the File Name box of the Form Properties dialog box shows the file to which the input data will be saved.

4. Click the Options button to open the Options For Saving Results Of Form dialog box, shown in Figure 3-15. Here you can set the name and location of the file to which the data is being saved and the format of the file. Additional information (for example, date, time, and user name) can be selected in the Saved Fields tab of the dialog box and included in the file.

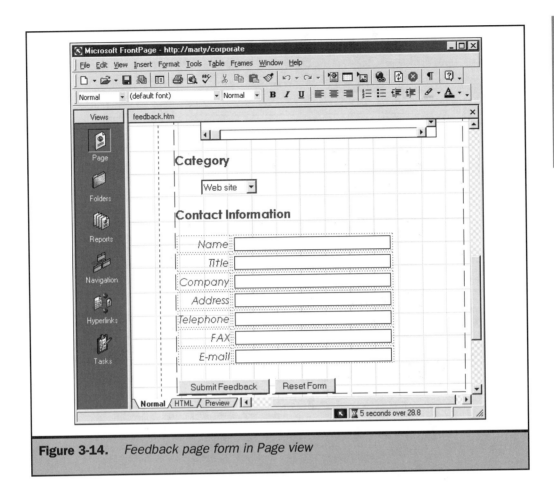

Figure 3-14.   *Feedback page form in Page view*

5. Close the Options For Saving Results Of Form dialog box and then the Form Properties dialog box. Then close the Feedback page in Page view.

The Search Page

In a large web site a table of contents does not always provide the quickest method for a user to find specific information. The Search page allows users to search your web using any of the keywords that describe the information they are looking for. The Search page uses the Active Elements Search Form to search the web and generate a results page. The search results page will contain hyperlinks to the web pages that match the search criterion. Figure 3-16 shows the results of a search of the Corporate web for the word "products."

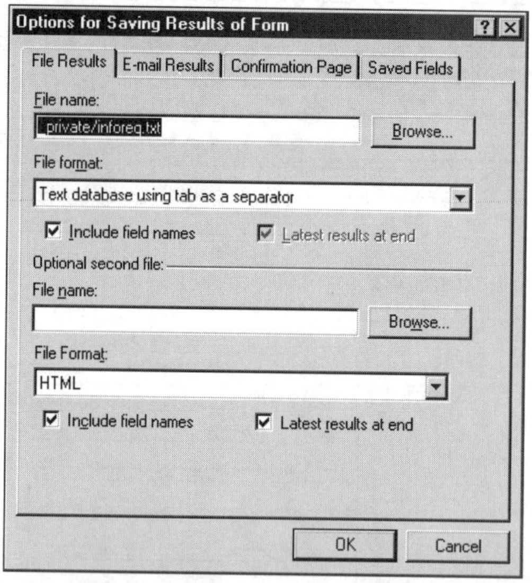

Figure 3-15. *Options for Saving Results of Form dialog box*

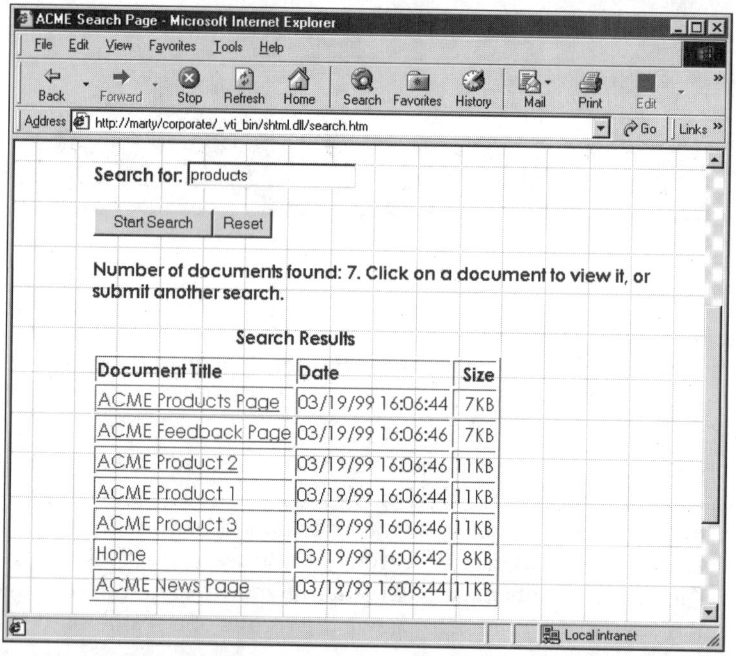

Figure 3-16. *Search results for the word "products"*

You can hide pages, such as style pages or pages that you are using only to include in other pages, from the Active Element Search Form by placing the pages in the special web folder Webname_private. The Search Form does not search this folder.

1. Open the Corporate web Search page in Page view (Search.htm in the Open File dialog box) as shown in Figure 3-17.

2. The body of the Search page is a simple form with a single text box and two buttons. The user enters the word(s) to search on in the text box and then clicks the Start Search button.

3. Right-click the form (the Search For text box), and select Search Form Properties from the context menu. In the Search Form Properties dialog box, shown next, you can set the labels for the text box and the buttons, and set the width of the text box. In the Search Results tab of the dialog box, you can set the options for the search results.

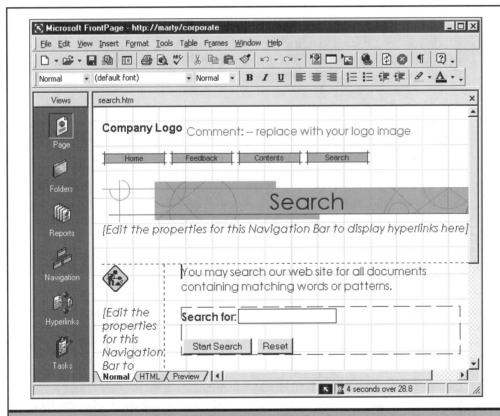

Figure 3-17.   *Search Page in Page view*

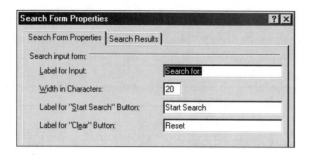

4. Click Cancel to close the Search Form Properties dialog box.

5. Click the Preview In Browser toolbar button and examine your web.

   Use the navigation buttons in the Corporate home page to look at other pages in the web. Go to the Search page and search for the word "press." After you generate a list of pages that match that criterion, go to the Feedback page and enter some constructive criticisms of the site. Notice that when you click the Submit button in the Feedback form, you will see a confirmation page that tells you that your feedback was received.

6. When you are finished viewing the Corporate web in your browser, close your browser, and then delete the Corporate web by selecting Delete Web from the File menu and clicking Yes in the Confirm Delete dialog box that will appear.

Note   *If you do not have Delete Web in your File menu, you can add it by opening the Tools menu and choosing Customize. Under the Commands tab of the Customize dialog box, select File in the Categories list. Scroll the command list until you see Delete Web, then drag Delete Web to the File menu and drop it just below Close Web.*

The Corporate web shows how easy it is to create a complete web site with the FrontPage wizards. To actually put the web on the World Wide Web, you would only need to add your content to the pages. In Chapter 12 you'll learn how to import word processor documents and other files into a FrontPage web.

Working with the Discussion Web Wizard

Discussion groups provide a means for people to have online conversations. They provide a simple method for you to link comments about a single subject, or to find comments about a specific subject in the discussion group. You can create a separate discussion web or incorporate a discussion group in another web by using the Discussion Web Wizard:

1. Choose New and then Web from the File menu, or click the down arrow next to the New toolbar button and select Web. The New dialog box will open. Click Discussion Web Wizard, enter **http://*server*/Discussion,** where *"server"* is the

name of you host server, in the Specify The Location Of The New Web box, and click OK. The first Discussion Web Wizard dialog box will explain how the wizard works.

2. Click Next. The second dialog box will ask you the features of a discussion group that you want to include, as you can see in Figure 3-18. Your choices include the following:

- **Submission Form** is the form used to submit comments to the discussion and is required for a discussion group.

- **Table Of Contents** provides a means of organizing and finding previously submitted comments by subject. If you want readers to read and comment on what previous contributors have submitted, then you need to include a table of contents.

- **Search Form** is an alternative way for readers to find previously contributed information. It allows a reader to find a contribution containing words other than those in the subject.

- **Threaded Replies** links multiple comments on the same subject. This allows the reader to go directly from one comment to the next on a given subject.

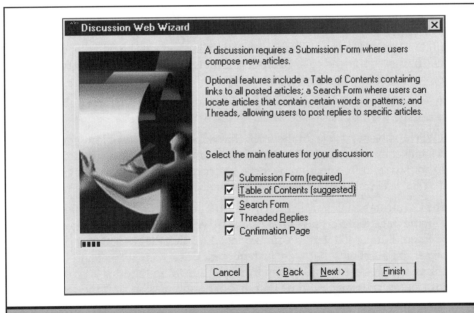

Figure 3-18.   *Discussion Web Wizard's second dialog box*

■ **Confirmation Page** shows the person making a submission what the system has received.

3. Check all of the options if they are not already checked, so you can look at them, and click Next. The third dialog box will open and ask for the title you want to use and the folder name for the discussion group messages. Accept **Discussion** for the title, and accept the default folder name (note that discussion folder names must begin with an underscore).

4. Again click Next. The fourth Discussion Web Wizard dialog box will ask for the fields you want to start with on the submission form such as the default fields named "Subject" and "Comments." You will be able to add more later in Page view.

5. Keep the defaults and click Next. The fifth dialog box will ask if you want to restrict the contributors to the discussion group.

6. Select No, Anyone Can Post Articles, and click Next. Also accept the defaults in the next six dialog boxes by clicking Next in each of them, noting each time the content being generated for the Discussion Group web. (You may want to choose a web theme, which you can do when the choice is offered to you.) Click Finish in the final dialog box.

7. Click Navigation view and double-click the single box in the right pane of Navigation view to open the Discussion Group Home page in Page view. Here you can open any of the pages and make any changes you desire. To try a page, though, you need to look at it in a browser. Since one of the defaults chosen was to use frames, you need to use Netscape Navigator 2.0 or later, or Internet Explorer 3.0 or later, to see the frames.

8. Preview your web in your Internet browser, and your Discussion Group web Home page will appear as shown in Figure 3-19.

9. Click Post A New Article. In the form that appears enter a subject, your name, and some comments, and click Post Article. (If you get a message saying you are about to send information over the Internet and other people might see it, click Yes.) The confirmation should appear showing the subject you entered.

10. In the Confirmation page, click the Refresh The Main Page hyperlink. Back at the Home page that you saw in Figure 3-19, you should again see the subject you entered under Contents. You may need to click the Refresh button in your browser to see articles that were just entered. Click your subject and that message will appear in the bottom frame, as shown in Figure 3-20. You will see the name, the date and time you made the submission, and the comments you entered. Depending on the options you selected for your discussion group, you may see other information about the person who submitted the comment as well.

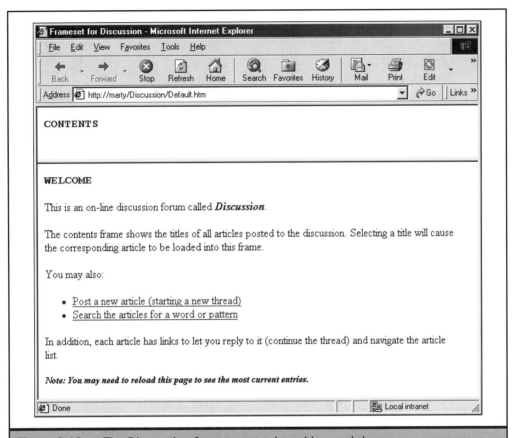

Figure 3-19. *The Discussion frames page viewed in a web browser*

The navigation bar in the bottom frame now has several new entries: Contents, Search, Post (to start a new thread), Reply (to add a comment to an existing thread), Next and Previous (to go forward and backward, respectively, in the current thread), and Up (to go to the next thread).

11. Try these new navigation bar entries by making several submissions, both independent and in reply to another submission, so you can see how the navigation works. When you are done, close the browser and delete the web.

A discussion group can be a powerful means of communication, and FrontPage offers an easy way to create one.

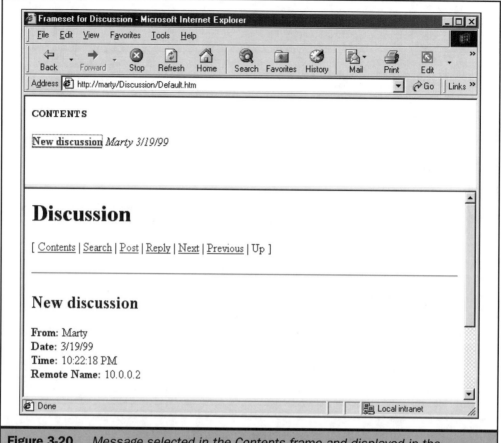

Figure 3-20. *Message selected in the Contents frame and displayed in the Discussion frame*

Using the Import Web Wizard

If FrontPage 2000 is the first version of FrontPage that you've used, you may have a number of existing webs that you will want to convert to FrontPage webs. The process is extremely simple when you use the Import Web Wizard.

1. Open the New dialog box as you have previously, click Import Web Wizard, and enter a location for the new web. Click OK and the first wizard dialog box will be displayed.

2. In the Import Web Wizard dialog box, shown in Figure 3-21, select a source for your web—either from your local computer or network, or from the World Wide Web. If you choose a source on your local computer or network, enter the

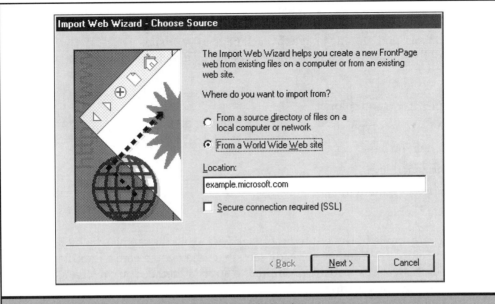

Figure 3-21. *Import Web Wizard opening dialog box*

complete path name of the folder where the web is located, or click the Browse button to locate the folder. Select the Include Subfolders check box. If you choose the World Wide Web, enter the complete URL and whether it requires a secure connection. Then click Next.

3. If you select a folder on your computer, then the next dialog box will display a list of the files located in the selected folder. Select the files you want to *exclude* from the new FrontPage web (if any) and click the Exclude button. Click Next and then click Finish.

4. If you select a web site, then the next dialog box will display a set of limits that you can impose on what you import. Select the limits that you want to impose, click Next, and then click Finish.

That's all there is to it. Your imported web will be displayed in the FrontPage ready for you to work on.

Themes

FrontPage 2000 comes with a selection of 13 themes that can be applied to an entire FrontPage web. Themes apply and control many different elements of a web page and they consistently apply these elements to *every* page in a web.

Having coordinated graphic elements, background images, and navigation bars gives a unifying feel to your web site. Visitors will see familiar color schemes, navigation tools, and graphic images at each page in your site.

Some of the elements that are applied to pages by a theme include

- Text colors
- Bullet styles and colors
- Font size and type
- Navigation bars
- Horizontal lines
- Page background images
- Page banners

Themes are applied to an entire FrontPage web using the themes dialog box that you saw in Figure 3-3. You have already seen that when you create a FrontPage web using one of the wizards, you are prompted to apply a theme. You can change or remove this theme at any time.

Each FrontPage theme can be modified by selecting or deselecting one of the top-three check boxes that are available for each theme. Those check boxes allow you to include Vivid Colors, Active Graphics, or a Background Image. The bottom check box, Apply Theme Using CSS, lets you choose whether to apply the theme using cascading style sheets (CSS), which uses special HTML commands to apply the styles associated with the theme. CSS is discussed further in Chapters 11 and 13.

Assigning Themes to FrontPage Webs

You can assign a theme to your FrontPage web whether or not that web already has a theme applied to it. So, for example, if you generate a FrontPage web using a template or wizard, you can change the theme of that web. Or if you create a web from scratch, you can also assign a theme to it. The process is the same regardless of whether your web already has a theme.

1. Open (or create) a FrontPage web. A web page without formatting or themes tends to leave the pages looking a bit barren, as you can see in Figure 3-22. You can, however, always elect to format pages one at a time. You will learn to do this in Chapter 6.

2. Open the Format menu and choose Theme. The Themes dialog box that you saw in Figure 3-3 will open.

3. Click All Pages to apply the theme to all pages in the web, select a theme, and view the results in the Sample Of Theme area. You can experiment with any theme by selecting different combinations of the theme effects check boxes before you apply the theme. Note some of the objects that are included in a theme:

   - A banner at the top of the page

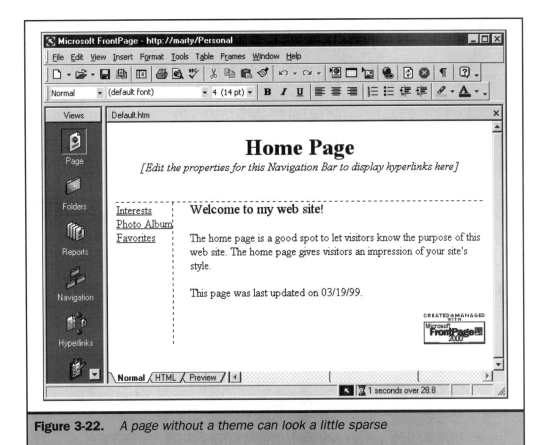

Figure 3-22.   *A page without a theme can look a little sparse*

- Navigation buttons at the top of the page
- A horizontal line above the bottom navigation buttons
- A matching set of different-sized bullets for bullet lists
- A color scheme that color coordinates page text, banner, bullets, and horizontal line
- A unified color scheme for links, followed links, and active links

4. Below the list of Themes there are four check boxes, which add special effects to a selected theme or apply them using CSS. As soon as you click one of the first three check boxes, the effect of that selection is applied immediately in the Sample Of Theme area. (You do not see any effect from using CSS.)

- Choosing the Vivid Colors option brightens the color scheme and generally transforms your site from subtle to brash.

- Choosing the Background Image check box replaces the solid color background with a tiled graphic image.

While you can test the effects of the Vivid Colors and Background Image check boxes in the Sample Of Theme area, you will not see the full effect of active graphics when you select the Active Graphics check box. This option transforms navigation buttons in your web pages into dynamic hover buttons. To test these hover buttons, you will have to apply your theme and open your web page using a browser that interprets Java applets. In Figure 3-23, the Hover Button effect causes the half-circle to appear as the mouse is moved over the button.

5. After you decide which theme and theme options to apply to your web pages, click OK. Then look at the effect in your web pages by opening them in Page view or in your browser.

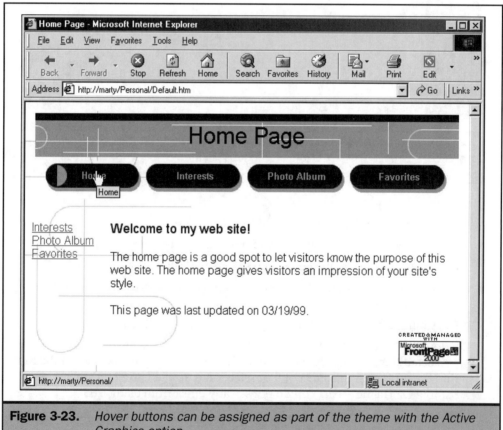

Figure 3-23. *Hover buttons can be assigned as part of the theme with the Active Graphics option*

Assigning Themes to Web Pages

Themes can be assigned to a single web page as well as to an entire FrontPage web. You assign themes to pages by selecting the page and then choosing Selected Pages in the Themes dialog box. When you do that, you affect only the selected web page.

Overall, the purpose of a theme is to provide a cohesive, unifying look and feel to your entire web site. Therefore, themes are usually applied to entire webs. However, there are a number of reasons why you might want to assign themes to an individual page. You could decide that one or more pages in your web should not look like they are part of the overall web site. These pages might include legal disclaimers, pages that provide information that isn't integral to the overall message of the web, or pages that you want to stand out from the rest of the web.

To apply a theme to a single web page, open it in Page view and edit the theme assigned to the page with the following steps:

1. With your web page open in Page view, right-click anywhere in the page and select Theme from the context menu.

2. The Themes dialog box opens. By default, the Themes dialog box will first display the theme that is applied to the entire FrontPage web.

   The buttons in the upper-left of the Themes dialog box allow two options. You can

   - Apply the theme you choose to all page, or

   - Apply the theme you choose to just this page by choosing Selected Pages.

3. From the theme list box choose to:

   - Use the web's default theme, which is automatically applied to a new page

   - Install an additional theme

   - Have no theme, or

   - Use one of the 13 themes that come with FrontPage 2000.

4. Once you have previewed your theme in the Sample Of Theme area of the Themes dialog box, click OK to apply the theme. The selected theme and theme options are applied to the open page.

There are a couple of other ways to see what theme is applied to a page, and remove a theme from a page. You can remove themes in the Page Properties dialog box. With your web page open in Page view, right-click anywhere on the page and choose Page Properties from the context menu. If a theme has been applied to the web page, the Page Properties dialog box has a Custom tab (see Figure 3-24) that lists the applied theme in the User Variables section. You can delete a theme by selecting the theme from the User Variables list and clicking the Remove button.

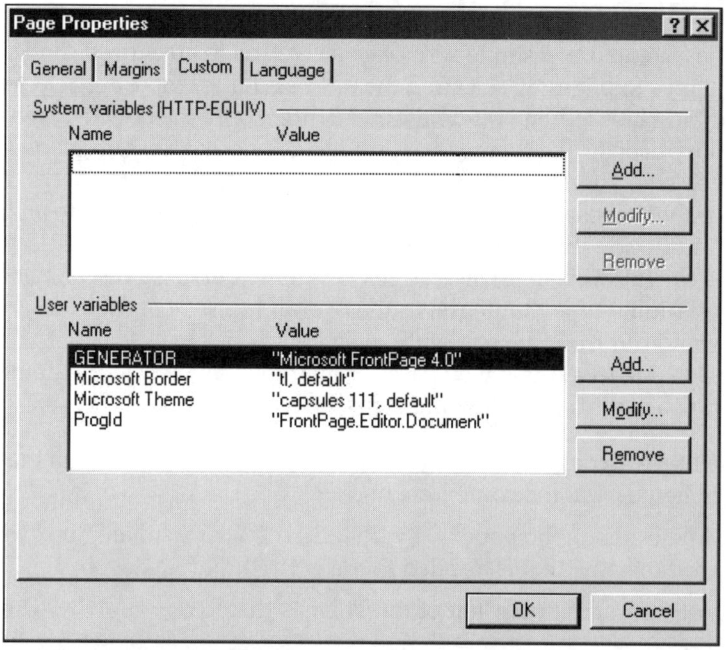

Figure 3-24. *A page's applied theme is shown in the Custom tab of the Page Properties dialog box*

You can also view or remove themes in the HTML tab of Page view (click HTML in the bottom left of the Page view window). The HTML code

```
<meta name="Microsoft Theme" content="capsules 111, default">
```

indicates that the Capsules theme has been applied to a page. You can remove a theme by selecting this line of HTML code in the HTML tab and pressing the DEL key.

Along with applying a new theme to an open web page, you can also edit many of the page format elements using page formatting. For example, you can change font color, font size, and paragraph alignment. However, other formatting options cannot be changed after applying a theme, such as the background and the default text and hyperlink colors. If you open the Themes dialog box from a page with an existing theme, there is a Modify button that lets you change the colors, graphics, and styles used in a theme and then save it as a new theme or a replacement for an existing theme.

Themes have many advantages, including the fact that they create attractive, professional, coordinated, and useful web pages very quickly. The downside is that your ability to fine-tune the look and feel of your web site is slightly constricted by themes.

As your expertise with FrontPage 2000 grows, you may decide to use the predefined themes to provide layout and design ideas, but then use other tools to create coordinated pages that are completely unique to your site.

Shared Borders

Shared borders are sections of a web page set aside for content that will appear on each page of your web. Shared borders are *borders* because they are at the top, bottom, left, or (rarely) right side of a page. They are *shared* because they include content that is shared by every page in a web.

Shared borders often include navigation bars. All the FrontPage webs generated by wizards or templates include navigation bars in the shared borders. Here are some examples of other useful shared borders:

- A top shared border with page titles
- A bottom shared border with copyright information, site contact information, and other text or images you want to appear on the bottom of every page in your site
- A left shared border with general information you want to place in every page in your site, such as links

Tip *Shared borders are rarely placed on the right side of web pages because your users may not see them. Depending on the size and resolution of the users' screen, and the size of their browser window, the right side of your web pages may not be visible to them unless they use the horizontal scroll bar to see it. Since shared borders often include navigation bars, you will normally want the shared border to be visible as soon as your web page downloads.*

All FrontPage themes assign some combination of shared borders to web pages. These shared borders can be changed. So, for example, even though a theme may apply three shared borders to every page in a FrontPage web, you can change it so only two shared borders appear on a given page.

If you did not create your FrontPage web from a template or wizard, you can still assign shared borders to your web. But FrontPage will not insert navigation bars in your shared borders unless you assign page relationships for your web (or generate the web from a template or wizard).

Assigning Shared Borders to a FrontPage Web

Global changes can affect the layout of shared borders in every page. Use the following steps to see how this works:

1. Open or create a FrontPage web; choose Folders, Navigation, or Hyperlink view; and select Shared Borders from the Format menu. (You may have to fully extend the menu.) The Shared Borders dialog box opens, as shown Figure 3-25.

2. Use the Top, Left, Right, and Bottom check boxes in the Shared Borders dialog box to select or turn off any of the four borders; use the two Include Navigation Buttons check boxes to add navigation buttons to the borders. If All Pages is selected, the borders you select will be applied to or removed from every page in your web by default, although you can turn them off or change them for specific pages.

Tip   *The shared borders you assign in the Shared Borders dialog box will override any shared borders assigned by a theme.*

3. When you have chosen which shared borders to add or remove, click OK. The shared borders are applied immediately to the pages in your web that do not have specific shared borders.

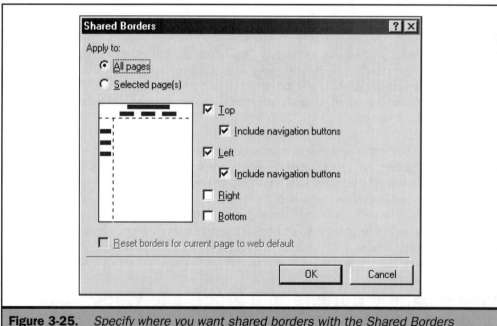

Figure 3-25.   *Specify where you want shared borders with the Shared Borders dialog box*

Assigning Shared Borders to a Web Page

Shared borders can be edited and customized for individual web pages. For example, you can apply a bottom shared border to some but not all pages in your web:

1. Open the page in Page view on which you want to customize the shared borders.

2. Right-click in the page and select Shared Borders from the context menu.

3. Choose the Current Page option in the Shared Borders dialog box, and define additional shared borders or remove current shared borders by selecting or clearing the applicable check boxes, as you can see in Figure 3-26.

After you create a new shared border for a page, the content of that shared border is available to other pages.

Editing the Content of Shared Borders

You can define a maximum of four shared borders for a FrontPage web. You can elect to apply or not apply different borders to different pages, but you can make only

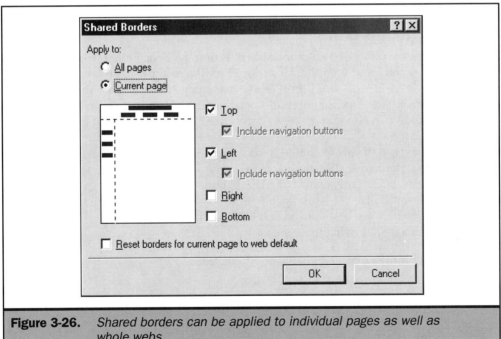

Figure 3-26.   *Shared borders can be applied to individual pages as well as whole webs*

limited changes to the content of shared borders on individual pages. If you want to place different content on each web page (and you will), do so independently of shared borders. The purpose of shared borders is to place the same content on multiple pages.

Think of shared borders as being similar to headers and footers in printed documents. They are there to include content that you want to repeat on each page. Therefore, when you edit the content of a shared border in one page, for the most part you change that content for every page to which the shared border is applied.

The content of the shared borders is edited in Page view:

1. Click the content of any shared border to edit it.

2. You can add text to any shared border by simply typing it in. For example, type **Copyright 1999, Acme Instruments** in the bottom shared border.

3. Click outside the shared border when you are done entering or editing its contents.

After you edit a shared border for a particular page, that shared border content will be applied to other pages. In Figure 3-27, a bottom shared border has been assigned to a page in a web.

Editing Navigation Bars

Navigation bars are generated automatically in FrontPage. They include hyperlinks to other pages within your web site. How does FrontPage know the relationship between pages in your web site? FrontPage uses the page relationships shown in Navigation view to place navigation buttons. The hierarchy you assign when you create a web (shown in Navigation view) determines the options available to you for navigation bars.

To assign navigation bars to shared borders, you must choose the Use Navigation Buttons option described earlier. If you created your FrontPage web using a wizard or template, or independently choose the Use Navigation Buttons, navigation bars are created automatically. The actual page-to-page relationships that are utilized by the navigation bars are best viewed and changed in Navigation view. Try defining new relationships by following these steps:

1. Open a FrontPage web and choose Navigation view.

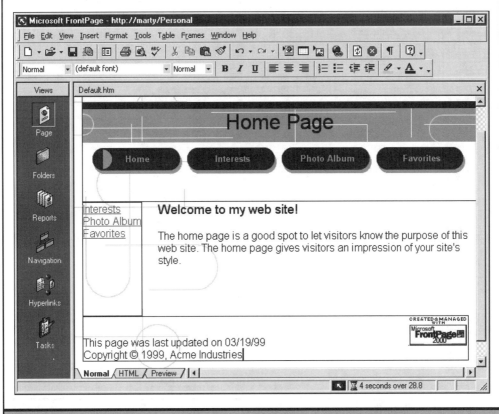

Figure 3-27.   *A bottom shared border can function as a repeating footer in a web*

2. Drag web pages from the Folder List (left pane) into the Navigation pane (on the right) as shown in Figure 3-28.

3. You can define the relationship between pages by where you place the pages in relation to each other.

The view shown in Figure 3-28 is the default portrait view of a web hierarchy and the one referred to in the following points. Using the Navigation toolbar, which you can open from the view menu, you can switch to landscape view, but it is of little value.

■ A page that is connected to and below another page in Navigation view is referred to as a *child* page.

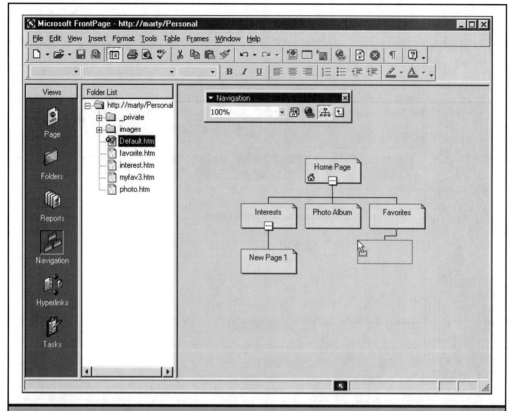

Figure 3-28.   *You can define and change navigation bar relationships in Navigation view*

- A page that is connected to and above another page is a *parent* page.
- Pages that are connected by a horizontal line are referred to as *same level* pages. These relationships determine the buttons that can be included in navigation bars.

Once you have defined page relationships in Navigation view, you can assign navigation bars in Page view:

1. Open a web page in Page view.
2. Click a shared border in which you will place or edit a navigation bar.

3. If a navigation bar already exists, double-click it. If there is no navigation bar, select Navigation Bar from the Insert menu. The Navigation Bar Properties dialog box appears as shown in Figure 3-29.

4. In the Hyperlinks To Add To Page area, choose one of the six options: Parent Level, Same Level, Back And Next (navigates between pages on the Same Level that are next to each other in Navigation view), Child Level, Top Level, or Child Pages Under Home.

5. Regardless of which option you choose, you can include a link to the home page or the parent page for the open page by selecting one or both of the Additional Pages check boxes.

6. The Orientation And Appearance area of the dialog box lets you define the layout and type of navigation buttons that will appear on your navigation bar. Horizontal and vertical layouts are previewed in the small preview area on the left side of the Orientation And Appearance area of the dialog box. The Buttons option generates graphic navigation buttons, while the Text option creates text links.

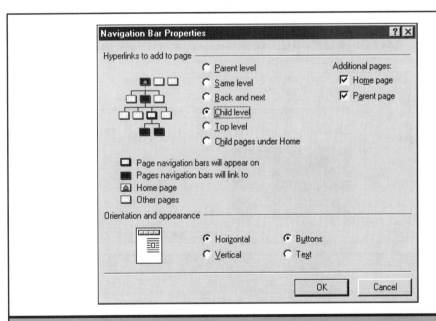

Figure 3-29.   *Use the Navigation Bar Properties dialog box to select the relationships implemented in the navigation buttons*

7. When you have selected all your navigation bar options, click OK. In Figure 3-30, horizontal button-style navigation bars have been generated in a page with links to pages on the same level.

By combining FrontPage web templates and wizards with themes, shared borders, and navigation bars, you can create professional and sophisticated integrated web sites.

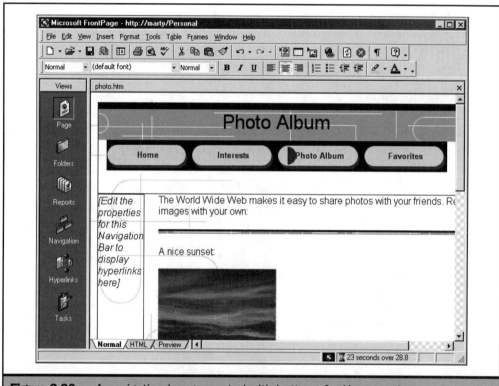

Figure 3-30.   *A navigation bar generated with buttons for Home and same-level pages*

The Complete Reference

Chapter 4

Using Templates

A s you now know, wizards and templates provide easy ways to create webs with FrontPage. In Chapter 3 you saw how to use wizards to create complete webs and pages by answering questions about the web you want to build. In the first part of this chapter, you'll see how to use templates to build both webs and pages without input from you, and the results that they produce. In the second part of this chapter, you'll learn how to create your own page templates. This will allow you to easily create new webs or add pages to existing webs without having to re-create a design or layout each time.

Web Templates

FrontPage provides templates at both the web level and the page level. Begin looking at the web level by loading FrontPage. When this is complete, if you are not in Folders view, click on Folders in the Views bar. Then click the arrow to the right of New on the toolbar, and choose Web. The New dialog box will open and display the templates and wizards that you can use. There are five web templates:

- One Page Web
- Customer Support Web
- Empty Web
- Personal Web
- Project Web

Using the One Page Web Template

The usual starting place for creating a general-purpose web is with the One Page Web template. This template creates a web folder structure for your server, with a single page. Do that now with these instructions (the New dialog box should be open on your screen):

1. Click One Page Web in the Web Sites tab of the New dialog box.

2. Enter the server and folder names where you want the new web stored in the Specify The Location Of The New Web drop-down list box. For the lack of any other name, type **Onepage**, and then click OK.

3. Click Folders in the Views bar. As you can see in Figure 4-1, this creates a web with a single page, the home page Default.htm.

4. Double-click Default.htm to open the home page in Page view. You will see a blank page. Just to keep track of it, type **Home Page**.

You can easily add pages to a web created with the One Page Web template in Page, Folders, or Navigation view, but in Navigation view you can also easily and

GETTING STARTED

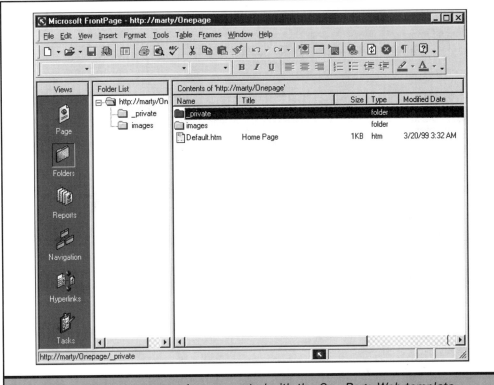

Figure 4-1. *The structure and page created with the One Page Web template*

graphically specify the relationship of new pages with existing pages. Try the following instructions and see how new pages are integrated into the web that was created in Navigation view.

1. After you generate a new One Page Web, click Navigation in the Views bar, click on the Home Page icon in the right pane, and then click New Page on the toolbar. (You can create as many pages as you need by clicking this button.) The first page you generate is called "New Page 1" and is a subsidiary page to the Home Page.

2. Create a second page with the New Page button, and continue to click New Page to generate four additional pages for a total of six in addition to the home page.

3. Edit the navigational relationships between pages by dragging the pages in the right (Navigation) pane of the Navigation view such that pages 4 and 5 are under page 2, and page 6 is being moved under page 4, as shown in Figure 4-2.

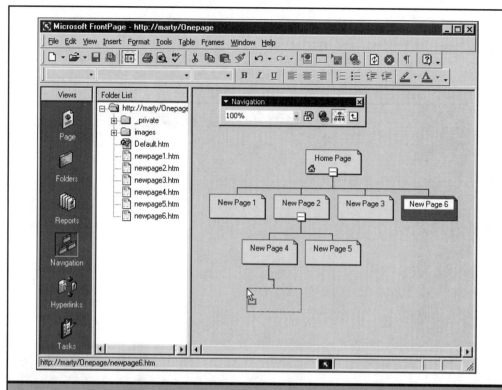

Figure 4-2. *Dragging a page into a new position in Navigation view*

Tip

Right-click an empty area of the right pane of Navigation view, and choose Zoom | Size To Fit to see all the pages if they are out of the window. If it is open, you can also use the Navigation toolbar, as shown in Figure 4-2.

4. Click the Home Page to select it, open the Format menu, choose Shared Borders, make sure All Pages is selected, click Top and Bottom, and then click OK.

5. Double-click the Home Page to open it in Page view. Click the top comment for the top shared border, press LEFT ARROW, open the Insert menu, open the extended menu, select Navigation Bar, choose Child Level, click OK, and press SHIFT+ENTER. This puts three buttons at the top of the Home Page to allow you to easily get from the home page to New Pages 1, 2, and 3, as shown next. You can see how easy it is to build a multipage web starting with a One Page Web template.

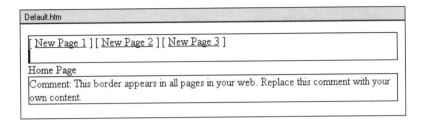

Note	*You replace the comments with your text by clicking on the comment and typing your text.*

6. When you are ready, open the File menu, choose Delete Web, click Remove This Web Entirely…, and click OK.

As you create your own webs, you'll probably use the One Page Web template often to build the small or custom webs that you'll need.

Applying the Empty Web Template

If you are going to import web content (see Chapter 12 for more on this subject) and a FrontPage structure in which to place it, then the Empty Web template is the way to start. This template creates a web folder structure for your server, but does not generate any web pages. Do that now with these instructions:

1. Click New | Web on the toolbar, click Empty Web in the New dialog box, enter a server and folder name, and click OK.

2. Click Folders in the View bar and you will see that the folder structure has been created for the web, but no pages, as here:

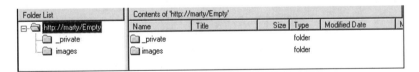

Why go to all this trouble for an empty web? FrontPage needs the folder structure to perform its functions. Since most webs have a number of pages and other elements, such as forms, the folder structure is used for organizing the web and making it easy to use and maintain. You can easily add pages to this web just as you did with the One Page Web.

3. Open the File menu and choose Delete Web, click Remove This Web Entirely…, and click OK.

Creating a Personal Web

FrontPage's Personal Web template creates a five-page web to publicize a person or small organization. See what this web is like by building it with the following steps:

1. Open the New dialog box, click Personal Web, enter a server and folder name, and click OK. The new web appears and if you look at Folders view, you will see the five pages (the five .htm files) that you can customize, as shown here:

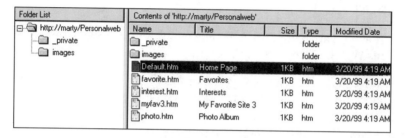

2. Double-click the Home Page (the Default.htm file) to open it in Page view. The page that opens has a lot of features incorporated in it, some of which are shown in Figure 4-3. These features are only suggestions and can be removed or customized. They provide a starting set of elements that you can use or delete depending on your needs, and you can add any other features that you want. Among the important features are the following:

   ■ **Shared Borders** at the top of the page and on the left side contain text or features such as navigation bars that start out the same on all pages, but can be customized on an individual page.

   ■ **Page title** in the top shared border contains a graphic with the page title text overlaid. To change the text, you must change the page title ("Home Page" in this case) in Navigation view by right-clicking the page and choosing Rename. Changing the name in the Page Property dialog box or editing the text on the page does not permanently change the title.

   ■ **Navigation bars** below the title (which needs to be edited to be displayed) and on the left of the page are buttons or lines of text that are hyperlinks to other pages in the web. You can edit a bar by right-clicking in the rectangle that encompasses it and then choosing Navigation Bar Properties. The Navigation Bar Properties dialog box will open, where you can change the hyperlinks used for navigation and the orientation and appearance of the buttons. You'll work with this dialog box later in the chapter.

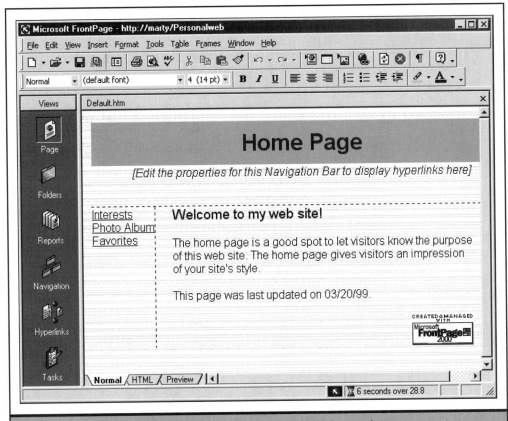

Figure 4-3.   *Home Page created with the Personal Web template*

Tip   *The Navigation Bar Properties dialog box allows you to determine the navigation bar buttons from among pages hierarchically above (Parent Level), below (Child Level), or on the same level in the Hyperlinks To Add To Page area of the dialog box. This allows you to direct how the navigation bar will be built.*

- **Plain text** is text that you can replace with your own words by simply editing it as you would in a word processor. For example, Michael Smith might replace "Welcome to my Web site!" with "Welcome to Michael Smith's Web Site!"

- **Hyperlinks** are marked with underlines. They are links to other pages in your web site.

- A **Background image** may be included in the page. This is a small graphic file that is *tiled* or repeated across the background of the web page.

- **Text font and colors** have been assigned. These, along with the background image, are part of a theme that has been attached to this web.

- **Timestamp** is placed on the page using the Date and Time option of the Insert menu. It will automatically display the date the page was last updated or edited. You can change the time stamp properties by double-clicking the date to open the Date and Time Properties dialog box, shown here:

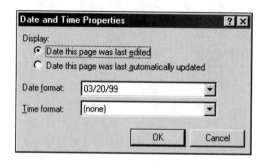

- **FrontPage 2000 logo** is on the bottom-right of the home page. You can delete this logo or edit it with the Picture toolbar by double-clicking it.

When you are done looking at the Home page, choose Open from the Page view File menu to view other pages that were generated by the Personal Web template. Then close Page view and delete the web you created. The "simple" personal web you can create with the Personal Web template is a good starting point for many webs and offers a number of useful features. Consider using it as you create your own webs.

Using the Project Web Template

The Project Web template creates a multipage web, shown in Figure 4-4, that is used to keep people up to date on a project. It lists a project's staff members, schedule, and status, and provides independent page headers and footers, an archive, a search engine, and a discussion bulletin board. (You've seen how some of these features are used in the webs you created with wizards in Chapter 3.) Follow these steps to look at some of the features that are unique to this template:

1. Open the New dialog box, select Project Web, enter a server and folder name for the web, such as "Project," and click OK. A new web will be created and will appear. In Navigation view it will look like Figure 4-4.

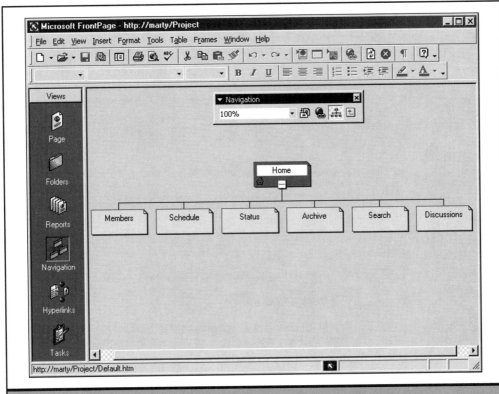

Figure 4-4. *Project web, as the Project Web template creates it*

2. Double-click the Home icon in Navigation view to open Page view. The page shown in Figure 4-5 will be displayed.

Shared Borders in the Project Web

In the previous chapter you explored shared borders and again saw them added to a web in the One Page Web discussion earlier in this chapter. See how shared borders can be edited here. The Project web has three shared borders that can be edited.

1. Edit the navigation bar in the top shared border by double-clicking it. This opens the Navigation Bar Properties dialog box.

2. In the Navigation Bar Properties dialog box, select the Child Level option from the Hyperlinks To Add To Page area and the Horizontal and Text options from the Orientation And Appearance area. Leave the two check boxes (Home page and Parent page) selected, as shown in Figure 4-6. Click OK.

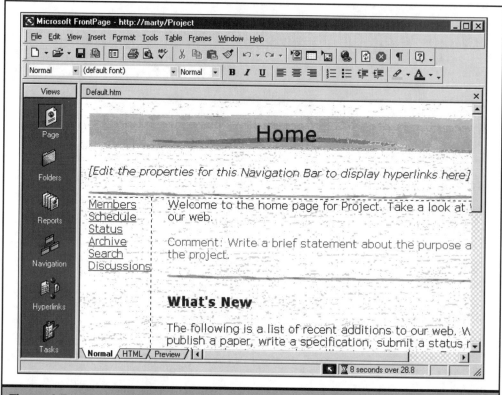

Figure 4-5.   *Project Web home page with title and navigation bars*

The names that appear in a navigation bar are the names of the other pages in the web as determined by the Navigation Bar Properties dialog box. To change the actual words used in the navigation bar, you must change the page names in Navigation view by clicking slowly twice (not double-clicking) on a page and entering a new name followed by pressing ENTER.

3. Scroll to the bottom of the page. Note the bottom shared border as shown next. It has the automatic Date and Time component (although it is showing only the date here).

> Copyright or other proprietary statement goes here.
> For problems or questions regarding this web contact [ProjectEmail].
> Last updated: March 20, 1999.

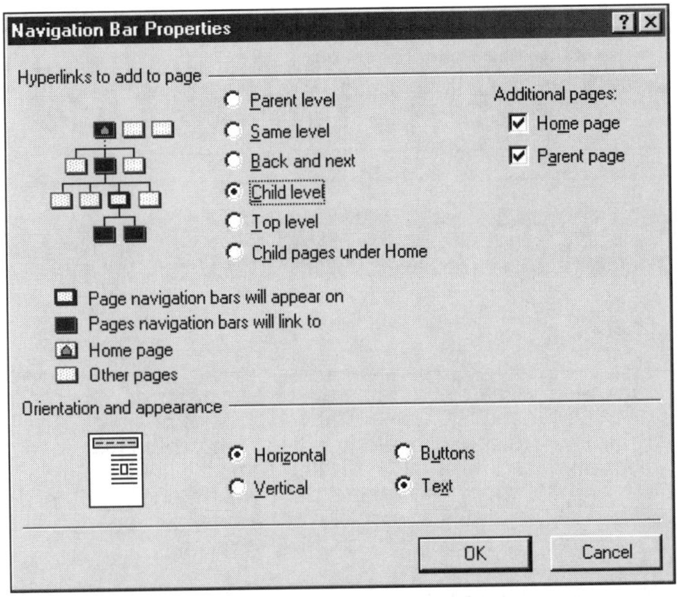

Figure 4-6. *Changing the hyperlinks references in a navigation bar*

4. Open and review the Members, Schedule, Status, and Archive pages. On each you'll see the shared borders, as well as other features you saw on the Personal Web Home Page.

Note *Since you chose Child Level in the Navigation Bar Properties dialog box, you only have Home in the navigation bar of the pages below the Home page. If you change it for the subsequent pages, you won't have any links on the Home page (try it and see), so you must find a combination that works for both page types.*

Searches and Discussion Groups

The Project web that you created incorporates two other FrontPage-created features—text searches and discussion groups—that add interactivity to the web. You saw how these features worked in the Corporate Presence web you created in Chapter 3. To review how these work in the Project web:

1. Open the Project Web Search page in Page view by choosing Open from the File menu and double-clicking Search.htm. Your screen should look like Figure 4-7. This page includes a one-field form that allows you to search the documents in the current web for a particular text string that you have entered in the form.

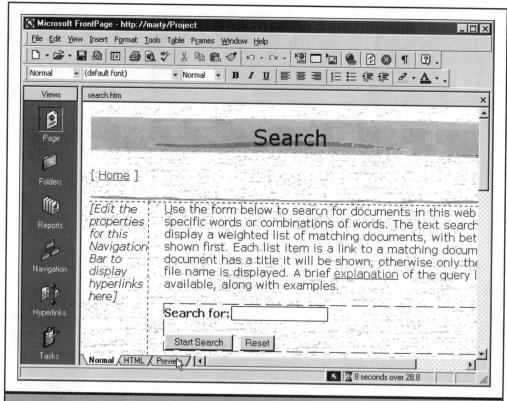

Figure 4-7. *Search page for doing text searches*

This search form is another FrontPage component. You can edit its characteristics by right-clicking in the search area and choosing Search Form Properties. The bottom part of the Search page contains instructions on how to structure a search query.

2. Close the Search page and open the Project Web Discussions page (Discuss.htm), which contains links to two discussion groups (Requirements and Knowledge Base). The discussion groups are separate. They allow people to enter comments, and others to comment on their comments, thereby creating threads on a given subject. Most online forums follow this format.

3. To get a better perspective of the Project web, click Preview In Browser on the toolbar and follow the navigation buttons to look at the various pages. When you are finished viewing the Project web, close your browser. Then delete the Project web.

A web that has been created with the Project Web template provides an excellent communications tool, not only for projects, but also for any team, operation, or department.

Applying the Customer Support Web Template

The Customer Support Web template, shown in Figure 4-8, makes a lot of information available to users in several ways and allows users to provide information to you in two ways. In doing this, the web uses FrontPage features you have already seen, but with different twists. We'll look at those differences next.

1. Create a Customer Support web using the Customer Support Web template in the New dialog box Web Sites tab. In Navigation view your result should look like Figure 4-8.

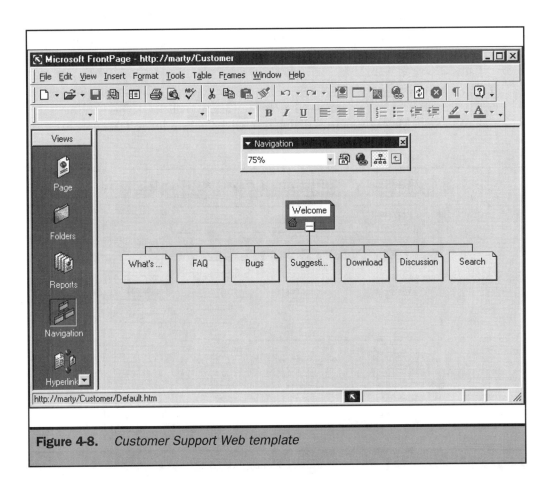

Figure 4-8. *Customer Support Web template*

2. Open the Welcome page, the home page for this web. This page has a top, bottom, and left shared border, with navigation bars in the top and left.

3. Close the Welcome page and then open, look at, and close the What's New and FAQ (frequently asked questions) pages. These pages, well-designed for their purposes, are simply combinations of text and hyperlinks with the included header and footer.

4. Open the Customer Support—Bugs page (Bugrep.htm). If you scroll down the page, you'll see a special form for collecting errors in computer software (*bugs*). As with all other features in a wizard- or template-created web, you can customize this, changing the text, size, and content of the fields.

5. To experience changing one of the fields on the form, right-click the drop-down list box that displays Windows 98, and choose Form Field Properties. The field's Properties dialog box will open, as shown in Figure 4-9. Here you can change the name of the field in the top text box and change the choices the field presents to the user by using the Add, Modify, and Remove buttons.

6. Click Windows NT or Windows 2000 to select it and click Modify. In the Modify Choice dialog box delete "or Windows 2000" and replace it with "4.0." Click OK.

7. Click Add to open the Add Choice dialog box. Type **Windows 2000** in the Choice text box, leave other settings as they are, and click OK. Back in the Drop-Down Menu Properties dialog box, click the Windows 2000 entry to

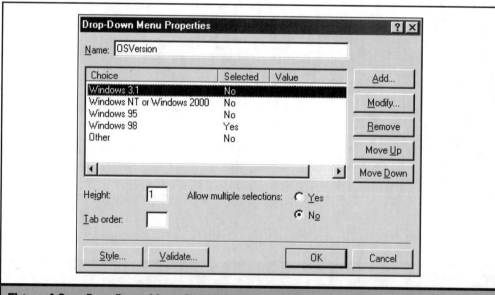

Figure 4-9.   *Drop-Down Menu Properties dialog box*

select it, and then click Move Up to move the new entry above Other and below Windows 98.

8. Click OK to close the Drop-Down Menu Properties dialog box and then close and save the Bugs page; open, look at, and close the Suggestions From Customers page (Suggest.htm), which contains the results of another form. Then open the Customer Support Download page (Download.htm).

The purpose of the Download page is to allow users to transfer software or documents to their computers from your server. This is done with the FTP (file transfer protocol) Internet protocol.

9. Close the Download page and then open, look at, and close the Discussion and Search pages. These contain a discussion group and a search form similar to those you saw in the Project web.

10. Open your Customer Support web in a browser and try its features, submitting a bug report and a suggestion. This will show you how these work. You should see a confirmation page.

11. After you enter and submit input in the Suggestions and Bugs pages, return to FrontPage and select Refresh from the View menu or by clicking the toolbar button. Then use Page view to open and view the Buglist.htm and Feedback.htm results pages.

12. When you are done, delete the Customer Support web.

 As noted in Chapter 3, these webs are deleted when you are done looking at them because they take a fair amount of disk space (the Customer Support web, as it is created by the template, takes over 500KB and the corporate web is almost 700KB).

Page Templates

The Web templates create webs with many different page types and features on each page. Sometimes, though, what you want is a single page. For that purpose, FrontPage provides page templates. In this section you'll see some of the more useful page templates. Begin with these steps:

1. In FrontPage create a new web using the Empty Web template; name its folder **TestPages**. In Navigation view, add a home page by clicking New Page on the toolbar.

2. Double-click the Home Page icon to open it in Page view.

3. Open the File menu, choose New, and select Page. The New dialog box appears with the General tab selected, as shown in Figure 4-10.

Note *The New Page toolbar button gives you a new page using the Normal Page template (a blank page); it does not open the New dialog box where you can choose other templates.*

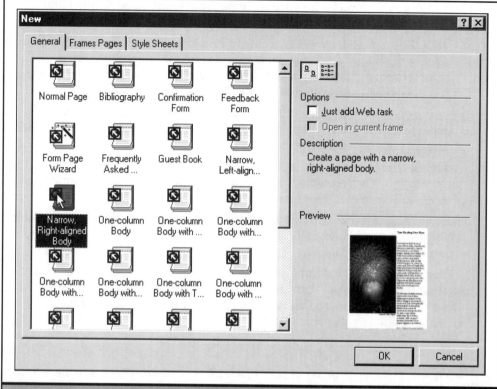

Figure 4-10. *The templates and wizard available to use with a new page*

The 25 templates (and one wizard) listed in the New dialog box General tab represent a tremendous resource that you can use to build your own webs. Chapter 2 provided a brief description of all the page templates and wizard. Let's look at five of them. As each template is discussed, use the template to create a page and look at the results, at least in Page view, and possibly in your browser. You can add a page like the Search Page to a web by opening the web in FrontPage, opening Page view, and then creating a new page with the template or wizard you want to use.

Feedback Form Template

The Feedback Form template creates a general-purpose form page, as you can see in Figure 4-11, that allows a user to send you comments. The template creates several types of fields, gives them names, and generates files needed to capture the information submitted and to save it in the Feedback.txt file in the _Private subfolder under the web's folder. (If you use the default folder scheme and your web is named TestPages, then the full path for Feedback.txt with the Microsoft Personal Web Server is C:\Inetpub\Wwwroot\ TestPages_Private\Feedback.txt.)

Note *Both "folder" and "directory" describe the container of disk files. In this book, we'll use "folder" when talking about the file structure in FrontPage and other Windows 98 applications, and "directory" when referring to the real or "virtual" file structure on many servers such as Windows NT.*

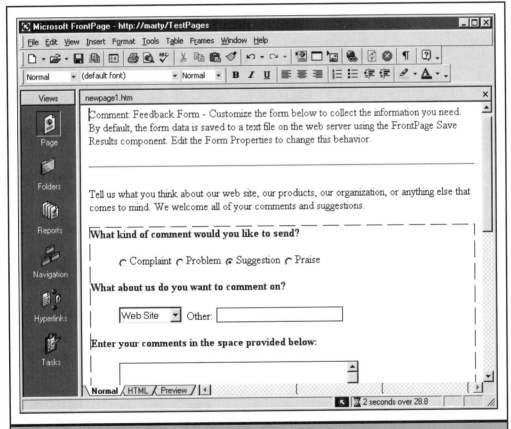

Figure 4-11. *Form page created with the Feedback Form page template*

Confirmation Form Template

A *confirmation page* is used to show someone submitting information to you that his or her submission was received. When you create a submission form—for example, a feedback form or a registration form—FrontPage automatically generates a default confirmation page. You can create a custom confirmation page by using the Confirmation Form template, but you must specify that you want to use your own confirmation page in the Form Properties dialog box of the submission form (from a form's context menu, click Form Properties, click again Options, select the Confirmation Page tab, and fill in the URL of the confirmation page). In Hyperlinks view, you can see the link between the submission form and the confirmation page it uses.

The Confirmation Form template creates a confirmation page, as shown in Figure 4-12. This page contains fields from the form the user submitted. You can add fields to a confirmation page by using the Component | Confirmation Field option on the Insert

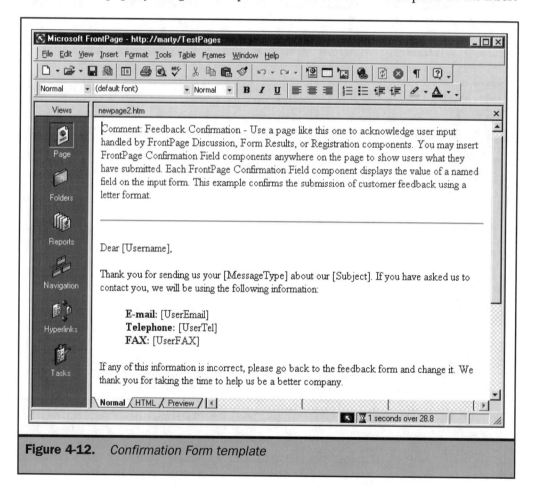

Figure 4-12. *Confirmation Form template*

menu, as well as change the text and move the existing confirmation fields. The only requirement is that the name of a field on a form must be the same as the name used in the confirmation page. Several submission forms can share the same confirmation page if the forms use the same field names.

 You must know the field names from the submission form when you are building the confirmation page, because the Insert | Component | Confirmation Field, option, which requires the field name, does not allow you to browse for them.

Search Page Template

The Search Page template provides all the text search features that you saw in the webs earlier in this chapter. It is completely self-contained, including the query language instructions, as you can see in Figure 4-13. When you include this page in a web, it will search all of the text in the web without any further effort on your part.

When visitors to your web site use your search page, they will receive a list of pages with content that matches their search criteria, as shown in Figure 4-14. The visitor can click the entries in the list of pages to view the page they want.

Table of Contents Template

The page, or more likely a portion thereof, created by the Table of Contents template is probably one of the more useful page templates. When you have finished adding all of the pages to a web, giving them each names and creating links from a home page, add a table of contents page, or incorporate its contents on another page. This will not look like much in Page view, but when you open the page in a browser, you'll have a complete table of contents of all the pages in the web.

Figure 4-15 was created from a web that contained the pages created with templates discussed in the preceding sections, including the home page of the web. To do this, a shared border with a page banner (to supply the page title) and a navigation bar (to supply the links to the other pages) was added to all pages of the web. After creating the Contents, you need to open the Table of Contents Properties dialog box and specify the filename of the home page, as shown here:

Table of Contents Properties

Page URL for starting point of table:

`Default.htm`   Browse...

Heading font size: `3`

Options:

☑ Show each page only once

☑ Show pages with no incoming hyperlinks

☑ Recompute table of contents when any other page is edited

OK   Cancel

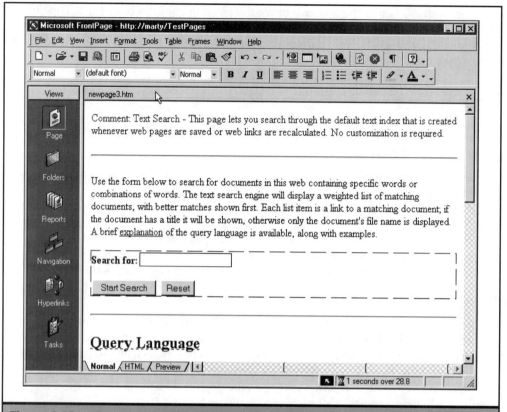

Figure 4-13. *Text search page created with the Search Page template*

The Narrow, Right-Aligned Body Page Template

The templates you have examined so far used components like search boxes, tables of contents, and input forms. These templates generated valuable features by using the components. There are other page templates that do not use components or any usable text. They provide layout features that you can use to design your web pages. Narrow, Right-aligned Body is one such template.

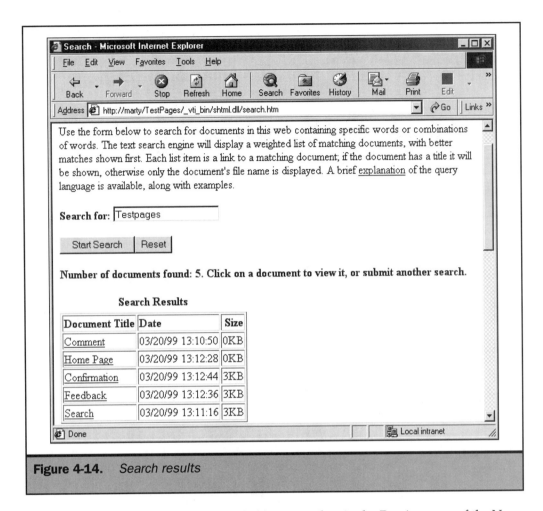

Figure 4-14.   *Search results*

You can preview the layout provided by a template in the Preview area of the New dialog box. Figure 4-10 earlier in this chapter shows the Narrow, Right-aligned Body template.

The page generated by the Narrow, Right-aligned Body template is a two-column, three-row table. The lower-left table cell has a large, impressive graphic. The upper-right cell has a heading, and the lower-right cell is full of nonsense (or Greeked)

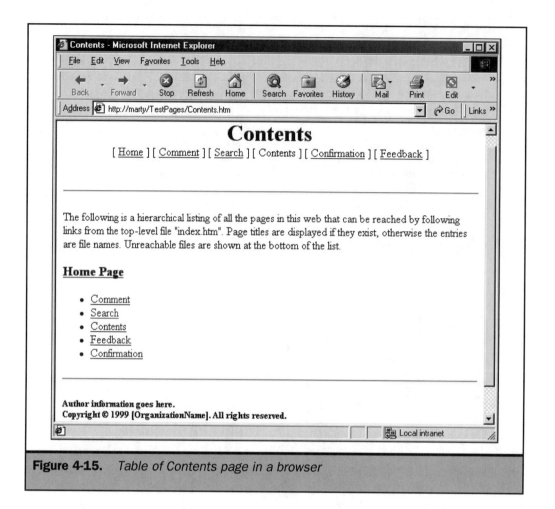

Figure 4-15. *Table of Contents page in a browser*

text, both of which you will replace with your own content. You will explore tables in detail in Chapter 8, but for now you can still use this template to design pages.

When visitors see your web page, they will not see the dotted lines that define the cells in Page view. Figure 4-16 shows how this page looks in the Preview tab, where table cell boundaries are not visible.

Before going on to create your own templates, close and delete the TestPages web you have been using.

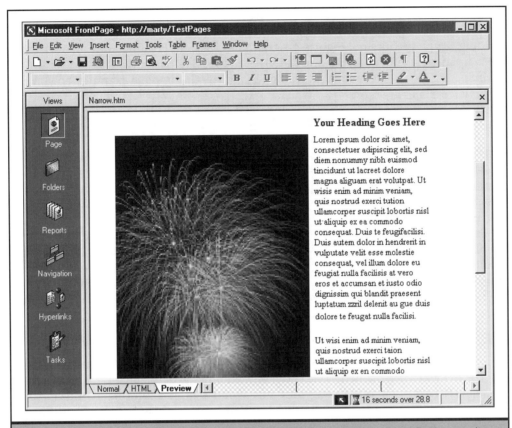

Figure 4-16. *Viewing a page generated by the Narrow, Right-aligned Body template*

Creating Your Own FrontPage Templates

As you have been working with templates, you have probably had some ideas for templates that you wished were available. If you are setting up an intranet, this is especially true, because it makes excellent sense to have a template for the entire organization to use to get a consistent web across the company. In any situation where several similar webs are needed, you can use a template to create them. If you are creating a large web with a number of pages that look alike, you can create a page template that will speed up the process.

In the next couple of sections you'll look at the types of templates you can create and their common characteristics, and then see how to build the different types. Building templates does not require programming, as does creating your own wizards, but templates do require getting the right files in the right place. We'll spend some time clarifying the file management and leading you through complete examples so you can see how templates are built.

Types of Templates

Templates are model or prototype webs or web pages, identical in every detail to an actual web or web page. The only thing that distinguishes them is that they are in a special folder. You can view a template in a browser and use it like any other web or web page. In fact, a template is just a web or web page that has been set aside to serve as a model for other webs or web pages.

Because they are stored in different folders, think of web templates and page templates as two distinct types of templates, although there are many similarities. *Page* templates generally create a single page that becomes part of a separately created web, although a page template can include additional linked pages. A *web* template creates a full FrontPage web with one or more interconnected pages. This means that it includes all of the folder structure that is a part of FrontPage. In both cases, though, you create the web or the page in the same way that you would create any other web or page. When the web or page is the way you want it, you then place it in a special folder set up for templates with the extension TEM. For example, Test.tem is a folder containing the files for a template named "Test." The files within the template folder are just the normal HTM extension HTML web files plus an INF template information file and a DIB file, which is a thumbnail of the template that appears in Page view's New dialog box Preview section.

FrontPage Folder Structure

The TEM template folders that come with FrontPage 2000 are stored in different folders depending on whether they are pages, webs, frames, or styles. If you used the default installation, these folders have the path

C: \Program Files\Microsoft Office\Templates\1033\

Figure 4-17 shows the contents of the Pages and Webs folders within that path.
If you have installed the Microsoft Personal Web Server 4.0 or are using it with Windows 98 along with the default installation, you have a folder with the path

C:\Inetpub\Wwwroot

This folder is the root directory for the webs that you want to let people access with MSPWS on your computer. The folder can store all of the FrontPage webs that you

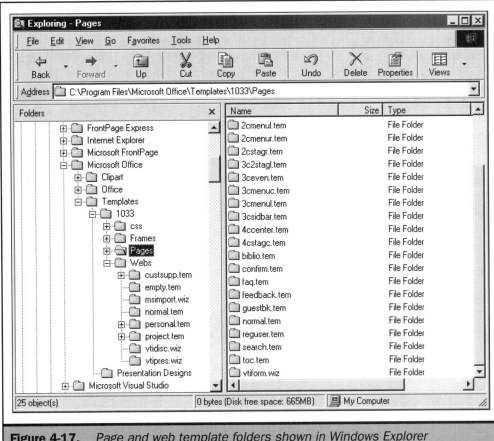

Figure 4-17.   *Page and web template folders shown in Windows Explorer*

create. It is *not* used to store templates, but comes into play when you create them, as you'll see later in this chapter.

Open your C:\Program Files\Microsoft Office\Templates\1033\Pages folder now, and then open one of the TEM template folders. Within the template folder you should see at least three files, like this:

Name	Size	Type
1center.dib	15KB	DIB File
1center.htm	3KB	Microsoft HTML Doc...
1center.inf	1KB	Setup Information

One of these files is an HTM web file that, if you double-click it, will open your default browser and display the web page produced by the template. In any other folder, this file would be considered just another web page; there is nothing to distinguish it except the folder it is in. The other files within the template folder are an INF setup information file and a DIB image file, which is a thumbnail of your page template automatically generated by FrontPage and used in the Preview area of the New dialog box. Look at the INF file next.

The INF (Setup Information) File

The INF (Setup Information) file is used to hold descriptive information about the template. It is similar to a Windows INI file and is read by Page view and FrontPage when they are working with templates. The INF file must have the same name as the TEM folder it is in; so, for example, the Test.tem folder will contain the Test.inf file.

In the Pages folder, open the 1center folder and then double-click the 1center.inf file. If the INF file type is not associated with an application that can read it on your computer, select Notepad as that application. Notepad will open and display the file's short contents, like this:

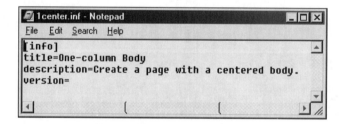

The Setup Information File [info] Section

The INF information file will always have an [info] section with at least two items in it—the title of the template and its description—as you just saw. These items are used in the New dialog box to provide the name of the template and its description (as you can see in Figure 4-18).

If the INF file is not included, FrontPage uses the base name of the template folder ("Test" if the template folder is Test.tem) as the title and leaves the description blank.

Under most circumstances, the INF file will automatically be created for you, as you will see in later sections of this chapter. When it isn't created automatically, you must be aware that the format of the INF file is important and must match what you saw earlier. There must be a section named "[info]," and it must contain the title and description lines spelled correctly and with the equal signs. Whatever is on the right of the equal sign is data that will appear in the Description area or below the icon representing its title of the New Page or New FrontPage Web dialog box. Each of the fields in the [info] section can be up to 255 characters long, including the attribute

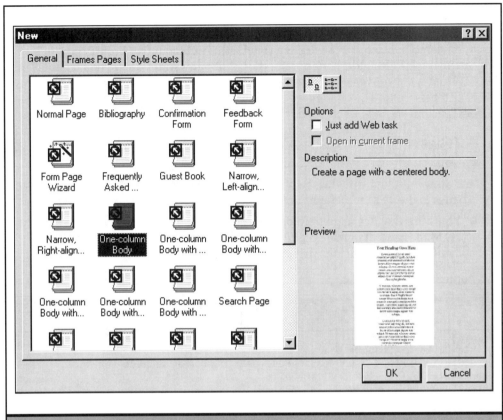

Figure 4-18.   *Page template descriptions reflect the description in the Setup information file*

name ("title" and "description") and an equal sign. As a practical matter, though, to be completely visible within the New dialog box, the title should be fewer than 30 characters, and the description should be fewer than 100 characters.

Tip   *If you do have to create an INF file, the easiest way is to copy an existing file and change the name, title, and description.*

For page templates, which are displayed in Page view, only the [info] section of the INF file is used. For web templates, with one or more pages within them, the INF file can have additional sections, including [FileList], [MetaInfo], and [TaskList], that are used when the template is loaded into a server.

The File Information [FileList] Section

The [FileList] section, which is shown in Figure 4-19, tells FrontPage how you want the files in the template stored in a web. If a [FileList] is not included, FrontPage loads all of the files in the TEM folder, but does nothing with any subfolders. The filenames in the TEM folder are converted to all lowercase and become URLs in the web. Also, any JPG or GIF files in the TEM folder are placed in the Images subfolder of the web. The [FileList] section should be included if you have any of the following situations:

- You have subfolders to the TEM folder containing files you want in the web.
- You want to specify the URL and/or the case it uses.
- You want to indicate the specific files in the TEM folder to be placed in the web (files in the TEM folder and not in [FileList] are ignored).
- You want the files to go to folders in the web other than the root folder for the HTM files and the images subfolder for the JPG and GIF files. The other available subfolders are _private and cgi-bin.

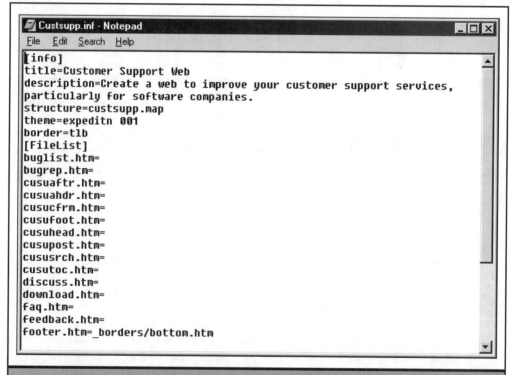

Figure 4-19.   *A Setup Information file (INF) with a [FileList] section*

When you use the [FileList], you must list all of the files you want transferred. If you do not want to change the filename or the path, list just the filename with an equal sign after it. If you want to specify the path, you need to switch from the MS-DOS/Windows use of the *backslash* between subfolders on the *left* of the file list to the URL use of a *slash* between subfolders on the *right* side, as shown in the last line of Figure 4-19.

The Information File [MetaInfo] Section

The [MetaInfo] section can be used to store configuration variables used in the Substitution component (discussed in Chapter 10). In this way the [MetaInfo] section supplies the custom configuration variables that would otherwise have to be manually loaded into the Parameters tab of the FrontPage Web Settings dialog box for each web (opened by selecting Web Settings from FrontPage Tools menu). For example, you might provide the following company information for all users of a template:

```
[MetaInfo]
CompanyName=Exciting Travel, Inc.
CompanyAddress=1 Main St., Some Town, WA 98100
```

The Information File [TaskList] Section

The [TaskList] section is used to provide a list of tasks to be placed in the FrontPage Tasks view for a web template. The tasks in the list have the following format:

TaskNumber=TaskName | Priority | CreatedBy | URL | Cookie | Comment

The elements in the task list are separated by a vertical bar and are described in Table 4-1. Figure 4-20 shows a Tasks view Task Details dialog box in which you can see how the elements are used.

Adding tasks to a web template adds significantly to its value and can reduce the amount of support that is needed to help organizations use your template.

Home Page Renaming

As a default, FrontPage names the home page in its webs Default.htm if you are using MSPWS. On an NCSA server (a common UNIX-based server), the name "Index.htm" is implied for the home page and can be left off the URL for a web. For example, the URL **http://www.fairmountain.com/wine** opens the Index.htm page in the Wine web on the Fairmountain NCSA server. Depending on the server to which the web is eventually uploaded, the implied name for a home page can differ. On a CERN server (another UNIX server), it normally is Welcome.htm, and on a Windows NT Internet Information Server, it is Default.htm. When FrontPage creates a web from a web template, it will

Element	Description	Comments
TaskNumber	A unique number or a key	For example, "t01," "t02," "t03," and so on
TaskName	A short task description	A three- or four-word phrase used as the task name
Priority	An integer describing relative importance	1 = High, 2 = Medium, 3 = Low
CreatedBy	Name of template	Used in the Created By field of the dialog box
URL	The URL for the task	The page or image that the task refers to
Cookie	The location on the page where work is required	Only bookmarks are supported, in the form #bookmark
Comment	Description of task	A longer description of what needs to be done (cannot contain new-line characters)

Table 4-1. *Description of [TaskList] Elements*

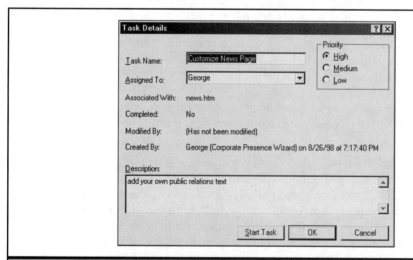

Figure 4-20. *The elements of a task in the Task Details dialog box*

automatically rename any file named "Index.htm" to the name appropriate for the current server. FrontPage, though, *does not change any links to the home page.* To use the automatic renaming feature, you can make all links to the home page be a special ./ (period-slash) link that will force the server to locate the correct home page. If you do not want to use the automatic renaming feature, put the following line in the [info] section of the INF information file:

NoIndexRenaming=1

Creating Page Templates

FrontPage 2000 makes it easy to create customized page templates. These templates can then be reused, just like the page templates that come with FrontPage. FrontPage 2000 even generates a thumbnail graphic illustrating your page that you can see in Page view's New Page dialog box.

Building a single-page template is simplicity itself. Just create a normal web page with the material you want on it, and then save it as a template. That's all there is to it! Before you go on, though, try it for yourself:

1. Load the CD that comes with this book in your drive, choose Open from the File menu, locate the Hometem.htm file in the \Book\Chap04 folder on the CD, and double-click it. The page opens in Page view.

2. From the File menu, click Save As. In the Save As Type drop-down list, select FrontPage Template. Click Save. The Save As Template dialog box will open.

3. Change the title to **Home Page Template**, name it **hometem**, type **Create a custom home page.** (including the period) in the Description box, as shown next, and click OK.

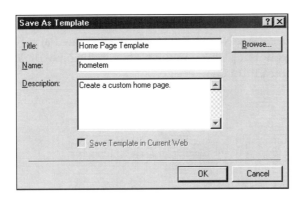

4. A New copy of FrontPage will open and display your new template in Page view, as shown in Figure 4-21. Note that the path is within the Windows folder and different from any template folder you have seen above.

5. Close the copy of FrontPage displaying the new template, open Windows Explorer, and locate the new template. With the default folder structure, it will be in

C:\Windows\Application Data\Microsoft\FrontPage\Pages\hometem.tem.

If you do not see the template name appear in the \Pages subfolder, press F5 to refresh Windows Explorer.

6. Open the Hometem.tem folder. You should see the three files that were automatically created when you saved the page as a template. These are the HTM web file, the INF information file, and the DIB image file (which is used for a thumbnail picture of the template in the New dialog box. Double-click the INF (Setup Information) file. It should open and reflect your entries in step 4 above, as shown next.

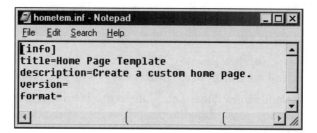

7. Close Notepad and return to the original copy of FrontPage in Page view. Open the File menu, choose New | Page, and select Home Page Template. Figure 4-22 shows what your template should look like in the New dialog box with the description and a thumbnail image.

8. Double-click Home Page Template, and a new page based on your template will open ready for you to customize. When you are ready, save the page with a unique name, and close the web.

Although this example was very simple, you can see that with your template you should be able to substantially reduce the time it will take to create additional pages, and that all of the pages you create using templates will be very consistent. In Chapter 5 you'll see how to create graphics you can use in a web, and in Chapter 6 you will learn about the various elements you can use to customize your web pages and templates. In Appendix B you can read about creating a web template, which is not as easy as creating page templates.

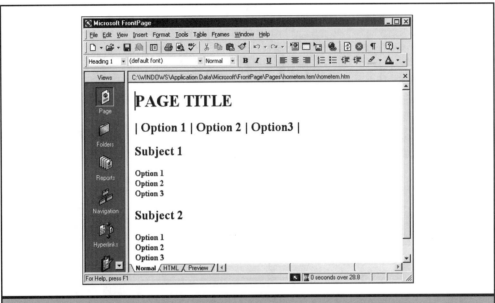

Figure 4-21.   *Folders and files created when a web page is saved as a template*

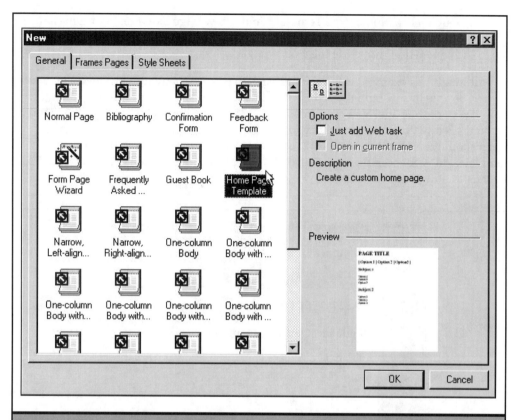

Figure 4-22. *List of templates include the newly created template with a thumbnail preview view*

The Complete Reference

FrontPage 2000

Chapter 5

Creating Graphics for FrontPage Webs

Y ou can buy FrontPage 2000 either as a stand-alone product or as a component of Office 2000 Premium Edition. The stand-alone package includes Microsoft Image Composer for producing graphics to be used in a web, while Office 2000 Premium Edition includes Microsoft PhotoDraw, which can be used for the same purpose. This chapter includes discussions of both products.

Using Microsoft Image Composer

Microsoft Image Composer is a graphic image program that is bundled with the stand-alone version of FrontPage 2000. In this section you'll look at Image Composer in some depth with an eye to creating and editing graphics that you can use in the webs you create.

Image Composer is a full-featured application for creating and manipulating bitmapped images. As the name implies, a *bitmapped image* is one that is composed of numerous bits that are of various colors and transparencies. Bitmapped images can be created by using many different "paint" programs, by scanning a photograph into your computer, or by taking a photograph with a digital camera. There are also many libraries of clip art and bitmapped images, including image files that come with FrontPage 2000 (you'll explore these later in this chapter) that you can use and modify. Image Composer has its own file format with the extension.MIC, but it can open and save images in a number of different bitmapped formats including

- Adobe Photoshop (*.PSD)
- Altamira Composer (*.ACC)—open only
- CompuServe GIF (*.GIF)
- FlashPix (*.FPX)
- JPEG (*.JPG)
- Microsoft Picture It! (*.MIX)
- Portable Network Graphics (*.PNG)
- Targa (*.TGA)
- Tagged Image File Format (*.TIF, *.TIFF)
- Windows bitmap (*.BMP, *.DIB)—.DIB open only

The Image Composer Window

The Image Composer window, which is shown in Figure 5-1, contains a number of unique features. In addition to the normal toolbar below the menus at the top, there is a *toolbox* running down the left edge. At the bottom of the toolbox is the *Color Swatch*, which shows the current color you are working with. Within the working area of the window there is a white area called the *composition space*, which shows the desired area of the image you're working on. At the bottom of the window is the status bar, which shows the *x* and *y* coordinates of the current mouse position on the right, the position and size of the currently selected object, and other information. Within the Image Composer window there is an open dialog box called a "palette." This particular palette is automatically opened when the Arrange tool is selected in the toolbox and allows you to select various options for that tool.

 The area of the composition space is the only area that is saved when you save to a GIF, JPEG, Targa, TIFF, FPX, MIX, PNG, or Windows BMP format. Only the Image Composer's MIC or Adobe Photoshop PSD format saves the entire composition you are working on.

Image Composer Toolbar and Menus

The Image Composer toolbar contains standard Windows buttons from the leftmost button through the Undo arrow. To the right of the Undo arrow are nine buttons or drop-down menus unique to Image Composer. They are described in Table 5-1.

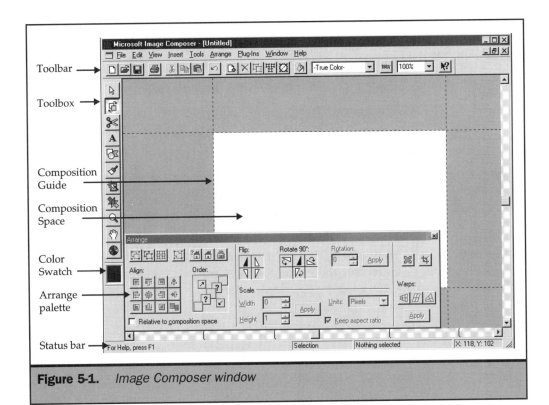

Figure 5-1.   *Image Composer window*

Icon	Name	Description
	Insert Image File	Opens the Insert From File dialog box, allowing you to select an image that you want to add to the current composition
	Delete	Deletes the current selection
	Duplicate	Duplicates the current selection
	Select All	Selects all of the objects currently displayed in Image Composer
	Clear Selection	Removes the focus from the currently selected object
	Color Fill	Assigns the color in the Color Swatch to all selected objects
-True Color-	Color Format	Allows the selection of the color palette that you want to use
100%	Actual Size	Returns the display to actual size
100%	Zoom Percent	Zooms the display to a selected percentage of actual size

Table 5-1. *Image Composer's Unique Toolbar Buttons*

Image Composer's menus include a number of standard Windows options, plus options that duplicate the toolbar and toolbox buttons and tools, and a few unique options not available elsewhere. The latter are described as they are used later in this chapter.

Image Composer Toolbox and Palettes

The tools in the toolbox allow you to manipulate the objects you are working on in many ways, including arranging, painting, warping, and coloring existing objects, plus adding shapes and text as additional objects.

The first tool in the Image Composer toolbox is the Selection tool. This tool is not associated with a palette or dialog box. It is used only to select individual objects in the workspace.

ARRANGE TOOL AND PALETTE   With the Arrange tool and palette, you can size, crop, rotate, flip, order, align, group, ungroup, flatten, and position the selected object(s).

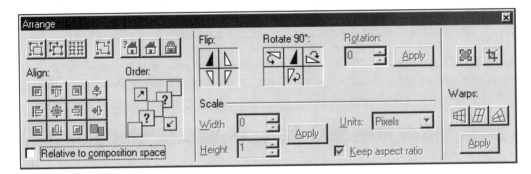

CUTOUT TOOL AND PALETTE   The Cutout tool and palette allow you to erase pixels from an individual object in the image on the screen (called a *sprite*), selecting them either by shape or by color.

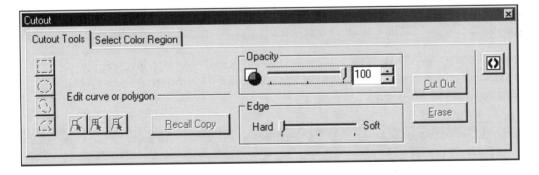

TEXT TOOL AND PALETTE   The Text tool and palette allow you to create or edit a block of text; to select the font, font size, and font style from those available on your computer; and to set the opacity.

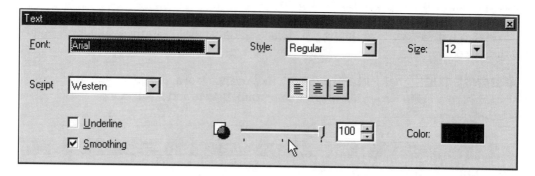

 SHAPES TOOL AND PALETTE   The Shapes tool and palette allow you to create rectangles, ovals, curves, and polygons; to set the opacity of a shape; and to edit the points or nodes in a curve or polygon.

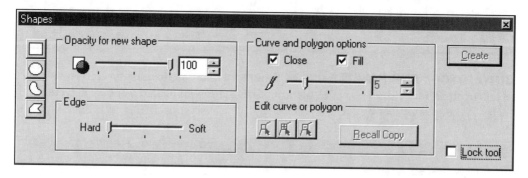

 PAINT TOOL AND PALETTE   With the Paint tool and palette, you can apply colors and effects to selected pixels within a sprite, using various tools, point sizes, and opacity.

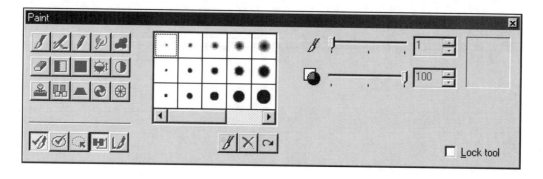

EFFECTS TOOL AND PALETTE   The Effects tool and palette allow you to apply specific transformations to the selected object. The transformations include bending an object, adding outlines around it, changing the sharpness of the image, and changing the properties of the object's color.

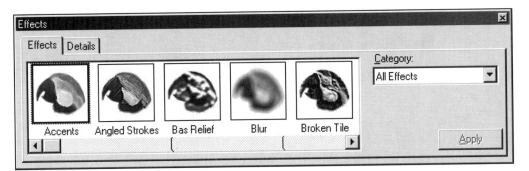

 TEXTURE TRANSFER TOOL AND PALETTE   The Texture Transfer tool and palette allow you to copy selected attributes of one sprite (including fill color or pattern) to another overlapping sprite. For example, you can use this tool to transfer a design or pattern into a text sprite.

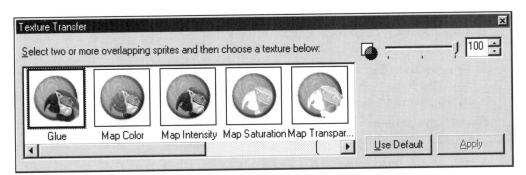

 ZOOM TOOL   Clicking the Zoom tool in the toolbox changes the mouse pointer to a magnifying glass (with a plus sign in it), which, when clicked anywhere in the workspace, increases the magnification of the objects by 100 percent. (Return to actual size by clicking Actual Size on the Image Composer toolbar.) Holding down the CTRL key on your keyboard while you click with the Zoom tool decreases the magnification (zooms out) in varying increments.

 PAN TOOL   Clicking the Pan tool in the toolbox changes the mouse pointer to a grabber hand with which you can move or pan the contents of the window's workspace. (The Pan tool moves the entire workspace, not individual objects—do that with the Selection tool.)

COLOR TUNING TOOL AND PALETTE   The Color Tuning tool and palette allow you to change the color of an object by shifting a color through changes to its brightness, contrast, hue, and saturation; by changing the highlights and shadows on the object; or by changing the dynamic range of a color.

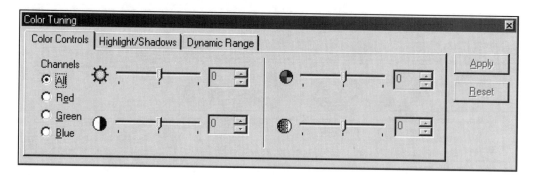

 COLOR SWATCH AND COLOR PICKER   Clicking the Color Swatch below the toolbox opens the Color Picker dialog box (referred to as the *Color Picker*), shown in Figure 5-2, which allows you to choose a color for the objects you create or whose color you want to change, or to create a custom palette from which you can choose colors. You can choose a color in the Color Picker in three ways:

- Click inside the large color square on the left of the dialog box, which is called a *color matrix* and shows hue and blackness.

- Drag the triangles or *handles* on the edges of the color matrix. The handle on the left is the *blackness* handle, the one on the top is the *hue* handle, and the one on the right is the *whiteness* handle.

- Drag any combination of the Red, Green, or Blue sliders, or click the corresponding spinners.

The Red, Green, Blue (RGB) color model is the most common and is the default when you first start Image Composer. You can alternatively pick the Hue, Saturation, Value (HSV) model, which better corresponds with the edge markers in the color matrix on the left of the dialog box.

 Beneath the sliders of the True Color tab of the Color Picker is a button with an eyedropper icon. If you click this button, the mouse pointer changes into an eyedropper that you can move to any color on your desktop (not just within the Image Composer window) and click a color to capture it for application in Image Composer.

Next to the Eyedropper button is a box that displays the *x* and *y* coordinate (in pixels) of the pixel that the eyedropper is over.

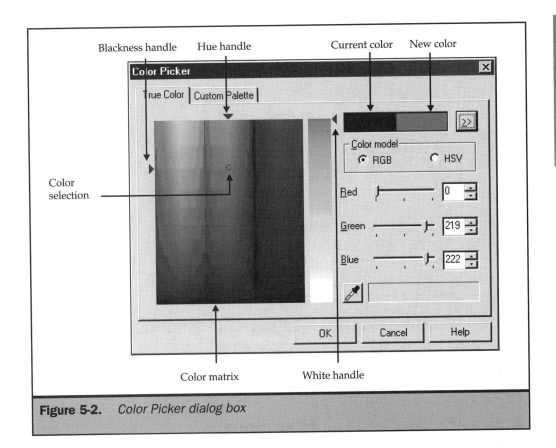

Figure 5-2. *Color Picker dialog box*

Note *Color Picker only determines the current color. It does not apply it to an object. To do that, you must either create an object while the color you want is selected, or use the Color Fill button on the toolbar to apply the current color in the Color Swatch to selected objects.*

The Custom Palette tab allows you to create your own palettes, as shown in Figure 5-3. If you click New and then name a palette, a set of empty color positions is created. You can then automatically generate the number of colors to fill those positions, or you can double-click a color position and open another dialog box from which you can choose a color for that position. If you close the Color Picker with the Custom Palette tab open, the Color Picker will reopen displaying the Custom Palette tab, so it is easy to use it if you choose to do so.

Tip *Experiment by using the tools and their palettes. If something undesirable occurs, simply click Undo on the toolbar or press CTRL+Z to undo the last command. Be sure to save your work before starting to experiment, so you can return to a beginning state.*

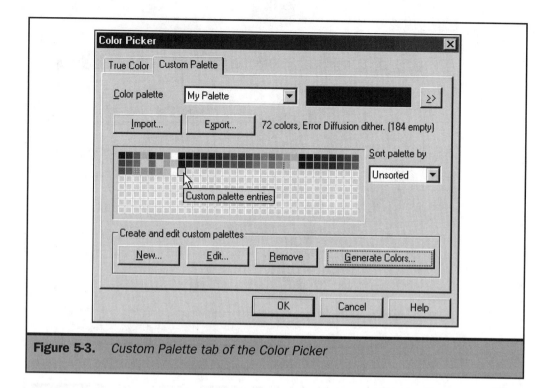

Figure 5-3. *Custom Palette tab of the Color Picker*

Working with Image Objects or Sprites

In Image Composer there are at least four ways to produce an initial image:

- Insert an image from a file on your disk, from a scanner or digital camera, or from an image on a PhotoCD
- Copy the image from another application through the Clipboard
- Create text with the Text tool
- Create shapes with the Shapes tool

Each image that you insert or create by one of these methods becomes a separate object that contributes to the final *composition* that you are creating. These image objects are called *sprites* in Image Composer and are the building blocks that you can manipulate with the various tools and features that you have been reading about. Although you can group sprites and manipulate them together, until you do the grouping, each sprite is independent and can be selected, moved, and otherwise manipulated separately.

When you add a second sprite to a composition, it may or may not overlap the first sprite, but in either case the two sprites are on separate *layers* in a *stack* of sprites. For this reason, the opacity of a sprite becomes an important property. When you move a sprite, you can do so in three dimensions, as you will read about later in this chapter.

Setting Up Image Composer

Before you insert or create sprites in Image Composer, you need to set the defaults to reflect the way you want your final composition to look. There are two aspects to this—the image size and the default color. Begin the creation of an Exciting Travel web page title by setting the image size and the default color with the following instructions:

1. Open the Windows Start menu, choose Programs, and then choose Microsoft Image Composer (if it is not already running).

2. Open the File menu and choose Composition Setup to open the Composition Setup dialog box.

3. If it isn't already selected, drag across the number in the Width numeric box and type **508**.

4. Press TAB to move to the Height numeric box and type **78**.

5. Click OK to close the dialog box and return to Image Composer.

6. Click the Color Swatch below the toolbox to open the Color Picker.

7. Click the True Color tab and select pure blue by using either the sliders or the spinners to set Red to **0**, Green to **0**, and Blue to **255**.

8. Click OK to close the dialog box and return to Image Composer. Your composition space should be a wide, short band in the middle of the workspace, and your Color Swatch should show the pure blue, as you can see (except for the color) in Figure 5-4.

Inserting Sprites

The easiest way to begin to work with Image Composer is by bringing in an existing image. Since Image Composer comes with a number of images you can use, as well as a collection of clip art, this is also very convenient. Bring in several existing images by using the following instructions. You will then manipulate the resulting sprites in later sections of this chapter.

1. Open the Insert menu and select Clip Art.

2. In the Search For Clips box, type **champagne** and press ENTER. A champagne bottle with its cork blowing off will appear, as shown next.

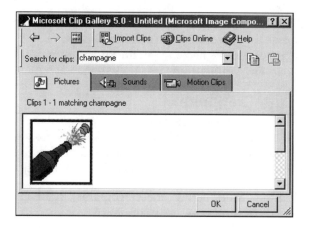

Note *If you cannot find the champagne clip art, you will need to rerun Microsoft Image Composer Setup and perform a Custom installation to install the optional clip-art library. If you cannot find the clip art used here (and at the time this is written we cannot be sure what clip art will be on the final distribution FrontPage CD), you can use the file Title0.mic in the \Book\Chap05\IngComp\ folder on the CD that comes with this book.*

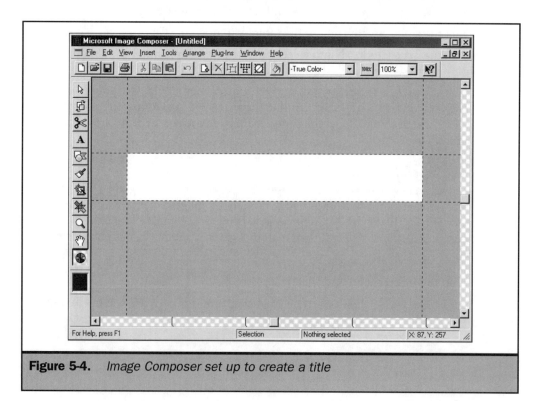

Figure 5-4. *Image Composer set up to create a title*

3. Click OK, and a very large champagne bottle appears on your screen, as in Figure 5-5. Select the Zoom tool, hold down the CTRL key, and click in the middle of your screen. The champagne bottle will decrease in size.

4. Again open the Insert menu, choose Clip Art, type **Travel** in the Search For Clips text box, and press ENTER. Scroll down, click the picture of the pyramids, and click Insert.

5. Use the same technique as in the previous step to insert clip-art pictures of the Golden Gate Bridge, the Acropolis, and the Taj Mahal. For the Golden Gate Bridge and Taj Mahal clip-art pictures, select the leftmost images.

You now have five objects, or sprites, in your workspace: the champagne bottle and four famous-landmark travel images, many of them on top of one another. It doesn't look like much at the present, but in the next several sections, you'll manipulate the sprites so that they become a border for your title.

Selecting Sprites

To do anything with sprites, you must select them. When you bring a sprite into Image Composer, it is automatically selected, but when you bring in a second sprite, you can

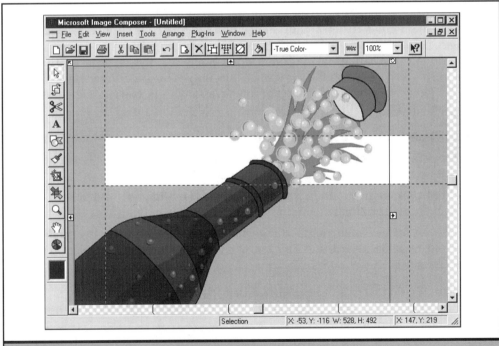

Figure 5-5.   *First sprite brought into Image Composer*

select the first, if it is not covered by another sprite, by clicking it. When a sprite is selected, it has a box drawn around it called a *selection box,* with eight small boxes called *sizing handles* (one on each side and one more in each corner), like this:

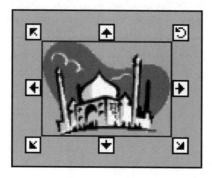

 When a sprite is selected, you can move it by placing the mouse pointer inside the selection box until it becomes a four-headed arrow, and then dragging the sprite where you want it. You can also size a sprite by moving the mouse pointer to any of the seven sizing handles with a straight arrow until the mouse pointer becomes a two-headed arrow, and then dragging the side or corner in the direction in which you want to change the sprite. By pointing on the eighth sizing handle (the one in the upper-right corner with the circular arrow) and dragging, you can rotate the sprite either clockwise or counterclockwise.

Currently the last clip-art image you inserted is selected. It was the last sprite brought in and is therefore on the top layer. Other sprites are on different layers in the stack. To select a sprite hidden by one or more layers above it, you can use one of the following methods:

- Click any part of the sprite that is exposed.
- Press TAB to select the next layer down. When the bottom sprite is selected, pressing TAB again will select the top layer.
- Right-click an image, and choose commands like Bring To Front or Send To Back from the context menu.
- Use the Arrange menu and Arrange palette commands and tools, such as To Front, Send Backward, and To Back, to change the position of a selected sprite in the stack.

You'll notice that there is a slight difference between how the positioning commands are named in the context menu and in the Arrange palette. Here they are along with their definitions:

Context Menu	Arrange Palette	Definition
Bring To Front	To Front	Move to the top (layer closest to the viewer)
Send To Back	To Back	Move to the bottom (layer furthest from the viewer)
Bring Forward	Bring Forward	Move toward the top one layer
Send Backward	Send Backward	Move toward the bottom one layer

Although a layer may be selected, you cannot see it unless it either is the top layer or is not covered by a higher layer.

Although you cannot see a layer, if you can select it (and you always can by pressing TAB), you can move it by pointing inside the selection box and dragging.

Use the following steps to practice selecting the sprites you have in your workspace:

1. Click the Pan tool in the toolbox to select it, and then use it to move the workspace so the sprites are away from the top and left edges.

2. Click the Selection tool, and press TAB slowly five times to select each sprite.

3. Click the part of an image that is below another image. This sprite is currently selected, even though it is partially covered by a sprite on a higher level.

4. Right-click the sprite on the top of the stack, and select Send To Back from the context menu.

5. Select the top image in your stack, and click the Arrange tool. In the left third of the palette there is a section titled "Order." If you place the mouse over the white squares, you will see that you can use it to rearrange your sprites, like this:

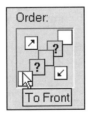

6. In the Order section, click the arrow in the upper-left labeled "Send Backward." The top image will go behind the image beneath it, but will still be selected. It

has gone from the top of the stack to the second from the top position. Click the Send Backward arrow again, and the selected travel image will move to the third position.

7. Click the white box in the upper-right of the Order section labeled "To Back." The selected sprite will move to the very back of the stack.

Although the concept of a stack of sprites with the upper ones hiding the lower ones seems like it might be difficult to work with, Image Composer has a powerful set of tools that makes it easy.

Moving, Sizing, Duplicating, and Rotating Sprites

The objective is to place the travel images and champagne on either end of the composition space that will become the title block for the web that you want to create. To do that, you must reduce the size of all the objects, move and rotate the travel images, and duplicate, flip, and move the champagne bottle to get this final image:

SIZING SPRITES   Image Composer also has a powerful set of tools for manipulating sprites. Begin using them by sizing and moving the travel images as follows:

1. With the champagne bottle selected, click the Units drop-down list in the Scale area of the Arrange palette and select Percent.

2. Drag over the "100" in the Width spinner and type **12**. Make sure that Keep Aspect Ratio is checked, as shown next, and click the Apply button that is in the Scale area (notice that there are three Apply buttons on this palette). The champagne bottle will become comparatively small.

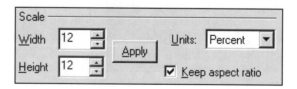

3. Drag the champagne bottle to the left side of the composition space.

4. Repeat steps 1 and 2 to size each of the other famous landmark images to 40 percent of their original size, and then drag them from the pile so all five images are visible, as shown here:

SIZING, DUPLICATING, AND FLIPPING THE CHAMPAGNE Next, duplicate the champagne bottle so there is a copy at either end of the title, and then flip the right-hand copy, so the two are pointing in opposite directions. Here's how:

1. With the champagne bottle selected, click Duplicate on the toolbar. A second champagne bottle appears, slightly offset from the original.

2. Drag the second champagne bottle to the right side of the composition space, about a quarter of an inch from the end.

3. With the right-hand champagne bottle selected, click the Flip Horizontally tool in the Arrange palette, as you can see next. The champagne bottle flips so that it is pointing to the left.

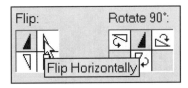

4. Open the File menu and save your work as **Title0.mic** in the default C:\Multimedia Files\My Media folder.

MOVING AND ROTATING THE IMAGES ON THE LEFT Now move two of the travel images to the left end, and rotate them to fit the space.

Use the Zoom tool to increase or decrease the magnification of the composition space so that you can best see the sprites.

1. Drag the Pyramids sprite so that it is slightly overlapping the upper portion of the left champagne bottle (the exact positioning is not important).

2. With the Pyramids image selected, click the up arrow in the Rotation spinner in the Arrange palette until you get **25**, and then click the Apply button adjacent to the spinner. The image will rotate to the right.

3. Click To Back in the Arrange palette (the upper-right white square in the Order section), causing the Pyramids image to go behind the champagne bottle, like this:

4. Drag the Golden Gate Bridge image so that it is below the Pyramids image.

5. With the Golden Gate Bridge still selected, set the Rotation spinner to **25** and click Apply.

6. Click To Back in the Arrange palette so that the Golden Gate Bridge goes behind the other images. Adjust the positioning of the travel sprites and champagne bottle until you are happy with them, similar to what you can see next:

7. Open the File menu, choose Save As, change the File Name to **Title1.mic**, and click Save to again save your work.

FLIPPING AND POSITIONING THE IMAGES ON THE RIGHT The final task with the travel images is to flip and position the final two on the right.

1. Drag the Taj Mahal so that it slightly overlaps the upper portion of the right-hand champagne bottle, and click To Back in the Arrange palette to place it behind the champagne bottle.

2. With the Taj Mahal still selected, set the Rotation spinner to **–25** and click Apply.

3. Select the Acropolis, rotate it **–25** degrees, position it in the lower right of the composition space, and send it to the back.

4. Adjust the size and positioning of the travel images and champagne bottle on the right until you are satisfied with them. It should resemble this:

5. When you are happy with the travel images and champagne bottles, choose Select All from the Edit menu, open the Arrange menu, and choose Flatten Selection. This creates one sprite on one level out of the six sprites and six levels that previously existed. It is easier to work with a single sprite as you build the remainder of the title block. Click OK in the message box that informs you this action cannot be undone unless you click Undo before completing another action.

6. Open the Arrange menu and choose Lock Position to keep the travel images and champagne bottles in their current position. Click Save on the toolbar to save your work once more.

Adding Text Sprites

Text sprites are simply any text that you create with the Text tool and place in the workspace. One aspect of creating text sprites is selecting the font that you will use. You can, of course, use any font, but FrontPage also includes some on its CD.

FONTS ON THE FRONTPAGE CD   The fonts available on the FrontPage CD include several that are unique and possibly interesting for a web page. See what is available and copy one to your hard disk for use in the title block you are building.

1. With the FrontPage 2000 CD in its drive, open the Windows Explorer, select your CD-ROM drive, and then select the \ImgComp\Common\Mmfiles\Fonts folder. Within that folder you'll see a number of folders, each with a different font, as you can see in Figure 5-6.

2. Open several of these folders, and double-click one or more fonts to see what they look like. For example, Calisto MT (file Calist.ttf) is shown in Figure 5-7.

3. Open the Windows Start menu, choose Settings | Control Panel, and then double-click Fonts. Your Fonts folder will open, showing you the fonts that you have available on your hard disk.

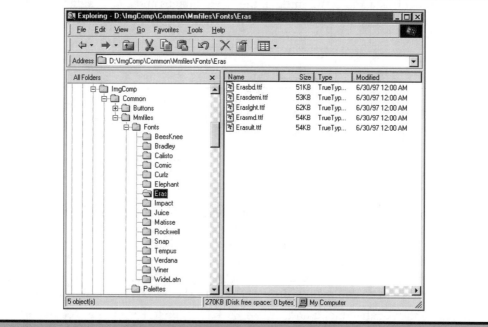

Figure 5-6. *Fonts available on the FrontPage CD*

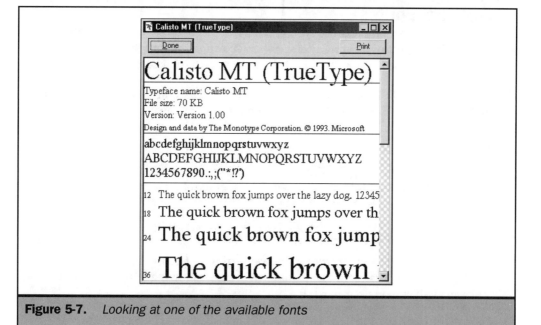

Figure 5-7. *Looking at one of the available fonts*

4. Scroll down through your fonts and see if you have Eras Demi. If you do not have it, open the File menu and choose Install New Font. Specify your CD-ROM drive, and then select the \ImgComp\Common\Mmfiles\Fonts\ Eras folder. Five fonts will appear, as you can see in Figure 5-8.

5. Select Eras Demi for use in the title block you are creating, and select any of the other fonts that you want (use CTRL to select more than one font). Click OK to copy those fonts that are not already installed on your computer.

6. Close the Fonts folder window, Control Panel, and Windows Explorer to get back to Image Composer.

CREATING TEXT SPRITES   Creating text sprites is fairly easy. Use your new font to create the Exciting Travel name:

1. Click the Text tool to open the Text palette.

2. Click the Font down arrow to open the Font drop-down list box.

3. Select Eras Demi ITC, accept the default Regular style, set the size to **30** points, and select the Align Center button, as shown next. Make sure 100% opacity is set (the slider below the alignment buttons).

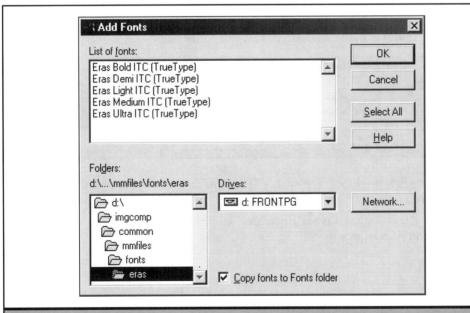

Figure 5-8.   *Fonts to be copied from the CD*

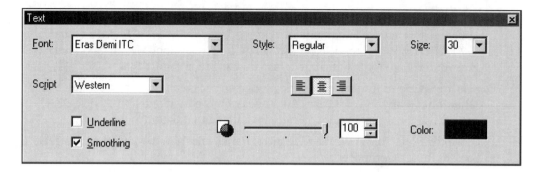

4. Draw a marquee with the text cursor starting in the upper left of the composition space, but to the right of the images. Click and drag to the lower-right corner of the composition space, but do not cover the images on the right, as shown next:

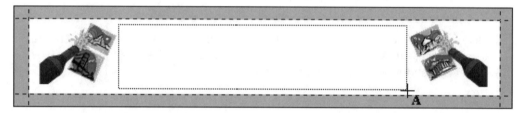

5. Type **Exciting Travel**. If the text does not quite fit in the marquee you drew, you can click and drag the left and right sides of the marquee using the middle sizing handle to make it larger, as you can see here:

6. Click the Selection tool. The words "Exciting Travel" appear as a sprite that can be moved or resized.

7. Drag the text so that it is approximately centered in the composition space, as the next illustration shows.

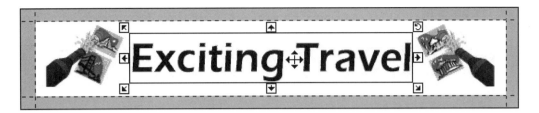

8. To resize the width of the text sprite, drag its left-middle sizing handle to the right or left until it is just adjacent to the right edge of the left travel images. Then drag its right-middle sizing handle to the left or right until it is just adjacent to the left edge of the right travel images. You can also adjust the height of the sprite by dragging on the top-center and bottom-center sizing handles. The final results should look like this:

9. Using Save As from the File menu, save your work as **Title2**.

ENHANCING TEXT SPRITES   There are, of course, many things that you can do to "enhance" text from its original two-dimensional appearance. Two possibilities are to add an outline and to add a drop shadow.

1. Reselect the title text if it isn't still selected, and click the Effects tool to open that palette.

2. In the Effects tab of the Effects palette, open the drop-down list box in the upper right and choose Outlines.

3. Choose the Edge icon and click the Details tab. Make sure that the Thickness is **1** and the opacity is **100**, and click the color swatch in the palette. The Color Picker dialog box will open.

4. Move the Red slider all the way to the right, making Red **255**. Leave the Green and Blue sliders all the way to the left, so they are **0**. Click OK.

5. Back in the Effects Detail tab, click Apply. A thin red border appears around the letters.

6. Keeping the text selected, click the Effects tab and choose Drop Shadow. Then click the Details tab.

7. Choose the Southeast drop shadow effect, shown here:

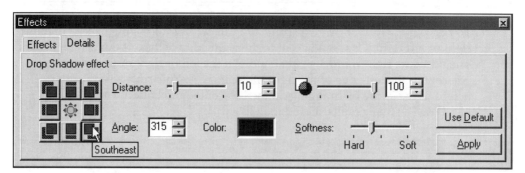

8. Click the color swatch in the Details tab and set Red at **60**, Green at **0**, and Blue at **100** in the Color Picker to create purple; click OK.

9. Again in the Effects Details tab, click Apply to give a small drop shadow to the characters, as shown in Figure 5-9.

10. Again use Save As to save your title block with the name **Title3.mic**.

The reason for all the separate files is that it lets you go back and work with the title at any stage of the process.

Adding Shapes

The final element you need to add to the title block you are building is some confetti around the title and champagne bottles. Do that by creating several geometric shapes, reducing their size, coloring them, and flipping and rotating them.

CREATING GEOMETRIC SHAPES   Use the Shapes tool to create several geometric shapes in different colors. You will then use the shapes to make confetti.

1. Click the Shapes tool to open the Shapes palette shown next. This palette allows you to create four types of shapes: rectangles and squares, ovals and circles, curved lines or curved shapes, and polygons or multi-straight-sided shapes.

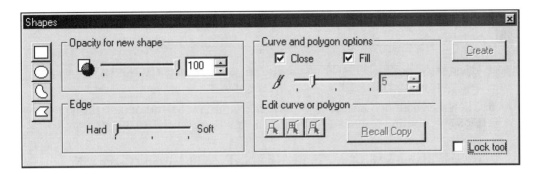

2. Click the Color Swatch below the toolbox to open the Color Picker. Create yellow, which is Red **255**, Green **255**, and Blue **0**. Click OK.

3. Click the Rectangle tool in the Shapes palette, and draw a small square in the workspace below the composition space by pressing and holding SHIFT while drawing the shape (holding down SHIFT keeps the sides equal). When the square is complete, click Create to finish it.

Figure 5-9. *Finished text with a border and drop shadow*

If you don't like your first square, simply click it to select it and press DEL. *Then you can try again.*

4. Open the Color Picker, change the current color to pure red (Red **255**, Green and Blue **0**), and click OK.

5. Click the Oval tool, and draw a circle the same size as and next to the square by again holding down SHIFT. When you are done, click Create and you'll see the circle.

6. Change the current color to pure green (Red and Blue **0**, and Green **255**).

7. Click the Polygon tool, and draw a small triangle next to and the same size as the square. Do this by clicking an initial point, moving the mouse a very short distance, clicking a second point, moving a short distance perpendicular to your first move, and clicking a third point. A triangle will be formed by drawing three lines between the points. Click Create when you are ready.

8. Change the current color to pure blue (Red and Green **0**, Blue **255**).

9. Click the Curve tool.

10. Draw a double curlicue going from bottom right to upper left as follows. Click an initial point; move a short distance to the upper left and then click the top of the first curlicue. Move slightly to the right and back down, and click at the bottom of the first curlicue. Move to the left and click at the outside of the first curlicue; then move to the upper left and click at the top of the second curlicue. Move slightly to the right and back down, and click at the bottom of the second curlicue. Move to the left and click at the outside of the second curlicue; then move up to the upper left and click a final point. Click Move Points on the left under Edit Curve Or Polygon in the Shapes palette. Click Close under Curve And Polygon Options to uncheck it, and set the curve line width (the slider on the right) to **4**, as shown here:

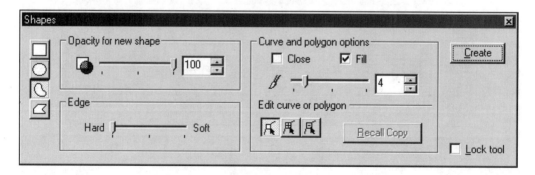

GETTING STARTED

11. Click and drag the points on your curlicue to better shape it. When your double curlicue is ready, click Create. Your result should look something like this (don't worry about perfection!):

12. Click the Arrange tool, and use the Arrange palette to reduce the size of the curlicue, square, circle, and triangle so each is about the size of the cork on the champagne bottle, as shown here:

Note *Use trial and error in sizing your shapes. Try a percentage reduction and if it isn't correct, immediately press CTRL+Z to undo it, and then try another percentage.*

MANIPULATING SHAPES The objective is to use the four shapes you have created to produce the random look of confetti around the name. Do that by duplicating, flipping, rotating, and placing these objects.

1. Move the shapes so they are close together and select the four shape sprites by "rubber banding" them. Point the mouse above and to the left of the shapes and drag below and to the right of them. When you release the mouse button, you'll see that all of the shapes are selected. (If for some reason one or more of the sprites did not get selected, you can press and hold SHIFT while clicking the unselected sprites.) Drag the selected sprites below the composition space.

2. Click Duplicate on the toolbar, and then drag the copy off to the right. Do that seven more times to create a total of nine sets of four shapes. You will next flip and rotate these objects so that they look like this:

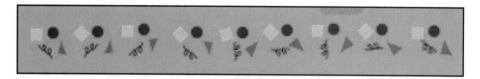

3. Zoom in on the second set of sprites. Click the curlicue in the second set, and use the Arrange palette to flip it horizontally. Flip the third curlicue vertically, and flip the fourth both vertically and horizontally.

4. Rotate the fifth, sixth, seventh, and eighth curlicues by 45, 135, 225, and 315 degrees, respectively.

5. Flip and then rotate the triangle as you did the curlicue.

6. Individually select the second, fourth, sixth, and eighth squares (you can't do it all at once) and rotate them 45 degrees.

7. Position the sets of shapes on the composition space around the title block. Move the individual pieces and even duplicate some more if you want to give it a random "confetti" look, something like what you see here:

8. When you are done positioning, save your work under the name **Title4.mic**, and then save it again under **Webtitle.mic**.

9. Click Select All on the toolbar to select all of the pieces of the title block, open the Arrange menu, and choose Flatten Selection. You are reminded that this cannot be undone. Click OK. Save your work another time under the name **Webtitle.mic**.

10. Open Windows Explorer and locate the two files Title4.mic and Webtitle.mic. They should be in c:\Multimedia Files\My Media if you used the default path. You'll notice a very significant difference in their size. In my case (yours could be different), Title4.mic was 1,134K and Webtitle.mic was 113K.

Tip   *If you can't see the file size in the Windows Explorer, open the View menu and choose Details.*

11. In Image Composer, open the File menu and choose Save As. In the Save As dialog box, open the Save As Type drop-down list box, choose TIFF and click Save. A message box will open telling you that the file format you are using will

flatten the sprites and crop the result to the composition space. Since you want to do that in this case, click OK. Repeat this Save As process two more times, and choose JPEG and GIF as the types.

12. Look in Windows Explorer and you'll see the file sizes reduced once more. In my case, the GIF file was 14K, the JPEG file was 21K, and the TIFF file was 58K.

> **Note** *The flattening process is important for saving file space on your disk, but once you flatten, you cannot reverse the process—and it is very difficult to do much editing of a flattened file. You can create the same size TIFF and JPEG files from an unflattened MIC file as you can from a flattened one.*

Working with Other Tools

While the Exciting Travel title block is complete, there are several tools that you haven't yet used. Try several of these in the next sections of this chapter.

Applying Patterns and Fills

The Texture Transfer tool and palette allow you to apply patterns to a sprite in your workspace. You can change the color assigned to a sprite (or sprites) to the color in the Color Swatch by selecting the sprite(s) and clicking Color Fill on the toolbar.

> **Note** *You can only apply a pattern or a fill to an existing sprite. You must create the sprite first, and then add the pattern or fill.*

1. In Image Composer open the File menu and choose New. The title block will be removed from your screen, and a new, blank composition space will open in Image Composer. Since you are not working on an end product, but just want to try out some of the tools, you don't care about the size of the composition space.

2. Click the Shapes tool, draw a rectangle about 2 × 4 inches (it's not important where it is, so long as you can see it—and the size can really be anything that you want it to be). Click Create. A rectangle will appear filled with the last color you used (pure blue in this book).

3. Click the Effects tool to open the Effects palette.

4. If it is not already selected, click the rectangle you just drew, and then select Gradient from the Category list on the right of the Effects tab.

5. Click the Details tab. Open the Gradient Name drop-down list box, choose Gold, and then click Apply. Your Image Composer window should look like Figure 5-10.

6. Open the Gradient Name list again, choose Sunrise, and click Apply. Your rectangle will now look like a sunrise.

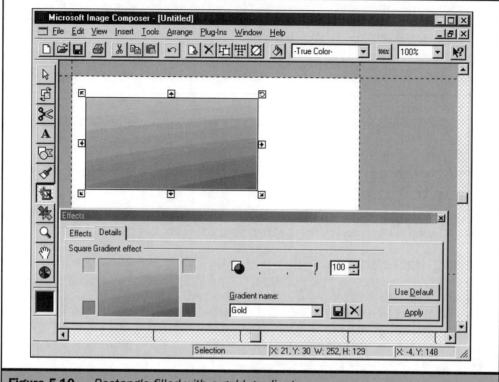

Figure 5-10. *Rectangle filled with a gold gradient ramp*

7. Click the Effects tab, select Patterns in the Category drop-down list, click Hue/Blackness, and click Apply. A rainbow of colors going to black at the bottom will fill your rectangle.

8. Click the Text tool, and draw a text marquee slightly narrower than the width of your rectangle. Based on your last use, the font should be Eras Demi Bold 28 point; if it isn't, make the necessary changes and type **This is text!** If the text box is not large enough, you can drag the right side handle to enlarge it. Move the text with the Selection tool so that it is roughly centered in the rectangle you created earlier.

9. Open the Texture Transfer palette with the Texture Transfer tool. Choose Tile from the list of texture icons. In the composition space, click the colored rectangle outside the text to select the rectangle with the rainbow colors. Then hold down the SHIFT key and click the text.

10. Click Apply in the Texture Transfer palette (the text will seemingly disappear). Click outside the rectangle to deselect it, then click the text and drag it off the rectangle, and you'll see that the text has exactly the same coloration as the part of the rectangle it covered, which you can get some idea of (it's in shades of gray!) in Figure 5-11.

11. Select the rectangle, change the current color to white (click the Color Swatch to open the Color Picker, move all three color sliders to **255**, and click OK), and click Color Fill on the toolbar. (This sets up the rectangle to use in the next section.)

Using the Paint Tool

The Paint tool, unlike most other bitmapped paint programs, only works within a sprite you have created elsewhere. The Paint tool (or any of the tools in the Paint palette) cannot create its own sprites; it can only color those that already exist.

1. Click the Paint tool to open the Paint palette. If your white rectangle is no longer selected, it may have disappeared into the white composition space. If

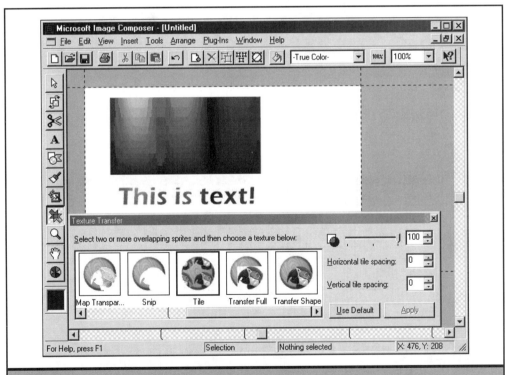

Figure 5-11. *Text after having the rectangle's colors transferred to it*

so, click in the general vicinity of where your rectangle was and it will reappear. In any case, the rectangle should be selected.

2. Change the current color to pure red, select the Paintbrush tool, click the fourth brush size from the left in the second row, and paint a line across the top of your rectangle.

3. Change the current color to a bright yellow (Red and Green **255**, Blue **0**), select the Airbrush tool, use the slider or spinner on the right to change the brush size to **40**, and draw another line in your rectangle, a little beneath the first line you drew.

4. Change the color to pure blue, select the Pencil tool, leave the default size, and draw a third line below the first two, so your Image Composer window looks something like Figure 5-12.

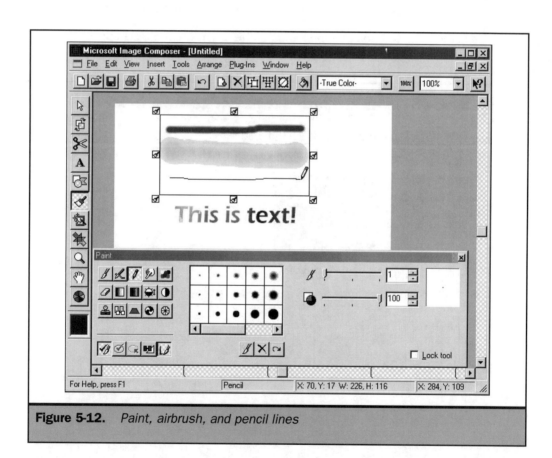

Figure 5-12.   *Paint, airbrush, and pencil lines*

5. Click the Smear tool, and smear areas of your three lines. Note that the color you start with gets smeared into the other color(s). Your results should look something like this:

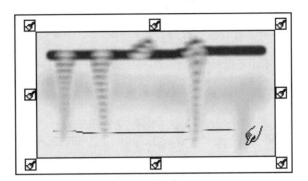

6. Click the Erase tool, and erase some of the lines and smears that you created earlier. (You can hold down SHIFT to get a straight erasure.) Here is how our results look (compare with the preceding illustration of the smeared lines):

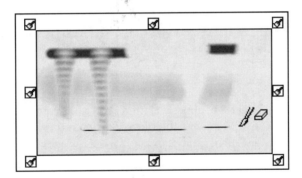

There are several other Paint and toolbox tools that are beyond the scope of this book, but use the examples of experimentation that you have seen here to try these for yourself. We think you'll agree that the Microsoft Image Composer is a comprehensive tool for creating graphics that you can use in your web pages.

Animating Graphics with GIF Animator

Microsoft GIF Animator is an animation program that is included with Microsoft Image Composer. You can open GIF Animator from the Tools menu in Microsoft Image Composer.

Animated GIF images are composed of several different images. The animation effect is created by displaying the series of images one after the other, with each image shown for only a short time. When animated GIF images are included in a web page, they seem to move. In reality, different images are being displayed in the same space. The first step in creating an animated GIF image is to create or import more than one graphic.

For this section of the chapter, you can either use the Title3.mic, Title4.mic, and Webtitle.mic files you created above with steps 1 through 6 below or open the file Atitle.mic from the CD that came with this book and jump to step 7. In either case you will use the confetti graphics you just composed to build an animated banner for Exciting Travel.

1. In Microsoft Image Composer open the file Title3.mic. Click Select All on the toolbar, open the Arrange menu and choose Flatten Selection, and click OK to do that. Open the File menu, choose Save As, enter the name **Title3f.mic**, and click Save. Repeat the Save As process with the name **Atitle.mic**.

2. Open the file Title4.mic, save it as **Title4a.mic**, and delete all of the confetti except those pieces on the very top of the title, like this:

3. Click Save, click Select All, choose Flatten Selection from the Arrange menu, click OK to do it, and then save the file as **Atitlea.mic**.

4. Click Copy from the toolbar, open Atitle.mic, drag the bottom edge of the composition space down so that it is roughly four times its original height, right-click the enlarged composition space, choose Paste, align the new title below the original one, and save it again as Atitle.mic.

5. Again open Title4.mic, save it as **Title4b.mic**, delete just the confetti on the bottom, as shown next, save it, select all, flatten, and then save as **Atitleb.mic**. Copy the title, open Atitle.mic, paste and align the third title, and save Atitle.mic.

6. Open Webtitle.mic, select all, copy, open Atitle.mic, paste and align the final title, and save Atitle.mic. Your final file should look like Figure 5-13

7. Select Microsoft GIF Animator from the Tools menu in Image Composer.

Tip

You can also open the GIF Animator from the Microsoft Image Composer Programs menu.

8. Click the GIF Animator title bar, and drag the GIF Animator window to the right, far enough so you can see at least some of each of your sprites, and click Main Dialog Window Always On Top, as shown in Figure 5-14.

Note

Selecting the Main Dialog Window Always On Top check box in the GIF Animator Options tab allows dragging from the Image Composer window to the GIF Animator window without having to tile the windows.

9. Click the top sprite, and drag it into the first frame in the GIF Animator (you can see this process in Figure 5-14).

Figure 5-13. *Four title sprites ready for animation in Atitle.mic*

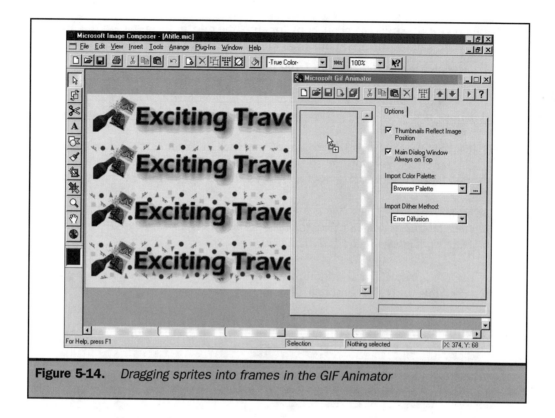

Figure 5-14. *Dragging sprites into frames in the GIF Animator*

10. Drag the remaining sprites, one at a time, into additional frames in the GIF Animator, as shown in Figure 5-15.

When you have placed all the images in frames in the GIF Animator, you are ready to define how you want GIF Animator to manage your image files, what kind of animation (transition) effects you wish to use, as well as individual attributes of the different image frames.

Defining Animation Options

The Options tab in the GIF Animator allows you to control a number of aspects of how your individual image frames will display. You can leave the settings in the Options tab at their default settings. The Thumbnails Reflect Image Position check box lets you see each image in the frame as it will actually appear. Keeping the Main Dialog Window Always On Top check box selected will keep the GIF Animator window on top of your desktop. This way, you can leave Image Composer and the GIF Animator windows open, and drag images from Image Composer into the GIF Animator. If this becomes confusing, you can deselect this option.

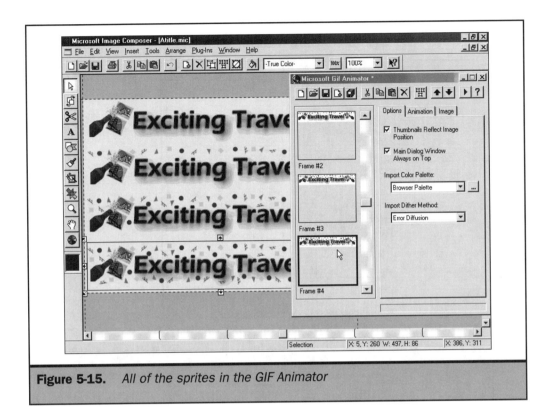

Figure 5-15.   *All of the sprites in the GIF Animator*

The Import Color Palette drop-down menu lets you choose between a color palette that works efficiently with web browsers, or a custom palette. The default setting for the Import Color Palette is Browser Palette. Unless you have some special reason to use a custom color palette, you should use the Browser Palette. The Browser Palette works fine for web graphics and creates efficient animated files that download quickly. The Optimal Palette option creates a palette for each frame in your animation, which makes the file larger and downloading slower.

You can choose a dithering method from the Import Dither Method drop-down menu:

■ The Solid option works well for line art and images with few colors.

■ The Pattern option works for 8 to 16 colored images and downloads quite quickly.

■ The Random option is used with images (like photos) that have many colors. It will slow down your animated file.

■ The Error Diffusion option provides the highest-quality dithering.

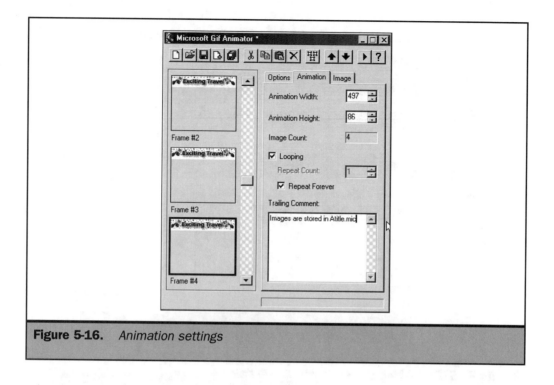

Figure 5-16.   *Animation settings*

Choose Error Diffusion for this example. It's a little slower to download, but it will handle the gradation fills best. When you have looked at and set the animation options, click the Animation tab in the GIF Animator window.

Defining Animation Effects

The main thing you control in the Animation tab of the GIF Animator, shown in Figure 5-16, is how many times you want your animation to play. You can set your animation to play once or any number of repetitions up to 99999 times. Or you can set your animation to play until you turn it off.

Normally, you will not adjust the Animation Width and Animation Height spinners. These values are calculated automatically by the GIF Animator so that all your image frames will fit in the animated GIF image. You will only change the values in these spinners if you want to crop your image (by making the values smaller) or create white space around your image (by making the values in the spinners larger). The Image Count area simply tells you how many frames you have.

You define the actual animation effects by the settings you choose for Looping:

1. Click the Looping check box so that your animation will run more than once.

2. Click the Repeat Forever check box to play your animation continuously. You could also enter a number in the Repeat Count spin box to define a finite number of repetitions.

3. In the Trailing Comment area enter a note to yourself that tells where you got the images for this animation, as shown in Figure 5-16.

When you have defined your Animation options, click the Image tab in the Microsoft GIF Animator window.

Image Settings

The Image tab of the GIF Animator lets you define how long frames will display, and what type of transition effect will be applied when frames change. You can also define a transparent background color in this tab using the Local Palette shown next, so your animation will appear to have no background on a web page.

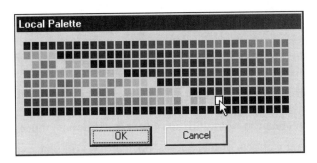

1. Apply the image effects you select to all your frames by clicking Select All on the GIF Animator toolbar. You could also use CTRL+click to choose individual frames to apply effects to.

2. Enter a value of **15** in the Duration spinner. That will display each (selected) frame for 15/100ths of one second.

3. Choose Restore Background from the Undraw Method drop-down list box, and preview this transition effect by clicking Preview (second from the right on the toolbar at the top). You will see your animation carried out over and over. Figure 5-17 shows the transition from Frame 2 to Frame 3 of the animation. You can stop your animation by clicking the black square button (second from the left) in the Preview window.

The options and their effects for the Undraw method are as follows:

■ The Undefined draw method adds no transition effects as your frames display in a browser.

■ The Leave effect creates a shadowing or fade effect between your frames. Both the Leave and Undefined effects create a somewhat messy-looking animation, since one frame is not erased before the next one is displayed.

Figure 5-17. *Previewing an animation*

■ The Restore Background effect redraws the original background as the current frame is displayed.

■ The Restore Previous effect redraws the previous frame as the current frame is being displayed. Both the Restore Background and Restore Previous effects create animation with smoother transitions between frames.

You will see the effects of these transitions when you place your animated GIF on a page and look at your animated GIF in the Preview tab of FrontPage's Page view or by using a browser.

4. When you have defined your animation, previewed it, and then closed the Preview box, click Save on the GIF Animator toolbar. Name your animated GIF **Atitle.gif** and then click Save.

Your animated GIF file can be placed on a page in FrontPage just like any other image file. When you view your animated GIF image in the Normal tab of FrontPage's Page view, you will only see the first frame. You can watch the whole animation in the Preview tab or by viewing your page in a browser.

Using Microsoft PhotoDraw

Microsoft PhotoDraw is a full-featured photo editing and drawing package that allows you to work with and combine both bitmap images and vector images. *Bitmaps* are produced by breaking a picture into tiny dots (their size being dependent on the resolution of the picture) and defining the properties of each dot. *Vector* images are produced with mathematical expressions that define an object in a picture. Photographs are bitmaps and most paint programs, including Microsoft Image Composer work with bitmaps. Mechanical drawing and illustration programs such as AutoCAD and CorelDRAW create vector-based images. If you have multiple objects in a bitmap image and you want to work with them separately, such as move them independently, then you must have separate layers within the bitmap and each layer must be transparent to the layers beneath it. This produces a very large file, so to keep a picture's file size reasonable in the final image, the layers are combined and can no longer be separately edited. In a vector picture, each object is a separate mathematical expression and can be edited separately or combined. The vector file is smaller than the layered bitmap file, but larger than the final combined bitmap.

PhotoDraw allows you to:

- Bring in a photograph through a scanner, a digital camera, or a file
- Bring in and modify clip art from a number of sources
- Touch up, change, or distort a photo, clip art, or other image
- Add, format, bend, and distort text
- Create lines and shapes, add outline and fill colors, rotate and flip the shapes, and apply special effects to them
- Combine the various photo, clip art, text, drawing, and painting capabilities to make a single picture

PhotoDraw has its own file format with the extension of .MIX, but it can open images with these formats:

- Microsoft PhotoDraw (*.MIX)
- Microsoft Picture It! (*.MIX)
- Adobe Photoshop (*.PSD)
- CorelDRAW (*.CDR)
- Encapsulated PostScript (*.EPS)
- FlashPix (*.FPX)
- CompuServe GIF (*.GIF, *.GFA)
- JPEG File Interchange Format (*.JPG, *.JPE, *.JPEG, *.JFIF)
- Kodak Photo CD (*.PCD)
- Macintosh PICT (*.PCT, *.PICT)
- Microsoft Image Composer (*.MIC)
- PC Paintbrush (*.PCX)
- Portable Network Graphics (*.PNG)
- Tagged Image File Format (*.TIF, *.TIFF)

- Windows bitmap (*.BMP, *.DIB, *.RLE)
- Widows Meta File (*.WMF, *.EMF

You can use PhotoDraw to save images in these formats:

- Microsoft PhotoDraw (*.MIX)
- Microsoft Picture It! (*.MIX)
- CompuServe GIF (*.GIF)
- JPEG File Interchange Format (*.JPG)
- PC Paintbrush (*.PCX)
- Portable Network Graphics (*.PNG)
- Tagged Image File Format (*.TIF, *.TIFF)
- Windows bitmap (*.BMP)

The full capabilities of PhotoDraw are beyond the scope of this book, but here you'll take a quick look at the PhotoDraw window and then see how to create banner headlines and buttons for use in web pages.

The PhotoDraw Window

The PhotoDraw window, shown in Figure 5-18, contains a number of unique features. In addition to the normal Standard and Formatting toolbars, there is a *Visual menu* below the normal menu at the top of the window and a *picture list* running down the left edge. The picture list contains a thumbnail representation of each picture currently open in PhotoDraw. To the right of the thumbnail is an arrow on which you can click to open an *object list* of objects that make up the picture. This list shows the objects in the order in which they are layered in the picture, and you can use the list to select a particular object or to reorder the layers.

In the center of the PhotoDraw window is the *workspace* where your image is created. In the workspace there is a white area called the *picture area*, which shows the desired area of the image you're working on. On the four corners of the picture area are picture guides, which by default are locked and therefore not visible. When they are unlocked you can drag them to change the size of the picture area. Surrounding the picture area is a gray *scratch area* to which you can temporarily drag objects, but unless you move the objects back to the picture area they will not be part of the final picture. At the bottom of the window is the status bar, which shows the position of the mouse pointer and the size of the picture area if there are no objects present, or the position and size of the currently selected object, and other information. Within the PhotoDraw window there is, on the right of Figure 5-18, an open dialog box called a *workpane*, which provides options for performing a given task. This particular workpane is opened when you select Text | Insert Text from the Visual menu and allows you to select various options for text selected in the workspace.

GETTING STARTED

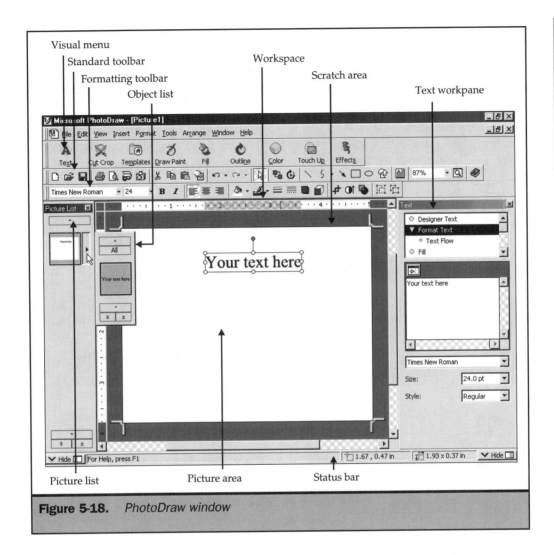

Figure 5-18.   *PhotoDraw window*

> **Note**
>
> *The picture area is the only area that is saved when you save to a GIF, JPEG, TIFF, FPX, PNG, or Windows BMP format and all objects are flattened into one object. Only PhotoDraw's MIX format saves the entire workspace you are using and keeps all objects separate.*

PhotoDraw Visual Menu and Workpanes

One of the most unique aspects of the PhotoDraw windows is the Visual menu. From it you can open a number of workpanes to control most of what you can do in PhotoDraw. While by default the Visual menu is immediately below the regular menu, you can move it anywhere—and even float it on your desktop. You can move the Visual menu by dragging the left end of the menu. The nine *task areas* on the Visual menu are described in Table 5-2.

Creating Text Banners

Many of the banner headlines used in web pages are nothing more than text. Within FrontPage you can create headline text up to 36 points in size using a wide variety of

Icon	Name	Description
A	Text	Insert, format, bend, make 3-D, and apply designer effects to text
	Cut Crop	Cut shapes out of, crop, and erase portions of objects or pictures
	Templates	Select a template to use from among web graphics, business graphics, cards, designer edges, and designer clip-art sets
	Draw Paint	Draw lines and shapes or paint an object
	Fill	Fill an object with solid color, texture, designer gradient, two-color gradient, or a picture
	Outline	Change the outline of an object to have soft or plain edges, or be created with artistic or photo brushes
	Color	Change the color of an object in terms of its brightness and contrast, tint, hue and saturation, colorization, color balance, or make it the negative of what it is or a grayscale
	Touch Up	Touch up a photo to fix red eye, remove dust and spots, despeckle, remove scratch, clone, smudge, or erase
	Effects	Add special effects to an object including shadow, transparency, fade out, blur or sharpen, distort, 3-D, and designer effects

Table 5-2. *The Task Areas Accessed with the Visual Menu*

fonts and styles. Within PhotoDraw you can turn text into a picture beginning with text of any size and any font by making it three-dimensional, by coloring it, bending it, and distorting it, all in several ways. Look at creating a text banner for a company named Exciting Travel.

Setting Up PhotoDraw

To begin any PhotoDraw picture you need to set the size of the final object, which is the *picture area* in PhotoDraw. To do so, start PhotoDraw and follow these steps:

1. Open the Start menu and choose Programs Microsoft PhotoDraw (if it's not already running). The Microsoft PhotoDraw window and a dialog box of the same name will open.

2. In the dialog box make sure Blank Picture is selected and then click OK. The New dialog box will open.

3. Click Banner and then OK. In the PhotoDraw window a thin white stripe will appear, as shown in Figure 5-19.

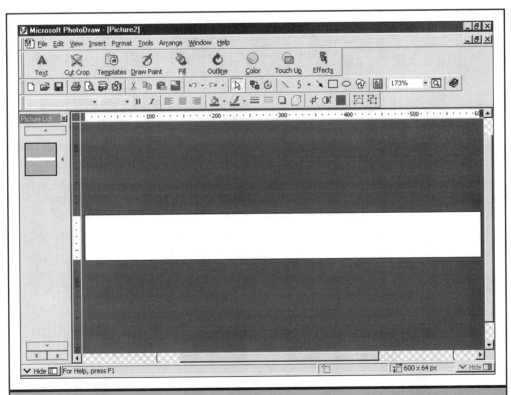

Figure 5-19. *Banner-shaped picture area in PhotoDraw*

Changing the Picture Area

The default banner area that is created is 600×64 pixels (see the size on the right of the status bar in Figure 5-19). As you have read in earlier chapters, 600 pixels is a good width to use in a web page in that it can be fully seen in most monitors, leaving room for scroll bars. The 64-pixel height is just a best guess at what a banner should be. You can change both height and width either by dragging or though a dialog box. Do both next.

1. Right-click in the picture area to open the context menu and then click Picture Setup. The Picture Setup dialog box will open like this:

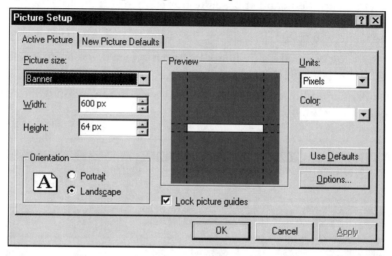

2. Open the Picture Size drop-down list and observe the many standard shapes you can choose (keep Banner as your choice). Open the Units drop-down list and observe the different units you can use (keep Pixels).

3. Click the New Picture Defaults tab and observe PhotoDraw's new picture defaults that were shown in Figure 5-18. Return to the Active Picture tab.

4. Click Lock Picture Guides to turn it off, leave all other settings as you found them when you opened the dialog box, and click OK.

5. Open the Zoom drop-down list on the right of the Standard toolbar and select 100%. Your banner will be reduced in size and you will see the picture guides as you can see here:

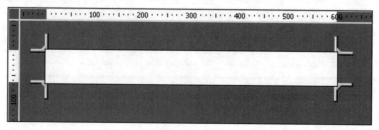

6. Place the mouse pointer over one or more of the guides and practice dragging the guide to change the size. Watch the size on the left of the status bar. Note that it is not easy to get an exact size.

7. Again right-click in the picture area and choose Picture Setup. Select Banner from the Picture Size drop-down list to return the picture area to the default banner size. Click Lock Picture Guides to turn that option on and click OK.

Often you will not know exactly the size you want the final picture to be, but it is best to start out with a rough guess so that you can see as you go along how what you are doing is fitting within that size.

Adding Text

In PhotoDraw you add text to a picture using the Text visual menu. The following steps describe this:

1. Click Text in the Visual menu and then click Insert Text. The Text workpane will appear on the right of the PhotoDraw window, and the words "Your text here" will appear in the picture area, as you can see in Figure 5-20.

2. Type **Exciting Travel** and those words will replace "Your text here" in both the picture area and the Text workpane.

3. Open the font drop-down list in the lower third of the Text pane. A scrolling list of fonts will appear, as shown next, which shows you what the font looks like. Scroll this list to see the fonts you have available (many of them were added when you installed Office 2000).

4. Choose Felix Titling as the font, select 30 points as the size, then move the mouse pointer to one of the edges of the box surrounding the text until it becomes a four-headed arrow, and drag the box so it is centered in the picture area, like this:

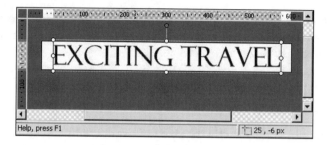

5. Open the File menu, choose Save As, select the folder you want to use, make sure the Save As Type is PhotoDraw, enter **Text1** as the filename, and click Save.

Changing Text

In selecting the font, size, and weight or style, you normally think you have done what can be done with text. PhotoDraw, though, has a number of other things that you can do with text to make it look a special way. Let's explore some of those options now.

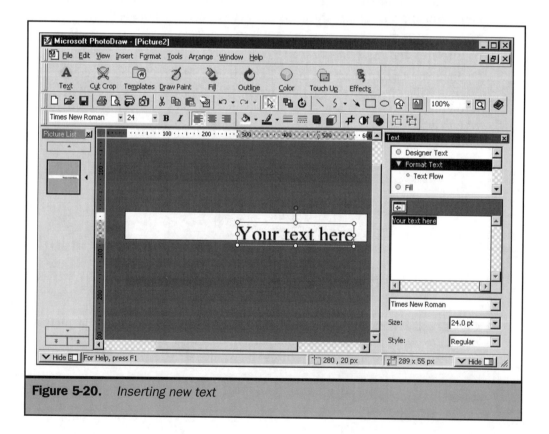

Figure 5-20.   *Inserting new text*

Tip

You can do so many things with text that it can sometimes become overpowering and possibly gaudy. In those instances it is good to remember the KISS (keep it simple…) principle

1. In either the Text workpane or the Text visual menu, click Designer Text to display 28 different ideas for changing text.

2. Click three or four of the Designer Text alternatives to see how they look with your text. When you are done, click Designer Text 5 (the third down on the left). Save that image as **Text2**.

Note

As you make changes to the text, they may take several seconds to take effect as they are being rendered for your screen. The length of time depends on the speed of your computer. While the rendering is taking place, a blue and white bar is rotating in the status bar.

3. Click Fill in the Text workpane, click texture in the Fill drop-down list, and then select several of the textures from the alternatives available. From the Fill drop-down list, select first Designer Gradient and then Picture, and for each of these, select several of the options to see how they look. As one choice, select Designer Gradient 17 and save it as **Text3**.

4. Click Outline in the Text workpane, make sure Plain is selected for the line type, click the third option in the lines labeled "Thin-Thin Line," and select a color for the outline. After a moment your text will have an outline added to it with a white space separating it from the original color with which you started this step.

5. Select Photo Brushes as the line type and click the arrow button on the left of the line type to open up the selection of lines, like this:

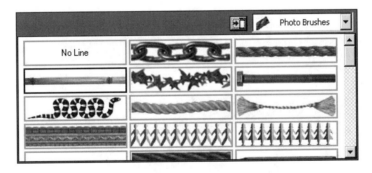

6. Choose several of the photo-brush outlines to see how they look. As one of your options, choose Bamboo as the outline. After several moments, you'll see your text outlined with bamboo. Save this as **Text4**.

7. In the Text workpane click Bend Text and select the Quarter Circle Down option, the top one on the right. This may take several moments minutes to

render. When it is done, your result should look like Figure 5-21, where the picture area no longer contains all of the text.

8. Right-click the picture area and select Lock Picture Guides to unlock them so you can enlarge the picture area. Drag one of the lower picture guides down until the picture area is larger than the text. Then, if necessary, drag one or both of the left and right guides out so the text is easily within the picture area, as shown next. Save this as **Text5**.

9. Open the Text visual menu and select 3-D Text. In the 3-D workpane choose the Designer 3-D 4 option (third down on the left). Again this will take a fair amount of time (several minutes) to render, and the result is not very attractive.

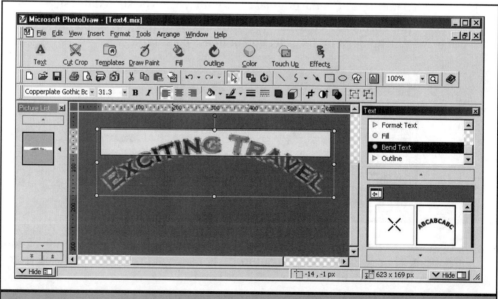

Figure 5-21.   *Bent text outside of the picture area*

10. Close Text5 without saving the changes and open Text1. Again select the Designer 3-D 4 option. This should appear relatively fast and look like something worthwhile. Stretch the containing box by dragging two opposite corners until the text fills the pictures area, as you can see here:

11. Save the 3-D image as **Text6**. Close Text6, open Text3, and apply one of the 3-D effects. Again, the result is not very attractive. Close the image without saving it.

12. Open Text3 again. Stretch the text to fit the picture area as you did above. Click Beveling and Extrusion in the 3-D workpane. Change the Extrusion depth to **10**. Click Rotate and Tilt; enter **25** in Tilt Left and Right, and **10** in Tilt Up and Down. This takes a bit of time to render, and the result is not very exciting. Try other combinations of extrusion, rotation, and tilt.

13. Close the current image without saving it. Close the Text workpane.

You can see that there are a great many things you can do to change the way text looks. Some of them are attractive and some, in my opinion, are not. There are, of course, many other combinations that were not tried here. You can try them on your own.

Working with Photographs

You can bring photographs into PhotoDraw by directly scanning them, by directly downloading them from a digital camera, or by opening a file that contains a photograph. Once the photo is in PhotoDraw you can size it, crop it (cut off the edges), touch it up, and distort it. In this section you'll look at scanning in a photo, bringing in several photo files, and making a number of changes to those photos.

Scanning in a Photograph

For this exercise I am going to scan in a photograph from the Princess Cruises 1999 Alaska Cruises catalog, which I am using with the permission of Princess Cruises. If you have a scanner, you can use any photographs that you have available (look at several magazines). If you don't have a scanner, the finished image is available on the CD that comes with this book as Princess.tif and in the \Book\Chap05\PhotoDraw\ folder.

It is important, if you scan or otherwise use material from a copyrighted publication such as the Princess Cruises catalog used above, that you get written permission for such use. (You can usually use clip art with the standard permission on the package.)

1. Load PhotoDraw if it is not already running. Either during startup or from the File menu, choose Blank Picture and click OK, or choose New, and in either case double-click Default Picture. PhotoDraw will display a 5 × 3¾-inch picture area that you saw in Figure 5-18.

2. Put the picture you want to scan in your scanner and make sure it is plugged in and turned on. You will also need to have a scanner driver loaded. In the case of newer HP scanners, an icon telling you the driver is loaded is displayed on the right of the taskbar.

3. Open the File menu and choose Scan Picture. The first time you do this you will get a message that a "new TWAIN device" has been found and you need to tell PhotoDraw about it. (TWAIN stands for "technology without an interesting name" and is the interface between scanners or cameras and software such as PhotoDraw.) If you get this message, click OK and the Options dialog box will open showing the Scanner/Camera devices that are present. If what it shows is correct, click OK again; otherwise click Modify, make the necessary changes, and then click OK. The Scan workpane will open.

4. Click Scan. After a moment your scanner should start. Again in the case of an HP scanner a percentage scale appears and shows you how far along the scanning is. When it is done the image should appear in PhotoDraw as you can see in Figure 5-22.

Cropping and Sizing a Photograph

Once you have brought a photograph into PhotoDraw, you will probably want to crop it and size it to fit your needs. Do that with the image you just scanned in with these steps:

1. Click the cropping tool in the formatting toolbar. The Crop workpane will open, allowing you to choose the shape to which you want to crop. Click the Square in the upper-right corner and then drag the corners and/or edges of the box surrounding the photo until you have the picture area you want to end up with, as shown in Figure 5-23.

 The cropped dimensions are shown on the right of the status bar as you are doing the cropping.

2. When you have the cropped image the way you want it, click Finish. The area of the picture that you cropped will disappear and the surrounding box will go

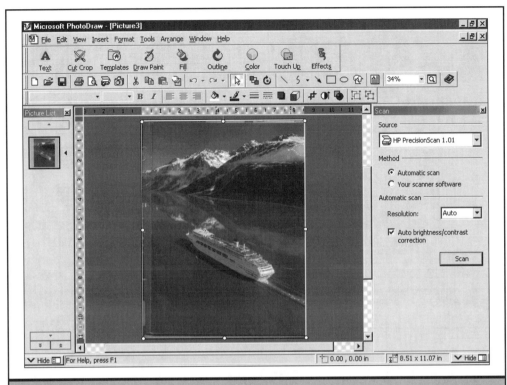

Figure 5-22.   *Picture scanned into PhotoDraw*

from a cropping box to a sizing box. This means that now when you drag an edge or a corner, the picture will get smaller, but the content will stay the same.

3. Open the Arrange menu and choose Arrange. The Arrange workpane will open with Size and Position selected. Make sure that Maintain Proportions is selected and then reduce the size to about 1 × ½-inch by changing the Height to .5 inches.

4. Right-click in the picture area outside the picture, choose Picture Setup, select Banner, and click OK. Drag the picture to within the banner, open the Zoom drop-down list, and choose 150%.

5. Drag the picture so the top border of the picture is on the top border of the banner. Then drag the lower-left corner of the picture up until the lower border of the picture is on the lower border of the banner (a height of about .43 inches or 64 pixels).

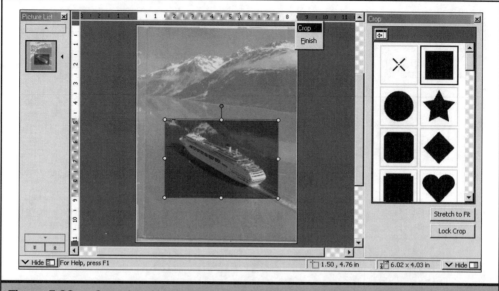

Figure 5-23. *Cropping the scanned photo*

Copying and Flipping a Photograph

One thing that might be done with this photo is to put mirror images on either side of one of the title texts. See how that is done next.

1. Right-click the picture and choose Copy. Right-click the picture area and choose Paste. A second image appears in the picture area.

2. In the Arrange workpane, click Flip and the four flip options appear. The top-right option occurs by flipping or pivoting the top left option on its right side, and the two bottom options occur by flipping the top two options on their bottom side.

3. Select the image you want to flip and click Flip Horizontal. The image will be flipped as shown in Figure 5-24.

Combining Photographs with Text

With two mirror images, you can match them on either end of a title. Here's how:

1. Close the Arrange workpane and adjust the scroll bars so you can see the entire length of the banner.

2. Drag the two images so they are on either ends of the banner.

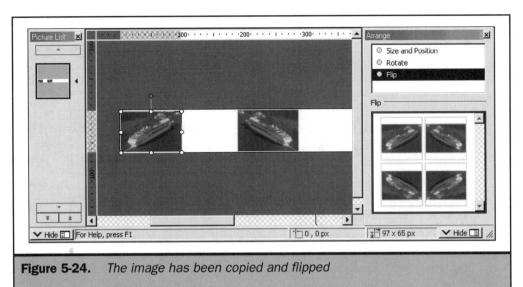

Figure 5-24.   *The image has been copied and flipped*

3. Open the Insert menu, choose From File, and find and double-click the Text6 file you created earlier. Drag the corners and sides of Text6 until it exactly fits in the area between the two pictures, like this:

4. Save this completed image as Banner1 and close the picture.

Using PhotoDraw's Photo Library

PhotoDraw comes with a large library of photographs that you can use in your pictures. Use them with these steps:

1. Select New from the File menu and double-click Banner. A new banner will appear.

2. Place the second PhotoDraw CD in your drive, open the Insert menu, and choose PhotoDraw Content. If necessary, locate the \Content\PDClips\Bldg_arc\ folder and then double-click Bk0106.mix, Big Ben and the Houses of Parliament.

3. Use the Zoom drop-down list to zoom out to 50%. Open the Arrange menu, choose Arrange, and with the Maintain Proportions selected, change the Height

to 64 pixels, the height of the banner. Drag the image down to the left end of the banner.

4. Again open the Insert menu, choose PhotoDraw Content, select the \Content\PDClips\Travel\ folder, and double-click Bk0089.mix, the Washington Monument. Make the height 64 pixels and drag the photo to the banner next to Beg Ben.

5. Repeat step 4 using the same folder, but double-clicking first Bk0105.mix (Eiffel tower) and then Bk0434.mix (Arc de Triomphe), and dragging them to the right end of the banner.

6. Close the Arrange workpane, open the View menu, and choose Fit To Picture Area to enlarge your banner to fill the workspace. Drag the four pictures so they are even and fill the two ends.

7. Open the Insert menu, select From File, and double-click the Text3 file you created earlier. Drag the sides and corners of the text so that it just fits between the photos, as you can see here:

8. Save this picture as **Banner2** and close the Picture.

Touching Up and Distorting Photographs

There are a great many additional things you can do to change a picture in PhotoDraw. Look at just a couple of them here and then try some of the others on your own.

1. Click New in the toolbar to open a new default picture area. Right-click the picture area, choose Picture Setup, change the picture size to Letter, and click OK.

2. Open the Insert menu, choose PhotoDraw Content, select the \Content\PDClips\ People\ folder, and double-click Ct0730.mix. A photo of a woman's face comes in. Roughly center the photo in the picture area.

3. In the Visual menu, choose Color | Brightness and Contrast. In the Color workpane, make sure Correct Selection is highlighted and click Automatic. The photo will be lightened.

4. Open the Effect drop-down list and choose Colorize. Click the eyedropper and then click a darker area of the hair to pick up that color. Select Correct By Painting, click the arrow opposite Brush to see the 24 brush options, but leave the Medium Circular 18 Point Brush default, and close the brush options.

5. Paint some of the areas of lighter hair to darken it, as shown in Figure 5-25.

6. Open the Touch Up Visual menu and select Fix Red Eye. (Ignore the fact that this photo does not have red eye, to see how this works.) Click in the areas of the eye that might have red eye and then click fix in the pop-up menu. You will get a message that says PhotoDraw could not locate the size and shape of the red eye area and that you must select Manual Red Eye.

7. Open the Effects Visual menu and choose Distort. In the Distort workpane, click Bulge. Interestingly, the result is pretty realistic in just creating a fuller face. Either click Undo in the toolbar or click No Distortion in the Distort workpane to remove the effect.

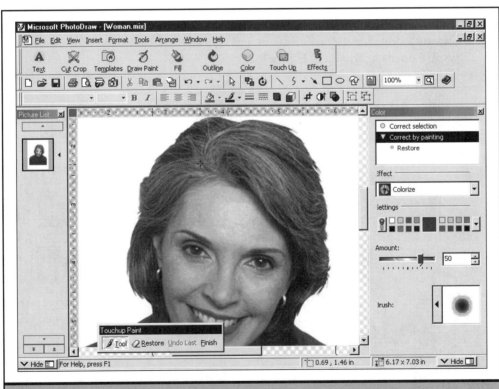

Figure 5-25.   *Darkening the hair in a photograph*

8. Click Wave2 to apply a really weird distortion, which you can see in Figure 5-26. If you wish, try some of the others. When you are done, close the picture without saving it.

Your imagination is the only limit to the changes you can make to photographs with PhotoDraw, but you will need to try them out to see how they work.

Creating Buttons

In web pages, buttons are used quite often, and having a distinctive button design adds uniqueness to the site. PhotoDraw supports this objective by providing templates for a number of ready-made buttons to which you can add your text, as well as the tools to make you own buttons.

Using Button Templates

PhotoDraw provides four categories of button templates with 13 designs within each category that you can customize to your own needs. See how to do this with these steps:

1. If you are just starting PhotoDraw, click Design Templates. If PhotoDraw is already loaded, open the File menu and choose New Templates. The Template wizard opens as shown in Figure 5-27.

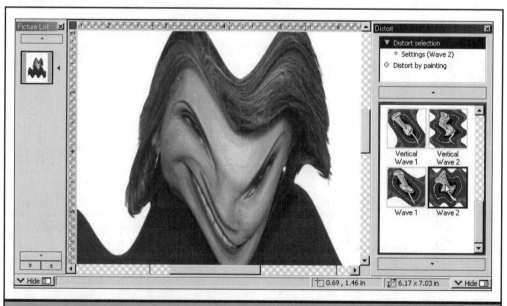

Figure 5-26.   *The Wave2 distortion applied to a photograph*

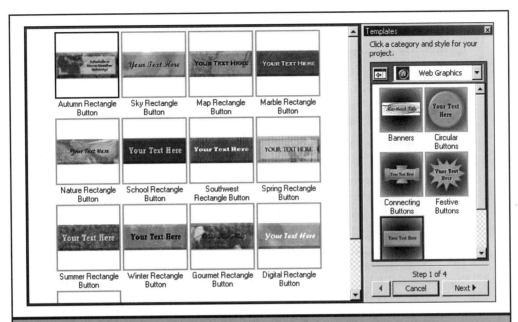

Figure 5-27. *Template wizard showing the web buttons available*

2. Click each of the four button template categories to see what is available. End up by selecting Rectangular Buttons and then click the design of your choice (I am using Map Rectangle here).

3. Click Next. This step allows you to replace the image used as the background for the button. Click Browse to look for an image in another file, or click an image in the existing file.

4. Click Next. Enter the text that you want on the button, such as **HOME**, change the font and style, and change the size to 12 points.

5. Click Next and then click Finish. The Template wizard will close and you will be in PhotoDraw. Here you can also change the text and image, save and print the button, and copy the button. Do the latter next.

6. Click the button outside the text area to select it, open the Arrange menu, and choose Arrange. In the Arrange workpane, make sure that Maintain Proportions is checked and then change the width to 1 inch. Re-center the word HOME in the new button size.

7. Right-click in the picture area and choose Picture Setup. Change the Width to 5 inches, the Height to .4 inches, and click OK. This gives you the necessary width for five buttons and makes the height the same as the new button size.

8. Open the Edit menu and choose Select All. Click Copy in the toolbar, click in the picture area to deselect the original button, click Paste, and drag the new button to the right of the original button in the picture area (its position should be Top: 0.00 and Left: 1.00).

9. Click again in the picture area, click Paste, and drag the new button to the right of the last button three more times to create a total of five buttons.

10. Click text in the second button, open the Text Visual menu, choose Format Text, and type **CRUISES**. Repeat that for the remaining three buttons, typing **AIR, LAND,** and **HOTEL**.

11. Close the Text workpane, open the View menu, and choose Fit to Picture Area. Open the Edit menu, choose Select all, and click Group in the Formatting toolbar. This prevents any of the words or buttons from moving relative to the others. The final result should look like this:

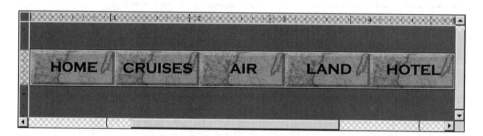

12. Save your buttons as **Travel Buttons** using the default PhotoDraw type. Then save the buttons again as **Travel Buttons.jpg**, click Yes to continue with the save and flatten all objects into one bitmap, and close the Picture.

The beauty of the button templates is that they are ready-made 3-D buttons and are a very fast way to create good-looking buttons. There are number of other places to get button templates, including in clip art and on a number of sites on the Internet, including Microsoft.

Creating Your Own Buttons

If you truly want your own unique buttons, you will have to create them yourself. That really isn't hard with PhotoDraw. Try it as your last exercise in this chapter.

1. Click New in the toolbar to open a default picture area. Right-click in the picture area and choose Picture Setup. Change the Width to 3 inches, the Height to .4 inches, and click OK.

2. Click the rectangle in the toolbar. The Outline workpane will open with the rectangle tool selected.

3. Draw a rectangle on the left end of the picture area that is 1 inch by .4 inches. Adjust the line width to 1 point with the slider at the bottom of the workpane, and choose white as the color of the border.

4. From the Arrange menu, open the Arrange workpane. Set the Width and Height to exactly 1 inch and .4 inches (turn off Maintain Proportions), and set the Top and Left Position to 0.00.

5. Open the Fill Visual menu and choose Texture. In the Texture workpane, choose an option you like. I am using Bronze. Leave the other settings at their defaults.

6. Open the Effects Visual menu, choose 3-D, and click Beveling and Extrusion. Choose Bevel1 (second option in the top row), set the Bevel Depth and Width to 10, and the Extrusion Depth to 50.

7. If necessary, reopen the Arrange workpane and reset the Width and Height to 1 and .4 and the Top and Left Position to 0.00.

8. Open the Text Visual menu and choose Insert Text. Type **HOME**, and accept the defaults of Copperplate Gothic Bold, 12 points, and Bold. Drag the text into the button and center it.

9. Press CTRL+A to select both the button and text and CTRL+C to copy it. Then Press CTRL+V twice to make two copies of the button and text. Change the text on the two new buttons to **LAST** and **NEXT**.

10. Make the necessary adjustments to the positioning and picture area, and then click Group in the toolbar. Finally, save the buttons as **Buttons** both as a .MIX file and as a .GIF. Your result should look like this:

There are, of course, many other things you can do to make buttons, from using other fills, to other shapes, to other ways of making them 3-D. Like many parts of PhotoDraw that have not been touched on here, these are left for you to explore. If you do, you'll find a wealth of capability waiting to be used.

The
Complete
Reference

Part II

Creating Web Sites

The
Complete
Reference

Chapter 6

Creating and Formatting a Web Page from Scratch

In Chapters 3 and 4 you saw how to build a web and its pages by using a wizard or a template. You learned that using a wizard or template is the easiest way to create a web that incorporates many FrontPage features. Occasionally, you may want to build a web from scratch. In this chapter, we'll do that (and consequently increase your knowledge of the parts of a web).

| Note | *This chapter uses a number of files that are on the CD included with this book. All files are in the folder \Book\Chap06 on the CD.* |

Planning a Web

Chapter 1 talked about the process of designing a web application or web site, and Chapter 2 listed the steps necessary to build a web. In both chapters planning was the first and probably most important step in making a good web—and the one most often shortchanged. Planning seeks to answer four questions:

- What are the goals of the web?
- What will its content be?
- How will it be organized?
- What do you want it to look like?

Suppose you work for a travel agency named Exciting Travel and have been given the task of creating an intranet web to communicate with the company's agents. Go through each of the four questions with that in mind. (With only small changes you could alternatively look at this as an Internet web to communicate with your potential clients.)

Whatever your need for a web site is, you should begin by defining your goals.

What Are Your Goals?

Setting the goals of a web is very important—if the goals are well thought out, you will probably end up with an effective web. Keep it simple. Having one or two obtainable goals for your web is better than having a number of goals that cannot all be met. Too many goals will scatter the focus of the web, making it much more difficult to accomplish any one of them.

For Exciting Travel, there is one primary goal for their intranet web: to give their agents a competitive advantage by providing access to a consolidated list of the latest travel offerings. (An Internet web goal might be to get the user to call Exciting Travel and inquire about a possible trip.) There is a secondary and supporting goal: to keep the web frequently updated so the agents will look at it often.

What Is the Content?

To accomplish Exciting Travel's goals, you'll need to include information about current travel specials over a broad range of travel options. The information needs to be complete enough to capture the agents' interest but concise enough for them to read quickly. Therefore, the content needs to include not only a brief description of current packages, but also general information the agents might need, such as the current exchange rates, climates, and current travel conditions.

How Is It Organized?

How well a web is organized determines how easily users can get the information they seek. The desired information should be within two or three clicks of your home page, and the path should be clear—users shouldn't have to guess how to get what they want. The home page mainly provides links to other pages. The pages below the home page contain the desired information and are a single click or link away from the home page. In a web site with a limited amount of content this is a relatively simple process, but a web site with a great deal of content requires more planning. The user will have to "drill down" into the web's structure, going from the general to the specific to reach the desired information. How you organize your content will determine the path the user follows. This path should be clear and logical, and should allow the user to jump back to the starting points without having to retrace every step. The home page's links to detailed information give relatively quick answers to those agents who are willing to take a couple of minutes, but following the links may not appeal to those who are in a hurry. For quick answers, you need to have some low-priced specials briefly but prominently listed on the home page.

Your web needs to be based on a simple and obvious tree structure, similar to the one shown in Figure 6-1, so that users always know where they are and how they got there. The lines connecting the pages show how the pages should be hyperlinked. In this example no page is more than three clicks from the homepage, and most of the content is within two clicks. The third-level pages within each second-level area are linked, but the user has to move back up the tree to reach the third-level pages in the other second-level area. While a cross-link between two third-level branches may seem like a quick way to get users from one place to another under certain circumstances, it is also a quick way to confuse users about where they are. It is often better to force users back up the tree and down another branch. If you never have more than two levels from your home page, it is not a big chore to backtrack. Besides, the previously

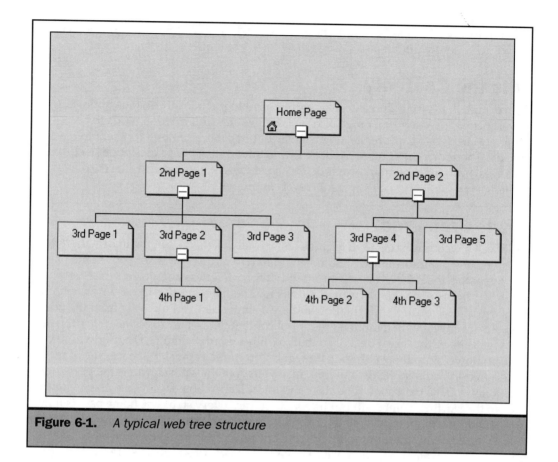

Figure 6-1. *A typical web tree structure*

visited pages are already on the user's disk in their browser's cache, so they can quickly backtrack.

Note   *Web browsers store the web pages and pictures they download in temporary files, called a cache, on the user's hard disk. This speeds up subsequent loading of the pages by reading from the hard disk rather than downloading the file over the Internet. The browsers check to see if the file on the web server is newer than the files in cache. If the pages are the same, the cached page is used. If the version on the web server is newer, it is downloaded. In Netscape 4.0 the users control the cache in the Preferences dialog box, opened by choosing Preferences from the Edit menu. The cache can be cleared anytime, and a time limit for saving cached files can be set. In Internet Explorer the cache ("Temporary Internet Files") is controlled from the General tab of the Internet Options dialog box, opened by choosing Internet Options from the View menu (IE 4.0) or the Tools menu (IE 5.0).*

> **Tip** *Each page in your web, regardless of the level, should have a direct link back to the home page. This allows users to quickly return to the starting point in one click.*

This tree structure can be expanded to hold hundreds or even thousands of pages, all within two or at most three clicks of the home page. The important thing is to remember that, no matter how small your web is at the beginning, a well-organized tree structure will allow you to expand your web to any size in the future.

What Will It Look Like?

With all the concepts just discussed, what will this web look like? This includes the graphic design as well as the structure of each page. It's best to begin with the structure and then add the graphic elements. This gives you the functionality first, and no web site, no matter how good-looking it is, will be successful if it isn't well structured and easy to use.

The best approach is to begin by sketching the primary types of pages that you will be using. Figure 6-2 shows one way that the information in this web could be laid out to satisfy the desired points brought out in the plan. To keep to the desired three levels, there will be three types of pages:

- A home page with a list of interesting specials and links to all second-level pages with the different types of travel
- A second-level page that contains the main content for a particular type of travel and links to the details for a particular travel type
- A third-level page with the details for a particular type of travel

All three types of pages will have the same footer, which will have a copyright notice, the date last updated, a postal address, and information on how to contact the webmaster (the person responsible for maintaining the web). Each second-level page and the third-level pages below it, of which there will be many, will share the same heading, which will be a navigation bar, or navbar, providing links to other pages. The home page will have a unique header and larger, separate sections with links in each.

The web will begin on the home page with major travel options such as cruises, land tours, hotels, and air travel. These will lead to a list of specific offerings for a travel option, such as a list of Alaskan cruises, on the second-level pages. Each entry will lead to the details of a specific offering, such as the specifics of a particular cruise, on the third-level pages. The "Current Specials" on the home page will link directly to the third-level details of those offerings.

The trick is to maintain a balance that doesn't overwhelm users with dozens of links on a page, or make them click until their finger drops to reach the information they want.

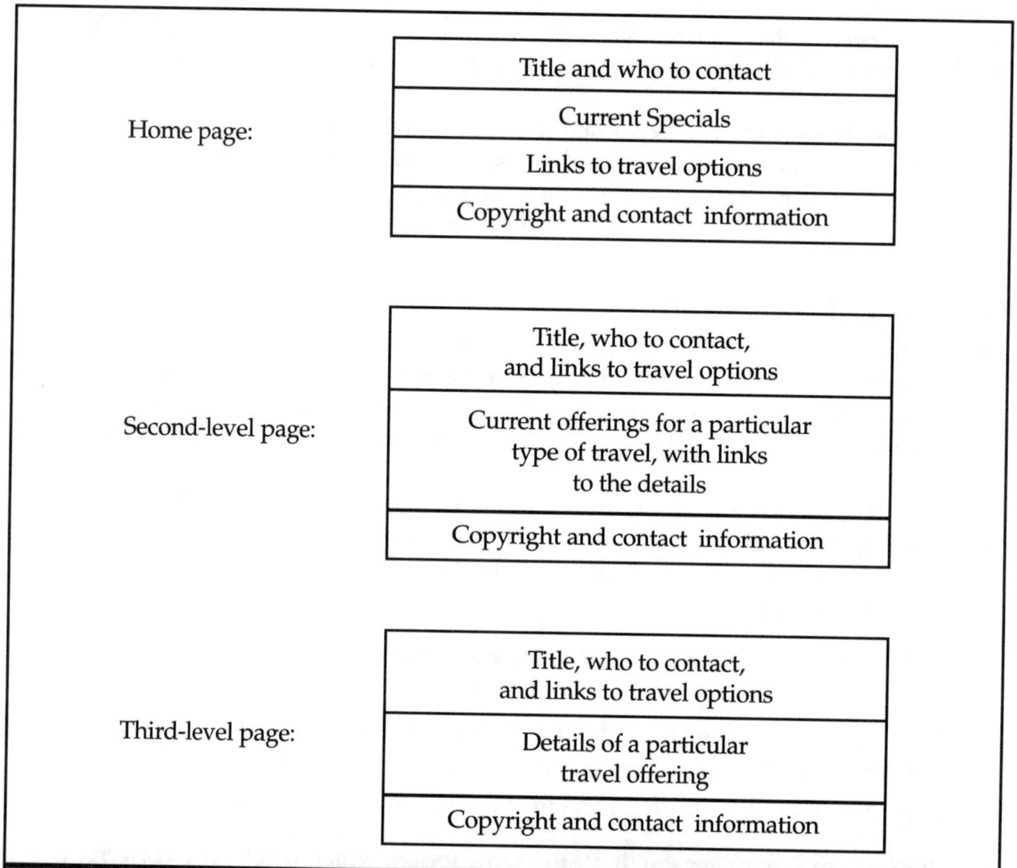

Home page:	Title and who to contact
	Current Specials
	Links to travel options
	Copyright and contact information

Second-level page:	Title, who to contact, and links to travel options
	Current offerings for a particular type of travel, with links to the details
	Copyright and contact information

Third-level page:	Title, who to contact, and links to travel options
	Details of a particular travel offering
	Copyright and contact information

Figure 6-2. *One way to lay out the Exciting Travel web*

This gives you a general view of what your web will look like, which is enough for the planning process. As you actually create the pages, you will fine-tune that look by placing pictures and positioning text.

Starting a Web

The Exciting Travel web will be created in this and the following several chapters. This chapter will look at working with text and pictures. Chapter 7 will deal with hyperlinks and hotspots, Chapter 8 will add tables and frames, Chapter 9 will work with forms, and Chapter 10 will address FrontPage Components. The reason for this approach is to focus on one topic at a time. As a result, you'll see areas, especially in this chapter, that may be better handled with, for example, a table or a FrontPage Component. That discussion will be put off until the appropriate chapter, so each topic can be fully developed without interfering with others.

Developing all but the simplest webs is a long and tedious chore. Look at this proposed travel web—there will be a second-level page for each type of travel, of which there are probably six to ten types. There are then probably six to ten offerings for each type. That means at a minimum there will be 36 third-level pages (not counting those that may be referred to directly from the home page), six second-level pages, and a home page—a total of at least 43 pages! You can let out your breath; in this chapter you'll only do one of each type of page. It is important to consider, though, how the page count explodes as you develop a web and how adding levels makes the web grow geometrically.

Tip   *Allow enough time to complete the development of a web. Material created electronically, such as Word text files and Image Composer or PhotoDraw pictures, is the easiest to work with, but you may need to use text for which you only have printed copies. One way to speed the process is to scan printed documents that you want incorporated (like travel brochures for the details of a travel offering) and then use optical character recognition (OCR) to convert them to text. Be sure to carefully edit any OCR-generated text (the process is less than perfect), and make sure you have written permission to reproduce other people's copyrighted material.*

Note   *It is recommended that you build this web site from scratch, but if you wish, you can download it from the CD that accompanies this book. As a third alternative, there is a Chap6txt.doc file on the CD that can be opened in Microsoft Word 95 or later and contains all of the text that is used on this web site. You can cut and paste this text between Word and FrontPage, saving you the typing.*

1. Start FrontPage. Open the File menu and choose New | Web.

2. Select the One Page Web from the New dialog box, enter the folder name **ExcitingTravel**, which becomes the web name, with the path you want to use (the path and folder name should look like **http://*servername*/ExcitingTravel**), and click OK.

3. In Navigation view, right-click the Home Page icon to open its context menu. Choose Properties to open the page's Properties dialog box. Observe, as shown next, that the URL for this page includes the page's filename of Default.htm. The filename of the home page should match the default for the server your web will be hosted on (check with the webmaster of your server if you're not sure). Default.htm is the default filename for the MSPWS and for Windows NT's Internet Information Services (IIS). Click OK to close the Page Properties dialog box.

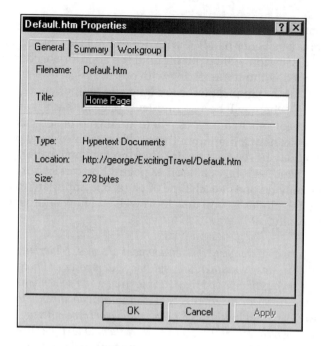

Note *FrontPage will detect the correct default filename for the selected server and name the home page accordingly. If you are developing your web on the MSPWS but intend to move it to another server later, you should set the default filename on the MSPWS to match the final web server. See Appendix A for instructions on how to set the default filename for the MSPWS.*

4. Click New Page on the toolbar. A new page will appear under the home page. Slowly click twice (don't double-click) in the title area of the new page, type **Second Level Page,** and press ENTER to revise the page name.

5. Again click New Page on the toolbar, click twice in the title area of the new page, and type **Third Level Page**. You should see three pages, one under the other, as shown in Figure 6-3.

Note *The web server that webs are developed on is often called the staging server. In this book the MSPWS is assumed to be the staging server. When the web is ready to go "live," it will be copied, or published, to a production server. All work on a web should be done and tested on the staging server before you publish it to the production server.*

There is a very good structural reason for organizing your web pages in folders. Web servers, like the MSPWS and Internet Information Services (IIS), allow you to create *virtual* directories. These are simply folders that are *aliased* or *mapped* to names that are easier to work with. For example, if you have set up FrontPage and the

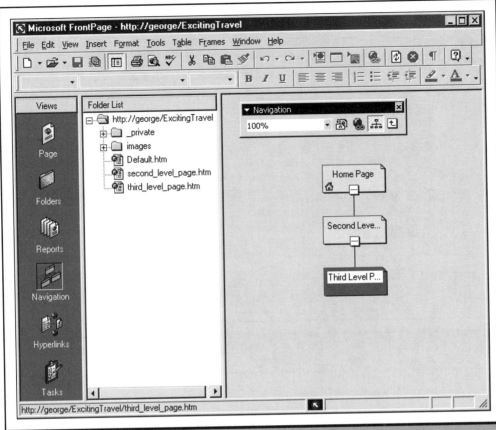

Figure 6-3. *The initial three pages in Navigation view of FrontPage*

MSPWS as recommended in Appendix A, the physical path to the Exciting Travel
folder is C:\Inetpub\Wwwroot\ExcitingTravel\, as displayed with the Windows
Explorer in Figure 6-4. This can be mapped to the virtual directory /ExcitingTravel. In
your web you can reference any pages in the ExcitingTravel folder using the
/ExcitingTravel virtual directory rather than the full path.

When you installed the MSPWS, certain virtual directories were created by default.
The most important is the root directory of the web server. The physical path is, by
default, C:\Inetpub\Wwwroot\. This was mapped to the Home virtual directory. This
means the URL http://*servername*/ will load the web page whose path is
C:\Inetpub\Wwwroot\Default.htm. There can only be one Home virtual directory
with the MSPWS, while web servers like IIS can have multiple home directories, but

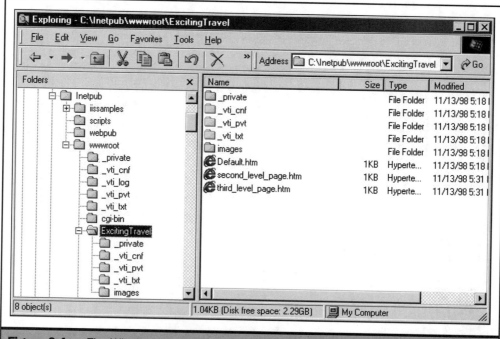

Figure 6-4. *The Windows Explorer shows you where the MSPWS puts your new web*

each one must have a unique IP address. Figure 6-5 shows the MSPWS's Personal Web Manager with some of the virtual directories that are created by default (compare this to Figure 6-4).

> **Note** *The terms folder and directory are interchangeable. FrontPage and Windows use "folder," while Windows NT uses "directory." The MSPWS Internet Services Administrator also uses "directory."*

Using virtual directories also allows you to set different levels of permissions for web pages. If you have some web pages that you want to be available to the public, but others that you want to limit access to, you can place the restricted pages in a separate folder and control access to the folder. In a FrontPage web, the _private folder serves this purpose. Chapter 21 covers security on the web in more detail.

The next step in creating your web is to add text and pictures to your pages. In Chapter 7 you will add the hyperlinks that will give the web a structure.

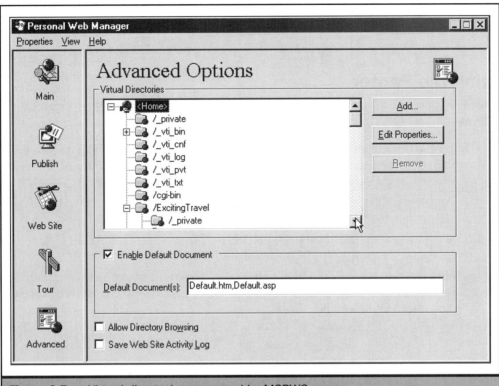

Figure 6-5. *Virtual directories managed by MSPWS*

Note *By creating the three pages in FrontPage Navigation view you automatically established a relationship among the pages, as shown by their relative position and the lines between them. This relationship will be used in creating the automatic links in a navigation bar. Since you will be working with hyperlinks and hotspots in Chapter 7, you won't do anything more with links in this chapter.*

Adding and Formatting Text

The text will be entered in sections corresponding to the home page sections shown in Figure 6-2—for example, the title, the footer (copyright and contact information), and the current specials. Where applicable, this information will be entered and formatted on the home page and then copied to other pages. Begin by entering the footer using FrontPage's Shared Borders feature.

All of the text that you are asked to enter in this chapter is on the CD that accompanies this book in the \Book\Chap06\ folder and Chap6txt.doc file. You can open that file in Microsoft Word and then cut and paste the text between Word and FrontPage.

Entering the Footer

The footer goes at the bottom of all the pages and contains the copyright notice and information on how to contact the webmaster. To create the footer:

1. In Navigation view, open the Format menu and choose Shared Borders. In the Shared Borders dialog box, select the Bottom check box, make sure All Pages is selected, and clear all the other check boxes, as shown in Figure 6-6. Click OK.

2. Double-click the Home Page icon in the Navigation pane to open the home page in Page view.

3. Select the line on the home page that begins "Comment: This border appears…", type the word **Copyright**, and press the SPACEBAR.

4. With the cursor where you left it after step 3, open the Insert menu and choose Symbol. In the Symbol dialog box, select the copyright symbol, as shown next, click Insert, and then click Close.

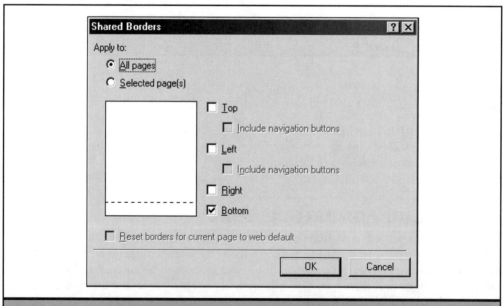

Figure 6-6.   Shared borders will put the same border contents on all pages

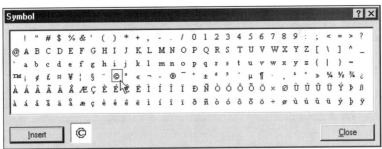

5. Press the SPACEBAR once again to insert a space after the copyright symbol, and then type the following information, just as it is shown here. Press SHIFT+ENTER (new line) at the end of the first two lines. Insert the bullet from the Symbol dialog box.

> **1996-99 Exciting Travel, Inc. All rights reserved.**
> **1234 W 13th, Ourtown, ST 99999 • (999) 555-1234**
> **Please send comments and suggestions to webmaster@excitingtravel.com.**

(Remember, if you don't want to type this text, it is in the Chap6txt.doc file in the \Book\Chap06 folder on the CD that comes with this book.)

Note
Using SHIFT+ENTER instead of ENTER reduces the amount of space between lines and helps group related material.

6. To see the new line and paragraph marks in Page view, click Show All on the right of the toolbar.

7. If you look at the paragraph style in the Style drop-down list box on the left of the Formatting toolbar, it should be Normal. This is a little large for the footer, so click the down arrow in the Style drop-down list, and select Heading 5. This reduces the size, but it is still easy to read, as you can see in Figure 6-7.

8. Click Save on the toolbar or press CTRL+S to save your home page with its new footer.

9. Open Folders view and double-click Second Level Page. You'll see that it has the same footer as the home page. Again, open Folders view and double-click Third Level Page. It also has the same footer.

You might need to refresh the Second Level Page and Third Level Page to see the shared border footer. With the page opened in Page view, click Refresh on the right of the toolbar. You now have the footer entered and correctly formatted on each page using shared borders. Next work on the home page title.

Creating the Home Page Title

The home page title is the introduction to a web. It needs to be inviting and to reflect the company. In this web it also needs to communicate how certain people can be reached. That is a big order and one that you'll revisit again in this chapter and in later

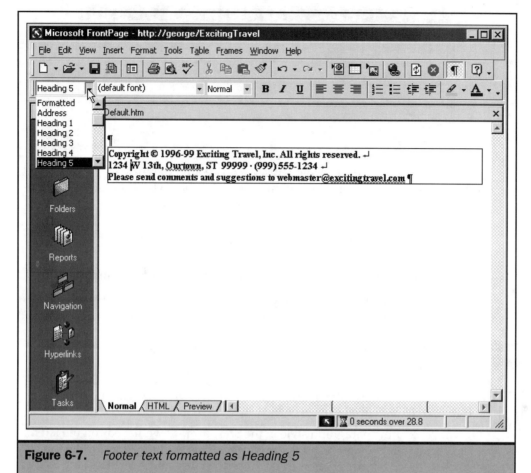

Figure 6-7.   *Footer text formatted as Heading 5*

chapters. To start out, create a text-only title with the following instructions. Later in the chapter you'll replace the text with the graphic you created in Chapter 5.

1. Open the Window menu, choose Default.htm and click above the footer to return to the top of the home page in preparation for creating the title.

2. Type the following text, pressing SHIFT+ENTER at the end of the first and fourth lines below, and pressing ENTER at the end of the second and sixth lines (the fourth and sixth lines are just continuations of the third and fifth lines). See Figure 6-8 to see what the final title will look like.

> **EXCITING TRAVEL**
> **"The Exciting Way To Go!"**
> **For the latest fares, contact Julie Bergan at 555-1234**
> **or John Donald at 555-1235**
> **or through e-mail at julieb@excitingtravel.com**
> **or jmd@excitingtravel.com**

3. Click anywhere in each of the two paragraphs you just typed, and then, for each paragraph, click Center on the Formatting toolbar.

4. Drag across the first two lines to select them, open the Style drop-down list, select Heading 1, click Bold, and then click Italic on the Formatting toolbar.

5. Drag across just the first line, open the Font Size drop-down list on the Formatting toolbar, and select 7 (36 pt) to increase the font size to the 36-point maximum.

6. Click Save on the toolbar to protect your work. Your final product should look like Figure 6-8. (The figures and illustrations in this book may look different than your screen because of differences in resolution.)

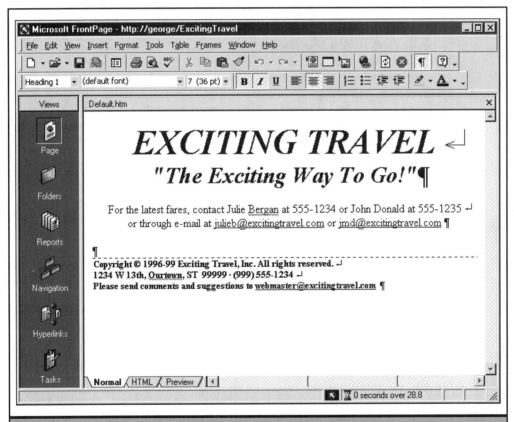

Figure 6-8. *The home page with the title and footer in its text form*

Listing the Current Specials

The current specials are promotional fares for a particular week. Listing them gives agents immediate access to the latest and lowest fares.

It is very important to keep the list of specials updated. First, it provides a reason for people to come back and look at the page. Second, it prevents information in the list from getting out of date.

To create the list of current specials:

1. With the insertion point on the line immediately following the two e-mail addresses in the title, press ENTER once to leave a blank line, and make sure that the paragraph style is Normal and the text is left-aligned.

2. Type the following text as it is shown. Press ENTER at the end of every other line. The intervening lines are continued on the next line (see Figure 6-9).

    CURRENT SPECIALS
    Super airfares to San Francisco: $75,
    LA: $175, New York: $275, & Miami: $375
    Hawaii, on the Kona beach, 1-bedroom deluxe condo,
    all amenities, $150 / night
    Fiji, air plus 6 nights in beautiful beachfront bungalow
    with breakfast, $850
    Disneyland, air, 1 day Disneyland pass, 2 nights hotel, rental
    car, and more, $285
    London, air, 5 nights first-class hotel, breakfast, 2 city tours,
    and more, $750
    (Some restrictions may apply to the above fares.)

A single paragraph cannot have more than one paragraph style, nor can a single paragraph contain more than one bulleted or numbered line. For that reason, all of the lines in both the Current Specials and Travel Options sections have ENTER placed at the end of each line, even though it takes more space.

3. Click line 1, and from the Style drop-down menu box, choose Heading 2.

4. Drag across lines 2 through 6, and click Bullets on the Formatting toolbar.

5. Drag over the last line, select 2 (10 pt) from the Font Size drop-down list, and then click Increase Indent on the Formatting toolbar.

6. Click Save. Your Current Specials section should look like Figure 6-9.

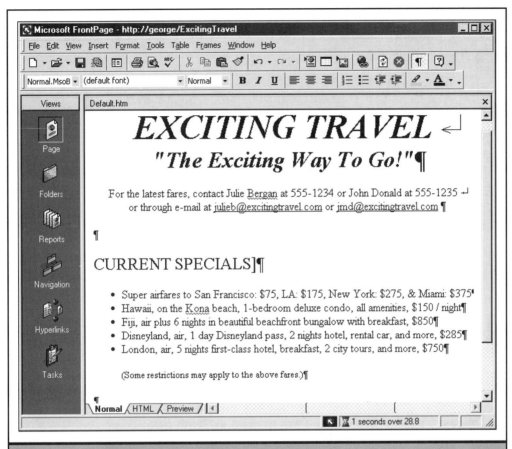

Figure 6-9. *The completed Current Specials section*

Adding the Travel Options

The Travel Options section provides a list, really an index, of the travel options that are available from this agency. In Chapter 7, you'll come back and make these links to the second-level pages.

To create the Travel Options section:

1. With the insertion point on the line immediately below the last line typed above, type the following text. Press ENTER at the end of every other line (the intervening lines are continued on the next line). You can copy the list of options on line 3 and use it on lines 6 and on.

If you press ENTER at the end of the last line typed, the next line will also be indented twice; if you press the DOWN ARROW key, the line will be left-aligned without the indents.

AVAILABLE TRAVEL OPTIONS
AIR TRAVEL: Domestic, Canada, Europe, So. America,
Africa, Asia, So. Pacific
CRUISES: Alaska, Panama Canal, Caribbean,
Europe, So. America, Asia, So. Pacific
TOURS: Domestic, Canada, Europe, So. America,
Africa, Asia, So. Pacific
HOTELS: Domestic, Canada, Europe, So. America,
Africa, Asia, So. Pacific
AUTO: Domestic, Canada, Europe, So. America, Africa,
Asia, So. Pacific
RAIL: Domestic, Canada, Europe, So. America, Africa,
Asia, So. Pacific

2. Click line 1 and choose the Heading 2 style.

3. Select lines 2 through 7, and click Numbering on the Formatting toolbar.

4. Delete all but one blank line between the last line of the travel options and the beginning of the footer.

5. Save the home page. The bottom of your home page should look like Figure 6-10.

This completes the text that you will need on the home page.

Building the Title for Pages 2 and 3

On all but the home page, you want to have a brief title or heading with the ways to contact the specialists and the links to other pages. This keeps the contacts in front of the agents and gives them the primary way to navigate or get around the web. Use the next set of instructions to enter the text related to these items on page 2 and copy them to page 3. Later in this chapter you'll do some graphics work on this, and in Chapter 7 you'll establish the actual links to implement the navigation.

1. On the home page, drag over the first four lines of text that represent the title of the web, and click Copy on the toolbar.

2. Open the Window menu and choose second_level_page.htm. After the page opens, click the top left corner to place the insertion point above the footer, and click Paste on the toolbar. The title appears on page 2.

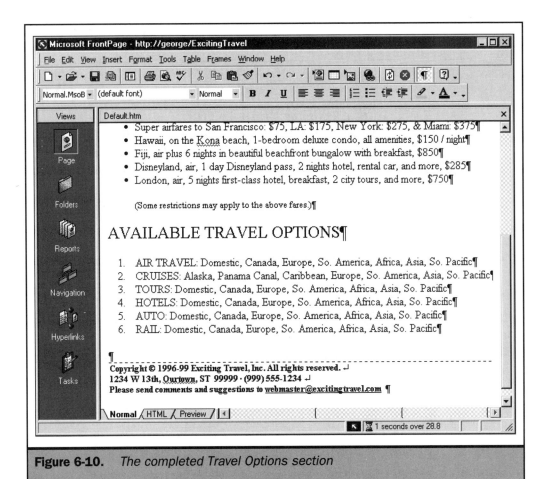

Figure 6-10. *The completed Travel Options section*

3. If you have an extra blank line above the just-pasted title, press CTRL+HOME to move the insertion point to the very top of the page, and then press DEL to delete the leading paragraph mark.

4. Select the words "Exciting Travel," and choose Heading 2 as the paragraph style. The size doesn't change, because you applied the special character size to these words. The size of the second line ("The Exciting Way To Go!") changes because it is part of the same paragraph, and you did not apply a special character size to it.

5. Open the Format menu, choose Font, and select Normal for the font size. This will change the first line to the actual Heading 2 size, as you can see next. Click OK to close the Font dialog box and resize your text.

"Normal" font size is not a particular size, but rather allows the default size of a given paragraph style to take precedence.

> ### EXCITING TRAVEL ↵
> ### "The Exciting Way to Go!"¶

6. Select the second line and press DEL twice to delete the line as well as the paragraph mark. This also changes the phone numbers and e-mail addresses to Heading 2.

7. Select the words "For the latest fares, c" (include the comma, the space following it, and the letter "c" from the word "contact") and type an uppercase **C**.

8. After the first phone number, type a space and **(julieb).** After the second phone number, add another space and type **(jmd)** to add the e-mail addresses.

9. Delete the new-line symbol and the remainder of the contact information.

10. Select all of the words in the title *except* **"Exciting Travel,"** open the Font Size drop-down list, and choose 3 (12 pt) so all of the contact information fits on one line like this (it may wrap to two lines with a different resolution):

> ### EXCITING TRAVEL ↵
> Contact Julie Bergan at 555-1234 (julieb) or John Donald at 555-1235 (jmd)¶

Note *The wavy red lines under the words "Bergan," "julieb," and "jmd" are the spelling checker telling you that these words are not in the spelling dictionary and may be misspelled. You can right-click on these words and get a list of alternative correctly spelled words, as well as commands to ignore the suspected misspelling or add the word to the dictionary.*

11. Click Align Left to left-align the title, and then move the insertion point to the first line after the title.

12. Type the following text, which in Chapter 7 will become a navbar with links to the rest of the web. (Note that there is a space, a vertical bar, and a space between each option.)

    | Home | Air Travel | Cruises | Tours | Hotels | Auto | Rail |

13. With the insertion point still in the future navbar, choose Heading 3 for the paragraph style. Press ENTER to add a blank line after the navbar if necessary. Your second-page heading should now look like Figure 6-11. Click Save to save the changes to page 2.

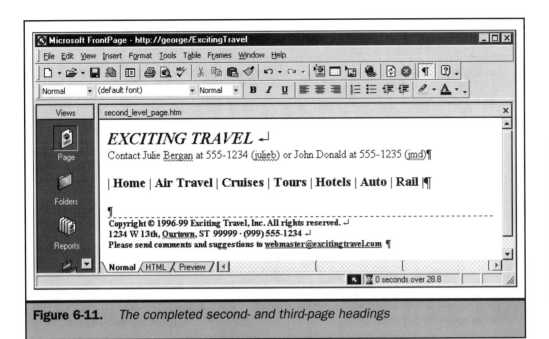

Figure 6-11.   *The completed second- and third-page headings*

14. Select the two title lines and the navbar, and click Copy on the toolbar.

15. Open the Window menu, choose third_level_page.htm, click the top left corner of the page to place the insertion point there, and click Paste on the toolbar. The heading appears on page 3.

16. If you have an extra blank line above the just-pasted title, press CTRL+HOME to move the insertion point to the top of the page. Then press DEL to delete the leading paragraph mark.

17. Click Save to save page 3.

Entering the Offerings for a Travel Option

The body of information on the second-level pages is a listing of specific offerings for a particular type of travel—for example, a geographically ordered listing of the cruises. That is, of course, a long list. For this example, to keep the typing to a minimum (remember you can use the Chap6txt.doc file on the CD that comes with this book), you'll work on the page for cruises, with only a couple of geographic areas and a couple of cruises in each.

1. Open the Window menu and choose Second_level_page.htm. When the page opens, place the insertion point at the end of the navbar, and press ENTER twice to leave a blank line.

2. Type **CRUISES**, choose Heading 1, click Center, and press ENTER.

3. Type **ALASKA**, choose Heading 3, click Align Left, and press ENTER.

4. Choose Heading 5 and click Increase Indent on the Formatting toolbar to format and indent the list of cruises.

5. Type the following cruise list, pressing SHIFT+ENTER after the second and fourth lines and ENTER after the last line (the first, third, and fifth lines are continued on the next line; see Figure 6-12):

> **Royal Caribbean, Legend of the Seas, 7 nights,**
> **Vancouver to Skagway & rtn, May-Sept**
> **Princess Cruises, Regal Princess, 7 nights,**
> **Vancouver to Skagway & rtn, May-Sept**
> **Holland American, Nieuw Amsterdam, 7 nights,**
> **Vancouver to Sitka & rtn, May-Sept**

6. Click Decrease Indent, choose Heading 3, type **SOUTH PACIFIC**, and press ENTER.

7. Choose Heading 5, click Increase Indent, and type the following cruise list, pressing SHIFT+ENTER after the second line and ENTER after the last line (the first and third lines are continued on the following lines):

> **Princess Cruises, Regal Princess, 12 days,**
> **Honolulu to Papeete, Oct. 6 only**
> **Royal Caribbean, Legend of the Seas, 10 days,**
> **Vancouver to Honolulu, Sept. 15 only**

8. Click Decrease Indent, choose Heading 4, and type the following notice:

> **Note: Excellent prices are available on these cruises, call for the latest ones.**

When you are done, your second-level page should look like Figure 6-12.

9. If you have more than one blank line between the last line entered and the beginning of the footer, delete the extra lines, and then save the page.

Importing the Details of a Travel Offering

The third level page contains the detailed description of one particular travel option. Since this is often better described by the travel provider, it may be helpful to use their material if you have permission to do so (check with your legal department or advisor on the need for this). You can do this by typing in the material, or in some cases it might be faster to scan it in.

Scanning text from brochures and other promotional pieces and then using optical character recognition (OCR) has a much lower success rate than if the text were on plain white paper. For small amounts of text, it is often easier to type it.

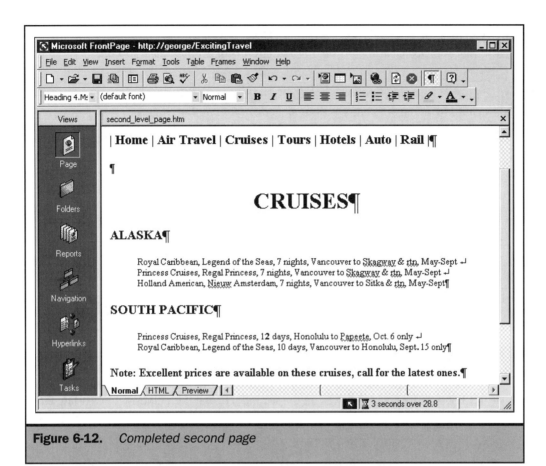

Figure 6-12.   *Completed second page*

In the following exercise you will use a combination of scanned and typed text to enter the information for the third page. If you have a scanner with OCR capability, you are encouraged to use it with something like a brochure or catalog—anything that is on slick paper with a mixture of text and pictures, and possibly with the text printed on a background image (the material can be about anything; it does not have to be related to travel). You'll then get an understanding of how that works. Of course, if you do not have access to a scanner, you can import the text used here from the Chap6txt.doc on the CD included with this book. That will at least give you experience importing.

The trip used for this detailed description is a cruise from Vancouver, BC Canada, to Skagway, Alaska, offered by Princess Cruises in their 1999 Alaska catalog (used by permission of Princess Cruises, a P&O Company). Several segments of text from this catalog will be scanned into Microsoft Word and then inserted into the Exciting Travel web.

You may use any text to replace that used here. If possible, use a scanner as directed, but if that is unavailable, import the Alaskax.doc files or the applicable portions of Chap6txt.doc on the enclosed CD.

FrontPage can import files from almost any word processor. Chapter 12 will cover in detail how to import word processor and other files into FrontPage.

To build the body of the third page by use of scanned and typed text, use the following steps:

1. Using your scanner and its software in the normal manner, scan an article of approximately 100 words. Use your OCR program (included with most scanners) to convert the text so that it can be read by Microsoft Word or your word processing program.

2. Similarly, scan and convert to text a table of approximately four columns and ten rows, and then scan and convert to text two articles of 20 to 30 words each.

3. In Microsoft Word or your word processing program, edit the articles and table for scanning errors and any changes that you want to make. Then save the articles.

4. From the second page of the Exciting Travel web in Page view, open the Window menu and choose Third_level_page.htm.

5. Place the insertion point at the right end of the navbar and press ENTER twice to leave a blank line below the navbar. Type the following text. Use SHIFT+ENTER at the end of the first line and ENTER on the second. Format these lines with Heading 2.

   Princess Cruises' Regal Princess
   7 Days, Vancouver to Skagway and Return

6. Move the insertion point below the heading you just typed, and then from the Insert menu, choose File. In the Select File dialog box, shown next, open the Files Of Type drop-down menu, and choose the type of word processor file you used.

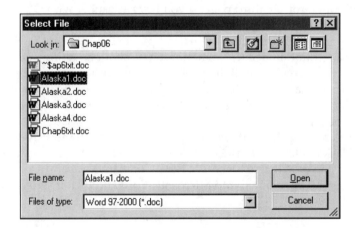

7. Locate the folder, select the name of your 100-word article, and click Open. (You may use the Alaska1.doc file on this book's CD.) You may be told that FrontPage needs to install a converter to display this file. If so, click Yes. The article will appear on your page, as you can see in Figure 6-13.

8. In a similar way, import your table (Alaska2.doc on CD) and then the two short articles (Alasks3.doc and Alaska4.doc).

9. If necessary, add or remove lines so that there is a single blank line before and after your two short articles.

10. On the second line after your short articles, type the following text:

    Material on this page originated from and is used with the permission of Princess Cruises.

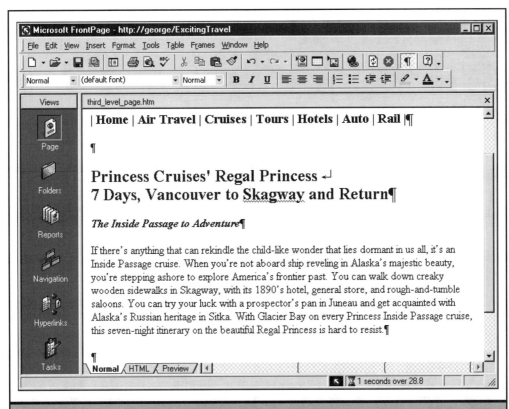

Figure 6-13. *Imported article*

Getting permission to use other people's work generally depends on whether it is to the advantage of the originator. For example, permission for the material used here from Princess Cruises was easy to get because it publicizes them and one of their cruises.

11. Select the line you just typed, and click Italic on the Formatting toolbar.

12. Leave one blank line between the line you just typed and the page footer, and then save the page. The bottom of the page should look like Figure 6-14.

The table in this example was created in Microsoft Word. When it was imported, FrontPage automatically generated an HTML table with the same rows and columns. In Chapter 8 you'll see how to create FrontPage tables.

This completes the entry of all the text you need in this web. Now let's look at sprucing up the text with pictures.

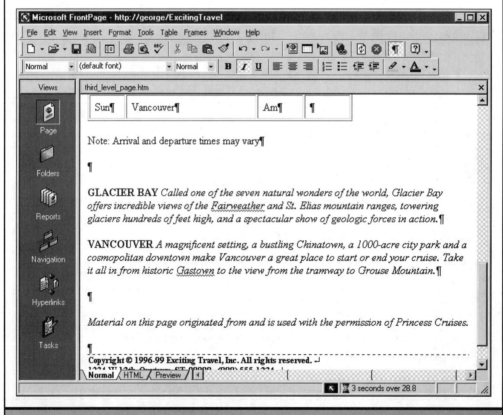

Figure 6-14.   *Text at the bottom of the third-level page*

Obtaining and Working with Pictures

There are three sources of pictures for a web:

- Programs like Microsoft Image Composer, Microsoft PhotoDraw, CorelDRAW, Windows Paint, or Adobe PhotoShop allow you to create your own pictures.

- Clip art from any number of sources including FrontPage, PhotoDraw, and CorelDRAW give you ready-made images that you can immediately place into your work.

- Scanners allow you to scan existing photographs and other printed art and put the results into your work.

All of these have advantages and disadvantages. Using clip art is fast and easy, but it is often difficult to find exactly what you want. Scanned art gives you a lot of versatility, but you must have access to a scanner, and you must get permission from the art's creator to copy it. Creating your own art has the ultimate versatility, but it takes time and skill. This section will look at all three types of pictures.

Pictures can communicate a lot very quickly, and to some people they are far better at communicating than text. Therefore, make pictures an important part of your web, whether it is on the Internet or an intranet. Adding pictures to an intranet page is slightly different from adding them to an Internet page. Intranet pages, for internal consumption, usually emphasize information. Internet pages, for external consumption, usually emphasize selling. Also, LAN connections used by most intranets are much faster at downloading pictures than the modem connections generally used on the Internet. Just keep in mind the objectives of your web and the time pictures take to load.

Creating and Inserting Pictures

In creating pictures for your web pages, you are limited only by your skill, imagination, and time. You saw one example of this in Chapter 5 where you used Microsoft Image Composer or Microsoft PhotoDraw to create a title that you will use for your Exciting Travel web. There are of course an infinite number of ways to create your own graphic and a number of different programs. For now, though, use your Image Composer or PhotoDraw piece with these steps:

Tip *Before exporting a graphic from a graphics program to a web, it's best to size the graphic as desired. Even though you can resize it in FrontPage, you cannot add more pixels. Enlarging a graphic will make it appear jagged. Also, choose a moderate number of colors or even grayscale to reduce the file size and therefore the download time.*

1. With the CD that comes with this book in your CD drive, open the Windows Explorer and copy the following seven files from the \Book\Chap06 folder on

the CD to the C:\Inetpub\wwwroot\ExcitingTravel\Images folder on your hard disk as shown in Figure 6-15: Atitle.gif, Glacier.gif, Map.gif, Princess.gif, Vancouver.gif, and Webtitle.gif.

Note *There are several pictures in this group that are not directly used in the steps in this chapter. They are meant for you to experiment with as you see fit. For example, you might put the Glacier.gif and Vancouver.gif near the two small articles, and the Map.gif near the table, all on the Third Level page.*

2. In FrontPage Page view, open the Window menu and choose Default.htm. Select the words "Exciting Travel" at the top of the page (leaving the new-line symbol), and press DEL.

3. Open the Insert menu, choose Picture | From File. Open the Images folder in the ExcitingTravel web and double-click Webtitle.gif. (If you don't see the GIF files you just copied to the …\ExcitingTravel\Images\ folder, click the Select A File button in the lower-right and

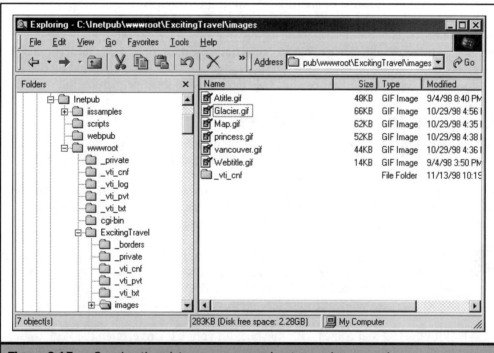

Figure 6-15. *Copying the pictures you are going to use in your web*

navigate to C:\Inetpub\wwwroot\ExcitingTravel\Images folder.) The title you created in Chapter 5 will be placed on your home page as shown here:

4. Save the changes to the home page. If you did not have the Webtitle.gif file in your Images folder, the Save Embedded Files dialog box will open, allowing you to save the images you are using in this web (the title, in this case) with the web files. Click OK.

Always save your images with your web files, so that when you copy the web to a server, they will all be together and FrontPage can do the copying for you.

Adding Horizontal Lines

Horizontal lines help separate sections of a web page. FrontPage provides an easy way to add such lines through the Insert menu. You can also add your own lines by placing them as pictures. Try both techniques now with these steps:

1. With the Exciting Travel home page displayed in Page view, place the insertion point on the blank line just above "CURRENT SPECIALS."

2. Open the Insert menu and choose Horizontal Line. A horizontal line will appear on your page.

3. Delete the original blank line (the horizontal line creates its own line ending). You now have a line separating the top two sections on your home page, like this:

> For the latest fares, contact Julie Bergan at 555-1234 or John Donald at 555-1235 ↵
> or through e-mail at julieb@excitingtravel.com or jmd@excitingtravel.com¶
>
> _____
>
> **CURRENT SPECIALS** ¶

4. Move the insertion point down to the left end of the line that reads "AVAILABLE TRAVEL OPTIONS." Press ENTER to create a blank line just above it. Here you'll add a horizontal line graphic that comes with FrontPage.

5. Open the Insert menu, choose Picture | Clip Art, type **Lines** in the Search For Clips list box, and press ENTER. A number of different lines appear.

6. Click the line that you want to use (the first line was used here) to open a fly-out menu as you can see in Figure 6-16.

7. Click Insert Clip and close the Clip Art Gallery. The line will appear on your home page like this:

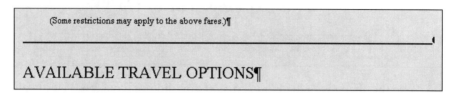

8. Save your home page and click OK to save the embedded file that is the last line you just placed.

Placing Clip Art

Clip art gives you that quick little something to jazz up a page. There are many sources of clip art, and some are bundled with FrontPage and Microsoft Office, Corel WordPerfect, and CorelDRAW. To add a firecracker next to the CURRENT SPECIALS heading by using art from the CorelDRAW clip-art collection or any other piece of clip art you have available:

1. Open your graphics package such as CorelDRAW, and import a firecracker-like piece of clip art (you can use the Firecracker.tif file in this book's CD).

2. While still in your graphics package, export your firecracker as a .TIF file, sizing it quite small (I used 59×53 pixels) and with 256 colors.

3. In Page view with the Exciting Travel home page, move the insertion point to the left edge of the CURRENT SPECIALS heading.

4. From the Insert menu, choose Picture | From File, click Select A File On Your Computer in the lower right, and select the path and filename of the file you want to use. Click OK when the file is selected.

The Picture dialog box gives you several methods of locating a picture file. To get an image from the Internet, click the Use Your Web Browser...button; to get an image from a file, click the Select A File... button. Also, you can type or select a URL in its box, or use the list box to get images from your current web.

5. If necessary, select the graphic, which opens the Picture toolbar, choose the Set Transparent Color tool, and click the background color to remove it. The final result should appear, as shown next:

6. Save the home page. The Save Embedded Files dialog box again appears, allowing you to save the graphic to the current FrontPage web. Click OK to do so and then close the dialog box.

It's easy to get carried away with adding small clip-art images. They are neat and don't use much memory (the firecracker image you see here is only 2K compared with the title, which is over 5K), so people think that they add little to the load time. But if you put a bunch of them on a page, such as one for every paragraph, all of a sudden you have a problem.

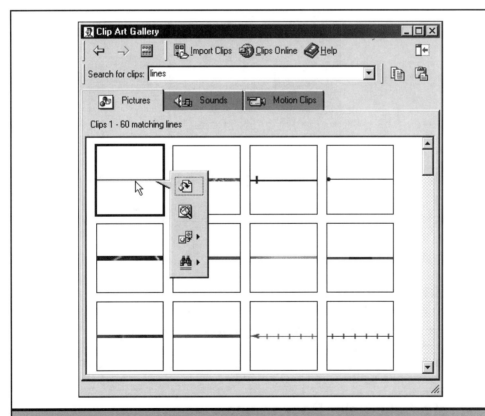

Figure 6-16.   *Selecting a horizontal line from FrontPage's clip art*

Adding Colored Text

FrontPage makes it very easy to color text and, as with clip art, it is easy to get carried away. Also it is very important that whatever you use does not impair readability. You want the color to have a high contrast with its background. Use the following steps to see how to make text some color other than black:

1. In the Exciting Travel home page, which should be open in Page view on your screen, drag across the words "The Exciting Way to Go!" including the quotation marks.

2. On the Formatting toolbar, click the down arrow on the right of the Font Color button to open the color palette shown next.

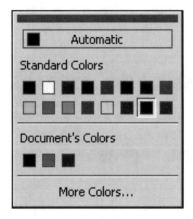

3. Double-click the lime green, the second selection in the second row, to give these words an electrifying color.

4. Select the words "Current Special" and, using the above process, make them red.

5. Once again save your home page.

Adding a Background

The default background used by FrontPage is white, which you have seen in all the figures and illustrations so far in this chapter. You can change this to any color you wish or to a background image by using the Page Properties dialog box. Again, you have to be aware of the load-time impact as your background gets more sophisticated. There are several possibilities for a background.

Creating a Solid-Color Background

Begin by looking at solid-color backgrounds:

> **Tip** *If you keep to black for your text—and there is no reason you must—then your backgrounds should be very light colors. In any case you should maintain a very high contrast between the background and text colors so they are easy to read.*

1. With the Exciting Travel home page in Page view, open the File menu, choose Properties, and then the Background tab. The Page Properties dialog box Background tab will appear as shown in Figure 6-17.

2. Click the down arrow for the Colors Background drop-down list. A palette of 16 colors, the default color, the colors currently in use in the document, and a More Colors option are displayed, as you saw with font colors.

3. By selecting More Colors, you display the More Colors dialog box, shown in Figure 6-18. You can use any of the predefined 127 colors, or you can use one of the 15 shades of gray. You can also create your own colors with the Custom button, which opens the Color dialog box where you can use either of two numerical schemes, or more simply by clicking a color in the color selector and then adjusting the brightness on the right. One possible color is the light yellow you can see being selected in Figure 6-18.

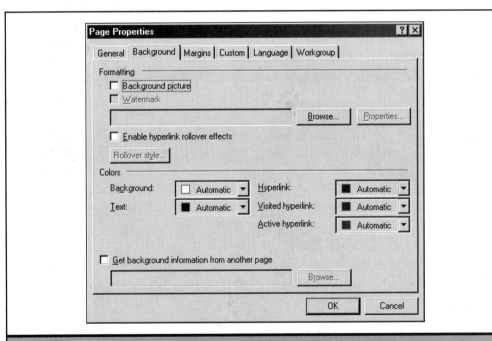

Figure 6-17. *The Page Properties dialog box Background tab*

4. Select a color of your own, and then click OK. The color appears in the Page Properties dialog box; click OK again. The color appears on the web page.

Tip *Be sure to check how both Netscape Navigator and Microsoft Internet Explorer display any custom color you create. Some colors may end up being dithered and won't look right.*

5. If either your page title or the firecracker now show a different background, click the graphic to select it and open the Picture toolbar. Select the Set Transparent Color tool, and click the color you want to be transparent.

6. Save your home page.

Tip *If you want to make the background the same on several pages in a web, then, after getting the first page the way you want it, open the second page, open its Page Properties dialog box Background tab, click Get Background Information From Another Page, and select the first page. Click OK.*

Using a Textured Background

Another choice for a background is one of the many textured backgrounds available on the Internet and from other sources. FrontPage offers several choices for a textured background.

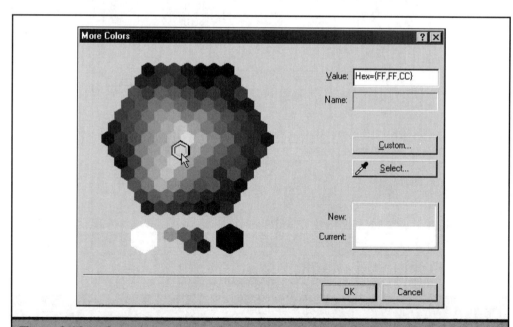

Figure 6-18.   *Selecting a color in the Colors dialog box*

Most textured backgrounds are made by tiling a small graphic. You can make your own with any small image, optimally 96×96 pixels. If the image has a repeatable pattern, it is possible to get it to be reasonably seamless, as FrontPage has done in its samples.

To add a textured background:

1. Select Second_level_page.htm from the Window menu of Page view.
2. Right-click a blank area of the page, choose Page Properties, then the Background tab, and click Background Picture.
3. Click Browse, click Clip Art, type **Backgrounds** in the Search For Clips drop-down list, and press ENTER.
4. Select one of the options presented, click Insert Clip, and then click OK in the Page Properties dialog box. The background appears as shown in Figure 6-19.

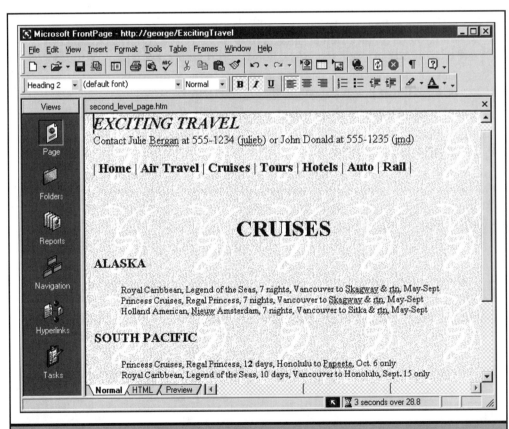

Figure 6-19. *A textured background on the second-level page*

5. Save your second-level page and click OK to save the embedded file that is the background image.

Using a Single Background Image

You can also use a single background image to cover a page. In most circumstances this is not advised, because the image is quite large (the image used in this example is over 1000KB) and therefore will take a very long time to download. Also, it is hard to get a single text color that shows up well against a multicolored image. Nevertheless, if you know that all your readers have high-speed connections, as they might in an intranet, a single background image can be quite striking. Try it:

1. Select Third_level_page.htm from the Window menu of Page view.

2. Open the Page Properties dialog box, click Background Picture in the Background tab, and browse to locate a large photographic image. (The image I've used is Princess.tif on the CD, scanned from the Princess Cruises catalog.) Click OK to close the dialog boxes and import the image.

3. After you have imported an image, reopen the Page Properties dialog box Background tab, open the Text color drop-down list, and select White.

4. Click OK to close the Page Properties dialog box. Your background image with white text over it will appear as shown in Figure 6-20.

5. Save your third-level page, clicking OK to save the image with the web.

Using Scanned Images

Using scanned images on web pages is very similar to using other pictures, except for what you can do to the image before bringing it into FrontPage. For example, you can scan an image into Adobe PhotoShop, where you can crop it or otherwise edit it. To try that, follow these steps:

1. Using your scanner and its software in the normal manner, scan a picture that you want to bring into your web (I used an image of the *Regal Princess* from the Princess Cruises catalog). This will create a .TIF or other bitmap file (the Princess.tif file used above).

2. Open Adobe PhotoShop or another program that can edit bitmap files, and crop the image to the size you want. Do any other editing and then resave the file as either a GIF or JPEG file (see discussion in Chapter 1).

3. In Page view, use the Windows menu to open the second-level page.

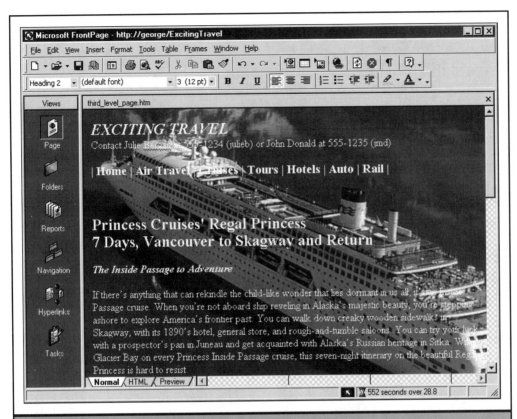

Figure 6-20. *A single image used as a background image (image used by permission of Princess Cruises)*

4. Place the insertion point to the left of the word "CRUISES." Open the Insert menu, choose Picture | From File, and then double-click the file you want to import (you can use the Princess.gif file that you copied from the CD). Your result will look something like Figure 6-21.

5. Save the second-level page, and click OK in the Save Embedded Files dialog box. Also, close Page view by selecting Close from the File menu for all open pages and then close FrontPage.

You can use some of the other pictures that you copied off the CD to place other scanned images in this web site.

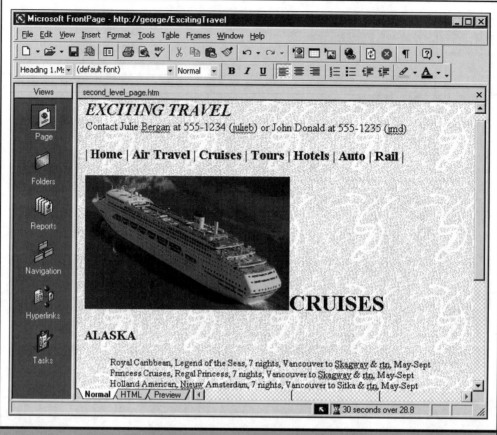

Figure 6-21. *Second-level page with a scanned image placed on it (image used by permission of Princess Cruises)*

Text and pictures are the foundation of any web, whether you create the web or it is created with a template or wizard. In Chapter 7 you'll see how to add hyperlinks, or just "links," to both text and pictures.

Chapter 7

Adding and Managing Hyperlinks and Hotspots

When you open a web page in a browser, you have access to only the single page in the address given to the browser. There is no way to get to another page without giving the browser its address, unless there is a hyperlink on the first page that provides the address of, and therefore takes you to, the other page.

A *hyperlink* or *link* is an object, either text or graphic, that, when you click it, tells the browser to move to a bookmark on the same page or to open another page. The hyperlink, when clicked, gives the browser an address called a uniform resource locator (URL). The browser then opens the page at that address. The page can be part of the current web, part of another web at the same site, or part of any web at any site anywhere on the Internet, anywhere in the world (unless your intranet limits you to its domain).

A hyperlink is an essential part of a web page. It is the element that allows the page to be interconnected with other pages, producing the "web." Hyperlinks are also why the language behind web pages, HTML, is called *Hyper*text Markup Language. Hyperlinks provide the first and most important level of interactivity in a web page: they give users a choice of where to go when they are done with the current page.

When a hyperlink is viewed in a browser, it is normally a different color than the surrounding text, and it is usually underlined (the person controlling the browser can determine what color a hyperlink is and whether it is underlined). Also, when you move the mouse pointer over a hyperlink, the pointer normally turns into a pointing hand, and either the full or partial URL related to that link is displayed in the status bar at the bottom of the window, as you can see next. (This shows a full path, C:/Inetpub/wwwroot/ExcitingTravel/Default.htm. A partial URL would be just the page name, Default.htm.)

In this chapter you will see how to add hyperlinks to text and graphics, how to assign areas of a graphic, or hotspots, to a hyperlink, and how to manage the hyperlinks in a web page.

Adding Hyperlinks to Text and Graphics

Hyperlinks can be assigned to anything you enter on a web page. Any piece of text—be it a word, a phrase, or a paragraph—or any graphic, from a bullet to a large image, can be assigned a link. While there are many similarities, there are also some differences, so let's look separately at assigning hyperlinks to text and to graphics.

Assigning Hyperlinks to Text

Within a web, hyperlinks provide the principal means of getting from one page to another and back again. Begin by assigning hyperlinks for that purpose:

1. If it isn't already loaded, start FrontPage. In FrontPage, open the ExcitingTravel web that you created in Chapter 6, and then open the three pages, one after the other, in Page view.

A fast way to open a web you have recently worked on is, for example in this case, to open the File menu and select Recent Webs | http://yourserever/ExcitingTravel.

2. Display the Home page in Page view, and then scroll the page so you can see the Available Travel Options.

3. Drag across the word "CRUISES" in the second line to select that word. You'll make this word a link to the Second Level page displaying a list of cruises.

4. Click Hyperlink on the toolbar. Alternatively, you can choose Hyperlink from the Insert menu or press CTRL+K. In any case the Create Hyperlink dialog box will open, as you can see in Figure 7-1.

5. The Second Level page is the one that you want to link to, so double-click the filename (Second_level_page.htm). The Create Hyperlink dialog box will close. When you return to the Home page, you'll see that the word "CRUISES" has changed. If you move the highlight off it, you'll see that it has changed color and is underlined (unless someone changed the defaults in the Page Properties dialog box) like this:

> 1. **AIR TRAVEL**: Domestic, Canada,
> 2. <u>CRUISES</u>: Alaska, Panama Canal,
> 3. **TOURS**: Domestic, Canada, Europ

6. Right-click CRUISES and choose Hyperlink Properties to again open the hyperlink dialog box, now called Edit Hyperlink. You'll see that the page name Second_level_page.htm has been assigned to this link. Click Cancel to close the dialog box.

7. Click Save on the toolbar to save the Home page.

8. Press and hold CTRL while clicking (this will be called "CTRL+click" in the future) CRUISES to follow the hyperlink and see where it will take you. You should end up on the Second Level page. (If you didn't, you somehow did not select the correct page in step 5.)

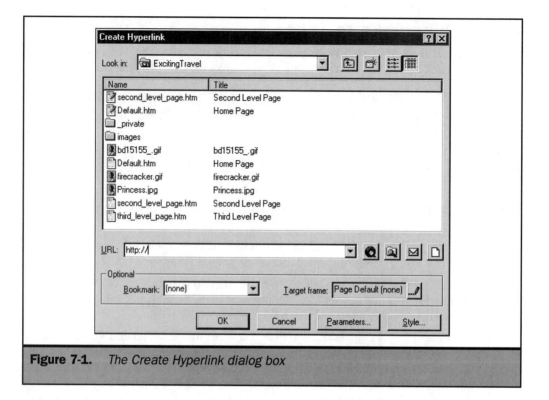

Figure 7-1.   *The Create Hyperlink dialog box*

Note   *When you choose a page as a link, you are not taken to any particular part of the page. The page is just opens. If you are opening the page for the first time in a session, then you'll be taken to the top of the page. If you have previously opened the page in the current session and scrolled down it, then when you return, you'll be taken to wherever you scrolled. This may or may not be what you want. You can control where you go on a page through bookmarks, which are discussed in "Establishing Bookmarks" later in this chapter.*

Creating or Activating a Navbar

Once you are on the second page, you need a way to return to the Home page (ignore for the moment that there is a Window menu). To do that you need a link back to the Home page as well as to other pages. This is what a navigation bar, or "navbar," is used for. In Chapter 6 you mocked up a navbar and put it in both the second-level and third-level pages. One way to provide the links back to the Home page and to other pages is simply to activate the words in the existing navbar mockup. An alternative is to let FrontPage build a navbar for you. Let's look at both these approaches next.

ACTIVATING THE NAVBAR MOCKUP   Activating the navbar mockup is the same as turning any word into a hyperlink, as you can see with these steps:

1. Drag across the word "Home" in the navbar, and click Hyperlink on the toolbar. (From now on this will just be called the "Link" button.)

2. Double-click the Home Page filename to establish that as the destination of the link.

3. Since you'll copy the navbar to other pages, drag across Cruises in the navbar, click Link, and double-click the Second Level Page filename. Home and Cruises are the only two navbar elements you can activate at this time, so your navbar should look like this:

EXCITING TRAVEL

Contact Julie Bergan at 555-1234 (julieb) or John Donald at 555-1235 (jr

| Home | Air Travel | Cruises | Tours | Hotels | Auto | Rail |

HAVING FRONTPAGE CREATE A NAVBAR   FrontPage uses the relationships established and shown in Navigation view to create a navbar for you. See how with these steps.

1. Click Navigation in the Views bar. The Navigation view of your Exciting Travel web should look like Figure 7-2. If for some reason your Second Level and Third Level pages are not as shown in Figure 7-2, you can drag them from the Folder List to the Navigation pane and they will automatically be connected to the page above where they are being dragged.

2. In the Navigation toolbar, the Included In Navigation Bars button, the second one from the right, allows you to turn a particular link in the automatic navbars on or off. If you select the Second Level page and click the Included In Navigation Bars button, both the Second Level and Third Level pages are removed from the Automatic navbars and become gray in color. Try this for yourself with different pages selected. When you are done, make sure that all pages are included in navbars and that your Navigation view looks like Figure 7-2.

3. Double-click the Second Level Page in the navigation pane to open that page in Page view. When the page opens, move the insertion point to the blank line under the manual navbar. If there isn't one, add one by placing your insertion point at the end of the manual navbar and press ENTER.

4. Open the Insert menu and choose Navigation Bar. In the Navigation Bar Properties dialog box, shown in Figure 7-3, select the Child Level option and

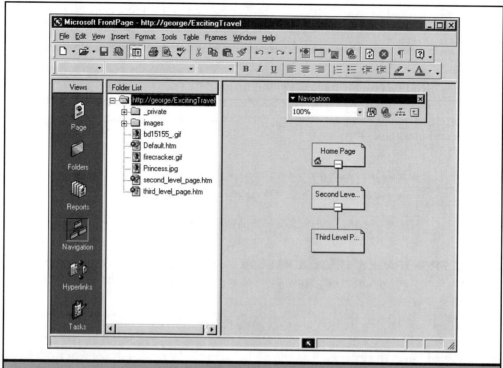

Figure 7-2.   *The relationships displayed in Navigation view establish the links in an automatic navbar*

Home Page check box. Also, make sure that Horizontal orientation and Text appearance option buttons are selected. Click OK.

Note   *In the Orientation And Appearance section of the Navigation Bar Properties dialog box, you can choose to have the hyperlinks displayed as either graphical buttons or text. For the buttons to be displayed as graphics, you must apply a theme to the web. Otherwise, as in this example, the links will be displayed as text even if Buttons is selected.*

As you can see in Figure 7-4, a navigation bar is inserted on the page displaying the links you established in Navigation view and selected in the Navigation Bar Properties dialog box.

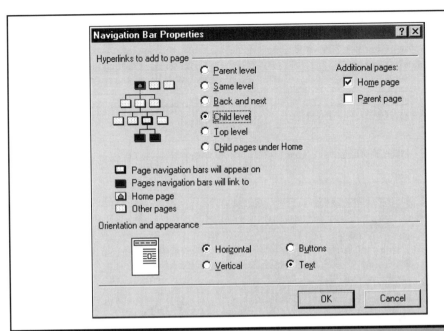

Figure 7-3.   *Establishing the hyperlink and other properties of the automatic navbar*

In step 4 of the preceding exercise, you chose to create links to the Home page and Child pages in the navbar. If you were to repeat these steps on the Third Level page navbar, since it doesn't have a child page, the navbar with the same settings as the Second Level page would have only one link, back to the Home page. The Third Level page does have a parent page—the Second Level page—and you'll want to provide a link to that page. You'd do that by changing the navbar properties on the Third Level page to include the Parent Page. Do that with these steps:

1. Open the Window menu and select the Third Level page. On that page place the insertion point immediately below the mockup of a manual navbar. Add a blank line if required.

2. Open the Insert menu and choose Navigation Bar. In the Navigation Bar properties dialog box, click Same Level to pick up any future pages that are created at the third level, and click Home Page and Parent Page to create links

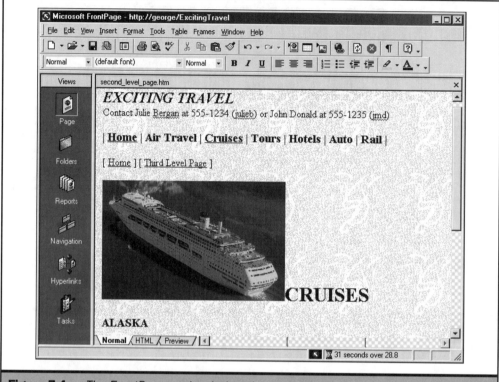

Figure 7-4. *The FrontPage navbar below the manual one*

to those pages. Also click Text and make sure Horizontal is selected, and then click OK. A navbar with Home and Up will appear.

3. Save both your Second Level and Third Level pages.

Establishing Bookmarks

Since some web pages can be quite long and you may want to direct exactly where on a page a link will take the user, you need to identify a spot on a page where a link will end up. This is done with the use of bookmarks. *Bookmarks* are objects (text or graphics) that have been selected as destinations for a link. Follow these steps to create a bookmark:

You must identify the bookmark before you establish the link, unless you want to go back and edit the link after it is established.

1. Return to the Second Level page and drag across the heading "ALASKA" below the image of a cruise ship.

2. Open the Insert menu and choose Bookmark. The Bookmark dialog box will open, as shown here:

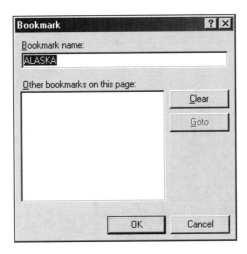

3. Click OK to make the word "ALASKA" a bookmark. You'll see a dashed line appear under "ALASKA."

4. Drag across the heading "SOUTH PACIFIC," open the Insert menu, choose Bookmark, and click OK in the Bookmark dialog box. A dashed line will appear under the selected words.

Selecting the bookmarks is only half the procedure; you must also establish the links to the bookmarks. Before going back to the Home page to do that, establish the link to the Third Level page.

Linking to the Third Level Page

The Third Level page is a detailed description of one Alaska cruise listed on the Second Level page. Therefore, set the line that lists the cruise as the link to the page that describes it, using these steps:

1. With the Second Level page displayed, scroll the page so you can see the list of cruises under the Alaska heading.

2. Drag across the line that begins "Princess Cruises, Regal Princess..."

3. Click Link on the toolbar to open the Create Hyperlink dialog box, and then double-click the Third Level Page filename. Your Second Level page with the activated navbars, the two bookmarks, and the link to the third page should look like Figure 7-5.

4. Click Save on the toolbar to save the second page.

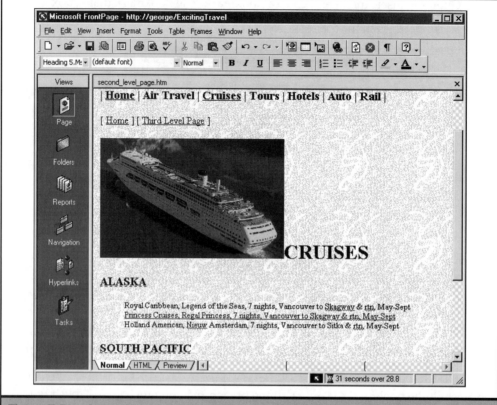

Figure 7-5. *Second Level page with links and bookmarks*

5. CTRL+click the Princess Cruises link you established in step 3 to follow the hyperlink. Your Third Level page should open.

6. Clean up the page and recapture some room by selecting and deleting the manual navbar mockup, leaving the navbar created by FrontPage on the Third Level page, as you can see in Figure 7-6.

7. Click Save on the toolbar to save the third page.

8. CTRL+click the word "Home" in the navbar to return to the Home page.

You have now followed the links you established from the first to the second page, from the second to the third page, and from the third page back to the first. You can see that they provide a good means of navigating a web. Later in the chapter you'll try them out in a browser, where all you'll need to do is click them.

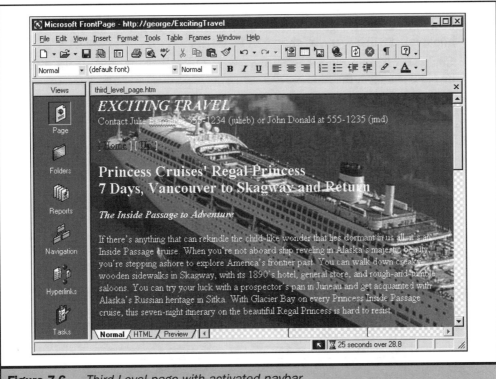

Figure 7-6.   *Third Level page with activated navbar*

Using Bookmarks in Links

On the Home page use the two bookmarks you set to create two detail links within the Cruises travel options:

1. On the Home page, scroll the page so you can see the numbered list of travel options.

2. Drag across the word "Alaska" in the list of cruise destinations, as you can see here:

> 1. AIR TRAVEL: Domestic, Canada,
> 2. CRUISES: Alaska, Panama Canal,
> 3. TOURS: Domestic, Canada, Europ

3. Click Link on the toolbar to open the Create Hyperlink dialog box.

4. Click the Second Level Page filename in the list of pages, and then click the down arrow to the right of the Bookmark drop-down menu. Your two bookmarks will appear, as shown in Figure 7-7.

5. Click ALASKA to select that bookmark, and then click OK to close the dialog box and establish the link.

6. Drag across the words "So. Pacific" (in the same lines as the Alaska you selected in step 2 above), click Link, select the Second Level page filename, open the bookmarks, and click SOUTH PACIFIC. The URL in the bottom of the Create Hyperlink dialog box now includes the bookmark, like this:

7. Click OK to close the dialog box and to set the link.

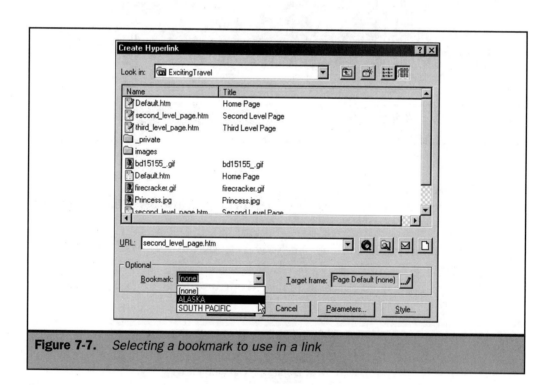

Figure 7-7.   *Selecting a bookmark to use in a link*

Setting Links to Other Than Web Sites

All of the links that you have created so far have been to other pages within this single web application. Later in this chapter you'll make a link to another web site and web. FrontPage allows you to make a link to:

- An existing page in the current web
- A new page in the current web
- Another web
- A bookmark in either the current web or another web
- A frame in either the current web or another web
- A file on a local hard disk
- An e-mail address to send e-mail

A link to an e-mail address using the mailto link is commonly found in the footer on a web page. This allows the user to easily contact the webmaster or the page's creator by using e-mail. FrontPage will create a mailto link when you enter text that looks like an e-mail address (two text strings, without spaces, separated by the @ character). In the footer for each page in your Exciting Travel web is the e-mail address webmaster@excitingtravel.com. FrontPage has created the mailto link, as you can with these steps:

1. Scroll to the bottom of the Home page in Page view, so you can see the copyright and other information in the footer.

2. Right-click "webmaster@excitingtravel.com," and then select Hyperlink Properties.

3. In the URL text box on the Edit Hyperlink dialog box you can see that the URL for the hyperlink is mailto:webmaster@excitingtravel.com, as shown in Figure 7-8.

4. Click OK to close the Edit Hyperlink dialog box, and then click Save on the toolbar to save the Home page.

You now have a number of links, so it is time to see if they work.

Testing Your Links in a Browser

The only way to know if your links are really working is to try them in a browser:

1. If you didn't save each of the three pages in the preceding steps, do that now.

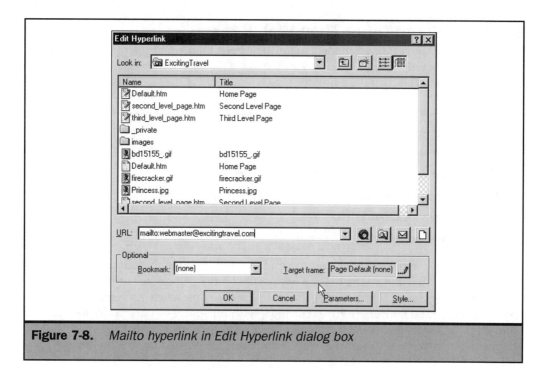

Figure 7-8.   *Mailto hyperlink in Edit Hyperlink dialog box*

You can tell if a page has been saved since it was last changed by looking in the Window menu. If the page has an asterisk beside it, it needs to be saved.

2. Your Home page should still be displayed in Page view. Open the File menu and choose Preview In Browser. That dialog box will open as you can see here:

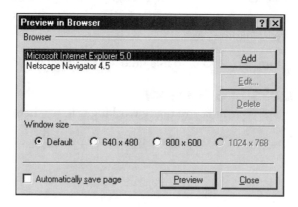

3. Select the Browser and Window Size you want to use and click on Preview.

> **Tip**
>
> *You should always look at your work in both 640x480 and 800x600 resolution. Remember that you have no control over the user's browser resolution, so your work must look good in both resolutions.*

4. If your web browser is already open, you can enter the address or URL for your web in the Address drop-down list. The address should be in the form *servername/webname/*. In Page view you can find this in the Page Properties dialog box for any page in a web (right-click the page and choose Page Properties). In Folders or Navigation views it's in the Properties dialog box (right-click the page and choose Properties). For example, here is the URL (a file in this case) for the Home page in its Page Properties dialog box opened from Page view:

Location:	http://george/ExcitingTravel/Default.htm
Title:	Home Page
Base location:	

> **Note**
>
> *If you include a page filename in the URL when you open a browser, you will open that page, which may not be the home page. You do not need to include the page filename if you want to open a home page.*

> **Tip**
>
> *You can drag across the URL in the FrontPage Page Properties dialog box, press CTRL+C to copy it to the clipboard, open a browser, click the Address box, and press CTRL+V to paste the URL there.*

5. If you have previously opened the Exciting Travel web in your browser, click Refresh on the browser's toolbar to make sure you are using the latest files.

6. Scroll down the page until you can see the Available Travel Options. Move the mouse pointer until it is over the word "CRUISES." The mouse pointer will turn into a pointing hand, and the URL for the second page will be shown in the status bar at the bottom of the window, as you can see in Figure 7-9.

7. Click CRUISES and your second page will be displayed. Your first hyperlink has now opened the Second Level page.

8. Click Home in either navbar. Your Home page should again be displayed.

9. If you are not already there, scroll down so you can see the Available Travel Options, and then click So. Pacific. The South Pacific heading will be positioned as far up in the window as information below it allows (if there is enough

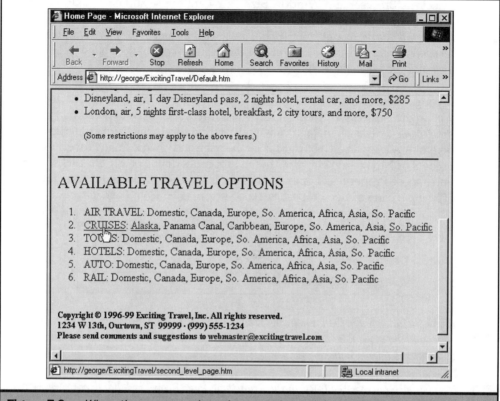

Figure 7-9. *When the mouse pointer is over a hyperlink, its URL is displayed in the status bar*

information below the bookmark, the bookmark will be at the top of the window), as shown in Figure 7-10.

10. Click the line beginning "Princess Cruises, Regal Princess." The Third Level page will open.

11. Click Up in the navbar, and you'll be returned to the Second Level page. Notice how the page is positioned at its top.

12. Click Home on the navbar. When the Home page opens, it will be positioned at its top.

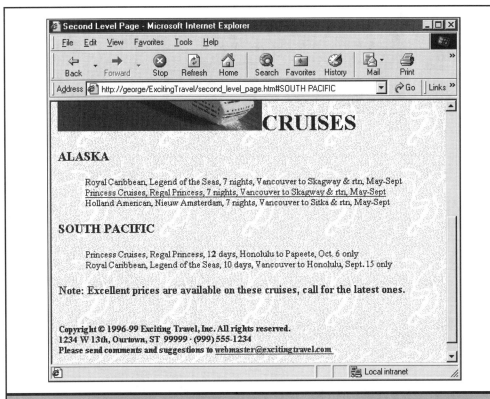

Figure 7-10.   *A bookmark in a link will position the bookmark toward the top of the window*

13. Scroll to the bottom of the Home page, and click the webmaster address. Your e-mail system should start and display a new message window with the webmaster address in the To text box, as you can see in Figure 7-11.

14. Close down your e-mail system without sending a message, and then close your browser and return to Page view.

All of your links should have worked, providing an excellent navigation system around your web. If you find that a link did not work, right-click it, click Hyperlink Properties to open the Edit Hyperlink dialog box, and correct where the link is

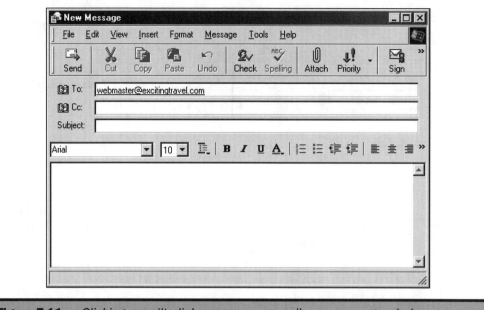

Figure 7-11. *Clicking a mailto link opens your e-mail new message window*

pointing. Checking your work in a browser not only confirms that your links work as expected, it also gives you a visual check of the page design. You cannot count on the appearance of a page in Page view carrying over to your browsers. Check your work on your browsers often.

Assigning Hyperlinks to a Graphic

Although text makes for good links, graphics have even greater possibilities. You can assign a single link to a graphic, or you can divide a graphic into sections, called *hotspots*, and make each section a separate link. All of the concepts that you learned about with text links also apply to graphics. You can have links to the existing web, both with and without bookmarks. You can have external links to web sites as well as to other types of Internet sites. You can make either a single graphic that has been divided or multiple graphics into a navbar, and you can test graphic links in your browser.

Making a Graphic a Single Link

Making a graphic a single link is very much like what you did with a piece of text. To do this for a graphic:

1. In Page view, open the Second Level page. Scroll the page down, if necessary, so you can see the picture of the ship.

2. Click the picture so it is selected with little boxes in the four corners and the middle of each side, like this:

3. Click Link on the toolbar to open the Create Hyperlink dialog box, and then double-click the Third Level page to establish that as the destination of the link.

Now when you move the mouse pointer over the graphic, you'll see "third_level_page.htm," the address for the third page, in the status bar.

Linking a Graphic to an External Web

Linking a graphic or text to an external web requires nothing more than specifying the external web's URL in the link:

1. Scroll the Second Level page down so the insertion point is on the blank line just above the footer.

2. Insert a horizontal line (you can use a FrontPage-created line from the Insert menu, as is done here, or you can place a graphics line).

3. If a blank line appears above the horizontal line, delete it. If necessary, add a blank line below the horizontal line.

4. On the next line, type **OUTSIDE SOURCES**, format it as a Heading 2, press ENTER, and type

    Check these additional sources for cruise information:

    Format it as a Heading 4, and press ENTER.

5. Insert two or three small images that can be used for links and center them, as shown in Figure 7-12. (You can use the art on the CD that come with this book; see \Book\Chap07 folder for this purpose.) You may want to make the background transparent. If so, click the picture, select Set Transparent Color from the Picture toolbar, and click the background color that you want to get rid of.

6. Click one of your images to select it (say the Royal Caribbean logo as an example), and then click Link to open the Create Hyperlink dialog box. If the insertion point isn't already there, click the URL text box to the right of the "http://".

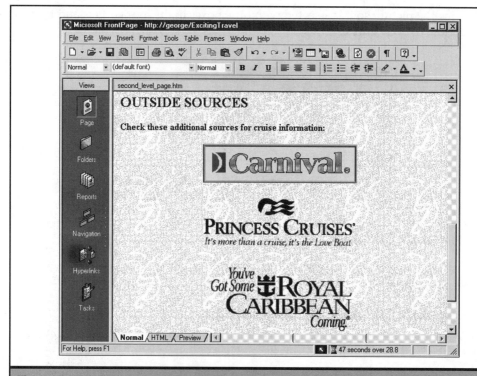

Figure 7-12. *Graphics set up for external links**

*"Carnival" and the "reverse-C" are registered service marks of Carnival Cruise Lines. Used with the permission of Carnival Cruise Lines. "Princess Cruises" and the "Lady with wind-blown hair" are registered trademarks of Princess Cruises. Used with permission of Princess Cruises. "Royal Caribbean" and the "Crown & Anchor" are registered trademarks of Royal Caribbean Cruises Ltd. Used with permission of Royal Caribbean Cruises Ltd.

7. Type, for example, **www.rccl.com/** and click OK. You should see the URL in the status bar when you move the mouse pointer over the graphic.

If you click the Use Your Web Browser button in the Create Hyperlink dialog box, locate the Web site you want to link to, and then return to the Create Hyperlink dialog box, the URL will be automatically copied to the URL text box in the Create Hyperlink dialog box.

Adding Hotspots to Graphics

FrontPage has a feature that allows you to divide a graphic into sections that can be rectangles, circles, or polygons, and to assign each of those sections a different link. Each linked, or clickable, section is called a *hotspot*. When FrontPage generates the actual web that is downloaded by the user, it creates an *image map* of the graphic and all of its hotspots. To create a graphic with hotspots:

1. Open the Home page of the Exciting Travel web in Page view and, if necessary, scroll down the page until you see the Available Travel Options.

2. Drag across the words "AIR TRAVEL," and click Link on the toolbar.

3. Click New Page on the right of the URL text box, and click OK to accept the Normal Page template. This will create a new page in the current web and link it to the selected object. A new page is generated and opened in Page view.

4. Separately, you can copy the title and navbar for the page. For now, enter several blank lines to leave room for the header, and then type

   Click the area of the world for which you want air fares.

   (including the period), format it as Heading 3, and then press ENTER.

5. Open the Insert menu, choose Picture, and from a clip-art collection, insert a world map on the page and center it, as shown in Figure 7-13.

6. Select your world map and then use the tools on the right in the Picture toolbar, which is by default at the bottom of the FrontPage window, to draw the hotspots on the map. For example, select the Rectangle tool and draw a rectangle around

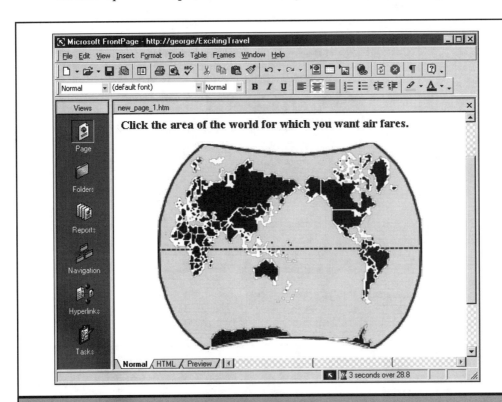

Figure 7-13. *A new page created with a world map*

the United States. When you complete the rectangle and release the mouse button, the Create Hyperlink dialog box will open. You have all the normal choices for a new link including an existing page, with or without a bookmark, any other site on the Internet, or a new page. If you create a new page, be sure and save it to give it a name that can be used for the link.

7. When you have completed drawing the shapes you want over the various areas of your map, you'll see all of the shapes on your map. The shapes will not be visible in a browser. When you move the mouse pointer over one of the areas, you'll see the URL, absolute or relative, in the status bar, as you can see in the lower left of Figure 7-14.

8. Right-click an area of the map that you have not drawn a hotspot over, choose Picture Properties, and in the Default Hyperlink section's Location text

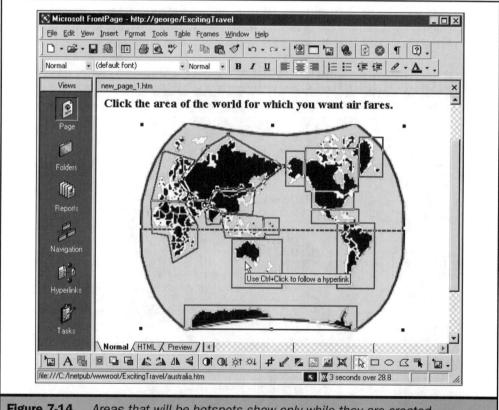

Figure 7-14. *Areas that will be hotspots show only while they are created*

box, enter the link that you want used if someone clicks outside of a hotspot, like this:

9. Click OK or Cancel to close the Picture Properties dialog box.

10. To see the hotspots uncluttered by the map, click Highlight Hotspots on the Picture toolbar. The map will disappear, leaving only the shapes you drew, as you can see here:

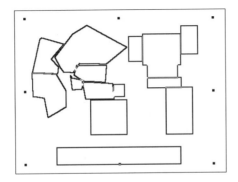

11. Turn off Highlight Hotspots, save your new Air Travel page as Air.htm, save the associated image, return to your Home page, save it, and then save any other pages that have not been saved.

Testing Your Graphic Links in a Browser

Once again it is prudent to open your browser and see how your links are working:

1. Open your browser with the Exciting Travel Home page displayed, and click Refresh on the toolbar to make sure you are looking at the most recent copy of your web.

2. Scroll down the Home page until you can see Available Travel Options, and then click AIR TRAVEL. Your new Air Travel page will open and display the map you placed there.

3. Move the mouse pointer around the map to see the various hotspots you created and their URLs in the status bar. Click several to see that they work, and then use Back to return to the Home page.

4. Click CRUISES to open the second page, click the image of the ship, and your third page should open (click Refresh if this doesn't work).

5. Click Up on the navbar to return to the second page.

6. Scroll down the page until you can see the two or three graphics you added, one of which you assigned a link to an external web.

7. If you are connected to the Internet and entered the Royal Caribbean URL, click it, and the Royal Caribbean web will open as you can see in Figure 7-15. You have been transported out of your web and to the Royal Caribbean web in Miami, Florida.

8. Close your browser. If you have any problems, edit the links to see what the trouble is. When all your links are working, click Hyperlinks in the Views bar.

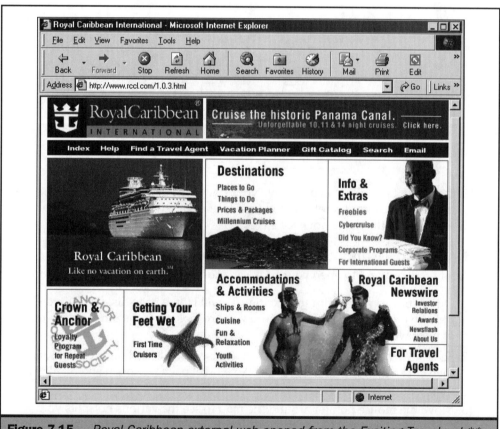

Figure 7-15.   *Royal Caribbean external web opened from the Exciting Travel web***
** Royal Caribbean home page used with the permission of Royal Caribbean Cruises Ltd.

Managing Hyperlinks

The Exciting Travel web displayed in Hyperlinks view now looks very different than it did when you started this chapter, as you can see in Figure 7-16. With this ability to display your links, FrontPage is an excellent tool for managing them. Besides the obvious visual checking that you can do in Hyperlinks view, it has the ability to verify that link exists through the Verify Hyperlink button on the Reports toolbar. FrontPage also has a command in the Tools menu that helps you in link management: Recalculate Hyperlinks updates the display of all links as well as the server databases used by the Include and Search components. To check out your links:

1. Click Reports in the Views bar. The Reports toolbar should open automatically with the Reports view. If it did not open, open the View menu and choose Toolbars | Reports.

2. Click Verify Hyperlinks on the bottom right of the Reports toolbar. You are given a choice of verifying all hyperlinks or just selected ones and given a tip that all

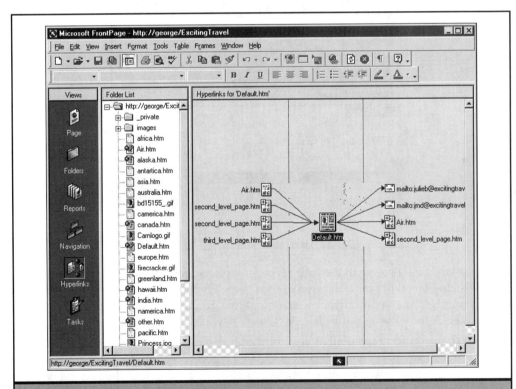

Figure 7-16.   *Hyperlink view showing the links to and from the home page*

open modified pages should be saved. Accept the default of verifying all hyperlinks and click Start. Each of your links is checked (if you are not currently connected to the Internet, your system will attempt to connect if you have an external link) and, if broken, entered on the Broken Hyperlinks report shown next.

Status	Hyperlink	In Page	Page Title
Broken	http://Mideast	Air.htm	Click the area of the world f...
Broken	http://Seasia	Air.htm	Click the area of the world f...
OK	http://www.rccl.com/1.0.3.html	second_level_page.htm	Second Level Page

Broken Hyperlinks

3. Select a broken link and click Edit Hyperlinks in the Reports toolbar. The Edit Hyperlink dialog box will open, as shown next, allowing you to replace the current link with a new one. You can change all pages with this link, or only selected ones.

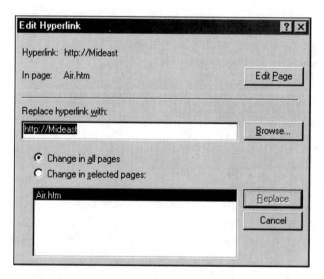

4. If you click Browse in the Edit Hyperlink dialog box, the Select Hyperlink dialog box will open. Here, as in the Create Hyperlink dialog box, you can select a page in the current web, enter any URL, browse for a site on the Web, search for a file on your disk, or create a new page.

5. When you have fixed all of your broken links, return to Hyperlinks view for your Home page, and select Recalculate Hyperlinks from the fully extended Tools menu. You are told what the process will do, and that the process will take several minutes as shown next. Click Yes to proceed. When the process is complete, your web will be redisplayed in FrontPage with any repairs it was able to do.

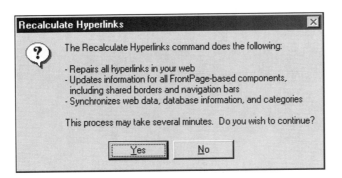

Note *When you have broken a link, the icon for the linked page is broken in Hyperlinks view of FrontPage, like this:*

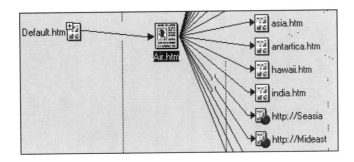

You have seen in this chapter how easy it is to establish links in FrontPage both with text and with graphics, both within a web and externally, and how you can manage those links with some powerful tools. Next, we'll look at the great tools FrontPage provides to add and work with tables and frames in your webs.

Chapter 8

Using Tables and Frames

So far in this book, you have used the full width of a web page for placing all text and graphics. Good layout designs can be accomplished this way, but it does not allow for text or graphics to be placed in independent columns, and the only way to align text within a line (other than at the ends) is to add spaces with the Formatted paragraph style. FrontPage has two features that allow you to break up some or all of a page into sections that can contain text or graphics. These two features are tables and frames. You can also position page elements using cascading style sheets, which are covered in Chapter 11, but support for style sheets is available only in the latest browsers. Tables and frames are supported in older browsers, which means your design is more likely to appear as you intended.

Tip   *Normally, browsers ignore multiple spaces in text; only the first space is displayed. The two exceptions to this are when the spaces are formatted with the Formatted paragraph style and when the nonbreaking space HTML character ( ) is inserted from the Symbol dialog box (the first character in the first row). Using HTML code is covered in Chapter 12.*

Designing with Tables

Tables allow you to divide a portion of a page into rows and columns that create *cells* by their intersection. Tables can be used to systematically arrange information in rows and columns, or they can be used to lay out text and graphics on a page. In web design, tables are probably the most important tool for creative page layout. Just a few of the ways that you can use tables are as follows:

- Tabular data display, with and without cell borders
- Side-by-side columns of text
- Aligning labels and boxes for forms
- Text on one side, graphics on the other
- Placing borders around text or graphics
- Placing graphics on both sides of text or vice versa
- Wrapping text around a graphic
- Adding colored backgrounds to text or graphics

When you create a table, you can determine the number of rows and columns in the table, the horizontal percentage of a page that will be used by the table, the percentage of the table's width in each column, and whether the table has a caption. After a table has been created, you can add or remove rows and/or columns, you can combine adjacent cells, and you can add to or remove from a cell or groups of cells any formatting available to the table's contents. Within the percentage limits set for the table and column, a cell will automatically expand both horizontally and vertically to contain the information placed in it.

Although you can create a table based on a percentage of the screen, with columns as a percentage of the table, there are often problems getting the table to display the way you want. If you use fixed pixel widths based on the minimum 640×480 screen, you'll be able to create a more consistent look. Each method has advantages and you will probably use both, depending on the function of the table.

Displaying Tabular Data in a Table

The classic table, such as you might create in a spreadsheet application, segments text into rows and columns. To build such a table, take the following steps:

1. If it's not already loaded, start FrontPage.

2. In FrontPage, open the File menu and choose New | Web.

3. In the New dialog box, select the One Page Web option. In the Specify The Location Of The New Web combo box, select your web server and type **/Wine** for the title of the new FrontPage web, and then click OK.

4. Click the Folders view in the Views bar, and then double-click the Home Page (Default.htm) in the Contents, or right, pane.

5. Press ENTER to move down the page one line and leave room at the top.

6. Open the Table menu and choose Insert | Table. The Insert Table dialog box will open, as shown in Figure 8-1. This shows the default values.

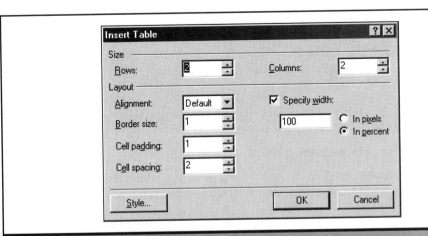

Figure 8-1. *Insert Table dialog box*

If your dialog box has different values in it, change them to match the values here. In the dialog box, take a look at the options available when you create a table; they are described in Table 8-1.

7. Click OK. A two-row, two-column table is displayed with the cursor in the first column of the first row. Select the table by opening the Table menu and choosing Select | Table, and then remove it by pressing DEL. If the carriage return you entered in step 5 is also removed, press ENTER to place a blank line at the top of the page.

8. Click the Insert Table button on the toolbar. In the drop-down list that opens, click the second cell from the left in the second row, as shown next. A four-cell table appears on your page.

The Insert Table button on the toolbar offers a quick method for creating a table using the defaults, while the Insert Table option in the Table menu allows you to set the properties for the table when it is created.

You can create a table with more rows or columns than shown in the Insert Table drop-down list by dragging past the edge of the list. The box will expand to display the number of rows and/or columns you select.

Working with Table Properties

Table properties affect all of the cells in a table and establish how the overall table will look. To see that for yourself:

1. In the new table that was just created, type **1** in the upper-left cell, press TAB to move to the cell on the right, and type

   This is a longer statement

   Your table should look like the one shown next. The table takes up almost 100 percent of the window's width, and the two cells in each row split that width.

1	This is a longer statement

Option	Description
Rows	Specifies the number of rows in the table.
Columns	Specifies the number of columns in the table.
Alignment	Aligns the table on the left, center, or right of the page. Default alignment is the same as left alignment.
Border Size	Sets the number of pixels in the border. A 0-pixel border will not appear in a browser, but you'll see a dotted line in FrontPage. The default is 1.
Cell Padding	Sets the number of pixels between the inside edges of a cell and the cell contents on all four sides. The default is 1.
Cell Spacing	Sets the number of pixels between adjacent cells. The default is 2.
Width	Sets the width to be a fixed number of pixels or a percentage of the window size, if Specify Width is selected. Otherwise, the table is the sum of the cells, which are individually sized to contain their contents within the size of the window. If the percentage method is selected, each cell is given an equal percentage of the table.

Table 8-1. *Table Properties*

2. Press DOWN ARROW twice to move out of the table, and then press ENTER to leave a blank line.

Tip *Pressing TAB in the last cell of a table will insert a new row at the bottom of the table.*

3. Open the Table menu and choose Insert | Table. In the Insert Table dialog box, click Specify Width to clear it, and then click on OK. A second, much smaller table appears.

4. Type **1**, press TAB, and type

   This is a longer statement

   Press TAB again to move to the left cell in the second row, type **2**, press TAB once more, and type

   This is a statement

Each column in the table is as wide as the cell in that column with the longest content, as shown in Figure 8-2.

5. Right-click the second table to open the context menu. You can see that it has both Table Properties and Cell Properties options. Choose Table Properties, opening the dialog box shown in Figure 8-3. Like the dialog box (shown in Figure 8-1) opened with the Insert Table option in the Table menu, it allows you to set the table's Alignment, Border Size, Cell Padding, Cell Spacing, and Width. You can also choose a height for the table, a background image or color, and colors for the table's border. The Float option allows text to wrap around the table by placing the table at the left or right edge of the page. This dialog box does not allow you to specify the number of rows and columns.

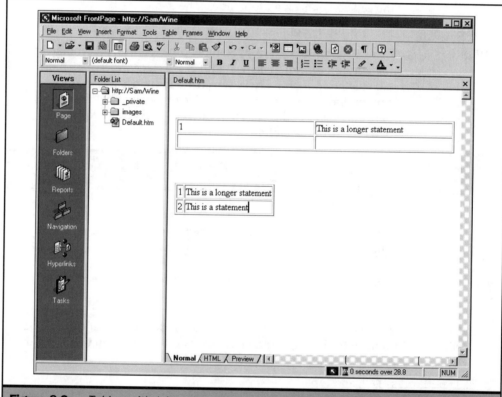

Figure 8-2.   *Tables with (above) and without (below) a specified width*

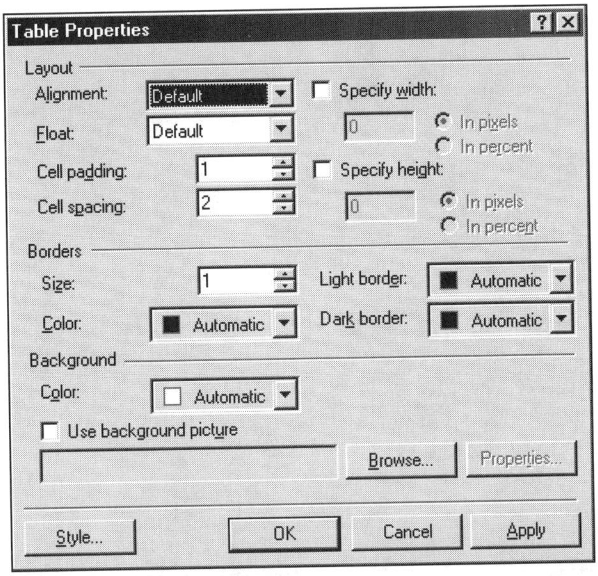

Figure 8-3. *Table Properties dialog box*

6. Change Border Size to **5**, Cell Padding to **6**, Cell Spacing to **8**, and click OK. Your table should look like this:

| 1 | This is a longer statement |
| 2 | This is a statement |

7. Right-click the upper-right cell in the upper table (Figure 8-2) and select Cell Properties. The Cell Properties dialog box will open, as you can see in Figure 8-4. Take a moment and look at the options it contains. They are described in Table 8-2.

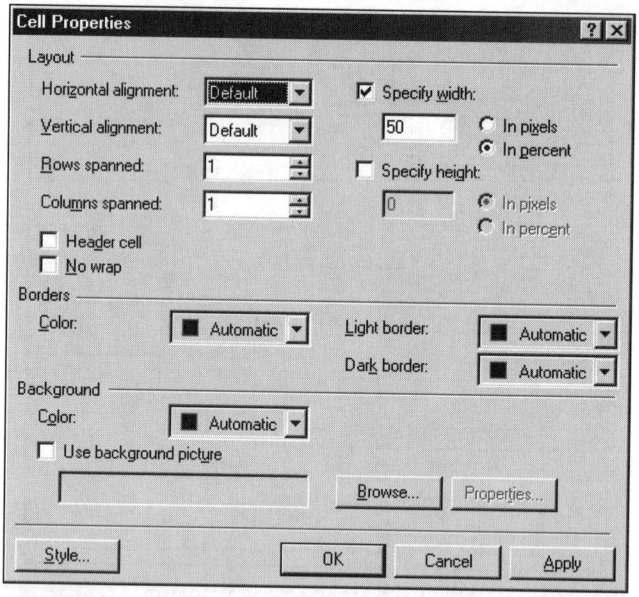

Figure 8-4. *Cell Properties dialog box*

Applying Cell Properties

Cell properties apply to just the one or more selected cells in a table, as shown in the following steps.

If you change the cell width, you should do so for an entire column, and you should make sure that the sum of the cell widths in a row does not exceed 100 percent, or you will get unpredictable results.

1. In the Cell Properties dialog box, change Horizontal Alignment to Center, Vertical Alignment to Top, and click OK. You should see the contents of the cell you selected (at the end of the previous section) change accordingly.

Cell padding and spacing may prevent much movement, especially vertically, in a cell when you change the alignment.

Option	Description
Horizontal Alignment	Horizontally aligns the contents of the cell. It can be Left, Center, or Right. Left is the default.
Vertical Alignment	Vertically aligns the contents of a cell. It can be Top, Middle, Baseline, or Bottom. Middle is the default. Baseline aligns the baseline of text in a cell with the baseline of the largest text in the row.
Rows Spanned	Joins adjacent cells to make a single larger cell that spans two or more rows.
Columns Spanned	Joins adjacent cells to make a single larger cell that spans two or more columns.
Header Cell	Identifies the cell as the label for a row or column and makes the text in the cell bold. (You can also do this with the paragraph or character formatting options.)
No Wrap	Indicates that the web browser should not wrap the text in the cell; otherwise, the text will be wrapped if the browser window is too narrow to display the text.
Specify Width	Sets the width to be a fixed number of pixels or a percentage of the table size, if Specify Width is selected. Otherwise, the cell width is automatically sized to hold its contents.
Specify Height	Sets the height to be a fixed number of pixels or a percentage of the table size, if Specify Height is selected. Otherwise, the cell height is automatically sized to hold its contents.
Borders	Sets the color used for the border, which can consist of one or two colors. Use the Border drop-down to specify a single-color border, and use any two of the three drop-downs to specify a two-color border, which will have a three-dimensional effect.
Background	Sets the background for a cell. This can be either an image, for which you can browse and set its properties, or a background color.

Table 8-2. *Cell Properties*

2. Select the bottom row in the upper table by pointing to the border of the table and clicking when the pointer changes to a heavy arrow. Then right-click the selected row, choose Cell Properties, change Columns Spanned to **2**, and click OK. Your table should look as shown next. The leftmost cell does span the two upper cells, but you have an extra cell on the right.

1	This is a longer statement

To select either a row or a column, move the mouse pointer to the outer edge of the table—the left edge for a row, the top edge for a column—until the mouse pointer changes to a heavy arrow, and click. If you drag the heavy arrow, you can select multiple rows or columns.

The width of your columns may be different than the illustration due to differences in screen resolution.

3. Press CTRL+Z or choose Undo Edit Properties from the Edit menu to undo step 2. In a moment you'll see another way to do this that is probably more what you want.

4. Select the top row of the upper table, open the Cell Properties dialog box, increase Rows Spanned to **2**, and click OK. The top two cells come down and push the bottom two to the right, like this:

1	This is a longer statement		

5. Click the Undo button on the toolbar, click the top left cell, open the Cell Properties dialog box, click Specify Width and In Pixels, type **40** for the width, and click OK. Both cells in the first column increase, as you can see in the following illustration.

1	This is a longer statement

6. Click Undo, click the bottom right cell, and open the Table menu. Look at the options in this menu, which are described in Table 8-3.

Option	Description
Draw Table	Creates a table by enabling you to draw the outside border and then the column and row borders.
Insert Table	Opens the Insert Table dialog box, where you can select the properties of a table to place at the current insertion point. If the insertion point is in the cell of another table, a second table is placed in that cell.
Insert Rows Or Columns	Opens the Insert Rows Or Columns dialog box, where you can select the number of rows or columns above, below, to the left, or to the right of the current selection.
Insert Cell	Inserts a new cell to the left of a selected cell, pushing any cells on the right farther to the right.
Insert Caption	Inserts a blank line, with an insertion point for typing text, immediately above the active table. This line is aligned with and attached to the table. If you select or delete the table, the caption is also selected or deleted. The initial alignment is for the caption to be centered on the table, but it can also be left- or right-aligned on the table.
Delete Cells	Deletes the selected cells.
Select Table, Column, Row, or Cell	Selects a particular area so that it can be merged, split, or deleted. You can also select a cell by pressing ALT while clicking the cell.
Merge Cells	Joins two or more selected cells in a row or column—including an entire row or column—into a single cell that spans the area originally occupied by the cells that were merged.
Split Cells	Opens the Split Cells dialog box, where you can split the selected cell into multiple rows or multiple columns.
Distribute Rows or Columns Evenly	Equalizes the width or height of the selected rows or columns.

Table 8-3. *Table Menu Options*

Option	Description
AutoFit	Reduces the width of each column in a table to the minimum width needed to display the longest content in the column. This has the same effect as clearing the Specify Width check box in the Cell and Table Properties dialog boxes.
Convert Text to Table	Opens the Convert Text to Table dialog box, where you convert selected text into a table. You should use commas (or another punctuation character) to separate columns, and paragraphs to separate rows. See the Tip in the "Building a Tabular Table" section later in this chapter for a detailed explanation of why you should not use tabs to separate columns.
Convert Table to Text	Converts a table into text with the contents of each cell becoming a separate paragraph.
Table, Cell, or Caption Properties	Opens the Table, Cell, or Caption Properties dialog box.

Table 8-3. *Table Menu Options (continued)*

To select multiple cells not in a row or column, press and hold CTRL while clicking the additional cells.

Employing the Table Menu Options

The Table menu provides some important options for working with tables. To see for yourself:

1. In the Table menu choose Insert | Table, accept the existing settings in the Insert Table dialog box, and click OK. You should now have a 2 × 2 table in the cell of your original table, as shown here:

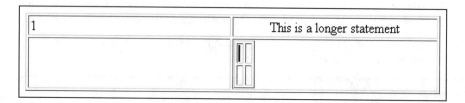

2. Click Undo and click the upper-left cell in the same table. Open the Table menu and choose Insert | Rows Or Columns. The Insert Rows Or Columns dialog box will open:

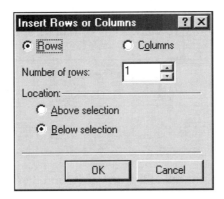

3. Accept the default options, Rows, 1, and Below Selection, and click OK. A new row appears in the middle of the table.

4. Reopen the Table menu and choose Insert | Rows Or Columns again. Click Columns, Left Of Selection, and then OK. A new column appears on the left so that your table now looks like this:

	1	This is a longer statement

5. Open the Table menu and choose Insert | Cell. A new cell appears in the table, pushing the right cell in the row out to the right. The insertion point also moves to the new cell, like this:

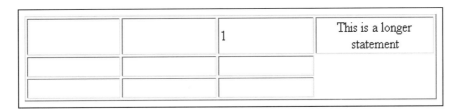

6. From the Table menu choose Select | Cell, or ALT+click the cell, and then choose Delete Cells from the Table menu. The new cell disappears.

7. From the Table menu choose Insert | Caption. An insertion point appears above and centered on the table. Type

This is a Caption

8. Select the bottom row of the first table. Then, from the Table menu, choose Merge Cells. The bottom row now only contains a single cell, as shown next:

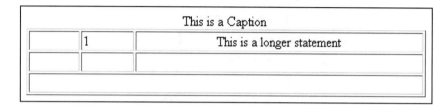

9. Click in the upper-right cell of the first table, and then choose Split Cells in the Table menu. The Split Cells dialog box will open:

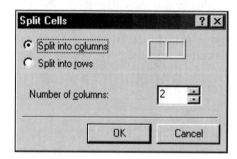

10. Accept the defaults and click OK. Your original cell is now split into two, as shown here:

11. From the Table menu, point on Select, choose Table, and press DEL. Your table disappears. Click Undo to bring it back.

Tip   *Tables can be selected from the Table menu and by double-clicking in the left margin of the page opposite the table.*

12. Open the Table Properties dialog box and set the Border Size to **0**; then click OK. There in now no indication that your text is being formatted by a table. Click Undo.

Drawing a Table

The Table menu and Table Properties dialog box allow you to create complex tables easily, but you can also simply draw a complex table, as described next.

1. Place the cursor in the blank line between the two tables and press ENTER, and then press UP ARROW once.

It's a good practice to leave a blank line between tables when working on them, as FrontPage makes it difficult to insert lines between tables. It is easier to remove extra lines when your table layout is completed.

2. Open the Table menu and choose Draw Table. The Table toolbar will be displayed, and the cursor turns into a pencil. Table 8-4 describes the Table Toolbar options.

3. Place the cursor between the two existing tables, and drag it horizontally across the page, and then vertically so that the new table is approximately the height of the second table. The exact dimensions are not important.

4. Place the cursor on the top border of the table approximately in the center. Drag down to the bottom border.

5. Create three rows in the right column by pointing to the column divider you just created and dragging to the right table border twice. Don't worry about the height of the rows.

6. Click Distribute Rows Evenly on the toolbar, and the three rows will be adjusted to equal heights, as shown here:

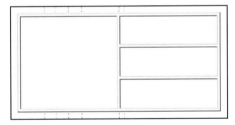

7. Draw a line dividing the second row in the right column into two columns.

8. Draw two lines dividing the third row in the right column into three columns. The first new column will align with the column divider in the row above it, as shown next.

Button	Option	Description
	Draw Table	Allows you to draw the overall dimensions of a table, and row and column borders.
	Eraser	Removes rows and columns from a table.
	Insert Rows	Inserts rows without opening the Insert Rows Or Columns dialog box.
	Insert Columns	Inserts columns without opening the Insert Rows Or Columns dialog box.
	Delete Cells	Deletes the selected cells.
	Merge Cells	Merges the selected cells.
	Split Cells	Opens the Split Cells dialog box.
	Align Top	Aligns the cell's contents with the top of the cell.
	Center Vertically	Centers the cell's contents vertically.
	Align Bottom	Aligns the cell's contents with the bottom of the cell.
	Distribute Rows Evenly	Equalizes the height of the rows in the table.
	Distribute Columns Evenly	Equalizes the width of the columns in the table.
	Fill Color	Changes the background color of the selected cell, row, column, or table.
	AutoFit	Reduces the width of each column in a table to the minimum width needed to display the longest content in the column.

Table 8-4. *Table Toolbar Options*

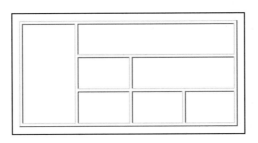

9. Point on the right column border of the first column. The cursor will turn into a double-headed arrow.

10. Drag the column border to the right to make the column wider.

11. Select the Eraser tool in the Table toolbar, and drag it across the right column divider in the bottom row (not the table border) so that the right column of the bottom row is divided into two columns, like this:

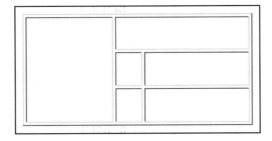

12. Click the Eraser tool to deselect it, and then point on the top border of the table, over the second column. When the pointer turns into a heavy arrow, click to select the column.

13. Press SHIFT and move the pointer to the right, over the column that wasn't selected, and click again. The first column of the table should *not* be selected, and the remaining two columns should be selected.

14. Click Distribute Columns Evenly Table on the toolbar. Your drawn table should now look similar to this:

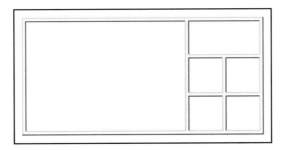

15. Select the table and then press DEL to remove it.

Through the preceding exercises you saw the incredible flexibility in FrontPage's table capability. And it is all WYSIWYG; you instantly see the table you are building very much as it will appear in a browser. Next, build a real table and then look at all three of your tables in a browser.

Building a Tabular Table

This web was called "Wine" earlier in the chapter because you are about to build a table of wines as might be prepared by a winery. To do so:

1. Click below the bottom table, press ENTER to leave a blank line, and then open the Insert menu and choose File.

2. Select your CD-ROM drive and open the file Wine.txt in the \Book\Chap08 folder. Select Normal Paragraphs With Line Breaks in the Convert Text dialog box and click OK.

Note   *Which option you select in the Convert Text dialog box is determined by the format of the file you are inserting. The Wine.txt file was created in Notepad and is correctly inserted with the Normal Paragraphs With Line Breaks option. Try the various options when importing files to see which works best.*

3. Select all the text that was inserted, open the Table menu and choose Convert | Text To Table.

4. In the Convert Text To Table dialog box, select the Other option button, delete the period in the text box, and type ; (a semicolon). Click OK. Figure 8-5 shows the table created from the text file. Several of the words in the table have been underlined by FrontPage's spell checker. They are spelled correctly, but the words do not exist in the FrontPage dictionary. Right-click the underlined words and choose Ignore All or Add from the context menu.

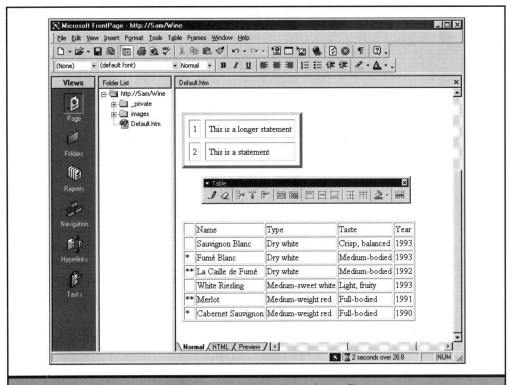

Figure 8-5. *Table created from semicolon-delimited text file*

Tip *HTML doesn't support tabs, so if you import a text file that uses tabs to separate (or delimit) each column's contents, the tabs will be removed and the table will not be created correctly. It is best to use a punctuation character that doesn't appear in the text file. The semicolon was used in this example since commas and hyphens appear in the text. In this example, periods could be used instead.*

5. Select the bottom (blank) row of the table, if you have one, and delete it.

6. Right-click the table and choose Table Properties. Choose Center alignment, enter a cell padding of **4**, turn off Specify Width if it is selected, and click OK.

7. Select the top row, right-click a cell in the first row, open the Cell Properties dialog box, click Header Cell and Left Horizontal Alignment, and click OK.

8. From the Table menu, point on Insert, and choose Caption. Click the Bold button and select 4 (14 pt) from the Font Size drop-down list, both on the Format toolbar, and then type

Fair Mountain Wines Currently Available

9. Select the first row of the table, and then click the down arrow of the Fill Color (Auto) button in the Table toolbar. Select Cyan from the Color drop-down list (the third color square from the left in the second row).

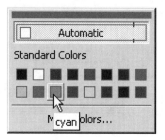

10. Select the remaining rows of the table, and then open the Cell Properties dialog box. Select Yellow from the Background Color drop-down list and click OK. When you are done, your table should look like the one in Figure 8-6. You may

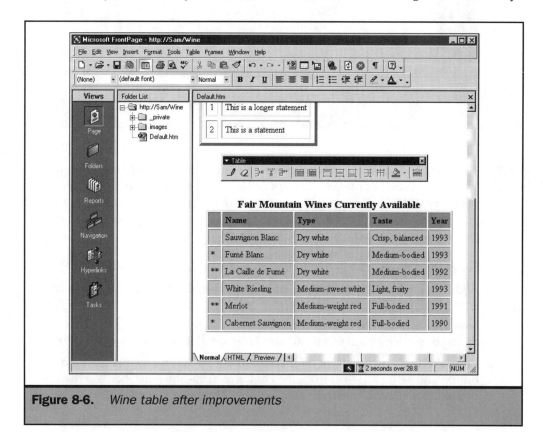

Figure 8-6.   *Wine table after improvements*

have further ideas about how to improve the table. Try them. You can always click on Undo if you don't like a change.

11. Click the Save button to save the tables you have built.

12. Open the File menu and choose Preview In Browser. Select your browser in the Preview In Browser dialog box and click Preview. Figure 8-7 shows the Fair Mountain Wines table in Internet Explorer 5.0. Close your Wine web in FrontPage and your browser when you are done.

13. If you have some other browser, open it and view your tables page. Close your other browser when you are done.

Support for tables has improved greatly in current browsers. There used to be considerable differences in how various browsers display tables—if they even did. You need to view your work in various browsers to decide how these differences affect you. In the Internet arena, Netscape and Microsoft have the lion's share of the market, and both support tables quite well.

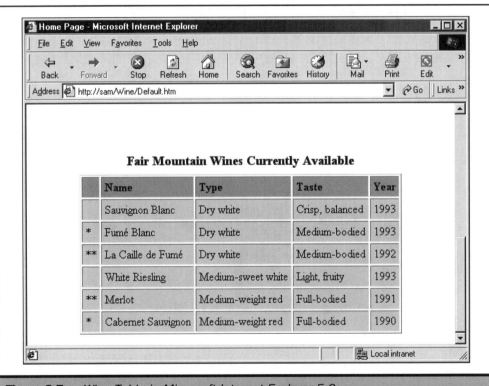

	Name	Type	Taste	Year
	Sauvignon Blanc	Dry white	Crisp, balanced	1993
*	Fumé Blanc	Dry white	Medium-bodied	1993
**	La Caille de Fumé	Dry white	Medium-bodied	1992
	White Riesling	Medium-sweet white	Light, fruity	1993
**	Merlot	Medium-weight red	Full-bodied	1991
*	Cabernet Sauvignon	Medium-weight red	Full-bodied	1990

Figure 8-7. *Wine Table in Microsoft Internet Explorer 5.0*

Using a Table to Enhance a Layout

While tabular tables are the classical way that you think of tables, in web page design tables are extensively used to lay out a page. Seldom are you aware that there is a table behind the layout. You can see how this works by creating a page in your Exciting Travel web:

1. In FrontPage, open your Exciting Travel web, and then open the file second_level_page.htm in Page View.

2. Open the File menu and choose Save As. Name the page **second_level_table.htm** and save it in your Exciting Travel web. This prevents any of your changes from affecting your original page.

3. Select the Draw Table tool on the Table toolbar; then draw a table around the graphic of the cruise ship. When you are done drawing the table, the graphic will be pushed below it.

4. Draw a horizontal line to create a new row at the bottom of the table, as shown in Figure 8-8.

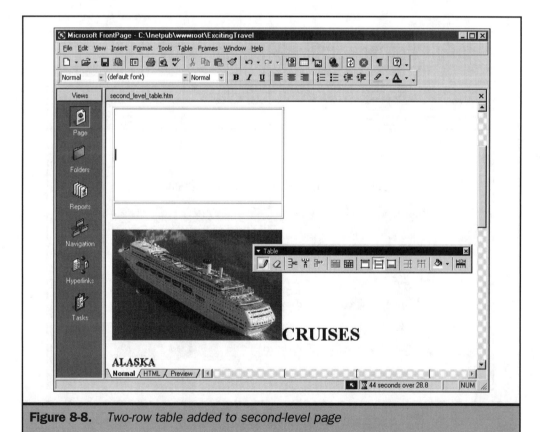

Figure 8-8. *Two-row table added to second-level page*

5. Click the Draw Table tool to deselect it, and then drag the graphic into the top row of the table.

6. In the bottom row of the table type **The Love Boat** and format it as Heading 3.

7. Open the Table Properties dialog box; select Left in the Float drop-down menu and a Border Size of 0. Click OK. Now the text will wrap around the table, as shown in Figure 8-9.

8. Save your work then open the File menu and choose Preview In Browser. Select your favorite browser and click Preview. Figure 8-10 shows the page in Internet Explorer 5.0.

9. Close your browser and the Second Level Table page.

Using a table is the easiest way to add a caption to an image, as you saw in this example. The importance of tables in web page design is also apparent if you look at

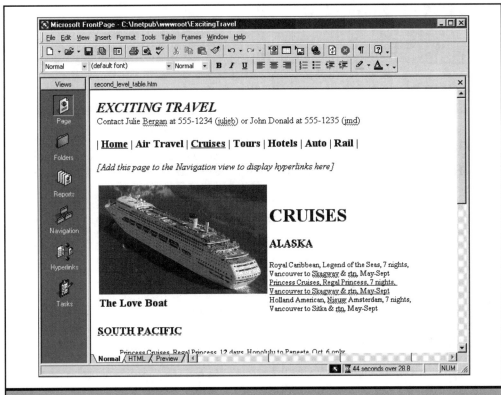

Figure 8-9.   *Text wrapped around the table with graphic*

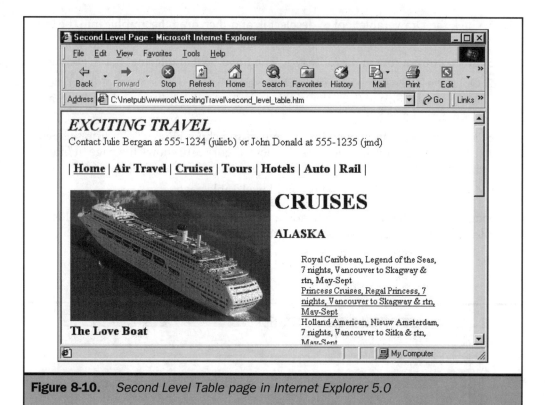

Figure 8-10. *Second Level Table page in Internet Explorer 5.0*

the types of pages that can be created from the New dialog box. Every page type that has more than one column uses tables to create the effect.

You may have some other ideas of how to apply tables to this page. Try them. Play with your ideas until you have the look you want—that is how good designs are created. FrontPage's table capability gives you an extremely powerful tool to create what you want.

Laying Out with Frames

While both frames and tables divide a page into sections, they do so in very different ways with very different results. *Tables* are typically a smaller section of a page that has been divided, while *frames* are actually several pages that have each been allocated a section of the viewing window. This structure of pages along with the HTML is called a *frames page*. (In previous versions of FrontPage the frames page was known as a *frameset*.) In FrontPage, frames are built by use of the Frames page templates. The Frames page templates establish a structure of blank pages and the HTML to view them, in frames within a single window.

> **Note**
>
> *Frames pages created quite a bit of excitement when they were first introduced. This has died down to some extent, and some sources now recommend that they not be used at all. Because frame pages actually load several pages, the total loading time is longer than for a single normal web page. There has also been a tendency to overuse frame pages. Regardless, they are a useful tool for the web designer. They should simply be used with care. Ask yourself if the pages you are creating really benefit from frame pages, and avoid using them simply for a whiz-bang effect.*

Explore FrontPage's frames capability by building a frames page for your Exciting Travel web. Create the frames page with these steps:

1. Open the File menu and choose New | Page. In the New dialog box, click the Frames Pages tab, shown in Figure 8-11.

   In the Frames Page tab there are a list of the frames page templates, a description of the template, and a preview of the frames page.

2. Click the Header, Footer, and Contents frame page template icon. The preview shows that this frames page displays four separate web pages: a header, a footer, a contents page, and the main page. Click OK. Figure 8-12 shows the frames page in FrontPage.

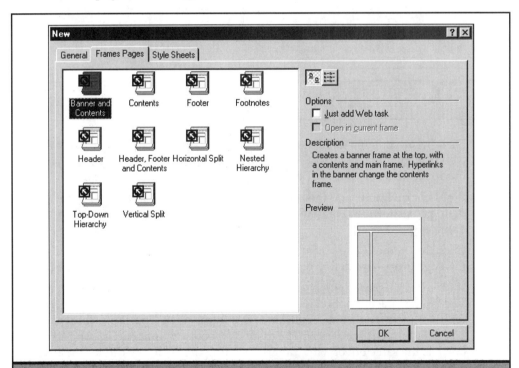

Figure 8-11.   *Frames Pages tab of the New dialog box*

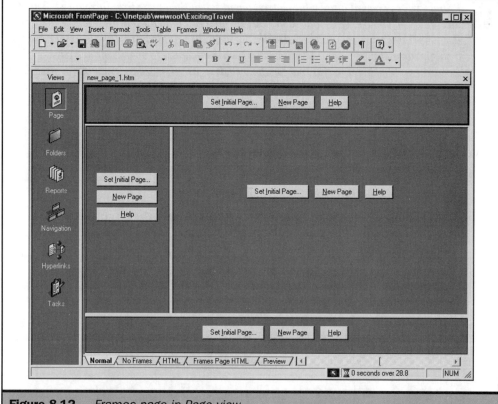

Figure 8-12. *Frames page in Page view*

Each frame contains three buttons: Set Initial Page, which you use to set the web page that will be displayed in the frame by default; New Page, which you use to create a new page to be displayed in the frame; and a Help button.

3. Right-click a frame, and then select Frame Properties. The Frame Properties dialog box shown in Figure 8-13 is displayed. The options are described in Table 8-5.

4. Click the Frames Page button in the Frame Properties dialog box. This displays the Page Properties dialog box that you have used before.

With a frames page there is an additional tab, Frames, which has two options. The Frame Spacing option is similar to the border width of a table; it sets the width of the borders between frames in a frame page. The Show Borders check box determines if borders will be displayed between frames. Clearing this check box has the same effect with frames as setting the border width to 0 in a table.

5. Click Cancel to close the Page Properties dialog box; then click Cancel to close the Frame Properties dialog box.

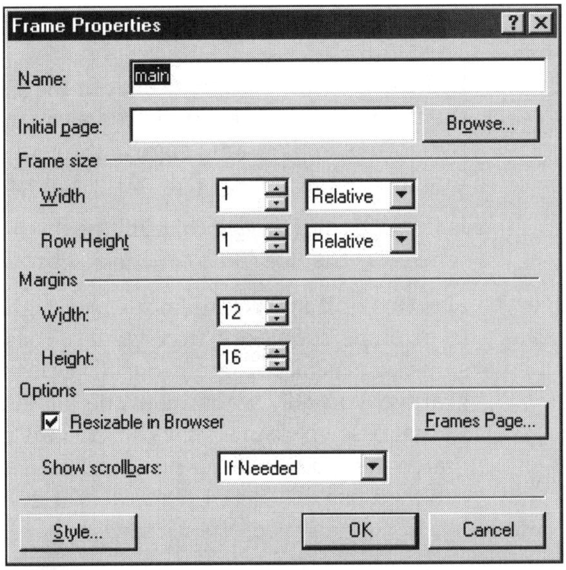

Figure 8-13. *Frame Properties dialog box*

6. In the Top (header) frame, click New Page. A new blank page is opened in the Top frame.

7. Right-click the new page in the Top frame and choose Shared Borders. In the Shared Borders dialog box, select the Current Page option and then clear the Bottom check box. Click OK.

Tip   *It's usually not a good idea to use shared borders with frame pages. Information may be duplicated and navigation can be complicated by having redundant links. If you are using shared borders in your web, you will usually want to turn off the feature for your frame pages.*

8. Open the Insert menu and choose Picture | From File. In the Picture dialog box, locate the Webtitle.gif file and double-click it. This will insert the graphic onto the new page.

9. Drag the bottom border of the Top frame down until the entire graphic is visible. Select the graphic and click Center on the toolbar.

10. In the Bottom (footer) frame, click New Page. This will create a new page with the Shared Borders footer containing the copyright and other information.

The default page for the Main frame (the right pane in the center of the frames page) will be a variation of the existing home page. Since the Exciting Travel graphic has been placed in the Top frame, you will make a copy of the home page and then remove the graphic, as explained in the following steps.

Option	Description
Name	Is the name of the frame itself, not the page displayed in the frame. This is the name used as a target by hyperlinks in the frame page and the one that determines in which frame a page will be displayed.
Initial Page	Is the URL of the page that will be displayed in the frame when it is first loaded by the user's browser.
Frame Size	Has two options, Width and Row Height, that can be set to pixel, percent, or relative values. These function the same way as table dimensions. If your frame contains a graphic, you may want the frame to be no larger than it. In that case you can set the dimensions of the frame to match the graphic using pixel values. The other frames can then use relative or percent values.
Margins	Sets the margins, in pixels, of the selected frame.
Resizable In Browser	Determines if the frame can be resized in the user's browser. If this option is cleared, the user cannot resize the frame.
Show Scrollbars	Has three selections: If Needed, which displays scroll bars if the page content is larger than the space available; Never, which will never display scroll bars regardless of the page content; and Always, which will always display scroll bars. The correct settings for these options depends on the page content being displayed in the frame. If it is a menu, you would want the scroll bars to be displayed as needed, and you would probably want the user to be able to resize the frame. If the frame is displaying a header with a graphic, and you've sized the frame to the graphic using the Frame Size options, then you might want to disable both these options.

Table 8-5. *Frame Properties*

11. Open the home page (Default.htm) in Page view. Save the page with the filename **Fr_main.htm**. This prevents any changes you make from affecting the home page.

12. Delete the Exciting Travel graphic and any blank lines at the top of the page, and then save the page again.

13. Open the frames page in Page view then click Set Initial Page in the Main frame (the right pane in the center of the frames page). In the Create Hyperlink dialog box that opens select the modified home page (Fr_main.htm) and click OK.

14. In the Contents frame (the left frame in the center of the frames page) click New Page.

15. Right click the new page in the contents frame and choose Shared Borders. In the Shared Borders dialog box select the Current Page option and clear the Bottom check box. Click OK.

16. In the Contents frame page type **AIR TRAVEL**, press ENTER, then type **CRUISES**.

17. Select AIR TRAVEL then click the Hyperlink button on the toolbar. In the Create Hyperlink dialog box select Air.htm, then check that the Target Frame is set to Page Default (Main). If it isn't, click the Change Target Frame button and select Page Default (Main) in the Target Frame dialog box, shown here. Click OK to close the Target Frame dialog box (if you opened it) and the Create Hyperlink dialog box.

18. Select CRUISES, open the Create Hyperlink dialog box, select Second_level_page.htm, check that the Target Frame is set to Page Default (Main), and click OK. Your screen should look similar to Figure 8-14.

19. Open the File menu and choose Save As. The Save As dialog box for frame pages, shown in Figure 8-15, includes an outline of the frames page (in the center-right pane). This indicates which frame will be saved. To save the frames

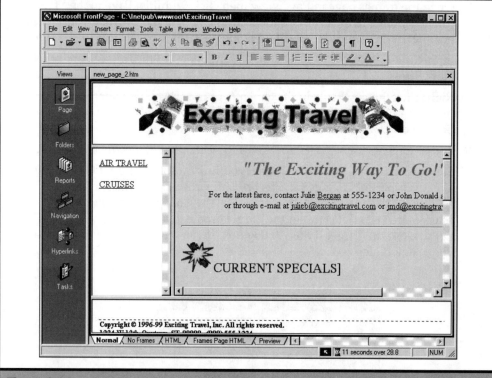

Figure 8-14. *Frames page in FrontPage*

page itself, there must be a border around the entire page, as shown in Figure 8-15. Save your frames page with the Title Frames Page and the File Name Frames.htm.

After the frames page is saved, the Save As dialog box will be displayed again, this time with one of the individual pages in the frame selected. The title and filename you enter will apply to the page in the selected frame.

20. Save the page in the Bottom (footer) frame with the Page Title **Frames Page Footer** and the File Name **Fr_footer.htm**.

21. Save the page in the Contents frame with the Page Title **Frames Page Contents** and the File Name **Fr_contents.htm**.

22. Save the page in the Top (header) frame with the Page Title **Frames Page Header** and the File Name **Fr_header.htm**.

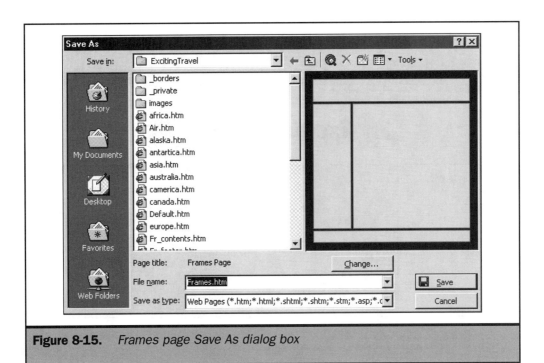

Figure 8-15. *Frames page Save As dialog box*

23. Open the File menu and choose Preview In Browser. Figure 8-16 shows the frames page in Internet Explorer 5.0.

24. In your browser, point on the vertical border between the left and right frames in the middle of the page. When the cursor changes into a double-headed arrow, drag the border to the left.

25. Point on the horizontal borders of the header or footer frame. The cursor will not change to a double-headed arrow because, by default in the Header, Footer, and Contents frames page template, these frames cannot be resized.

26. Click the Cruises hyperlink in the Contents frame. The Cruises page (second_level_page.htm) is displayed in the Main frame. Close your browser.

One problem with frame pages is that not all browsers support them. Frames were introduced in Netscape Navigator 2.0, and Microsoft followed suit in Internet Explorer 3.0. Support for frames was made official with the adoption of HTML 3.2 early in 1997. Older versions of these browsers, as well as other browsers, do not support frames.

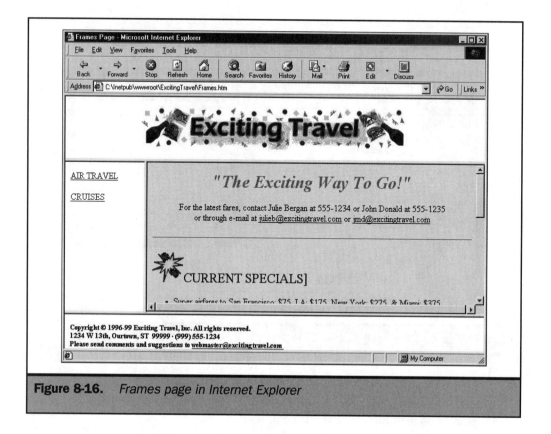

Figure 8-16. *Frames page in Internet Explorer*

Some people still use these older browsers, so you must assume a small, but possibly significant, percentage of your audience will not be able to view your frame pages correctly.

This problem is dealt with by creating a No Frames page. If the user's browser does not support frames, the No Frames page is displayed instead. FrontPage will automatically create a No Frames page when a frames page is created, as you can see by clicking the No Frames tab at the bottom of the page when a frames page is open. Figure 8-17 shows the default No Frames page. You can use this page either to direct the user to download a browser that supports frames by creating hyperlinks to Microsoft's or Netscape's browser-download pages on their web sites, or to re-create your frames pages without frames. This is a case where you could use tables to place the categories list in one column and other pages in a second column. Your table could have one row with two columns.

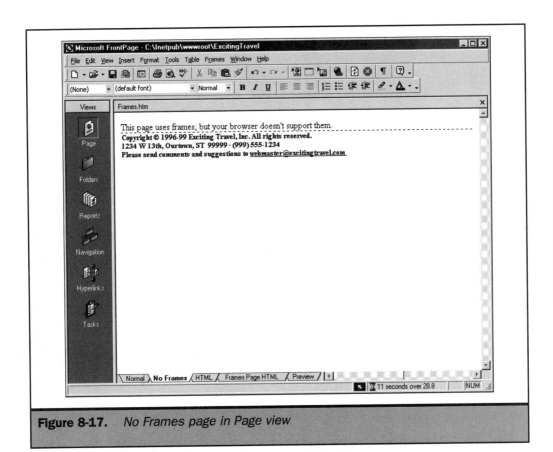

Figure 8-17.   *No Frames page in Page view*

Frames provide some powerful layout capabilities, especially the ability of a frame to scroll and the target frame concept. Based on the default target frames, anything that you open by clicking a link in a Contents frame will appear in the Main frame.

Tables and frames provide real depth to your ability to create sophisticated, state-of-the-art web pages in FrontPage. And you can do it very easily and with true WYSIWYG ability to see the final results.

The Complete Reference

Chapter 9

Working with Forms

n Chapters 6 through 8, the focus has been on how to present text and graphic information to users of your web. In this chapter, the tables will be turned—you'll learn how to get information back from users. *Forms* are the obvious mechanism for collecting user input and are the focus of this chapter. FrontPage Components, the focus of Chapter 10, also provide a means for collecting user input and are instrumental in the use of forms. Both forms and FrontPage Components have classically (meaning "last year," in terms of the Web) required either programming or the use of canned programs on a web server. FrontPage has replaced this with its Server Extensions and Components, which save you from any programming or from using canned programs with their arcane HTML calls. FrontPage then goes further by giving you powerful tools to perform these functions in a WYSIWYG environment. See for yourself, starting with using forms.

Using Forms

Forms in a web are very similar to those on paper, as you saw in Chapter 2. You are given boxes to fill in, options to select, and choices to make. The advantages of computer forms over paper forms are that computer forms can be easily modified, you don't have to decipher someone's handwriting, and the data starts out in computer form, so it does not have to be retyped into a computer. As with paper forms, though, the design of a form is very important if you want the user to fill it out willingly and properly. The three cardinal rules of forms are

- Keep it simple.
- Keep it short.
- Make it very clear what the user is supposed to do.

FrontPage provides a comprehensive Form Page Wizard to lead you through the development of a form. In addition, FrontPage has a complete set of tools both in the toolbar and in the Insert menu to allow you to create any form you can dream up. You'll work with both of these in this chapter, beginning with the Form Page Wizard.

Creating Forms with the Form Page Wizard

To create a form, you need to figure out what questions to ask and what fields are necessary for the user to answer them. Go through that process with the idea of creating a questionnaire for prospective project team members. First use the Form Page Wizard to generate the form; then examine and modify the results.

Generating the Form

Like the other wizards you have seen, the Form Page Wizard asks you a series of questions, which it then uses to build a form. To work with the Form Page Wizard, follow these steps:

1. If necessary, start FrontPage.

2. In FrontPage, create a new one-page web and name it **Forms**.

3. Click Page view on the Views bar, open the File menu and choose New | Page. Select Form Page Wizard in the New dialog box and click OK. The Form Page Wizard's introductory dialog box will appear telling you about web forms, what the wizard will do, and what you can do with the result. Click Next after reading this.

4. You are asked for the Page Title and Page URL (or filename). Type **Project Team Questionnaire** for the Page Title and **Project.htm** for the Page URL. Click Next when you are done.

5. The Form Page Wizard dialog box that opens will eventually show the questions that you are asking on your form. Currently it is blank. Click Add to select the first question.

6. In the next dialog box (shown in Figure 9-1), there is a list of types of questions at the top. Click Contact Information. As you can see in Figure 9-1, a description of the fields that will be placed on the form appears in the middle of the dialog box, and the actual question is displayed at the bottom, where you can change it as you want. Accept the default and click Next.

7. You are then asked to select the specific fields that you want on the form for your first question (see Figure 9-2). All of these are related to an individual contact. For the Name entry you can use one, two, or three fields. Leave the check boxes that are selected as is and click First, Last, which is the two-field choice. Also click Postal Address and Home Phone, and then click Next, leaving the suggested name for the group of variables (Contact) as is.

8. You are returned to the list of questions, which now shows the contact information question you just selected. Use steps 5 through 7 to include questions dealing with Account Information and Personal Information. In the dialog box that appears once you choose Account Information, select the As First And Last Names Fields option for the Username, and then accept the other defaults. For the Personal Information dialog box you don't want to repeat the Name field, so clear the Name check box; but you do want to accept the other defaults.

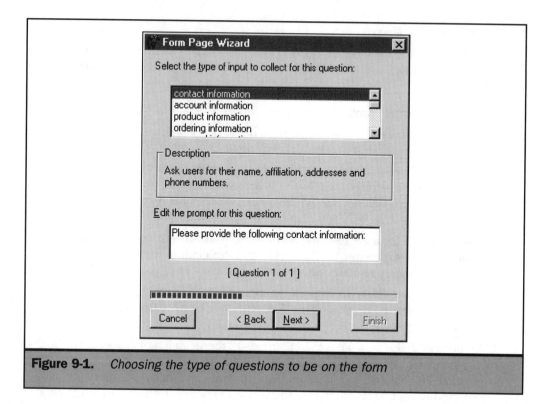

Figure 9-1. *Choosing the type of questions to be on the form*

Note *After you are done using the Form Page Wizard, you can add to, change, and delete what the wizard has produced.*

9. Click Add in the dialog box that shows the list of questions, select the One Of Several Options question, and change the prompt in the lower section of the dialog box to

Choose the city where you want to be located:

Click Next, and enter **New York, Austin,** and **San Francisco** as three separate labels on three lines in the upper list box (press ENTER after the first and second label). Then click Radio Buttons, enter the word **Location** as the variable name, and click Next.

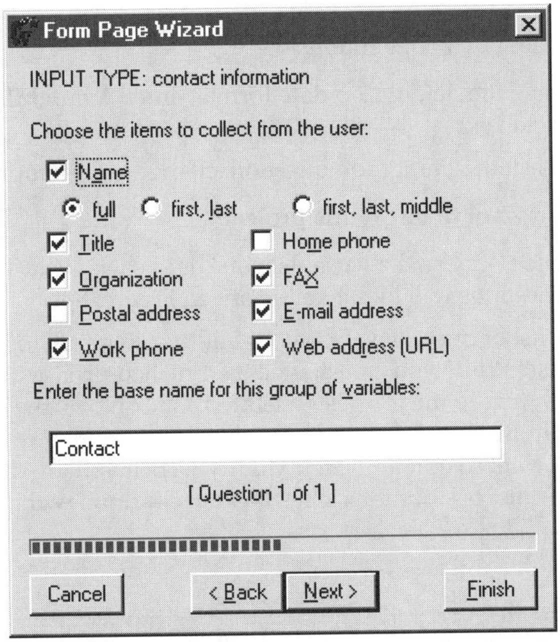

Figure 9-2. *Selecting the specific fields to use for gathering contact information*

10. Click Add, select the Any Of Several Options question, and change the prompt to

  Select two areas you want to be associated with:

  Click Next and enter

  Initial design

  Detail plan

  Project management

  Plan implementation

  Evaluation

  on five separate lines. Enter **PreferredAreas** as the name for the group of variables, and click Next.

11. Click Add, select the Date question, change the prompt to

     Enter the date you are available:

     click Next, leave the default top date format, enter **Availability** for the variable name, and click Next.

12. Click Add, select the Paragraph question, change the prompt to

     Why do you want to be on this project?

     click Next, enter **Why** as the variable name, and click Next. When you are done, your list of questions will look like the one in Figure 9-3.

13. Look at your list of questions. Do you want to change any of them or reposition them in the list? While you can change the finished product, it is easier to change it now, before the form is generated. Click No. 6, the availability date. Click Move Up twice to move the date ahead of the city question. Click any question you want to edit and click Modify. When you are done editing and are returned to the list of questions, click Next to continue with the form creation.

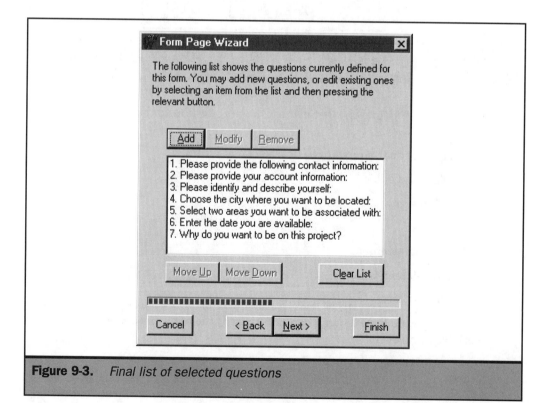

Figure 9-3. *Final list of selected questions*

14. You are asked how the list of questions should be presented. Leave the defaults of: As Normal Paragraphs, no Table Of Contents, and Use Tables To Align Form Fields. Then click Next.

15. You are asked how you want to save the results of the questionnaire. Choose Save Results To A Text File, enter the filename of **Proj_ans** for the results file, click Next, and then click Finish to generate the form page, which appears as shown in Figure 9-4 (with the Folder List closed). Scroll down the form in Page view to see all the types of form fields created.

16. Save your form either by clicking Save on the toolbar or by opening the File menu and choosing Save. Then click OK.

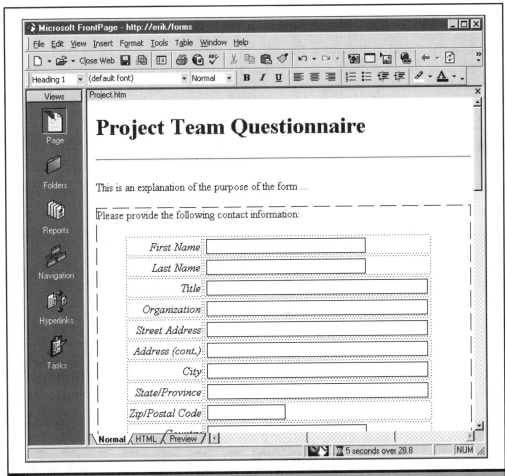

Figure 9-4. *The form as generated by the wizard*

Tip *If you want to transfer the results of a web form to a database or spreadsheet, you can use a text file to collect the information. You can choose a comma-, tab-, or space-delimited file (tab probably being the best for exporting from FrontPage), which is fairly easy to import into most products. In Chapter 18 you will learn how to record the form results directly to a database. In Chapter 12 you will see how database and spreadsheet information can be displayed in web pages.*

Forms can be formatted by use of either a table or the Formatted paragraph style. The Formatted style was often used in the past for two reasons: it is the only paragraph style that can display more than one consecutive space, which can then be used to align the form fields; and many browsers did not support tables. Most browsers now support tables, and this is the preferred method for aligning forms. Using tables greatly simplifies aligning the labels and fields in a form, and it allows you to use any available font.

Reviewing and Editing a Form

As with most documents that you create, you'll want to go through your form in detail and make any necessary changes. In the real world, you would need to replace the introductory paragraph with an explanation of the form. This should tell users how the form will be used and why they should fill it out. In this case you might use something like "This form will be used to qualify prospective members of the Project Team. If you are interested in being a member, please fill out this form."

You can customize many areas of the form. The things that you can do are discussed in the following sections.

CHANGING THE FIELD'S LABEL OR TEXT Change the label or text on the left of each field by simply typing over or adding to the existing text. This may change the width of the table column. For example, add **& Middle** to the first label, and you'll get the column width change, as shown next. Click Undo to restore your form.

Please provide the following contact information:

First & Middle Name:	
Last Name:	

Tip *If you use the Formatted paragraph style to format your form, changing the label for one field may necessitate adjusting other fields to restore the form's alignment. If you use a table to format the form, the realignment will occur automatically.*

CHANGING THE FIELD'S ALIGNMENT   Change the alignment by opening the Cell Properties dialog box for the cell and changing the horizontal or vertical alignment. You can select the entire column to change the alignment for all the labels or fields at one time. If you are using the Formatted paragraph style, you change the alignment by adding or deleting spaces.

 If you use the Formatted style and change the paragraph style on the form fields from Formatted to any other style, you'll lose all the leading spaces that produce the original field alignment. This can easily happen if you backspace up to the first paragraph. If this happens to you, click Undo to quickly recover.

DELETING A FIELD   If you want to delete a field and its label, select the table row and press DEL. You can also select either the label or field individually and press DEL. This leaves the table row available for replacing the label or field. Delete an entire section by selecting the question, labels, and fields, and pressing DEL.

CHANGING A FIELD'S PROPERTIES   Right-clicking a field (not its label) and selecting Form Field Properties opens the field's Properties dialog box, shown next (the dialog box displayed depends on the type of field selected):

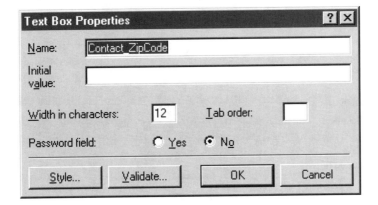

Here you can

- Change the field's name (not the label displayed on the web page)
- Establish an initial value, such as a state abbreviation if most people filling out a form are from one state
- Determine if the field contains a password so its contents can be encrypted

■ Set the order in which the fields will become active when the user presses TAB (this feature doesn't work with all browsers)

■ Set the width of the text box, which can also be changed by dragging the end of a field, as shown here:

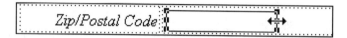

Changing the width of a text box does not affect the maximum number of characters the field can contain. To do that, you use the Form Field Validation dialog box. Right-click a form field and select Form Field Validation. For a text field the Text Box Validation dialog box shown in Figure 9-5 is displayed. The Max Length text box displays the maximum number of characters the field will accept, regardless of the

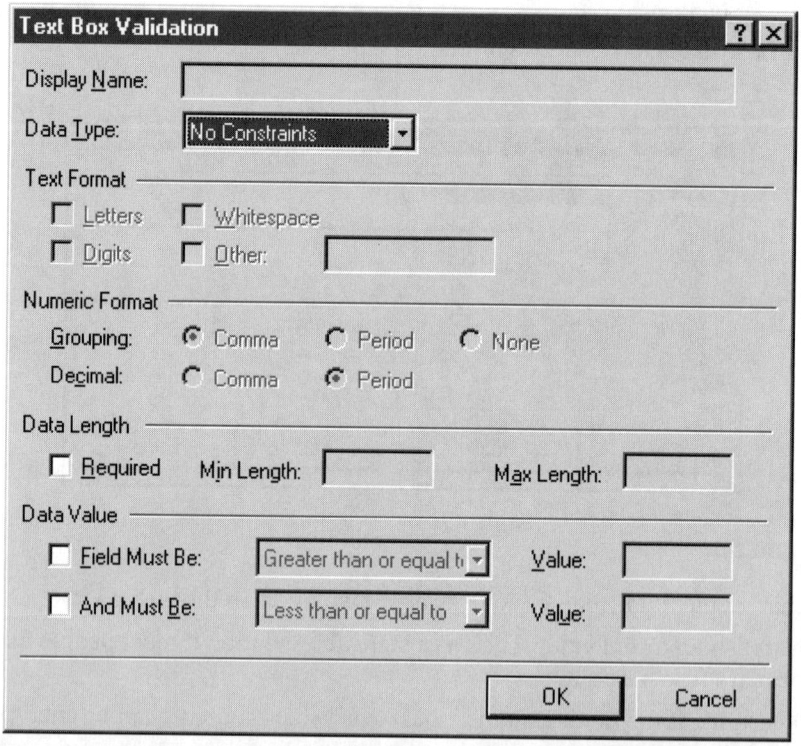

Figure 9-5. *Text Box Validation dialog box*

width of the field. If the maximum length is greater than the width, the text will scroll in the text box until the maximum length is reached. The other options in the Validation dialog box will be covered later in the chapter in the section "Validating a Form." For now, close any open dialog boxes.

> **Tip** *Even if you set the field width and maximum length to the same number, all the text might not fit in the text box without scrolling. This is because the width of a character as determined by the HTML is not always the same as a character displayed on the screen. Test your form fields in a browser by entering the maximum number of characters and setting the width accordingly.*

CHANGING THE FIELD'S PLACEMENT   The table created with the Form Page Wizard has two columns, each with one label and one field on each of its lines. You may want to have more than one field on a line, such as the State and Zip fields. To do that, you need to split a single cell into multiple cells, like this:

1. Reduce the width of the State/Province field (not the label or the table) to about a third of its original size by selecting it and dragging the right selection handle to the left.

2. With the cursor in the same cell, select the cell by choosing Select | Cell from the Table menu.

3. Right-click the selected cell and select Split Cells. Accept the default Split Into Columns, and then enter **3** in the Number Of Columns spinner and click OK.

4. Cut and paste first the "Zip/Postal Code" label and then separately cut and paste the "Zip/Postal Code" form field into the new cells.

5. Right-click the cell containing the "Zip/Postal Code" label, and open the Cell Properties dialog box.

6. Set the Horizontal Alignment to Right and click OK. Your form fields should look like this:

| *State/Province* | | *Zip/Postal Code* | |

7. Select the vacated row and select Delete Cells from the Table menu to remove the row.

VALIDATING A FORM   Fields in a form often need to be limited to specific types of information, such as allowing only numbers (no letters), or requiring that a field not be left blank. Form validation has traditionally been done on the web server by the form handler (*server-side* validation). This has the disadvantage of requiring the form to be sent to the server, validated, and then sent back to the user if the validation fails. Besides the time involved, server-side validation places a greater demand on the web server's resources. If your web site is receiving a large number of hits each day, this can slow down the server. Validating a form before it's sent (*client-side* validation) has the advantages of speeding up the process and placing less demand on the web server.

Note

Client-side validation is performed by the web browser. FrontPage generates a JavaScript or VBScript script (see Chapter 15) that is run by the browser to validate the form. JavaScript (the default) is supported by both Netscape and Microsoft, while VBScript is supported mainly by Microsoft. Some browsers do not support either scripting language. If the browser being used does not support the scripting language used, the client-side validation is ignored. This is another reason to encourage visitors to your web sites to upgrade to the latest versions of either Netscape Navigator or Communicator, or to Microsoft Internet Explorer.

Validation criteria for one-line and scrolling text boxes are set by use of the Text Box Validation dialog box that you saw in Figure 9-5. The options are explained in Table 9-1.

Radio buttons are validated by use of the Radio Button Validation dialog box, shown next, which allows you to make the field required and to set a display name for error messages.

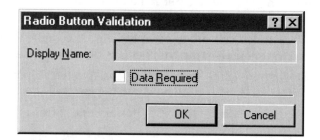

Drop-down lists, or menus, have an additional validation option: Disallow First Item, as shown next. When this is selected, the first item in the drop-down menu cannot be chosen. This enables you to place an instruction or comment, rather than an option, as the first item in the drop-down list.

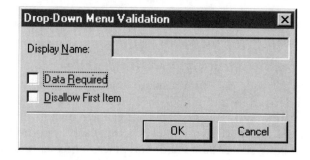

Option	Description
Display Name	Displays the name when an error message is generated. If no name is entered, the contents of the Name field in the form field's Properties dialog box is displayed.
Data Type	Sets the type of data that will be accepted: No Constraints (any characters), Text (alphanumeric characters), Integer (numbers, including "," and "-", without decimals), or Numbers (numbers with decimal places).
Text Format	Sets the acceptable format for the form field data: Letters, Digits (numbers), Whitespace (spaces, tabs, returns, and new-line characters), and Other. If Other is selected, you must type the characters (such as hyphens or commas) that will be accepted in the text box.
Numeric Format	Sets both the Grouping and Decimal numeric punctuation characters. Grouping characters can be Comma (1,234), Period (12.34), or None (1234). Decimal sets the character used as a decimal point: either a Comma or a Period. You cannot use the same character for both Grouping and Decimal.
Data Length	Sets the acceptable length of the data. Required means that the field cannot be left blank. Min Length and Max Length set the minimum and maximum number of characters that can be entered, respectively.
Data Value	Sets a test for the data entered. The value entered in the Value text box is used for the comparison. You can set two tests for each field: Less Than, Greater Than, Less Than Or Equal To, Greater Than Or Equal To, Equal To, or Not Equal To.

Table 9-1. *Text Box Validation Dialog Box Options*

You can validate all the fields in a form except check boxes and push buttons by right-clicking them and selecting Form Field Validation. A dialog box, such as the one shown next, is displayed for each form field that fails the validation criteria, which was generated by making the First Name field required and then submitting the form with the field left blank. In this case, the Display Name field in the Text Box Validation dialog box was set to "First name." If the Display Name field had been left blank, the error message would have displayed the form field name "Contact_FirstName."

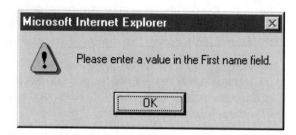

Make the First and Last Name fields required with these steps:

1. Right-click the First Name form field, and select Form Field Validation from the context menu.

2. In the Text Box Validation dialog box, select Required for a Data Length, enter **First name** as the Display Name, and click OK.

3. Repeat steps 1 and 2 for the Last Name form field, using **Last name** as the Display Name.

4. Save the page and then open it in your web browser. Without entering any information, click Submit Form. The validation error dialog box shown above is displayed.

5. Click OK to close the validation error dialog box, and then type any characters in the First Name field of the form. Click Submit Form again. The validation error dialog box will now state that a value is needed for the Last Name field.

6. Click OK to close the validation error dialog box; then close your browser.

CHANGING THE FORM'S PROPERTIES   A *form* is a group of fields enclosed within a dashed border on a page. From the context menu of any field in the form, click Form Properties to open the Form Properties dialog box shown in Figure 9-6. This allows you to set the following properties:

- The form handler, labeled "Where to store results:," will return the contents of a form to you. You have a choice of a file (the default), an e-mail, a database, a custom script that you create, and the Discussion or Registration Form Handlers for those types of web forms.

- The Form Name.

- The Target Frame in which you want the form to appear.

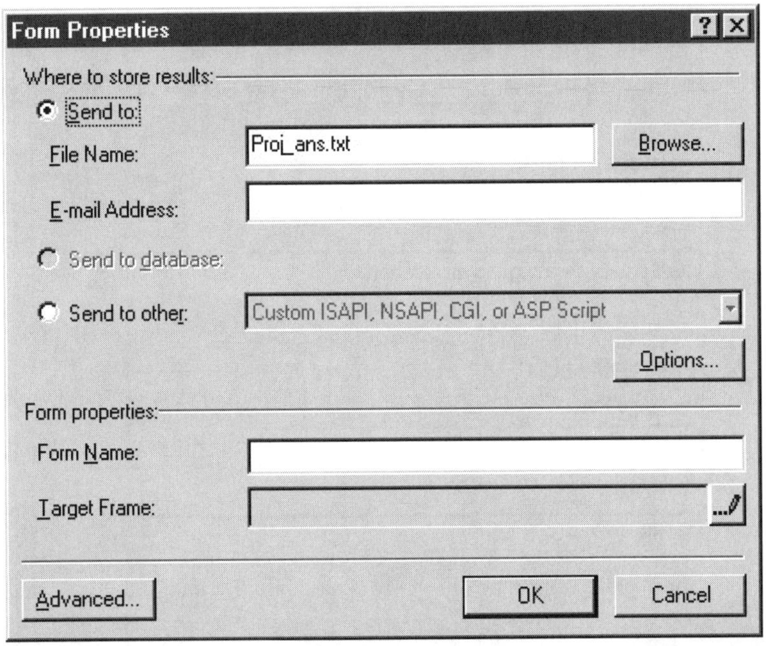

Figure 9-6. *Form Properties dialog box*

■ The Options for the form handler. By clicking Options, you open the Options For Saving Results Of Form dialog box, shown in Figure 9-7. Here you can change the name and format of the results file, include (or exclude) the field names, add fields and data, and set up a second file to save the results with its format and the selection of fields to be included. The E-mail Results tab allows you to change the address and format of the results e-mail, and to set the Subject and Reply-to Line values. The Confirmation Page tab establishes the URL for a confirmation page to be sent on the receipt of a form and establishes the Validation Failure Page to be displayed if the form fails the server-side validation. In the Saved Fields tab you can select the form fields to be saved and add information to the results file.

If the Send To Other option is selected in the Form Properties dialog box, clicking Options displays the Options for Custom Form Handler dialog box shown next. The Action is the URL of the script that will process the form input. This can either be the default or a custom script. The Method is either Post or Get; Post is the default. The Encoding Type sets how the form data will be encoded; this should be left blank to use

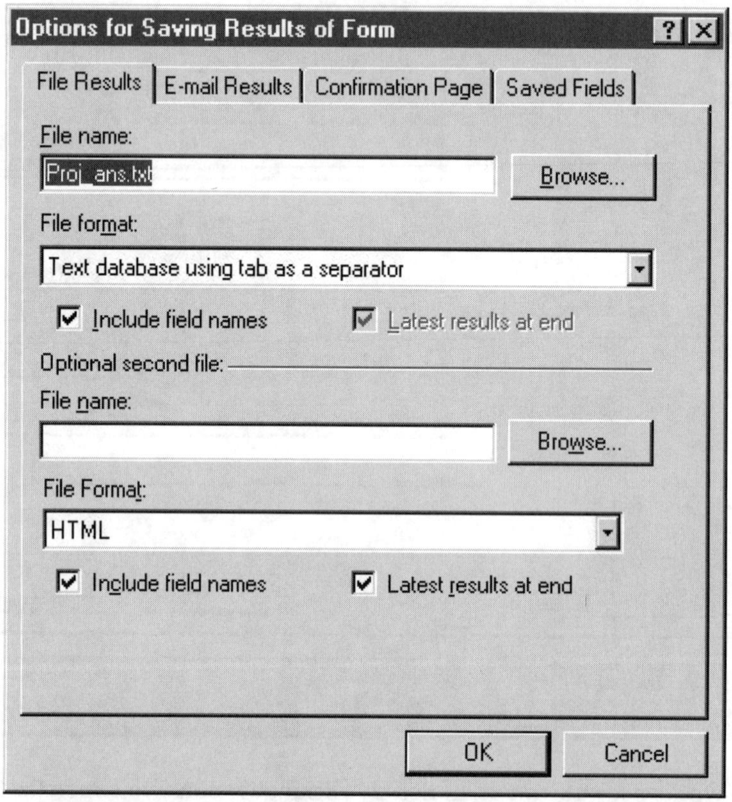

Figure 9-7. *Options For Saving Results Of Form dialog box*

the default. You should use the defaults for both the Method and Encoding Type fields unless you have a specific reason for changing them. The finer points of these options relate to the HTTP protocol itself.

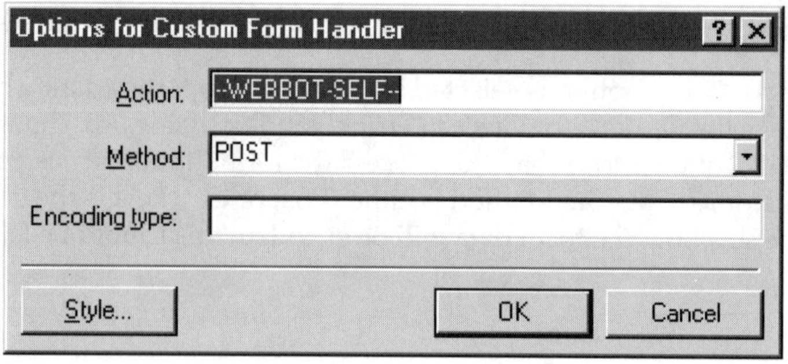

Clicking Advanced in the Form Properties dialog box displays the Advanced Form Properties dialog box, where you can add hidden fields. The hidden fields are information you want to appear in the data collected from the form but not on the form itself.

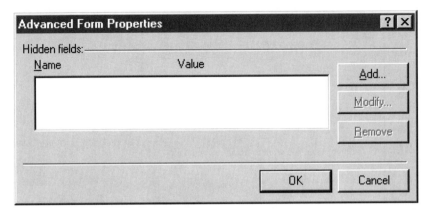

With the Add, Modify, and Remove buttons, you can add a field name and a value that appear in the data. For example, if you use the same form on several web pages, you could add a field named "Source" that identifies where this set of data originated, like this:

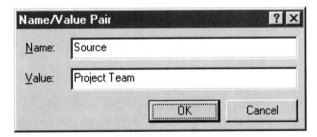

The lower part of the form in Figure 9-4 contains different types of fields, as shown in Figure 9-8. Each of these fields has slight variations in its Properties dialog box. Open each of these in turn and look at their differences. Note the following features:

- The group of radio buttons is a single field, and the value is the button selected.
- Each of the check boxes is its own field, and the value is "on" if a box is selected.
- In the scrolling text box, you can select the number of lines as well as the width. The total content, though, can be far greater than you might think by looking at the width and number of lines (five lines of 35 characters, or 175 characters total), since each line can contain up to 256 characters, not just the 35 characters per line used here.

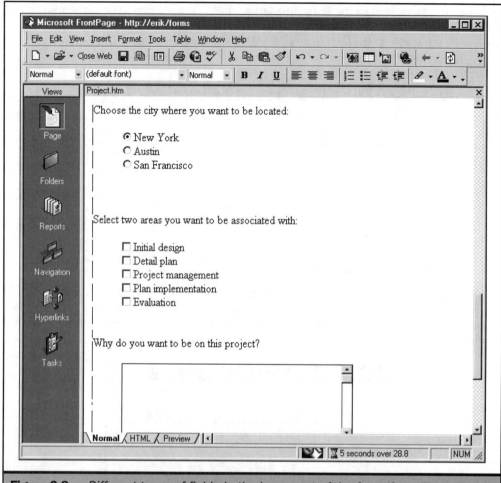

Figure 9-8. *Different types of fields in the lower part of the form (from Figure 9-4)*

- You can change the label on the push buttons. Push buttons can submit or reset a form (erasing any entries made and not submitting the form), or link the form to a custom script (using the Normal option).

The Normal option in the Push Button Properties dialog box is a new feature, supported by HTML 4.0. This option allows the button to call a script, rather than the normal form handler. When the button is clicked, the form data is passed to the script. Scripting is covered in Chapter 15.

Given the considerable customization that can be done to a wizard-created form, if your form looks anything like a form the wizard can build, it will probably save you time to use the wizard. The wizard also makes the necessary settings for handling the form results that you otherwise would have to remember to do. Next you'll see what it is like to build a form from scratch. Before going to that, close any open dialog boxes and save your project form one more time.

Building Forms from Scratch

As good as the Form Page Wizard is, there will always be the need for forms that are different enough from the standards that it is worthwhile building them from scratch. Now that you're familiar with wizard-created forms, take on the building of a form from scratch, and see the differences in the following exercise using the Forms toolbar, shown here. (Display the Forms toolbar by choosing Forms from the View menu and dragging the blue title bar of the flyout menu away from the menu to create a "floating" toolbar.)

Here you will build a request for literature, which could be built with a wizard, but this design calls for it to be laid out with Formatted text quite differently from what the wizard would do.

1. With the Project Team Questionnaire still open in FrontPage, click New Page on the toolbar to open a blank page.

2. Open the Page Properties dialog box by selecting Properties on the File menu, and type **Literature Request** for the title. Click OK to close the dialog box.

3. At the top of the new page, type **Literature Request**, center it, and format it as Heading 1.

4. Insert a horizontal line under the title by use of the Horizontal Line option on the Insert menu.

5. On the first line below the horizontal line, select the One-Line Text Box tool from the Forms toolbar. A text box will appear within the dashed line representing a form followed by the Submit and Reset form buttons.

6. Place the cursor to the left of the Submit button, and press ENTER to move the buttons to a separate line.

7. Right-click the text box, and from the context menu, select Form Field Properties to open the Text Box Properties dialog box, type **First** for the name, change the width to **25**, leave the other defaults as shown next, and click OK.

8. Move the insertion point to the left of the new text box, select the Formatted paragraph style, type **First Name:**, and leave a space before the text box.

9. Move the insertion point to the right of the text box, leave two spaces, type **Last Name:**, leave a space, and insert a second one-line text box named **Last** with a width of **25**. Click OK, press RIGHT ARROW, and then SHIFT+ENTER to start a new line within the form.

10. Type **Company:**, leave four spaces, insert a one-line text box named **Company**, change the width to **63** characters, click OK, and press RIGHT ARROW and then SHIFT+ENTER. (The 63 characters make the second line equal to the first line on *my* screen; yours may be different. You can change this number if you want.)

11. Type **Address:**, leave four spaces, insert a one-line text box named **Address1** with a width of **25**, and click OK.

12. Press RIGHT ARROW, leave two spaces, type **Address 2:**, leave a space, insert a one-line text box named **Address2** with a width of **25**, click OK, and press RIGHT ARROW and then SHIFT+ENTER.

13. Type **City:**, leave seven spaces, insert a one-line text box named **City** with a width of **25**, press RIGHT ARROW, leave two spaces, type **State:**, leave a space, insert a one-line text box named **State** with an initial value of **WA**, change the width to **9** characters, press RIGHT ARROW, leave two spaces, type **Zip:**, leave a space, insert a one-line text box named **Zip** with a width of **12** characters, and press RIGHT ARROW and then SHIFT+ENTER.

14. Type **Phone:**, leave six spaces, insert a one-line text box named **Phone** with a width of **25**, press RIGHT ARROW, leave two spaces, type **E-mail:**, leave four

spaces, insert a one-line text box named **Email** with a width of **25**, and press RIGHT ARROW and then SHIFT+ENTER.

15. Click Check Box on the Forms toolbar, give it the name **Literature**, accept the defaults shown next, and click OK. Press RIGHT ARROW, but do not enter a space, and then type

    Click here if you wish literature.

    (include the period). Leave six spaces. (The number of spaces you need in order to make the right end line up may be different.)

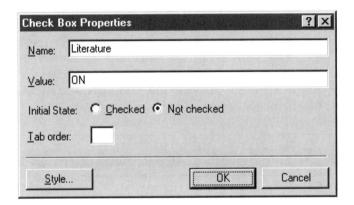

16. Type **Which products?**, leave a space, and click Drop-Down Menu on the Forms toolbar. In the Drop-Down Menu Properties dialog box, type **Lit_Products** for the Name, and click Add to open the Add Choice dialog box. Type **Portable model** and click Selected as the Initial State, as shown next.

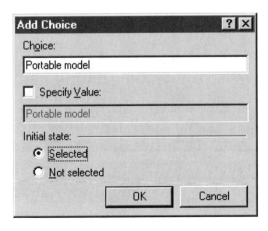

17. Click OK and then click Add twice more to add the choices of **Desktop model** and **Floor model**. In both cases, leave the Initial State as Not Selected. In the Drop-Down Menu Properties dialog box, click Yes to Allow Multiple Selections, so that your dialog box looks like Figure 9-9.

18. Click OK. Select both the "Which products?" label and the drop-down menu box by dragging across them, and press CTRL+C to copy them to the Clipboard. You'll use this twice again. Move the insertion point to the end of the line and press SHIFT+ENTER.

19. Insert a check box named **Use**, accept the defaults, and click OK. Press RIGHT ARROW and immediately type

    Click here if you use our products.

    Leave five spaces (the number of spaces you need to align the labels may be different on your system), and press CTRL+V to paste in your "Which products?" label and drop-down menu. Right-click the drop-down menu, choose Form Field Properties, change the Name to **Use_Products**, and click OK. Move the insertion point to the end of the line and press SHIFT+ENTER.

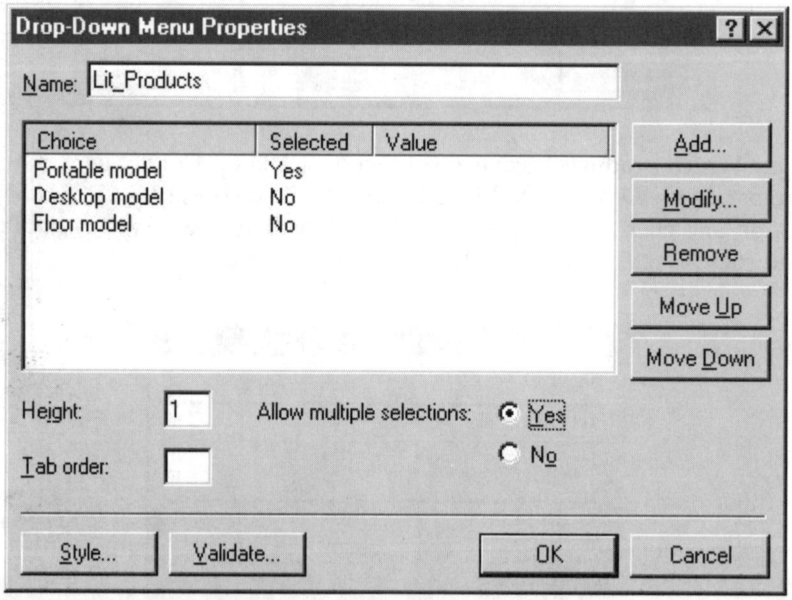

Figure 9-9. Drop-Down Menu Properties dialog box

20. Insert a check box named **Plan**, accept the defaults, and click OK. Press RIGHT ARROW, and immediately type

      Click here if planning our products.

      Leave four spaces and press CTRL+V to paste in your "Which products?" label and drop-down menu.

21. Right-click the drop-down menu. If FrontPage finds any words in the drop-down menu text that are not in the dictionary, the Spelling context menu is displayed. Select an option on the context menu for each word found. When the spell-check is complete, right-clicking the drop-down menu will display the standard context menu. From there, choose Form Field Properties, change the Name to **Plan_Products**, and click OK. Move the insertion point to the end of the line and press SHIFT+ENTER.

22. On the new line, type

      What is your company size?

      Leave three spaces, and click Radio Button on the Forms toolbar. In the Radio Button Properties dialog box, enter a Group Name of **Size**, a Value of **Less than 50**, an Initial State of Not Selected, as shown next, and then click OK.

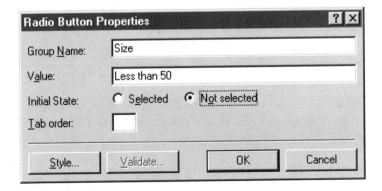

23. Press RIGHT ARROW, and immediately type

      Less than 50

      Leave three spaces, insert a Not Selected radio button with a Group Name of **Size** and a Value of **50 to 500**, press RIGHT ARROW, and immediately type

      50 to 500

Leave three spaces, insert a third Not Selected radio button with a Group Name of **Size** and Value of **Over 500**, press RIGHT ARROW, type

Over 500

and press SHIFT+ENTER.

24. Type

Please give us any comments you wish:

Click Scrolling Text Box on the Forms toolbar, type a Name of **Comments** in the Scrolling Text Box Properties dialog box, enter a width of **36**, and click OK.

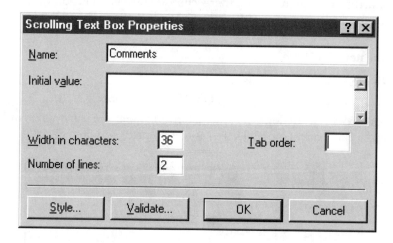

25. Right-click Submit and open the Push Button Properties dialog box. Type a Name of **Submit** and a Value/Label of **Submit Form**. Make sure the Button Type is Submit, as shown next, and click OK.

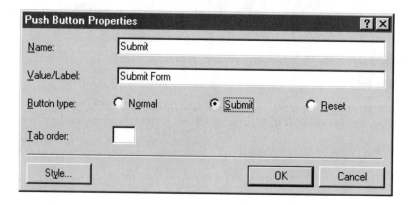

Tip   *Push buttons are placed in forms by use of the Push Button button on the Forms toolbar.*

26. Right-click Reset and open the Push Button Properties dialog box. Name the button **Reset** with a Value/Label of **Reset Form**, select a Button Type of Reset, click OK, save your form with a File Name of **Literature.htm**, and you're done! The result should look like Figure 9-10.

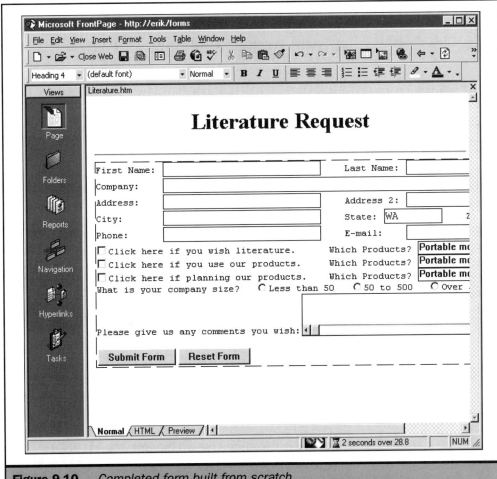

Figure 9-10.   *Completed form built from scratch*

27. Well, almost done. You still need a handler to process the input from the form. Right-click the form and choose Form Properties. In the Form Properties dialog box, the Send To radio button should be selected.

28. In the File Name text box, type **_Private/Literate.txt** for the filename, and then click Options. In the File Results tab of the Options For Saving Results Of Form dialog box, select Text Database Using Tab As A Separator for the File Format, and turn off Include Field Names. In the Saved Fields tab, select User Name For Additional Information To Save, and select the first option after None in the Date Format drop-down list, then click OK twice to get back to your form. Now you are done, so save your form once more.

Note	*Much of the spacing and wording in this form was done interactively—in other words, by use of the "try it and see what it looks like" approach. The beauty of a WYSIWYG form editor is that you can immediately see what the form you're building looks like and change it if needed.*

Part of the purpose of this "from scratch" example was to see what the Form Page Wizard does for you. You must admit it's a lot. The wizard saves you the hassle of naming, spacing, and layout, not to mention the setup of the form handling. For longer forms like this, the Form Page Wizard offers a lot of advantages.

Handling Form Input

The next step is to look at your forms in a browser. The web called Forms should still be active on your screen and should have three pages: a blank page named Home Page, a Project Team Questionnaire page built with the Form Page Wizard, and a Literature Request form built from scratch. To use the web, you'll need to put some links on the Home page to the two forms. To do that and then try out the forms in a browser, follow these steps:

1. In FrontPage, open the Home Page in Page view. At the top of the page, type **Forms Examples**, format it as Heading 1, and press ENTER.

2. On the next line, type **Form Page Wizard**, format it as Heading 4, select the three words you just typed, and click Hyperlink on the toolbar. In the Create Hyperlink dialog box, select Project Team Questionnaire (Project.htm), and click OK. Move the insertion point to the end of the line and press ENTER.

3. Type **Custom Form**, format it as Heading 4, select the words, and click Hyperlink on the toolbar. In the Create Hyperlink dialog box, select Literature Request (Literature.htm), and click OK. Your Home page should now look like Figure 9-11. Save this page, put a "Home" link back to the Home page at the bottom of each form, and save each of them.

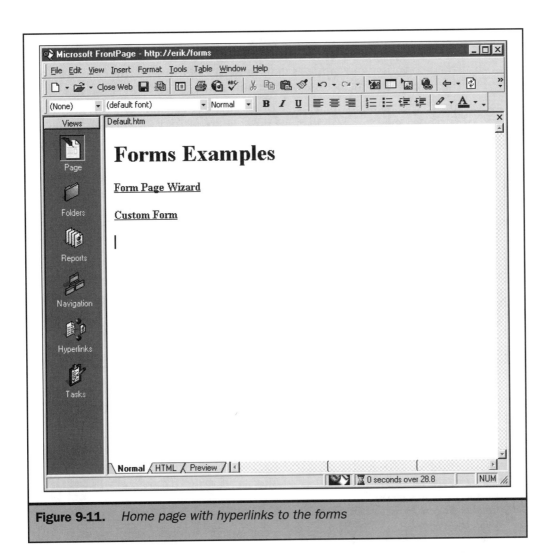

Figure 9-11. *Home page with hyperlinks to the forms*

4. Open your favorite browser and display the Forms web. Select the Form Page Wizard to open the Project Team Questionnaire, and submit it without filling in the First Name field. Immediately an error message is displayed, as shown here:

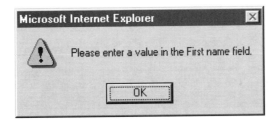

5. Fill out the form and submit it again. Almost immediately you'll see another benefit of FrontPage—an automatic confirmation form is created for you and is used here to verify your input, as you can see in Figure 9-12. Click the Return To The Form link at the bottom of the confirmation page.

6. Use the Home Page link to get back to the Home page, and then select Custom Form to open the Literature Request form. Fill it out and click Submit Form. Again you'll see the automatic confirmation report. Click Return To The Form, and then close your browser.

> **Note**
>
> *The "beautiful" symmetry of the form in FrontPage Page view (previously shown in Figure 9-10) has not carried over to the browser, as shown in Figure 9-13. If you look at the form in different browsers, you'll notice different spacing. The user can also change the spacing by selecting different fonts in the browser. In a table, the form's appearance would be much improved.*

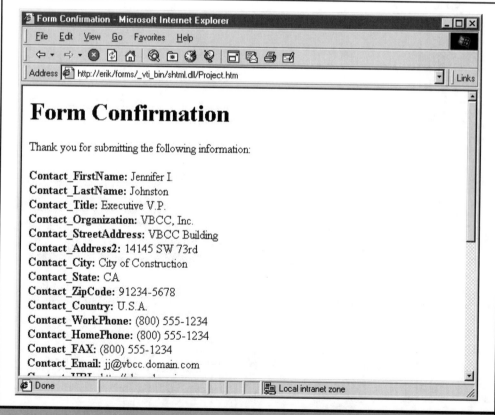

Figure 9-12. *Automatic confirmation page created by FrontPage*

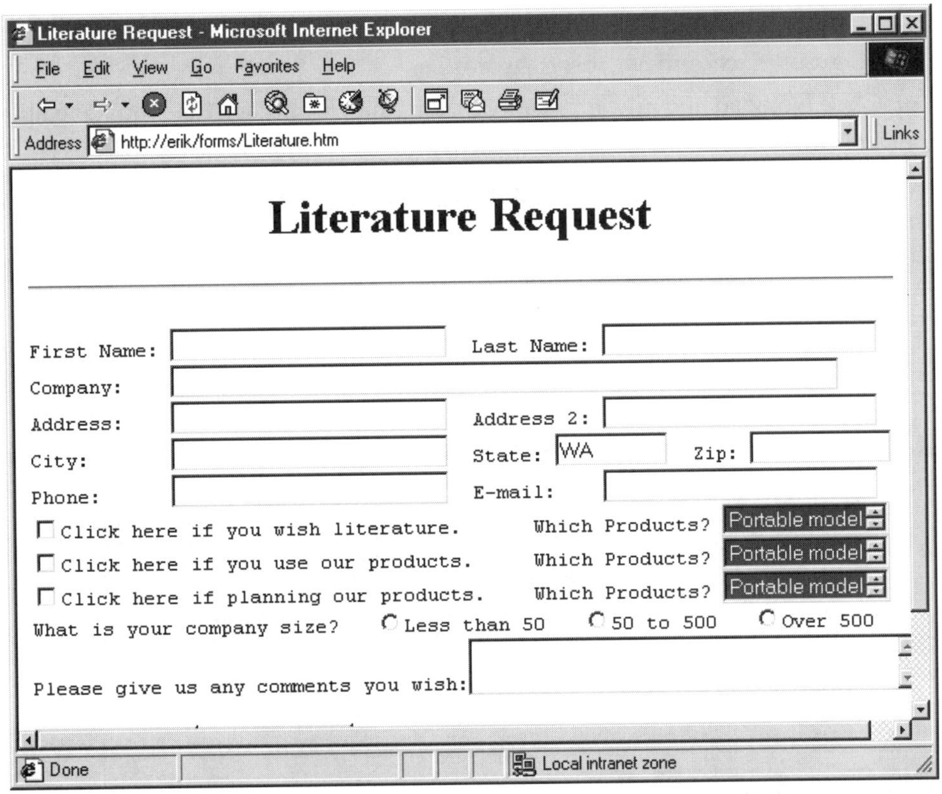

Figure 9-13.   *Literature Request form loses its symmetry in a browser (Internet Explorer)*

7. Open the file that was created by the WebBot Save Results Component from the Project Team Questionnaire. If you used the default directories when you installed FrontPage, this should be located at C:\Inetpub\Wwwroot\Forms\ Proj_ans.txt. Use Windows Explorer or My Computer to locate it, and then double-click it to open it in Notepad. What you see should look something like this:

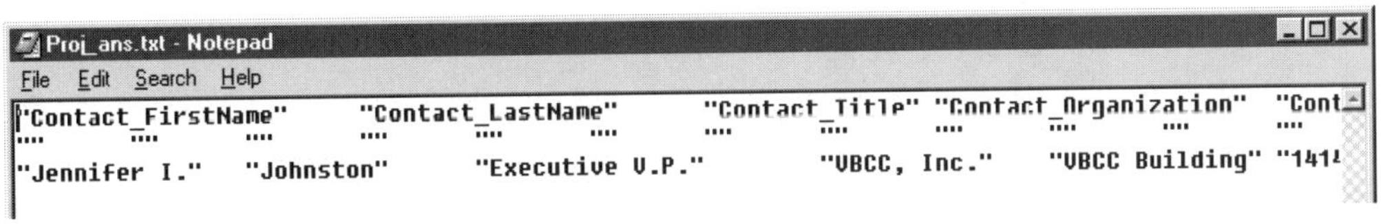

8. You can also open the files saved from either form in a database program or in a spreadsheet. Figure 9-14 shows the Project Team Questionnaire data in Microsoft Excel and Microsoft Access.

9. Close Notepad and any applications other than FrontPage that you have open. In FrontPage, close your Forms web.

As you can see, FrontPage not only provides significant power for creating a form, but it also does a lot to get the data collected on the form back to you. Also, in the data collection area, a form created with the Form Page Wizard does not necessarily have an advantage over a properly set up custom form. In Chapter 18 you'll learn how to insert the form data directly into a database.

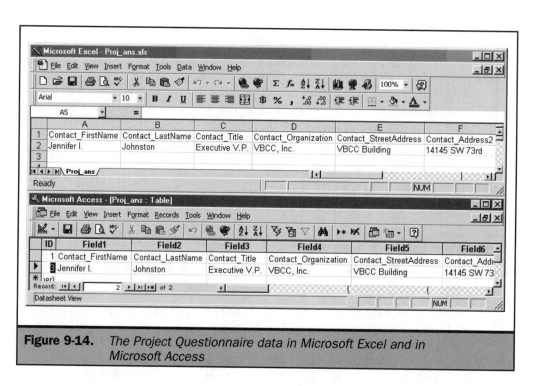

Figure 9-14. *The Project Questionnaire data in Microsoft Excel and in Microsoft Access*

Chapter 10

Using FrontPage Components

As you have read in earlier chapters, a component is a way you can add automation to your web, often to provide interactivity with the user. Some components are buried in other features, such as the form-handling components that you saw in Chapter 9, while others are stand-alone tools that you can use directly. The stand-alone components, shown in the following illustration of the Insert menu Component fly-out, are the subject of this chapter (they are also listed in Chapter 2's Table 2-8). The Banner Ad Manager, Hover Button, and Marquee components in the Components fly-out will be covered in Chapter 19. There are four additional components you can use that are opened from the Insert menu rather than from the Component fly-out. These are the Date and Time component, opened with the Date and Time option; the Comment component, opened with the Comment option; the Navigation Bar component, opened with the Navigation Bar option; and the Page Banner component, opened with the Page Banner option. The Navigation Bar component was discussed in Chapter 7.

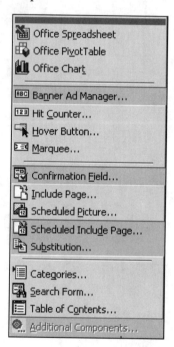

The Advanced fly-out in the Insert menu contains one additional component, the HTML component, which allows you to include an HTML command that is not otherwise supported directly on a web page. This component will be discussed in Chapter 13.

Note   *In earlier versions of FrontPage, the FrontPage components were referred to as WebBots or bots. In some cases Microsoft still uses this term, and it appears in the code generated by FrontPage. For all practical purposes, the terms WebBot, bot, and component can be used interchangeably.*

Incorporating Components in Your Webs

See how you can incorporate FrontPage Components in your own webs by trying out several of the stand-alone components in the following sections. Begin by opening a new One Page Web named **Components** and then opening its Home page in FrontPage Page view.

Comment Component

The Comment component allows you to insert notes that you want to be visible while the web is in Page view, but invisible or hidden while the web is being viewed in a browser. To see how that works, follow these steps:

1. On the blank home page in Page view, type

   This is normal text.

   (include the period) and press ENTER.

2. From the Insert menu, choose Comment. The Comment dialog box opens, as shown next. Here you can type any text you want to see in Page view but not in a browser.

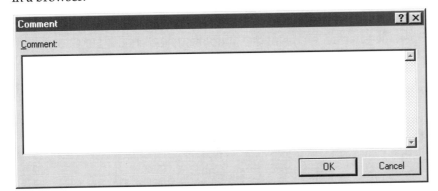

3. Type

   This is comment text that should not be visible in a browser.

   (include the period) and then click OK. The comment text will appear in Page view as shown next.

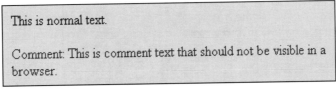

This is normal text.

Comment: This is comment text that should not be visible in a browser.

4. Save your web page, open it in a browser, and all you'll see is the normal first line.

Hit Counter Component

Hit counters were popular in the past, but most are actually useless for compiling any real information about traffic on a web site. What they record is *page views,* the number of times a particular web page has been loaded by a browser. Advertisers are generally more interested in *visits,* the actual number of people who access a site. One visit will have a number of page views. If the visitor reloads a page, the hit counter will record it as a separate hit, which is what limits the hit counter's usefulness. Hit counters can be fun to have on a page, though, especially if you don't take them seriously.

> **Note**
>
> *For an excellent explanation of web site statistics, see* Web Site Stats *by Rick Stout (Osborne/McGraw-Hill, 1997). The included CD-ROM contains versions of popular web-tracking software, which are much more useful than the hit counter. If you intend to have advertising on your site, you will need to provide better statistics than the hit counter can provide. These statistics come from analyzing the web server logs, as explained in Stout's book.*

Adding a hit counter to a page requires only a few steps:

1. In Page view, move the cursor to the line after your comment.
2. Open the Insert menu, point on Component, and choose Hit Counter. The Hit Counter Properties dialog box is displayed.

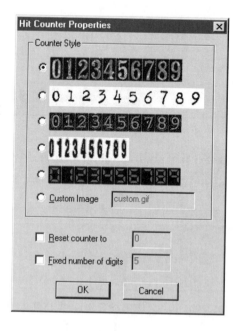

In the Hit Counter Properties dialog box, you can select the type of numbers to be displayed, the starting number for the counter, and a fixed number of digits to be displayed. Each digit is actually a graphic; you can use the ones included with FrontPage, download others from the Web, or create your own. The Reset Counter To option lets you set the starting number for the counter. The Fixed Number Of Digits option will always cause the number of digits selected to be displayed. If you accept the default of 5, the first visit will be 00001; when the count reaches 99999, the next visit will roll the counter over to 00000 again.

Tip

To create you own counter graphic, you create a single GIF file with the numbers 0 to 9. Each number is 10 percent of the total width of the graphic. If your graphic is 120 pixels wide, zero would be the first 10 percent of the graphic (12 pixels), one would be the next 10 percent, and so on.

3. Select any of the Counter Style options, and click the Fixed Number Of Digits check box. Accept the default of 5. Click OK. In Page view a text placeholder is inserted.

4. Save the page and refresh it in your browser. The hit counter will appear similar to this:

> This is normal text.
>
> 0 0 0 0 1

5. Minimize your browser, close the open page in Page view, and close the Components web.

Confirmation Field Component

The Confirmation Field component allows you to build a confirmation page that echoes the contents of a web form that has been submitted. Such a page would replace the automatic confirmation form you saw in Chapter 9 (Figure 9-12). To build a confirmation page for your Literature Request form:

1. In FrontPage, open the Forms web you created in Chapter 9, and then open the Literature Request form in Page view.

2. In Page view, create a new Normal page. On the new page you'll create a brief confirmation letter. Begin by putting a heading on the page, such as

   Great Products Company

   formatting it as Heading 1, centering it, and then pressing ENTER.

3. Click Align Left on the toolbar; then at the left margin, type **To:** and press SHIFT+ENTER.

4. Open the Insert menu and choose Component | Confirmation Field. In the Confirmation Field Properties dialog box, type **First**, as shown next, and then click OK.

5. Leave a space, again open the Confirmation Field Properties dialog box, type **Last**, click OK, and press SHIFT+ENTER for a new line.

There is no easy way to get a list of field names—you need to either remember them or write them down as you are creating a form, or open the Properties dialog box for each field. A suggestion has been made to Microsoft that a "Browse" feature be added to the Confirmation Field Properties dialog box.

6. Repeat step 4 to enter confirmation fields for **Company**, **Address1**, and **Address2** all on separate lines ending with SHIFT+ENTER.

7. Again repeat step 4 to enter confirmation fields for **City**, **State**, and **Zip** all on one line, with a comma and a space between "City" and "State," and a space between "State" and "Zip."

8. Enter two blank lines and type the body and ending of the letter, something similar to that shown in Figure 10-1. Follow this with a link that says **Return to the form** and points to the Literature Request form. When you are done, save the confirmation letter with a page title of **Literature Request Confirmation** and a filename of **Litreqcf.htm**.

9. Open the Literature Request form, right-click the form, choose Form Properties, click Options, and then click the Confirmation Page tab. Click Browse, and double-click Literature Request Confirmation. Your Options For Saving Results Of Form dialog box should be as shown next. Click OK twice. Save the Literature Request form and close any open pages.

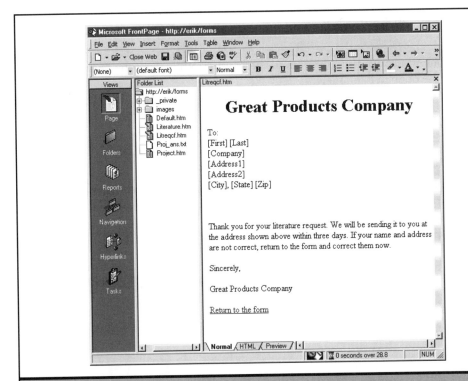

Figure 10-1.   *Literature Request Confirmation letter in FrontPage Page view*

10. In your browser, open the Forms web, click Custom Form, fill out the form, click Submit Form, and you'll see a confirmation letter similar to the one shown in Figure 10-2.

11. Close your browser and your Forms web.

For more on confirmation forms, see the "Confirmation Form Template" section of Chapter 4.

Include and Scheduled Include Page Components

The Include Page component allows you to include one web page on another. For example, if you wanted a section with identical contents on every page, you could put the contents on a web page and then include that page on all others in the web. Future changes to the contents of that page would then automatically appear on all the pages that include the page. The Scheduled Include Page component allows you to include one page on another for a given period. When the time expires, that page is no longer included.

To try this, follow these steps:

1. In FrontPage, open the Components web, and double-click the Home page to open the page in Page view.

2. Click New Page on the toolbar to create a new page. At the top of the page, type

   This is a page heading, it should be on all pages.

   (include the period) and format it as Heading 2. Save this page with the page title **Included Header** and a filename of **Inchead.htm**.

3. Return to the Home page, place the insertion point at the top of the page, open the Insert menu and choose Component | Include Page to open the Include Page Component Properties dialog box.

4. Click Browse to get a list of pages in the current web.

5. Double-click the Included Header page, and then click OK to return to the web page. You should see the heading appear on this page and the WebBot icon appear when you move the mouse pointer over it, as shown next:

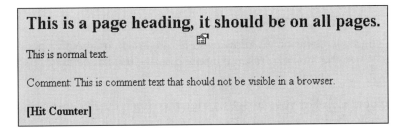

The real beauty of using the Include Page component is that not only are you saved from retyping or copying the heading onto each page, but also changes you make need only be typed once. The Scheduled Include Page component works like the Include Page component, except that it has a start and stop date and time, as will be demonstrated next, with the Scheduled Image component.

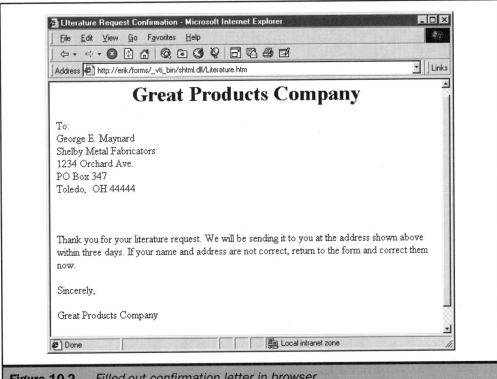

Figure 10-2. *Filled-out confirmation letter in browser*

Scheduled Image Component

The Scheduled Image Component allows you to display an image on a page for a fixed period. When the time expires, the image disappears. To see how this works, take these steps:

1. In Folder List select your Images folder, then open the File menu and choose Import. In the Import dialog box click Add File. In the Add File To Import List dialog box open your Clipart folder (C:\Program Files\Common Files\ Microsoft Shared\Clipart by default), then open the Cagcat50 folder. Select the first file (An01124_2.wmf). Click Open and then OK. (If you do not have the file An01124_2.wmf, you will need to do a custom installation of FrontPage 2000 and choose to install additional clip art. For this exercise you can choose any available image.)

2. On the Home page of the Components web in Page view, move the insertion point to the end of the comment line and press ENTER to create a blank line between the comment and the hit counter.

3. Open the Insert menu and choose Component | Scheduled Picture. In the Scheduled Picture Properties dialog box, shown in Figure 10-3, click the first Browse to open the Picture dialog box. In the Picture dialog box, double-click Images. Select An01124_2.wmf (or the picture you imported in step 1) and click OK.

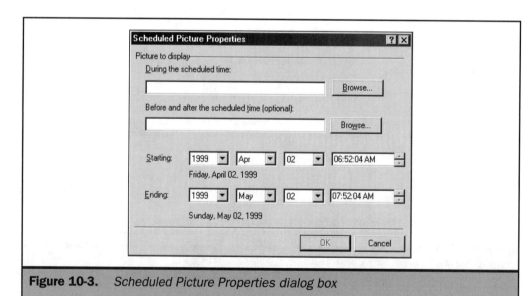

Figure 10-3.   *Scheduled Picture Properties dialog box*

4. Set the ending time for a couple of minutes past the current time in the Ending Date And Time spinner. (The default is to display the image for one month.) Click OK. You should see the image appear in Page view.

```
┌───────────────────────────────────────────────────────────────┐
│  Ending date and time: ────────────────────────────────        │
│                                                                 │
│   ┌─────────┐ ┌─────────┐ ┌─────────┐ ┌──────────────────┐     │
│   │ 1998  ▼ │ │ Oct   ▼ │ │ 04    ▼ │ │ 09:00:00 AM    ▲ │     │
│   └─────────┘ └─────────┘ └─────────┘ └──────────────────▼┘     │
│                                                                 │
│   Sunday, October 04, 1998                                      │
└───────────────────────────────────────────────────────────────┘
```

5. Save your web page and open your browser and the Components web. If necessary, click the Refresh button in the Internet Explorer Standard toolbar or the Reload button in the Netscape Navigator Navigation bar.

    You should see your lion graphic, as shown in Figure 10-4.

6. After the time has expired, go back to FrontPage Page view displaying the Components web Home page, and click Refresh on the toolbar or select Refresh from the View menu.

    The lion graphic will be replaced with the message "[Expired Scheduled Picture]." If you return to your browser and refresh it, the graphic will also disappear from there.

7. Minimize your browser.

Page Banner Component

The Page Banner component is similar to the Include Page component; it allows you to select an image or text to use as a banner at the top of a web page. Banners are usually larger graphics that identify the site or the page contents.

If the web page does not use a theme or a shared border, then the page title is inserted, and choosing Image in the Page Banner Properties dialog box has no effect. If a theme has been applied, the theme's banner image is inserted when Image is selected. If the page has a top shared border, then a page banner is created automatically.

1. On the Home page in Page view, press CTRL+HOME and then press ENTER. Press UP ARROW if necessary to move the cursor to the top of the page.

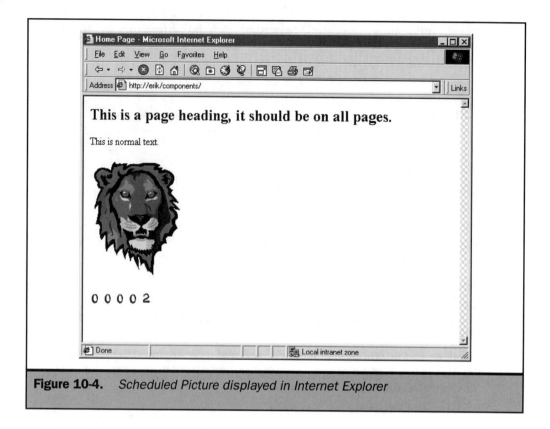

Figure 10-4. *Scheduled Picture displayed in Internet Explorer*

2. Open the Insert menu and choose Page Banner to open the Page Banner Properties dialog box, shown here:

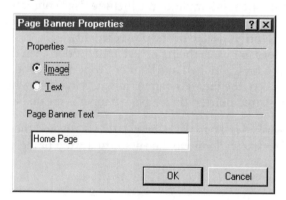

3. Select Text, type **Components Home Page** in the Page Banner Text text box, and click OK. The page banner text is inserted on the page.

4. Save your work.

Substitution Component

The Substitution component replaces a value on a web page with a configuration variable when the page is viewed by the user. A *configuration variable* contains specific information about either the current page or the current web. There are four predefined configuration variables, as shown in Table 10-1, and you can define additional ones in the FrontPage Web Settings dialog box Parameters tab opened from the Tools menu. You can see how this works with the following instructions:

1. In the Folders view, while it is still displaying the Components web, right-click the Home page (Default.htm), and choose Properties. The page's Properties dialog box will open with the General tab showing, as you can see in Figure 10-5.

2. If it isn't already open, click the General tab of the page's Properties dialog box so you can see the Location field. Click the Summary tab to see the Created By and Modified By fields, and to both see and change the Comments scrolling text box, as shown in Figure 10-6.

3. In the Comments scrolling text box, type

   This is a great web!

   click Apply, and then click OK to close the Properties dialog box.

4. At the bottom of the Home page in Page view, type

   This page was last modified by

   leave a space, open the Insert menu, point on Component, and click Substitution. The Substitution Properties dialog box will open.

Variable	Description
Author	Name that is in the Created By field of the FrontPage current page's Properties dialog box Summary tab (opened from the File menu, Properties option).
Modified By	Name of the person who most recently changed the page, contained in the Modified By field of the FrontPage current page's Properties dialog box Summary tab.
Description	Contents of the Comments scrolling text box of the FrontPage current page's Properties dialog box Summary tab.
Page URL	Filename in the Location field of the FrontPage current page's Properties dialog box General tab.

Table 10-1.   *Configuration Variables*

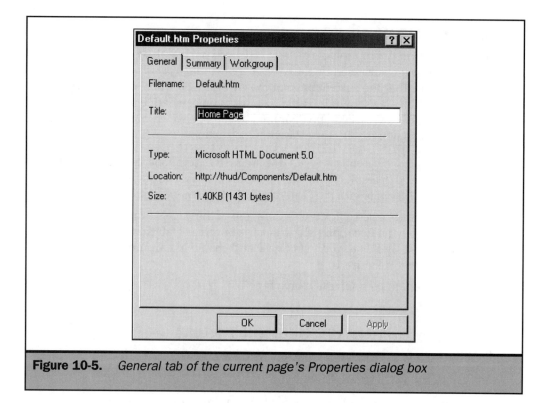

Figure 10-5. *General tab of the current page's Properties dialog box*

5. Click the down arrow to see the list of variables shown next. Click Modified By and then OK. You'll see the name of the person who last modified the page appear on the Home page in Page view.

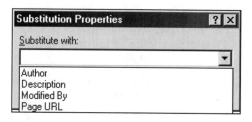

6. Leave a space and then type

    who left these comments:

    leave a space, and from the Substitution Properties dialog box, choose Description. Click OK.

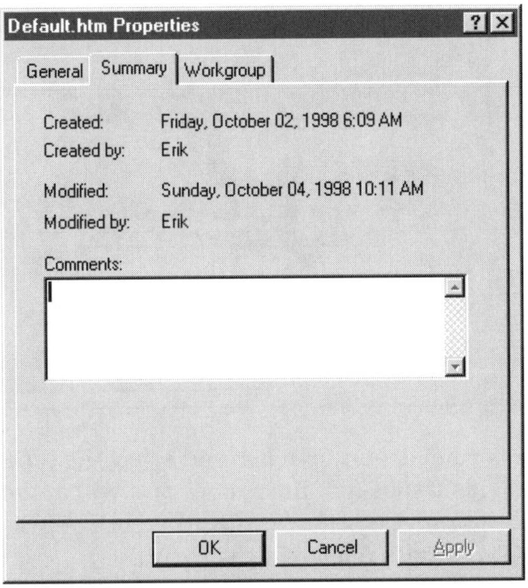

Figure 10-6. *Summary tab of the current page's Properties dialog box*

CREATING WEB SITES

The comments you left should appear, as you can see here:

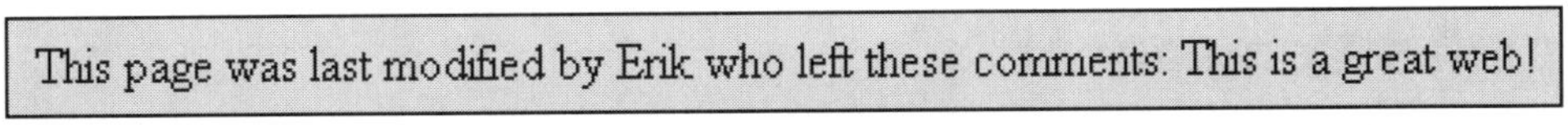

This page was last modified by Erik who left these comments: This is a great web!

Date and Time Component

The Date and Time component inserts either the date (and optionally, the time the page was last saved), or the date and time (optional) the page was last automatically updated and saved. Also, the page is automatically updated when an included page is updated, even if there were no changes to the active page. To see this, follow these steps:

1. In Page view, move the cursor to the line below your Substitution component comments, and then type **This page was last saved on**. Leave a space and don't include the period.

2. Open the Insert menu, and choose Date and Time to display the Date and Time
   Properties dialog box.

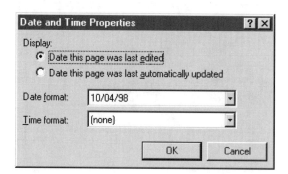

3. Open the Time Format drop-down list, and select the time format that ends
   with "AM TZ." This stands for "time zone" and will automatically insert the
   time zone your computer is set to, as the difference between Greenwich Mean
   Time (GMT). (GMT is also referred to as Zulu.).

4. Click OK. The date and time your page was last saved should appear,
   as shown here:

> This page was last saved on 04/02/99 08:14:29 AM -0800

5. Save your work and close your Components web.

Categories Component

The Categories component provides an automated method for creating hyperlinks to
web pages, based on the content of the pages. This is accomplished by assigning each
page to a category. The Categories component then creates the links to the page based
on the category. When a page is added or removed from a category, the hyperlink is
also updated. The first step is to create Master Categories for your web:

1. Open your Forms web in FrontPage.

2. In Folders view, right-click the Home page (Default.htm) and choose
   Properties.

3. In the Default.htm Properties dialog box, select the Workgroup tab, shown in
   Figure 10-7.

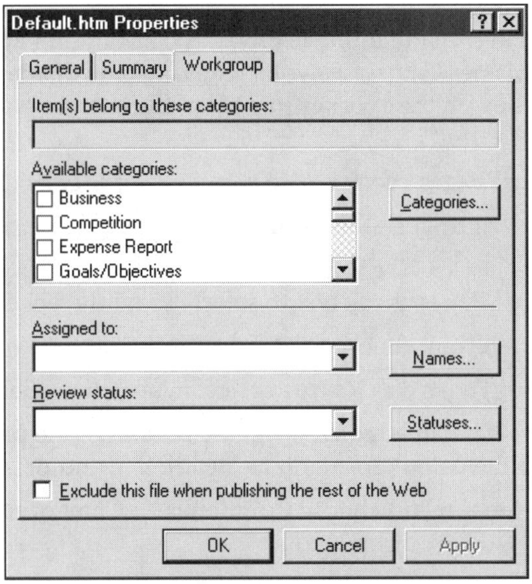

Figure 10-7.   *Workgroup tab of the current page's Properties dialog box*

4. Click the Categories button to open the Master Category List dialog box, shown next.

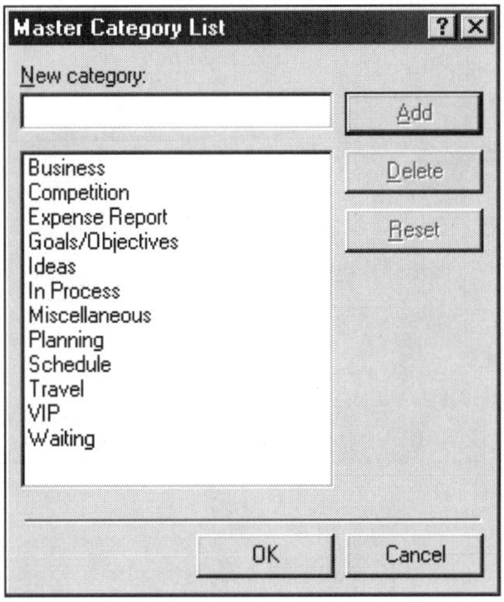

5. In the New Category text box, type **Wizard Pages** and click Add.

6. Delete any text in the single-line text box, type **Manual Pages**, click Add, and then OK. The Master Categories you created will be displayed in the Available Categories list box on the Workgroup tab of the current page's Properties dialog box.

7. Click the Manual Pages check box to select it, and then click OK.

8. In Folders view, right-click Literature.htm, choose Properties, and then the Workgroup tab.

9. Click the Manual Pages check box to select it, and then click OK.

10. Right-click Project.htm, choose Properties, and then the Workgroup tab.

11. Click the Wizard Pages check box to select it, and then click OK.

12. Open the Home page in Page view. At the bottom of the page, type **Wizard Pages:** (include the colon), format it as Heading 3, and press ENTER.

13. Open the Insert menu and choose Component | Categories. The Categories dialog box, shown here, is opened.

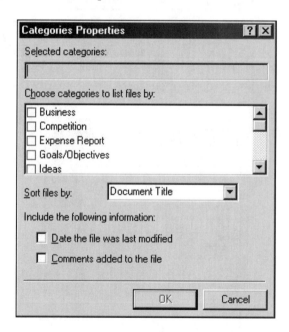

The Categories dialog box displays the Master Categories you created previously and several options for how the hyperlinks will be displayed. You can choose to display the hyperlinks sorted by either the date the page was last modified or by the page title, using the Sort Files By drop-down. You can also include the date the page was last modified and/or any comments for the page (comments are added using the Summary tab of the current page's Properties dialog box).

14. Click the Wizard Pages and the Date The Page Was Last Modified check boxes to select them. Accept the other defaults and click OK.

15. Save your work and then open the Forms web Home page in your browser. A hyperlink, showing the page title of the web's wizard page and the date it was last modified, is displayed, as shown in Figure 10-8.

16. In the FrontPage Page view, press CTRL+END to move the cursor to the bottom of the page, and type **Manual Pages:** (include the colon). Format it as Heading 3 and press ENTER.

17. Open the Insert menu and choose Component | Categories.

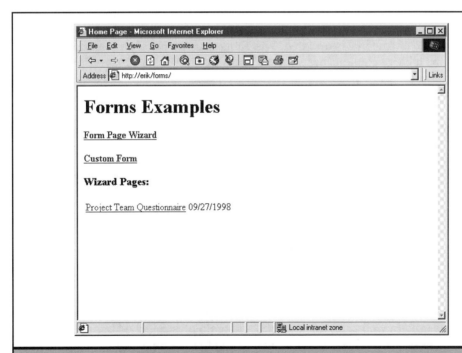

Figure 10-8.   *Hyperlink created with AutoLinks component in Internet Explorer*

18. In the Categories Properties dialog box, select Manual Pages in the Choose Categories To List Files By list box and Document Title from the Sort Pages By drop-down list. Click OK.

19. Save your work and refresh the Forms Home page in your browser. A hyperlink to the Home and Literature Request pages is displayed.

20. In Folders view, right-click Literature.htm, choose Properties, and then the Workgroup tab.

21. Click the Wizard Pages check box, and then OK.

22. Open the Literature Request page in Page view, save your work, and then refresh the Forms Home page in your browser. A new hyperlink for the Literature Request page appears under the Wizard Pages heading. Since the Literature Request page is assigned to both categories, it appears in both hyperlink lists.

23. Close your browser and the Forms web.

Table of Contents Component

The Table of Contents component creates and maintains a table of contents for a web, with links to all the pages in the web. Whenever the web's contents are changed and resaved, the table of contents is updated. The Table of Contents component builds the structure of the table of contents based on the links that are on each page. For example, if the home page has three pages directly linked to it and the second page has two other pages linked to it, the following structure would be built:

Home Page

    First Page

    Second Page

        Linked Page One

        Linked Page Two

    Third Page

If there are pages in the web that are not linked to other pages, they are listed at the end of the table of contents.

Chapters 3 and 4 discuss (and have several examples of) the Table of Contents component as used in web and page wizards and templates. See the "Using the Corporate Presence Wizard" section in Chapter 3 and the "Table of Contents Template" section in Chapter 4.

When you add the Table of Contents component to a page, you do not see the full table of contents. It is only when you open the page in a browser that the full table is displayed.

When you select the Table of Contents component from the Insert menu, the Table Of Contents Properties dialog box will open, as shown here:

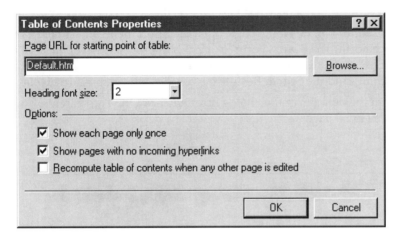

The options in this dialog box are as follows:

- **Page URL For Starting Point Of Table** should be the home page of the web, unless you want a subsidiary table of contents for a section of a web.

- **Heading Font Size** is the size of the top entry in the table. Each subsidiary entry is one size smaller.

- **Show Each Page Only Once** prevents a page that has links from several pages from being listed under each page.

- **Show Pages With No Incoming Hyperlinks** allows unlinked pages to be listed.

- **Recompute Table Of Contents When Any Other Page Is Edited** forces the table to be rebuilt if any page in the web is changed. Since this can take a significant amount of time, you may not want to do this. A table of contents is also rebuilt every time the page it is on is saved, which should normally be adequate.

 Using the Table of Contents component can be a good way to initially establish a link from the home page to all the other pages in the web.

Search Form Component

The Search Form component creates a form in which users can enter any text that they want to search for in the current web. After users enter such text and click the Search button, the Search Form component carries out the search and returns the locations where the text was found. To look at how this is done, take these steps:

1. Open your Components web in FrontPage; then open the Home page in Page view.

2. At the bottom of the Home page, open the Insert menu and choose Component | Search Form. The Search Form Properties dialog box will open, as shown in Figure 10-9. The Search Form Properties tab displays the selections for searching, and the Search Results tab sets how the results are displayed.

3. Accept the defaults in this dialog box and click OK. The search form will appear on the Home page.

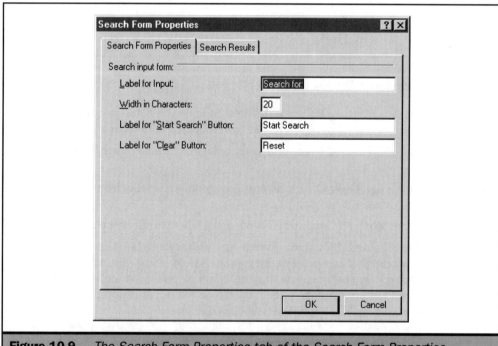

Figure 10-9.   The Search Form Properties tab of the Search Form Properties dialog box

4. Save the web page, open the page in your browser, and the search form will appear at the bottom of the page.

5. In the Search For text box, type **home** and click Start Search. In a moment, you will get the results, which should look like this:

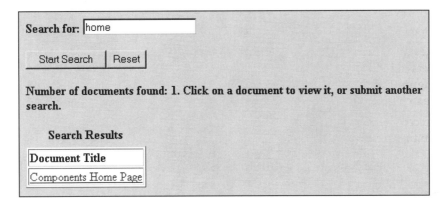

6. Close your browser and your Components web.

If you want a page not to be found by the Search Form Component (like style pages and included pages), place the pages in the _private folder of the current web; that folder is not searched. If you're using FrontPage's default folder structure and the Components web, the full path to the private folder for that web is
C:\Inetpub\Wwwroot\Components_private.

FrontPage components represent a high level of sophistication that gives you significant power to build the web you want. Much of the "gee whiz" that you saw in the wizards and templates in Chapters 3 and 4 came from these tools.

The
Complete
Reference

FrontPage
2000

Chapter 11

Advanced Formatting Techniques

In the preceding chapters you have seen many ways to lay out, format, and enhance a web page. These are, for the most part, classic techniques that have been available to web authors for some time. FrontPage 2000 brings you several advanced techniques for doing this. The purpose of this chapter is to cover these advanced techniques, including:

■ Customizing existing themes

■ Creating and using style sheets

■ Positioning and wrapping text around objects

■ Adding Dynamic HTML animation effects

■ Easily choosing Web-safe colors

Customizing Existing Themes

If you have used the themes that are available in FrontPage and looked at the many alternatives, you may have come to the conclusion that while there are many neat elements in a number of the themes, no one theme is exactly the way you would like it to be. You can solve this by customizing one of the existing themes to add your own logo; change the styles, colors, and graphics used; and then save the theme with your name. In this way you create your own theme.

At the present there is not a way to create your own theme from scratch. Supposedly in 1999 Microsoft will release a FrontPage 2000 System Development kit, or SDK, that will have that capability, but it was not available to the authors.

Modifying a Theme

You begin the process of creating a customized theme by picking an existing theme, hopefully one that is close to what you want, and opening it for modification.

1. With FrontPage open in any view, open the Format menu and choose Theme. The Themes dialog box will appear as shown in Figure 11-1.

2. Click each of the themes in the list and look at them with and without their Vivid Colors, Active Graphics, and Background Picture options.

If you cannot find a theme you like, you can choose Install Additional Themes from the top of the themes list to have more sample themes to choose from (you need to have your Office or FrontPage 2000 CD in your drive).

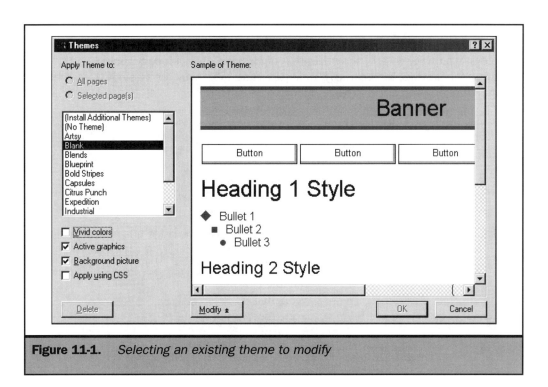

Figure 11-1.   *Selecting an existing theme to modify*

3. Select the theme and accompanying options that come closest to the theme you want to create.

4. Click Modify. An additional set of buttons opens, as you can see next, that allows you to modify the colors, graphics, and text styles in the selected theme and then save the resulting theme with a new name.

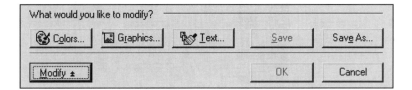

See how to change each of these elements in the next several sections.

Changing the Colors in a Theme

The colors in a theme control the coloration of all parts of a web page including the background, headings, hyperlinks, banner text, and table borders. See how to set these with the following steps:

1. Click Colors. The Modify Theme dialog box opens as shown in Figure 11-2. It provides three ways to set the colors used in a theme: ready-made color schemes, a color wheel, and custom color selection.

2. With the Color Schemes tab selected, click a number of the ready-made schemes and then scroll the Sample Of Theme preview box to see how the colors are applied.

3. Click the Color Wheel tab. Drag the small circle in the color wheel to see how the color schemes change. Also change the Brightness slider and observe its effects.

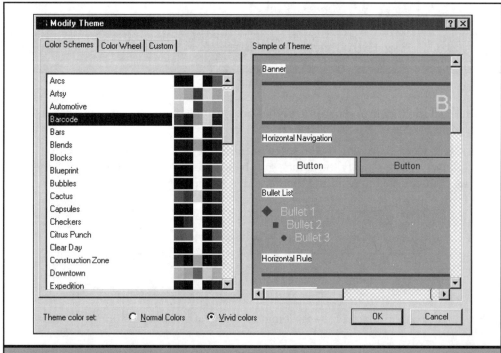

Figure 11-2. *Choosing or creating a color scheme*

4. Click the Custom tab. Click the down arrow under Item and observe the list of items on a web page for which you can set a particular color, as shown here:

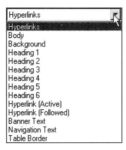

5. Select several of the page items one at a time—say, Background, Heading 1 and 2, and Banner Text—and choose a color to use for each.

6. Click the Color Schemes tab and you will see a new (Custom) scheme with the colors you chose.

7. Click OK to close the Modify Theme dialog box.

Replacing the Graphics in a Theme

The graphics that can be used on a page and set in a theme include the background, the banner, bullets, and buttons. You can change any and/or all of these with the following steps:

1. Click Graphics. The Modify Theme dialog box again opens, but this time it allows you to change the picture and font used for a particular item on the page, as you can see in Figure 11-3.

2. Open the Item drop-down list to see the list that can be changed, like this:

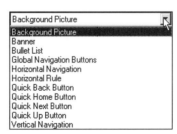

3. Select several items in the drop-down list and look at what you can select a picture for. In some cases—for example, Horizontal Navigation—there are three elements that need pictures (the regular button, the selected button, and the button that is hovered over).

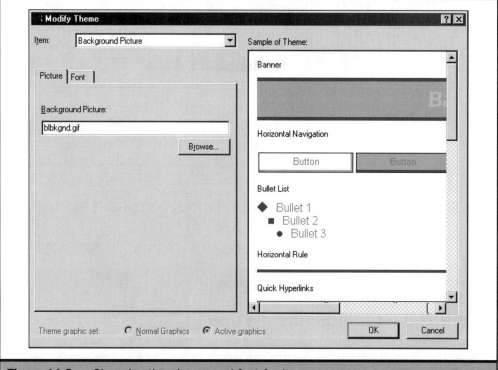

Figure 11-3.   *Choosing the picture and font for items on a page*

4. Click Browse and find an alternative graphic to use for the selected item. (The items for the current theme are in the \Windows\Temp\FrontPage TempDir\Mstheme\ folder.)

5. When you have selected a graphic to use for an item, click the Font tab. Here you can choose from a variety of fonts and select the style, size, and alignment you want to use.

6. After you have the graphics and fonts the way you want them for all the items you are using on the page, click OK to return to the Themes dialog box.

Applying Different Text Styles to a Theme

As you just saw, the Graphics button allows you to set the fonts, sizes, and font styles (bold, italic) to be used for text on the graphic items in a theme such as banners and buttons. The Text button allows you to do the same tasks for normal text (called

"Body") and headings on a web page. You can also create or modify a style sheet related to the theme. Explore theme text modification with these steps:

1. Click Text. The Modify Theme dialog box will open. In this case you can choose Body or one of the heading types and then select the font you want to use for that particular type of text.

2. Open the Item drop-down list. You can see that you have six levels of headings and Body to choose from:

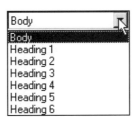

Note *Body text refers to regular text as well as hyperlinks (regular, followed, and active).*

3. With Body selected, scroll the sample until you see "Regular Text Sample," and then click several fonts you might like and see how the text looks in the sample area. For example, I like Eras. Once you find a family, look at the weights that are available and decide how you are going to assign those weights to the body and heading items. For example, here are the assignments I made, as shown in Figure 11-4:

- Heading 1: Eras Ultra
- Heading 2: Eras Bold
- Heading 3: Eras Demi
- Heading 4: Eras Medium
- Heading 5: Eras Medium
- Heading 6: Eras Medium
- Body: Eras Light

4. Select a text item (Body or one of the headings), and click a font. Repeat that for all the text items.

5. When you have completed selecting the font you want to use for all of the text items, click More Text Styles. The Style dialog box will open, like the one in Figure 11-5.

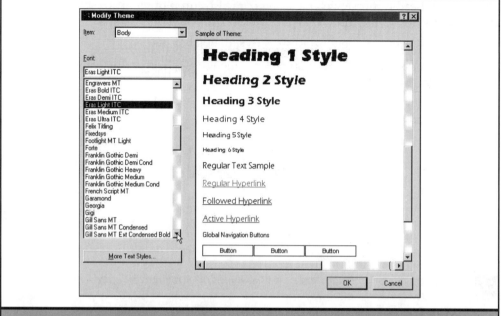

Figure 11-4. *Assigning fonts to types of text*

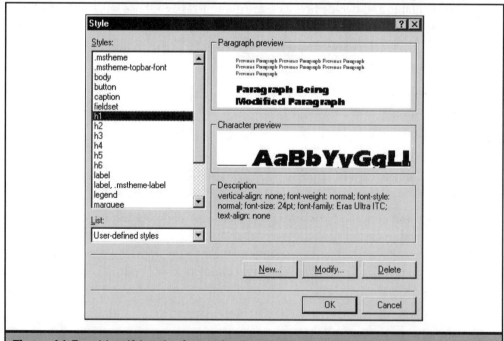

Figure 11-5. *Identifying the formatting in a particular style*

6. With User-Defined Styles selected in the List drop-down box, click Body in the Styles list. A description of that style will appear along with examples of it.

7. Click Modify to open the Modify Style dialog box and then click Format | Font. Here choose the font style, size, color, and effects that are to be used for the selected style. When you set the characteristics of the style, click OK twice.

Note   *The next section will describe style sheets, how to create them and use them in more detail.*

8. Repeat steps 6 and 7 for all the styles you want to modify. After defining all the styles, click OK to close the Style dialog box and click OK again to close the Modify Theme dialog box.

9. In the Themes dialog box, click Save As to save your changes under a new name. Enter a name and click OK. The new theme name will appear in the list of themes under the Apply Theme To area. Click Cancel to close the Themes dialog box.

10. Apply this theme by opening a new or existing web, open the Format menu, choose Theme, click Apply Theme To All Pages, select your new theme, and click OK. As you build the web pages, select the style you want to use for a particular item (heading, body text, and so on) from the style drop-down list on the left of the Formatting toolbar.

Themes are a very powerful device to maintain a constant look and feel when a number of people are creating parts of a web site or an intranet.

Creating and Using Style Sheets

Style sheets, which are also called cascading style sheets, or CSS, allow you to predefine a number of styles and then consistently apply them throughout a web site. This not only gives a consistent look to your site, it saves you time and allows you to change the entire site by simply changing the style sheet. As you saw above, you can use style sheets with themes, but you can also define your own style sheets and use them to control the webs you create.

There are two types of style sheets: *embedded style sheets* that apply only to the page on which they reside, and *external style sheets* that are linked to and used in a number of pages. How these two types of style sheets are created is different, although their usage is the same.

Note   *Early web browsers (before Internet Explorer 3.0 and Netscape Navigator 4.0) cannot use style sheets, and pages that are formatted with them probably will not look as they are intended. There are two style sheet standards: CSS 1.0, which covered formatting, and CSS 2.0, which covered the positioning and layering of page elements. Internet Explorer 3.0 supports CSS 1.0 and Internet Explorer 4.0 and later, and Netscape Navigator 4.0 and later, supports both CSS 1.0 and 2.0.*

Creating Embedded Style Sheets

An embedded style sheet is created in the page in which it will be used. Follow these instructions to do so:

> **Note**   *If the Style option is dim (not available) in the Format menu, it has been disabled. It can be enabled by opening the Tools menu, choosing Page Options, clicking the Compatibility tab, and clicking CSS 1.0 and CSS 2.0 under the Technologies section.*

1. Open, in Page view, the page in which you want the style sheet. Then open the Format menu and choose Style. A Style dialog box will open like the one you saw in Figure 11-5.

   In Figure 11-5 the Styles list shows user-defined styles, while here it shows HTML tags. If you select User Defined Styles in the List box, you will see it is empty. To build a style sheet, you can either choose an HTML tag to attach the style to or you can create a style from scratch. If you choose an HTML tag, then the style is automatically applied when the tag is used (for example the Body tag is automatically used in every web page, while the H1 tag is used whenever you use a Heading 1). With user-defined styles, you must manually apply them to the page element you select.

2. Click Body in the Styles list and then Modify to create a style for the body text on the page (you can also just double-click Body). The Modify Style dialog box opens showing a preview of the style and giving a description of it, which initially is blank.

3. Click Format and choose Font. The Font dialog box opens as you can see in Figure 11-6. Choose the font, font style, size, color, and effects you want (remember this is the body text, the majority of text on a page).

4. Click the Character Spacing tab. Open the Spacing drop-down list and see that you have expanded and condensed options, and in the spinner to the right you can set the amount of either by 1 point increments. In the Position drop-down list you can raise or lower the text from a normal baseline, and again with the spinner to the right you can set the amount in 1 point increments up to 10 points.

5. Click OK to close the Font dialog box, and then back in the Modify Style dialog box, again click Format and choose Paragraph. The Paragraph dialog box will open where you can select the paragraph alignment from the drop-down list, and set indentation, and line and word spacing from spinners.

6. Click OK to close the Paragraph dialog box. In a similar manner, look at the Borders and Shading, Bullets and Numbering, and Position dialog boxes.

7. When you are back in the Modify Style dialog box, click OK to return to the Style dialog box. Notice that you now have Body in your User Defined Styles, and its description is as you defined it.

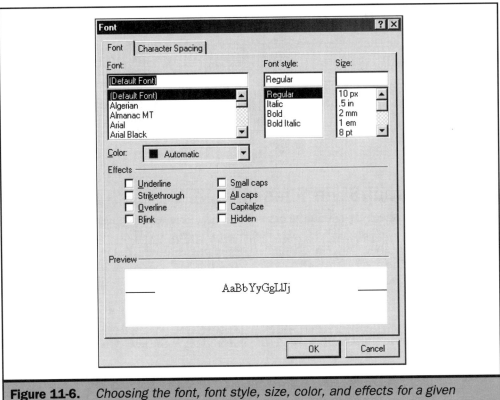

Figure 11-6. *Choosing the font, font style, size, color, and effects for a given text style*

8. To define styles for other tags, such as H1 (Heading 1), select All HTML Tags from the List drop-down box, click the tag in the Styles list, click Modify, and repeat steps 3 through 7.

9. To define your own style—for example, Red H1 for a red Heading 1—click New, enter the name such as **h1(red)**, click Format, and follow steps 3 through 7.

10. When you have defined all the styles you need, click OK to close the Style dialog box, and then save your page and close the web.

You'll see in a minute how to apply your new styles, but if you want to sneak a peek, open the Style drop-down list on the left of the Formatting toolbar and you'll see the standard styles at the top (Body is Normal) and your custom styles at the bottom of the list. For example, I defined the custom styles Special and H1(red), which are shown in this Styles list:

Creating External Style Sheets

An external style sheet gives you the benefit of being able to apply a set of styles to a number of pages, a whole web site, or even several web sites. Then, with a single change in the style sheet you can change all of the pages to which it is linked. External style sheets provide a very powerful means to maintain a consistent look to all of the pages in a site. Here are the steps to create an external style sheet:

1. Open the FrontPage File menu and choose New | Page. Click the Style Sheets tab, which will open as you can see in Figure 11-7. This tab allows you to either create a style sheet from scratch (the Normal Style Sheet) or to start with one of

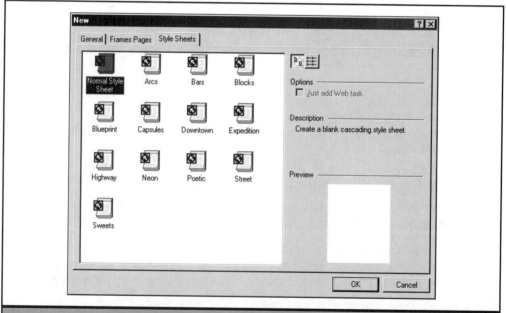

Figure 11-7. *Selecting a starting point for a style sheet*

12 ready-made style sheets, which are also used in the themes. The description will give you an idea of the style sheet. In any case, you can add to and modify the style sheet you start with.

2. Click Blueprint to see what you have when you start with a ready-made style sheet. Note from the description that you should have Century Gothic text and headers, purple hyperlinks, and a bright yellow background.

3. Click OK. A new page opens in Page view with a .CSS extension and displaying the HTML used in the page, as shown in Figure 11-8. Notice that there are no tabs at the bottom of the page. For this type of page, HTML is the only way you can look at it.

You can edit the style sheet in two ways: you can directly edit and add to the HTML on the page, being sure to follow the rules for writing HTML (see Chapter 13); or you can use the Style option in either the Format menu or the floating Style toolbar.

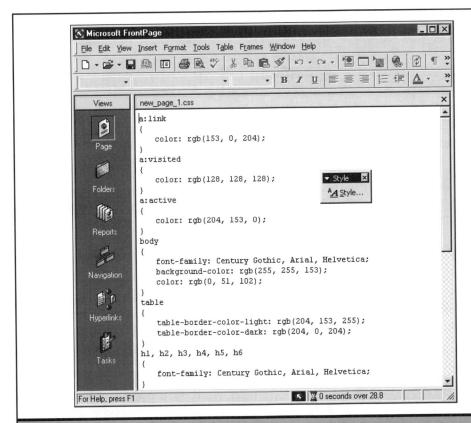

Figure 11-8. *An external style sheet in Page view shows the HTML behind the page*

4. Scroll down the page until you see first the group of heading styles and then the individual heading styles. The group defines the font to be used for all the headings, while the individual styles define their color.

5. Click Style in the floating Style toolbar. The Style dialog box will open with a number of user-defined styles, as you can see below, which you can add to or modify as you did in the previous section.

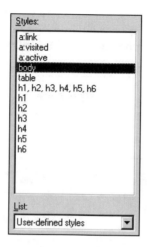

6. After you have made the additions and changes that you want to make, click OK to close the Style dialog. In FrontPage, open the File menu and save the page with a .CSS extension in your root web (C:\Inetpub\Wwwroot\ if you are using the Microsoft Personal Web Server). Close the web.

Had you used the Normal Style Sheet instead of a ready-made one, you would have opened a blank page and a blank style sheet to which you could add your own styles—either for HTML tags or user-defined styles.

Linking to External Style Sheets

For a page to use an external style sheet, it must be linked to the style sheet. Once that is done, the linked page behaves as though it is an embedded style sheet. All the styles in the external style sheet are available in the Style drop-down list in the Formatting toolbar. Here's how to link to an external style sheet:

1. With the page that you want linked to the external style sheet open in Page view, open and fully extend the Format menu and click Style Sheet Links. The Link Style Sheet dialog box will open.

2. If the URL list does not show any style sheets, click Add. The Select Hyperlink dialog box will open, followed almost immediately by the Select File dialog box. Select the drive and path to the folder in which you stored your style sheet (C:\Inetpub\Wwwroot is the default), and then double-click your style sheet.

The Select File and Select Hyperlink dialog boxes will close, and you will see the path to your style sheet in the Link Style Sheet dialog box, like this:

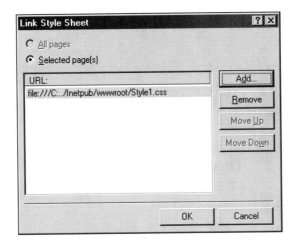

3. Click the link to select it, and then click OK to close it. The styles on the external style sheet are now available on the page.

The external style sheet does not have to be on your hard disk, it can be anywhere on your network or your intranet, and theoretically it could be on the Internet. The potential problem is that you would have to be connected to the Internet to access the styles.

Using Style Sheets

Using a style sheet, as has been implied, is very easy—you just select the style you want to use from the style drop-down list, like this:

1. Open either the page with an embedded style sheet or the page that is linked to a style sheet in Page view. (The external style sheet described above is used in the steps and figures below.)

2. Open the Style drop-down list on the Formatting toolbar and select Heading 1. Type the heading and press ENTER. The next line should be Normal or Body text. Type a line and again press ENTER.

3. From the style list, select Heading 2. Type the heading and press ENTER. Again, the next line is Normal style.

4. Type some text to be a hyperlink, select the text, click the Hyperlink button on the toolbar, and select a destination to which to link. The line will be formatted as a hyperlink.

5. Try out any other styles you have defined. Using these steps and the linked style sheet, my page looks like Figure 11-9. If you had different styles, yours, of course, will look different.

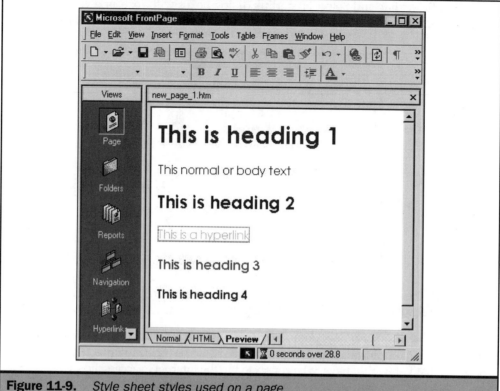

Figure 11-9.   *Style sheet styles used on a page*

6. Close your page without saving it.

   While it may be a bit of a hassle to set up a style sheet initially, you'll find it more than pays you back for the time you spend.

Positioning and Wrapping Text Around Objects

When you place an object like a picture on a web page with text, the default is for the picture to be flush left and for the text to flow from the bottom right corner of the picture from left to right and top to bottom, as you can see in Figure 11-10. (The pictures and text in this section are from Princess Cruises' 1999 Alaska Catalog and are used with the permission of Princess Cruises.) FrontPage gives you several tools to position objects in different ways on the page and to wrap text around the objects.

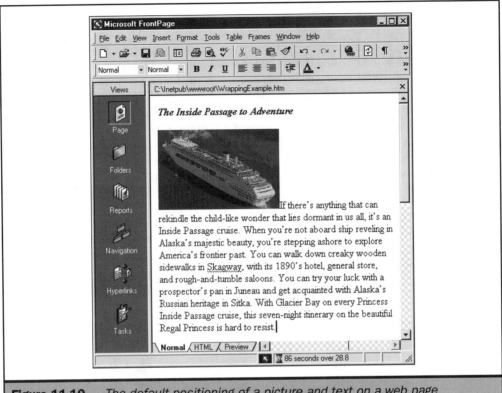

Figure 11-10. *The default positioning of a picture and text on a web page*

Positioning Objects on a Page

The default positioning of objects on a page can be changed through the positioning properties of the object. Simple positioning through the alignment controls on the Formatting toolbar is supported by all browsers. Use of tables for positioning is also supported by most browsers, but the advanced positioning described here requires web browsers that support CSS 2.0, specifically Internet Explorer 4.0 and above. This advanced positioning can be *relative* to the other objects on the page or *absolute* to a specific set of coordinates, and can be assigned a layer or *z-order* in the stack of objects on the page. Advanced positioning is done through the object's Properties dialog box, the Position dialog box, and the Positioning toolbar.

Note *Advanced positioning may conflict with Dynamic HTML and cause unpredictable results, so the two should not be used together.*

Using Absolute Positioning

Absolute positioning allows you to specify the exact pixel position for the upper left-hand corner of an object. You can do that by dragging an object to that position, or by specifying that position in either the Position dialog box or Positioning toolbar. When you place an object at an absolute position, it is taken out of the text stream and text will no longer flow around it or be impacted by its position—the text will be either above it or below it on a separate layer. Absolute positioning means that the object is located at a specific set of pixel coordinates independent of the screen resolution and therefore will not change even though the layout of text and other relative objects have changed with a different resolutions. So it is important to test a page with absolute positioning on all the common resolutions (640×480, 800×600, and 1024×768), as well as in both Netscape Navigator and Internet Explorer. The following steps demonstrate how absolute positioning works:

1. In FrontPage with nothing else open, open the File menu, choose Open, set the path to the \Book\Chap11\ folder on the CD that comes with this book, and double-click PositionExample.htm. A page similar to Figure 11-10 will open, but the picture will be on a different line from the text.

2. Click the picture to select it, open the Format menu, and choose Position (you must open the menu all the way to do this). The Position dialog box will open as shown in Figure 11-11.

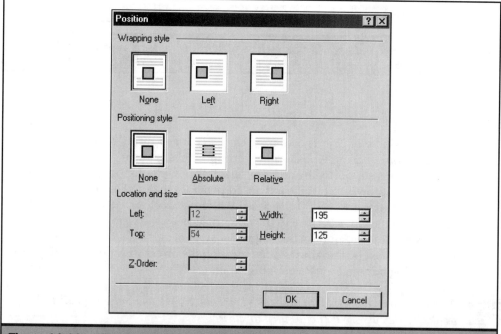

Figure 11-11.   *The Position dialog box provides options for positioning objects and wrapping text*

3. Click Absolute. Notice how the Left and Top location spinners become active. This is the number of pixels from the left edge and from the top edge of the page—its absolute position on the page. You can change that position by changing the numbers.

4. Change the left spinner to 130, and click OK to close the dialog box. The picture will now be on top of the text and in its approximate center, like this:

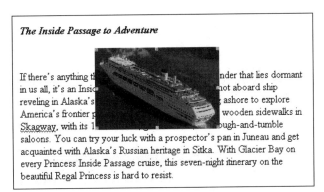

5. Open the View menu and choose Toolbars | Positioning. The Positioning toolbar will appear showing the position of the selected picture.

6. Move the mouse pointer to the picture, where it becomes a four-headed arrow. Drag the picture around. Notice that it is independent of the text and that the Positioning toolbar shows you your position in pixels, as you can see in Figure 11-12.

7. Save your page as Absolute.htm, open the File menu, choose Preview in Browser, and double-click Internet Explorer. Internet Explorer will open and display a slightly different positioning than what you had in FrontPage, as shown in Figure 11-13 (compare to Figure 11-12).

8. Return to FrontPage, open the File menu, choose Preview in Browser, and double-click on Netscape Navigator. Again, you have a slightly different positioning from that in both FrontPage and Internet Explorer 5.0.

9. Close Internet Explorer, Netscape Navigator, and your current page in FrontPage. Also close the Positioning toolbar.

You should also try different screen resolutions. The above figures were shot at 800x600; when I switched to either 1024x768 or 640x480, there did not seem to be a significant difference. But that will not always be the case. You need to test your pages at those resolutions, especially if you are using absolute resolution.

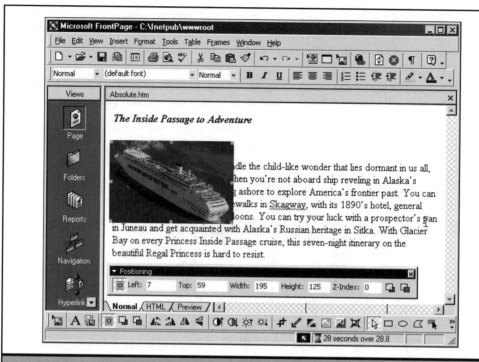

Figure 11-12. *The picture's absolute position reflected in toolbar*

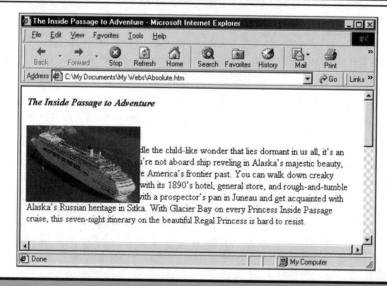

Figure 11-13. *Internet Explorer 5.0 showing a different absolute positioning*

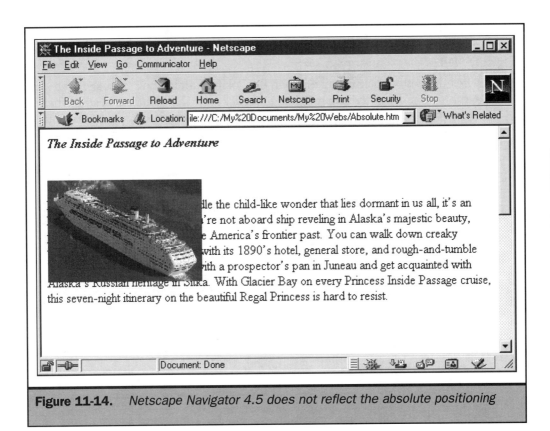

Figure 11-14. *Netscape Navigator 4.5 does not reflect the absolute positioning*

Using Relative Positioning and Wrapping Text

Relative positioning allows you to set the position of an object in relation to other objects on the page, so no matter how the size of the page changes, the objects will remain in the same relative position. This allows you to wrap text around a picture and keep it that way with various screen resolutions. This is demonstrated with the following instructions:

1. In FrontPage with nothing open, open the PositionExample2.htm file from the \Book\Chap11\ folder on the CD that comes with this book. A page will appear with two pictures and two pieces of text all from the Princess Cruises 1999 Alaska catalog (used with their permission).

2. Click the top picture to select it, open the Format menu, and choose Position (you must open the menu all the way) to open the Position dialog box you saw in Figure 11-11.

3. Click the Right wrapping style, Relative Positioning Style, and click OK. The picture of the boat will move over to the right and the text will move up and to the left of the picture.

4. Click the bottom picture, again open the Position dialog box, choose Left wrapping and Relative positioning, and click OK. The picture will stay where it is and the text will move up on the right, as you can see in Figure 11-15 (you may need to delete a line above the word "Vancouver" to fully move the text to the top of the picture).

5. Save this page as Relative.htm, and then preview the page in both Internet Explorer and Netscape Navigator, and in several resolutions. Figure 11-16 shows Netscape Navigator at 1024x768; Figure 11-17 shows Internet Explorer at 800x600.

6. Close both Internet Explorer and Netscape Navigator as well as your page in FrontPage.

At least in my case, only Internet Explorer displays the page the way it was intended to be displayed. You may have a different experience. This demonstrates the need to preview your pages in both browsers.

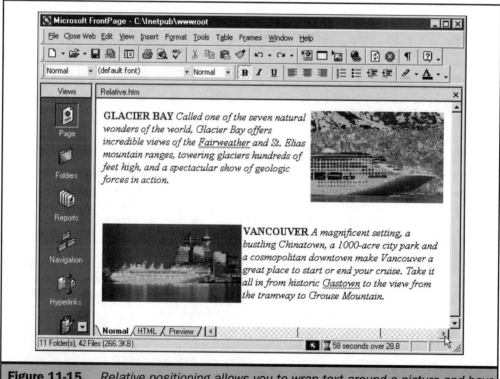

Figure 11-15. *Relative positioning allows you to wrap text around a picture and have it stay there*

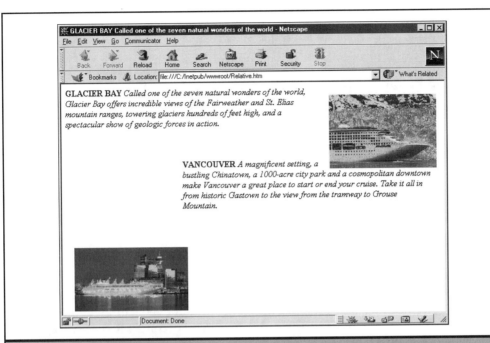

Figure 11-16. *Relative positioning in Netscape Navigator at 1024x786*

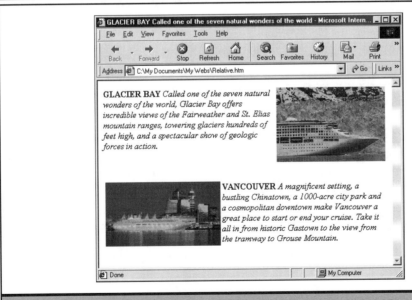

Figure 11-17. *Relative positioning in Internet Explorer at 800x600*

Note *The above placement of photos and text can also be done with a table, which would assure you that everyone would see it as you intended.*

Adding Dynamic HTML Animation Effects

Dynamic HTML allows you to animate most of the elements on a page. For example, you can have a paragraph "fly in" when a page is loaded or a button move or change when the mouse pointer hovers over it or clicks it. FrontPage 2000 allows you to easily apply Dynamic HTML. See how with these steps:

1. With nothing else open in FrontPage, place the CD that comes with this book in its drive, open the File menu, choose Open, and select \Book\Chap11\DHTMLexample.htm to open a page that you'll animate.

2. Select the title line, open the Format menu, and choose Dynamic HTML Effects. A floating toolbar will appear and ask you to choose an event to trigger the effect.

3. Click the down arrow next to Choose An Event to open its drop-down list. Here you can see that you have the choice of four events to trigger the animation. Click Page Load. The Apply list will become active and ask you to choose an effect.

4. Click the down arrow next to Choose An Effect to open its drop-down list. Here you have eight choices. Choose Drop In By Word. Your DHTML Effects toolbar should look like this:

5. Click the Preview tab and you should see your title drop in from the top of the page, one word at a time. Return to the Normal tab.

6. Select the first paragraph after the title. In the DHTML Effects toolbar, choose On Page Load, Apply Fly In, and From Right. Again go to the Preview tab and see the paragraph fly in after the title drops in. Return to the Normal tab.

7. Select the picture of the door. In the DHTML Effects toolbar, choose On Click, Apply Swap Picture, click Choose Picture, and then in the Select A File dialog box, open the \Book\Chap20\ folder and double-click Dooropen.gif.

 Note *Door.gif and Dooropen.gif are courtesy of Clip Art Universe at http://www.nzwwa.com/ mirror/clipart/.*

8. In the Preview tab, when you click the door, the door will open; when you click it again, it will close. Return to the Normal tab.

9. If the Highlight Dynamic HTML Effects button on the DHTML Effects toolbar is activated, you'll see a light blue selection box around the title and first paragraph. Also, when you put the mouse pointer in either of those boxes or on the door picture, you will get a tooltip telling you about the DHTML effect, as you can see in Figure 11-18.

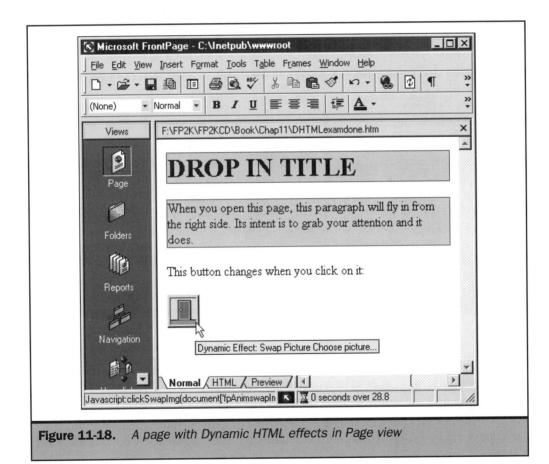

Figure 11-18.   *A page with Dynamic HTML effects in Page view*

10. Save this page as DHTMLdone.htm and them preview it in both Internet Explorer and Netscape Navigator. You'll find that both browsers do everything perfectly.

11. Close any open browsers, the DHTML Effects toolbar, and close your web page.

> **Tip** *You can apply multiple effects to a single page element. For example, the door could fly in and then change when you click it. (For some reason you have to select the entire picture for the Swap Picture effect and have the selection on the right edge of the picture for the fly-in effect; otherwise, the second effect cancels the first and you must handle the Swap Picture first.)*

The key to using Dynamic HTML is to experiment with it and see what you get in the Preview tab as well as in the two main browsers.

> **Tip** *You can copy animation effects with the Format Painter, located on the Standard toolbar.*

Easily Choosing Web-Safe Colors

FrontPage 2000 brings substantial improvement to applying Web-safe colors to graphics, backgrounds, tables, hyperlinks, and text and to picking up existing colors. In HTML, color is specified as a six-character hexadecimal (hex) value that is difficult to use. Earlier versions of FrontPage allowed you to select a color without having to use the hex value, but gave you only 48 colors that were Web-safe and then a more difficult way to pick any custom color. FrontPage 2000 gives you 134 Web-safe colors, a way to pick up an existing color from anything on your screen, even outside of FrontPage—for example, in a browser—as well as a way to create any custom color. If you create custom colors, they are available throughout FrontPage and are even maintained between editing sessions. Look at where and how color is created in FrontPage in the following instructions:

1. From the \Book\Chap11\ folder on this book's CD, open the Color.htm file in FrontPage. The page that opens gives you some text, a table, a hyperlink, and a horizontal line, plus the background on which to work with color.

2. Right-click the text and choose Font. In the Font dialog box there is a Color drop-down list. If you click the down arrow, a small color palette opens showing the 16 primary colors and allows you to choose more colors, like this:

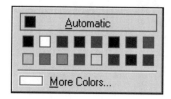

3. Close the Font dialog box, right-click the table, and choose either Table Properties or Cell Properties (the dialog boxes are the same; one applies to the entire table, the other to a single cell). The Table or Cell Properties dialog box opens and shows four of the Color drop-down controls—three for the border, and one for the background, as you can see next. If you open any of these drop-down lists, you'll see the 16-color palette from the previous step.

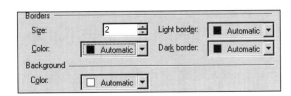

4. Close the Table or Cell Properties dialog box, right-click the horizontal line, and choose Horizontal Line Properties. Again you see the same Color drop-down control and if you open it you see the 16-color palette.

5. Close the Horizontal Line Properties dialog box, right-click any blank area of the page, and choose Page Properties. In the Background tab you see five Color drop-down controls—three for hyperlinks, one for the background, and one of text, like this:

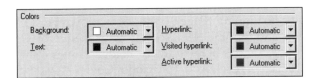

6. Click the Background color drop-down control to display the 16-color palette, and then click More Colors. The More Colors dialog box will open, as you can see in Figure 11-19. Here are the 134 Web-safe colors (127 in the hexagon and 7 below, since white is in the hexagon). When you click a color either in or below the hexagon, the color's hex value is displayed in the upper-right of the dialog box and if the color has an official color name, that is displayed beneath the hex value.

7. Click the eyedropper Select button. The mouse pointer turns into an eyedropper, and with it you can go anywhere on your screen, including outside of FrontPage. Hovering over a color will cause that color to be identified in the More Colors dialog box; clicking that color will select it.

Tip   *You can press ESC to return the eyedropper mouse pointer to a normal pointer.*

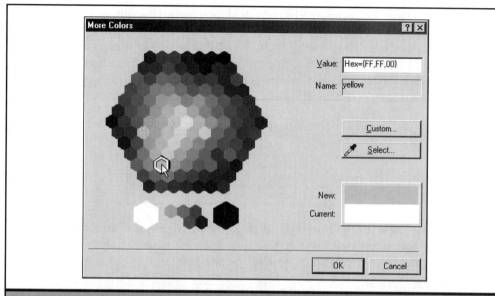

Figure 11-19.   *More Colors allows you to choose Web-safe colors*

8. Click Custom to open the Color dialog box, which is the same as the Color
   Selection dialog box in FrontPage 97 and 98, as shown next. Here there are 48
   Web-safe colors and the ability to pick any color there is by clicking the color
   matrix or by choosing one of the numeric color schemes. When you have
   chosen a custom color, click Add To Custom Colors; it will be displayed in the
   Custom Colors blocks in the lower left. Close the Color dialog box to return to
   the More Colors dialog box.

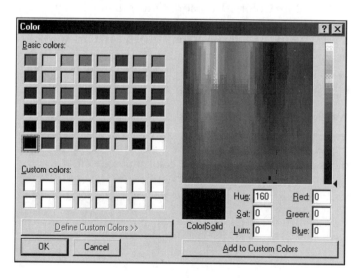

9. Choose a color and click OK to close the More Colors dialog box. Reopen the Page Properties | Background tab and open the Text color drop-down palette and specify a color using any of the schemes that have been discussed. Click OK to close the Page Properties dialog box again, reopen the initial color palette, and notice how a new section has been added entitled Document's Colors, like this:

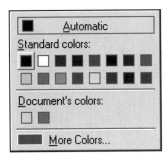

10. Close the open dialog boxes. Open any of the other Color drop-down controls' palettes and see that the document colors are repeated there.

11. Close all dialog boxes, close the Color page without saving it, and then close FrontPage.

The additional color features of FrontPage 2000 allow you to easily define a set of Web-safe colors and then use those colors anywhere in a web site. Like the other features in this chapter, the color features significantly enhance your ability to easily produce outstanding web sites.

Chapter 12

Importing and Integrating Office and Other Files

Y ou will probably want to augment your FrontPage web with files imported from other applications—if for no other reason than because the files you want already exist in another format. This is especially true with multimedia files, since FrontPage does not have the capability to create multimedia files. FrontPage has several ways of working with information created outside of it, including importing information onto an existing page, importing information onto a new page, and attaching or linking to a non-FrontPage file from a web. Let's look at this from the standpoint of Microsoft Office 2000 and other productivity applications. Working with multimedia files will be covered in Chapter 20.

Importing Microsoft Office 2000 and Other Productivity Files

FrontPage 2000 is part of Microsoft's Office family and thus is tightly integrated, and in the Premium Edition bundled, with the other Office products. If you use the Office products Word, Excel, PowerPoint, and Access, you can see a definite similarity to the menus, toolbars, and behavior of FrontPage. Of equal or even greater importance, though, is how easy it is to bring files created in the Office products into FrontPage. Here you'll look at several Office products and see how you can import information they create into FrontPage. If you use other productivity applications, such as those from Corel WordPerfect or Lotus, you will find that they are not as tightly integrated as the Office applications, but you can still easily import these files into FrontPage.

Note   *Microsoft Access is covered in depth in Chapter 18.*

Using Text from Microsoft Word and Other Word Processors

FrontPage can bring externally created text, especially Microsoft Word text, into a web in a number of ways. Among these are

- Pasting text from the Windows Clipboard onto an existing page in Page view.
- Inserting a file onto an existing page in Page view. The file can be in any of the file formats listed in Table 12-1.
- Opening a file onto a new page from within Page view. The file can be in any of the file formats listed in Table 12-1.
- Importing a file onto a new page(s) in either HTML format or its native format, if that format has been associated with its native editor in FrontPage. (Microsoft Word's DOC format is an example that has been.)
- Dragging and dropping a file into FrontPage.

File Format	Extensions
Hypertext Markup Language	.HTM, .HTML
Hypertext Templates	.HTT
Preprocessed HTML	.HTX, .ASP
HTML Documents	.HTM, .HTML, .HTX, .OTM
Lotus 1-2-3	.WK1, .WK3, .WK4
Microsoft Excel Worksheet	.XLS, .XLW
Recover Text from Any File	.*
Rich Text Format	.RTF
Text Files	.TXT
Windows Write	.WRI
Word (Asian Versions) 6.0/95	.DOC, .DOT
Word 2.x for Windows	.DOC
Word 4.0–5.1 for Macintosh	.MCW
Word 6.0/95 for Windows & Macintosh	.DOC
Word 97-2000	.DOC
WordPerfect 5.x	.DOC
WordPerfect 6.x	.DOC, .WPD
Works 4.0 for Windows	.WPS

Table 12-1.   *File Formats That Can Be Brought into FrontPage in Page View*

To see how these methods differ, you'll need documents from Microsoft Word or another word processing application to use as examples. You can find the Office 2000 product examples used in this chapter on the CD accompanying this book.

Pasting Text from the Clipboard

Probably the easiest way to bring in a small amount of text from almost any Windows application is through the use of the Windows Clipboard. To see how it works with FrontPage:

1. Place the CD that accompanies this book in your drive. Start Microsoft Word and from the \Book\Chap12 folder on the CD, open the file Word Document Example.doc, as shown in Figure 12-1.

2. Select all the text (CTRL+A), and copy it to the Windows Clipboard by pressing CTRL+C.

3. Close Microsoft Word and start FrontPage.

4. Create a new One Page Web, name it **Import**, and double-click its home page to open Page view.

5. In Page view, click the page to place the insertion point, and then press CTRL+V to paste the contents of the Clipboard there. Your result should look like Figure 12-2.

6. Press CTRL+A to select all of the text, and press DEL to get rid of it.

As you can see, only some of the formatting is retained when you bring text into FrontPage from the Windows Clipboard. The vertical spacing between paragraphs is changed and the numbering on the numbered list is gone. Also a 1-point border space has been added around each cell in the table.

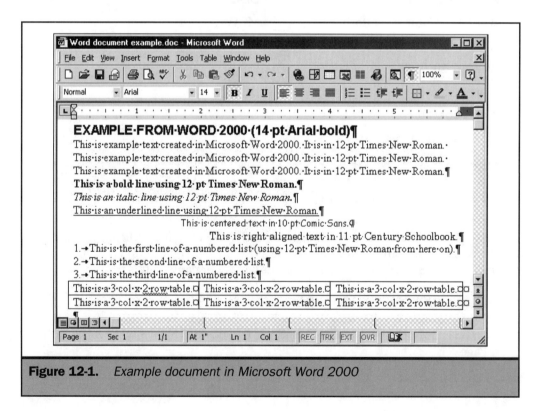

Figure 12-1.   *Example document in Microsoft Word 2000*

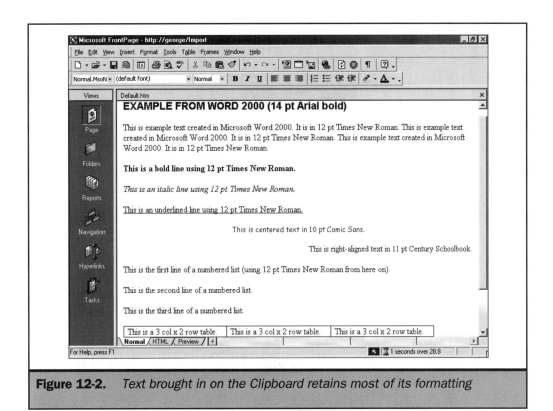

Figure 12-2.   *Text brought in on the Clipboard retains most of its formatting*

Note   *FrontPage and some browsers support the use of fonts other than the default Times New Roman. However, the font used must be installed on the user's computer to be displayed correctly, even if the browser supports the use of other fonts. More information about using fonts on the Web can be found at http://www.microsoft.com/truetype/.*

Inserting a File onto an Existing Page

You can insert a file onto an existing page by using any of the supported file formats. You'll look at the Word DOC, HTML, RTF, and TXT files next. The steps are similar for all the supported formats.

INSERTING TXT FILES   The Text (.TXT) option of inserting a file has several alternatives. To try them, follow these steps:

1. On the blank page in Page view, open the Insert menu and choose File. The Select File dialog box will open.

2. Click the DOWN ARROW in the Files Of Type drop-down list box. Here you can see some of the types of files you can bring into FrontPage:

```
HTML Files (*.htm;*.html)                              ▼

HTML Files (*.htm;*.html)                              ▲
Preprocessed HTML (*.htx;*.asp)
Rich Text Format (*.rtf)
Text Files (*.txt)
Hypertext Templates (*.htt)
Lotus 1-2-3 (*.wk1;*.wk3;*.wk4)
Microsoft Excel Worksheet (*.xls;*.xlw)
Word 6.0/95 for Windows&Macintosh (*.doc)
Word 97-2000 (*.doc)
Word (Asian versions) 6.0/95 (*.doc)                  ▼
```

3. Click Text Files, select Word Text Example.txt from the \Book\Chap12 folder on the CD, and click Open.

4. In the Convert Text dialog box, click Formatted Paragraphs, and then click OK. The text comes in using the FrontPage Formatted paragraph style, but all of the formatting from Microsoft Word is gone and it is treated as one paragraph with new-line (SHIFT+ENTER) breaks. If you turn on Show All on the right of the toolbar, you can see this, as shown in Figure 12-3.

   If you were to use the One Formatted Paragraph option, you would have no paragraph breaks, only new-line breaks throughout. With the Formatted Paragraphs option, you get paragraph breaks wherever you had a blank line or two paragraph breaks in the original text.

5. Click Undo, open the Insert menu, choose File, and double-click your TXT file. Select Normal Paragraphs With Line Breaks and click OK. The text comes in using FrontPage's Normal style, but again has no other formatting.
   If you were to use the Normal Paragraphs option, the only paragraph or line breaks you would get are if you had blank paragraphs in the original (or two paragraph marks together).

Tip *Notice that when you insert the TXT file with Formatted Paragraphs, the first paragraph is one line, that is, without word wrap. With the Normal Paragraphs With Line Breaks option, the text is wrapped to the width of Page view.*

6. Click Undo.

The text format does not give you much, unless you want to bring in some plain text in FrontPage's Formatted paragraph style.

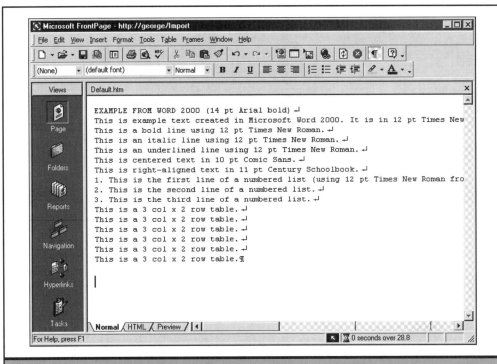

Figure 12-3.   *A text file inserted in TXT format with formatted paragraphs*

INSERTING A DOC FILE   As you saw in Table 12-1, many word processors use the .DOC extension for their files. In this example a Word 2000 file is used. The steps will be similar for any of the word processors supported by FrontPage.

1. With a blank page in Page view, open the Insert menu, choose File, and select the Word 97-2000 file type. Open the \Book\Chap12 folder on your CD.

2. Double-click Word Document Example.doc. The file will appear on the open page, as shown in Figure 12-4. Notice that the numbers are again missing on the numbered list.

If this is the first time that you are bringing a DOC file into FrontPage, you will be told that you need to install the import filter. In that case, insert your installation CD and follow the directions on the screen.

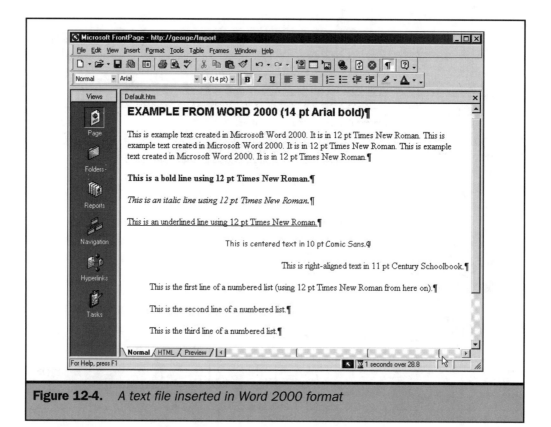

Figure 12-4. *A text file inserted in Word 2000 format*

3. At the left end of the heading that begins "EXAMPLE FROM WORD," type **Inserted DOC** to distinguish this page from others that you will create.

4. Open the File menu and choose Save As. Click Change, type **Inserted Word DOC File** for the Page Title, click OK, type **Worddoc.htm** as the File Name, and click Save.

An inserted DOC file retains some, but not all, of the formatting in the original document. There are two differences between the original and this HTML version—the numbers are missing from the numbered list, and the originally 11-point right-aligned line is 12 points (because there is no standard HTML size of 11 points; the closest standard sizes are 10 or 12 points).

INSERTING AN HTML FILE   An HMTL file (with a file extension of .HTM or .HTML) is the normal format of all text files on the Web, including FrontPage text files. For that reason it is the default when you insert a new file. The HTML files come into FrontPage nicely, as you can see.

Microsoft Word 97 and 2000 allow you to save files directly in HTML format (.HTM extension). Microsoft has a free add-in called Internet Assistant you can download for Word 6 or 7/95 that will do the same thing, at
http://support.microsoft.com/download/ support/mslfiles/Wdia204z.exe *(for Word 7/95 or Wordia.exe for Word 6). You may also read about this in the Microsoft Knowledgebase article ID Q153860. Open* ***http://www.microsoft.com/support***, *click Support Online, register as necessary, in Step 2 choose Specific Article ID Number (Example), and in Step 3 type the ID number.*

1. Open a New Normal Page from the File menu in Page view, open the Insert menu, choose File, and change the file type to HTML Files.

2. In the \Book\Chap12 folder on the CD, double-click Word HTML Example.htm. The file will appear on the open page, as shown in Figure 12-5. Inserting the HTML file has maintained more of the original formatting than any other method.

CREATING WEB SITES

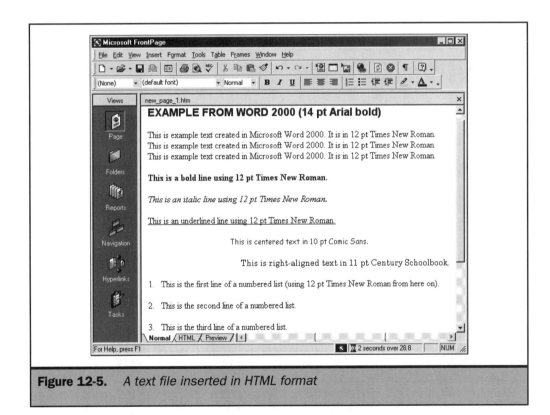

Figure 12-5. *A text file inserted in HTML format*

3. At the left end of the heading that begins "EXAMPLE FROM WORD," type **Inserted HTML** to distinguish this page from others that you will create.

4. Open the File menu and choose Save As. Click Change, type **Inserted Word HTML File** for the Page Title, click OK, type **Wordhtml.htm** as the File Name, and click Save.

INSERTING AN RTF FILE   RTF (Rich Text Format) was created to communicate the majority of text formatting. Many applications, not just word processing programs, have the ability to export files in RTF. To see how well FrontPage handles these files, follow these steps:

1. From Page view, click New on the toolbar to open a new page using the Normal template.

2. Open the Insert menu and choose File to open the Select File dialog box, choose Rich Text Format as the file type, and in the \Book\Chap12 folder on this book's CD, double-click Word RTF Example.rtf. The file will appear on the new page, as you can see in Figure 12-6.

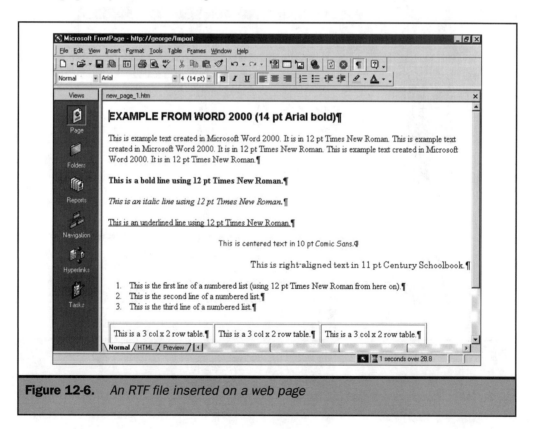

Figure 12-6.   *An RTF file inserted on a web page*

3. At the left end of the heading at the top, type **Inserted RTF**, select Save As from the File menu, click Change, type **Inserted Word RTF File** for the Page Title, click OK, type **Wordrtf.htm** for the File Name, and click Save.

The results of the RTF import are very good, the best of any so far, with the only exception being that the 11-point text is converted to 12 point.

Opening a File onto a New Page

The third way you can bring text files into a FrontPage web is through Page view's File menu Open command. This yields the Open File dialog box, shown in Figure 12-7, from which you can again select any of the supported file types. To explore this method:

1. Click New Page to open a new page in your web. From Page view, open the File menu and choose Open.

2. In the Open File dialog box that is displayed, select the Text Files type, open the \Book\Chap12 folder on the CD, and double-click the TXT version of your Word file.

3. Windows Notepad will open and display the text file. Here you can edit the file and then copy and paste it into a web page in FrontPage. The end result is similar to the text file you inserted earlier in this chapter, as shown in Figure 12-8.

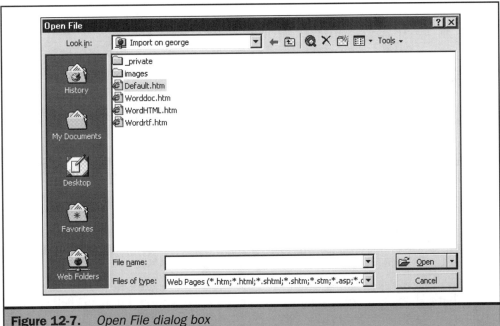

Figure 12-7. *Open File dialog box*

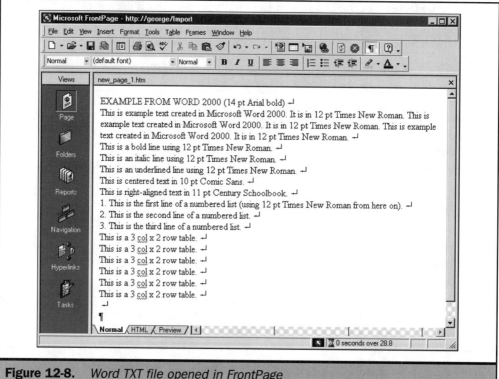

Figure 12-8. *Word TXT file opened in FrontPage*

4. At the left end of the heading, type **Opened Text**, select Save As from the File menu, click Change, type **Opened Word Text File** for the Page Title, click OK, type **Opentext.htm** for the File Name, and click Save.

5. Click New Page, from the File menu choose Open, in the Open File dialog box select the Web Pages file type, and double-click Word HTML Example.htm. Microsoft Word will open and the file will be displayed. Again you can edit and copy and paste it onto a new page in FrontPage. The result is just as you saw earlier (as shown in Figure 12-5).

6. Type **Opened HTML** at the left of the heading, select Save As from the File menu, click Change, type **Opened Word HTML File** for the Page Title, click OK, type **Openhtml.htm** for the File Name, and click Save.

7. Click New Page, choose Open from the File menu, in the Open File dialog box that is displayed, select the Rich Text Format file type, and double-click Word RTF Example.rtf. Again Microsoft Word will open and the file will be displayed. Here you can edit, cut, and paste it into FrontPage. The result is similar to the HTML page you brought into the web in step 5.

8. Type **Opened RTF** at the left end of the heading, select Save As from the File menu, click Change, type **Opened Word RTF File** for the Page Title, click OK, type **Openrtf.htm** for the File Name, and click Save.

9. Click New Page, choose Open from the File menu, select the Word 97-2000 file type in the Open File dialog box that is displayed, and double-click Word Document Example.doc. For a fourth time Microsoft Word will open and display the file. Copy and paste the file on a new page in FrontPage, where it looks like the HTML page.

10. Type **Opened DOC** at the left end of the heading, select Save As from the File menu, click Change, type **Opened Word DOC File** for the Page Title, click OK, type **Opendoc.htm** for the File Name/, and click Save.

11. Close any sessions of Microsoft Word that are open on your system.

You can see that the Open command opens the parent application for the file type where you can edit the file and then cut and paste it into FrontPage. In all but the text example, the resultant page is similar to the HTML example.

Importing a File onto a New Page

The fourth method for bringing text files into FrontPage is to use FrontPage's File menu Import command. Try that next:

1. In FrontPage Folders view, open the File menu and choose Import. The Import dialog box opens. (If you get the New dialog box, you need to create a One Page Web and then try to Import.)

2. Click Add File and the Add File To Import List dialog box opens. Click the down arrow in its Files Of Type drop-down list. Notice that you do not have all the choices here that you had in Page view Insert and Open methods, as you can see here:

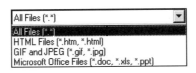

3. Choose HTML Files as the file type, select Word HTML Example.htm from the \Book\Chap12 folder on the CD, and then click Open. The file is added to the Import dialog box.

4. Click Add File again, select All Files as the type, and then double-click Word Document Example.doc, which represents the native Word for Windows format of your Word file.

5. With your Import dialog box looking like the one shown next, click OK.

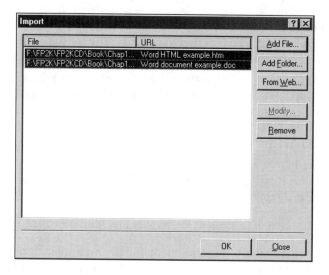

6. Back in Folders view, you will see two new pages. One is the DOC file, Word Document Example.doc, which has the Word icon, and the other is the HTML file with a modified Word icon. Both files are in their native format and have your heading or first line of text as their page title, like this:

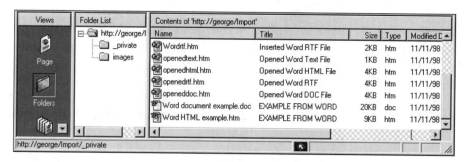

The ability to import a file in its *native format* is very important because it means that you don't have to convert it before you use the file. But this process has limitations. You'll see how this works next. Later in the chapter, in the "Bringing Files from Other Productivity Applications" section, you'll also see how this works with other applications.

1. Double-click the file with the Word icon in Folders view of FrontPage. Microsoft Word will load, and the file will be displayed and ready to edit as you saw in Figure 12-1.

2. Close Microsoft Word and double-click the Word HTML icon. Again Microsoft Word will load, and the file will be displayed.

The .HTM and .DOC extensions have been associated with Microsoft Word, and that application is opened to edit the file. These extension associations are determined by your Windows Registry.

3. Close Microsoft Word, open FrontPage's Tools menu, and click Options. In the Options dialog box, click the Configure Editors tab, shown next. You can use this dialog box to associate a file extension with the application that FrontPage will open to edit the file.

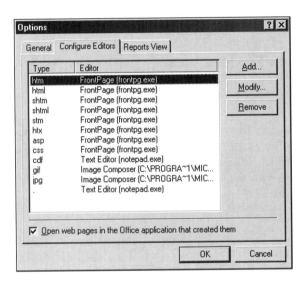

4. Click Add. The Add Editor Association dialog box will open. Enter a new file association that makes sense for you. For example, to add an association between the application CorelDRAW and the extension .CDR, type **cdr** as the File Type, press TAB, type **CorelDRAW** for the Editor Name, press TAB again, and then click Browse and locate the CorelDRAW application, as you can see in the following illustration. Click OK. If you don't have CorelDRAW, use an application that you do have for this example.

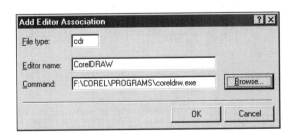

5. Your new application will appear in the Configure Editors tab of the Options dialog box. Click OK to close it.

There is one catch to using a file in its native format in a web—you are assuming that users have the application on their computer so they can view the file. This is made easier for Microsoft Office products, because Microsoft offers free viewers on its web site (http://www.microsoft.com/msdownload) that can be used with Microsoft Internet Explorer.

Drag and Drop

Another way to bring files into FrontPage is to drag and drop a file into Folders, Navigation, or Page views. We'll start with the Folders view.

Drag and Drop in Folders View

1. Open the Windows Explorer and select the \Book\Chap12 folder on this book's CD.

2. Select Folders view in FrontPage, minimize any running applications besides Windows Explorer and FrontPage, and then right-click an empty portion of the taskbar and click Tile Windows Horizontally. The Windows Explorer window and FrontPage window are arranged so that both are visible on your screen, as shown in Figure 12-9.

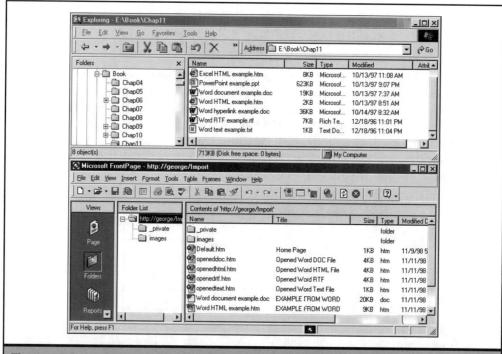

Figure 12-9.   *Windows Explorer and FrontPage arranged to drag and drop files*

3. Select the Word Text Example.txt file in the Windows Explorer, and then drag it onto the left pane of FrontPage, on top of the Import folder, as shown next. The pointer changes to an arrow with a plus sign, indicating the selected file will be copied to the new location. Release the mouse button to copy the file to the selected folder.

 In FrontPage's Folders, Navigation, Hyperlinks, and Page views, if the Folder List is turned on, you can drop the file into the selected folder.

4. Double-click the Word Text Example.txt file in FrontPage and it opens in Notepad. Close Notepad without changing the file before proceeding.

Dragging and dropping a file onto FrontPage has the same result as importing a file by use of the Import option on the File menu.

 Dropping an HTML file onto FrontPage imports only the HTML page; any images on the page are not imported and must be imported separately.

Drag and Drop in Page View

You can also use drag and drop to insert files into Page view. The result is the same as selecting File from the Page view Import menu, as you'll see next:

1. Arrange your screen (as was shown in Figure 12-9) so that both the Windows Explorer and Page view windows are visible.

2. Click New on the toolbar in Page view to open a new page.

3. In the Windows Explorer, select the Word Document Example.doc file, and drag it onto the new page in Page view.

4. Type **Dropped DOC** at the left end of the heading, select Save As from the File menu, click Change, type **Dropped Word DOC File** for the Page Title, click OK, type **Dropdoc.htm** for the File Name, and click Save.

5. If you have several open pages in FrontPage, close them now.

Bringing Files from Other Productivity Applications

By using HTML, RTF, or a file in its native format if you think the user can open it, you can bring files from many applications into FrontPage. Now you'll see how this works with Microsoft Excel and PowerPoint files.

Using Microsoft Excel Files

In Microsoft Excel, as in most spreadsheet applications, you can create both tabular information and charts or graphs, as shown in Figure 12-10. When you bring this material into FrontPage, you must use either the native format—which handles both types of data—and hope the user has the product or the viewer, or you must handle the two data types separately. Try this with Excel.

1. In Microsoft Excel, open Excel Example.xls, shown in Figure 12-10, from the \Book\Chap12 folder on this book's CD.

2. In Excel, open the File menu and choose Save As Web Page. The Save As dialog box will open, as shown in Figure 12-11. Here you can save either the current selection or the entire workbook. In the example here, the tabular data and the chart will be saved as one file.

3. Make sure that the Save As Type is Web Page. Click Change Title, type **Excel HTML Example** for the Page Title, and click OK. Click Web Folders, select your Import web (or go to the location where you have saved your webs), change the filename to **Excel HTML example.htm**, and click Save. Close Excel.

4. In FrontPage, click Refresh in the toolbar and the files will come into Folders view as shown in Figure 12-12.

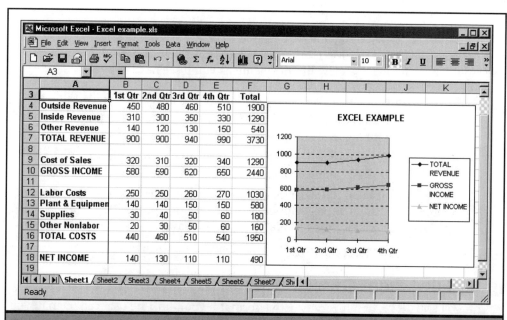

Figure 12-10.   *Excel example with both tabular and chart data*

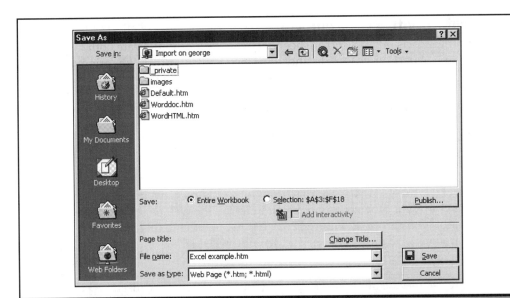

Figure 12-11.   *Excel Save As dialog box saving an entire workbook as a web page*

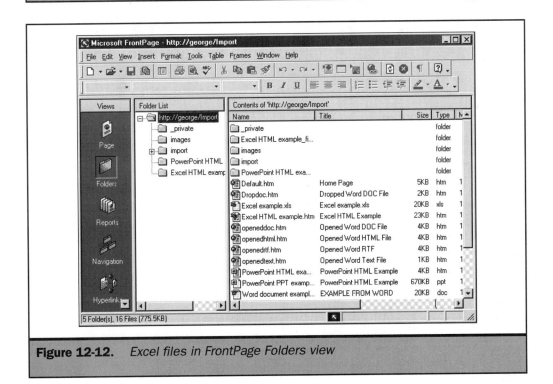

Figure 12-12.   *Excel files in FrontPage Folders view*

5. Notice in the Folder List that there is a new folder named Excel HTML Exampl_Files. Click this folder to open it. You will see two files, Filelist.xml and Image001.gif. The GIF file is the chart part of the Excel workbook, and the Filelist is XML (extensible markup language) code to tell your browser to combine the spreadsheet and chart portions of the Excel workbook. When you saved your Excel file as an HTML file, the chart was converted to a GIF image file and linked to the HTML page.

6. Double-click first the HTML page and then, after closing it, the native Excel file. In both cases, Excel will open and display the file with both the spreadsheet and the chart. Close Excel.

7. Select the Excel HTML Example.htm file in Folders view and click Preview in Browser. Your browser will open and display the web pages complete with its chart as you can see in Figure 12-13. If you open the Excel file (Excel Example.xls) in your browser and your browser is Internet Explorer 5, it will open; open Excel within it and display your workbook as shown in Figure 2-14.

You can also use the methods of bringing files into Page view discussed earlier in this chapter to insert all or part of your spreadsheet onto a web page in FrontPage.

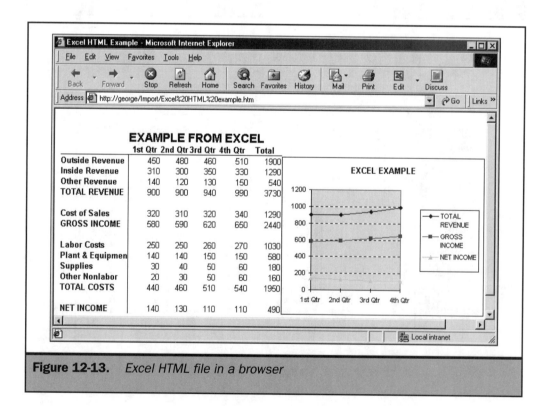

Figure 12-13. *Excel HTML file in a browser*

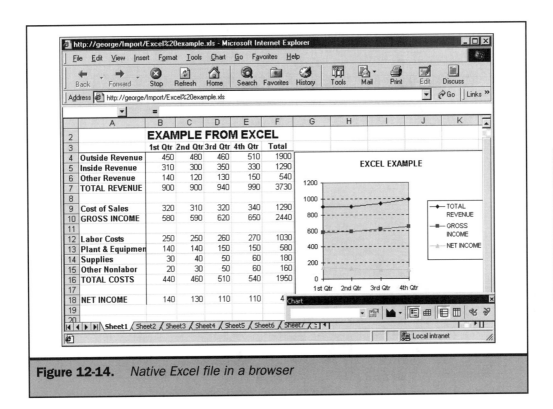

Figure 12-14. *Native Excel file in a browser*

Also, both spreadsheet tabular and chart data can be copied to the Clipboard and pasted onto a web page, and the files can be dragged and dropped into Folders view.

When you save an Excel spreadsheet as a web page and choose *Selection: Sheet and Add Interactivity*, and then open that spreadsheet in a browser, you will get an interactive spreadsheet where you can change the numbers and see both the totals and the chart change without having Excel on the browser machine. This is independent of FrontPage and allows you to save the changed spreadsheet back to Excel.

Bringing in PowerPoint Files

In PowerPoint, like Word and Excel, you have two choices for getting its files on the Internet: in native format and in HTML format. To look at each of these, follow these steps:

1. Load PowerPoint, choose Open An Existing Presentation in the PowerPoint dialog box, and click OK. In the Open dialog box, locate the PowerPoint Example.ppt in the \Book\Chap12 folder on this book's CD, and click Open.

2. Open the File menu and choose Save As Web Page. The Save As dialog box will open as shown here:

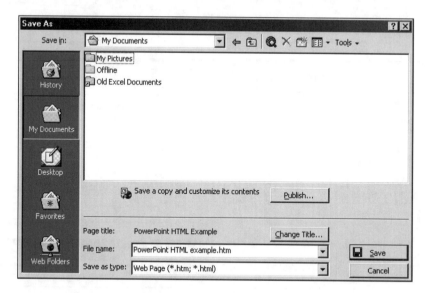

3. Click Change Title, type **PowerPoint HTML Example** for the Page Title, click OK, type **PowerPoint HTML Example.htm** for the File Name, specify the Import folder as the Save In location, and click Save.

PowerPoint 2000 Save As Web Page

The PowerPoint 2000 Save As Web Page command creates a complete web with a number of files that are placed in their own folder complete with fonts, a page for each slide, and a number of pictures. This web uses frames with an outline of the presentation in the left frame and the current slide and its graphics in the right frame. If you open this web directly in Microsoft Internet Explorer 5, as shown in Figure 12-15, you can see these frames as well as several custom buttons at the bottom of the window. The Outline button on the left turns the outline frame on or off, the next button expands or collapses the outline, then there are two buttons that move the slide show backwards and forwards, and finally on the right is a button that expands the slide to fill the screen. In full screen mode you click the slide to go to the next slide, press BACKSPACE to the previous slide, and press ESC to return to the normal browser window. If you right-click the slide, you get a context menu with a number of options.

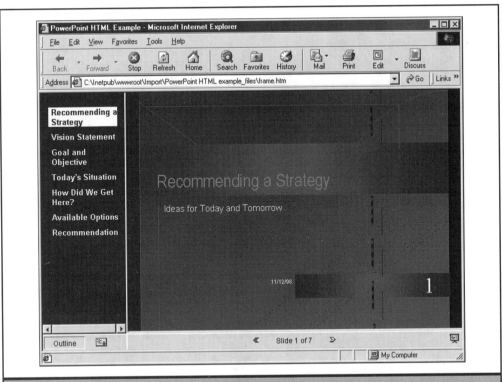

Figure 12-15.   *PowerPoint 2000 web page in a browser*

4. Using the Windows Explorer, open the folder in which you saved the PowerPoint HTML example, and observe the complete web that has been created, as you can see in Figure 12-16. Close the Windows Explorer and return to PowerPoint.

5. Open the File menu once more and choose Save As. Again select the Import folder being used in this chapter. Select Presentation (*.ppt) as the Save As Type, name the file **PowerPoint PPT Example.ppt**, and click Save. Close PowerPoint.

6. In FrontPage Folders view, click Refresh in the toolbar and you will see a PowerPoint HTML Example folder and both .PPT and .HTM files.

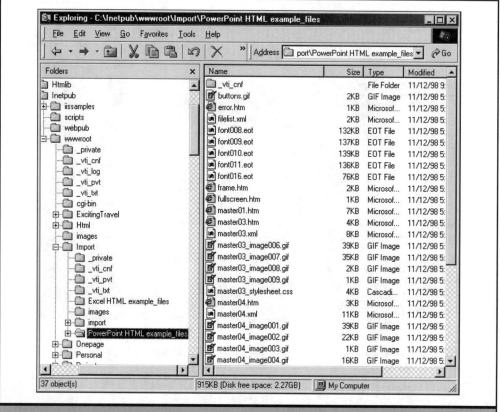

Figure 12-16.   *The complete set of files created for a PowerPoint web*

7. In FrontPage Folders view, double-click the PowerPoint HTML Example.htm file in the Import folder to open it in PowerPoint. What you get is your original presentation, as you do with the .PPT file. Close PowerPoint when you are ready.

8. Again in FrontPage Folders view, select the PowerPoint HTML Example.htm file and click View In Browser on the toolbar. You get the browser window shown in Figure 12-15. Close the browser.

9. Once more in FrontPage Folders view, select the PowerPoint PPT Example.ppt file and click View In Browser on the toolbar. Now you get just the PowerPoint presentation without the buttons or frames that incorporate the outline, as shown in Figure 12-17.

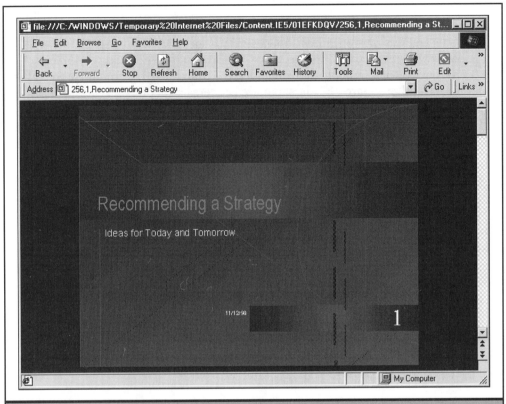

Figure 12-17.   *Normal PowerPoint presentation file in a browser*

All of the Microsoft Office applications, including Access and Outlook, have an impressive ability to create HTML and other files that are usable in a web and importable with FrontPage. This is a great way to quickly generate web content.

Using Legacy Files on an Intranet

An intranet provides an excellent opportunity to make good use of, or even improve, *legacy* (previously created) files. Manuals and sets of procedures are particularly good examples of this. Instead of maintaining 20 (or 50 or 500!) sets of company manuals that rarely get used except to settle an argument, maintain one set on your intranet. Here people can use a search capability to quickly find what they are looking for, whenever they want and wherever they are.

Manuals and sets of procedures almost surely exist as word processing files that can be easily transferred to FrontPage. Once you do that, you can add the Table of Contents Component to quickly index the files, the Search Form Component to search all of the text, and the Shared Borders to place headers and footers on each page with navbars, time stamps, and contacts.

Company reports and periodicals are also good candidates for your intranet—current editions and previous issues can be searched and read in one easily accessible place.

The availability of FrontPage's search capability to easily find information on an intranet could be the primary reason for putting information on it. In the same vein, the Table of Contents and Shared Borders can significantly improve usability of existing documents. In other words, putting your legacy documents on your intranet with FrontPage not only gives them a new way to be distributed and read, but features such as the Search, Table of Contents, and Shared Borders also make them substantially more usable, and therefore more likely to be used. Finally, and far from least important, putting information on an intranet ensures that everyone in the organization is getting the same and the latest information.

Looking at Imported Files in a Browser

You have seen how the Excel and PowerPoint files look in a browser, but look now at how the rest of the Import web you have built looks:

1. Open the very first "Home page" you created for this web in Page view. This should be your Home page with a filename of Default.htm. If you do not find it, use any other page to open Page view and create a new page. In either case, enter a title for the page of **Import Home Page**, formatted with Heading 1 and centered, and then open the Insert menu and choose Component | Table of Contents.

 This is a great demonstration of how the Table of Contents FrontPage Component can automatically create links to all the HTM pages and the DOC, XLS, and PPT files.

2. Accept the defaults for the Table of Contents Properties; this gives you a link to all of the HTM files (although they won't appear until you open the web in a browser), and click OK.

3. Save the Home page with the **Import Home Page** Title and the **Default.htm** page File Name. Click Hyperlinks in the Views bar. You should see all of the links for the Import Home Page as shown in Figure 12-18.

4. Click Preview In Browser on the toolbar. The Import Home Page will appear, as you can see in Figure 12-19.

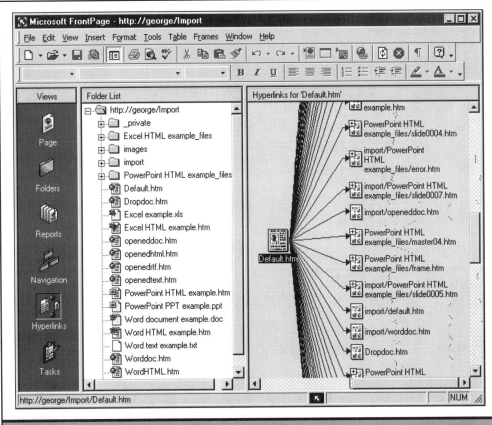

Figure 12-18.   *Hyperlinks created by the Table of Contents Component*

CREATING WEB SITES

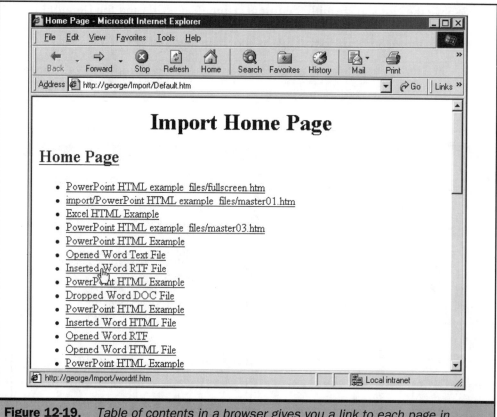

Figure 12-19.   *Table of contents in a browser gives you a link to each page in the web*

Links to seemingly duplicate pages are a result of the many secondary files in the PowerPoint example.

5. Click a number of the links to view the imported (or opened or inserted) files, using the browser's Back button to return to the Import Home page. You will not find many surprises. For example, the Word RTF example is shown in Figure 12-20.

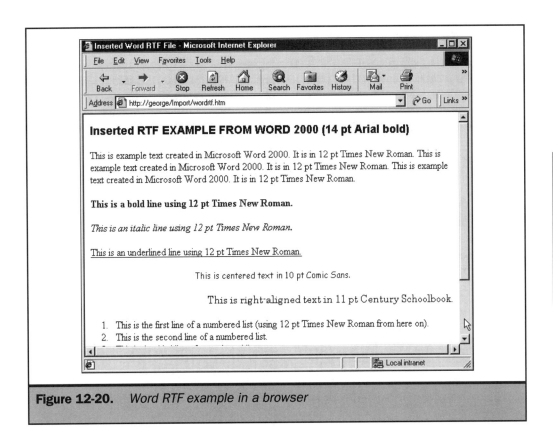

Figure 12-20.   *Word RTF example in a browser*

6. If you have a second browser, open the same web in it and go through each of the links. Note the differences. For example, if you try to open the PowerPoint HTML Example.htm in Netscape Navigator 4.5, you will get this message:

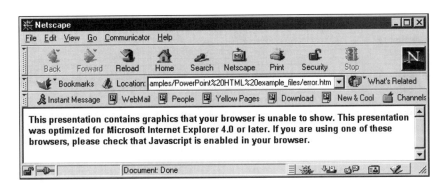

7. Close your browser(s).

Importing Hyperlinks

One of the better examples of Office 2000 integration is the ability of FrontPage 2000 to recognize and preserve hyperlinks that are present in imported files. Not only does FrontPage 2000 display the hyperlinks in FrontPage views, but when affected files are moved or renamed within the FrontPage web, FrontPage will update the hyperlink references in the Office 2000 files. Figure 12-21 shows an excerpt from Chapter 1 of this book saved as a Word document, including hyperlinks to references of other chapters in the book. After importing the file (Word Hyperlink Example.doc) along with the three chapter files (Chapter 11.doc, Chapter 15.doc, and Chapter 17.doc) into a FrontPage web, the hyperlink relationships are displayed in Hyperlinks view, as shown in Figure 12-22.

Importing files into a FrontPage web—whether they are text, tables, presentations, or databases—provides a great deal of ready-made content. When these files are artfully used, they can quickly give a web a lot of depth. As you are building a web site, remember the many existing files that are available. Their use in a web will further leverage their original investment.

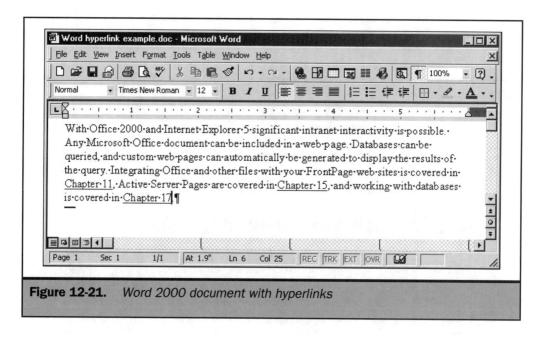

Figure 12-21. *Word 2000 document with hyperlinks*

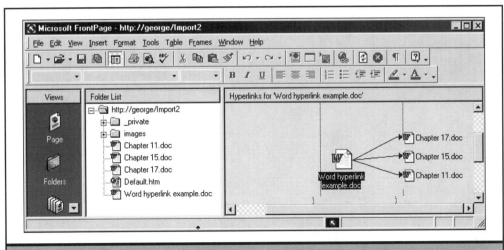

Figure 12-22.   *Hyperlinks carried over into a web being created in FrontPage*

The Complete Reference

FrontPage 2000

Part III

Working Behind the Scenes

The Complete Reference

FrontPage 2000

Chapter 13

Working with HTML

Throughout the previous chapters, you have read that by using FrontPage you don't have to learn HTML (Hypertext Markup Language), the programming language of the Web. You can build great web pages without ever learning HTML or even reading this chapter. But for those who either want to go further—to put the last bit of flourish on their web page—or who just want to understand the HTML behind their FrontPage-created web, this chapter will be useful. With access to FrontPage, you probably will not have to create many webs from scratch in HTML, so this chapter will not provide exhaustive coverage of that topic, nor will it cover every nuance of every HTML tag. Both areas are fully covered by sites on the Web, as listed at the end of this chapter. What this chapter will cover is how to understand the HTML that is generated by a FrontPage web and how to add specific capabilities to a FrontPage web with HTML.

Note   *The CD that comes with this book includes Stephen Le Hunte's HTML Reference Library, HTMLib. It is a valuable resource that provides, in Windows Help format, a detailed reference to every HTML tag and its attributes. It is strongly recommended that you install HTMLib and refer to it as you read this chapter.*

Note   *HTML is an evolving language that's a little out of control. With Netscape and Microsoft adding their own (sometimes, often? incompatible) tags, the standards committee is playing catch-up. Adding to this problem is that both Netscape and Microsoft are rushing ahead with new browsers with many more features. The best approach is to test your web on the browsers that you want to write for to make sure your web behaves the way you want it to.*

Introducing HTML

HTML is a series of tags that identify the elements in a web page. *Tags* or *markup tags* consist of a tag name enclosed in angle brackets and normally come in pairs. Tags are placed at the beginning and end of an element, generally text, that you want to identify, with the ending tag name preceded by a slash. For example,

```
<TITLE>This is a title</TITLE>
```

uses the Title tag to identify text that will be placed in the title bar of the browser window. Tags are not case sensitive, so they can be all uppercase, all lowercase, or a mixture. Tags are placed around text to control its formatting and placement on a page; to identify a hypertext link; to identify a graphic, sound, or video to be loaded; or to identify a particular area of a web page.

Tip   *Just because an HTML tag exists doesn't mean you have to use it. As in most other endeavors, the KISS principle applies to the use of HTML.*

In addition to a tag name, a tag may contain one or more *attributes* that modify what the tag does. For example, if you want to center a paragraph on the page, you would use this tag:

```
<P ALIGN=CENTER>This will be a centered paragraph</P>
```

`ALIGN=CENTER` is an *attribute* for the Paragraph tag.

Using Basic Tags

All web pages must contain a basic set of tags. These tags identify the document as being an HTML document and identify the major parts of the document. With the exception of DOCTYPE, these are the only tags that must be included in a web page to conform to the HTML standard. The Body tag is also used to identify the page defaults, such as the background color or image and the text color. The basic tags, some of which are shown in Listing 13-1, are described with their attributes in Table 13-1.

On the CD that accompanies this book, in the \Book\Chap13\ folder there is a folder named HTML that is a web with all of the listing and other files that are discussed in this chapter.

In the listings in this chapter, tags are shown in all capital letters and bold, while attributes are just all capital letters. Also, continuation lines are indented from their parents. These conventions are used solely for readability. Tags and attributes can be any mixture of cases, and there is no need to indent. HTML created by FrontPage is also indented and can be color-coded in the HTML tab for readability.

Listing 13-1
Basic set of
HTML

```
<!DOCTYPE HTML PUBLIC "-//W3C//DTD HTML 4.0//EN">
<HTML>
  <HEAD>
    <META NAME="GENERATOR" CONTENT="Microsoft FrontPage 4.0">
    <META NAME="Microsoft Theme" Content="global 101, default">
    <TITLE>Home Page</TITLE>
  </HEAD>
  <BODY BGCOLOR="blue" TEXT="white">
    <P>This is the text that is the body of this web document</P>
  </BODY>
</HTML>
```

Note

In the tables of tags and attributes in this chapter, tags are shown with their angle brackets, and attributes are indented from the left.

WORKING BEHIND
THE SCENES

Tag or Attribute	Description
`<!DOCTYPE ...>`	Identifies the document as adhering to the given HTML version. This tag is optional and often left off.
`<HTML>` `</HTML>`	Identifies the intervening text as being HTML.
`<HEAD>` `</HEAD>`	Contains the title and document identifying information. The `<TITLE>` tag is required in the `<HEAD>` tag.
`<TITLE>` `</TITLE>`	Identifies the title that is placed in the browser's title bar.
`<META ...>`	Assigns content to an element that can be used by a server or browser and cannot otherwise be assigned in HTML; "Microsoft FrontPage 4.0" is assigned to "GENERATOR" in Listing 13-1. Placed within the `<HEAD>` tag.
`<STYLE>` `</STYLE>`	Defines a style sheet that prescribes specific styles that are to use certain elements such as normal paragraph (`<P>`) and first-level headings (`<H1>`). See "Style Sheets" later in this chapter.
`<BODY>` `</BODY>`	Specifies the part of the page that is shown to the user and defines overall page properties.
ALINK	Identifies the color of the active link as either a color name or hexadecimal number representing a color value.
BACKGROUND	Identifies the background image that will be tiled if necessary to fill the window.
BGCOLOR	Identifies the background color that will be used, as either a color name or a hexadecimal number representing a color value.
BGPROPERTIES	Specifies that the background will not scroll with the window if `BGPROPERTIES=FIXED`.
LEFTMARGIN	Sets the left margin for the entire page and overrides any default margin (a margin of 0 will be exactly on the left edge).

Table 13-1.   *Basic Set of HTML Tags with Their Attributes*

Tag or Attribute	Description
LINK	Identifies the color of links that have not been used, as either a color name or a hexadecimal number representing a color value.
TEXT	Identifies the color of text on the page as either a color name or a hexadecimal number representing a color value.
TOPMARGIN	Sets the top margin for the page and overrides any default margin (a margin of 0 will be exactly on the top edge).
VLINK	Identifies the color of links that have been used, as either a color name or a hexadecimal number representing a color value.

Table 13-1.   *Basic Set of HTML Tags with Their Attributes* (continued)

Using Color

Color names that can be used with ALINK, BGCOLOR, LINK, TEXT, and VLINK as well as other tags with the Microsoft Internet Explorer 2.0 or 3.0 are Black, White, Green, Maroon, Olive, Navy, Purple, Gray, Red, Yellow, Blue, Teal, Lime, Aqua, Fuchsia, and Silver. Microsoft Internet Explorer 4.0 and on, and Netscape Navigator 3.0 and on, support 140 named colors (see **http://microsoft.com/workshop/author/,** click Show Toc, click HTML References Elements, and select <BODY>, BGCOLOR, Color Table). In addition to the named colors, a color value may be used that is a combination of three pairs of hexadecimal numbers, one pair (256 possibilities) each for Red, Green, and Blue. Over 16 million color values can therefore be generated, compared with the 16 to 140 color names. However, a great many of these colors will not display well in most browsers when used as solid colors.

One of the best sources for information on color and web browsers is *The DMS Guide to Web Color* at **http://www.oit.itd.umich.edu/projects/DMS/answers/ colorguide/.** The site includes palettes that can be used with Adobe Photoshop and Fractal Design Painter. The CD that comes with this book also has a Color Wizard that is part of Stephen Le Hunte's HTML Reference Library. The Color Wizard gives you three ways to visually create the three pairs of hexadecimal numbers for any color.

Note: The **http://microsoft.com/workshop/author/** URL is a comprehensive site on HTML authoring and is extremely valuable.

Setting Paragraph Styles

Paragraph styles include basic paragraph definition and alignment; headings; the line break; bulleted, numbered, and definition lists; preformatted (called "Formatted" in FrontPage) paragraphs; comments; and horizontal lines or rules. Unless the preformatted style is used, normal line endings, extra spaces of more than one, and tabs are ignored in HTML. Lines simply wrap to fit the space allotted for them unless you use the Paragraph tag. Listing 13-2 shows examples of paragraph styles. This listing is combined with the tags in Listing 13-1 to produce the web page shown in Figure 13-1. Paragraph styles are described in Table 13-2.

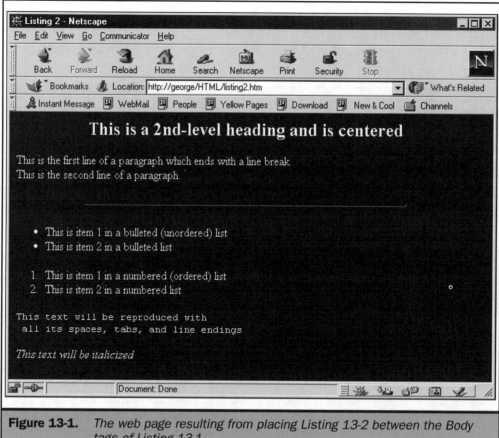

Figure 13-1.   *The web page resulting from placing Listing 13-2 between the Body tags of Listing 13-1*

sting 13-2 Example of using paragraph style tags

```
<H2 ALIGN=CENTER>This is a 2nd-level heading and is centered</H2>
<P>
  This is the first line of a paragraph which ends with a line
    break<BR>
  This is the second line of a paragraph.
</P>
<HR SIZE=3 WIDTH=70%>
<UL>
  <LI>This is item 1 in a bulleted (unordered) list
  <LI>This is item 2 in a bulleted list
</UL>
<OL>
  <LI>This is item 1 in a numbered (ordered) list
  <LI>This is item 2 in a numbered list
</OL>
<!-- This is a comment, it is ignored by a browser and not
  displayed -->
<PRE>This text will be reproduced with all its spaces, tabs, and
  line endings</PRE>
<ADDRESS>This text will be italicized</ADDRESS>
```


Tag	Description
<P> </P>	Identifies the start and end of a paragraph and its alignment with ALIGN= and LEFT, CENTER, or RIGHT.
<H*n*> </H*n*>	Identifies a heading in one of six heading styles (n = 1 to 6) and its alignment with ALIGN= and LEFT, CENTER, or RIGHT.
 	Forces a line break similar to pressing SHIFT+ENTER in FrontPage.
<HR>	Creates a horizontal rule or line where you can specify the alignment, color, shade, size (height), and width across the page.
<OL> </OL>	Contains an ordered (numbered) list.
<UL> </UL>	Contains an unordered (bulleted) list.

Table 13-2. *Paragraph Style HTML Tags*

Tag	Description
`<LI>`	Identifies an item in a numbered or bulleted list.
`<DL> </DL>`	Contains a definition list.
`<DT>`	Identifies a term to be defined, displayed on the left of a window.
`<DD>`	Identifies the definition of the term that immediately precedes it, indented from the left.
`<ADDRESS> </ADDRESS>`	Identifies a paragraph of italicized text.
`<BLOCKQUOTE> </BLOCKQUOTE>`	Identifies a paragraph that is indented on both the left and right, as you might do with a quotation.
`<CENTER> </CENTER>`	Centers all text and images contained within it.
`<!- -> or <COMMENT> </COMMENT>`	Identifies a comment that the browser will ignore and not display. `<COMMENT> </COMMENT>` is not used in Netscape Navigator.
`<DIV> </DIV>`	Identifies a division of a page for which the alignment is set with `ALIGN=` and `LEFT`, `CENTER`, or `RIGHT`.
`<PRE> </PRE>`	Identifies preformatted text in which all spaces, tabs, and line endings are preserved (called "Formatted" in FrontPage). The maximum number of characters in each line can be set with `WIDTH=` (generally 40, 80, or 132).

Table 13-2. *Paragraph Style HTML Tags* (continued)

 It is not necessary to have a `</P>` if it would be immediately followed by a `<P>`. All browsers will assume the last paragraph has ended when a new one starts.

 You can nest lists within lists and get automatic indenting.

Applying Character Styles

Character styles, which determine how one or more characters will look or behave, come in two forms. *Logical* character styles are defined by the browser and may be displayed in any way that the browser has established. *Physical* character styles have a strict definition that will be the same in all browsers. Examples of character style tags are shown in Listing 13-3, while Figure 13-2 shows how Microsoft Internet Explorer 5.0 and Netscape Navigator 4.5 display them. Note the lack of differences. Table 13-3 describes most character styles.

Listing 13-3
Examples of using character style tags

```
<B>This text is bold</B>
This text is normal size, <BIG>this is larger</BIG>
This text is normal size, <SMALL>this is smaller</SMALL>
<CODE>This is normally fixed-width font</CODE>
<EM>This text is normally italic</EM>
<FONT SIZE=5 COLOR=BLUE>This text is size 5 and in blue</FONT>
<I>This text is italic</I>
<S>This text is struck through</S>
<STRONG>This text is normally bold</STRONG>
<U>This text is underlined</U>
```

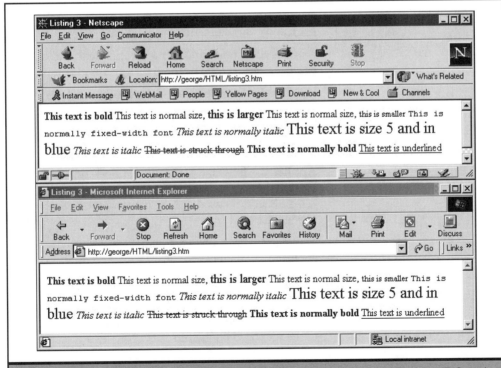

Figure 13-2. *Character style tags displayed in Microsoft Internet Explorer 5.0 and Netscape Navigator 4.5*

WORKING BEHIND
THE SCENES

Figure 13-2 demonstrates that browsers ignore line endings unless they are marked with `<P>`, `<BR>`, or other paragraph styles.

Tag	Description
`<B> </B>`	Applies the Bold physical character style to the enclosed characters.
`<BASEFONT>`	Establishes the font size and/or color and/or typeface for a web (`<STYLE>` is now often used in place of `<BASEFONT>`; see "Style Sheets" later in this chapter).
`<BIG> </BIG>`	Makes the enclosed characters one size larger.
`<BLINK> </BLINK>`	Applies the Blink physical character style to the enclosed characters; not used in Microsoft Internet Explorer 4.0 or earlier.
`<CITE> </CITE>`	Applies the Citation logical character style to the enclosed characters; normally italic.
`<CODE> </CODE>`	Applies the Code logical character style to the enclosed characters; normally a fixed-width font.
`<DFN> </DFN>`	Applies the Definition logical character style to the enclosed characters; normally italic.
`<EM> </EM>`	Applies the Emphasis logical character style to the enclosed characters; normally italic.
`<FONT> </FONT>`	Applies the font size and/or color and/or typeface specified to the enclosed characters; if `<BASEFONT>` is used, `<FONT>` size can be relative to the base font size.
`<I> </I>`	Applies the Italic physical character style to the enclosed characters.
`<KBD> </KBD>`	Applies the Keyboard logical character style to the enclosed characters; normally a fixed-width font.
`<S> </S>` or `<STRIKE> </STRIKE>`	Applies the Strikethrough physical character style to the enclosed characters.

Table 13-3. *Character Style HTML Tags*

Tag	Description
`<SAMP> </SAMP>`	Applies the Sample logical character style to the enclosed characters; normally a fixed-width font.
`<SMALL> </SMALL>`	Makes the enclosed characters one size smaller.
`<STRONG> </STRONG>`	Applies the Strong logical character style to the enclosed characters; normally bold.
`<SUB> </SUB>`	Applies the Subscript physical character style to the enclosed characters.
`<SUP> </SUP>`	Applies the Superscript physical character style to the enclosed characters.
`<TT> </TT>`	Applies the Typewriter Text physical character style to the enclosed characters; a fixed-width font.
`<U> </U>`	Applies the Underline physical character style to the enclosed characters.

Table 13-3.   *Character Style HTML Tags* (continued)

Displaying Characters

HTML defines that the less-than, greater-than, and ampersand characters have special meanings and therefore cannot be used as normal text. To use these characters normally, replace them as follows:

Less-than (<)	< or <
Greater-than (>)	> or >
Ampersand (&)	& or &

All other characters that you can type on your keyboard will be displayed as they are typed. In addition, HTML has defined a number of other characters that can be displayed based on entering an *escape sequence* where you want the character displayed (in FrontPage these characters are also available from the Insert | Symbol window). The escape sequence can take either a numeric or a textual format, as was shown with the three special characters just mentioned. In either case the escape sequence begins with an ampersand (&) and ends with a semicolon (;). In the numeric format, the ampersand is followed by a number symbol (#) and a number that represents the character. All characters, whether they are on the keyboard or not, can be represented with a numeric escape sequence. The textual format has been defined only for some characters and excludes most characters on the keyboard. Additional examples of the two formats are shown in Table 13-4.

Unlike the rest of HTML, escape sequences are case sensitive—for example, you cannot use < for the less-than symbol.

For complete lists of the escape sequences, see the Microsoft Internet Explorer Specification Character Set at **http://www.microsoft.com/workshop/author/**. At that site, click Show Toc, choose HTML References Character Sets, and select either ISO Latin-1 Character Set or Additional Named Entities for HTML.

Style Sheets

Style sheets, or *cascading style sheets* (CSS), allow you to define and apply paragraph and character styles to an entire document or web. Style sheets can be part of (embedded in) an HTML document within the Head tag using the Style tag, or can be a separate document referenced by the HTML page using the Link tag. Listing 13-4 shows the definition of a simple embedded style sheet that defines two heading and two paragraph styles.

Character	Name	Numeric Sequence	Text Sequence
...	Horizontal Ellipsis	…	…
■	Bullet	•	•
™	Trademark	™	™
©	Copyright	©	©
Æ	AE ligature	Æ	æ
Ä	a umlaut	ä	ä
É	e acute accent	é	é
Õ	o tilde	õ	õ

Table 13-4. *Samples of Character Escape Sequences*

Listing 13-4
Definition
and use of a
style sheet

```
<HTML>
  <HEAD>
    <TITLE>This is the title</TITLE>
    <STYLE>
      <!--
        H1.red { font-family: Arial; font-size: 18pt;
                 font-weight: bold; color: red}
        H1.blue { font-family: Arial; font-size: 18pt;
                  font-weight: bold; color: blue}
        P.main { font-family: Times; font-size: 12pt}
        P.special { font-family: Times; font-style: italic;
                    font-size: 12pt}
      -->
    </STYLE>
  </HEAD>
  <BODY>
    <H1 CLASS="red">This is a heading in red</H1>
    <P CLASS="main">This is a main paragraph</P>
    <H1 CLASS="blue">This is a heading in blue</H1>
    <P CLASS="special">This is a special paragraph</P>
  </BODY>
</HTML>
```

A style is a set of properties that can be attached to any HTML tag, such as <H1> (level-1 heading). In effect, you can redefine HTML tags. For example, to have all your level-1 heads display as 18 pt Arial bold in blue, you would redefine the level-1 head like this:

```
H1 {font-family : Arial; font-size : 18 pt
    font-weight: bold; color: blue}
```

You can also have classes of styles. For example, if you want some of your level-1 heads to be blue and some red, you could define two styles: H1.blue and H1.red, as shown above in Listing 13-4. The HTML to use the red style would then look like this:

```
<H1 CLASS=red>This heading would be in the H1.red style</H1>
```

Style sheets use a single tag, Style, and within that tag define the various styles you want to use. To keep older browsers that do not know how to handle styles from generating an error, comment tags are placed at the beginning and end of the definitions. These are ignored by the more recent browsers and keep the older browsers from choking on the style definitions.

For more information on the HTML related to style sheets, see the Style Sheets Reference section of the HTML Reference Library (HTMLib) on the CD that comes with this book, the Style Sheet resource page at W3C (**http://www.w3c.org/pub/Style/**), and Microsoft's web authoring site mentioned above (**http://www.microsoft.com/workshop/author/**).

Working with Images and Image Maps

Images are added to a web by use of the Image (<IMG>) tag, which specifies the path and filename of the image as well as a number of attributes such as size, positioning, margins, and border. One of the attributes, ISMAP, identifies the image as having an image map attached to it. The image map is a separate MAP file used by the server to relate areas of the image to URLs. To use ISMAP, you must include the Image tag in an Anchor tag (see the next section, "Adding Hyperlinks and Bookmarks"). A couple of examples are given in Listing 13-5 and shown in Figure 13-3. Many of the Image attributes are described in Table 13-5.

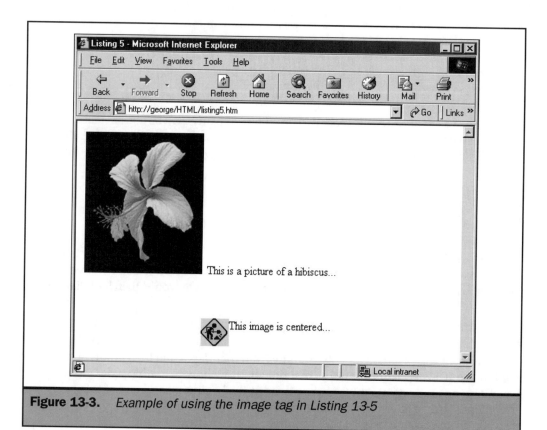

Figure 13-3. *Example of using the image tag in Listing 13-5*

Note

The   (which can also be) in Listing 13-5 is a nonbreaking space and is used with the Paragraph tags to create a blank line (paragraph) that HTML will not get rid of.

Listing 13-5
Examples of
using the
Image tag

```
<P><IMG SRC="hibiscus.jpg" ALT="A picture of a hibiscus"
  ALIGN="bottom" BORDER="2" HSPACE="3" WIDTH="166"
  HEIGHT="190"> This is a picture of a hibiscus ...</P>
<P> </P>
<P ALIGN="center"><IMG SRC="undercon.gif" ALT="Under
  Construction" ALIGN="top" WIDTH="40" HEIGHT="38">
  This image is centered...</P>
```

Note

Netscape Navigator 3.0 and above and Internet Explorer 4.0 and above will automatically scale the other dimension based on the current aspect ratio of the image if just one of the dimensions (HEIGHT or WIDTH) is given.

Tip

Specifying the HEIGHT and the WIDTH speeds up loading, because a quick placeholder will be drawn for the image, allowing the text to continue to be loaded while the image is drawn. Without these dimensions, the loading of the text must wait for the image to be drawn and thereby determine where the remaining text will go.

Attribute	Description
ALIGN	Positions text at the TOP, MIDDLE, or BOTTOM of the image, or positions the image on the LEFT or RIGHT of the text.
ALT	Identifies alternative text that is displayed if the image cannot be displayed.
BORDER	Specifies that a border of so many pixels be drawn around the image.
HEIGHT	Specifies the height, in pixels, of the image.
HSPACE	Specifies the blank space on the left and right of the image.
ISMAP	Indicates that the image has an image map.
SRC	Identifies the path and filename or URL of the image.
USEMAP	Identifies the name of the image map that is to be used.
VSPACE	Specifies the blank space on the top and bottom of the image.
WIDTH	Specifies the width, in pixels, of the image.

Table 13-5. *Image Tag Attributes*

Adding Hyperlinks and Bookmarks

Hyperlinks provide the ability to click an object and transfer what is displayed by the browser (the *focus*) to an address associated with the object. HTML implements hyperlinks with the Anchor tag (`<A> </A>`), which specifies that the text or graphic that it contains is a hyperlink or a bookmark or both. If the tag is a *hyperlink* and the contents are selected, then the focus is moved either to another location in the current page or web, or to another web. If the tag is a *bookmark,* then another Anchor tag may reference it and potentially transfer the focus to it.

An image used as just described assumes that the entire image is the hyperlink. An image may also be broken into sections, where each section is a link or a *hotspot*. To break an image into multiple links requires an *image map* that is implemented with the Map tag. The Map tag contains Area tags that define the shape of a specific area of the image and the link that it is pointing to.

Listing 13-6 provides some examples of the Anchor, Map, and Area tags, which are shown in Figure 13-4. Table 13-6 describes these tags and their attributes.

Listing 13-6
Examples of hyperlinks and bookmarks

```
<P>This is a link to the <A HREF="default.htm">Home
   Page.</A></P>
<P><A NAME="This ">This </A>is a bookmark.</P>
<P>This <A HREF="#This ">link </A>takes you to the bookmark.</P>
<P><MAP NAME="ComputerMap">
  <AREA SHAPE="POLYGON" COORDS="163, 121, 197,
    145, 91, 183, 55, 157" HREF="#Keyboard">
  <AREA SHAPE="POLYGON" COORDS="6, 90, 147, 87,
    148, 115, 46, 145, 2, 124" HREF="#Processor">
  <AREA SHAPE="RECT" COORDS="30, 6, 124, 70"
    HREF="#Screen"></MAP>
  <A HREF="computer.map">
    <IMG ALIGN="bottom" SRC="computer.gif" WIDTH="200" ISMAP
      USEMAP="#ComputerMap" HEIGHT="186"></A></P>
```

Note *The pointer in Figure 13-4 is pointing to the hotspot labeled "Screen," as shown at the bottom of the window.*

Note *The SHAPE attribute of the Area tag may be left out, and a rectangular shape will be assumed.*

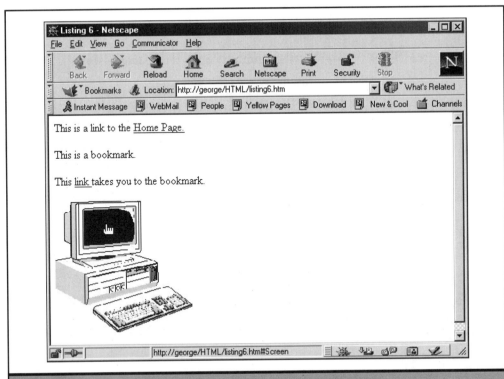

Figure 13-4.   *Hyperlinks and bookmarks defined in Listing 13-6*

Tag or Attribute	Description
`<A>  </A>`	Specifies the definition of a hyperlink.
HREF	Identifies the destination URL, which can be a bookmark, page, or web.
NAME	Identifies the bookmark at this location.
TARGET	Identifies a specific frame in the link destination.
TITLE	Identifies a name for a link that is displayed when the mouse passes over the link; otherwise the link address is displayed.

Table 13-6.   *Anchor, Map, and Area Tags and Their Attributes*

Tag or Attribute	Description
<MAP> </MAP>	Specifies the definition of an image map.
NAME	Identifies the name of the image map.
<AREA> </AREA>	Specifies the definition of one image area.
SHAPE	Identifies the type of shape being defined to be CIRC, CIRCLE, POLY, POLYGON, RECT, or RECTANGLE.
COORDS	Identifies the coordinates of the shape being defined using x and y positions in terms of image pixels for each point.
HREF	Identifies the bookmark or URL to which the focus is transferred.
NOHREF	Indicates that a given area causes no action to take place.

Table 13-6.   *Anchor, Map, and Area Tags and Their Attributes* (continued)

Defining Forms

A form in HTML is defined by the input fields that it contains. Each input field is defined by its type, name, and potentially a default value. There are a number of field types around which you can wrap text and formatting to get virtually any form you want to define. One example is shown in Listing 13-7 and displayed in Figure 13-5. Table 13-7 describes the tags and attributes related to forms.

Listing 13-7
Example of a form

```
<H1>This is a form</H1>
<FORM ACTION="saveresults" METHOD="post">
  <PRE>
    Name: <INPUT TYPE=TEXT SIZE=50 MAXLENGTH=256 NAME="Name"><BR>
    Address: <INPUT TYPE=TEXT SIZE=50 MAXLENGTH=256
      NAME="Address"><BR><BR>
    Send Data? Yes <INPUT TYPE=RADIO NAME="Send" Value="Yes">
      No <INPUT TYPE=RADIO NAME="Send" Value="No">
    For what product? <SELECT NAME="Product" MULTIPLE SIZE="1">
      <OPTION VALUE="Floor" SELECTED>Floor model
```

```
        <OPTION VALUE="Desk">Desk model</SELECT><BR>
     Check if a member <INPUT TYPE=CHECKBOX NAME="Member"
       Value="TRUE">
     <BR><BR>
     <INPUT TYPE=SUBMIT VALUE="Send It"> <INPUT TYPE=RESET
       VALUE="Forget It">
   </PRE>
</FORM>
```

Note
The Microsoft Internet Explorer 3.0 does not correctly display the <SELECT NAME="Product" MULTIPLE SIZE="1"> instruction. (It's fixed in Internet Explorer 4.0 and on.) The SIZE="1" says that only one of the multiple entries should be displayed, but IE 3.0 showed both "Floor model" and "Desk model." Netscape Navigator will correctly display this.

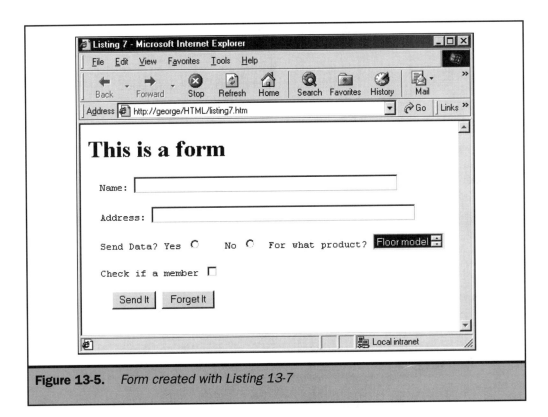

Figure 13-5.   *Form created with Listing 13-7*

Tag or Attribute	Description
`<FORM> </FORM>`	Specifies the definition of a form
`<INPUT>`	Identifies one input field.
TYPE	Specifies the field type to be CHECKBOX, HIDDEN, IMAGE, PASSWORD, RADIO, RESET, SUBMIT, TEXT, or TEXTAREA.
NAME	Specifies the name of the field.
VALUE	Specifies the default value of the field.
ALIGN	If TYPE=IMAGE, positions text at TOP, BOTTOM, or CENTER of image.
CHECKED	If TYPE=CHECKBOX or RADIO, determines if by default they are selected (TRUE) or not (FALSE).
MAXLENGTH	Specifies the maximum number of characters that can be entered in a text field.
SIZE	Specifies the width of a text field in characters, or the width and height in characters and lines of a text area.
SRC	Specifies the URL of an image if TYPE=IMAGE.
`<SELECT> </SELECT>`	Specifies the definition of a drop-down menu.
NAME	Specifies the name of a menu.
MULTIPLE	Specifies that multiple items can be selected in a menu.
SIZE	Specifies the height of the menu.
`<OPTION>`	Identifies one option in a menu.
SELECTED	Specifies that this option is the default.
VALUE	Specifies the value if the option is selected.

Table 13-7.   *Form Tags and Attributes*

Creating Tables

HTML provides a very rich set of tags to define a table, its cells, borders, and other properties. As rich as the original HTML table specification was, there have been many extensions to it by both Microsoft and Netscape. Since these extensions are not consistent between the two companies, they need to be used with caution. Listing 13-8 provides an example of the HTML for creating the simple table shown in Figure 13-6. Table 13-8 shows the principal table tags and their attributes.

```
<H2>A New Table</H2>
<TABLE BORDER=2 CELLPADDING=3 CELLSPACING=4 WIDTH=100%>
  <CAPTION ALIGN=CENTER>THIS IS THE TABLE CAPTION</CAPTION>
  <TR><TH ALIGN=LEFT WIDTH=25%>Cell 1, a header</TH>
    <TD COLSPAN=2 WIDTH=25%>Cell 2, This cell spans two
      columns</TD>
    <TD WIDTH=10%>Cell 3</TD>
    <TD WIDTH=10%>Cell 4</TD></TR>
  <TR><TD WIDTH=25%>Cell 5, 25%</TD>
    <TD WIDTH=25%>Cell 6, 25%</TD>
    <TD WIDTH=25%>Cell 7, 25%</TD>
    <TD WIDTH=10%>10%</TD></TR>
  <TR><TD ROWSPAN=2 WIDTH=25%>Cells 9/13, These cells were
    merged</TD>
    <TD WIDTH=25%>Cell 10</TD>
    <TD WIDTH=25%>Cell 11</TD>
    <TD WIDTH=10%>Cell 12</TD></TR>
  <TR><TD WIDTH=25%>Cell 14</TD>
    <TD WIDTH=25%>Cell 15</TD>
    <TD WIDTH=10%>Cell 16</TD></TR>
</TABLE>
```

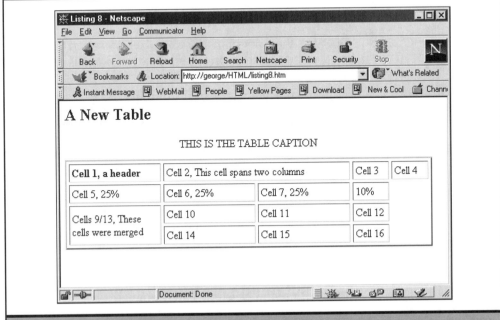

Figure 13-6. Table created with Listing 13-8

Tag or Attribute	Description
`<TABLE> </TABLE>`	Specifies the definition of a table.
`ALIGN`	Specifies that the table will be aligned on the `LEFT` or `RIGHT` of the page, allowing text to flow around it.
`BACKGROUND`	Specifies that a URL containing an image be used as a background; works in Internet Explorer 3.0 and above and Netscape Navigator 4.0 and above.
`BGCOLOR`	Specifies a background color for an entire table.
`BORDER`	Specifies the size, in pixels, of a border to be drawn around all cells in a table.
`BORDERCOLOR`	Specifies a border color if a border is present; works in Internet Explorer 3.0 and above and Netscape Navigator 4.0 and above.
`BORDERCOLORLIGHT`	Specifies the lighter of 3-D border colors if a border is present; not used in Netscape Navigator.
`BORDERCOLORDARK`	Specifies the darker of 3-D border colors if a border is present; not used in Netscape Navigator.
`CELLSPACING`	Specifies the amount of space, in pixels, between cells; a default of 2 is used when not specified.
`CELLPADDING`	Specifies the amount of space, in pixels, between the cell wall and its contents on all sides; a default of 1 is used when not specified.
`COLS`	Specifies the number of columns in the table.
`FRAME`	Specifies which of the outside borders of a table are displayed—`VOID` (none), `ABOVE` (only the top), `BELOW` (only the bottom), `HSIDES` (horizontal sides), `VSIDES` (vertical sides), `LHS` (left-hand side), `RHS` (right-hand side), `BOX` (all); not used in Netscape Navigator.
`HEIGHT`	Specifies the height of a table as either a certain number of pixels or a percentage of the window.
`RULES`	Specifies which of the inside borders of a table are displayed—`NONE`, `BASIC` (horizontal rules between the heading, body, and footer sections), `ROWS`, `COLS`, `ALL`; not used in Netscape Navigator.

Table 13-8.   *Table Tags and Attributes*

Tag or Attribute	Description
STYLE	Specifies a style sheet for the table.
WIDTH	Specifies the width of a table as either a certain number of pixels or a percentage of the window.
\<TR\> \</TR\>	Identifies the cells in a single row of a table. BACKGROUND, BGCOLOR, BORDERCOLOR, BORDERCOLORLIGHT, BORDERCOLORDARK, HEIGHT, and STYLE are the same as described for \<TABLE\>.
ALIGN	Specifies that the text in the cells of this row is aligned on the LEFT, CENTER, or RIGHT of each cell.
VALIGN	Specifies that the text in the row can be aligned with the TOP, CENTER, BASELINE, or BOTTOM of the cells; if not specified, text is center-aligned. Not used in Netscape Navigator.
\<TD\> \</TD\>	Identifies a single data cell in a table. BACKGROUND, BGCOLOR, BORDERCOLOR, BORDERCOLORLIGHT, BORDERCOLORDARK, HEIGHT, WIDTH, STYLE, and VALIGN are the same as described for \<TABLE\> or \<TR\>.
ALIGN	Specifies that the text in this cell is aligned on the LEFT, CENTER, or RIGHT of the cell.
COLSPAN	Specifies the number of columns a cell should span.
ROWSPAN	Specifies the number of rows a cell should span.
NOWRAP	Specifies that the text in the table cannot be wrapped to fit a smaller cell, forcing the cell to enlarge.
\<CAPTION\> \</CAPTION\>	Identifies the caption for a table.
ALIGN	Specifies that the caption is aligned to the LEFT, CENTER, or RIGHT of the table; not used in Netscape Navigator.
VALIGN	Specifies that the caption should appear at the TOP or BOTTOM of the table; not used in Netscape Navigator.

Table 13-8.   *Table Tags and Attributes* (continued)

Tip   *A table without the BORDER attribute will not have a border, but will take up the same space as if it had a border of 1. Therefore, specifying a border of zero (0) will take up less space.*

Incorporating Frames

HTML frames allow the definition of individual panes or *frames* within a browser window. Each frame contains a separate page that can be scrolled independently of the other frames. HTML defines frames in terms of *frame pages,* which contain Frameset tags, which in turn contain Frame tags. In a frame page, the Frameset tag replaces the Body tag and provides the overall structure of the frames to be created in a browser window. Similarly, the Frame tag is used to define the structure of a single frame. Figure 13-7 shows a simple frame page that was created with the tags displayed in Listing 13-9. (The banner, contents, and main pages are separately defined to contain the information you see.) The tags and attributes related to frames are described in Table 13-9. Because the browser in Figure 13-7 correctly displays frames, the body message "This page uses frames, but your browser doesn't" is not displayed.

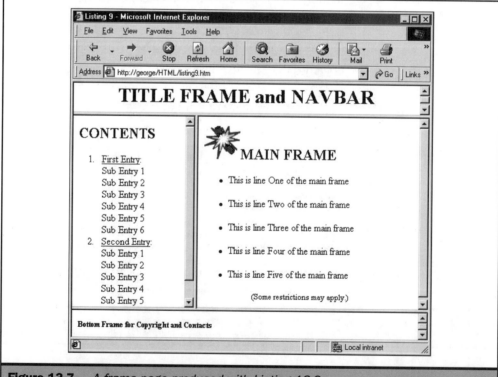

Figure 13-7.   *A frame page produced with Listing 13-9*

sting 13-9
ame page
with
Frameset
and Frame
tags

```
<HTML>
  <HEAD>
    <TITLE>Frameset 1</TITLE>
  </HEAD>
  <FRAMESET ROWS="12%,*,12%">
    <FRAME SRC="frtop.htm" NAME="top" NORESIZE>
      <FRAMESET COLS="35%,65%">
        <FRAME SRC="frconten.htm" NAME="contents">
        <FRAME SRC="frmain.htm" NAME="main">
      </FRAMESET>
    <FRAME SRC="frbottom.htm" NAME="bottom" NORESIZE>
    <NOFRAMES>
      <BODY>
        <P>This web page uses frames, but your browser doesn't</P>
      </BODY>
    </NOFRAMES>
  </FRAMESET>
</HTML>
```

Tag or Attribute	Description
`<FRAMESET> </FRAMESET>`	Specifies the definition of a set of frames.
COLS	Identifies the number of vertical frames (columns) in the frameset and their absolute or relative size (see comments on this attribute).
ROWS	Identifies the number of horizontal frames (rows) in the frameset and their absolute or relative size (see comments on this attribute).
FRAMEBORDER	Turns the border around a frame on (FRAMEBORDER="Yes" or "1") or off (="No" or "0").
FRAMESPACING	Identifies extra space, in pixels, inserted between frames; not used in Netscape Navigator.
BORDERCOLOR	Specifies the color of the frame border; not used in Internet Explorer 3.0, but is in 4.0.

Table 13-9.   *Frame Tags and Attributes*

Tag or Attribute	Description
`<FRAME> </FRAME>`	Specifies the definition of a single frame.
FRAMEBORDER	Turns the border around a frame on (`FRAMEBORDER="Yes"` or `"1"`) or off (`="No"` or `"0"`).
FRAMESPACING	Identifies extra space, in pixels, inserted between frames.
MARGINWIDTH	Identifies the size, in pixels, of the left and right margin in a frame.
MARGINHEIGHT	Identifies the size, in pixels, of the top and bottom margins in a frame.
NAME	Identifies the name of the frame so it can be referred to by `TARGET` attributes.
NORESIZE	Prevents the frame from being resized by the user.
SCROLLING	Turns the appearance of scroll bars on or off with `SCROLLING="Yes"/"No"/"Auto"`; `Auto` is the default.
SRC	Identifies the URL of the web page that will occupy the frame.
BORDERCOLOR	Specifies the color of the frame border; not used in Internet Explorer 3.0, but is in 4.0 and on.
`<NOFRAMES> </NOFRAMES>`	Specifies HTML that will be displayed by browsers that cannot display frames, but ignored by browsers with frame capability.
`<IFRAME> </IFRAME>`	Specifies the definition of a floating frame; `WIDTH`, `HEIGHT`, `HSPACE`, `VSPACE`, and `ALIGN` are the same as described for `<IMG>`.

Table 13-9. *Frame Tags and Attributes* (continued)

Note *If FRAMEBORDER and FRAMESPACING are specified in the Frameset tag, they will automatically apply to all the Frame tags contained within it and only need to be specified for the Frame where a change is desired.*

The TARGET *attribute, which you have seen with other tags, is used to load pages into specific frames.*

Internet Explorer 3.0 introduced *floating frames.* These are individual frames that can be placed anywhere in a standard HTML document. If the browser does not support floating frames, the HTML within the <IFRAME></IFRAME> tags is displayed on the page in the usual manner.

 No tags that would be within a Body tag can precede the first Frameset tag, although Frameset tags can be contained within another Frameset tag.

Within the ROWS and COLS attributes are a list of values separated by commas, one for each horizontal frame ("row") or vertical frame ("column") in the frameset. These values can be

- The absolute width of a column or height of a row, in pixels. For example,
  COLS="200, 100, 300"
  sets up three columns that, from left to right, are 200, 100, and 300 pixels wide, respectively.
- A percentage of the window's width for a column or the window's height for a row. For example,
  ROWS="15%, 85%"
  sets up two rows, one taking 15 percent of the window and the other, 85 percent.
- A relative value to the other rows or columns. For example,
  COLS="*, 2*"
  sets up two columns, the right one getting twice as much space as the left one (this is the same as using "33%, 67%").
- Any combination of absolute, percentage, and relative. For example,
  ROWS="100, 65%, *"
  sets up three rows: the top is 100 pixels high, the middle is 65 percent of the window, and the bottom gets the remaining space.

 Using absolute pixel values with the ROWS and COLS attributes can result in some weird-looking frames, due to the many differences in screen sizes and resolutions.

Using Multimedia

Multimedia is the inclusion of audio, video, and animation pieces in a web. You can simply offer a user a multimedia file to be downloaded by clicking its link, and then, depending on the availability of players, the file can be automatically or manually played. If you want to make multimedia an automatic part of a web (called *inline* audio or video)—for example, to automatically play an audio piece when a web opens—you must use some extensions to HTML. These include the <BGSOUND> tag for playing inline audio and the DYNSRC attribute for the Image tag to play inline audio-video. Also <MARQUEE>, which is a scrolling bar of text across the window, is included here as a form of animation. These HTML extensions are *only* supported by Microsoft Internet Explorer 2.0 or later, and to a lesser extent by NCSA Mosaic. Netscape Navigator 3.0 and above support the <EMBED> tag, which allows you to include audio and video files with one of the Netscape plug-ins. Netscape plug-ins for standard audio and video files are included with Navigator 3.0 and above, and more can be found on the Netscape web site (**http://home.netscape.com**). Internet Explorer 4.0 and on also supports the <EMBED> tag. Listing 13-10 provides some examples of using multimedia with Internet Explorer, and Table 13-10 describes the related tags and their attributes.

Listing 13-10
Examples of the HTML to use multimedia

```
<BGSOUND SRC="all.wav" LOOP=2>
<IMG SRC="hibiscus.jpg" DYNSRC="goodtime.avi" CONTROLS
   START=MOUSEOVER>
<MARQUEE BEHAVIOR=SLIDE, DIRECTION=RIGHT>The marquee will
   scroll this text</MARQUEE>
```

Tag or Attribute	Description
<BGSOUND>	Specifies a sound to be played automatically as a page is loaded. Not used in Netscape Navigator.
SRC	Identifies the URL of the WAV, AU, or MID file that will be played as soon as it is downloaded.
LOOP	Identifies the number of times the sound will play; if LOOP=-1 or INFINITE, the sound will play until the page is closed.
<IMG>	Specifies a video or animation clip is to be played.
DYNSRC	Identifies the URL of the inline video AVI file to be played. Not used in Netscape Navigator.
START	Identifies when the file should start playing (START=FILEOPEN or MOUSEOVER); FILEOPEN is the default, and MOUSEOVER means the file will start playing when the mouse is moved over the alternative image.

Table 13-10. *Multimedia Tags and Attributes*

Tag or Attribute	Description
CONTROLS	Specifies that the video player control panel should be displayed.
LOOP	Identifies the number of times the video will play; if LOOP=-1 or INFINITE, the sound will play until the page is closed.
LOOPDELAY	Identifies how long to wait, in milliseconds, between repetitions in a loop.
SRC	Identifies the image to display if the browser cannot play the video.
<MARQUEE> </MARQUEE>	Specifies the definition of a scrolling bar of text across the browser window. Not used in Netscape Navigator.
ALIGN	Identifies the alignment of the text in the marquee to be at its TOP, MIDDLE, or BOTTOM.
BEHAVIOR	Identifies how the text should behave. BEHAVIOR=SCROLL means the text will continuously scroll from one side to the other; =SLIDE means it will move from one side to the other and stop; =ALTERNATE means the text will continuously bounce from one side to the other. SCROLL is the default.
BGCOLOR	Identifies the background color.
DIRECTION	Identifies the direction that the text will scroll (=LEFT or =RIGHT); LEFT is the default.
HEIGHT	Identifies the height of the marquee in either pixels or percentage of the window.
HSPACE	Identifies the right and left margins of the marquee in pixels.
LOOP	Identifies the number of times that the text will loop; if LOOP=-1 or INFINITE, the sound will play until the page is closed.
SCROLLAMOUNT	Identifies the number of pixels between successive loops of text.

Table 13-10.   *Multimedia Tags and Attributes* (continued)

Tag or Attribute	Description
SCROLLDELAY	Identifies the number of milliseconds between successive loops.
VSPACE	Identifies the top and bottom margins of the marquee.
WIDTH	Identifies the width of the marquee, either in pixels or as a percentage of the window.
<EMBED>	Specifies a sound or video file to be played by the appropriate plug-in; SRC, WIDTH, HEIGHT, BORDER, HSPACE, and VSPACE are the same as for <IMG>.

Table 13-10. *Multimedia Tags and Attributes* (continued)

Note *The Image tag attributes in Table 13-10 are in addition to the regular Image tag attributes listed in Table 13-5, which can all be used with video and animation clips.*

Understanding FrontPage-Generated HTML

Many of the example listings in the "Introducing HTML" section have been created with FrontPage and only slightly modified to fit the needs of the section. Let's look at three more examples of increasing complexity and get a feeling for the HTML generated by FrontPage. First, though, we'll explore the ways of looking at FrontPage's HTML.

How to Look at FrontPage HTML

You have at least two ways to look at the HTML generated by FrontPage: in Page view and in your browser. If you have more than one browser, you can look at the HTML in each. Use the following steps to see the differences among the views:

1. Load FrontPage if it's not already loaded. Click New in the File menu and choose Web. Click One Page Web, name it **SimpleHTML**, and click OK.

2. Double-click the Home Page to open it in Page view.

3. Enter a heading, a couple of short paragraphs with some formatting, and place an image with text after it, as shown in Figure 13-8. Save the page.

4. Click the HTML tab at the bottom of Page view. The HTML source will appear as shown in Figure 13-9.

Figure 13-8. *A simple web page*

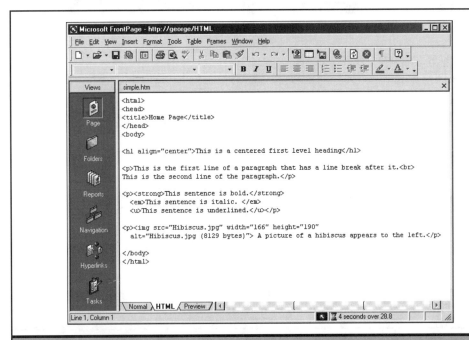

Figure 13-9. *HTML for the simple web page in Figure 13-8*

5. Click the Normal tab, make some small change to your web page like centering the image, and *without saving* the page, click the HTML tab again and you will see your change, like this:

```
<p align="center"><img src="Hibiscus.jpg" width="166" height="190"
   alt="Hibiscus.jpg (8129 bytes)"> A picture of a hibiscus appears to the left.</p>
```

Note *The highlighting allows you to see the effect on the HTML of the changes you make in FrontPage since the last time you saved the page.*

6. Close the HTML window and open the Simple HTML web in Microsoft Internet Explorer if you have it. Open the View menu and choose Source. Windows Notepad will open and display the HTML behind the Simple HTML web page, as you can see in Figure 13-10.

7. Close Notepad and Internet Explorer, and open Simple HTML in Netscape Navigator if you have it. Open the View menu and choose Page Source. A Netscape window will open as shown in Figure 13-11. Onscreen you can see that tags are one color, attributes another, and text a third.

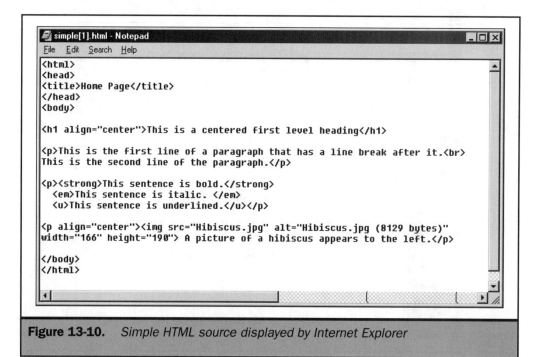

Figure 13-10. *Simple HTML source displayed by Internet Explorer*

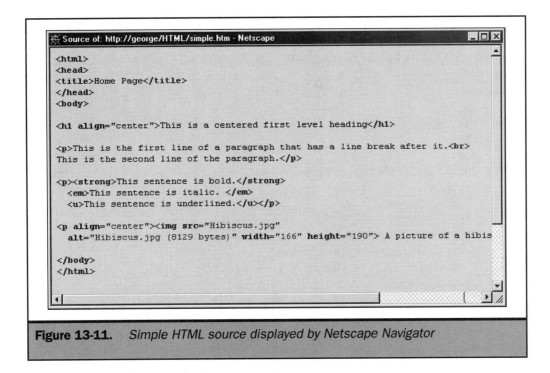

```
Source of: http://george/HTML/simple.htm - Netscape

<html>
<head>
<title>Home Page</title>
</head>
<body>

<h1 align="center">This is a centered first level heading</h1>

<p>This is the first line of a paragraph that has a line break after it.<br>
This is the second line of the paragraph.</p>

<p><strong>This sentence is bold.</strong>
  <em>This sentence is italic. </em>
  <u>This sentence is underlined.</u></p>

<p align="center"><img src="Hibiscus.jpg"
  alt="Hibiscus.jpg (8129 bytes)" width="166" height="190"> A picture of a hibis

</body>
</html>
```

Figure 13-11.   *Simple HTML source displayed by Netscape Navigator*

8. Close the Netscape window and Navigator, and reopen FrontPage Page view.

In the three views in which you have just seen the Simple HTML example, there are no major differences, although you may see some with other pages. In this example it just depends on your preference and what you want to do with what you are looking at. If you just want to look, Netscape and FrontPage offer the advantage of having different colors for the different HTML components, which Microsoft Internet Explorer does not offer. If you want to directly change the HTML, you can do that in FrontPage or Microsoft Internet Explorer with Notepad editor. In all three views you can select and copy the HTML to the Windows Clipboard, copy it to another editor, and then easily move the HTML from both FrontPage and Navigator to, for example, Notepad.

In the next several sections of this chapter, you will try all three methods (if you have both browsers). By the end of the chapter you'll be able to decide which you like best.

Looking at a Simple HTML Example

Take a closer look at the tags and attributes that were created by FrontPage in the Simple HTML example. Listing 13-11 shows the HTML for this example. It was copied to the Clipboard and then pasted in the manuscript for this book. The tags and

WORKING BEHIND THE SCENES

attributes were put in uppercase letters, the tags were made bold, and tags contained in other tags or lines that were a continuation of the previous line were indented. Otherwise this listing has not changed from that generated by FrontPage.

```
<HTML>
  <HEAD>
    <TITLE>Home Page</TITLE>
  </HEAD>
  <BODY>
    <H1 ALIGN="CENTER">This is a centered first level heading</H1>
    <P>This is the first line of a paragraph that has a line break
      after it.<BR>
      This is the second line of the paragraph.</P>
    <P><B>This sentence is in bold.</B>
      <I>This sentence is in italic.</I>
      <U>This sentence is underlined.</U></P>
    <P ALIGN="CENTER"><IMG SRC="Hibiscus.jpg" ALT="Hibiscus.jpg
      (8129 bytes)" WIDTH="166" HEIGHT="190">
      A picture of a hibiscus appears to the left.</P>
  </BODY>
</HTML>
```

There are no surprises in Listing 13-11. All of the tags and attributes were discussed in the "Introducing HTML" section earlier in the chapter. There are, however, a few interesting items to note:

- FrontPage uses the ALIGN=CENTER attributes of Heading and Paragraph tags instead of embedding the tags in a Center tag.

- The Bold (B) and Italic (I) tags are now used in FrontPage 2000. In previous versions of FrontPage, you would see the Strong and Emphasis tags.

- The HEIGHT and WIDTH attributes are added to the Image tag to establish the area to be occupied by the image and to allow the following text to be displayed while the image is loaded.

Looking at Exciting Travel HTML

For a second example, close your Simple HTML example and open the Exciting Travel home page you created in Chapters 6 and 7. The beginning of the web page is shown in Figure 13-12, and the HTML that creates it is provided in Listing 13-12 (to reduce the bulk and repetition, the middle three items in the bulleted list and the middle four items in the numbered list were removed, as was the bottom shared border).

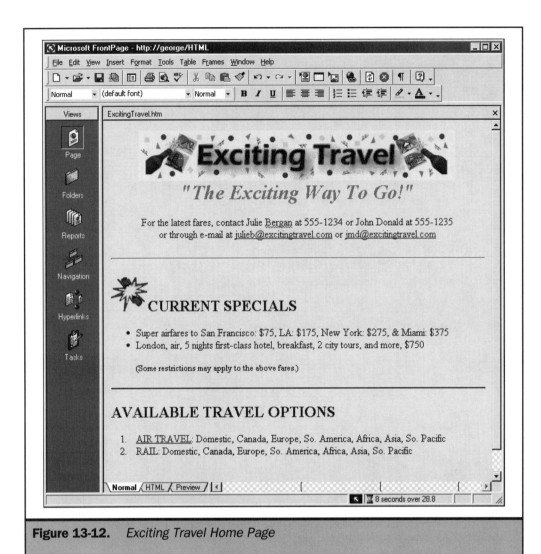

Figure 13-12. *Exciting Travel Home Page*

Listing 13-12
Exciting
Travel Home
Page

```
<HTML>
  <HEAD>
    <META HTTP-EQUIV="Content-Type" CONTENT="text/html;
    charset=windows-1252">
    <TITLE>Home Page</TITLE>
    <META NAME="GENERATOR" CONTENT="Microsoft FrontPage 4.0">
    <META NAME="ProgId" CONTENT="FrontPage.Editor.Document">
```

```
  <META NAME="Microsoft Border" CONTENT="none, default">
</HEAD>
<BODY BGCOLOR="#FFFFCC">
  <H1 ALIGN="center"><I><B>
    <FONT SIZE="7"><IMG BORDER="0" SRC="ExcitingTravel.gif"
      WIDTH="508" HEIGHT="78"><BR></FONT>
    <FONT COLOR="#00FF00">&quot;The Exciting Way To Go!&quot;
    </FONT></B></I></H1>
  <P ALIGN="center">
    For the latest fares, contact Julie Bergan at 555-1234
    or John Donald at 555-1235<BR>
    or through e-mail at <A
    HREF="mailto:julieb@excitingtravel.com">
    julieb@excitingtravel.com</A>
    or <A HREF="mailto:jmd@excitingtravel.com">
    jmd@excitingtravel.com</A></P>
  <HR>
  <H2>
    <IMG BORDER="0" SRC="firecracker.gif"
      WIDTH="59" HEIGHT="53">CURRENT SPECIALS</H2>
  <UL>
    <LI><P>
      Super airfares to San Francisco: $75, LA: $175, New York:
      $275, &amp; Miami: $375</LI>
    <LI><P>
      London, air, 5 nights first-class hotel, breakfast, 2 city
      tours, and more, $750</LI>
  </UL>
  <BLOCKQUOTE>
    <P>
      <FONT SIZE="2">(Some restrictions may apply to the above
        fares.)
      </FONT></P>
  </BLOCKQUOTE>
  <H2><IMG BORDER="0" SRC="bd15155_.gif" WIDTH="600"
    HEIGHT="10"></H2>
  <H2>
    AVAILABLE TRAVEL OPTIONS</H2>
  <OL>
    <LI><P>
      <A HREF="Air.htm">AIR TRAVEL</A>: Domestic, Canada, Europe,
      So. America, Africa, Asia, So. Pacific</LI>
```

```
    <LI><P>
        RAIL: Domestic, Canada, Europe, So. America, Africa, Asia,
        So. Pacific</LI>
    </OL>
    <P> </P>
    </BODY>
</HTML>
```

There is not much difference whether you look at the Exciting Travel Home Page HTML in Page view's HTML tab, or in either Microsoft Internet Explorer or Netscape Navigator. All three look like Listing 13-12 (with more or less formatting). Several items to observe in them are:

■ The use of the color value for the custom color you created. Without FrontPage to figure this out for you, you would have had to either be satisfied with one of the color names, or get and work with one of the unwieldy color charts.

■ The replacement of the quote (") character in your text with """ because the quote is considered a reserved character. You can use it in text, unlike the other reserved characters.

■ The Blockquote tag used to indent the "Some restrictions" paragraph. While this looks awkward in HTML, it works—looks don't count.

Looking at the Corporate Presence HTML

The Corporate Presence Wizard (and the web it creates), shown in Figure 13-13, is FrontPage's tour de force. It uses most of the features available in FrontPage, including many of the FrontPage active components. As a result the HTML has many unusual elements, as shown in Listing 13-13. These elements are used by the FrontPage Server Extensions (which are used with the Microsoft Personal Web Server and commercial web servers). In Listing 13-13, some repetition has been removed for brevity.

Note *There is a significant difference between the HTML that you see in the HTML tab of Page view and the HTML that you see in the browser. The reason is that in the browser the FrontPage active components, or formerly "WebBots," have been fully expanded with a significant amount of HTML, whereas in Page view you see only the component itself. Listing 13-13 shows what you see in a browser.*

Listing 13-13
Corporate Presence web Home page in a browser

```
<HTML>
    <HEAD>
        <TITLE>Home</TITLE>
```

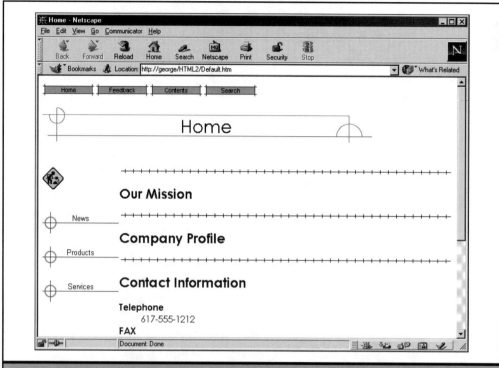

Figure 13-13.   *Corporate Presence web Home page in a browser*

```
<META NAME="GENERATOR" CONTENT="Microsoft FrontPage 4.0">
<META NAME="ProgId" CONTENT="FrontPage.Editor.Document">
<META NAME="Microsoft Theme" CONTENT="blueprnt 000, default">
<META NAME="Microsoft Border" CONTENT="tlb, default">
</HEAD>
<BODY BGCOLOR="#FFFFFF" TEXT="#003399" LINK="#3366FF"
  VLINK="#9900FF" ALINK="#000066"  >
  <!--msnavigation-->
  <TABLE BORDER="0" CELLPADDING="0" CELLSPACING="0" WIDTH="100%">
    <TR>
      <TD><!--mstheme--><FONT FACE="Century Gothic, Arial,
        Helvetica">
        <P><A HREF="../"><IMG SRC="_derived/home.gif" WIDTH="95"
          HEIGHT="20" BORDER="0" ALT="Home" ALIGN="middle"></A>
```

```
        <A HREF="search.htm"><IMG SRC="_derived/search.gif"
          WIDTH="95" HEIGHT="20" BORDER="0" ALT="Search"
          ALIGN="middle"></A></P>
        <P><IMG SRC="_derived/Default.gif" WIDTH="600"
         HEIGHT="60" BORDER="0" ALT="Home"><BR></P>
        <P> </P>
      <!--mstheme--></FONT></TD>
    </TR>
    <!--msnavigation-->
  </TABLE>
  <!--msnavigation-->
  <TABLE BORDER="0" CELLPADDING="0" CELLSPACING="0" WIDTH="100%">
    <TR>
      <TD VALIGN="top" WIDTH="1%"><!--mstheme--><FONT
        FACE="Century Gothic, Arial, Helvetica">
        <P><IMG SRC="images/undercon.gif" ALT="[Under
          Construction]" BORDER="0" WIDTH=40 HEIGHT=38></P>
        <P><A HREF="news.htm"><IMG SRC="_derived/news.gif"
          WIDTH="140" HEIGHT="60" BORDER="0" ALT="News"></A><BR>
          <A HREF="services.htm"><IMG SRC="_derived/services.gif"
            WIDTH="140" HEIGHT="60" BORDER="0"
ALT="Services"></A></P>
        <!--mstheme--></FONT></TD>
      <TD valign="top" WIDTH="24"></TD>
      <!--msnavigation-->
      <TD valign="top"><!--mstheme--><FONT face="Century Gothic,
        Arial, Helvetica">
        <P><!--webbot bot="PurpleText"
          preview="Write an introductory paragraph." --> </P>
        <P> </P>
        <H2><!--mstheme--><FONT COLOR="#660066">Our Mission
          <!--mstheme--></FONT></H2>
          <!--msthemeseparator-->
        <DL>
          <Dt><STRONG>Telephone</STRONG> </DT>
          <DD><!--webbot bot="Substitution"
            s-variable="CompanyPhone"
```

```
            startspan -->617-555-1212<!--webbot bot="Substitution"
              endspan i-checksum="13173" --></DD>
        <Dt><STRONG>Postal address</STRONG> </DT>
        <DD><!--webbot bot="Substitution"
          s-variable="CompanyAddress"
          startspan -->123 Web Way, Cambridge MA
            02138<!--webbot bot=
          "Substitution" endspan i-checksum="8844" --></DD><BR>
        </DL>
      <!--mstheme--></FONT><!--msnavigation--></TD>
    </TR>
    <!--msnavigation-->
  </TABLE>
  <!--msnavigation-->
  <TABLE BORDER="0" cellpadding="0" cellspacing="0" WIDTH="100%">
    <TR>
      <TD><!--mstheme--><FONT face="Century Gothic, Arial,
      Helvetica">
      <P> </P>
      <H5><!--mstheme--><FONT COLOR="#660066">
        Send mail to <A HREF="mailto:someone@microsoft.com">
        someone@microsoft.com</A><BR>
      <!--mstheme--></FONT></H5>
      <!--mstheme--></FONT></TD>
    </TR>
    <!--msnavigation-->
  </TABLE>
</BODY>
</HTML>
```

Some of the major observations in Listing 13-13 are as follows:

■ The HTML uses that are unique to FrontPage commands within comments, <!- - mstheme - - and <! - - msnavigation - - >, to provide instruction to the FrontPage server extensions to implement the use of themes and the navbar.

■ The <! - - webbot bot="PurpleText"...- - > annotation active component, which is sprinkled throughout the listing, provides text that is only visible while authoring—not in the browser.

- The <! - - webbot bot="Substitution"...- - > active component provides a useful and observable function by being a single source of information, like the company address and phone number, that can be used throughout the web.

If there is one feeling that you should come away with after looking at the HTML generated by FrontPage, it is a much greater appreciation for FrontPage and what it saves you in creating web pages. Just the amount of reduced typing is mind-boggling, but more important are all the automatic features, where you simply don't have to worry about some minutiae that is important to the browser but to no one else. For example, the following items are totally handled by FrontPage:

- The hexadecimal triplet for the custom color in the theme

- The height and width of images

- The particular font size for a piece of text

- Making sure you have all the ending tags for all your beginning tags

- Translating some characters into their escape sequence

Adding Capability to a FrontPage Web with HTML

Besides understanding the HTML that FrontPage generates, the other reason to learn about HTML is to be able to augment FrontPage when it doesn't provide an HTML- supported function. First look at how you'd add HTML to FrontPage, and then look at two examples of added features: one to add a floating frame, and the other to modify a table.

How to Add HTML to FrontPage

There are three ways to add HTML to FrontPage:

- Directly edit the HTML produced by FrontPage outside of FrontPage and resave it. This technique should be strongly discouraged, because it potentially removes the ability to maintain the web with FrontPage, and there is now an excellent way to add HTML within FrontPage.

- Use the HTML tab in Page view, which allows you to see and edit the HTML that describes a given page.

■ Use the Insert HTML component, which is available anywhere on a normal page in Page view, by positioning the insertion point where you want to add the HTML, opening the Insert menu, and choosing Advanced | HTML. The HTML Markup dialog box will open and allow you to directly enter HTML.

In the two examples that follow you'll use the latter two approaches for adding HTML, and you can decide which you like best. The HTML tab, though, provides much more flexibility and a complete picture of the HTML behind a page. The Insert HTML component allows you to encapsulate the HTML you are adding and keep it separate from the FrontPage-generated and -checked HTML.

 Through FrontPage 98, FrontPage had a bad habit of changing HTML that you entered to fit its own rules. Thankfully FrontPage 2000 fixed that and no longer changes HTML that you enter.

Inserting HTML to Display a Floating Frame

A *floating frame* is a single window that can contain text or graphics and that can be anywhere on a web page. There is no way in the WYSIWYG (normal window) of FrontPage to create a floating frame. While you could easily do this using the HTML tab, use the Insert HTML component to add a floating frame to a web page with these instructions:

1. Open a new single page in FrontPage, open Page view, and with the insertion point in the upper-left corner, type **This hibiscus is in a floating frame:**.

2. Format it as Heading 1, and move the insertion point to the next line.

3. Open the Insert menu and choose Advanced | HTML. The HTML Markup dialog box will open.

4. In the text box, type (you do not have to use any capital letters, and you can use any GIF or JPG image you have in place of the hibiscus):

```
<IFRAME NAME="hibiscus" WIDTH="166" HEIGHT="190"
SRC="hibiscus.jpg">If this browser supported
floating frames you would see a
hibiscus.</IFRAME>
```

so your dialog box looks like that shown next:

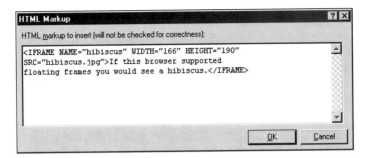

5. Click OK to close the dialog box. When you return to the normal Page view window, you will not see the floating frame that you added. It is encapsulated in a FrontPage component (see Figure 13-14), as you can see if you click the HTML tab.

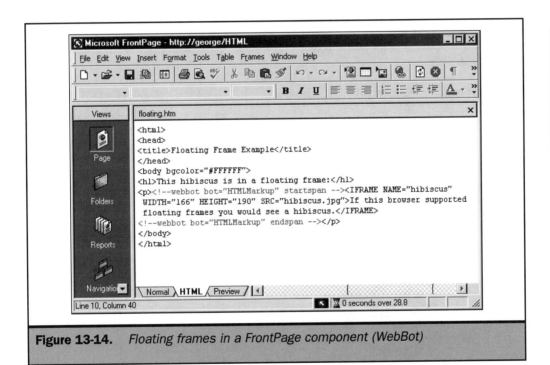

Figure 13-14. *Floating frames in a FrontPage component (WebBot)*

6. Save the page, and then open it in Microsoft Internet Explorer 3.0 or later (Netscape Navigator as late as 4.5 does not support floating frames). You should see the image of the hibiscus (or whatever image you used) in a floating frame, as shown in Figure 13-15. In a browser that does not support floating frames, the text "If this browser supported floating frames you would see a hibiscus." is displayed, like this:

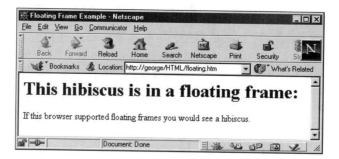

7. Close your browser and Page view. Also close any webs you have open in FrontPage.

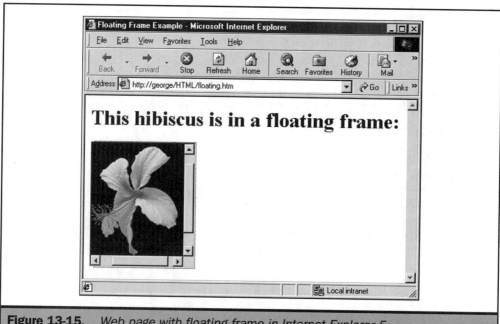

Figure 13-15. *Web page with floating frame in Internet Explorer 5*

Inserting HTML to Modify a Table

The table that you saw in Figure 13-6 had an outside border or frame around the entire table and individual borders around each cell. In Page view Normal tab, you control how a table looks with the Table Properties dialog box, where the border controls allow you to change the size and color of the border, but not turn off the outer frame while leaving the cell borders. You can do that with HTML. Next use the HTML tab to remove the borders of any simple table. For illustration purposes the table created earlier in this chapter and shown in Figure 13-6 is used, but you can use any table with the following steps.

Note
In the Page view Normal tab, you can achieve the same effect of cell borders without a table border by first turning off all borders in the Table Properties dialog box by making the Borders Size 0. Then Select the cells you want to have borders, open the Cell Properties dialog box, click Style, click Format, choose Border, click Box, make the Width something larger than 0, and click OK three times. The HTML technique is easier!

1. From FrontPage either create a new web, or open an existing web with a table in it (on this book's CD it is Listing8.htm in the \Book\Chap13\HTML\ folder). In either case, open Page view.

2. If necessary, create a simple 4x4 table with some simple text in each cell (like "Cell 1," "Cell 2," and so on).

3. Right-click the table and choose Table Properties. In the Table Properties dialog box, make the Borders Size **0**, close the Properties dialog box, and look at the results in the Preview tab. Reset the border to **2** and then, one at a time, make each of the border colors white (or the same color as the background), and look at the results. You can see that either all the borders are showing or all the borders are not visible. When you are done, return the Table Properties dialog box to its default settings.

4. Open the HTML tab and click between <table and border to place the insertion point there.

5. Type **frame="void"** (including both quotation marks). Make sure there is a space on either side of the newly typed material. Your results should look like this:

```
<h2>A New Table</h2>
<table frame="void"| border="2" cellpadding=
    bgcolor="#FFFFFF" bordercolordark>
    <caption align="center">THIS IS THE TABLE
    <tr valign="bottom">
```

6. Click Save on the toolbar to save your page, and then click the Preview tab or look at it in a browser. Your result should resemble the table in Figure 13-16.

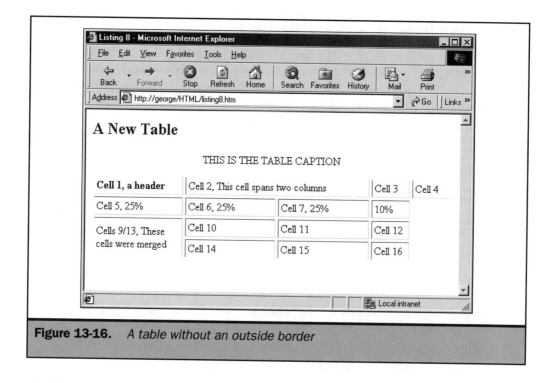

Figure 13-16. *A table without an outside border*

7. Close your browser and FrontPage.

With the two examples here and the HTML reference earlier in the chapter, you can see how easy it is to add significant capability to your FrontPage webs.

HTML Authoring Resources

There are a number of excellent resources on HTML authoring available on the Web. The following is a list of the ones that are most important.

*URLs change very quickly. While every effort was made to get the following URLs correct when this book went to print, they probably will have changed by the time this book reaches the bookstores. If you are having trouble with a URL, drop off right-hand segments, delineated by slashes, until it works. Microsoft's site is changing faster than anybody's, so if one of their URLs isn't working, don't be surprised. The best work-around is to go to **http://www.microsoft.com** and work forward.*

A Beginner's Guide to HTML by NCSA (the National Center for Supercomputing Applications at the University of Illinois at Urbana-Champaign, original creators of Mosaic, the first of the web browsers from which Netscape Navigator, Microsoft Internet Explorer, and others have descended, last updated November 9, 1998 available at
http://www.ncsa.uiuc.edu/General/Internet/WWW/HTMLPrimer.html

Composing Good HTML, by James "Eric" Tilton, last updated July 13, 1998, available at
http://www.cs.cmu.edu/~tilt/cgh/

Style Guide for Online Hypertext by Tim Berners-Lee (the originator of the World Wide Web), last updated May 1995, available at
http://www.w3.org/hypertext/WWW/Provider/Style/All.html

Web Etiquette by Tim Berners-Lee, last updated May 1995, available at
http://www.w3.org/hypertext/WWW/Provider/Style/Etiquette

A Basic HTML Style Guide by Alan Richmond (NASA GSFC), last updated September 16, 1994, available at
http://guinan.gsfc.nasa.gov/Style.html

Elements of HTML Style by Jonathan Cohen, last updated August 2, 1995, available at
http://www.book.uci.edu/Staff/StyleGuide.html

Microsoft offers a number of documents that provide support of HTML authoring for the Internet Explorer. These can be found at
http://microsoft.com/workshop/
with a detailed explanation of Internet Explorer HTML and DHTML support at
http://microsoft.com/workshop/author/

Netscape's HTML resources for use with Navigator include a number of documents, some also referenced here, indexed at
http://developer.netscape.com/docs/index.html
Netscape's complete *HTML Tag Reference,* last updated January 26, 1998, at
http://developer.netscape.com/docs/manuals/htmlguid/index.htm
Netscape's HTML tags sorted by Navigator release is very useful, last updated August 1997, at
http://developer.netscape.com/docs/manuals/

World Wide Web Consortiums (W3C) HTML 3.2 Specification, dated January 14, 1997, available at
http://www.w3.org/TR/REC-html32.html

World Wide Web Consortium's (W3C) *HTML 4.0 Specification,* last updated April 24, 1998, available at
http://www.w3.org/TR/REC-html40

One of the most valuable HTML references on the Internet is *The HTML Reference Library* by Stephen Le Hunte. This is a very extensive Windows 3.1, or alternatively, Windows 95/98, Help System for HTML. It is a gold mine of information and is available on the CD included with this book or for download from
http://subnet.virtual-pc.com/le387818/
This site is mirrored for North American users at
http://www.terminalp.com/htmlib/
You may also be placed on a mailing list to be notified of updates to the library by sending an e-mail request to
htmlib@htmlib.demon.co.uk.

There are also a number of other good books on the Web and HTML authoring. Among them are

HTML: The Complete Reference by Thomas Powell (Osborne/McGraw-Hill, 1998)

Beyond HTML by Richard Karpinski (Osborne/McGraw-Hill, 1996)

Dynamic HTML in Action by Michele Petrovsky (Osborne/McGraw-Hill, 1998)

The World Wide Web Complete Reference by Rick Stout (Osborne/McGraw-Hill, 1996)

HTML Programmer's Reference by Thomas A. Powell and Dan Whitworth (Osborne/McGraw-Hill, 1998)

The Webmaster's Guide to HTML: For Advanced Web Developers by Nathan J. Muller (Osborne/McGraw-Hill, 1996)

The Complete Reference

FrontPage 2000

Chapter 14

Advanced Markup Languages

In the previous chapter, you learned how HTML, the primary language of the World Wide Web, works with FrontPage. In this chapter, you will explore the next generation of markup languages: Dynamic HTML (DHTML), Extensible Markup Language (XML), and Virtual Reality Modeling Language (VRML). These languages have moved from the frontiers of the Web to the mainstream. Each offers extended capability for the web developer, making the days of pure HTML webs an increasingly distant memory.

FrontPage simplifies using DHTML, but support for XML and VRML is limited to the ability to edit scripts in the Page view HTML tab. This chapter first looks at FrontPage's support for DHTML and then provides an overview of XML and VRML.

Dynamic HTML

Dynamic HTML moves HTML to the next level of functionality by making every object on a web page dynamic and interactive. It's hard to underestimate the impact this technology will have on web design. With it, HTML becomes a real programming language. DHTML is based on the Document Object Model (DOM). This concept makes every element of a web page an object with properties that can be modified. It allows content to be modified in real time, without the user reloading the page in their browser from the server. Cascading style sheets (CSS), which were introduced in Chapter 13, are also a part of the Document Object Model. In addition to setting styles for text, CSS enables absolute positioning of elements on a web page.

Note
The basic DHTML standard is defined in the HTML 4.0 Recommendation of the World Wide Web Consortium (W3C). Unfortunately, as with most other developments on the Web, support varies by manufacturer. Both Netscape and Microsoft support the W3C Recommendation to some degree, but with some significant differences. Fortunately, DHTML degrades gracefully; that is, pages that use it will appear normal to the user even if their browser doesn't fully support DHTML. They will just lack the interactivity of full DHTML support.

Data binding is another advanced concept of DHTML. It allows data to be cached on the client and then filtered for presentation without reloading the data from the server. The user can filter or sort the data so that only information that meets specific, user-defined criteria is displayed in the order the user wants. The user can change the criteria without reloading the page from the server, speeding up the process and using fewer server resources.

Scriptlets are an evolving idea, the basic concept being small, reusable pieces of code that can be used throughout a web application. Internet Explorer 4 introduced the concept, but with the release of Internet Explorer 5 Microsoft now recommends that DHTML behaviors be used instead. Of course, this creates a compatibility problem, as IE 4 doesn't support DHTML behaviors.

At this time, it appears that Microsoft has developed the better implementation of DHTML. It adheres more closely to existing standards and provides more flexibility. For example, Microsoft's implementation supports both VBScript and JavaScript, while Netscape's supports only JavaScript. Part of this is probably based on Netscape's apparent desire to have as little to do with Microsoft technologies as possible. This is a business decision. As a web developer, you need to be concerned with functionality.

In this section you will see how Microsoft has implemented DHTML. This is the version supported by FrontPage and Internet Explorer 5. As a result, the example you create may not function in Netscape Navigator. This doesn't mean that DHTML cannot be used with Netscape, only that you will need to check your specific DHTML code carefully in the browsers your intended audience uses.

Event Handling

In HTML there is very limited support for handling events, such as moving the mouse pointer over an object. The only event that is really handled is clicking a hyperlink or form button. In DHTML this has been greatly expanded. Table 14-1 lists the names of the mouse events Microsoft's flavor of DHTML supports, and the actions that trigger them. Table 14-2 lists the keyboard events and actions.

Mouse Event	Action Triggered When
onmouseover	The mouse pointer is placed on an object.
onmouseout	The mouse pointer moves off an object.
onmousedown	Any mouse button is pressed.
onmouseup	Any mouse button is released.
onmousemove	The mouse pointer is moving over an object.
onclick	The left mouse button is clicked on an object.
ondblclick	The left mouse button is double-clicked on an object.
oncontextmenu	The right mouse button is clicked on an object (supported by IE5 only).
ondrag	An object is being dragged with the mouse (supported by IE 5 only).

Table 14-1.   *Microsoft-Supported DHTML Mouse Events*

Mouse Event	Action Triggered When
ondragend	The left mouse button is released after dragging an object (supported by IE 5 only).
ondragstart	The dragging of an object starts (supported by IE 5 only).
ondragenter	An object being dragged enters a specified target area (supported by IE 5 only).
ondragover	An object being dragged is over a specified target area (supported by IE 5 only).
ondragleave	An object being dragged leaves a specified target area (supported by IE 5 only).
ondrop	The left mouse button is released while dragging an object over a specified target area (supported by IE 5 only).

Table 14-1. *Microsoft-Supported DHTML Mouse Events* (continued)

Note
The events listed in Tables 14-1 and 14-2 are by no means all the events that can be used with DHTML. Microsoft currently lists 59 distinct events that can trigger DHTML actions, and you can expect the list to grow to include every conceivable event. However, many of these events are currently only supported in Internet Explorer 5, with partial support in Internet Explorer 4 and Netscape's browsers. Unless you're writing for an intranet where Internet Explorer 5 is the required browser, using these events is not very practical at this time.

Keyboard Event	Action Triggered When
onkeypress	A key is pressed and released. Holding a key down will generate multiple onkeypress events.
onkeydown	A key is pressed. Holding the key down will not generate multiple events.
onkeyup	A key is released.

Table 14-2. *Microsoft-Supported DHTML Keyboard Events*

These events are used to trigger actions in the web page. For example, you could change the color or size of an object when the user points to it. FrontPage contains several ways to use DHTML without having to program the event and action, as you will see in the next section.

Animating Text with DHTML

Animating text—making it move on a page—can be done a number of ways. Internet Explorer 4 supports the HTML Marquee tag (covered in Chapter 19), and this is a common use for a Java applet. DHTML does this also, and this is a good place to start your exploration of DHTML in FrontPage. Begin with these steps:

1. In FrontPage, create a new One Page Web named **Advmarkup**.

2. Open the home page (Default.htm) in Page view and type **DHTML Moves Me**; then format it as Heading 2.

3. Open the Format menu and choose Dynamic HTML Effects. This displays the DHTML Effects toolbar, shown here:

This toolbar allows you to apply DHTML effects to the selected object. In the On drop-down list, you select the event that will trigger the effect. The Apply drop-down list displays the available effects, and the third drop-down list allows you to set any available properties of the chosen effect. You can remove any effect by clicking Remove Effect, and the button at the far right of the toolbar toggles between whether or not the DHTML effect is highlighted in FrontPage.

You can also display the DHTML Effects toolbar by opening the View menu and choosing Toolbars | DHTML Effects.

4. With the cursor still on the same line as your text, click the down arrow in the On drop-down list in the DHTML Effects toolbar and choose Page Load.

Note   *The DHTML Effects toolbar provides limited support for DHTML events. To fully utilize DHTML with FrontPage, you will need to manually edit the code using the Page view HTML tab. Chapter 15 introduces web scripting languages, and Chapters 16 through 18 provide further examples of web scripting.*

5. Click the down arrow in the Apply drop-down list and choose Zoom.

6. Click the down arrow in the third drop-down list and choose Out. Your page should look similar to Figure 14-1.

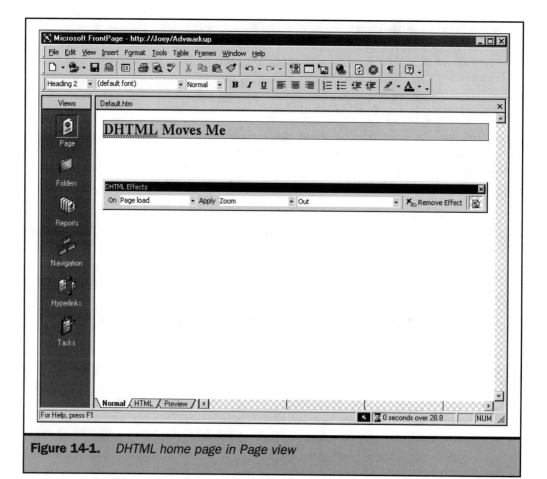

Figure 14-1. DHTML home page in Page view

7. Save your page and then open it in Internet Explorer. Your text will start out large and then decrease in size.

8. Repeat steps 5 through 7, choosing different types of animation from the Apply drop-down list and refreshing the page in your browser after each change.

9. In Page view, with the cursor still on the same line as your heading, select Mouse Over from the On drop-down list in the DHTML Effects toolbar.

10. Select Formatting from the Apply drop-down list, and then select Choose Font from the third (Effects) drop-down list. The Font dialog box, shown here, is displayed.

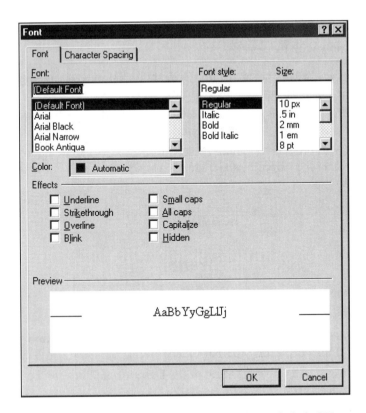

11. Select Arial Black from the Font scrolling list box and click OK.

12. Save your page and then load it in Internet Explorer. The Zoom Out effect runs when the page is first loaded.

13. Point to the heading and the font will change to Arial Black. When you move the mouse pointer off of the heading, it will return to the default font.

As you can see, FrontPage greatly simplifies using DHTML. You do not need to do any programming to add DHTML to your webs. You can also use these DHTML effects with any object, not just text. DHTML is also much more flexible than extended HTML tags, such as the Marquee tag, because it is a script, not a tag with limited predefined attributes. FrontPage support for other DHTML features is enabled in much the same way as animating objects.

Collapsible Lists

Collapsible lists are any type of lists (bulleted, numbered, and so on) where the list items below the top level of the hierarchy are not displayed until the user clicks a list item. This next exercise will show you how easy it is to create a collapsible list with FrontPage and DHTML. Begin now with these steps.

1. In Page view, place the cursor on the first line below your heading; then type **Dynamic List** and format it as Heading 3. Press ENTER.

2. Click Bullets on the Formatting toolbar and type **Item 1**. Press ENTER, type **Description 1**, and press ENTER again.

3. Type **Item 2**, press ENTER, type **Description 2**, press ENTER again, and then type **Another Description**. Press ENTER twice to end the list. Your list should look similar to this:

> **Dynamic List**
>
> - Item 1
> - Description 1
> - Item 2
> - Description 2
> - Another Description

4. Place your cursor at the beginning of the Description 1 line, and click Increase Indent on the Formatting toolbar twice.

5. Place the cursor at the beginning of the Description 2 line, and click Increase Indent twice.

6. Place the cursor at the beginning of the Another Description line and press Increase Indent four times. Your list should now look similar to this:

> **Dynamic List**
>
> - Item 1
>   - o Description 1
> - Item 2
>   - o Description 2
>   - ▪ Another Description

7. Right-click Item 1 in the list and select List Properties. In the List Properties dialog box, select Enable Collapsible Outlines and Initially Collapsed, as shown next. Click OK.

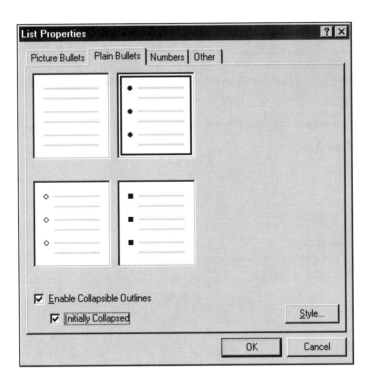

Tip   *The Enable Collapsible Outlines and Initially Collapsed check boxes are available on all the tabs of the List Properties dialog box.*

8. Save your page and then reload it in Internet Explorer. The list should appear with two list items: Item 1 and Item 2.

9. Click Item 1 in the list and Description 1 should now be displayed.

10. Click Item 2. When Description 2 is displayed, click it also. This displays the last item in the list, Another Description, as shown in Figure 14-2.

11. Click Item 2 to collapse the items below it in the list hierarchy—Description 2 and Another Description.

DHTML makes adding advanced features, such as dynamically changing text and collapsible lists, extremely easy in your webs. In the next section you'll see how to add

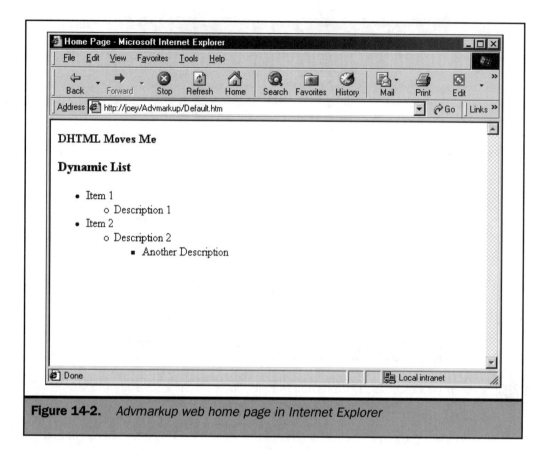

Figure 14-2. *Advmarkup web home page in Internet Explorer*

clickable form field labels, which make your web pages behave more like an actual Windows application.

Clickable Form Field Labels

In Windows dialog boxes you can select a check box or option button by clicking the label for the box or button. With web forms you have to actually click the check box or option button to select it. You can use DHTML to make web form labels function in the same way as Windows dialog boxes. Do that now with these instructions.

1. In FrontPage Page view, place the cursor on the first line after your list.

2. Open the Insert menu and choose Form | Check Box.

3. Press HOME and type **This is a label** (leave a space at the end). Press RIGHT ARROW and then SHIFT+ENTER.

4. Drag across the label and check box to select them; then open the Insert menu and choose Form | Label.

5. Save your page and then open it in Internet Explorer.

6. Click the label and a checkmark appears in the check box. Click the label again and the checkmark is removed (the check box is cleared).

Another DHTML effect that adds a dynamic element to your work is page transitions, as you will see next.

Page Transitions

Page transitions are effects that can be applied to a web page when the user enters or exits a page, or when the user enters or exits your site. You apply a page transition to the active page from the Page Transitions dialog box, shown next.

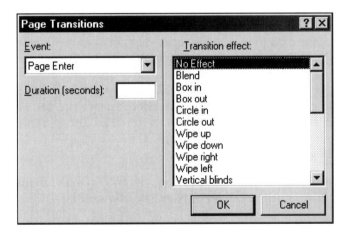

Page transitions can be triggered by four events, selected from the Event drop-down list in the Page Transitions dialog box:

■ **Page Enter** invokes the transition when the page is loaded.

■ **Page Exit** invokes the transition when the user leaves the page.

■ **Site Enter** invokes the transition when the user enters your site by loading any page.

■ **Site Exit** invokes the transition when the user leaves your site by loading a page that is not on your site.

You can specify the amount of time for the transition (in seconds) by entering a value in the Duration (Seconds) text box. The transition effect is selected from the Transition Effect scrolling list box. You will see how this works with these steps.

1. In FrontPage, open the Format menu and choose Page Transition.

2. Select Page Enter in the Event drop-down list, if it's not already selected, and then type **10** in the Duration (Seconds) text box.

3. Select Vertical Blinds in the Transition Effect scrolling list box, and then click OK.

4. Save your page, and then load it in Internet Explorer. Each time you load the page you will see the page transition effect.

To learn more about Dynamic HTML, visit Microsoft's Site Builder Network (*http://microsoft.com/sitebuilder/*). *Here you will find detailed explanations and examples of DHTML in their Workshop area. You can learn more about Netscape's implementation of DHTML on their web site (**http://developer.netscape.com/ openstudio/**).*

Positioning

Another feature of DHTML is the ability to precisely position an object on a web page. Tables are often used to position items in relation to each other, but there is little control of where the table is placed on the page. With HTML, tables can be positioned left, right, or center, and the size of the table can be defined, but that is about the limit of what you can do. DHTML extends this by allowing you to place an object, not just a table, at a specific offset from the top left corner of the page. You can also set how text will wrap around the object, much like text is wrapped around a graphic or table using the ALIGN attribute of the IMG or TABLE tags. The following exercise will show you how this works. Begin with these steps.

1. Create a new page in your Advmarkup web and save it with the Page Title **DHTML Positioning** and the File Name **Position.htm**.

2. Open the Insert menu and choose Picture | Clip Art. In the Clip Art Gallery dialog box Pictures tab, select Animals.

3. Right-click the image of the lion (the first graphic in the first row) and choose Insert. The image of the lion is placed in the upper-left corner of your page, the default location.

4. Click the image of the lion to select it; then open the Format menu and choose Position. The Position dialog box, shown next, is displayed.

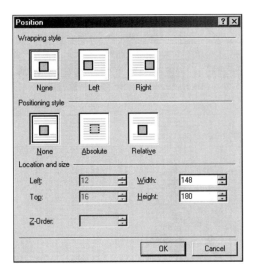

The Wrapping Style options set how text will wrap around the object (the lion graphic in this case), the Positioning Style options allow you to choose no positioning (None), Absolute (an exact location on the page), or Relative (positioned relative to other objects on the page) positioning. When either Absolute or Relative positioning is selected, the Location And Size options become available. Left and Top are used to specify the position of the object from the upper-left corner of the page. Width and Height are the size of the object. The default values are the size of the object in pixels.

Z-Order sets the *layer* of the object. With style sheets, objects on a page can be placed in layers, so that one object can be placed behind of or on top of another object. Imagine that each object (text, graphics, and so on) is printed on clear plastic, like an overhead transparency. One sheet contains the text for the page, and another sheet contains the graphic. If the text is the top sheet and the graphic is on the bottom sheet, you will see the graphic behind the text. If you reverse the order, the graphic will cover part of the text. This concept is familiar if you have worked with page layout programs such as Adobe PageMaker, but it is a new concept for the Web.

5. In the Position dialog box, select None for Wrapping Style and Absolute for Positioning Style; then type **50** in the Left Location And Size spinner and **50** in the Top Location And Size spinner. Click OK. Figure 14-3 shows the lion graphic absolutely positioned in Page view.

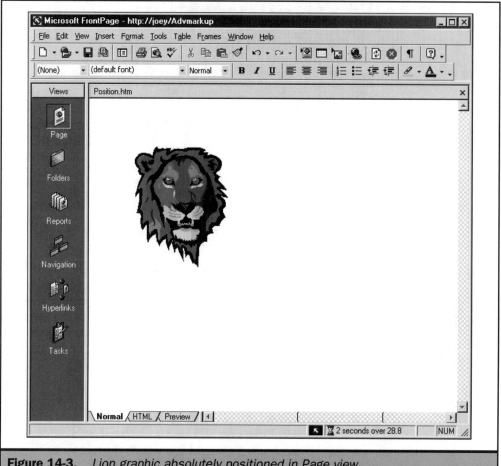

Figure 14-3. *Lion graphic absolutely positioned in Page view*

6. Press CTRL+HOME to move the cursor to the top of the page; then type **This is a picture of a lion** and format it as Heading 3.

7. With the cursor still on the line you just typed, open the Format menu and choose Position. In the Position dialog box, select Absolute for Positioning Style. Notice that the text has both a width and height, as shown in the Width and Height Location And Size spinners. This is another new concept for a web page; the width displayed is the full width of the page, not just the width of the text. If you visualize the text as being on a separate piece of paper the width of the page and then placed on top of the web page, the concept is clearer.

8. Type **50** in the Left Location And Size spinner and **75** in the Top Location And Size spinner; then type **0** in the Z-Order spinner. Click OK. Figure 14-4 shows what your page should now look like. The text has been absolutely positioned and the graphic has moved down.

9. Select the lion graphic, open the Format menu, and choose Position. In the Position dialog box, type **25** in the Left Location And Size spinner, **-75** in the Top Location And Size spinner, and **–1** in the Z-Order spinner. Click OK. Your page should look similar to Figure 14-5. The text is on the layer in front of the graphic.

Figure 14-4.   *Text and graphic absolutely positioned*

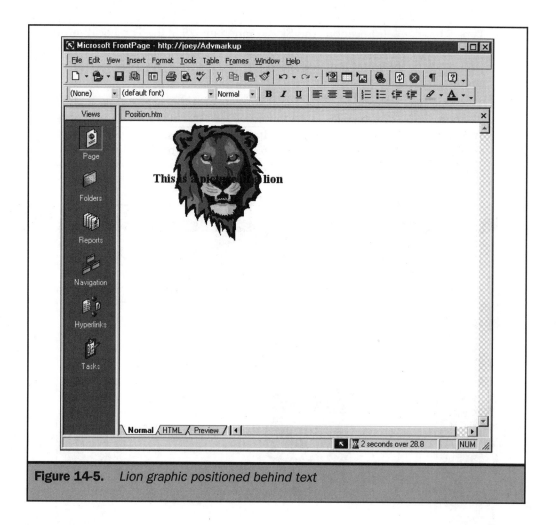

Figure 14-5. *Lion graphic positioned behind text*

10. Click the lion graphic; then open the View menu and choose Toolbars | Positioning. The Positioning toolbar, shown here, is displayed.

This toolbar duplicates most of the functions of the Position dialog box. The two buttons on the right end of the toolbar move the selected object forward one layer or back one layer.

11. With the lion graphic still selected, click Bring Forward on the Positioning toolbar. This changes the Z-Order of the layers and places the text behind the graphic.

12. Save your work, including the embedded graphic, and then open your DHTML Positioning page in Internet Explorer, as shown in Figure 14-6, where you can see the layers effect.

Dynamic HTML greatly extends the power of HTML. You can use it without any programming with FrontPage's built-in support. The current disagreements over standards of DHTML as implemented by FrontPage limit its usefulness, but like every

Figure 14-6.   *DHTML Positioning page in Internet Explorer*

other web development, a standard will be defined and newer releases of browsers will eventually include support for the W3C standard.

Extensible Markup Language

Extensible Markup Language (XML) is one of the latest additions to the web developer's toolkit. Like all new web technologies, it suffers from lack of support among browsers. A proposed standard is being reviewed by the World Wide Web Consortium (W3C), but it can take some time before a proposed standard becomes a recommendation. Nevertheless, the technology will become increasingly important in advanced web applications.

A simple definition of XML, in comparison to HTML, is that HTML defines what information will look like, while XML describes the information itself. For example, in HTML, `<H2>One Flew Over The Cuckoo's Nest</H2>` would display the text as a Heading 2 without giving any indication what the information is. In XML, the line might be written as `<BookTitle>One Flew Over The Cuckoo's Nest</BookTitle>`. The XML code by itself does not indicate how the information should be displayed; rather it describes what the information is. An important difference between HTML and XML is that a tag (`<H2>` in the preceding example) in HTML is described as an *element* in XML (`<BookTitle>` in the preceding example). The difference is more than a matter of semantics. Since XML is dealing with data rather than formatting, the information enclosed by the opening and closing elements is the data that can be referenced by the name of the element.

XML Syntax

XML syntax can look very much like standard HTML, but there are enough differences to quickly get you into trouble. These are:

- **XML is case-sensitive.**   In HTML, <UL>, <Ul>, and <ul> all are interpreted as the same thing, the opening tag for an unordered list. In XML, each would be interpreted a distinct element, and the author would determine what each element meant.

- **XML does not ignore spaces.**   HTML ignores extra spaces; if there are two or more spaces in the HTML code, all except the first is ignored. Since XML treats the content between the opening and closing elements as data, all spaces are relevant.

- **All elements must be closed.** In HTML, you can use a single paragraph tag, <P>, without explicitly closing it, </P>. In XML, all elements must be closed. If an element is empty, such as `<BookTitle></BookTitle>`, XML provides a shorthand in the form <BookTitle/>. Either example is correct XML syntax.

- **All element attributes must be in quotes.** In HTML `<img src="some.gif" width=150 height=100>` is acceptable syntax. In XML, this would have to be written as `<img src="some.gif" width="150" height="100"/>`. The XML syntax also includes a forward slash (/) to properly close the element.

XML Data Structures

Since XML is a language for describing data, how it structures data is a logical place to begin to understand the language. XML creates a hierarchical data structure. If you're familiar with databases, this is familiar territory. If not, a little review is in order. (Chapter 18 covers databases in more detail.) In precomputer days, every library had a card catalog. In the card catalog, each book in the library's collection was represented by a paper card that had the book's title, author, and other information about it. (This same information is now usually available online at the library.) Listing 14-1 shows how this information could be structured in XML.

Listing 14-1
Sample
XML Data
Structure

```
<Books>
    <Title>Liberty Ship</Title>
    <Author>Sherod Cooper</Author>
    <Publisher>Naval Institute Press</Publisher>
</Books>
<Books>
    <Title>The Summer of the Paymaster</Title>
    <Author>Alfred Nielsen</Author>
    <Publisher>Norton</Publisher>
</Books>
```

The information enclosed by the `<Books>` and `</Books>` elements is all the information about a single book. Even though this looks similar to the HTML code you looked at in the previous chapter, there are significant differences. The title of each book is enclosed in the `<Title>` and `</Title>` element. This looks like the <TITLE> HTML tag, but it is completely different. Since it is used within an XML data structure it is not interpreted in the same way as the HTML tag.

XML data is described as being *well formed* or *valid*. The difference is whether or not a Document Type Definition (DTD) is included with the data. If a DTD is included, the XML data is valid. Without a DTD, it is well formed. A DTD enables the XML data to be validated against the rules defined in the DTD. Well-formed XML data describes itself. As long as the syntax of XML is adhered to, the data is assumed to be valid. Listing 14-2 is a partial sample DTD for the XML data in Listing 14-1.

Listing 14-2
Sample
XML DTD

```
<!ELEMENT Books (Book)*>
<!ELEMENT Book (Title, Author, Publisher)>
<!ELEMENT Title (#PCDATA)>
...
```

In Listing 14-2, the first line defines a single Books element that contains zero or more Book elements. The second line defines a single Book element that contains one Title, Author, and Publisher. The third line defines a single Title element that contains only text. If the DTD in Listing 14-2 were included with the XML data in Listing 14-3, the XML data would fail the validation test since there isn't a Publisher. If it were well formed, that is, without a DTD, it would be accepted.

Listing 14-3
Sample XML
data

```
<Books>
  <Title>The Summer of the Paymaster</Title>
  <Author>Alfred Nielsen</Author>
</Books>
```

When a DTD is included, it would be referenced on the web page with the code

```
<?xml version='1.0'?>
<!DOCTYPE Books SYSTEM "Books.dtd">
```

where Books.dtd is the name of the DTD file.

Using XML

Once your XML data and DTD are created, the question is what can you do with them? Quite a bit, actually. In a broad sense, XML allows visitors to your web to manipulate information. For example, suppose the user wanted to find all the books about ships in your XML data. You could create a form that would allow the user to enter "ship" as a search word. The search would return the information about the book *Liberty Ship*.

At this point in the evolution of XML, however, it's also reasonable to ask if there are other, possibly easier ways to do this. In the next four chapters, you will learn about web scripting, Active Server Pages (ASP), and integrating databases with your webs. Many of the techniques in these next chapters are also applicable, and necessary, to successfully use XML. But XML is not yet a standard—it is a proposal. In the process of becoming a standard (actually, the W3C releases a recommendation, but this in effect becomes the standard), it could very well change in ways that would require you to modify parts of your work. There is also the problem of browser support. Being an early implementer of a new technology can be exciting, but there is also a downside to being on the "bleeding edge."

In practical terms, most of what XML promises can be accomplished with "mature" web technologies—those that have been accepted for at least a year. As XML evolves, though, it will push the envelope beyond what is now possible, or make certain tasks easier. A great deal more information about XML, including practical examples, is available on Microsoft's SiteBuilder Network (**http://microsoft.com/sitebuilder/**). This is the best place to start really digging into XML before deciding to what extent you want to use this technology.

Virtual Reality

The concept of virtual reality has been around for quite a while. It was a central theme of William Gibson's seminal virtual reality science-fiction novel *Neuromancer*, published in 1984. (Gibson also added the word *cyberspace* to the language.) Since then the concept has been popularized in a number of books and movies. In the strictest sense, virtual reality is a system that supplies all the sensory information that we normally assimilate to perceive the world around us. In practical terms, no such systems exist at the consumer level, though there are a variety of goggles and helmets that provide a taste of true virtual reality. These are mostly used with computer games. Advanced systems in research laboratories allow the user to experience such feats as walking through and around 3-D molecules.

In the context of the Web, the term "virtual reality" means the ability to display 3-D objects and to change the viewer's viewpoint of the object. So at this time, "true" virtual reality doesn't exist on the Web; rather, there are two-dimensional "slices" of 3-D objects. When enough objects are brought together, a "world" can be created.

Note *Although the phrase "virtual reality" is used throughout this section, in practical terms we're really talking about 3-D modeling. At this point in its development, creating true virtual reality worlds is beyond the capability of most computer systems. However, the basic concepts dealt with here will eventually grow into true virtual reality worlds. Check back in about ten years.*

To create any form of virtual reality on the Web, a language that can mathematically describe the world and browsers that can interpret the language are required. In 1993, Mark Pesce and Tony Parisi developed the first Virtual Reality Modeling Language (VRML) and created Labyrinth, the first 3-D browser. Since then there has been interest in the subject, with web sites, browsers, and programming tools becoming increasingly widespread. Despite the interest in the subject, virtual reality has failed to enter the mainstream of web activity. Like some other aspects of technological innovation, the idea arrived before the supporting infrastructure.

The standard language of web-based virtual reality is VRML 2.0 (VRML 1.0 is considered obsolete and there are too many differences in the languages to provide backward compatibility). Microsoft also has its own flavor of virtual reality called Chromeffects. Neither language is directly supported by FrontPage. Virtual reality objects are added to FrontPage webs in a manner similar to graphics—an object is placed in the web with the supporting code to display it correctly. This also allows you to download virtual reality objects from the Web and use them in your webs with no further understanding of virtual reality concepts. However, a basic understanding of the concepts behind VRML, whichever flavor you use, is helpful.

VRML Concepts

Virtual reality begins by describing a 3-D space with height, width, and depth. These are represented by three axes—x (width), y (height), and z (depth). Coordinates using these three axes can define any point in the 3-D space. The point of origin, from which all three axes are considered to start, is the lower-left corner. The value of the x-axis increases as the point moves to the right of the origin, and the value of the y-axis increases as the point moves toward the top of the space. On the z-axis, the value of a point increases as it moves towards the viewer from the origin and decreases as it moves away from the viewer, behind the origin. This is represented by a negative number. This system for defining a 3-D space is the Cartesian coordinate system. In VRML 2.0, these distances are referenced in meters (3.2808 feet). The coordinates for the origin are 0 0 0. For a point one meter behind the origin on the z-axis, the coordinates would be 0 0 –1. In this space, a point of origin and a radius, for example, can describe a sphere.

These coordinates are used to describe all the objects within the 3-D space. Along with any visible objects, this includes light sources and the viewpoint—the point in space from which the scene is being viewed. Once the objects are defined in the Cartesian space, things get interesting. What is the surface of the object like? Is it reflective, like a mirror, or textured, like a baseball? Is the light source a point source, like the sun, or is it more diffuse, like the sun through fog? Virtual reality modeling languages have to deal with all these concepts.

Any viewer of television is familiar with the practical results of virtual reality or 3-D modeling, seen most often in the form of "flying logos." The key difference between this type of 3-D modeling and what we call virtual reality on the Web is the ability of the user to interact with the objects—to be able to change the viewpoint so that they can walk around objects, for example. This interactivity is also one of the problems with web-based virtual reality. As described earlier, virtual reality objects and worlds are created mathematically. When the viewpoint is moved, these objects have to be recalculated, and this level of computation is not simple. To create any sort of believable experience requires massive amounts of computing power, as well as a very fast video card. With VRML browsers, this computation takes place on the client, not the server, and most home computers aren't up to the task.

Chromeffects

A significant development in the world of virtual reality (though many VRML purists may disagree) is Microsoft's Chromeffects technology. What makes Chromeffects significant is the fact that it is being integrated in Windows. Rather than the user having to download browser plug-ins, etc., the tools for working with and viewing basic 3-D and virtual reality effects will already be incorporated on the user's system. In one very real sense, this serves to weaken other virtual reality technologies, which can be expected to bring protests; at the same time, it does give developers a widely supported standard to work with.

Chromeffects builds upon both DHTML and XML for its implementation on the Web. Currently it is supported only in Internet Explorer 5, so, as with other new technologies, actually using it in your webs is somewhat risky. You probably cannot count on most of your audience being able to view the effects. Figure 14-7 shows an interactive sample of Chromeffects from the Microsoft SiteBuilder Network (**http://microsoft.com/sitebuilder/**). In this demo application you can set actions that trigger the rotation of the object and change colors.

| Tip | *Microsoft's SiteBuilder Network has been mentioned several times in this chapter as a resource. Whatever else may be said about Microsoft, they provide an incredible amount of information for working with their technologies. Given the speed at which the Web changes, access to this type of information is essential for anyone who wants to do serious web work. The site definitely belongs in your browser's bookmarks or favorites.* |

This chapter has provided an overview of the newest web technologies. DHTML made it to the level of a standard with the release of the W3C HTML 4.0 Recommendation, XML is still in the discussion stage, and Chromeffects is Microsoft, once again, marching to their own tune. Each has a place in your web toolkit, though you need to evaluate for yourself how quickly you should begin to use them in your work. As always, supporting the browsers your audience uses is critical to successful implementation. At a minimum, you should be aware of these technologies and their usefulness so that you are prepared to use them when you feel user support reaches critical mass.

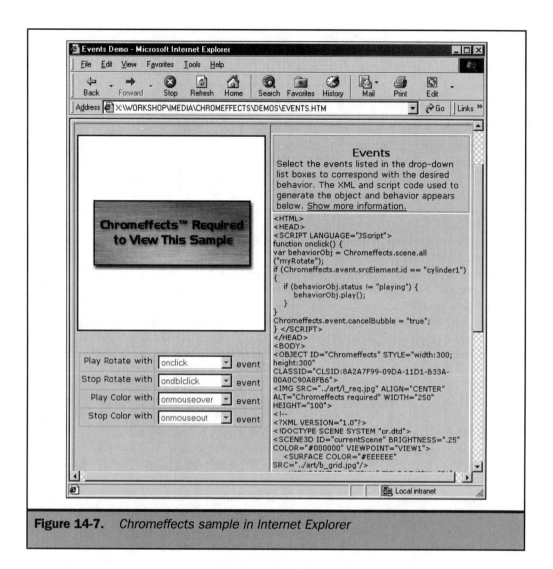

Figure 14-7.   *Chromeffects sample in Internet Explorer*

In the following chapters you will work with technologies that are more firmly established and so can be used with confidence that the majority, if not all, of your audience will see your work the way you intend it to be seen.

The Complete Reference

FrontPage 2000

Chapter 15

Web Scripting Languages

531

The use of scripting languages on the Web is one of the major reasons we now refer to web *applications,* rather than simply web pages or web sites. Scripting languages enable true interactivity in web applications. A *scripting language* is a computer programming language in a simple text format. HTML itself is a scripting language.

The general difference between scripting languages and other programming languages is in how they are treated when executed. Programming languages, like Java and Visual Basic, create a *bytecode* file that is executed by the operating system. (Java and Visual Basic are covered in Chapter 19.) A bytecode file is a binary (all 0's and 1's) file containing instructions that are directly used by the operating system. *Scripts* are text files that are interpreted at the time they are executed and converted into the bytecode the system needs. This explanation is a bit simplified. Java *applets,* for example, are bytecode files compiled from the text source file, but they are still interpreted at run time by the browser's Java interpreter, rather than directly by the computer's operating system. A good working definition is simply that scripts are text files that you can edit directly, unlike a Java applet or an ActiveX control, which must be compiled before it can be used.

JavaScript and VBScript (Visual Basic Script or Visual Basic Scripting Edition) are the two primary scripting languages used on the Web. Perl (Practical Extraction and Report Language) preceded them as the dominant web scripting language, but is no longer as popular, for several reasons. Most importantly, it can only be executed on the server, requiring the data to make a round-trip over the Internet and using the server's processing time. This is because current web browsers do not include Perl interpreters. Both JavaScript and VBScript can run on the client (the user's computer), where the transit time and server overhead are eliminated, or on the server. This is an important consideration—client-side processing is much faster for the user. Perl is also primarily a UNIX programming language. This wasn't a problem in the early development of the Web, as most web servers were running the UNIX operating system. Today, Windows NT and Internet Information Services have an ever increasing share of the market. Development of Perl for Windows NT has always lagged behind Perl for UNIX, making it much less useful for Windows NT web servers.

Note *Microsoft has developed its own variant of JavaScript called JScript. Information about JScript can be found at **http://msdn.microsoft.com/scripting/**. The examples in this book use the industry standard JavaScript.*

A short time ago these languages were primarily doing simple tasks, such as validating form input (as you'll see in the next section). Their future is much more glorious—they are the glue that binds Java applets, ActiveX controls, and other types of program and data files into powerful web-based desktop applications.

The Web is bursting with an avalanche of products that will allow you to create webs that are completely interactive. Users are able to see web pages tailored to their needs rather than static presentations of information. Data contained in remote databases or other applications can be accessible, not as raw data the user has to wade through, but as concise presentations that can be manipulated on the user's desktop. In Chapters 18 and 19 you will learn how to bring these elements together in your webs.

At the center of these developments are the scripting languages. They accept information from the user, control the flow of data between objects, and prepare the output of the processing. Currently, JavaScript has greater support than VBScript, so that's where we'll start.

JavaScript

JavaScript was developed by Sun Microsystems Inc., with involvement from the early stages by Netscape. At the time (late 1995), Netscape was developing a prototype scripting language named LiveScript, but chose to abandon the name and combine their efforts with Sun. Support for JavaScript began with Netscape Navigator 3.0 and Internet Explorer 3.0. VBScript is still only supported by Internet Explorer.

*There are plug-ins available for Netscape's browsers, such as ScriptActive from Ncompass Labs (**http://www.ncompasslabs.com/**), that add support for VBScript. However, it's not reasonable to expect your audience to purchase and install a plug-in to support your pages. JavaScript remains your best choice for client-side scripting.*

The best way to understand JavaScript is to look at some code. FrontPage makes this easy to do, as it will generate either JavaScript or VBScript for you. In the next section you will use FrontPage to generate a JavaScript script that will validate a form.

JavaScript and VBScript are the subjects of entire books. JavaScript Essentials, *by Jason J. Manger (Osborne/McGraw-Hill, 1996), is an excellent choice for JavaScript.*

Form Validation with JavaScript

Form validation, the process of checking the data in each field of a form to be sure it is the correct type, formerly was done on the server using a language such as Perl. This was done through the common gateway interface (CGI). You may be familiar with the term *CGI script* to describe this type of programming. This had the disadvantage of requiring a round-trip over the Internet and of using the server's processing time. With client-side form validation, the process is speeded up because the work is done on the user's computer, rather than on the server.

With FrontPage you use the Form and Field Properties dialog boxes to define the criteria for validation, and the script is created for you—you don't need to know a thing about either scripting language. These steps will take you through the process:

1. In FrontPage, click the down arrow next to New on the toolbar and then click Web.
2. In the New dialog box, select One Page Web, name it **Scripting**, and click OK.
3. Open the home page (Default.htm) in Page view.
4. At the top of the page, type **Form Validation** and format it as Heading 1.
5. Move the cursor to the next line, and click One-Line Text Box on the Form toolbar.

Tip *You can make the Form menu a floating toolbar by dragging it from the Insert menu. Open the Insert menu, point on Form, and then point on the bar at the top of the Form menu and drag it from the Insert menu.*

6. Press HOME to move the cursor to the beginning of the line, and type **Enter some text:** (leave a space after the colon). Format the text as Formatted.

7. Press RIGHT ARROW one or more times to move the cursor to the end of the text box and before the Submit and Reset buttons. Press SHIFT+ENTER.

8. Click One-Line Text Box on the Form toolbar once more and then press HOME.

9. Type **Enter a number:** (leaving two spaces after the colon), press RIGHT ARROW, and then press SHIFT+ENTER.

10. Open the Page Properties dialog box and change the Title of the page to **Form Validation**. Click OK and then save your work.

Your page should look similar to Figure 15-1. Before setting the validation criteria for the form, check which scripting language is set as the default.

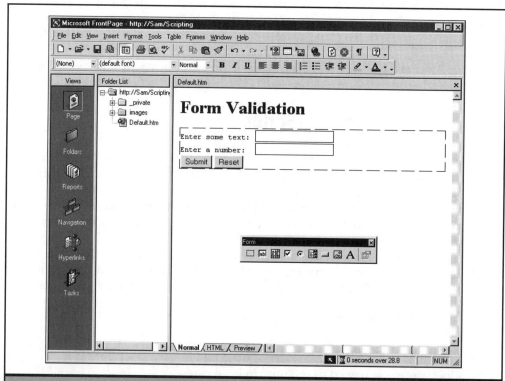

Figure 15-1.   *Form Validation Page*

11. Open the Tools menu and select Web Settings.

12. In the Web Settings dialog box, click the Advanced tab. JavaScript should be displayed in the Default Scripting Language Client drop-down menu, as shown in Figure 15-2. (VBScript is the other choice.) The default scripting language selected here is used by all the pages in your web.

You can run one scripting language on the client (the browser) and another on the server itself. Since only Internet Explorer supports VBScript, JavaScript is the default for client-side scripting. Microsoft's Personal Web Server and Internet Information Services support both scripting languages, so you can choose either for server-side scripting.

13. Click OK and then right-click the first one-line text box in the form. Select Form Field Validation from the context menu.

14. In the Text Box Validation dialog box, select Text from the Data Type drop-down menu, and then click the Letters check box.

15. In the Display Name text box, type **Text Field**. This is the name for the field that will be used in the validation error messages. Click OK.

16. Right-click the second one-line text box, and select Form Field Validation from the context menu.

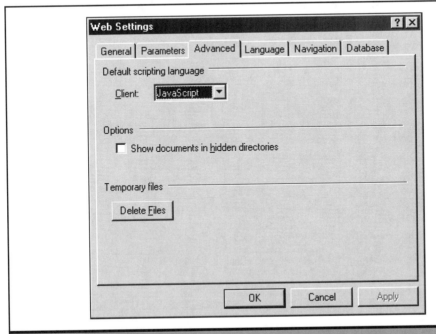

Figure 15-2. *FrontPage Web Settings dialog box Advanced tab*

17. Select Integer from the Data Type drop-down menu, and type **Numeric Field** in the Display Name text box.

18. Under Data Value, select the Field Must Be check box, and type **5** in the Value text box.

19. Select the And Must Be check box, and type **10** in the Value text box. Your Text Box Validation dialog box should look like Figure 15-3.

20. Click OK and then save the page.

21. Open the page in your browser, type **11** in the Enter A Number text box, and click Submit. You should see an error message similar to this:

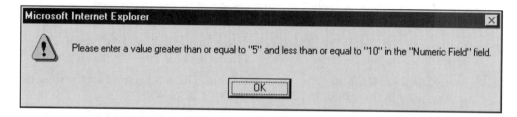

Figure 15-3. *Text Box Validation dialog box*

22. Click OK and then select Source from the View menu in Internet Explorer, or Document Source from the View menu in Netscape Navigator. At the beginning of the HTML listing, you will see the JavaScript script that generated the error message. The JavaScript portion of the file is shown in Listing 15-1.

Note *Some of the characters may appear as small boxes in the source code listing. This is due to the character set supported by the text viewer displaying the code. If the supported character set doesn't include a character, it is replaced by a small box in the display. This doesn't affect the functionality of the script.*

Listing 15-1
JavaScript
Form
Validation

```
<script Language="JavaScript"><!--
function FrontPage_Form1_Validator(theForm)
{
  var checkOK = "ABCDEFGHIJKLMNOPQRSTUVWXYZabcdefghijklmnopqrstuvwxyz
    ƒŠŒ šœ ŸÀÁÂÃÄÅÆÇÈÉÊËÌÍÎÏÐÑÒÓÔÕÖØÙÚÛÜÝÞßàáâãäåæçèéêëìíîïðñòóôõöøùú
    ûüýþÿ";
  var checkStr = theForm.T1.value;
  var allValid = true;
  for (i = 0;  i < checkStr.length;  i++)
  {
    ch = checkStr.charAt(i);
    for (j = 0;  j < checkOK.length;  j++)
      if (ch == checkOK.charAt(j))
        break;
    if (j == checkOK.length)
    {
      allValid = false;
      break;
    }
  }
  if (!allValid)
  {
    alert("Please enter only letter characters in the \"Text Field\" field.");
      theForm.T1.focus();
    return (false);
  }
  var checkOK = "0123456789-,";
  var checkStr = theForm.T2.value;
  var allValid = true;
  var decPoints = 0;
  var allNum = "";
  for (i = 0;  i < checkStr.length;  i++)
  {
    ch = checkStr.charAt(i);
    for (j = 0;  j < checkOK.length;  j++)
      if (ch == checkOK.charAt(j))
```

WORKING BEHIND
THE SCENES

```
        break;
    if (j == checkOK.length)
    {
      allValid = false;
     break;
    }
    if (ch != ",")
      allNum += ch;
  }
  if (!allValid)
  {
    alert("Please enter only digit characters in the \"Numeric
    Field\" field.");
    theForm.T2.focus();
    return (false);
  }
  var chkVal = allNum;
  var prsVal = parseInt(allNum);
  if (chkVal != "" && !(prsVal >= "5" && prsVal <= "10"))
  {
    alert("Please enter a value greater than or equal to \"5\" and
      less than or equal to \"10\" in the \"Numeric Field\" field.");
    theForm.T2.focus();
    return (false);
  }
  return (true);
}
//--></script>
```

If you've ever done any programming, the JavaScript script in Listing 15-1 will look familiar to you. If you haven't, it may look very strange. The best way to understand what it does is to step through the script and look at each section, as follows.

The JavaScript Form Validation Script

Don't worry if the JavaScript code looks indecipherable. The function of each section of a program is understandable once you begin to understand the type of shorthand it's written in. In this section you will look at each piece of the code and see what it does and how it fits in with the other pieces to make a complete script.

Note   *Programming, like writing in any language, has a lot of room for style, and programmers tend to develop their own styles. There are rules for good programming, such as adding comments to explain each section, that make code easily understood. The JavaScript code in this section was generated by FrontPage using the rules defined by the team that programmed this feature of FrontPage. This is not the only way the script could have been written, but it is a good example of JavaScript scripting.*

In the rest of this section the script has been dissected to explain the purpose of each section of code. In doing so, the formatting has been changed somewhat. Listing 15-1 contains the correct syntax for the script.

```
<script Language="JavaScript"><!--
```

The script begins by declaring the programming language using the <SCRIPT> tag. The entire body of the script is within the opening and closing <SCRIPT> tags. If the browser doesn't support the scripting language, then the entire script is ignored. The Language property is required to inform the browser which language is being used (either JavaScript or VBScript). There is also an optional property, SRC, which identifies the location of the script (as a URL) if it's not included on the HTML page. This allows you to create a library of scripts that can be used by many web pages without requiring you to include the script on each page. There is also a <NOSCRIPT> tag that is used to define the HTML that will be displayed if the script isn't supported. It is placed after the script in the HTML document.

Note
You will notice a slight shift in terminology used to describe the components of scripting languages as compared to pure HTML. In Chapter 13 we used the terms "tags" and "attributes" to describe the basic HTML commands and their modifiers. Scripting languages approach the terminology of more conventional programming languages, so we use a hybrid set of terms. "Tag" is still used to describe a basic scripting language command, but the term "property" is used to describe how a certain tag can be modified (analogous to "attribute" in pure HTML-speak).

After the <SCRIPT> tag is an opening HTML comment tag (<!--) matched by the closing comment tag (-->) at the end of the script. Without these tags the entire text of the script would be displayed in browsers that don't support the <SCRIPT> tag.

```
function FrontPage_Form1_Validator(theForm)
```

This next line declares the function name and its arguments in the form `function functionName (arguments)`. In this case the `functionName` is `FrontPage_Form1_Validator`, and the single argument is `theForm`. A *function* is a series of JavaScript statements that performs a task and optionally returns a value. The function statements are enclosed within the { and } brackets. An *argument* is a value that is passed to the function. What this value can be will depend on the purpose of the function. For example, if the purpose of the function was to multiply two numbers, then the two numbers would be the arguments passed to the function. Since the arguments are represented by variables (which can be considered a container for the value), they could be passed from the web page through a form as variables, which is what is being done in this script. The argument `theForm` refers to the values you enter in the form text boxes and then submit. The script intercepts the values before the form handler and checks them against the rules established by the function. If they meet the criteria, they are passed on to the form handler; if not, then an error message is generated, as you saw earlier, and the form handler never receives the data. Since the form handler will be on the server, this prevents unnecessary traffic and server time.

Note   *Functions cannot be nested, that is, a function cannot be defined inside another function.*

```
{ var checkOK = "ABCDEF...";
   var checkStr = theForm.T1.value;
   var allValid = true;
```

These three lines define the variables that are used by the function in the form `var variableName = variableValue`. The first variable, `checkOK`, is a text string consisting of all the acceptable characters that can be returned by the first form field. (The list has been shortened here.) The second, `checkStr`, is the value entered in the first text box, `T1`. `T1` is the default name given to the form field when you created it in FrontPage. If you had given the field a different name, that name would be used in defining the variable. This variable illustrates a JavaScript naming convention— defining an object as a hierarchical string with each level of the hierarchy separated by a period. In this case the hierarchy is the form itself, the field in the form, and the value contained in the field. Each level of the hierarchy is a property of the preceding level, so, in this example, `T1` is a property of `theForm`.

This is one method by which data is passed between the HTML page and the script. To the script, the form is an object and so can have properties that can be processed. JavaScript can also recognize events, such as a mouse click or placing the mouse pointer over a defined area, and execute a function based on the event. The third variable, `allValid`, is a flag that will be used later in the script to determine if the data will be passed to the form handler. It is defined as TRUE, meaning that the script is interpreting the data entered in the first text box as valid. If the data fails to meet the criteria for the field, the value of the variable will be changed to FALSE, which will trigger the error message.

```
for (i = 0;   i < checkStr.length;   i++)
   { ch = checkStr.charAt(i);
     for (j = 0;   j < checkOK.length;   j++)
   if (ch == checkOK.charAt(j))
        break;
   if (j == checkOK.length)
   { allValid = false;
        break;  }}
```

This section of the script is the part that does most of the work. The first line is a For-Next loop. The variables i and j are counters that are used to determine which character in the text string is being evaluated. What's happening is that the text string entered in the text form field is being *parsed;* that is, the text string is being looked at one character at a time, and compared with the legal characters defined in the checkOK variable. At each step each counter is incremented by 1 (i++ and j++) until the last character in each string is reached (i < checkStr.length; and j < checkOK.length;). The variable checkStr.charAt(i) holds the character at position i that has been entered in the text box. The variable checkOK.charAt(j) holds the character at position j in the string of legal characters. When the first loop is started, the character at position i in the input string is compared with the character at position j in the string of legal characters. For the first iteration, each of these is 0 (zero), since that is the first position as far as the computer is concerned. (If the input string was ten characters long, the computer would count them as zero to nine, not one to ten.)

The first character in the input string is loaded into the variable ch, and ch is compared with the first character in checkOK. If the characters don't match (if the character isn't A), j is incremented (j++) and the first character in the input string is compared with the second legal character (B). This continues, with j being incremented each time, until a match is found or the end of the string of legal characters is reached. If a match is found, the loop stops (break;) and i is incremented so that the next character in the input string can be checked. Then the process starts over, with j being reset to zero (j = 0;) so that the entire string of legal characters will be checked.

If no match is found, meaning the character entered in the form field is invalid, the process stops and the value of the variable allValid is changed to FALSE. This happens if the end of the string of legal characters is reached without finding a match (j == checkOK.length). If the character is determined to be invalid, the steps shown next are executed.

```
if (!allValid)
  { alert("Please enter only letter characters in the \"Text
    Field\" field.");
theForm.T1.focus();
    return (false);}
```

The first line in the preceding code tests the value of the variable allValid. This line can be read as "If allValid is NOT TRUE, then..." (the exclamation mark is the notation for the logical NOT operator). As you saw in the previous code, allValid is defined as TRUE at the beginning of the script, and the value is changed only if an illegal character is encountered. The "then" is defined by the next line, which causes an alert message box to be displayed, as you saw earlier when you entered the number "11" in the numeric text box and clicked Submit. This is a built-in function of JavaScript, so all you have to do is define the text that will appear in the alert ("Please enter only letter..."). The next line contains a very useful JavaScript function, the focus() method, written in the form *object*.focus(). What this does is make the form field where the error occurred in the selected object active (in this case, the cursor is placed in the text box). Once you click OK in the alert message box, your browser will return you to the first form field so you can fix the error. The form field (theForm.T1) is the object. Finally, the script returns the value FALSE (return (false);). This value can be used by the statement that called the function, or it can be ignored. In this case it will prevent the data from being sent to the form handler.

If all the characters inputted pass the test, then the first loop ends when the last character in the checkStr variable has been checked. The script then begins the test for the data entered in the second text box.

```
var checkOK = "0123456789-,";
 var checkStr = theForm.T2.value;
 var allValid = true;
 var decPoints = 0;
 var allNum = "";
```

Like the test for the first form field, this one also begins by defining the variables. Then similar loops and tests are started with the new variables.

```
for (i = 0; i < checkStr.length;  i++)
  { ch = checkStr.charAt(i);
     for (j = 0;  j < checkOK.length;  j++)
       if (ch == checkOK.charAt(j))
          break;
     if (j == checkOK.length)
     { allValid = false;
        break; }
     if (ch != ",")
        allNum += ch;
  }
  if (!allValid)
  {
     alert("Please enter only digit characters in the \"Numeric
        Field\" field.");
     theForm.T2.focus();
     return (false);
  }
```

The next test determines if the number entered is within the range specified.

```
var chkVal = allNum;
  var prsVal = parseInt(allNum);
  if (chkVal != "" && !(prsVal >= "5" && prsVal <= "10"))
  { alert("Please enter a value greater than or equal to \"5\" and
    less than or equal to \"10\" in the \"Numeric Field\" field.");
    theForm.T2.focus();
    return (false);
  }
```

The work in this section of code is done by the third line. After the second line converts the number string to an integer (`var prsVal = parseInt (allNum);`), three checks are performed: is it a null value (was a value entered), is it equal to or greater than five, and is it equal to or less than ten. The second line is necessary because the program can interpret a number in two ways: as a text string and as an actual number. This line converts the text to a number so that it can be used for the tests that follow. The `!=` operator is the logical NOT EQUAL, so that the expression could be read as "is the value in the form field NOT EQUAL to null." The `&&` operator is the logical AND. The third line could be read as "if the number is NOT equal to null AND it's not equal to or greater than five AND it's not equal to or less than ten, then display the alert error message." Focus would then be returned to the second form field box.

```
  return (true);
  }
  //--></script>
```

These last two lines clean up and end the script. If both values have passed all the tests, the value TRUE is returned, and the data is sent to the form handler. The last line contains three elements: the `//` is the JavaScript Comment tag, which is required at the end of the JavaScript script; the `-->` is the HTML closing comment tag; and finally the HTML `</SCRIPT>` tag ends the script.

Once a script has been created, there also has to be a method for calling the script. For the form validation script, the call is contained in the `<FORM>` HTML tag. This next line of code shows how the JavaScript validation script is called by the form:

```
<form method="POST" name="FrontPage_Form1" action="_vti_bin/
shtml.dll/Jsform.htm" onsubmit="return FrontPage_Form1_Validator
(this)"webbot-action="--WEBBOT-SELF--">
```

The HTML form code should look reasonably familiar to you (Chapter 13 contains an explanation of the HTML used for forms). The JavaScript validation script is called with the JavaScript command `onsubmit`, like this, `onsubmit="return FrontPage_Form1_Validator(this)"`

The value of the `onsubmit` attribute is the name of the JavaScript function, defined at the top of the JavaScript script. The argument being passed to the script (in the parentheses at the end of the function name) is `this`, which indicates the active form. In this manner, it's possible for multiple JavaScript forms on a single page to use the same validation script, provided the field names are identical.

JavaScript is case-sensitive, so form and field names must be exact, including upper- and lowercase letters, in both the form and the script itself.

You'll be using the Form Validation page again with VBScript, so leave your current FrontPage and browser windows open. You can close Notepad or your text viewer.

VBScript

VBScript is similar to JavaScript. It is based on Microsoft's Visual Basic programming language, which gives Visual Basic programmers a bit of a head start. The problem with VBScript is lack of support among browsers. Currently only Microsoft's Internet Explorer includes support for VBScript, and it's unlikely that Netscape will add support anytime soon, so your client-side VBScript scripts will have a limited audience. VBScript could be your first choice if you are planning an intranet and you can specify Internet Explorer as the browser everyone must use. Otherwise it's hard to see why you shouldn't simply go with JavaScript for client-side scripting. There are enough differences in the languages to make learning both of them a burden.

For server-side scripting, VBScript offers advantages if your web server is Windows NT based. Visual Basic is more tightly integrated with Windows NT than Java and so is probably the best choice for more advanced programming. Because VBScript is a subset of Visual Basic, this reduces the learning curve. If you're using an operating system other than Windows NT, Java must be your choice for server-side programming, since Visual Basic is not supported by other operating systems. (You can also use other languages like C++, but these languages are beyond the scope of this book.) As you can see, there are several factors that must be considered in choosing a scripting language, and the reality is that you need to have a basic knowledge of both.

You can see some of the differences in the two languages by changing the scripting language in the Advanced tab on the Web Settings dialog box. Do that now with these instructions:

1. In FrontPage, open the Tools menu and select Web Settings.

2. In the Web Settings dialog box, click the Advanced tab and select VBScript from the Default Scripting Languages Client drop-down menu. Click Apply. The FrontPage dialog box shown next will be displayed.

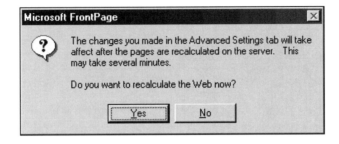

3. Click Yes. After the Scripting web is recalculated, click OK (the OK button will be inactive until the recalculation is done).

4. Load the Form Validation page in your web browser, and select Source or Page Source from the View menu, depending on which browser you are using.

Listing 15-2 shows the same form validation script as Listing 15-1, except that it is now written in VBScript. The flow of the script is pretty much the same, but the syntax has changed. You should still be able to follow what the script is doing.

Listing 15-2
VBScript form validation

```
<script Language="VBScript"><!--
function FrontPage_Form1_onsubmit()
  Set theForm = document.FrontPage_Form1
  checkOK = "ABCDEFGHIJKLMNOPQRSTUVWXYZabcdefghijklmnopqrstuvwxyz
    ƒŠŒ Šœ ŸÀÁÂÃÄÅÆÇÈÉÊËÌÍÎÏÐÑÒÓÔÕÖØÙÚÛÜÝÞßàáâãäåæçèéêëìíîïðñòóôõ
    öøùúûüýþÿ"
  checkStr = theForm.T1.value
  allValid = True
  For i = 1 to len(checkStr)
    ch = Mid(checkStr, i, 1)
    If (InStr(checkOK, ch) = 0) Then
        allValid = False
        Exit For
    End If
  Next
  If (Not allValid) Then
```

```
        MsgBox "Please enter only letter characters in the ""Text Field""
          field.", 0, "Validation Error"
        theForm.T1.focus()
        FrontPage_Form1_onsubmit = False
        Exit Function
      End If
      checkOK = "0123456789-,"
      checkStr = theForm.T2.value
      allValid = True
      decPoints = 0
      allNum = ""
      For i = 1 to len(checkStr)
        ch = Mid(checkStr, i, 1)
        If (InStr(checkOK, ch) = 0) Then
            allValid = False
            Exit For
        End If
        If (ch <> ",") Then
          allNum = allNum & ch
        End If
      Next
      If (Not allValid) Then
        MsgBox "Please enter only digit characters in the ""Numeric Field""
          field.", 0, "Validation Error"
        theForm.T2.focus()
        FrontPage_Form1_onsubmit = False
        Exit Function
      End If
      If ((checkstr <> "" and Not IsNumeric(allNum)) Or (decPoints > 1))
        Then MsgBox "Please enter a valid number in the ""T2""
        field.", 0, "Validation Error"
        theForm.T2.focus()
        FrontPage_Form1_onsubmit = False
        Exit Function
      End If
      prsVal = allNum
      If ((prsVal <> "") And (Not (prsVal >= 5 And prsVal <= 10)))
        Then MsgBox "Please enter a value greater than or equal to
        ""5"" and less than or equal to ""10"" in the ""Numeric
        Field"" field.", 0, "Validation Error"
        theForm.T2.focus()
        FrontPage_Form1_onsubmit = False
        Exit Function
      End If
      FrontPage_Form1_onsubmit = True
    End Function
    --></script>
```

The Microsoft Script Wizard

The examples in the previous sections used scripts created with the Text Field Validation dialog box and generated by the FrontPage Server Extensions. This is a good method if all you want the script to do is validate a form. Both languages are much more useful than that, as you will see in the next two chapters.

There are two methods you can use to add scripts to your webs. The first is to use FrontPage to generate the script, as you did in the previous sections. The advantages of this method are that the script can be easily modified from within FrontPage and you do not need to be a proficient JavaScript or VBScript programmer to create scripts. The second is to create the script manually using either the Script Wizard, shown in Figure 15-4, or by writing the script using the HTML tab of FrontPage's Page view. The advantage with this method is that the page will use slightly less server resources when it is called, as the WebBot code doesn't need to be interpreted.

Which method you use will depend on how comfortable you are with writing scripts manually and how often you expect the code to be modified. You can combine the benefits of each method by using FrontPage to generate the script, opening it using

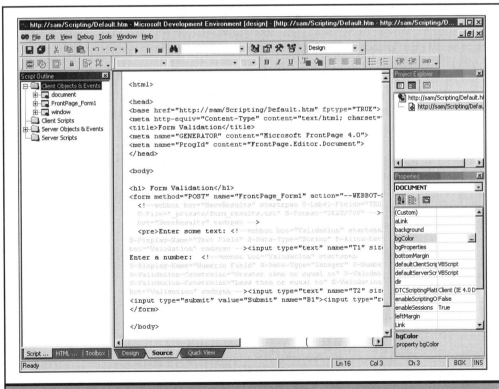

Figure 15-4. *Microsoft Script Wizard*

your browser's View | Source option, and then copying and pasting it into your page, overwriting the FrontPage WebBot code. The script will no longer be editable from within FrontPage (except by using the HTML tab in Page view), but will use slightly less server resources.

The Script Wizard allows you to edit HTML and Active Server Pages (ASP) files, much like the FrontPage Page view. (Active Server Pages is the subject of the next two chapters.) In this section, only the script editing functions of the Script Wizard will be covered. To see how the Script Wizard works, follow these steps:

1. With your Form Validation page still open in Page view, open the Script Wizard by opening the Tools menu, pointing on Macro, and then clicking Microsoft Script Wizard.

Note *The Script Wizard may not be installed on your system. In that case a dialog box will be displayed stating that the Script Wizard is not installed and asking if you want to install it now. Click Yes.*

In Figure 15-4, the leftmost pane of the Script Wizard displays the Script Outline window. (If the Script Outline isn't displayed, click the Script Outline tab at the bottom of the window.) The Script Outline window shows the objects and scripts on a page. This pane can also display the HTML Outline window or the Toolbox by selecting the appropriate tab at the bottom of the window.

The center pane is the Text or Code Editing window. When the Source tab is selected, this displays the source code of your page. This view is similar to FrontPage when the HTML tab is selected in Page view. Design and Quick View (selected with the tabs at the bottom of the window) are similar to the Normal and Preview tabs in FrontPage Page view.

The upper-right pane is the Project Explorer window. This window displays the outline of the current project. Below it is the Properties window where the available properties and values of the selected object are displayed and can be edited.

In the Client Objects & Events folder in the Script Outline window, shown in detail here, there are three objects: Document, FrontPage_Form1, and Window. The Document object represents the properties of the page itself. The FrontPage_Form1 object is the form you created in FrontPage, and the Window object refers to the browser window.

2. In the Script Outline window, click the plus sign (+) to the left of the FrontPage_Form1 object to expand the tree. This displays a list of the available events for the object and the defined objects within the selected object. In this case, the two text boxes (T1 and T2) are displayed along with the form buttons (B1 and B2). Expanding the tree for a text box or button will display a list of events available for that object.

> **Note**   *The Script Wizard uses the default scripting language selected within FrontPage. In this case, that is VBScript. The events listed in the expanded tree are VBScript events. If JavaScript was set as the default scripting language, the available JavaScript events would be listed.*

If you double-click on an event, the basic scripting code for the event is inserted into your page. Right-clicking an event will display a context menu. Selecting Goto Definition from the context menu will place the cursor in the Code Editing window at the code for the selected event. If the event doesn't exist in your page it will be inserted. Scripts are usually placed just before the closing </HEAD> tag. The other context menu options allow you to Show Events, Sort the events either alphabetically or by declaration on the page, and Sync Script Outline.

3. Double-click onsubmit in the event list for the FrontPage_Form1 object. The following code will be inserted in the page:

```
<SCRIPT ID=clientEventHandlersVBS LANGUAGE=vbscript>
<!--
Sub FrontPage_Form1_onsubmit
End Sub
-->
</SCRIPT>
```

This is the basic code for the event handler. It does not define the action to be taken when the event occurs; it only creates the skeleton code for your subroutine. The name of the VBScript function is FrontPage_Form1_onsubmit. You must write the VBScript script that defines the action to be executed when the form is submitted. This code goes between the VBScript Sub (after the name of the function) and End Sub statements.

4. Open the Edit menu and choose Undo or press CTRL+Z to remove the onsubmit code from your page. In the Code Editing window you can see that the VBScript validation script is not present (which you saw using your browser's View | Source option). What is on the page is the FrontPage WebBot code that the FrontPage Server Extensions use to generate the validation script when the page is requested.

The term Components is now used in FrontPage to describe what were formerly WebBots. However, the term WebBot still appears in the code generated by FrontPage. Usually the only time you will encounter the term WebBot is when you are working with the HTML tab of FrontPage Page view or the Script Wizard.

5. Click on the Form tag in the Code Editing window. The Properties window (in the lower-right corner of the Script Wizard) will display the properties and their values for the form, as shown next.

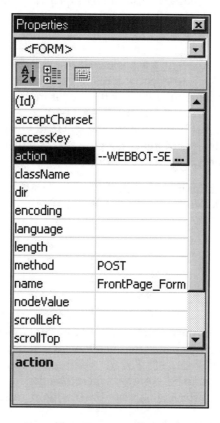

You can edit any of the properties using the Properties window. For the Action property (shown selected in the preceding illustration), clicking on the small box with the ellipsis (...) displays the Open dialog box so that you can select a file for the output of the form.

6. Select Method in the Properties window. A downward-pointing arrow appears in the value cell for the Method property. This opens a drop-down menu displaying the two choices for Method, either Post or Get.

7. Select Name in the Property window. Since this property is a user-defined value, there are no choices or dialog boxes presented. You simply enter the name of the form in the value cell for the property.

8. Close the Script Wizard without saving any changes to your page.

To make the most of the Script Wizard requires an advanced knowledge of the selected scripting language. If you do choose to write your own scripts, rather than having them generated by FrontPage, you will find it a valuable tool. For example, the Script Wizard also contains extremely useful script debugging tools. You can insert *breakpoints* in your script that stop the execution of the script so that you can identify where errors are occurring. You can also view the values of your variables during execution. These features make debugging a script much easier.

Each of the technologies covered in this chapter could easily fill a book of its own, and, in fact, each does. The purpose here was to give you an overview of them so that you could make an informed decision about which technologies you want to add to your own webs. At a minimum, a working knowledge of JavaScript will be beneficial to web designers. If you plan to use server-side scripting on Windows NT servers, VBScript is also a must. If you want your webs to stand out in the crowd, these tools are part of your future.

The
Complete
Reference

Chapter 16

Active Server Pages

The Web is no longer just a collection of static, unchanging web pages. It has become a truly interactive medium, with input from users controlling the information that is displayed in their browser. Scripting languages were the first step in bringing this shift about, and Active Server Pages (ASP) has taken the concept to the next level.

Active Server Pages is a server-side scripting environment that includes built-in objects and components. These objects and components enable a degree of interactivity that was extremely difficult, if not impossible, to achieve previously. Using ASP effectively requires more hands-on programming than other features of FrontPage, but, as you will see in this and the following chapters, there are many benefits in using this technology to bring true interactivity to your webs.

> **Note** *Active Server Pages is a Microsoft technology; it is a component of Internet Information Servicer 3.0 and later (running under Windows NT), and Microsoft's Personal Web Server. ASP is installed by default with IIS 4.0 and PWS 4.0. In previous versions of IIS and PWS, the ASP libraries had to be explicitly installed. ASP can be used with UNIX web servers with Chili!ASP, an ASP clone available from Chili!Soft, Inc. (http://www.versicom.com).*

Active Server Pages Overview

ASP is a combination of *objects*—programming code and data that are treated as a single element, and *components*—programs that perform common tasks. ASP components are actually ActiveX components (see Chapter 19). You can also create your own ActiveX components to use in your webs with ASP, or acquire them from other vendors. Using objects and components greatly simplifies normally complex tasks. Active Server Pages files have an .ASP file extension, rather than .HTM or .HTML.

> **Tip** *Extensive ASP documentation can be installed with both IIS and PWS. The functionality possible with ASP means that there is a certain amount of complexity that goes with it. If you intend to use ASP to any extent, you should become very familiar with the documentation.*

A scripting language, such as VBScript or JavaScript, holds all the pieces together and controls the program flow of the web page. These scripts are normally executed on the server, though you can use a combination of client-side and server-side scripting on a web page. Typically, you would use server-side scripting to create the web page and client-side scripting for tasks such as form validation, as you saw in the previous chapter.

> **Note** *Although either VBScript or JavaScript can be used as the primary scripting language, the examples in this chapter use VBScript as the default language. In the case of server-side scripting, VBScript offers the advantage of being tightly integrated into the*

Windows NT and IIS operating environment. This, or PWS running under Windows, is the default web server environment assumed in this book. Also, Visual Basic is one of the primary languages for creating ActiveX components. Since VBScript is a subset of Visual Basic, staying within the Visual Basic family reduces your learning curve. JavaScript is still the preferred choice for client-side scripting, since only Microsoft's browsers support VBScript.

An ASP application is the root directory of the web application and all the files and subdirectories in the root directory. In addition, the root directory must be a virtual directory (see Chapter 6 for an explanation of virtual directories). By default, FrontPage will create most of the required virtual directories and set the proper permissions when you create a new FrontPage web. There are still a few settings that will have to be done manually, but most of the work is done for you.

Note   *When talking about permissions on NT-based web servers, there are two sets that must be considered. First, NT Server itself has permissions that are applied to the directories and files. Second, the web server software, either the PWS or IIS, also has permissions that must be set. Setting NT Server permissions is beyond the scope of this book and is itself the subject of entire books. Two excellent references are Tom Sheldon's Windows NT Security Handbook (1996) and Microsoft Internet Information Server 4, The Complete Reference (1998), both published by Osborne/McGraw-Hill. This chapter will focus on configuring the Microsoft Personal Web Server, which has fewer permission settings than IIS. The reason there are fewer permissions with the PWS is that Windows 95 and 98 (the normal operating systems for the PWS) are inherently less secure than Windows NT.*

In an ASP web application, any ASP page that is requested must be processed by the ASP library on the server before it is sent back to the requesting browser. In other words, the ASP file must be executed. This is where the "Active Server" part comes in. The ASP library interprets the scripting code and outputs a standard HTML page that is then sent in response to the browser's request. If the root directory of the ASP application is not a virtual directory and the scripts or execute permission isn't set, the ASP web application will not work. In that case your browser will display an HTTP error page, as shown in Figure 16-1.

Before actually creating an ASP web, you need to make sure support of ASP is enabled in FrontPage.

1. Open FrontPage if it's not already open, open the Tools menu, choose Page Options, and click the Compatibility tab. The Page Options dialog box shown in Figure 16-2 will be displayed.

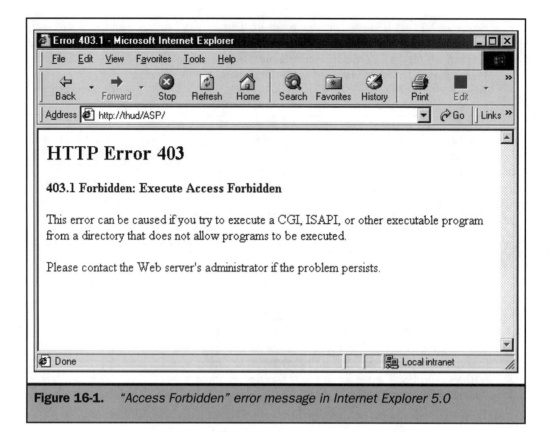

Figure 16-1. *"Access Forbidden" error message in Internet Explorer 5.0*

At the bottom of the Page Options dialog box is a list of technologies that FrontPage can support. By default these are all selected, giving the maximum support in FrontPage for current web technologies.

2. Check that the Active Server Pages check box is selected; if not, select it. Click OK to close the dialog box.

3. Create a One Page Web and name it **ASP**.

4. In Folders view, right-click Default.htm and choose Rename.

5. Rename the Default.htm file **Default.asp**. The dialog box shown here will be displayed. Click Yes.

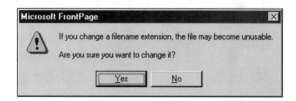

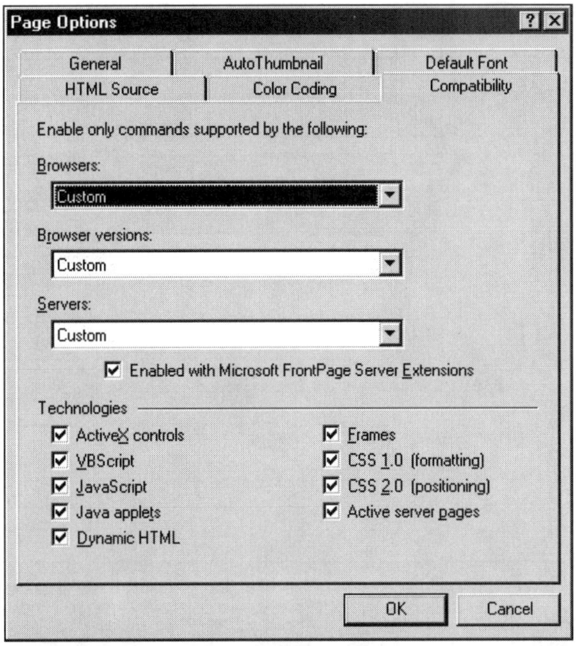

Figure 16-2.   *Page Options dialog box*

There are two additional settings you should also check before actually starting work on your ASP web. These are the default document and the permissions applied to the ASP web.

6. Open the Personal Web Manager by right-clicking the PWS icon in the taskbar system tray and then clicking Properties. You can also open the Personal Web Manager by clicking Start on the taskbar, pointing on Programs, then Internet Explorer, Personal Web Server, and choosing Personal Web Manager.

7. In the Personal Web Manager, click the Advanced button. Your Personal Web Manager should look similar to Figure 16-3. The Enable Default Document check box should be selected, and the Default Document(s) text box should contain Default.htm and Default.asp, separated by a comma.

8. Click the ASP icon in the Virtual Directories scrolling list box, then click Edit Properties. The Edit Directory dialog box shown next will be displayed. Enter

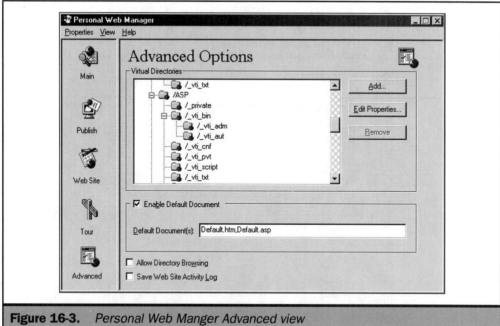

Figure 16-3. *Personal Web Manger Advanced view*

the full path to your ASP directory in the Directory text box. By default this will be **C:\Inetpub\Wwwroot\ASP**. Both the Read and Scripts check boxes should be selected.

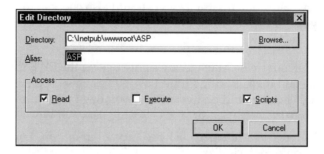

For a web with only HTML pages, only the Read permission needs to be selected. Since ASP pages contain server-side scripts, the Scripts permission also needs to be selected. The Execute permission is only required when the directory will contain programs that need to run on the server.

9. Close the Edit Directory dialog box and the Personal Web Manager.

Now that your web server is properly configured for ASP web applications, you're ready to unleash their interactivity.

ASP Objects

Active Server Pages contains six built-in objects, described in Table 16-1. These allow you to handle events, such as triggering an action to take place the first time a user loads a page from the web, getting information from a user, or setting properties for the user's session.

ASP objects and components can have collections, events, methods, properties, and parameters associated with them. Individual objects and components will have one or more of these, but not all of them. *Collections* are data associated with a particular object. *Events* trigger an action by an object. *Methods* define the action that will be performed by the object. *Properties* are attributes of the object or component. *Parameters* are usually the name of an object that is the target of an action. Each of these will be explained in detail throughout this chapter.

In ASP applications you use variables to hold values that are used in the web application. A *variable* is simply a name that serves as a reference to the value assigned to it. For example, you can assign the text string "Hello World" to a variable named

Object	Description
Application	Sets properties or information that is shared by all users accessing the web application.
ObjectContext	Commits or aborts a transaction started by a script on an ASP page. The transaction itself is handled by the Microsoft Component Services (formerly Transaction Server).
Request	Handles information passed from the browser to the server.
Response	Sends information from the server to the browser.
Server	Provides access to server-side properties and operations.
Session	Sets properties or information for a single user accessing the web application. A session starts when users load the first page from the web and ends when they leave the web or the session time-out value is reached.

Table 16-1. *ASP Objects*

"Heading." When you reference the variable Heading in a web page, the text string "Hello World" will be displayed on the web page. Using variables to hold values allows you to set a value used in many places in your web in a single reference. To make a change that affects all the pages in your web, you only have to make a single change to the page where the variable is defined. Variables also allow you to pass values between web pages or between objects. In the following sections you will see how these are applied to ASP objects and components.

Application and Session Objects

In an ASP web application you may want to set values that apply either to every user or to a single user. These values are set by use of the Application and Session objects. The Application object sets properties or information that is shared by all users of a web application. These are any *global* values, or variables you want to set for the entire web application, and are said to have *application scope*. Session objects set *local* values, or variables restricted to a single user, and are said to have *session scope*.

Session state is only maintained for browsers that support cookies; if cookies are not supported, a new session starts every time the user loads a page in the web. See the section "The Cookies Collection" for more information about cookies.

Application objects are set by use of the Global.asa file, an optional text file that is placed in the root directory of the web application. Session objects can be set in the Global.asa file or on an ASP web page. The next step in building your ASP web application is to create a Global.asa file for it.

The .ASA extension used by the Global.asa file stands for "Active Server Application."

The Global.asa File

The Global.asa file is unique to ASP web applications. It is optional, but you cannot use Application objects without it. The Global.asa file is not visible to users; it is only used to store Application and Session objects. The file must be named Global.asa, there can be only a single Global.asa file for an ASP web application, it must be in the root directory of the web application, and the root directory must be a virtual directory with Scripts permission. To create a Global.asa file, first configure FrontPage to be the default editor for .ASA files.

The Global.asa file is a text file and can be edited using a text editor, such as Notepad. In previous versions of FrontPage, a text editor was required as the Global.asa file could not be edited from within FrontPage. In FrontPage 2000 you can safely edit the Global.asa file using the Page view HTML tab.

1. Open the Tools menu and choose Options. In the Options dialog box, click the Configure Editors tab.

2. Click Add to open the Add Editor Association dialog box, shown here correctly configured.

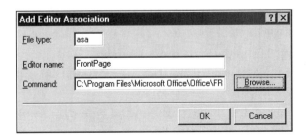

3. Type **asa** in the File Type text box and **FrontPage** in the Editor Name text box.

4. In the Command text box, enter the full path to the FrontPage program file. By default this is C:\Program Files\Microsoft Office\Office\frontpg.exe. Click OK twice.

You can find the location of your FrontPage program file by selecting one of the existing FrontPage configurations in the Configure Editors list box and clicking Modify. The path to your installation will be in the Command text box.

5. Create a new page in your ASP web and then click the HTML tab in Page view. In the HTML tab you'll see that FrontPage has created the basic HTML coding for a normal web page. This coding is not included in the Global.asa file, so you need to remove it.

6. Press CTRL-+A to select all the text in the Page view HTML tab, and then press DEL.

7. Type

```
<script language=VBScript runat=server>
Sub Application_OnStart
    Application("Heading") = "Hello World"
End Sub
</script>
```

8. Open the File menu and choose Save. In the Save As dialog box, select All Files (*.*) in the Save As Type drop-down list and change the File Name to **Global.asa**, then click Save.

WORKING BEHIND
THE SCENES

Note *You will not be able to open the Global.asa page in your browser. This is a unique file and both the PWS and IIS will not allow it to be opened by a browser. This is a security measure as this file will usually contain information about your server's configuration that you do not want the public to see.*

9. From the Window menu, click Default.asp. Click the Page view Normal tab.

10. Press CTRL+HOME to place the cursor at the top of the page.

11. Select Heading 2 from the Style drop-down list.

12. Click the HTML tab in Page view. The cursor should be on the line
    `<h2> </h2>`.

13. Delete the nonbreaking space (` `) and type **<%= Application("Heading")
    %>** between the <h2> and </h2> tags.

14. Save your page, and then open the File menu and choose Preview In Browser.
    Select your preferred browser and click Preview. In your browser the words
    "Hello World" are displayed.

15. Still in your browser, view the source of the page. In Internet Explorer, open the
    View menu and choose Source. In Netscape Navigator, open the View menu
    and choose Page Source. Between the body tags (<BODY> and </BODY>) in
    the page source you will see the line

    `<h2>Hello World</h2>`

16. In the Page view HTML tab, look at the source for the Default.asp page.
    Between the body tags you will see the line

    `<h2><%= Application("Heading")%></h2>`

    In your Global.asa file you created an Application object named "Heading" and
    gave it the value "Hello World." When your browser requested the Default.asp
    page, ASP looked up the value of the Heading Application object and inserted
    it into the web page before it was sent to your browser. This is the key to how
    ASP works. When an ASP page is requested, the server processes any code
    (ASP objects, components, and scripts) and generates a normal HTML page that
    is then sent to the requesting browser. Since the script is processed on the
    server, the browser does not need to support the scripting language used.

Note *The "<%" and "%>" in the Page view HTML tab source code are VBScript server-side delimiters. These define the code between them as a VBScript script that is to be executed on the server.*

17. In Page view, change the line "Hello World" in the Global.asa file to **"Hello
    Brave New World"** and save the file.

Changes to the Global.asa file are not recognized by the web application until the file has been recompiled. This happens when the web application is first started, either by booting the server or stopping and starting the web application.

Note *With the PWS, only the service—not individual webs—can be stopped and started. With IIS and other web servers, each web can be started and stopped individually.*

18. Right-click the PWS icon in the taskbar system tray and choose Stop Service. Then right-click the PWS icon again and choose Start Service.

19. In your browser, click the Refresh (Internet Explorer) or Reload (Netscape) button. The heading in your browser will now reflect the change you made to the Global.asa file.

Note *It may be necessary to reboot your computer in order to see the changes in the Global.asa file when using PWS. With IIS, running under Windows NT, changes to the Global.asa file are reflected properly.*

As you can see, an Application object allows you to set values that are shared by all users of your web application. You can use the script `<%= Application ("Heading") %>` on any page in your web application, and format it with any HTML tags. You have a single place to change any Application value or property, which greatly simplifies the maintenance of your web.

Application Object Methods, Collections, and Events

The Application object has two methods, two collections, and two events that trigger it. The methods are Lock and Unlock. The syntax for using either method is

```
Application.method
```

The Lock method prevents more than one user from changing an Application object value at one time, while the Unlock method allows other users to change the value. If Unlock is not called, the Application object is unlocked when the ASP file finishes executing or the server time-out value is reached.

Note *Throughout this chapter you will be given the syntax for the ASP objects and components. In these syntax statements, words in bold (including opening and closing parentheses) are used exactly as written. Words in italic indicate that, in actual use, the word is replaced with a value. In the preceding example the actual use of the methods would be **Application.Lock** or **Application.Unlock**. When a vertical bar (|) is used in the syntax statement, such as **Session**.property | method, it indicates "or." That is, the correct syntax is either **Session**.property or **Session**.method, not **Session**.property.method. Optional elements are enclosed in square brackets, as in **Request.Cookies**(cookie)[(key) | .attribute], which indicates that the key and attribute* *parameters are optional. Unlike HTML created in FrontPage, your scripts will not be automatically checked for syntax errors, so it is very important to understand and use the correct syntax.*

The Application object events are Application_OnStart and Application_OnEnd. In the Global.asa file, you created a VBScript subroutine that used the Application_OnStart event to assign the text string Hello World to the Application object Heading.

The first line of the script,

```
<script language=VBScript runat=server>
```

identifies what follows as a VBScript script that is executed on the server. The next line,

```
Sub Application_OnStart
```

uses the SUB (subroutine) VBScript statement and the ASP Application_OnStart Application event to declare that what follows is a subroutine that is to be executed the first time any page in the web is requested by any user. This will be the first page loaded after the web application is started (normally web applications start by default when the computer is started). The following line creates the Application object and assigns its value:

```
Application("Heading") = "Hello World"
```

Finally, the subroutine and the script are closed with the END SUB VBScript statement and the closing HTML Script tag:

```
End Sub
</script>
```

Tip   *In creating ASP web applications, you will be using at least three different programming languages: a scripting language, HTML, and ASP. This can make for interesting debugging, as you first have to determine which language is causing the problem. When you are working with databases (see Chapter 18), you will also have SQL statements to contend with.*

The Application_OnEnd event is used in a similar manner. The action defined in the subroutine would be executed when the web application is shut down. This could be caused by either stopping the web server software, or by turning off or rebooting the computer. For example, if you used the Application_OnStart event to open a file for writing, you would need to close the file when the application shuts down. In that case you would create one subroutine to open the file and a matching subroutine to close the file. The subroutine to close the file would be triggered by the Application_OnEnd event.

The two Application object collections are Contents and StaticObjects. The Contents collection contains all the items that have been added to the Application object using script commands, as you did in your Global.asa file. The syntax for the Contents collection is

```
Application.Contents(key)
```

where *key* is the name of the item to retrieve. In your Global.asa file there is a single object in the collection: Heading with a value of Hello World. You displayed this value on your ASP page using

```
<h2><%= Application("Heading") %></h2>
```

You could also write this as

```
<h2><%=Application.Contents("Heading") %></h2>
```

The StaticObjects collection contains the items added using the <OBJECT> tag. This tag is usually used to embed ActiveX controls in a web page. (Chapter 19 will cover ActiveX controls.) In the Global.asa file it is used to create objects with either application or session scope. The <OBJECT> tag is not used within a script; it is a self-contained tag. The use of the <OBJECT> tag itself is explained in Chapter 19. The syntax for the StaticObjects collection is:

```
Application.StaticObjects(key)
```

As with the Contents collection, *key* is the name of the item being referenced.

The Session Object

A Session object is available to a single user. A session begins when the user first requests a page from the web application and ends when the user abandons the session (by requesting a page outside the web application) or the session times out (there is no activity for a specified period). A session can only be maintained by a browser that supports cookies. A *cookie* is a small file that is written to the user's hard drive to identify the client to the web server. A more in-depth explanation of cookies is in the section "The Cookies Collection."

Reading and writing cookies from an ASP web application is covered in the sections "Request Object" and "Response Object."

Session Object Properties, Collections, and Methods

The Session object has four properties, two collections, and a single method. The properties are CodePage, LCID, SessionID, and Timeout, and the method is Abandon.

The collections are Contents and StaticObjects. These collections are the same as for the Application object, with session, not application, scope. The syntax for the Session object is

```
Session.collection|property|method
```

The CodePage property sets the character set that the web application will use. These character sets are called *codepages*. A codepage contains all the characters, punctuation, etc., for a character set. The CodePage property can be set to any valid codepage on the web server, but will normally be left set to the system default. In North America and Europe this is usually ANSI codepage 1252. In Japan you would use OEM codepage 932 to display Kanji. The syntax for the CodePage property is

Session.CodePage(=*codepage***)**

where *codepage* is the numeric value of the codepage.

The LCID property is the Locale ID. This is used to localize the content to a specific country. The syntax for the LCID property is

Session.LCID(=*lcid***)**

where *lcid* is a valid Locale ID. For example, the LCID for the United States is L0409. A list of Locale IDs can be found in the Windows 98 Resource Kit.

The SessionID property is the unique numeric identifier that is created the first time a user loads a page from the web (the start of their session). To place the value of the SessionID property in the variable lngSID, you would use the syntax

```
lngSID = Session.SessionID
```

You can see how this works by displaying the Session ID on your ASP home page.

1. Open your Default.asp file in the Page view Normal tab and press CTRL+HOME.

2. Press DOWN ARROW once and type **The Session ID is**.

3. Click the HTML tab. The cursor should be in the line that you just entered in the Normal tab, which should look like this

   ```
   <p>The Session ID is </p>
   ```

4. Move the cursor to the end of the line, but before the closing paragraph tag, and type **<%= Session.SessionID %>**. The line should look like this

   ```
   <p>The Session ID is <%= Session.SessionID %></p>
   ```

5. Save the page, and then view it in your browser. You may have to Refresh or Reload your page. Figure 16-4 shows the ASP home page in Internet Explorer 5.0.

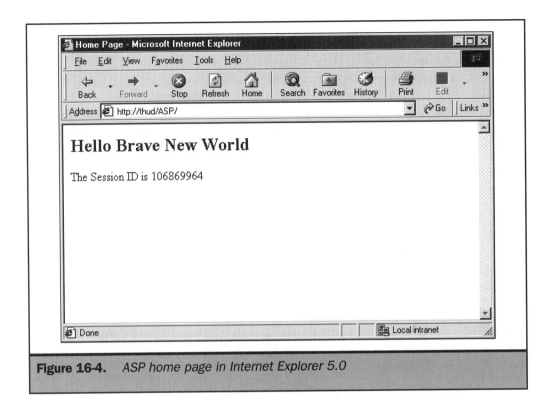

Figure 16-4.   *ASP home page in Internet Explorer 5.0*

The Timeout property is the time, in minutes, that the application will wait for user activity before abandoning the session. The default is 20 minutes. To change the time-out value to ten 10 minutes, you would use the syntax

```
Session.Timeout = 10
```

in your code.

The Abandon method is used to explicitly end a session. You could use this to free up system resources, rather than waiting for the time-out value to take effect. All running scripts are completed before the session is abandoned.

ObjectContext Object

The ObjectContext object is used to commit or abort transactions that are called from an ASP page using the Microsoft Component Services. It has two methods, SetComplete and SetAbort, and two events, OnTransactionCommit and OnTransactionAbort. The syntax is

ObjectContext.*method*

Microsoft Component Services is an environment for managing components on a server. A component is an application on a server that is shared by all the web applications. Component Services enable *multi-tier* applications, that is, applications that have a client component and a server component. A *transaction* is a process that succeeds or fails as a whole; there cannot be a half-completed transaction.

An accounting example shows why this can be critical for web applications. Say you want to move a sum of money from one account to another. For the transaction to be complete, one account must debit the amount and the other must credit it. If either fails, the transaction is incomplete. However, if one account was debited correctly and the process failed to credit the other, you have an accounting headache. When this procedure is done as a transaction, all the steps have to be completed before the transaction is committed. This prevents the situation where a one account is changed and the other is not.

The SetComplete method is used in a script to declare that the script is unaware of any reason for the transaction to fail. If all the components agree, then the transaction is committed. The SetAbort method will abort the transaction. These can be used as part of the logical test in the script. For example, the script can test for a condition and then branch to SetComplete or SetAbort, depending on the results of the test.

The OnTransactionCommit event is triggered when the transaction is committed. As you did with the Application_OnStart event, you can control a subroutine that will run when the transaction is committed. The OnTransactionAbort event is triggered if the transaction is aborted.

Request Object

When a user's browser sends a request to the web server, a great deal of information can be contained in the HTTP header. Along with the URL of the page that is being requested, the header will contain a text string that identifies the browser making the request. The HTTP header may also contain values from an HTML form, values appended to the URL, cookies, and information about the client certificate (if the request is being made over a secure connection). Secure connections over the Internet are covered in Chapter 21.

Request objects have five collections, listed in Table 16-2. These collections give you a great deal of control over a user's experience on your web. The syntax for the Request object is

```
Request[.collection|property|method](variable)
```

The Request object has a single property, TotalBytes, and a single method, BinaryRead. The TotalBytes property is read-only and contains the total number of bytes being sent by the client in the body of the request. The BinaryRead method returns the data sent as part of a POST request (used with the FORM tag). Normally you would use the Form collection to retrieve data sent using a POST request (see the section "The Form Collection"); the BinaryRead method retrieves the raw data in an array, rather than a name/value pair.

Collection	Description
ClientCertificate	Contains information about the user's client certificate.
Cookies	Contains the values of the user's cookies.
Form	Contains the values sent by an HTML form.
QueryString	Contains additional information stored in the URL string.
ServerVariables	Contains information from the HTTP header sent by the requesting browser.

Table 16-2. *Request Object Collections*

If you first call the BinaryRead method, calling Request.Form will generate an error. Conversely, if you call Request.Form first, calling BinaryRead will create an error.

In the following sections you will see how you can use these in your own webs.

If the collection name is omitted, all the collections will be searched for the named variable. This unnecessarily uses server resources and so should be avoided.

The ClientCertificate Collection

The ClientCertificate collection is not extensively used at this time. The user needs to have obtained a certificate from an issuing body, such as VeriSign, Inc. (**http://www.verisign.com**). The issuing body confirms that you are who you say you are and then issues you a certificate. This is a *personal ID certificate,* while servers will have *server IDs.* One valuable use of a personal certificate is that it can ensure that e-mail sent by the certificate holder is not a forgery. This can be important if the e-mail is business related. You can expect that the use of personal certificates will grow, particularly in the business world. The syntax for the ClientCertificate collection is

```
Request.ClientCertificate(key[subfield])
```

where *key* is the name of the certificate field to retrieve and *subfield* is a single field in the Subject or Issuer key. Table 16-3 lists the certificate fields and Table 16-4 lists the individual fields in the Subject and Issuer keys.

The Microsoft Personal Web Server does not support client certificates.

Key	Description
Certificate	Is a string containing all the certificate information.
Flags	Provide additional information about the certificate. There are two keys: ceCertPresent, which indicates a client certificate is present; and ceUnrecognizedIssuer, which indicates the issuer for the most recent certificate is unknown.
Issuer	Is a string containing all the information about the issuer of the certificate.
SerialNumber	Is the certificate serial number.
Subject	Is a string containing all the subfield values for the certificate.
ValidFrom	Is the starting date of the certificate.
ValidUntil	Is the expiration date of the certificate.

Table 16-3.   *ClientCertificate Collection Keys*

SubField	Description
C	Is the country of origin.
CN	Is the user's common name (Subject key only).
GN	Is a given name.
I	Is a set of initials.
L	Is the locality.
O	Is the company or organization name.
OU	Is the name of the organizational unit.
S	Is the name of a state or province.
T	Is the title of a person or organization.

Table 16-4.   *SubFields for ClientCertificate Issuer and Subject Keys*

The Cookies Collection

Properly used, cookies are a valuable tool for both the user and the webmaster. Improperly used, they can be a major problem for both.

Cookies have received a lot of publicity in the popular press, most of it bad. Some would have you believe that they can extract all sorts of personal information about a user and are a serious threat to the user's privacy. There's no question that cookies can be abused, but they are not magic. They cannot extract any information that the user doesn't supply. They are intended to simply identify the client to the web server. A typical cookie generated by an ASP session looks like this:

ASPSESSIONID=NTPHQYWDDUXWFNFO

As you can see, in its simplest form, a cookie is simply a long string of characters. Cookies can also contain a great deal more information, if the webmaster so chooses.

> **Tip** *On Windows computers, cookies are saved in the Windows folder in a folder named Cookies (usually C:\Windows\Cookies). Cookies are text files so you can view them in any text editor, such as Notepad. You can also delete them from a hard drive if you desire. Cookie filenames are usually in the form user@domain, so a cookie generated for someone named Sally who visited Microsoft's web site would be sally@microsoft.txt.*

Since cookies have become controversial, you should understand why they are used. In the first chapter, HTTP was described as stateless protocol, meaning that each request from a client to the server is a separate entity. When the same client makes another request (such as opening another page in a web), the server has no way of knowing that it is the same client. By writing a cookie to the user's computer, the web server can read it when the request is made and identify the client. It won't be able to tell who the user is unless the user has given information about him- or herself at some point. That information can be kept in a database and analyzed to see how users are using the web (how often they visit, how long they stay, what pages they view, and so on). Anonymity is highly prized by many web users, and cookies can be seen as a threat to that.

> **Note** *The current versions of both Netscape and Internet Explorer allow the user to disable cookies. In Internet Explorer 4.0, open the View menu, choose Internet Options, and select the Advanced tab. Under Security there are three options: Always Accept Cookies, Prompt Before Accepting Cookies, and Disable All Cookie Use. In IE 5.0, open the Tools menu, choose Internet Options, select the Security tab, and click Custom Level. In the Security Settings dialog box you can set cookies to Enable, Prompt before accepting, and Disable. You can apply these settings to temporary cookies (which are not stored on the computer's hard drive) and stored cookies. In Netscape Navigator, open the Edit menu, choose Preferences, and click Advanced. There are four options: Accept All Cookies, Accept Only Cookies That Get Sent Back To The Originating Server, Disable Cookies, and Warn Me Before Accepting A Cookie.*

Cookies can also make the users' lives easier. For example, users could request a custom home page that would have the areas of a site that the users are most interested in. The Microsoft site (**http://www.microsoft.com**), especially if you use Internet Explorer, makes extensive use of cookies. It will even automatically create a custom home page based on your page requests. This may offend some people—and that has to be considered in your own cookie use—but if you're visiting the site for information or downloads, it makes life easier.

 *A good source of information about cookies, both technical and philosophical, is Cookie Central at **http://www. cookiecentral.com**. Netscape has a cookie FAQ at **http://netscape.com/products/security/resources/faq/cookies.html**.*

The syntax for the Cookies collection is

```
Cookies(cookie)[(key)|.attribute]
```

The functions of the parameters are

- **Cookie**   The name of the cookie.
- **Key**   An optional parameter that identifies a values in a cookie *dictionary*, a collection of cookie values.
- **Attribute**   Contains information about the cookie itself. Currently there is a single attribute, HasKeys. This is a read-only value that indicates whether the cookie has key values.

Since a cookie first has to be written to a client, using cookies will be covered in more detail in the section "The Response Object Cookies Collection."

The Form Collection

The Request object Form collection provides a method to handle the responses the user enters in an HTML form. FrontPage itself provides several methods for processing form input, but using the Request object Form collection gives you basically unlimited options for doing the same thing.

The syntax for the Form collection is

```
Request.Form(name)[(index)|.Count]
```

The functions of the parameters are

- **Name**   The name of the form element
- **Index**   An optional number used if the form element has multiple values to determine which value is being referenced
- **Count**   The total number of values for a parameter

Using the Form collection can be demonstrated by use of the Literature Request form page you created in Chapter 9. Do that now with these steps (the ASP web should still be open in FrontPage):

1. Open the File menu and choose Import.
2. In the Import dialog box, shown here, click on the Add File button.

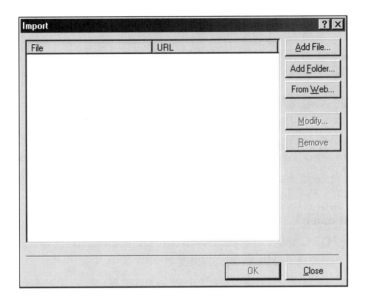

3. In the Add File To Import List dialog box, select the Literature.htm file in the Forms folder (C:\Inetpub\Wwwroot\Forms\ Literature.htm), click Open, and then OK.
4. Open the Literature.htm page in Page view, right-click the form portion of the page, and choose Form Properties.
5. In the Form Properties dialog box, select the Send To Other option, and then click Options. The Options For Custom Form Handler dialog box, shown next, is displayed.

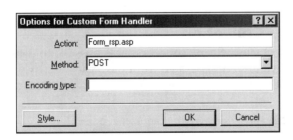

6. Type **Form_rsp.asp** in the Action text box, make sure the Method is Post, and then click OK twice. Save the page.

7. Create a new page, and then click Save on the toolbar.

8. In the Save As dialog box, type **Form_rsp.asp** for the File Name and **Form Response Page** for the Page Title. Click Save.

9. Type **Form Response Page** at the top of the page and format it as Heading 1.

10. Press ENTER and type **Your first name is:** (leave a space after the colon).

Note
When you are instructed to type a line that ends with a period or comma, do not include it unless specifically noted. If the line ends with a colon, always leave a space after the colon.

11. Click the HTML tab. The cursor should be at the end of the line you just typed in the Normal tab.

12. Position the cursor after the space at the end of the line and type **<%= Request.Form("First") %>**. The complete line should look like this

```
<p>Your first name is: <%= Request.Form("First") %></p>
```

13. In the Normal tab, move the cursor to the first blank line on the page and type **Your last name is:**.

14. Click the HTML tab and type **<%= Request.Form("Last") %>** at the end of the line you just typed. The complete line should look like this:

```
<p>Your last name is: <%= Request.Form("Last") %></p>
```

15. Save the Form Response Page.

16. Open the Literature Request page in your browser, fill out the First and Last Name fields on the form, and then click on Submit Form. The Form Response Page will open with your form entries displayed, as shown in Figure 16-5.

This example basically duplicates part of the Confirmation page you can create for a form in FrontPage. However, using ASP is much more flexible. You have total control over the layout of the page and can pass the values to another application, or even to the same page. In the next section, on the QueryString collection, you will see how you can allow the user to modify the page that contains the script.

The QueryString Collection

With the Request object QueryString collection, it is possible to pass values to a page in the URL itself. These values are separated from the basic URL by a question mark (?). The QueryString collection has the same basic syntax as the Form collection:

```
Request.QueryString(variable)[(index)|.Count]
```

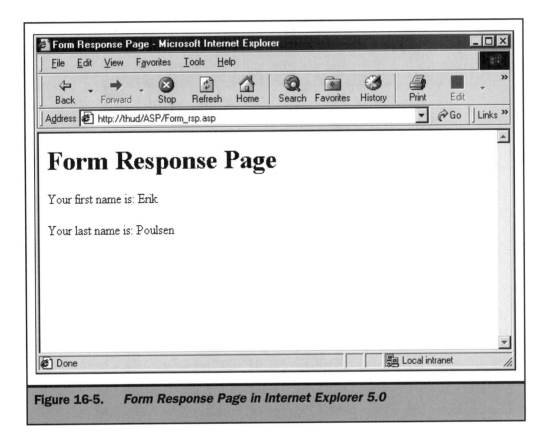

Figure 16-5.   *Form Response Page in Internet Explorer 5.0*

Note   *The QueryString collection is also used when a form uses the Get, rather than Post, method to send form data. With the Get method the data is appended to the URL instead of being included in the HTTP header.*

This next example will demonstrate how the user can customize a page—in this case, the same page that contains the script.

1. Create a new page in your ASP web, and then click Save on the toolbar.

2. In the Save As dialog box, type **Backgrounds.asp** for the File Name and **Backgrounds** for the Page Title. Click Save.

3. With the cursor at the top of the page, type **Would you like a blue background or a yellow background?** and format it as Heading 3.

4. Select the word "blue" and then click Hyperlink on the toolbar.

5. In the Create Hyperlink dialog box, click Backgrounds.asp. The filename will be copied to the URL drop-down list box.

6. Click the URL drop-down box and then press END. Type **?color=blue**. (Do not include the period.) Your Create Hyperlink dialog box should look like this:

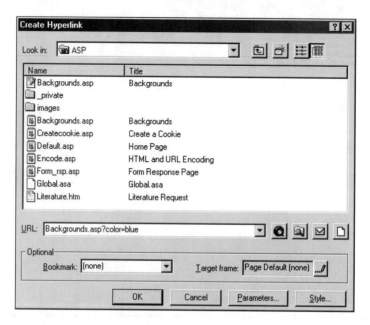

7. Click OK and then select the word "yellow."

8. Open the Create Hyperlink dialog box again and click Backgrounds.asp.

9. Click the URL drop-down box and then press END. Type **?color=yellow**. (Do not include the period.) Click OK.

10. Save the page.

In the next steps you are going to use a combination of VBScript, ASP, and HTML to allow the user to select a background color for the Backgrounds page. To do this, you will create two Body tags for the page, one for the blue page and one for the yellow page. You will use the VBScript Select Case statement to test the value of the color variable being passed in the URL to determine which Body tag is used. FrontPage will not allow multiple BODY tags so you need to have a single BODY tag with the attributes determined by the VBScript script. You will do this by creating a text string that will be appended to the BODY tag.

11. Click the HTML tab and place the cursor on the line between the closing HEAD tag and before the BODY tag.

12. Type **<% Select Case Request.QueryString("color")** and press ENTER.

13. Type **Case "blue"** and press ENTER.

14. Type **strBody = "bgcolor=blue text=yellow link=yellow"** and press ENTER.

15. Type **Case "yellow"** and press ENTER.

16. Type **strBody = "bgcolor=yellow text=blue"**, and press ENTER.

17. Type **End Select %>** and press ENTER.

> **Tip**
>
> *You could also use the VBScript If… Else…statements rather than Select Case. Select Case is a better choice if there are more than two choices as the If… Else… statement can get complicated. If there are more than two choices, or if you think that there may ultimately be more than two choices, you should use the Select Case statement. Planning ahead can save you from rewriting your code later.*

18. Place the cursor in the BODY tag at the end of the word "body" and press SPACE.

19. Type **<%= strBody %>**. (Do not include the period.) The complete BODY tag should look like this

    ```
    <body <%= strBody %>>
    ```

20. Your Backgrounds page code should look like Figure 16-6. Save the Backgrounds page.

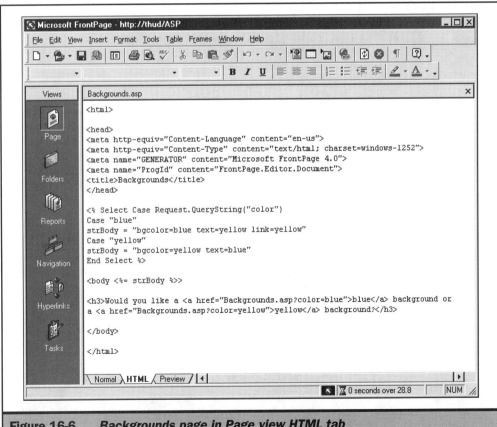

Figure 16-6. *Backgrounds page in Page view HTML tab*

21. Open the page in your browser and click the "blue" hyperlink. The page is displayed with a blue background and yellow text.

22. Click the "yellow" hyperlink. The page is now displayed with a yellow background and blue text.

If you load the Backgrounds page without a color specified (the URL doesn't include the question mark and either color=... value), both Case tests fail and strBody is an empty string. In this case the default Body tag is used. If you look at the source for this page in your browser, you will see how the Body tag is modified when a color is specified. This is an important concept, as it allows the page to degrade gracefully. That is, it doesn't self-destruct if a color value isn't specified. Whenever you are using ASP objects or scripting, you have to deal with what happens in all cases, such as if a browser doesn't support a feature you are trying to use.

These examples just scratch the surface of what is possible by use of the Request object's Form and QueryString collections. With a little imagination you can add a great deal of interactivity and customization with them.

The ServerVariables Collection

The ServerVariables collection gives you access to a plethora of information about the server environment. The syntax is straightforward:

```
Request.ServerVariables(variable)
```

The variables available in the ServerVariables collection are listed in Table 16-5. The variables in the ServerVariables collection are very useful for examining the server environment, but you will probably not use them as often as the Cookies, Form, or QueryString collections.

Variable	Description
ALL_HTTP	Contains all the HTTP headers sent by the browser.
ALL_RAW	Contains all the HTTP headers without processing. When ALL_HTTP is used, each header name is prefaced with HTTP_. With ALL_RAW the headers appear exactly as sent.
APPL_MD_PATH	Is the metabase path for an ISAPI application (a DLL file). The metabase is where Windows stores the configuration information for your web server (IIS or PWS).

Table 16-5. *Request Object ServerVariables Collection Variables*

Variable	Description
APPL_PHYSICAL_PATH	Is the physical path corresponding to the metabase path. This is the actual location of the file on your hard drive.
AUTH_PASSWORD	Contains the password entered in the browser's authentication dialog box. This variable is only available with Basic authentication.
AUTH_TYPE	Is the authentication method used by the server. This is set in the Internet Services Manager.
AUTH_USER	Is the raw authenticated username.
CERT_COOKIE	Is a unique ID for the client certificate.
CERT_FLAGS	Are flags set to indicate if a client certificate is present and if it was issued by a valid authority.
CERT_ISSUER	Contains the information for issuer of a client certificate.
CERT_KEYSIZE	Is the number of bits in the Secure Sockets Layer (SSL) key. This is 128 bits for domestic browsers and 40 bits for international browsers.
CERT_SECRETKEYSIZE	TheIs the number of bits in a server certificate private key.
CERT_SERIALNUMBER	Is the serial number of the client certificate.
CERT_SERVER_ISSUER	Is the issuing authority for the server certificate.
CERT_SERVER_SUBJECT	Is the contents of the subject field in the server certificate.
CERT_SUBJECT	Is the contents of the subject field in the client certificate.
CONTENT_LENGTH	Is the length of the content requested.
CONTENT_TYPE	Is the type of the content, such as Post or Get.
GATEWAY_INTERFACE	Is the version of the CGI (common gateway interface) on the server.

Table 16-5. *Request Object ServerVariables Collection Variables* (continued)

WORKING BEHIND
THE SCENES

Variable	Description
HTTP_*HeaderName*	Used to extract values not included in the default variables. An example is HTTP_UA_PIXELS, which returns the user's screen resolution. Not all variables are returned by all clients.
HTTPS	Contains ON or OFF depending on whether or not the request came through a secure channel.
HTTPS_KEYSIZE	Is the number of bits in the SSL key.
HTTPS_SECRETKEYSIZE	Is the number of bits in the server certificate private key.
HTTPS_SERVER_ISSUER	Is the issuing authority for the server certificate.
HTTPS_SERVER_SUBJECT	Is the contents of the subject field in the server certificate.
INSTANCE_ID	Is the ID for the current IIS instance of the client request.
INSTANCE_META_PATH	Is the path in the metabase for the current instance of the client request.
LOCAL_ADDR	Is the address of the server that received the request.
LOGON_USER	Is the NT user account that is used for the request. By default this is IUSR_*computername.* This account is created when IIS is installed on NT Server.
PATH_INFO	Virtual path information contained in the request.
PATH_TRANSLATED	Maps the virtual path to the physical path.
QUERY_STRING	All the information after the question mark in a request. This is the same information that is in the QueryString collection, but it is not parsed into separate elements.
REMOTE_ADDR	Is the IP address of the remote host.
REMOTE_HOST	Is the name of the remote host.

Table 16-5. *Request Object ServerVariables Collection Variables* (continued)

Variable	Description
REMOTE_USER	Is the username string sent by the client without any filtering.
REQUEST_METHOD	Is the request method, such as POSTPost, GETGet, and so on.
SCRIPT_NAME	Is the virtual path of the script being executed.
SERVER_NAME	Is the web server's name, DNS (Domain Name System) alias, or IP address.
SERVER_PORT	Is the server's port number handling the request. For web services this is normally port 80. A *port* is a reference to a process on the server, not a physical port.
SERVER_PORT_SECURE	A flag (either 0 or 1) that indicates if the request is secure. A 1 indicates a secure port is being used to handle the request.
SERVER_PROTOCOL	Is the name and version of the protocol processing the request.
SERVER_SOFTWARE	Is the name and version of the server software.
URL	Is the base portion of the URL.

Table 16-5.   *Request Object ServerVariables Collection Variables* (continued)

WORKING BEHIND
THE SCENES

Many of these server variables are used with Secure Sockets Layer (SSL) transactions, which require both a server certificate and a client certificate. Certificates and SSL are covered in Chapter 21. The Personal Web Server doesn't support SSL, so we will look at some of the other server variables in the next exercise. This next set of instructions will create a simple web page that displays some of the server variables:

1. In your ASP web, create a new page, and save it with the File Name **Server.asp** and the Page Title **Server Variables**.

2. Type **Server Variables** at the top of the page, and format it as Heading 2.

3. Press ENTER, open the Table menu, and choose Insert | Table.

4. In the Insert Table dialog box, specify **6** Rows, **2** Columns, a Cell Padding of **4**, and clear the Specify Width check box if it is selected. Click OK.

5. In the first cell of the first row, type **VARIABLE**, press TAB, and type **VALUE**.

6. Press TAB and type **PATH_INFO**.

7. Press DOWN ARROW and type **PATH_TRANSLATED**.

8. In the remaining three cells of the first column, type **SERVER_NAME**, **SERVER_PROTOCOL**, and **SERVER_SOFTWARE**, pressing DOWN ARROW between each entry. Your table should look like Figure 16-7.

9. Click in the second cell of the second row, and click the HTML tab.

10. The cursor should be in the table cell underneath the cell containing PATH_INFO. Delete the nonbreaking space ( ) and type **<%= Request.ServerVariables("PATH_INFO") %>**. The completed code for the table row should look like this:

```
<tr>
  <td>PATH_INFO</td>
  <td><%= Request.ServerVariables("PATH_INFO") %></td>
</tr>
```

11. Move the cursor to the table cell underneath the cell with the PATH_TRANSLATED label and type **<%= Request.ServerVariables("PATH_TRANSLATED") %>**.

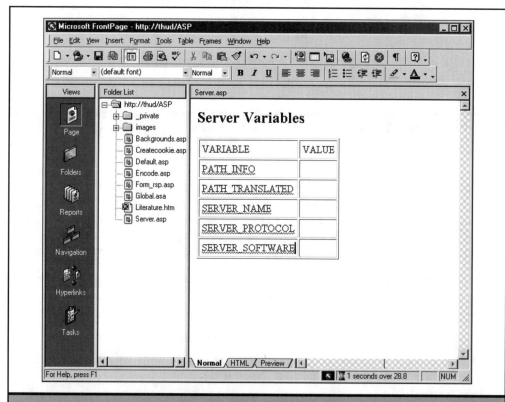

Figure 16-7.   *Server Variables page in Page view*

12. Move the cursor to the next cell with a nonbreaking space (under the SERVER_NAME label), delete the nonbreaking space, and type **<%= Request.ServerVariables("SERVER_NAME") %>**.

13. Move the cursor to the next cell with a nonbreaking space (under the SERVER_PROTOCOL label), delete the nonbreaking space, and type **<%= Request.ServerVariables("SERVER_PROTOCOL") %>**.

14. Move the cursor to the next cell with a nonbreaking space (under the SERVER_SOFTWARE label), delete the nonbreaking space, and type **<%= Request.ServerVariables("SERVER_SOFTWARE") %>**. Your page should look similar to Figure 16-8.

15. Save your Server Variables page, and then open it in your browser.

Figure 16-9 shows the Server Variables page in Internet Explorer. Some of the values in your table will be different, reflecting your server setup.

The Request object and its collections allow you to handle a great deal of input from the user. This is the key to creating truly interactive web applications. In the next section you will see how to use the Response object and its collection, properties, and methods to send output to the user.

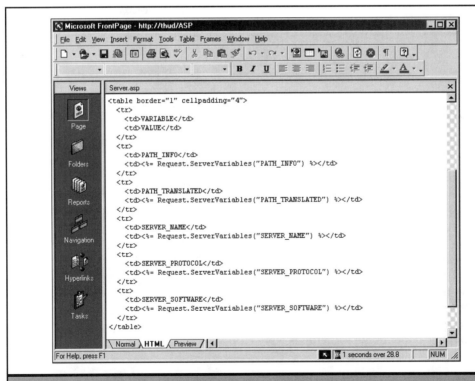

Figure 16-8. *Server Variables page in Page view HTML tab*

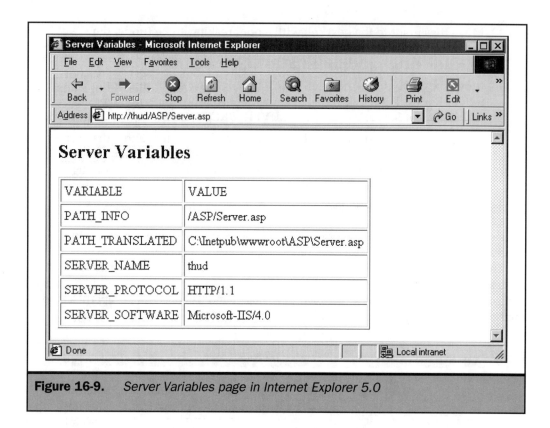

Figure 16-9.   *Server Variables page in Internet Explorer 5.0*

Response Object

The Response object is the complement to the Request object. The syntax is

```
Response.collection|property|method
```

The Response object has a single collection, Cookies; nine properties, listed in Table 16-6; and eight methods, listed in Table 16-7.

Of the various properties and methods in the Response object, the Redirect method is one of the most useful. It allows you to control what page is sent to the user's browser based on some form of input, such as a selection in a form. For example, earlier in this chapter you created a page to display data entered in the Literature Request form. What if you wanted to prevent users from seeing that page unless they had entered all the data in the form? With the Redirect method you could send users to the form page if any of the form fields were empty.

Property	Parameters	Description
Buffer	[=*TRUE*	*FALSE*]	When set to TRUE, the server does not send any output to the client until all the scripts on the page have been processed. When set to FALSE (the default), the output of each script on the page is sent as soon as it processed.
CacheControl	[= *cache control header*]	Determines if a proxy server will cache ASP files.
Charset	(*charset*)	Specifies the character set of a page where *charset* is the name of the character set.
ContentType	[=*content type*]	Specifies the type of data being sent to the client. The default content type is text/HTML. Other possible values include image/GIF and image/JPEG.
Expires	[=*minutes*]	Sets the length of time in minutes a page will be cached on the user's browser. If the user reloads the page before the Expires value is reached, the cached file is displayed. When the Expires value has been exceeded, the page will be reloaded from the server.
ExpiresAbsolute	[=[*date*][*time*]]	Sets a date and time a page is flushed from the user's browser. If a date is specified, but not a time, the page expires at midnight.
IsClientConnected		Is a read-only property that indicates whether or not the client is still connected.
Pics	(*PICSlabel*)	Inserts a PICS (Platform for Internet Content Selection) label to the response header. PICS is a system for rating Internet content.
Status	[=*status description*]	Sets a three-digit error code and a brief explanation, such as "403 Access Forbidden," as shown in Figure 16-1.

Table 16-6.   *Response Object Properties*

Method	Parameters	Description
AddHeader	*name, value*	Adds an HTML header to a page. This method is not recommended for use if another Response method will do the job.
AppendToLog	*string*	Adds the string value to the web server log for the request. The string cannot contain commas and has a maximum length of 80 characters.
BinaryWrite	*data*	Sends data to a browser without any conversion—for example, a graphics file.
Clear		Clears any buffered output. If this method is called, Response.Buffer must first be set to TRUE or an error will be generated.
End		Stops the processing of an ASP file. The current results are sent, and the rest of the scripting is ignored.
Flush		Sends any buffered output immediately. If this method is called, Response.Buffer must first be set to TRUE or an error will be generated.
Redirect	*URL*	Loads the page in the user's browser specified by the URL parameter.
Write	*string*	Sends the data specified in the string parameter. This can be any valid data type for your scripting language.

Table 16-7.   *Response Object Methods*

In actual use, forms normally use a JavaScript form validation script to prevent users from leaving any required fields blank, but this doesn't prevent users from entering the confirmation page URL in the browser's Address box and going to the page. With the Redirect method you could test for a valid value in the form field and send users to the form if there weren't one.

You will see an example of the Response.Redirect method in the next section.

The Response Object Cookies Collection

Earlier in this chapter you had an overview of cookies. In this section you will learn how to use them. The syntax for the Response object Cookies collection is

```
Response.Cookies(cookie)[(key)|.attribute]=value
```

The functions of the parameters are

- **Cookie**   The name of the cookie
- **Key**   An optional parameter that identifies a value in a cookie *dictionary*, a collection of cookie values
- **Attribute**   Information about the cookie itself
- **Value**   The actual value of the cookie

The Attribute parameter has five possible values, listed in Table 16-8. As you can see, you have a great deal of control over just what is in a cookie.

The best way to understand cookies is to start using them. In the following exercise, you'll create a form page for the user to enter the cookie values, a page to write out the cookie, and a page to display the cookie values. You will also use the Response.Redirect method to move the user seamlessly from the form page to the page that displays the cookie values. Do that now with these steps:

Note   *Your browser has to be set to accept cookies for this exercise to work correctly.*

WORKING BEHIND
THE SCENES

Name	Type	Description
Expires	Write-only	Sets the date on which the cookie will expire.
Domain	Write-only	Sets the domain to which the cookie is sent. This is usually the domain where the web page is located, but some advertisers require the cookie be sent to their domain, rather than to the issuing domain. Netscape allows the user to block this type of cookie.
Path	Write-only	Sets the path that the cookie will be sent. If this value is not set, the application path is used.
Secure	Write-only	Indicates whether the cookie is secure.
HasKeys	Read-only	Indicates whether the cookie has a dictionary.

Table 16-8.   *Response Object Cookies Collection Attribute Parameter Values*

1. In your ASP web, create a new page, and save it with the File Name **Createcookie.asp** and the Page Title **Create a Cookie**.

2. In the Page view Normal tab, type **Enter Cookie Values**, and format it as Heading 2.

3. Press ENTER and then insert a one-line text box from the Insert | Form menu or the Form toolbar.

4. Press HOME and type **Enter your name:** (leave seven spaces after the colon). Format the text as Formatted.

5. Press RIGHT ARROW to move the insertion point between the text box and the Submit button, and then press SHIFT+ENTER to move the Submit and Reset buttons to the next line.

6. Insert another one-line text box, press HOME, and then type **Enter a favorite food:** (leave a space after the colon).

7. Press RIGHT ARROW and then press SHIFT+ENTER. Your page should look similar to Figure 16-10.

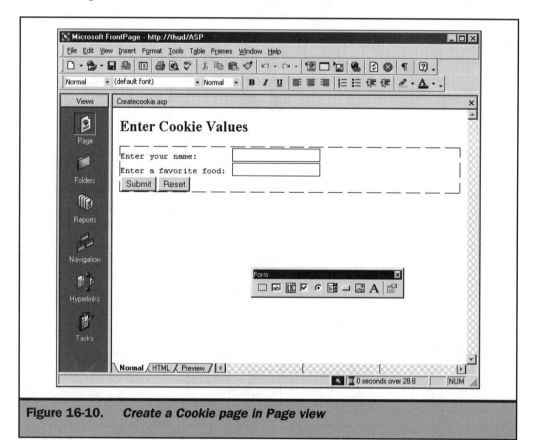

Figure 16-10. *Create a Cookie page in Page view*

8. Right-click the first form field and choose Form Field Properties. In the Text Box Properties dialog box, type **Name** in the Name text box, as shown next, and then click OK.

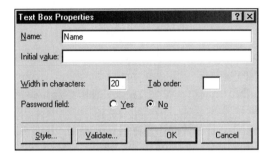

9. Right-click the second form field and choose Form Field Properties. In the Text Box Properties dialog box, type **Food** in the Name text box and then click OK.

10. Right-click the form and choose Form Properties. In the Form Properties dialog box, select Send To Other, and then click Options.

11. In the Options For Custom Form Handler dialog box, type **Writecookie.asp** in the Action text box, make sure Post is the Method selected, as shown here, and click OK twice.

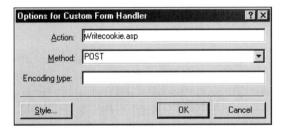

12. Save the page.

13. Create a new page, and save it with the File Name **Writecookie.asp** and the Page Title **Write a Cookie**.

14. Click the HTML tab, press CTRL+A to select all the text, and then press DEL.

15. Type
<% name = Request.Form("Name")
food = Request.Form("Food")
Response.Cookies("theCookie")("Name") = name
Response.Cookies("theCookie")("Food") = food
Response.Redirect "Readcookie.asp" %>
This script assigns the values entered in the Name and Food form fields to the

variables name and food, respectively. It then assigns the values in the name and food variables to the keys Name and Food for the cookie theCookie. Finally, it redirects the user to the ASP page that will read and display the values for the cookie theCookie. If the script is executed properly, the user will never see the Writecookie.asp page.

16. Save the page.

17. Create a new page and save it with the File Name **Readcookie.asp** and the Page Title **Read a Cookie**.

18. In the Page view Normal tab, type **Your Cookie Values Are:** and format it as Heading 2. Press ENTER.

19. Type **Name =** (leave a space after the equal sign), click the HTML tab and type **<%= Request.Cookies("theCookie")("Name") %>** after Name = and on the same line. There should be one space after Name = and before the VBScript delimiter.

20. Click the Normal tab, move the cursor to the line below Name = , and type **Food =** (again, leave a space after the equal sign).

21. Click the HTML tab, and type **<%= Request.Cookies("theCookie")("Food") %>** after Food = (and on the same line).

22. Save the page.

23. Open the Create A Cookie page (Createcookie.asp) in your browser.

24. Fill out the form and then click Submit. Your browser should display the Read a Cookie page as shown in Figure 16-11.

Cookies can be very useful to the webmaster, but you must also remember that not every browser will support them, either by design (an older browser that doesn't support cookies) or choice (the user has disabled them). If your web contains features that depend on cookies (such as user preferences or customizable web pages), it might be better to keep the user preferences in a database on your server and to have users log in when they visit your site.

Both methods have advantages and disadvantages, so you will have to decide what works best for your site.

Server Object

The Server object provides one property and four methods (listed in Table 16-9) that primarily provide utility functions. The syntax is

```
Server.method
```

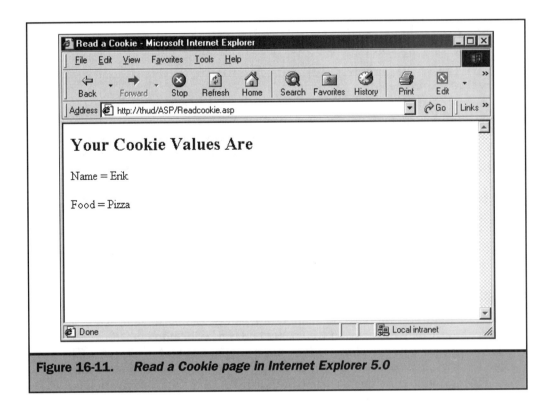

Figure 16-11.   *Read a Cookie page in Internet Explorer 5.0*

The MapPath method functions much the same way as the Request object PATH_TRANSLATED ServerVariable, converting a virtual path to a physical path. The CreateObject method is primarily used with ASP components and will be covered in the next chapter.

Method	Description
CreateObject	Creates an instance of an ASP component.
HTMLEncode	Encodes a text string into HTML so that reserved characters, such as < and >, are displayed correctly.
MapPath	Converts a virtual path to a physical path.
URLEncode	Encodes a text string so that it conforms to URL encoding rules.

Table 16-9.   *Server Object Methods*

The Server Object ScriptTimeout Property

The single Server object property is ScriptTimeout, and the syntax is

```
Server.ScriptTimeout = seconds
```

This value sets the length of time, in seconds, that the server will process a script before abandoning it. This is needed because an error in a script may cause it to run forever without ending, a situation sometimes known as an *infinite loop*. Obviously, this is not a good thing. The ScriptTimeout value prevents this from happening.

The Windows NT or Windows 98 Registry (a special system file that contains defaults for the operating system and applications) contains the default ScriptTimeout value, which is usually 90 seconds. The Server object ScriptTimeout property overrides the Registry setting for the script that calls it, but it cannot be set to a value shorter than the Registry entry.

The Server Object HTMLEncode and URLEncode Methods

The HTMLEncode and URLEncode methods are handy utilities for converting text strings so they display correctly on web pages and can be included in URLs.

HTML uses certain characters, such as < and >, to define HTML elements. These are known as *reserved characters*. If you attempt to use them as text characters in a web page, HTML will interpret them as HTML coding. The HTMLEncode method converts the reserved characters in the text string to special characters that will display correctly and not be interpreted as part of the HTML coding.

FrontPage will automatically convert reserved characters when they are entered on a page in Page view or are in an imported text file.

The URLEncode method provides a similar function for text strings that are to be included in a URL. As you saw with Request.QueryString, you can attach information to a URL and then use it to control actions on an ASP page. If the extended information contains spaces or other special characters, these will not be interpreted correctly.

You can easily create an ASP page that demonstrates how these two methods work with these instructions:

When you are instructed to type a line that ends with a period or comma, do not include it unless specifically noted. If the line ends with a colon, always leave a space after the colon.

1. Create a new page and save it with the File Name **Encode.asp** and the Page Title **HTML and URL Encoding**.

2. Type **HTML and URL Encoding** at the top of the page, and format it as Heading 2.

3. Press ENTER and then insert a one-line text box from the Insert | Form menu or the Form toolbar.

4. Press HOME and type **Enter some text:**.

5. Press RIGHT ARROW and then press ENTER.

6. Right-click the form field and choose Form Field Properties.

7. In the Form Field Properties dialog box, type **Text** in the Name text box, and set the Width In Characters to **40**. Click OK.

8. Right-click the form and choose Form Properties.

9. In the Form Properties dialog box, select the Send To Other option and then click Options.

10. In the Options For Custom Form Handler Action text box, type **Encode.asp** and click OK twice.

11. Click the first blank line below the form, and then click the HTML tab.

12. In the first blank line after the form code, type **<% strText = Request.Form("Text") %>**.

13. Click the Normal tab, move the cursor to the first line under the form, and type **Your text HTML encoded:**.

14. Press ENTER and type **Your text URL encoded:**.

15. Click the HTML tab, and locate the line <p>Your text HTML encoded: </p>, and type **<%= Server.HTMLEncode(strText) %>** before the closing paragraph tag.

16. Move the cursor to the line <p>Your text URL encoded: </p> and type **<%= Server.URLEncode(strText) %>** before the closing paragraph tag. Your code should look like this:

```
</form>
<% strText = Request.Form("Text") %>
<p>Your text HTML encoded: <%= Server.HTMLEncode(strText) %></p>
<p>Your text URL encoded: <%= Server.URLEncode(strText) %></p>
</body>
```

17. Save the page and then open it in your browser.

18. Type **Some text <P> <h3>** in the form text box and click Submit. Your browser should look similar to Figure 16-12.

If you look at the source for the HTML page displayed in your browser, you will see how the text was encoded for both HTML and the URL. For HTML, the text is written

Some text <P> <h3>

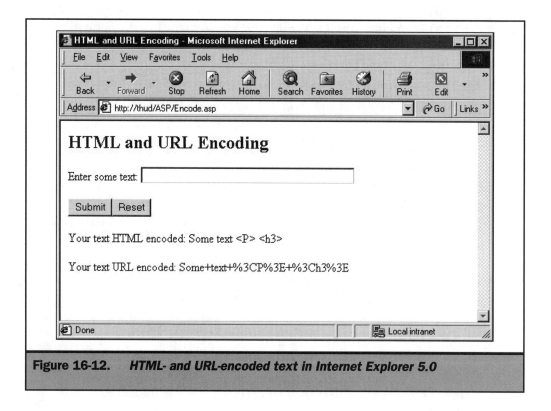

Figure 16-12.   *HTML- and URL-encoded text in Internet Explorer 5.0*

For the URL encoding it is written as

Some+text+%3CP%3E+%3Ch3%3E

In the HTML-encoded example, the less-than (<) and greater-than (>) symbols have been replaced with "<" and ">". For the URL-encoded example, the less-than and greater-than symbols have been replaced with "%3C" and "%3E," and spaces have been replaced with plus signs (+). The percent symbol (%) is used as an escape character, which indicates that what follows is the number of the ASCII character in hexadecimal.

The Active Server Page objects are extremely flexible and powerful. The examples given here have just scratched the surface of what you can do with them. ASP would be a great boon to the web builder even if the objects covered so far were all there was to it, but there's more. The ASP components covered in the next chapter will show how ASP is an open-ended structure for interactive web applications.

The Complete Reference

FrontPage 2000

Chapter 17

Advanced Active Server Pages

595

A ctive Server Pages components differ from the objects that have been covered so far in that they are really ActiveX components. (An explanation of ActiveX components can be found in Chapter 19.) ASP creates the structure to use these components on the server. You are not limited to the components included with ASP; you can integrate any ActiveX components. This is what makes ASP an open-ended system for interactive web applications.

There are six components included with the MSPWS and IIS. Additional components are available from Microsoft and other sources. Table 17-1 provides a brief description of the default components as well as additional components that will be covered in this chapter.

> **Note**   *The Counters, Content Rotator, Page Counter, and Permission Checker Components are not included with either MSPWS or IIS. They are available with the Internet Information Server Resource Kit (Microsoft Press, 1998). If you do not have these components installed, you will not be able to do the exercises using them. They are included here as it's reasonable to expect your web presence provider to have them installed.*

Component	Description
Ad Rotator	Automates the rotation of ad banners.
Browser Capabilities	Determines the features of the user's browser.
Counters	Creates an object that can control any number of individual counters.
Database Access	Provides connectivity to ODBC-compliant databases.
Content Linking	Links pages in a web application and creates tables of contents.
Content Rotator	Automates the rotation of HTML content.
File Access	Provides methods for accessing the computer's file system.
MyInfo	Contains personal information.
Page Counter	Tracks page hits.
Permission Checker	Checks user permissions to access files.

Table 17-1.   *Active Server Pages Components*

The Server.CreateObject Object and ASP Components

The components included with ASP are all objects that must be *instantiated* before they can be referenced. This simply means that an instance of the component must be created. This is done with the Server.CreateObject method by creating a variable that references the component. An example of the syntax is

```
Set objComponent = Server.CreateObject([Vendor.]Component[.Version])
```

Note *The Set statement is required in Visual Basic and VBScript when assigning a variable to an object.*

Tip *In creating variables, it is a good practice to use a three-character prefix that identifies what type of variable has been created. In the preceding example, objComponent, the prefix "obj" indicates that the variable references an object. Common prefixes are listed in Table 17-2. More information can be found in the MSPWS Help file VBScript Language Reference.*

Variable Type	Prefix
Boolean	bln
Byte	byt
Date/Time	dtm
Double	dbl
Error	err
Integer	int
Long	lng
Object	obj
Single	sng
String	str

Table 17-2.   *Prefixes for Variable Names*

WORKING BEHIND THE SCENES

By default, instances of objects have page scope. This means that they exist from the time they are created until the script on a page is completely processed. They can also be explicitly destroyed by setting the object variable to Nothing, for example: *objComponent* = Nothing. Instances of objects can be given session or application scope by creating them in the Global.asa file with the <OBJECT> tag. In the examples in this section, most of the objects will be used with page scope. The Counters and MyInfo Components will have application scope.

In the following sections, you will see exactly how Server.CreateObject is used with ASP components.

The Ad Rotator Component

Webs are created for a variety of reasons: some are produced by hobbyists, others by businesses to advertise their products or services. Many web sites are now being created to make a profit. (This is, in fact, the Holy Grail for most webmasters, as few web sites are actually making a profit, though this is changing.)

One way to generate revenue is to sell ad banners on your pages. These banners are graphics that usually provide links to the advertiser's own web site. Ad banners are typically sold by number of impressions or page views, or by click-throughs. *Impressions* are the number of times an ad banner is actually loaded by users. *Click-throughs* are the number of times users click the banner and jump to the advertiser's site. Good click-through rates run between 3 and 6 percent of impressions.

Once you begin selling ad banners on a site, you also have to manage them. Unless an advertiser buys all the impressions for a particular page, each page may have several ad banners, and you will need to rotate them constantly. Even if an advertiser does buy all the impressions for a page, they may have several banners that they want rotated. This would be a full-time job if done manually, which is why the Ad Rotator Component is so useful. It automates the process of rotating banners and even apportions impressions between them so that one banner could get 50 percent of the impressions, with the remaining 50 percent shared equally by two other banners.

The Ad Rotator Component uses a text file, the Rotator Schedule file, which contains the banner file information and schedule. You can also use a script, the Redirection file, that can be used to capture information when a user clicks a banner before redirecting the user to the advertiser's site.

There are three properties and a single method for the Ad Rotator Component; the properties are described in Table 17-3. The method is **GetAdvertisement** (*schedule file*).

Creating a Rotator Schedule File

The first step in using the Ad Rotator is to create a Rotator Schedule file. This is a text file that contains some basic information about all the ad banners and specific information about each banner. You create the schedule file in your text editor.

Property	Description
Border	Sets the width of the border around the ad graphic.
Clickable	Sets whether the ad graphic is a hyperlink.
TargetFrame	The name of the frame in which to display the ad, if used on a frame page.

Table 17-3.   *Ad Rotator Component Properties*

The syntax for the file is

```
Redirect URL
Width PixelsWidth
Height PixelsHeight
Border PixelsBorder
*
```

These first four items are the optional global values for the Rotator Schedule file. If they are not included, the first line of the file will contain a single asterisk (*) and the default values will be used. The function and default value of each parameter are described in Table 17-4.

Parameter	Default	Description
Redirect		URL of the file that redirects users when they click a banner and captures any information, such as click-throughs.
Width	440	Width in pixels of the ad banners.
Height	60	Height in pixels of the ad banners.
Border	1	Width in pixels of the border around each banner.

Table 17-4.   *Rotator Schedule File Global Parameters*

After the asterisk, you enter the information about each ad banner. The syntax is

```
BannerURL
AdvertiserURL
AltText
Impressions
```

The BannerURL is the location of the ad banner graphic; AdvertiserURL is the URL of the web page that is the target of the banner hyperlink; AltText is the alternate text for the banner graphic; and Impressions is the percentage of impressions the banner will receive. The actual value for the Impressions parameter is a number between 0 and 4,294,967,295. In determining the percentage of impressions for each banner, the component totals all the values for all the banners and then calculates the percentage. For example, if you had three banners with impressions values of 6, 3, and 3, the total would be 12. The first banner would get 6/12 of the impressions, or 50 percent, and the remaining two would get 3/12, or 25 percent, each.

Note   *The Rotator Schedule file must be available on a virtual path on the web server.*

Create a Rotator Schedule file with these steps:

Note   *In your Schedule Rotator file, substitute the name of your computer for servername. In the examples shown here, the computer name is sam.*

1. Open your text editor. In a new page, type

   Redirect /scripts/Adredirect.asp
   Width 468
   Height 60
   Border 1
   *
   images/banner1.gif
   http://*servername*/asp/default.asp
   FrontPage 2000
   1

   images/banner2.gif
   http://*servername*/asp/default.asp
   FrontPage 2000
   1

2. Save the file in your ASP directory with the name **Adsched.txt**.

3. In FrontPage, open your ASP web if it's not already open, and create a new page. At the top of the page, type **Ad Banner Rotation** and format it as Heading 2.

4. Save the page with the Page Title **Ad Banner Rotation** and the File Name **Banners.asp**.

Creating an Instance of the Ad Rotator Component

On the Banners.asp page, you need to create an instance of the Ad Rotator Component and then use the GetAdvertisement method to display a banner. Do that now with these steps:

1. In the Page view Normal tab, move the insertion point to the line below the heading.

2. Click the HTML tab, check that the cursor is on the line below your heading, and type

    ```
    <%
    Set objRotator = Server.CreateObject("MSWC.AdRotator")
    Response.Write(objRotator.GetAdvertisement("Adsched.txt"))
    %>
    ```

    Figure 17-1 shows the Ad Rotation script in the FrontPage HTML tab.

3. Save the page.

    In your script you use the Response.Write object to write out the value returned by the GetAdvertisement method. You will see the results of this later in this exercise.

4. Click Folders in the Views bar, and in the FrontPage Folder List, double-click the Images folder to open it. Then open the File menu and choose Import.

5. In the Import dialog box, click Add File.

6. In the Add File To Import List dialog box, select your CD-ROM drive, and open the Chap17 folder on the included CD.

7. Click the file Banner1.gif; then press and hold CTRL and click on Banner2.gif. Release CTRL, click Open, and then click OK.

8. Open the Banners.asp page in your web browser. It should look similar to Figure 17-2.

9. Click your browser's Refresh (Internet Explorer) or Reload (Netscape) button until the ad banner changes.

> **Note**
> *Even with two ad banners set to receive 50 percent of the impressions each, every refresh will not always change the banner displayed. On average, over a period of time, each banner should receive 50 percent of the impressions.*

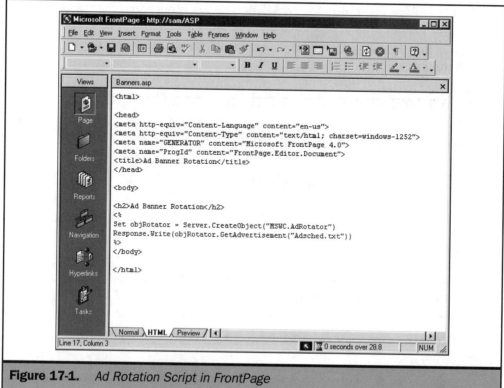

Figure 17-1.   *Ad Rotation Script in FrontPage*

10. View the source of the page in your browser.

By looking at the source, you can see the HTML code that is created by the Ad Rotator Component and written to the web page by the Response.Write object. Two HTML tags are used: the <A HREF> tag, which creates a hyperlink, and the <IMG> tag, which displays the graphic. Your hyperlink source should look similar to this (depending on which banner is being displayed):

```
<A
HREF="/scripts/Adredirect.asp?url=http://servername/asp/default.htm
&image=images/banner1.gif">...</A>
```

The hyperlink will not take you directly to the advertiser's web page; it first takes you to the Redirection file, which you will create in the next part of this exercise. You will use the Request.QueryString object to parse the URL for the final destination and

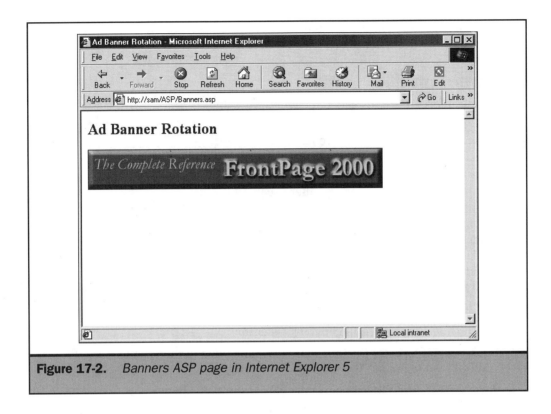

Figure 17-2. Banners ASP page in Internet Explorer 5

then use the Response.Redirect object to send the user there. First, though, the function of the FrontPage Scripts directory, where the Redirection file will be placed, needs to be explained.

The FrontPage Scripts Directory

In the examples of working with cookies, you created an ASP page, Writecookie.asp, that processed data from one page, Createcookie.asp, and then sent the user to another page, Readcookie.asp. When you're working with ASP files, this situation is not uncommon. You can create ASP pages in FrontPage, complete with HTML headers, to handle these tasks, but then you will always have the problem you experienced earlier if you use the Response.Redirect object. A better way is to use the Scripts directory created by default as a virtual directory with Execute and Scripts permission when you install the MSPWS or IIS.

The default path for the Scripts directory is C:\Inetpub\Scripts. As a virtual directory, it can be accessed from any page in any of your webs with the virtual path /scripts. For security, this directory does not have Read permission set. This is to prevent users from seeing any of the files located there. Without the Read permission, users cannot load any of the files in the Scripts directory in their browser. This is where you will save the Adredirect.asp Redirection file.

The Redirection File

In its simplest form, the Redirection file will have a single line:

```
Response.Redirect(Request.QueryString("url"))
```

However, you can use this file to do much more. For example, you could record each click-through in a database. Another use would be to use the VBScript Select Case statement to expand the URL provided by the Rotator Schedule file. Many advertisers use complicated URLs for their banner ads. Often they will include identifiers for the site hosting the banner and write out the information to their own databases. To avoid passing these long URLs between the Rotator Schedule file, the ASP page, and the Redirection file, you can use a single, short text string in the schedule file that is expanded to the complete URL in the Redirection file. This is what you will do with these steps:

1. Open the Adsched.txt file in your text editor.

2. Change the URL for the first banner to **Banner1**, and then change the URL for the second banner to **Banner2**.

3. Save the file, and then open a new file in your text editor.

4. Type

```
<%
Set AdUrl = Request.QueryString("url")
Select Case AdUrl
Case "Banner1"
AdUrl = "http://servername/asp/default.asp"
Case "Banner2"
AdUrl = "http://servername/asp/default.asp"
End Select
Response.Redirect AdUrl
%>
```

5. Save the file in the Scripts directory (C:\Inetpub\Scripts) with the name **Adredirect.asp**.

6. Reload the Banners.asp page in your browser, and click the ad banner. You will be taken to the ASP web home page you created earlier in this book.

7. Close the Banners.asp page in FrontPage.

The Ad Rotator Component is very flexible, and you don't have to use it just to rotate ad banners. You could rotate graphics with links to pages in your own site, or any other graphic content.

The Browser Capabilities Component

There is a great variety of browsers currently in use on the Internet, not just Microsoft and Netscape browsers. Many of the online services, such as Prodigy and MindSpring, use either proprietary or licensed browsers that are tailored to their needs. Even among Netscape and Microsoft you will find many different versions in use, and each version supports different features.

Microsoft supplies a text file, Browscap.ini, that lists the features of many different browsers. The default path for this file is C:\Windows\System\Inetsrv\Browscap.ini. It is worth opening this file in your text editor, as shown in Figure 17-3, just to get an idea of how many variations exist.

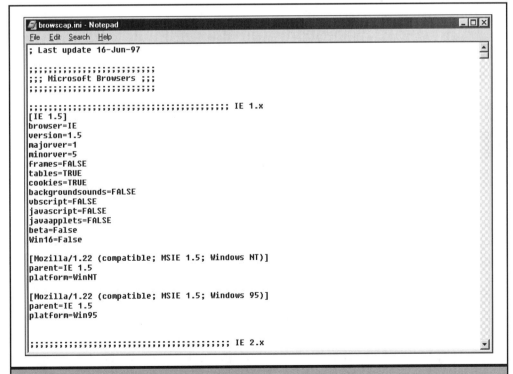

Figure 17-3.   *Browscap.ini file in Notepad*

Tip *An even more extensive Browscap.ini file is available from cyScape, Inc. (http://www.cyscape.com/asp/browscap).*

The latest browsers offer features that are unsupported by earlier versions, and some that are only supported by specific browsers. For example, only Internet Explorer supports client-side VBScript scripting. The problem for web designers is to decide which features to include in their webs. There's a tendency to want to use the latest and greatest, but what happens when the site is visited by a browser that doesn't support the features used?

The Browser Capabilities Component and the Browscap.ini file address this problem directly. Every browser identifies itself in the HTTP header sent by the browser (the USER_AGENT) when it requests a file from a web server. You can read this header, extract the browser and version, look up which features it supports in the Browscap.ini file, and tailor your web pages to the users' browser (or tell them to get an update).

Tip *It can be very educational to record the browser types and versions visiting your web site in a database, where you can analyze the data. If the majority of your users are using browsers that don't support frames, for example, then it's a good idea not to use them. If your audience is technically literate, you will probably find more current browsers than if your site is aimed at the general public.*

In this next exercise, you will create an ASP page that displays some of the major capabilities (or lack thereof) of the browser that has loaded it. Create the page with these steps:

Note *When you are instructed to type a line that ends with a colon, always leave a space after the colon.*

1. Create a new page in FrontPage, and save it with the Page Title **Browser Capabilities** and the File Name **Browsers.asp**.

2. At the top of the page, type **Your Browser's Capabilities** and format it as Heading 2. Press ENTER.

3. Type **The HTTP User Agent is:** and press ENTER.

4. Type **Your browser is:** (leave a space after the colon); then type **version #** and press SPACE.

5. Press ENTER, open the Table menu, and choose Insert | Table.

6. In the Insert Table dialog box, select **4** Rows, **4** Columns, **Center** Alignment, and a Cell Padding of **4**. The Specify Width check box should be cleared as shown next. Click OK.

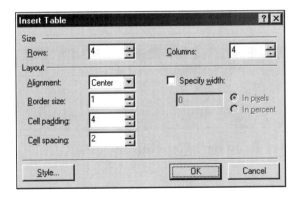

7. In the first cell of the first row of the table, type **Platform** and then press TAB twice.

8. Type **VBScript,** and then press TAB twice.

9. Type **Cookies**, press TAB twice, type **JavaScript,** and then press TAB twice.

10. Type **Tables**, press TAB twice, type **ActiveX Controls,** and then press TAB twice.

11. Type **Frames**, press TAB twice, and type **Java Applets**.

12. Save your page. It should look similar to Figure 17-4.

    In the next steps, you will use the Page view HTML tab to enter the ASP scripting on the page. You must make sure that each script matches the labels on the page.

13. Click the HTML tab, and then press CTRL+HOME.

14. Place the cursor on the first line after the BODY tag and type **<% Set objBrowser = Server.CreateObject("MSWC.BrowserType") %>**.

15. Place the cursor at the end of the line "The HTTP User Agent is:" but before the closing HTML paragraph tag (<P>).

16. Type **<%= Request.ServerVariables("HTTP_USER_AGENT") %>**.

17. Place the cursor one space after the colon in the line "Your browser is:" and type **<%= objBrowser.Browser %>**. Leave a space between your script and the word "version."

18. At the end of the same line (before the closing paragraph tag) type **<%= objBrowser.Version %>**.

    The remaining scripts will be placed in the appropriate HTML code for the table cells.

19. Place the cursor in the table row beneath the row with the label Platform. Delete the nonbreaking space ( ) that is there and type **<%= objBrowser.Platform %>**.

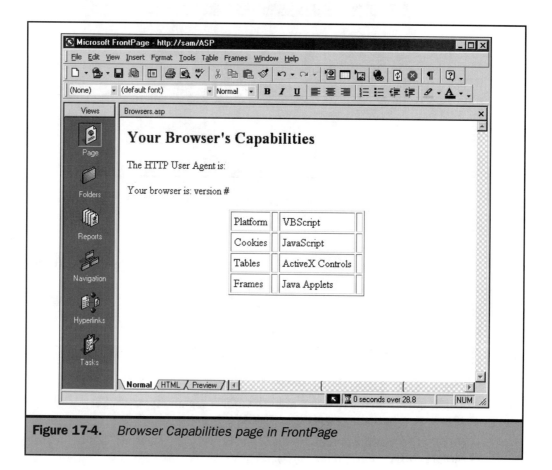

Figure 17-4.   *Browser Capabilities page in FrontPage*

20. In the table cell below the label VBScript, delete the nonbreaking space and type
    <%= objBrowser.VBScript %>. At this point the first row of your table should
    look like this:

```
<tr>
<td>Platform</td>
<td><%= objBrowser.Platform %></td>
<td>VBScript</td>
<td><%= objBrowser.VBScript %></td>
</tr>
```

The remaining rows of the table will be filled out in the same manner: deleting the nonbreaking spaces and entering the script in the cell below the label in the HTML tab.

21. In the table cell below the label Cookies, type **<%= objBrowser.Cookies %>**.

22. In the table cell below the label JavaScript, type **<%= objBrowser.JavaScript %>**.

23. In the table cell below the label Tables, type **<%= objBrowser.Tables %>**.

24. In the table cell below the label ActiveX Controls, type **<%= objBrowser.ActiveXcontrols %>**.

25. In the table cell below the label Frames, type **<%= objBrowser. Frames %>**.

26. In the table cell below the label Java Applets, type **<%= objBrowser.Javaapplets %>**.

27. Save your page. It should look similar to Figure 17-5.

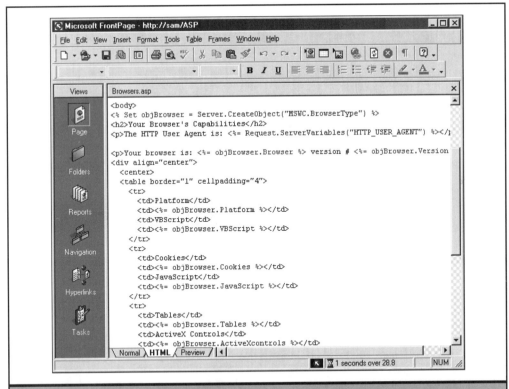

Figure 17-5.   *Browser Capabilities page in Page view HTML tab*

28. Open the Browser Capabilities page in all your browsers. Figure 17-6 shows the page in Internet Explorer, and Figure 17-7 shows the page in Netscape Navigator.

Tip   *If your browser displays "Unknown" in the table fields, it means that your browser is newer than your Browscap.ini file. You can get an updated file at* **http://www.cyscape.com/ asp/browscap** *or* **http://www.backoffice.microsoft.com/downtrial/moreinfo/bcf.asp.**

Note   *Both Internet Explorer and Netscape identify themselves as "Mozilla," though Internet Explorer also says "compatible." "Mozilla" was the code name of Netscape's original browser. The name remains a part of Internet lore for backward compatibility. When this book went to press, an updated Browscap.ini file that correctly identifies Internet Explorer 5.0 was not available. For this reason, IE 5 is incorrectly identified as "Netscape version #4.00" in Figure 17-6.*

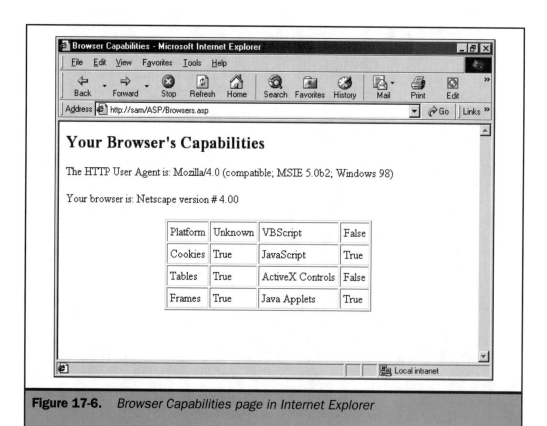

Figure 17-6.   *Browser Capabilities page in Internet Explorer*

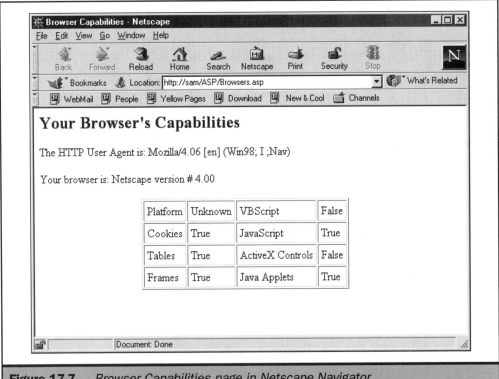

Figure 17-7.   *Browser Capabilities page in Netscape Navigator*

The Counters Component

This component is not included with either MSPWS or IIS. You will not be able to complete this exercise unless you obtain and install the Counters Component. The component is available with the Internet Information Server Resource Kit from Microsoft Press.

The Counters Component creates a collection of counters for your web application. Unlike the FrontPage Hit Counter Component, the ASP Counters Component collection can contain any number of individual counters. However, the counters are not

WORKING BEHIND
THE SCENES

incremented automatically; you must increment them programmatically. This allows you to have different pages or actions by a user increment the same counter, or to set up individual counters for pages or actions. The FrontPage Hit Counter also displays the value as a GIF file, while the Counters Component allows you to display the counter value in any format that you desire. The Counters Component has four methods, listed in Table 17-5.

In this exercise, the Counters Component will have application scope, so you will need to instantiate it in your Global.asa file. Do that now with these steps.

1. Open your Global.asa file in Page view; then click the HTML tab.

2. Move the cursor to the first blank line at the bottom of the Global.asa file and press ENTER, so that there is a blank line at the end of the file.

3. Type **<object runat=Server scope=Application id=objCounter progid="MSWC.Counters"></object>;** then press ENTER and save the Global.asa file.

> **Note**
>
> *When changes are saved to the Global.asa, they will not be implemented immediately. First, all active user requests will be processed and the server stops accepting any more requests; then all active sessions are deleted. The Global.asa file will then be recompiled. This could take some time on a production server, depending on the amount of traffic. You can force the Global.asa file to be recompiled by stopping and starting your IIS web server.*

4. Close your Global.asa file; then create a new page, type **Counters** at the top, and format it as Heading 2. Press ENTER.

5. Type **This page has been loaded times.**, press ENTER, and type **The home page has been loaded times.**

Method	Action
Get	Returns the value of the specified counter.
Increment	Increases the value of the specified counter by one.
Remove	Deletes the specified counter.
Set	Sets the specified counter to a specific value.

Table 17-5. *Counters Component Methods*

6. Click the HTML tab and press CTRL+HOME. Type **<% objCounter.Increment("Counters") %>** and press ENTER.

7. Place your cursor between "loaded" and "times" in your first line of text and type **<%= objCounter.Get("Counters") %>**. Leave a space on each side of the code.

8. Save your page with the Page Title **Counters** and the File Name **Counters.asp**. Open the page in your browser, as shown in Figure 17-8.

You do not need to explicitly create a counter file; it will be created the first time it is referenced. The counters are stored in a text file named Counters.txt, which is located in the same directory as the Counters Component. By default this is C:\Windows\System\ Inetsrv\. It is a plain text file and so can be modified in your text editor. The format of the file is *countername:value*. At this point of the exercise, the counter.txt file would consist of Counters:1, or however many times you've incremented the Counters counter. The first line on the Counters page

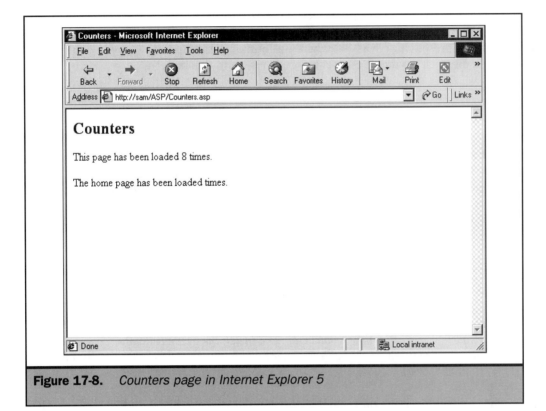

Figure 17-8.   *Counters page in Internet Explorer 5*

increments the Counters counter each time the page is loaded. Next add a counter for the home page.

9. In your Counters.asp page place, your cursor between "loaded" and "times" on the second line of text and type **<%= objCounter.Get("Default") %>**. Leave a space on each side of the code, and then save your page.

10. Open your ASP home page (Default.asp) in Page view HTML tab.

11. Press CTRL+HOME and type **<% objCounter.Increment("Default") %>**; then press ENTER.

12. Save your home page, and then open it in your browser. Click Refresh or Reload a few times, and then open your Counters page (Counters.asp) in your browser. You should now see values for both the Counters page and your home page.

The Counters Component can be very useful. You can have any number of counters on your site; they can be incremented by almost any action with the Increment method, and they return a value that can be used in other scripts. For example, you could create a script that compared a counter value to a preset value and then branched on the result. If the preset value was 100 when the counter value equaled 100, you could display a message saying "You are the 100th visitor to this page!".

The Database Access Component

So far you've seen a number of ways Active Server Pages can be used to add interactivity and features to your webs. The total of all the features you've learned about so far actually does not equal the functionality of the Database Access Component. This component allows you to make your web applications totally database driven.

The Database Access Component is the subject of Chapter 18 and so will not be covered in this chapter.

The Content Rotator Component

 This component is not included with either MSPWS or IIS. You will not be able to complete this exercise unless you obtain and install the Content Rotator Component. The component is available with the Internet Information Server Resource Kit from Microsoft Press.

The Content Rotator Component is very similar to the Ad Rotator Component. The primary difference is that the Content Rotator doesn't use a redirection file. However, since any valid HTML can be inserted with the Content Rotator, you can include hyperlinks in the HTML. You can also rotate graphics using the <IMG> tag.

The Content Rotator uses a Content Schedule file to hold the HTML that will be rotated, and it has two methods, ChooseContent and GetAllContent. ChooseContent selects one of the HTML strings to display, and GetAllContent retrieves all the HTML content in the Content Schedule file. The format of the Content Schedule file is

```
%% [#Weight] [//Comments]
HTMLString
```

The first line of each entry in the Content Schedule file must begin with two percent signs (%). Weight is an optional number between 0 and 65,535 that determines the relative weight of the HTML string. If the weight is 0, the HTML string will never be displayed. If a weight isn't specified, the default value is one. Optional comments are indicated by two forward slashes (//) and must be on a single line. If a comment is longer than one line, each additional line must begin with two percent signs followed by two forward slashes.

The first step in using the Content Rotator is to create a Content Schedule file. This is a text file that you create in your text editor rather than in FrontPage. You will do that with these steps:

1. Open your text editor, such as Notepad, and create a new file.

2. Type **%% #2 //A favorite quote** and press ENTER.

3. Type **<p><font color="blue">"Even if you're on the right track, you'll get run over if you just sit there."</font>
** and press ENTER.

4. Type **- Will Rogers<p>** and press ENTER twice.

5. Type **%% #1** and press ENTER, then type **<p><font color="red">"A thought is an idea in transit."</font>
** and press ENTER.

6. Type **- Pythagoras</p>** and press ENTER. Save the file in your ASP folder (C:\Inetpub\Wwwroot\ASP by default) with the filename **Cntsched.txt** and close your text editor.

7. Open your ASP home page (Default.asp) in FrontPage and click the HTML tab.

8. Place your cursor before the closing </BODY> tag and type
   **<%
   Set objQuote = Server.CreateObject("MSWC.ContentRotator")
   Response.Write(objQuote.ChooseContent("Cntsched.txt"))
   %>**

9. Save your page and then open it in your browser. Figure 17-9 shows the page in Internet Explorer.

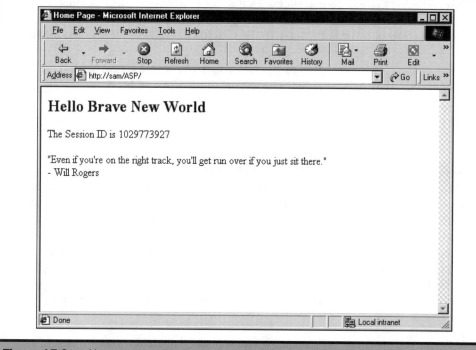

Figure 17-9.   *Home page with a quote displayed with the Content Rotator Component*

Any valid HTML can be displayed using the Content Rotator Component, so you could also use it to randomly display a hyperlink, graphic, and so on.

The File Access Component

The File Access Component accesses the VBScript FileSystemObject object to allow you to read and write to text files on the server's hard drive. The functionality of this component exceeds what is possible with FrontPage's capabilities.

The syntax for instantiating the File Access Component is

```
Set objName = CreateObject("Scripting.FileSystemObject")
```

The FileSystemObject object has two methods: CreateTextFile and OpenTextFile. The syntax for the CreateTextFile method is

> `[object.]`**`CreateTextFile(`**`filename[, overwrite[, unicode]])`

Each parameter is described in Table 17-6. The syntax for the OpenTextFile method is

> `[object.]`**`OpenTextFile(`**`filename[, iomode[, create[, format]]])`

Each parameter is described in Table 17-7.

> **Note** *Since this is a VBScript object that is being instantiated, and not an ASP Server object, the correct syntax is CreateObject(), not Server.CreateObject().*

The VBScript TextStream object is used to write data to the file and to close the file. The syntax is

> **`TextStream.`**`property|method`

TextStream has two methods: WriteLine and Close. In actual use, TextStream is replaced by a variable representing an object. Listing 17-1 shows how the CreateTextFile method could be used to create a simple text file, and Listing 17-2 shows how OpenTextFile could be used.

Parameter	Description
Object	Optional name of a FileSystemObject.
Filename	Name of the file to create.
Overwrite	Optional value, either TRUE or FALSE, that indicates if an existing file can be overwritten. The default is FALSE so that existing files won't be overwritten.
Unicode	Optional value, either TRUE or FALSE, that determines if the file will be Unicode or ASCII format. The default is FALSE, which creates an ASCII file. (*Unicode* is an international standard used to provide a uniform encoding scheme for written characters and text, generally used when more than one character set is present.)

Table 17-6. *CreateTextFile Method Parameters*

Parameter	Description
Object	Optional name of a FileSystemObject.
Filename	Name of the file to create.
Iomode	Optional value, either ForReading or ForAppending, that indicates if the file is being opened for reading or for writing.
Create	Optional value, either TRUE or FALSE, that indicates if a new file can be created if the specified filename doesn't exist. The default is FALSE, which doesn't allow a new file to be created.
Format	Optional value, either TristateTrue, TristateFalse, or TristateUseDefault, that indicates the format of the opened file. The default is TristateFalse, which opens the file as an ASCII file. TristateTrue opens the file as a Unicode file.

Table 17-7. *OpenTextFile Method Parameters*

Listing 17-1
Using the
CreateTextFile
method

```
Set objFile = CreateObject("Scripting.FileSystemObject")
Set objTextFile = objFile.CreateTextFile("Myfile.txt", False)
ObjTextFile.WriteLine("This is where your text goes.")
ObjTextFile.Close
```

Listing 17-2
Appending to
a text file

```
Set objFile = CreateObject("Scripting.FileSystemObject")
Set objTextFile = objFile.OpenTextFile("Myfile.txt", ForAppending,
False)
ObjTextFile.WriteLine("This is where your text goes.")
ObjTextFile.Close
```

The MyInfo Component

The MyInfo Component is used to store general information about the web. It is instantiated in the Global.asa created in the default virtual root when the MSPWS is installed (C:\Inetpub\Wwwroot\Global.asa). The code is

```
<object runat=Server scope=Session id=MyInfo
progid="MSWC.MyInfo"></object>
```

Like the Global.asa file itself, there can only be one MyInfo object associated with a web. With IIS you normally create values for the object created by the MyInfo Component using the web server interface. The MSPWS doesn't include access to these properties, but you can both set them and read them using an ASP script. The syntax for setting a property is

```
MyInfo.property = "textstring"
```

You read the values with

```
MyInfo.property
```

The default properties for the MyInfo Component are listed in Table 17-8. You can also create other properties in the collection using the syntax shown above.

Property	Description
PageType	Returns a number corresponding to the type of web. The numerical values are as follows: 1 = About My Company 2 = About My Life 3 = About My School 4 = About My Organization 5 = About My Community
PersonalName	Is the web owner's name.
PersonalAddress	Is the web owner's address.
PersonalPhone	Is the web owner's phone number.
PersonalMail	Is the web owner's e-mail address.
PersonalWords	Is additional information entered by the web owner.
CompanyName	Is the web owner's company name.
CompanyAddress	Is the web owner's company address.
CompanyPhone	Is the web owner's company phone number.
CompanyDepartment	Is the web owner's company department name.

Table 17-8. *MyInfo Properties*

Property	Description
CompanyWords	Is additional company information entered by the owner.
HomeOccupation	Is the web owner's occupation.
HomePeople	Is a list of people living with the owner.
HomeWords	Is additional information entered by the web's owner.
SchoolName	Is the web owner's school name.
SchoolAddress	Is the web owner's school address.
SchoolPhone	Is the web owner's school phone number.
SchoolDepartment	Is the web owner's school department or class.
SchoolWords	Is additional information about the web owner's school.
OrganizationName	Is the name of the web owner's organization.
OrganizationAddress	Is the organization's address.
OrganizationPhone	Is the organization's phone number.
OrganizationWords	Is information about the organization.
CommunityName	Is the web owner's community name.
CommunityLocation	Is the community's location.
CommunityPopulation	Is the community's population.
CommunityWords	Is additional information about the community.
URL(n)	Is the nth URL in a user-defined list and corresponds to the nth link description in the URLWords property.
URLWords(n)	Is a text string containing the nth user-defined description of a hyperlink corresponding to the nth URL in the URL(n) property.
Style	Is the relative URL of a style sheet.
Background	Is the background of the site.
Title	Is the title of the home page.
Guestbook	Is –1 if a guest book is available for the web. Otherwise, it is 0. The default is an empty string (" ").
Messages	Returns –1 if a private message form is available for the web. Otherwise, it is 0. The default is an empty string (" ").

Table 17-8.   *MyInfo Properties (continued)*

Normally a web will not require all the possible properties to contain valid data. If the web is an educational site, the properties relating to the school (SchoolName, etc.) would be used, but not the company (CompanyName, etc.) or home (HomeOccupation, etc.) properties. Some properties—HomePeople, for example—would be information that you would not normally want exposed. It is not necessary to enter any information in the MyInfo object. It is available to use if you so desire.

The Page Counter Component

 This component is not included with either MSPWS or IIS. You will not be able to complete this exercise unless you obtain and install the Page Counter Component. The component is available with the Internet Information Server Resource Kit from Microsoft Press.

The Page Counter Component offers a slight advantage over the FrontPage Hit Counter in that you have more control of the object. Similar to the Counters Component, it stores the values in a file named hitcnt.cnt, which is located in the Windows directory by default. It has three methods, listed in Table17-9, and is instantiated with

```
Set objName = Server.CreateObject("MSWC.PageCounter")
```

The Hits and Reset methods can be applied to the page the object is instantiated on, or a virtual path to a page can be specified with the syntax

```
objName.Hits(virtualpath)
```

and

```
objName.Reset(virtualpath)
```

Method	Description
Hits	Is the number of times the URL has been hit.
PageHit	Increments the number of hits.
Reset	Sets the value of Hits to zero.

Table 17-9. *Page Counter Component Methods*

If no virtual path is specified, the current page is used.

FrontPage's Hit Counter, the ASP Counters, and Page Counter Components provide ample methods of recording hits on your sites. Which one(s) you use, if any, is a matter of personal choice. You should remember, though, that none of these provide the data integrity you get by analyzing your web server's actual log files.

The Permission Checker Component

This component is not included with either MSPWS or IIS. You will not be able to complete this exercise unless you obtain and install the Permission Checker Component. The component is available with the Internet Information Server Resource Kit from Microsoft Press.

The Permission Checker Component uses IIS security to determine if a user has permission to access a web page. It has a single method, HasAccess, which will return either TRUE or FALSE. It is instantiated with the syntax

```
Set objName = Server.CreateObject("MSWC.PermissionChecker")
```

After an object variable has been instantiated, it is referenced using the HasAccess method like this

```
objName.HasAccess(filename)
```

You can use either a physical or virtual path for the filename.

IIS supports three types of user authentication, listed in table 17-10.

Authentication	Description
Anonymous	All users are logged on using the default IIS NT user account, which is normally IUSR_*servername*. This account is created by default when IIS is installed. Since all users are allowed access with this account, there are no permissions to check.
Basic	Sends the username/password combination in plain text.
NT Challenge/Response	Sends the username/password combination in an encrypted format.

Table 17-10. *Internet Information Services User Authentication*

NT Challenge/Response is the most secure of the methods since it is an encrypted format. Unfortunately, it is only supported by Internet Explorer. This makes it the best choice for an intranet, where you can specify the browser that must be used, but pretty much unusable for normal web access.

 NT Challenge/Response is usually referred to as NTLM (NT LanManager). When an error is encountered using this method, the error message will usually reference NTLM.

In configuring IIS, directories open to the public are given Anonymous access permission. To use either Basic or NTLM authentication, you must also disable the Anonymous permission. Chapter 21 covers security in more detail.

The Content Linking Component

The Content Linking Component is used to generate tables of contents for a web. It uses a Content Linking List, a text file containing the URLs of the pages, to accomplish this. This method is actually more cumbersome than the navigation features in FrontPage, which don't require you to create a text file listing all the pages. However, FrontPage's navigation features are of limited use with ASP pages (Navigation view doesn't support Active Server Pages), so it is a viable method for navigation.

As usual, you create an instance of the Content Linking Component using the Server.CreateObject statement. The syntax is

```
Set objLinks = Server.CreateObject("MSWC.Nextlink")
```

Once the object is instantiated, each method is called with the URL of the Content Linking List passed as a parameter, for example, **GetListCount(***listURL***)**. Where an index number is required, the syntax is

```
GetNthDescription(listURL, i)
```

where *i* is the index number. The methods for the component are explained in Table 17-11.

The Content Linking List is a simple text file. Each line of the file contains the URL of the page, a description of the page, and an optional comment. Each item is separated by a tab (this allows you to use spaces within the description and comment), and each line ends with a carriage return. The URL can be a relative or virtual path, but it cannot be an absolute URL. An absolute URL would begin with http:, //, or \\.

You will see how this works in this next exercise. Begin by creating a Content Linking List for your ASP web.

1. In your text editor, create a new document.

Method	Description
GetListCount	Returns the number of items in the Content Linking List.
GetNextURL	Returns the next URL in the Content Linking List.
GetPreviousDescription	Returns the previous description in the Content Linking List.
GetListIndex	Returns the number in the Content Linking List for the current page. The first page is number 1.
GetNthDescription	Returns the description of the item with the specified index in the Content Linking List.
GetPreviousURL	Returns the URL of the previous item in the Content Linking List.
GetNextDescription	Returns the description of the next item in the Content Linking List.
GetNthURL	Returns the URL of the item with the specified index in the Content Linking List.

Table 17-11.   *Content Linking Component Methods*

2. Type **Backgrounds.asp**, press TAB, type **User Input Changes Page Background Color**, press TAB, and type **This is a comment**.

3. Press ENTER, type **Banners.asp**, press TAB, and type **Rotate Ad Banners Using ASP**. Press ENTER.

4. Type **Browers.asp**, press TAB, and type **Check Your Browser's Features**. Press ENTER.

5. Type **Createcookie.asp**, press TAB, and type **Create A Cookie**. Press ENTER.

6. Type **Counters.asp**, press TAB, and type **Page Counters and More**. Press ENTER.

7. Type **Server.asp**, press TAB, and type **View Your Server Variables**. Press ENTER.

8. Save your text file in your ASP directory (C:\Inetpub\Wwwroot\ASP\ by default) with the filename **Links.txt**, and then close your text editor.

9. Open your ASP home page (Default.asp) in FrontPage, if it's not already open, and then click the HTML tab.

In the next part of this exercise, you will create a VBScript loop that uses the Content Linking methods to read your links file and create a hyperlink to each page.

10. Place your cursor at the beginning of the line containing the closing BODY tag (</BODY>) and press ENTER, and then UP+ARROW.

11. Type **<ul>** and press ENTER. This will display the index as a bulleted list.

12. Type

```
<%
Set objLink = Server.CreateObject("MSWC.NextLink")
intCount = objLink.GetListCount("Links.txt")
i = 1
Do While (i <= intCount)
%>
```

This first section of the script instantiates the Content Linking Component; it then reads the number of records in the Content Linking List (Links.txt) and places the number in the local variable intCount. The variable i is then initialized with the number one. The value of i will be incremented by one in each iteration of the Do While loop. When i exceeds the value of intCount, the loop will end. Each iteration of the loop will write a hyperlink to a page listed in Content Linking List. Continue with these steps:

13. Type

```
<li><a href="<%= objLink.GetNthURL(("Links.txt"), i) %>">
<%= objLink.GetNthDescription(("Links.txt"), i) %></a>
```

This script first formats the output as a list item (<LI>); it then writes URL as the target of the hyperlink, and Description as the displayed text, from the item in the Content Linking List that corresponds to the value of i. When the value of i is 1, the first item in the Links.txt file, the URL, and Description for your Backgrounds.asp page will be written to your home page. You will finish the loop and the bulleted list in the next step:

14. Type

```
<%
i = (i + 1)
Loop
%>
</ul>
```

15. Save your work and then open your ASP home page in your browser. Figure 17-10 shows the page in Internet Explorer.

The Content Linking Component is not as flexible as Navigation view, but does provide a useful alternative.

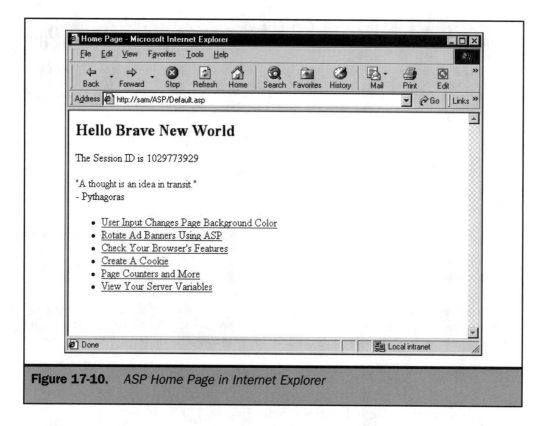

Figure 17-10.   *ASP Home Page in Internet Explorer*

The Server-Side Include Statement

Active Server Pages have one other element that duplicates to some extent a FrontPage
feature. This is the Include statement. It functions much the same as the FrontPage
Include Page Component. It has two methods, Virtual and File. The syntax is

```
<!--#Include method = "filename"-->
```

With the Virtual method, the filename is a virtual path; the File method requires an
absolute path to the file.

Tip   *Included files are generally given the extension .INC to indicate how they are to be used,
but this is not required.*

Active Server Pages are a huge leap forward in bringing true interactivity to web
applications. In the next chapter you will see how this functionality, coupled with
database connectivity, can be used to create state-of-the-art web applications.

The Complete Reference

FrontPage 2000

Chapter 18

Working with Databases

U p to this point you have learned how to create webs that contain information that is basically static. In the previous chapters you learned how to integrate the capabilities of Active Server Pages to greatly expand the interactivity of your webs, but the content was still mainly static. In this chapter you will see how to take your webs to the next level—using databases to provide the information displayed on your web pages. This is a tremendous advantage over traditional webs.

Webs that are database driven, where the content is coming from a database rather than static pages, allow for a great deal of user interactivity while simplifying the task of the web administrator. For example, an e-commerce site needs to display information about products and prices. If the web is static, a price change requires you to manually find all the pages that contain the old price and change it to the new price. If the web is database driven, the price is updated in the database and all pages will show the new price the next time the page is loaded. Using a database to provide content also reduces the number of pages in a web. If a company's product line contains 100 items, and each one is displayed on a single page, there would be 100 pages to maintain. With the content being drawn from a database, there would only be a single page, which would be a template for displaying the information about the selected product.

The focus of this chapter is to provide you with an understanding of databases and how to add them to your webs using FrontPage and Active Server Pages. Each of these subjects really requires a book of its own. The information here, however, will give you an overview of how the pieces fit together and show you how to get started using databases with your webs. The first step is to understand what a database is.

Understanding Databases on the Web

A *database* is an organized collection of information. This can be a simple list of names and telephone numbers, or a complete collection of all the information about a company—its products, salespeople, sales, and inventory. In a database, all the information about one item, such as the name and telephone number for one person, is a *record*. Each record is made up of a number of *fields* or *columns*. In a list of names and telephone numbers, each name is one field, and the telephone number associated with the name is another field in the record. A collection of records is a *table*. A simple *flat-file* database is made up of one table, while a *relational* database has two or more tables with one or more relationships, or *links*, between fields in the tables. In the database table shown here, there are four records, each consisting of five fields. Each row in the table is a record; each column is a field. At the top of each column is the field name for that column. The CustomerID field provides a unique number to identify each record. You may have customers with the same name, or in the same city and state, so you need a way to uniquely identify each customer. There should be at least one field in each record that contains a unique value to identify that record. This field is the *primary key* for the table.

Customers : Table					
	CustomerID	**Name**	**Address**	**City**	**State**
▶ +	1	Clark's Hardware	1200 Spruce St.	Lake City	WA
+	2	Tom's Tools	2714 E. Ocean Ave.	Ventura	CA
+	3	Bulldog Hardware	3609 Bulldog Lane	Athens	GA
+	4	Downtown Tools	3787 Main St.	West Caldwell	NJ
✱	(AutoNumber)				

Record: ◀◀ ◀   1   ▶ ▶◀ ▶✱ of 4

> **Tip**
>
> *With many databases, the names displayed at the top of the column, as shown in the previous illustration, do not have to match the actual field name. This can cause confusion if the displayed name and the actual field name are different. Your database queries must use the actual field name, not the displayed name if it is different. The FrontPage Database Results Wizard, described in the section of the same name, will display the correct field names. In Access you can also find the actual field names by looking at the table in Design view.*

Simple flat-file databases are of limited use. Relational databases, on the other hand, can contain millions of records that can be sorted and organized by use of complex criteria. Relational databases get their name from the fact that relationships are created between fields in two or more tables. Figure 18-1 shows the relationships between the tables in the North Beach Tools database that will be used in this chapter. This is a very simple relational database whose purpose is to introduce you both to relational databases and to integrating a relational database into a web.

The North Beach Tools database contains four tables, described in Table 18-1. The Orders table has a relationship with fields in each of the other three tables. These are one-to-many relationships, which means that the contents of a field must be unique in one table, but can appear many times in the other table. In Figure 18-1, this is shown by a 1 next to the field with the unique value and by the symbol for infinity (∞) next to the field that can have many occurrences of the same values. For example, the Customers table contains a unique CustomerID to identify each customer. This is the "one" side of the relationship. The Orders table contains a record for each order the customer places, so there can be a number of records for each customer. This is the "many" side of the relationship. There can also be one-to-one relationships, but these are less common.

The benefit of a relational database is that by linking a unique field in one table to a field in another table, all the information in the first table is made available to the second table without having to be entered each time. The North Beach Tools database illustrates this. The database has tables for customers, products, sales staff, and orders. In a simple flat-file database, each record in the Orders table would have to contain all the information about the customer, the product, and the salesperson, as well as the information about the order itself. In a relational database, each record in the Orders table would contain only the information unique to the order. The information about the customer, product, and salesperson is collected from the appropriate table as

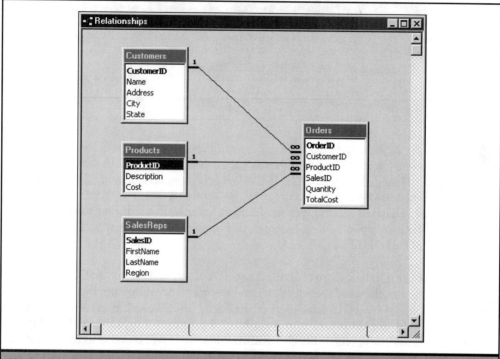

Figure 18-1. *Relationships in the North Beach Tools database*

Table	Description
Customers	Contains the information relating to individual customers
Products	Contains the information describing each product
SalesReps	Contains the information relating to each salesperson
Orders	Contains the information for each order

Table 18-1. *Tables in the North Beach Tools Database*

needed. This greatly reduces the size and complexity of the database. For example, to record a price change for a product, only one field in one table (the Price field in the Products table) needs to be changed. From that point on, every new record in the Orders table will reflect the new price. Relational databases also reduce the total size of the database by avoiding the duplication of information, an important consideration when the database contains thousands or millions of records.

There are two primary database programs that you would use with FrontPage in creating webs. These are Microsoft Access and Microsoft SQL Server. Access (included with Office 2000 Premium Edition) is an excellent database for applications where the number of queries is limited. If the database will be queried often (more than a few hundred times a day), or will contain thousands of records, Access is not up to the task. SQL Server, on the other hand, is a robust, full-featured client/server database application that can handle millions of records.

Note	*You can use any Open Database Connectivity (ODBC) compliant database with your webs. These include Microsoft's Visual FoxPro and Oracle Corporation's (http://www.oracle.com) Oracle databases. ODBC is covered in the section "Open Database Connectivity (ODBC)" later in this chapter.*

Microsoft Access

If you are new to relational databases, Access is an excellent place to start. It contains a number of features, such as wizards, that guide you through the process of creating relational databases. Access is a good choice for a small office intranet. You can also use Access to develop your databases and then upsize them to SQL Server using its Upsizing Wizard. Access 2000 was used to develop the database that will be used in the examples in this chapter. Access is still a desktop database, however, designed for single users. It is not a real client/server database, like SQL Server, so it is of limited use for web applications.

Tip	*A few excellent resources for learning more about Access are Access 2000: The Complete Reference, by Virginia Andersen (Osborne/McGraw-Hill, 1999); Access 2000 for Busy People, by Alan Neibauer (Osborne/McGraw-Hill, 1999); and Access 2000 Answers! Certified Tech Support, by Edward Jones and Jarel M. Jones (Osborne/McGraw-Hill, 1999).*

Microsoft SQL Server

SQL Server is a *Structured Query Language* (SQL) database. SQL (pronounced "sequel") is a programming language for creating, managing, and querying large relational databases. A brief overview of SQL itself is provided in the section "Structured Query Language Statements." SQL Server can easily handle millions of records and tens of thousands of queries per day. For large corporations, this is a common scenario. It lacks Access's interface and is not so user friendly. For example, drive space for the databases must be configured manually when the database is created, rather than dynamically as needed, as with Access. However, you can use Access as a front end to SQL Server tables (the back end). This gives you the best of both worlds. A detailed discussion of SQL Server is beyond the scope of this book, nor is it necessary in order to understand how to integrate databases into your webs. You should understand, though, that any serious database work requires a serious database programmer. Large databases, such as SQL Server, are complex applications, and while the basic concepts of relational databases are easy to understand, in actual use the design of the database structure can be quite complex. This is an important point. Poor relational database design will haunt you and, as more records are added to the database, the problems will become harder to resolve. Just as a building has to have a properly constructed foundation, so must your database.

You can learn more about SQL Server and other large relational databases, as well as gain a better understanding of how to design relational databases, from SQL: The Complete Reference, by James R. Groff and Paul N. Weinberg (Osborne/McGraw-Hill, 1999).

Open Database Connectivity (ODBC)

The Open Database Connectivity standard was developed as a way to allow databases to be accessed by different programs—not just the database program that created the data. For example, by using ODBC, you can access a database file using Microsoft Word. This is an important feature for organizations that have data in a number of different database formats, as well as for using databases on the Web. In effect, the ODBC driver is an interpreter between the data stored in the database and the program that is querying the data.

To use an ODBC-compliant database on the Web or with a database program other than the one that created the database itself, the proper ODBC driver must be installed. In the case of web-based databases, the ODBC driver for the database being used must be installed on the web server. To run the examples you will create in this chapter, you will need the Access ODBC driver installed on your computer. This driver, along with ODBC drivers for other popular database programs, can be found on the Microsoft Office 2000 CD, the Windows 98 CD, and on Microsoft's web site at **http://www.microsoft.com/ data/download.htm**.

How the Web Server Handles a Request

When a web browser makes a database request (by requesting a page with a database call), a number of things happen before the data is returned and displayed by the browser:

1. The request for a database page is sent by the browser to the web server.

2. The web server reads the requested page and passes the name of the data source and the SQL statement to the ODBC driver.

3. The ODBC driver executes the SQL statement on the specified data source.

4. The data source returns the results of the SQL statement to the ODBC driver.

5. The ODBC driver passes the query results to the web server.

6. The web server formats the query results and sends the file to the web browser.

With a properly configured server with adequate resources, the delay introduced by this process is unnoticeable to the user. This is one reason Microsoft's Access database and other desktop databases are unsuitable for large-volume web sites—they cannot process multiple database queries fast enough. Another bottleneck is the server's hard drive. Database work involves numerous database file reads. Slow hard drives will also be unable to process requests quickly enough for the process to remain transparent to the user when the server is experiencing high traffic volumes. If at all possible, use a client/server database, such as SQL Server, and fast hard drives, such as Fast-Wide SCSI drives.

Data Source Name (DSN)

A *Data Source Name* (DSN) allows a user with the correct permissions to use a database over a network. This can be an intranet, extranet, or the Internet. The DSN contains the location and type of the database, the time-out and other system values, and the user name and password. There are three types of data source names:

- **User** Allows a single user on the local computer to access a data source.
- **File** Allows all users with the same ODBC drivers installed to access a data source.
- **System** Allows all users to access a data source.

The File DSN is a plain text file, which is easily transported between computers. This makes it useful while you're developing applications.

There are several ways that you can define a DSN to use a database with FrontPage. If you import a database file into a FrontPage web, you will be prompted for a DSN as part of that process. You can also set a DSN, using the Windows Control Panel. You will see how both of these methods work in the following sections.

Note *In FrontPage, a DSN is also called a database connection. These terms are used interchangeably in this chapter, but in general use, DSN is preferred.*

A web application does not care where the database is physically located or what type of database it is as long as it has a valid DSN and the correct ODBC drivers are installed. Depending on the database program you are using, you may not be able to import the file into your FrontPage web. Access databases can be easily moved around, but this is much harder to do, if not impossible, with a database program such as SQL

Server. With larger web sites, the database program may be running on its own server, creating a situation where it's physically impossible to have the database itself as part of the FrontPage web.

There's also the question of accessing the database for updates and maintenance. For a small web with a few hundred visitors a day, an Access database that is part of the FrontPage web is a viable solution. The database can be maintained on a local computer and uploaded to the server as needed. As the web grows, and traffic increases, this solution may start to provide unacceptable results. It may then be necessary to upsize the database to a more robust database program. This creates its own problems since it may require access to the server that your web presence provider, for valid security reasons, is unwilling to provide. This could add a step between you and your database, requiring you to go through your provider for certain database tasks. These issues will have to be resolved with your web presence provider.

One of the benefits of the DSN system is that these changes will not necessarily mean major changes to your web application. Since the database is referenced through the DSN, not its physical location or type, only the DSN properties would need to be updated.

The FrontPage Database Results Wizard

Now that you've learned the basics of how databases are integrated into webs, it's time to put theory into practice. In this section, you will import the files you need to get started into the ASP web. Create your database web with these steps:

1. Open the ASP web in FrontPage if it's not already open.

2. In the Folders List, select the root folder, open the File menu, and choose New |
Folder. Name the folder **NBT**.

3. Open the File menu again and choose Import. In the Import dialog box, click
Add File.

4. In the Add File To Import List dialog box, select your CD-ROM drive; then open
the \Book\Chap18\ folder and select **NorthBeachTools.mdb**. Click Open and
then OK. The Add Database Connection dialog box, shown here, is displayed.

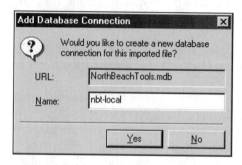

5. Type **nbt-local** in the Name text box and then click Yes.

The function of the Add Database Connection dialog box is to create a DSN (or database connection) for the database. FrontPage does this by adding the DSN properties to the Global.asa file. (If you open your Global.asa file, you will see the changes made.) This method has the advantage of being very simple for the user to implement. The disadvantage is that the DSN is only valid for the web application that uses that Global.asa file (in this case your ASP web). This can create a problem if you need to access the database using a DSN from outside the web application. This situation may arise in a network environment where the database may be accessed from several workstations. A System DSN is a better choice in this case. How to do this is explained in the section "Defining a System DSN."

6. A message box, shown here, is displayed recommending that your database be stored in the folder "fpdb", which FrontPage creates automatically (if it doesn't already exist) when you import a database file. Click Yes.

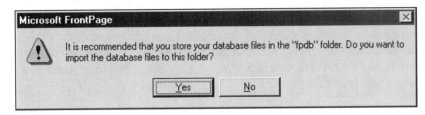

The fpdb folder is the preferred location for a database in a FrontPage web. The only difference between this folder and any other folder you might create is the default permissions assigned to it. When you create a new folder, such as the NBT folder you created in step 2, the default permissions allow scripts to be run and allow the contents of the folder to be browsed. You can see this by checking the properties of the folder.

7. Right-click the NBT folder and choose Properties.

8. In the NBT Properties dialog box, shown here, the Allow Scripts To Be Run and Allow Files To Be Browsed check boxes are selected. New folders inherit the permissions of their root folder. In this case, the root folder has both script and browsing permissions, so the NBT folder inherits them. This dialog box allows you to change the permissions for a folder.

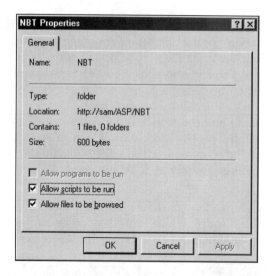

On your local computer, the Allow Files To Be Browsed check box can be selected, but your production web should not allow file browsing. File browsing permits Internet users to read the file structure of your web server. It's a significant security issue, and one you should be aware of.

Your database folder, however, should not allow either of these permissions. You want to keep your database itself as far from the public as possible. This is one reason you may not want your database to be included in your FrontPage web if at all possible. When FrontPage creates the fpdb folder, by default it will not allow either script or browsing permissions. You can check this by looking at the properties of the fpdb folder.

Defining a System DSN

The DSN you created for the North Beach Tools database when you imported it into your ASP web is similar to a file DSN. The properties of the database connection are added to your Global.asa file. This means you can access your database from within the web application that the Global.asa file belongs to. However, this connection isn't valid outside the web application.

Creating the DSN from within FrontPage is not the only method, or always the best method. Nor will you always want to or be able to import a database into your FrontPage web. Moving an Access database around is fairly simple, but the same is not true for other databases, such as SQL Server. A System DSN is often the best choice. Define a System DSN for the North Beach Tools database with these steps:

1. Open the Windows Start menu, point on Settings, and select Control Panel.

2. In the Control Panel, double-click ODBC Data Sources (32bit). Select the System DSN tab in the ODBC Data Source Administrator dialog box, as shown in Figure 18-2.

The Northwind database is a sample database application included with Access 2000. It is not installed by default with Access, but it's a good idea to do so. If you're new to databases, it's an excellent starting point for learning.

The ODBC Data Source Administrator dialog box is used to set User, System, and File Data Source Names; to display information about the installed ODBC drivers; and to configure the Connection Pooling and Tracing options. *Connection Pooling* improves performance by reusing idle database connections, rather than creating a new connection for each user. In this way the minimum number of database connections will be open at any time. Since each open connection uses server resources, pooling the connections reduces the server's workload. *Tracing* creates a log of database calls, which is useful for debugging. Tracing is disabled by default, as it can generate very large files.

3. In the System DSN tab, click Add. The Create New Data Source dialog box, shown next, is displayed.

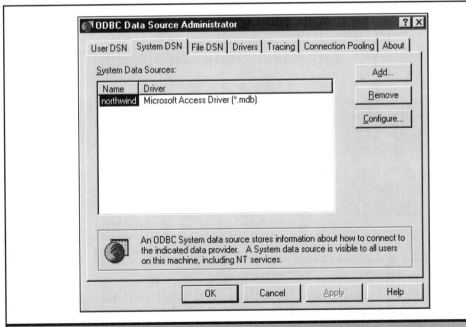

Figure 18-2. *The ODBC Data Source Administrator dialog box System DSN tab*

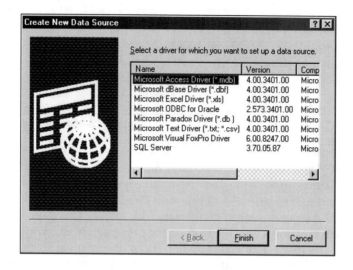

You may have different drivers in your dialog box, depending on which drivers are installed on your system or server. You must have the Access driver installed to use the North Beach Tools database.

4. Select the Microsoft Access Driver and click Finish. The ODBC Microsoft Access Setup dialog box, shown next, is displayed.

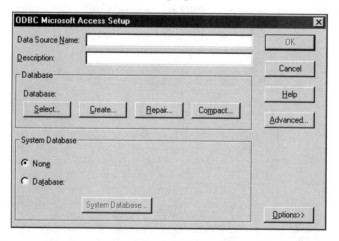

5. Type **NBT** in the Data Source Name text box, press TAB, and type **North Beach Tools Access database** in the Description text box.

6. Click Select, locate your sample database in the Select Database dialog box (the path should be C:\Inetpub\Wwwroot\ASP\fpdb\NorthBeachTools.mdb), and click OK.

7. Click Advanced to open the Set Advanced Options dialog box, shown next. If your database is password protected, enter the account information in the

Login Name and Password text boxes. The properties of the DSN are displayed in the Options scrolling list box. Click OK twice.

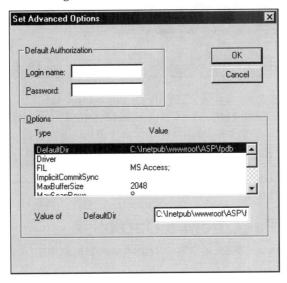

8. The System DSN tab in the ODBC Date Source Administrator dialog box will now display the North Beach Tools System DSN (NBT).

9. Click the Connection Pooling tab, shown next.

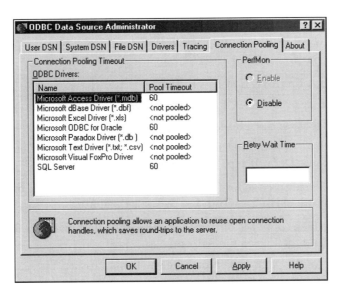

10. Double-click the Microsoft Access Driver in the ODBC Drivers list box. The Set Connection Pooling Attributes dialog box, shown next, is opened.

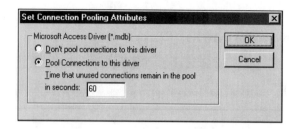

11. Select the Pool Connections To This Driver option, leave the default time-out at 60 seconds, and click OK. The Connection Pooling time-out value is the length of time a connection can be idle before it will be closed.

12. Click OK and then close the Control Panel.

The North Beach Tools database now has a System DSN, which you will use to access the database from the web page.

Creating a Web Page from a Database

The next step is to create a page to display the information from a database. First create a home page for the NBT folder:

1. In FrontPage Page view, click New Page on the toolbar.

2. At the top of the page, type **North Beach Tools** and format it as Heading 1. Press ENTER.

3. Type **Products** and format it as Heading 2. Move the cursor to the next line and click Bullets on the toolbar.

4. Type **View All Products** and press ENTER.

5. Type **Find A Product** and press ENTER.

6. Type **Add A Product** and press ENTER.

7. Type **Modify or Delete A Product** and press ENTER.

8. Click Bullets to end the bulleted list.

9. Save the page in your NBT folder with the Page Title **North Beach Tools** and the File Name **Default.asp**. Your page should look similar to Figure 18-3.

Next you will create a page for the Database Results Region. This page will display in a table all the products in the North Beach Tools database.

1. Create a new page in the NBT folder and save it with the Page Title **All Products** and the File Name **Allprod.asp**.

2. At the top of the page, type **North Beach Tools Product Line**, format it as Heading 2, and press ENTER.

3. Open the Insert menu and select Database | Results. The first dialog box of the Database Results Wizard is displayed, as shown here:

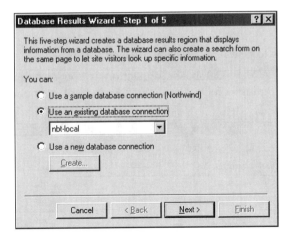

This dialog box allows you to select the type of DSN you want to use. The first option, to Use A Sample Database Connection (Northwind), can be used with the Northwind sample database if you installed it with Access 2000. The second

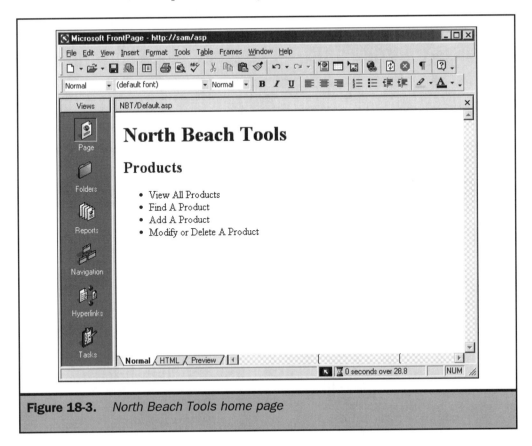

Figure 18-3.   *North Beach Tools home page*

option, Use An Existing Database Connection, lists any database connections in your Global.asa file. Your nbt-local DSN is displayed in the drop-down list. The third option is to Use A New Database Connection.

4. Select the Use A New Database Connection option, and then click Create. The Web Settings dialog box Database tab, shown here, is opened.

The nbt-local connection is listed along with a question mark in the Status column. The question mark is displayed until the connection has been verified.

5. Select the nbt-local connection and click Verify. The question mark should change to a green check-mark. This indicates that the database connection has been verified.

6. Click Add. This opens the New Database Connection dialog box, shown next.

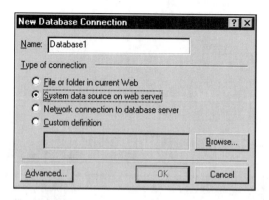

There are four options for selecting the location of the database. File Or Folder In Current Web allows you to use a file or folder in the current web that you haven't already created a data connection for. If you select this option, you would also click Browse to select the file or folder for the data connection. Selecting System Data Source On Web Server allows you to use any DSN that has been configured on the web server. Network Connection To Database Server allows you to use a DSN for a database that exists on a server other than the web server, where your FrontPage web would be located. The fourth option, Custom Definition, allows you to establish a connection using a text file, such as a file DSN. There are obviously a number of ways to establish a data connection, but in actual use you will not need or use all the available options. The next steps will look at how each of the first three options work, but you will use System Data Source On Web Server for the rest of the exercise.

7. Select the File Or Folder In Current Web option, and then click Browse. The Database Files In Current Web dialog box, shown next, is displayed. Here you can select the file or folder containing the database, and FrontPage will create a data connection for that database in the current web.

8. Click Cancel; then select Network Connection To Database Server and click Browse. The Network Database Connection dialog box is displayed. This dialog box allows you to use a connection to a database located on a server on the network. This is a common scenario for large databases. A database program such as SQL Server can require a great deal of server resources. Putting both a large web application, or several web applications, and the database program on the same server can create bottlenecks in the delivery of your content.

 Much of the configuration of your web and database will depend on your web presence provider. You will need to know which database programs they support, their policies regarding user access, and the configuration of their servers.

9. Click Cancel, select the System Data Source On Web Server option, and then click Browse. The System Data Sources On Web Server dialog box, shown here, is displayed. In this dialog box, you should have the NBT System DSN you created earlier. If you installed the Northwind sample Access database when you installed Access, you will also have the Northwind DSN.

10. Select NBT and click OK. Click Advanced. This displays the Advanced Connection Properties dialog box. Here you can set the user name and password for the database, if required, and the connection and command time-out values. You can also set other parameters that your database supports.

```
Advanced Connection Properties                    [?][X]
Authorization
    Username: [        ]       Password: [        ]
Timeouts
    Connection: [15]          Command: [30]
Other parameters
    Name        Value                      [ Add...   ]
                                           [ Modify...]
                                           [ Remove   ]

    [ Move Up ] [ Move Down ] [ Clear List ]

                              [   OK   ]  [ Cancel ]
```

11. Click Cancel. In the New Database Connection dialog box, type **NBT** in the Name text box and click OK. Even though you selected the NBT DSN in the New Database Connection dialog box, you can rename the connection using the Name text box in the New Database Connection dialog box.

12. In the Web Settings dialog box, select the NBT connection and click Verify. After the connection is verified (the question mark changes to a green checkmark), click OK.

13. In the Database Results Wizard dialog box, the NBT database connection should be displayed in the Use An Existing Database Connection drop-down list. Click Next.

14. Select the Record Source option if it's not already selected, and then select Products in the drop-down list. Click Next.

WORKING BEHIND THE SCENES

15. After the database is connected, a list of the fields in the selected table, Products, is displayed, as shown here.

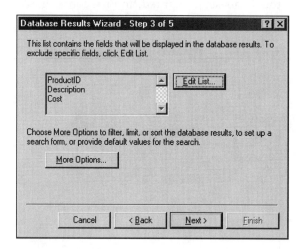

16. Click Edit List. The Displayed Fields dialog box, shown next, is displayed. You use this dialog box to select the fields in the database table to be displayed in the results set (also referred to as a *recordset*), and the order that will be displayed. You will display all the fields in this example and use the default order, so click Cancel.

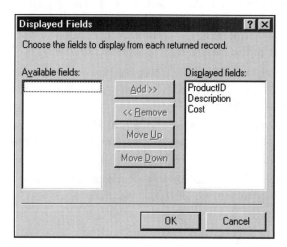

17. Click More Options to display the More Options dialog box, shown next. Here you can set the criteria for the database query, the field that will be used to order the returned records, set defaults for the search criteria, limit the number

of records that are returned, and create a message to be displayed if no records are returned by the query.

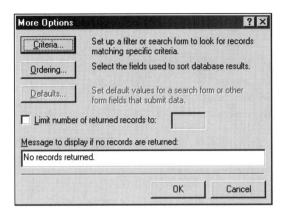

18. Click Ordering, which displays the Ordering dialog box. Select Description in the Available Fields list; then click Add. The results set will be sorted on the values in the Description field of the Products table. By default this will be an ascending sort (A–Z) as indicated by the yellow triangle pointing up next to Description in the Sort Order list. You can change the sort order to descending by selecting the sort order field and clicking Change Sort. The yellow triangle would then point down.

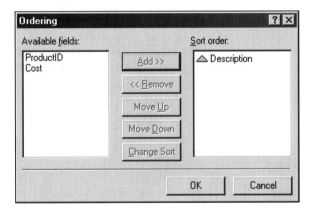

19. Click OK; then type **There were no matches for your search** in the Message To Display If No Records Are Returned text box. Click OK and then click Next.

20. In the Database Results Wizard, you can now select how to display the results set, either as a table, a list, or a drop-down list. The options displayed are

determined by the formatting option selected. You will use the Table option, but first look at the List options.

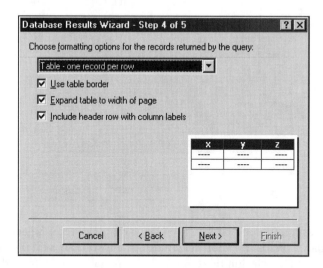

21. Select List – One Field Per Item in the Choose Formatting Options For The Records Returned By The Query drop-down list. You can choose whether or not to have labels for all field values and whether or not to have a horizontal rule as a separator between records. In the List Options drop-down list, you can choose how to format the list—with paragraphs, line breaks, bullets, and so on.

22. Select Drop-Down List – One Record Per Item in the Choose Formatting Options For The Records Returned By The Query drop-down list. This option allows you to populate a drop-down list from the database query. In the Display Values From This Field drop-down list, you select the field whose contents will be displayed. You select the value to be returned in the Submit Values From This Field drop-down list. This allows you, for example, to display a product description to the user and return the product's ID number in the form.

23. Select Table – One Record Per Row in the Choose Formatting Options For The Records Returned By The Query drop-down list.

24. Clear the Expand Table To Width Of Page check box. The other two options, Use Table Border and Include Header Row With Column Labels, should be selected.

25. Click Next. The final page of the Database Results Wizard dialog box allows you to group the records returned. You can either display all the records returned by

the query or break them into smaller groups. The option you select will depend on how many records you expect to be returned by the query. The North Beach Tools database contains only a few records in each table, so no results set will be very large. If you expect the query to return more records than can be easily displayed on a web page—no one wants to scroll through dozens of records—you should break the results set into smaller groups.

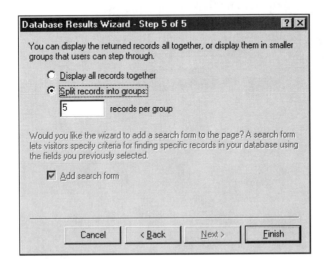

26. Select the Display All Records Together option and click Finish. Figure 18-4 shows what your All Products page should now look like.

27. Change the title for the first column by selecting ProductID and typing **Product Number**.

28. Right-click the table cell that will display the cost of each item (this is the cell with <<Cost>> in it as a placeholder) and choose Cell Properties. Change the Horizontal Alignment to Right and click OK.

29. Place the cursor on the first line after the Database Results region and type **NBT Home**; then select it and click Hyperlink on the toolbar.

You will manually create the hyperlinks for your ASP pages as FrontPage's Navigation view will not create links for Active Server Pages.

30. In the Create Hyperlink dialog box, open the NBT folder, if necessary, and select Default.asp. Click OK; then save your page.

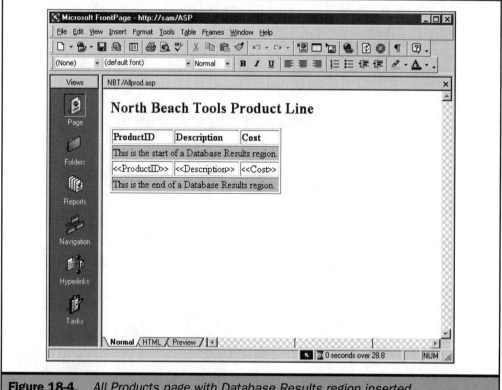

Figure 18-4. *All Products page with Database Results region inserted*

31. Open the File menu and choose Preview In Browser. Figure 18-5 shows the All Products page in Internet Explorer 5.0.

In FrontPage you saw placeholders for the selected fields. In your browser the actual data in the database table is displayed. You can format the table in Page view, as you did by changing the horizontal alignment in the Cost cell. The Database Results region will automatically create as many rows as are required to display the results set.

In this case, all the records and all the fields in each record were read by the query. More often you will want to select a specific record or group of records based on some criteria. You will do this next, but first look at the SQL query created by FrontPage.

Structured Query Language Statements

SQL is the language you use to query and maintain your database. It consists of about 30 commands, but you can accomplish quite a bit with just a few main commands.

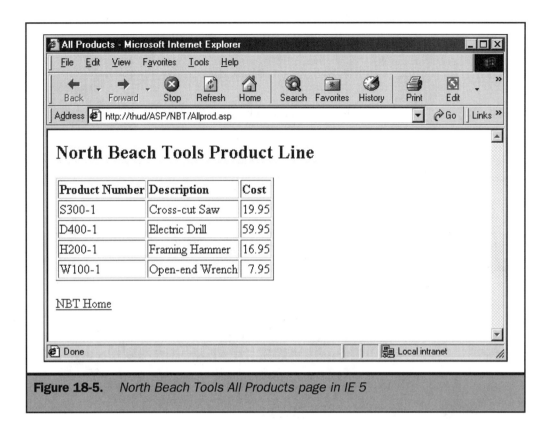

Figure 18-5.   *North Beach Tools All Products page in IE 5*

Table 18-2 describes the principal SQL commands that are used to query and maintain a database.

Every SQL statement begins with a SQL command followed by the database fields that are the target of the command and, optionally, selection criteria. To see how this works, look at the SQL query you created for the All Products page.

1. In FrontPage Page view, with the All Products page open, click the HTML tab. As you can see, FrontPage generated quite a bit of code to read the database and display the results set.

2. Scroll down the page until you reach a section of code between opening and closing VBScript delimiters (<% and %>), as shown in Figure 18-6.

   The first line of code in this section should be

   ```
   fp_sQry="SELECT * FROM Products ORDER BY Description ASC"
   ```

This line of code assigns the SQL query to a local variable, fp_sQry. The query itself is a text string, as indicated by the quotes around it. This string is passed to the

SQL Command	Description
SELECT	Retrieves from a database the records that meet the specified criteria
INSERT	Creates a new record in the database
DELETE	Removes an existing record
UPDATE	Modifies an existing record
FROM	Identifies the database table that is the object of the query
WHERE	Identifies the criteria for the query

Table 18-2.   *Principal SQL Database Statements*

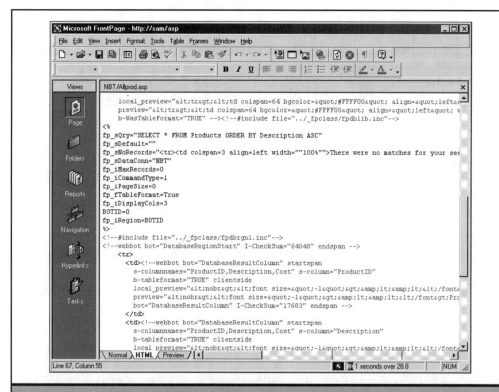

Figure 18-6.   *All Products page in the Page view HTML tab*

database through your data connection (DSN), which is assigned to the local variable fp_sDataConn in the fourth line of the VBScript code.

The words in all caps are SQL keywords. SELECT defines the operation—to return the fields specified from the database table. In this case, all the fields in the table are selected by using the asterisk wildcard. FROM identifies the table (the Products table) that is the target of the SELECT command. ORDER BY identifies the field (Description) that will set the sort order, and ASC sets an ascending sort.

Note *In SQL it's a good practice to use the syntax* table.field *to identify a field in a table, even though FrontPage doesn't do this. The SQL statement could be written as* SELECT Products.* FROM Products ORDER BY Products.Description ASC. *The example here is about as simple as a SQL query can be. When building complex queries where you join several tables, the* table.field *syntax will make your life easier.*

FrontPage does a good job of keeping you from actually having to write SQL statements. Using dialog boxes and wizards, it will create most of the SQL queries you will need. It is important, however, to understand how the queries work. Advanced queries, drawing from multiple tables, will require you to do some programming manually. You will get firsthand experience writing SQL statements later in this chapter.

Using Search Criteria

One of the benefits of using a database with your web is the ability to create custom searches of your data. FrontPage greatly simplifies this task by allowing you to use a value entered in an HTML form in the SQL query it creates. In this next exercise, you will use this technique to select a single North Beach Tools record. Do that now with these steps:

1. Create a new page; then type **Search North Beach Tools** at the top of the page and format it as Heading 2. Press ENTER.

2. Open the Insert menu and choose Form | One-Line Text Box.

3. Press HOME and type **Description:** (leave a space after the colon). Press RIGHT ARROW and then ENTER.

4. Right-click the Description text box and choose Form Field Properties.

5. In the Text Box Properties dialog box, type **SearchWord** in the Name text box, and then click Validate.

6. In the Text Box Validation dialog box, select Required for the Data Length, type **24** in the Max Length text box, and then type **Description** in the Display Name text box. Click OK twice.

Note *The maximum number of characters allowed in the Description field of the North Beach Tools database Products table is 24. This determines the maximum number of characters allowed in the search form.*

7. Right-click the form and choose Form Properties. Select the Send To Other option, and then click Options.

8. In the Options For Custom Form Handler dialog box, type **Results.asp** in the Action text box. Click OK twice.

9. Save the page in your NBT folder with the Page Title **Search North Beach Tools** and File Name **Search.asp**.

10. Create a new page, type **Search Results** at the top of the page, and format it as Heading 2. Press ENTER.

11. Open the Insert menu and choose Database | Results.

12. In the first page of the Database Results Wizard, select the Use An Existing Database Connection option, and then select NBT from the drop-down list. Click Next.

13. Select the Record Source option then select Products from the Record Source drop-down list. Click Next.

14. Click More Options. The More Options dialog box shown here is displayed.

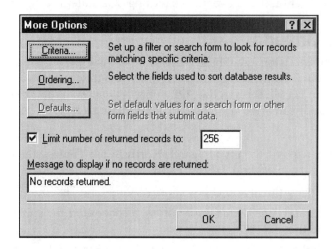

15. Click Criteria. In the Criteria dialog box click Add. The Add Criteria dialog box shown next is displayed.

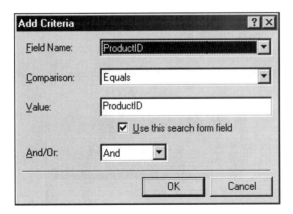

16. In the Add Criteria dialog box select Description from the Field Name drop-down list then select Contains from the Comparison drop-down list.

    The Comparison drop-down list contains the types of comparison operators that can be used in your database query. For example, Equals allows you to find exact matches to your search criteria while Not Equals allows you to exclude records that match your criteria. The Contains comparison, which you are using in this exercise, allows partial matches. For example, using the search string "boat" would match "sailboat," "boating," and so forth. If you wanted to limit the search to exact matches, you would use Equal in place of Contains.

17. Type **SearchWord** in the Value text box. This is the name of the form field that you created on your Search page that will contain your criterion.

18. Select the Use This Search Form Field checkbox, if it's not already selected. You are using a single criterion in this exercise so you can ignore the setting in the And/Or drop-down list. Click OK. The Criteria dialog box now contains the criterion for your Search Results page, as shown here. Click OK.

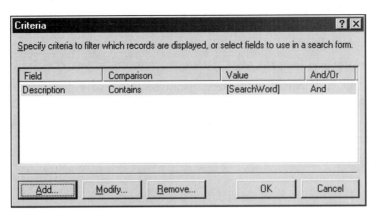

WORKING BEHIND THE SCENES

19. In the More Options dialog box, type **There are no records to display.**, including the period, in the Message To Be Displayed If No Records Are Returned text box.

20. Click Defaults to display the Defaults dialog box, shown here.

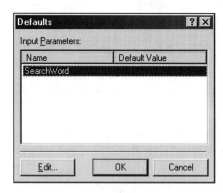

Setting a default for the parameter will ensure that the parameter variable is replaced by a value in the SQL query. You are not going to enter a default value for the parameter as the only link to the Search Results page will be from the form on the Search page. In other words, the Search Results page will not be displayed unless a parameter is first entered in the Search form. Later in this exercise you see, using the ASP Response object Redirect method, how to ensure that the Search Results page can't be opened without a valid search parameter.

21. Click OK two times; then click Next.

22. Select List – One Field Per Item in the Choose Formatting Options For The Records Returned By The Query drop-down list. Both the Add Labels For All Field Values and Place Horizontal Separator Between Records check boxes should be selected.

23. Select Line Breaks in the List Options drop-down list and click Next.

24. Clear the Add Search Form check box, if it's selected, and click Finish. Your Search Results page should look similar to Figure 18-7.

25. Place the cursor on the first line after the Database Results region and type **NBT Home**; then select it and click Hyperlink on the toolbar.

26. In the Create Hyperlink dialog box, open the NBT folder, if necessary, and select Default.asp.

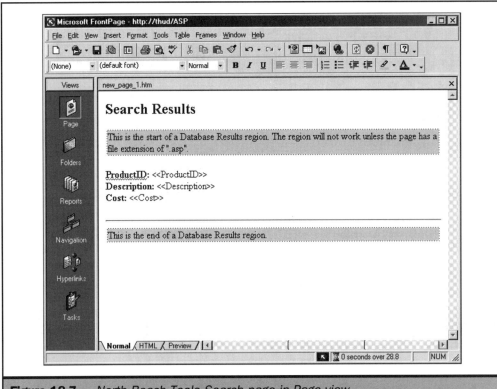

Figure 18-7. *North Beach Tools Search page in Page view*

27. Save your page with the File Name **Results.asp**, and then open it in your browser. Figure 18-8 shows the page in Internet Explorer 5.

    Since you didn't specify a search phrase before loading the Search Results page, all the records are displayed. This is the same result, with different formatting, as your All Products page. This page is designed to display only the records that match specified search criteria, which are entered in the form on your Search page.

28. In FrontPage, click the HTML tab and press CTRL+HOME. Press ENTER and then UP ARROW. The ASP code must be before the <HTML> tag or the redirect will not work. You cannot redirect to another page after the HTML header is written.

29. Type

```
<% If Request.Form("SearchWord") = "" Then
Response.Redirect "Search.asp"
End If %>
```

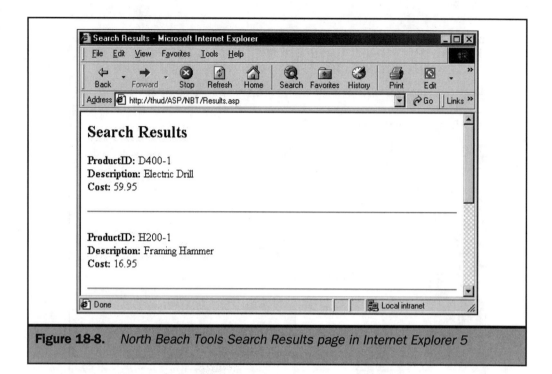

Figure 18-8.   *North Beach Tools Search Results page in Internet Explorer 5*

30. Save your page; then refresh the Search Results page in your browser. You will be redirected to the Search page, shown in Figure 18-9.

31. In the search form text box, type **saw** and then click Submit. Figure 18-10 shows the search results.

32. Close your browser and the open pages in FrontPage.

FrontPage now greatly simplifies the task of creating parameterized queries, as this exercise has shown.

Writing to a Database

There are a number of scenarios in which you would want the user to be able to write to a database on your web server—for example, a user survey where the user answers a series of questions. By writing their responses directly to a database, the results can be easily compiled and analyzed. An organization may have a number of remote staff people who need to access and update a database. This might be a business where salespeople need to record sales data from remote locations, such as the customer's place of business.

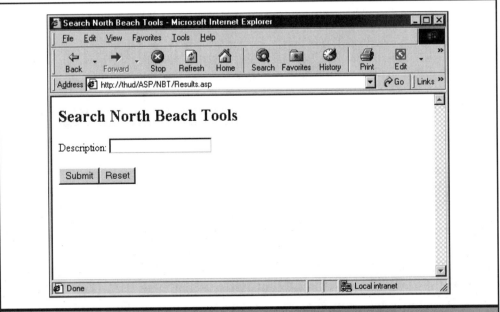

Figure 18-9. *North Beach Tools Search page in Internet Explorer 5*

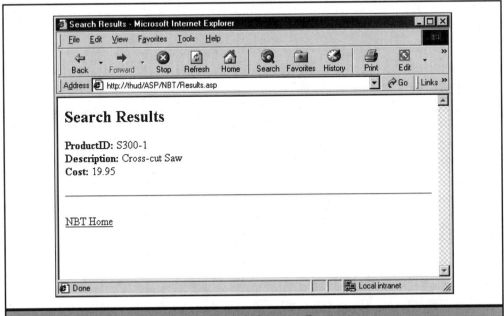

Figure 18-10. *Search results in Internet Explorer 5*

> **Note**
> *Allowing a user to write to a database on your web server raises some serious security concerns. Authorized users, such as employees, can be given this type of access with methods that are more secure than using a web interface. One simple method using the Web is to have the database that is written to located separately, with its own DSN, rather than in the main database. At regular intervals the two databases could be synchronized. How to do this will depend on the database application. If no public access to the database is required, there are network methods that use the Internet without a web interface, such as a Virtual Private Network (VPN). These techniques are beyond the scope of this book. Chapter 21 covers security on the Web in more detail.*

In this next exercise, you will create a page that allows the user to add a product to the North Beach Tools database. Security issues will be kept to a minimum; the purpose here is to learn how FrontPage's database tools work. Do that now with these steps.

1. Create a new page; then type **Add A Product** at the top of the page and format it as Heading 2. Press ENTER.

2. Save the page in your NBT folder with the Page Title **Add A Product** and the File Name **Addprod.asp**.

3. Open the Insert menu and choose Form | One-Line Text Box.

4. Press HOME and type **Product ID:** with two spaces after the colon. Format it as Formatted, press RIGHT ARROW, and then press SHIFT+ENTER.

5. Type **Description:**, with one space after the colon, and insert a one-line text box. Press SHIFT+ENTER.

6. Type **Cost:**, with eight spaces after the colon, and insert a one-line text box. Press ENTER.

7. Right-click the first text box (Product ID) and choose Form Field Properties.

8. In the Text Box Properties dialog box, type **ProductID** in the Name text box and then click Validate.

9. In the Text Box Validation dialog box, select Text from the Data Type drop-down list, and select Required for Data Length.

10. Type **4** in the Min Length text box and **8** in the Max Length text box; then type **Product ID** in the Display Name text box. Click OK twice.

> **Note**
> *Eight characters is the maximum length allowed in the ProductID field of the North Beach Tools database Products table.*

11. Right-click the second text box (Description) and choose Form Field Properties. Type **Description** for the Name, then click Validate.

12. In the Text Box Validation dialog box, select Text from the Data Type drop-down list, and select Required for Data Length.

13. Type **4** in the Min Length text box and **24** in the Max Length text box; then type **Description** in the Display Name text box. Click OK twice.

14. Right-click the third text box (Cost) and choose Form Field Properties. Type **Cost** for the Name and then click Validate.

15. In the Text Box Validation dialog box, select Number from the Data Type drop-down list, and select Required for Data Length.

16. Type **Cost** in the Display Name text box and click OK twice.

Note   *This is minimal validation for the form. When creating your own databases and forms, you will want to have client-side validation that will trap all possible errors. It is much easier to deal with form validation than arcane error messages returned by the ODBC driver.*

17. Right-click the form and choose Form Properties. In the Form Properties dialog box, select Send To Database, and then click Options. The Options For Saving Results To Database dialog box Database Results tab, shown in Figure 18-11, is opened.

18. Select NBT from the Database Connection To Use drop-down list. FrontPage will connect to the database and populate the Table To Hold Form Results drop-down list.

19. Select Products in the Table To Hold Form Results drop-down list. Leave the URL Of Confirmation Page and URL Of Error Page text boxes blank for this exercise. In actual use you would probably want to specify both pages.

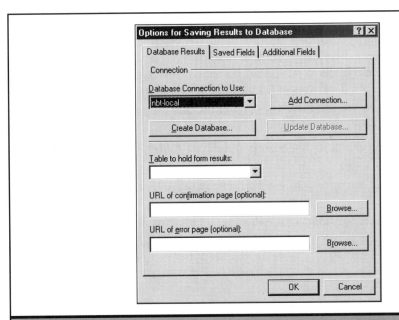

Figure 18-11.   *Options For Saving Results To Database dialog box Database Results tab*

20. Click the Saved Fields tab. Select Cost in the Form Field column of the Form Fields To Save list box, and then click Modify. The Modify Field dialog box, shown here, is displayed.

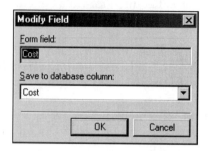

21. Select Cost from the Save To Database Column drop-down list; then click OK.

 A field in a database table can be referred to as either a column or field. The term used will depend on the database.

22. Select Description, click Modify, select Description from the Save To Database Column drop-down list, and click OK.

23. Select ProductID, click Modify, select ProductID from the Save To Database Column drop-down list, and click OK.

24. Select the Additional Fields tab. Here you can select additional information, such as a time stamp, to also be written to the database. The North Beach Tools database Products table doesn't contain fields to hold any of these values, so you will leave them blank. You should remember this feature, however, when designing your own databases as they can be very useful.

25. Click OK twice. Place the cursor on the first line after the form and type **NBT Home**; then select it and click Hyperlink on the toolbar.

26. In the Create Hyperlink dialog box open the NBT folder, if necessary, and select Default.asp. Click OK.

27. Save your page; then open it in your browser. Figure 18-12 shows the page in Internet Explorer.

28. In your browser, type **S400-1** in the Product ID text box and press TAB.

29. Type **Radial-arm Saw** in the Description text box and press TAB.

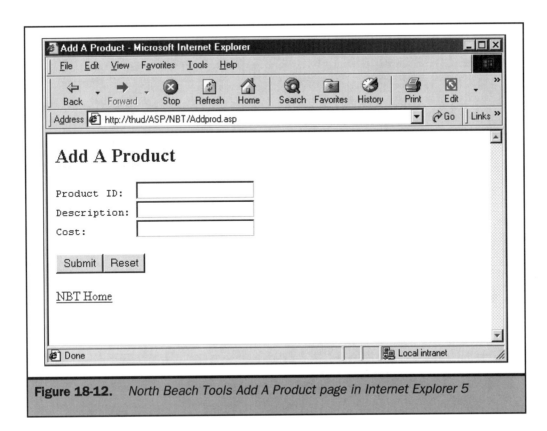

Figure 18-12.   *North Beach Tools Add A Product page in Internet Explorer 5*

30. Type **129.75** in the Cost text box and click Submit. Figure 18-13 shows the default Form Confirmation page in Internet Explorer.

31. Open the North Beach Tools database in Access; then open the Products table. You will see that the information you entered in the form has been added to the Products table, as shown here.

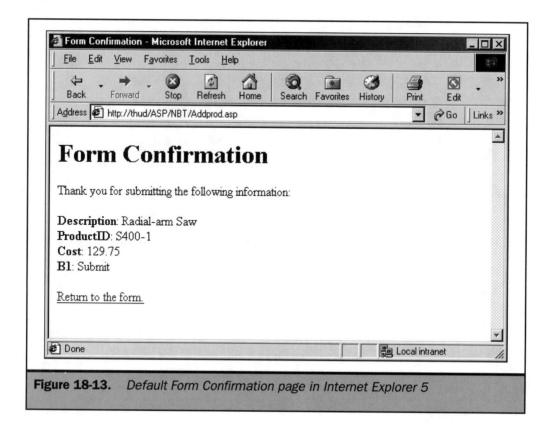

Figure 18-13.   *Default Form Confirmation page in Internet Explorer 5*

32. Close the North Beach Tools database and Access. Open the North Beach Tools All Products page in your browser, shown in Figure 18-14.

This illustrates one of the prime advantages of a database-driven web—a change made to information in the database will appear on your web pages the next time they are loaded without any further human intervention.

The FrontPage Database Results Wizard can create most of the code you need to work with databases. However, this method has both advantages and disadvantages. You can see one of the security issues by looking at the source for the All Products page in your web browser. (In Netscape, select Page Source from the View menu; in Internet Explorer, select Source from the View menu.) At the beginning of the database region, you will see code like this:

```
<!--webbot bot="DatabaseRegionStart" startspan
    s-columnnames="ProductID,Description,Cost" s-columntypes="202,202,4"
```

```
s-dataconnection="NBT" b-tableformat="TRUE" b-tableborder="TRUE"
b-tableexpand="FALSE" b-tableheader="TRUE" b-listlabels="TRUE"
b-listseparator="TRUE" i-ListFormat="0" b-makeform="TRUE"
s-recordsource="Products" s-displaycolumns="ProductID,Description,Cost"
s-criteria s-order="[Description] +"
s-sql="SELECT * FROM Products ORDER BY Description ASC" b-procedure="FALSE"
```

Letting the user see some of the information in this code is a serious security problem. This code gives the user the DSN of your database, the field names and types, as well as the SQL statement you are using. The SQL statement will normally reveal the table and field names of your database. This is information you want to keep hidden from the user. If someone wants to break into your system and do damage, giving them detailed information about your database makes their job much easier.

When you're working with databases, FrontPage provides an interface that greatly simplifies the job. Unfortunately, it's not a perfect system. It can be used for many web applications quite successfully, but there are some drawbacks. To really master

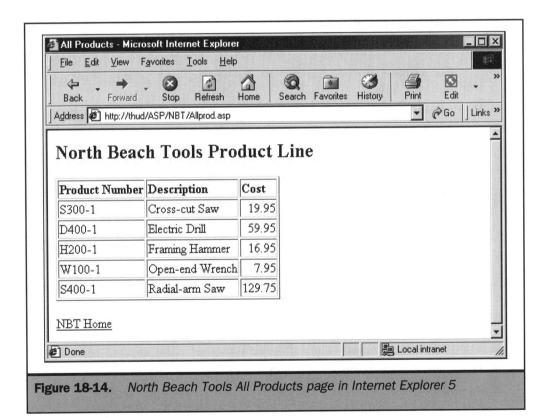

Figure 18-14. *North Beach Tools All Products page in Internet Explorer 5*

database and web integration, you need to understand how FrontPage and ASP are working together. FrontPage's database tools are based on the Active Server database component, so mastery begins with understanding how it works.

The ASP Database Access Component

The Active Server Pages Database Access Component uses ActiveX Data Objects (ADO) to manipulate information in a database. The actual version used in ASP and FrontPage is ADODB, a version of ADO optimized for Microsoft's OLE DB drivers. ADO is an extremely powerful tool for integrating databases and webs.

Note   *This section will introduce this technology, but it cannot be a thorough explanation of it. For more information, visit Microsoft's Universal Data Access web site (**http://www.microsoft.com/data/**).*

Since ADODB is an ASP component, it is used in much the same way as the ASP components you worked with in previous chapters. There are three primary ASP objects for working with databases:

- **Connection object** provides the connection to the database.
- **Command object** provides the instructions for the data source specified by the Connection object.
- **Recordset object** contains the results of the Command object. This can be a single or multiple records.

With these objects you can open a database connection, execute a query against the database, and store the results of the query. Listing 18-1 is the minimal code required to open a database, execute a command, and handle the results. The parts of this listing are explained in the following sections.

Listing 18-1
Minimum
ASP code for
reading a
database

```
Set objConnection = Server.CreateObject("ADODB.Connection")
objConnection.Open ConnectionString
Set Recordset = objConnection.Execute("SQL Statement")
objConnection.Close
```

The remaining objects are:

- **Error**   Returns errors from an ADO operation.
- **Field**   Allows you to work with data from a single column of a recordset.
- **Parameter**   Used to hold values for queries and stored procedures.

- **Property** Contains information about dynamic characteristics of ADO objects. ADO objects have built-in and dynamic characteristics—built-in characteristics are set by ADO, and dynamic characteristics are contained in the specific ADO object.

The Connection Object

The Connection object is used to handle communication between the data source and the web server. The connection must be opened before the data source can be accessed and should be closed when the operation is completed. The methods used with the Connection object are listed in Table 18-3, and the properties are listed in Table 18-4.

As with all the Active Server Pages components, you must create an instance of the Connection object before you can use it (the first line in Listing 18-1). Once the Connection object is created (or *instantiated*), you can use it until you close it or it times out. Each open connection uses system resources, so you generally want to close your connections as soon as the database operation is completed, as shown in the last line of Listing 18-1.

The Open Method

When you call the Open method, the database and its parameters (such as login name and password) are specified. You generally do this with either a DSN or with the

Method	Description
BeginTrans, CommitTrans, RollbackTrans	Used for database transactions. A *transaction* is a group of related changes to tables, so that any changes are made to all the tables at the same time. BeginTrans creates a new transaction, CommitTrans makes any changes and closes the transaction, and RollbackTrans cancels any changes and closes the transaction.
Close	Ends the connection.
Execute	Runs the specified query or procedure.
Open	Creates the connection to the data source.
OpenSchema	Returns the database *schema* information. A schema is like a blueprint of the database.

Table 18-3. *Connection Object Methods*

Property	Description
Attributes	Contains attributes of an object. With the Connection object it is used with CommitTrans and RollbackTrans to determine if a new transaction is started when they are called. This feature is not supported by all databases.
CommandTimeout	The time, in seconds, the command will wait to be executed. The default is 30 seconds. If this value is exceeded, the command will return an error message.
ConnectionString	The properties of the connection being created.
ConnectionTimeout	The time, in seconds, the connection will wait to be executed. The default is 15 seconds. If this value is exceeded, the Connection object will return an error message.
CursorLocation	Allows either a client-side or server-side cursor. A cursor marks the current position in a multirecord recordset.
DefaultDatabase	Sets the default database for the connection.
IsolationLevel	Used with the BeginTrans method to set how transactions interact with each other—for example, whether uncommitted transactions are visible to all users. Also, higher isolation levels can be given priority over lower isolation levels.
Mode	Sets permissions for using the database.
Provider	The name of the connection provider. With ASP this is usually ADODB. By default it is MSDASQL (the Microsoft ODBC provider for OLE DB).
State	Returns the current state of an object, either open or closed.
Version	The ADO version number.

Table 18-4. *Connection Object Properties*

ConnectionString property. The ConnectionString property can be either defined when the database is opened or created as a Session object in the Global.asa file. The parameters of the ConnectionString property are listed in Table 18-5.

Parameter	Description
Provider	Name of the ODBC driver used for the connection.
Data Source	Name of the data source being opened.
User ID	User name for the data source connection.
Password	Password for the login account.
Filename	Name of a file to open. If a file is specified, the Provider attribute is not used; the appropriate provider will be opened by the specified file.

Table 18-5.   *ConnectionString Property Parameters*

The ConnectionString is written as a series of name=value pairs separated by semicolons, similar to this:

```
DSN=NBT;DBQ=C:\Inetpub\Wwwroot\ASP\NBT\fpdb\NorthBeachTools.mdb;
DriverId=25;
FIL=MS Access;MaxBufferSize=512;PageTimeout=5;
```

For security, you should create a user account for the database that has read-only permission, and use this account for all web-based queries. If it is necessary for the user to write to the database, you should consider creating a separate database with read-write permission. You can then synchronize the databases offline. The time and money spent creating and populating a database application is usually very significant. Obviously, you want as much security as possible for your investment.

Note   *In this chapter, discussion of security has been kept to a minimum to focus on database connectivity and because setting up user accounts is more a function of the database and server, not FrontPage or ASP. In the real world, you should use the maximum amount of security practical with your database.*

The Command Object

The Command object is used to define the command that will be applied to the data source. It has two methods, CreateParameter and Execute. CreateParameter is used to create a new parameter for the Command object and assign values to it. As with the Connection object, the Execute method is used to run the command against the data source. In fact, you can often use the Connection.Execute object to perform the same function as the Command.Execute object. The third line of Listing 18-1 uses the

Connection object, rather than the Command object, to execute the query. The Command object is more flexible and so should generally be used.

The Command object has seven properties, listed in Table 18-6.

> **Note** *ASP SQL statements are passed to the ODBC driver as text strings. The ODBC driver converts them into the proper syntax for the data source. Commonly used queries can be defined as stored procedures, which are part of the database. Calling a stored procedure is faster than passing a text SQL statement. Consult your database documentation to see how to create stored procedures.*

You can also use the Command object without first opening the Connection object by setting the ActiveConnection property of the Command object to a valid connection string. This method is not recommended if you are making more than one call per page, because it opens a new connection for each command, rather than reusing an existing connection.

Property	Description
ActiveConnection	The active data source connection for the command.
CommandText	The query, *stored procedure* (a precompiled query), or a database table name that will be run against the data source.
CommandTimeout	The time, in seconds, the command will wait to be executed. The default is 30 seconds. If this value is exceeded, the command will return an error message.
CommandType	The type of command (text, table name, stored procedure, or unknown). Specifying a CommandType speeds up the command execution.
Name	Assigns or returns the name of an object.
Prepared	Sets whether to compile the command before executing it. This will slow the first execution of the command, but will speed up subsequent executions.
State	Returns the current state of an object, either open or closed.

Table 18-6. *Command Object Properties*

The Recordset Object

Most SQL queries in your web will return some form of data, such as one or more fields from one or more records. (SQL statements that insert or update a record will return a value indicating success or failure.) With FrontPage and ASP, the Recordset object is used to store the information returned by executing the SQL query. Because the Recordset object is used for holding the records returned by a database query, it has a large number of methods and properties. These are needed so that you can manipulate the data in the recordset. The Recordset methods are listed in Table 18-7, and the properties are listed in Table 18-8.

Method	Description
AddNew	Creates a new record in the recordset, but doesn't write it to the database until the Update or UpdateBatch method is called.
CancelBatch	Cancels a batch update.
CancelUpdate	Cancels any changes made to a record before calling the Update method.
Clone	Creates a copy of a Recordset object.
Close	Used to close an open recordset.
Delete	Removes the current record from a recordset.
GetRows	Places the selected fields from multiple rows in an array.
Move	Changes the position of the current record in a recordset.
MoveFirst	Makes the first record in the recordset the current record.
MoveLast	Makes the last record in the recordset the current record.
MoveNext	Makes the next record in the recordset the current record.
MovePrevious	Makes the previous record in the recordset the current record.
NextRecordset	Closes the current recordset and opens the specified recordset.
Open	Opens a cursor in the specified recordset. Cursors are described in the section "Recordset Cursors."
Requery	Updates the recordset by rerunning the query on the database.

Table 18-7. *Recordset Object Methods*

Method	Description
Resync	Refreshes the current recordset from the database.
Supports	Indicates if the recordset supports a certain type of functionality. The recordset functionality is determined by the type of cursor used.
Update	Saves the current record to the database.
UpdateBatch	Saves all pending updates to the database.

Table 18-7.   *Recordset Object Methods* (continued)

Property	Description
AbsolutePage	Specifies the page to move to. A *page* is a group of records in a recordset. If the recordset contains ten records, it could be divided into two pages with five records on each page.
AbsolutePosition	Makes the specified record in the recordset the current record. The first record is numbered as 1.
ActiveConnection	Sets the Connection object or connection string for the recordset.
BOF and EOF	Returns a TRUE or FALSE value, indicating you are moving before the first record or after the last record in the recordset.
Bookmark	Used like bookmarks in a word processor to identify a record. You can then make the bookmarked record the current record by using the bookmark.
CacheSize	Determines the number of records in a recordset that are cached in memory locally.
CursorLocation	Allows either a client-side or server-side cursor. A cursor marks the current position in a multirecord recordset.
CursorType	Sets or returns the cursor type being used in the Recordset object.
EditMode	Indicates if the record is being edited and if any changes have been saved.

Table 18-8.   *Recordset Object Properties*

Property	Description
Filter	Used to apply additional criteria to a recordset so that only a subset of the recordset is used.
LockType	Sets or returns the type of lock on a recordset. Locks are covered in the section "The LockType Property."
MaxRecords	Specifies the number of records to return in a recordset. By default this value is 0, which returns all the records. If the query is very general, the number of records returned may be excessively large. Setting the MaxRecords value to a reasonable number will prevent the recordset from becoming unmanageable.
PageCount	Indicates the number of pages in a recordset.
PageSize	Returns the number of records per page in a recordset.
RecordCount	Returns the number of records in a recordset.
Source	The source of the recordset, which can be a Command object, SQL statement, table name, or a stored procedure.
State	Returns the current state of an object, either open or closed.
Status	Used during batch updating to determine the status of records affected by the update.

Table 18-8.   *Recordset Object Properties* (continued)

Recordset Cursors

A cursor in a recordset is a pointer to the current record. There are four types of cursors that you can use. They are listed in Table 18-9.

The Forward-only cursor (the default) is used when you expect a single record to be returned in the recordset (for example, when you are selecting a record based on a field that contains a unique value), or you don't need to move backwards through a recordset (you are only making a single pass through the recordset). The Static cursor is used when the user needs to be able to move freely through the recordset. On the web these are the cursors you will use most often. If the user is allowed to modify the database, you will need to use either the Dynamic or Keyset cursors.

The LockType Property

Locks are placed on database records to prevent the user from performing certain actions—for example, to prevent the user from modifying data in the recordset. The types of locks available are shown in Table 18-10. You should always use the ReadOnly lock, unless the user specifically needs to be able to update a database record.

Cursor Type	Description
Dynamic	Allows full movement through the recordset and allows the user to see additions, changes, and deletions made by other users.
Keyset	Allows full movement through the recordset, but prevents you from seeing other users' additions and prevents other users from deleting your records. All changes are still visible.
Static	Creates a copy of the records in the recordset. This is useful for searching the data and creating reports. Full movement is allowed, but additions, deletions, and changes are not visible.
Forward-only	The default; this is identical to the Static cursor, except that only forward movement is allowed. This is the fastest method for reading a single pass through a recordset.

Table 18-9. *Recordset Object Cursor Types*

The Adovbs.inc File

Both cursor types and lock types are usually passed to the database as numeric values. This makes the resulting code hard to read, unless you've memorized the numeric values for each cursor and lock type. Microsoft provides a file with ASP that maps these numeric values to text strings that you can use in your code. This file is named Adovbs.inc, and you can use it with your ASP pages by including it on each page using the ASP Server-Side Include command. Table 18-11 lists the cursor and lock types, their numeric values, and the text string you can use in your code.

Lock Type	Description
ReadOnly	Prevents the user from modifying the data
Pessimistic	Locks a record as soon as it starts being edited
Optimistic	Locks a record being edited when the Update method is called
BatchOptimistic	Used like the Optimistic lock when doing batch updates

Table 18-10. *Recordset Object Lock Types*

Cursor or Lock Type	Value	Text String
Forward-only cursor	0	adOpenForwardOnly
Keyset cursor	1	adOpenKeyset
Dynamic cursor	2	adOpenDynamic
Static cursor	3	adOpenStatic
Read-only lock	1	adLockReadOnly
Pessimistic lock	2	adLockPessimistic
Optimistic lock	3	adLockOptimistic
Batch Optimistic lock	4	adLockBatchOptimistic

Table 18-11.   *Cursor and Lock Numeric and Text Values*

There is also a comparable file if you are using JavaScript as the default server-side scripting language. The filename is Adojavas.inc.

In the next section you will see how the Connection, Command, and Recordset objects, along with some of their methods and properties, are used to create database-based web pages.

Using ASP to Create Web Database Pages

Previously you used the FrontPage Database Results Wizard to integrate database information on a web page. You can do the same thing using ASP objects and VBScript. There are two advantages to this. The first is that you can tailor your code to your application. The Database Results Wizard generates generic code that works fine most of the time, but doesn't allow you to change the code in any way. (If you change the FrontPage-generated code, FrontPage overwrites your changes the next time the page is saved.) The second is that FrontPage-generated code reveals sensitive information about your database to the user. The disadvantage is that entering the code by hand is slower and you will have to also create any error checking needed.

In the following exercise, there is a minimum of error checking. This is to focus on the core functionality of using ASP's database connectivity. In actual use you would need to check for error conditions and deal with them.

This next exercise will introduce you to the process of creating a database web page using ASP. You will create pages that allow you to modify and delete a record in the database. You will also learn how to populate a form from a database. Begin now with these steps:

1. Open a new page in FrontPage; then type **Modify Or Delete A Record** and format it as Heading 2. Press ENTER.

2. Insert a One-Line form text box and press HOME. Type **ProductID:** (leave a space after the colon).

3. Press RIGHT ARROW and then ENTER. Right-click the ProductID text box and choose Form Field Properties.

4. Type **ProductID** in the Name text box; then click Validate.

5. Select Text in the Data Type drop-down list; then select Required for Data Length.

6. Type **8** in the Max Length text box, and then type **ProductID** in the Display Name text box. Click OK twice.

> **Note** *The ProductID field is the primary key for the Products table. This means that it is a unique value, while both Description and Cost allow duplicate values. That is, many records may have the same price or the same description, but each ProductID must be unique. This is enforced by the database itself. You want this form to send a unique value that will be inserted into the SQL query so that only a single record will be returned.*

7. Right-click the form and choose Form Properties.

8. Select Send To Other; then click Options. Type **Modify2.asp** in the Action text box. Click OK twice.

9. Save your page in your NBT folder with the Page Title **Modify Or Delete A Record** and the File Name **Modify.asp**.

10. Open the File menu and choose Import.

11. Click Add File and locate the Adovbs.inc file. The default location is C:\Program Files\Common Files\System\ADO\Adovbs.inc.

> **Note** *If you don't have the Adovbs.inc file installed, you can use the appropriate numeric values from Table 18-11 in the following exercises.*

12. Select the Adovbs.inc file in the Add File To List dialog box, click Open, and then click OK.

13. Create a new page, click the HTML tab, and press CTRL-HOME to move the insertion point to the top of the page.

14. Type **<!-- #Include File="Adovbs.inc"-->** and press ENTER.

Note *You could also place the Adovbs.inc file in a virtual directory and use <!—#Include Virtual="/virtual directory/Adovbs.inc"-->. This would allow you to have a single copy of the Adovbs.inc file that can be referenced by all your webs that include the virtual directory.*

15. Click the Normal tab. With the cursor at the top of the page, type **Record To Modify Or Delete**, and format it as Heading 2. Press ENTER.

16. Insert a One-Line text box, press HOME, type **ProductID:** (with three spaces after the colon), and format it as Formatted.

17. Press RIGHT ARROW and then SHIFT+ENTER. Type **Description:** (with one space after the colon), and insert a one-line text box.

18. Press SHIFT+ENTER, type **Cost:**, with eight spaces after the colon, and insert a one-line text box. Press ENTER.

19. Right-click the ProductID text box and choose Form Field Properties.

20. Type **ProductID** in the Name text box; then type **Placeholder** in the Initial Value text box, and click OK.

Note *You will not use any validation for this form because you will be entering code in the HTML tab later in this exercise. Not having the validation code will make it easier to locate the correct placement for the code. This form will be used to collect data to be written to the database, so in actual use you would have client-side validation. The validation rules would be determined by the database structure.*

21. Right-click the Description text box and choose Form Field Properties. Type **Description** in the Name text box, type **Placeholder** in the Initial Value text box, and click OK.

22. Right-click the Cost text box and choose Form Field Properties. Type **Cost** in the Name text box, type **Placeholder** in the Initial Value text box, and click OK.

23. Right-click the form and choose Form Properties. Select Send To Other and click Options.

24. Type **Modify3.asp** in the Action text box and click OK twice.

25. Right-click the Submit form button and choose Form Field Properties.

26. In the Push Button Properties dialog box, type **Action** in the Name text box, and then type **Update Record** in the Value/Label text box.

27. Check that the Submit Button type option is selected and click OK.

28. Right-click the Reset form button and choose Form Field Properties.

29. Type **Action** in the Name text box, type **Delete Record** in the Value/Label text box, and then select the Submit Button Type option. Click OK. Your page should look similar to Figure 18-15.

30. Save your page with the Page Title **Record To Modify Or Delete** and the File Name **Modify2.asp**.

In the next section of this exercise, you will enter VBScript and ASP code to populate the form you created in the previous steps. It is very important that this code be placed in the correct location on the page and that the syntax be correct. The pages are included on the CD in the \Books\Chap18 folder. Check your own work against these pages if you encounter any errors.

1. With your Modify2.asp page still open in FrontPage, click the HTML tab.

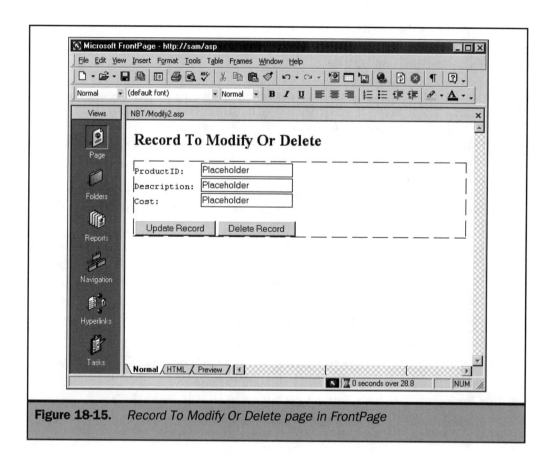

Figure 18-15. *Record To Modify Or Delete page in FrontPage*

2. Place the cursor on the first line after the opening <BODY> tag and type

```
<%
strProductID = Request.Form("ProductID")
SQL = "SELECT Products.* FROM Products WHERE Products.ProductID = '" &
strProductID & "'"
Set objConnection = Server.CreateObject("ADODB.Connection")
objConnection.Open "NBT"
Set objCommand = Server.CreateObject("ADODB.Command")
Set RS = Server.CreateObject("ADODB.Recordset")
objCommand.CommandText = SQL
objCommand.CommandType = adCmdText
Set objCommand.ActiveConnection = objConnection
RS.Open objCommand, , adOpenForwardOnly, adLockReadOnly
%>
```

Because the SQL statement is a VBScript text string, it has to be formatted by use of VBScript's rules for formatting text strings. First, the entire string must be contained within double quotes ("). The ProductID value for the WHERE clause will be passed by the form on the Modify.asp page and so must be inserted into the SQL text string. It is easiest to assign this value to a local variable, strProductID, before inserting it into the SQL string.

The variable strProductID must then be *concatenated* with the SQL string. Concatenation joins two strings into a single string. The ampersand (&) is the VBScript operator that does this in the second line of the code you entered. The type and placement of the single and double quotes around the concatenated string are critical. In the section of the SQL string '" & strProductID & "'" there is first a single quote (') and then a double quote ("). When the SQL string interpreted, there must be single quotes around the text. This is the purpose of the single quote. The double quote ends, or delimits, the first part of the SQL string.

Next comes the concatenation operator, then the strProductID variable, followed by another concatenation operator, a double quote, a single quote, and the final double quote. There are really three strings that are being concatenated into a single string. If the value of the strProductID variable was ABC, the final concatenated SQL string passed to the ODBC driver would be "SELECT Products.* FROM Products WHERE Products.Product.ID = 'ABC'". ABC is enclosed in single quotes and the entire string is enclosed in double quotes.

If the variable was numeric, rather than text, you would not use the single quotes. This is because anything in single quotes is interpreted as text, and anything without single quotes is interpreted as a number.

The remaining code establishes the parameters of the data connection. In actual use it is easier to have this code in an Include file. This simplifies maintenance by creating a single source. In the Include file you could either use the numeric values for the cursor and lock parameters, or map just the ones you need to text strings (shown in Table 18-11). It would not be necessary to include the Adovbs.inc file in that case.

3. Find the HTML for the first form text box. The line will look like this:

```
<input type="text" name="ProductID" size="20" value="Placeholder">
```

You will replace the text "Placeholder" with the value returned for ProductID by the SQL query.

4. Select the word Placeholder, but not the quotes around it. Type **<%= RS("ProductID") %>**. The line should now look like this:

```
<input type="text" name="ProductID" size="20" value="<%= RS("ProductID") %>">
```

5. Replace the text Placeholder in the HTML for the Description form text box with **<%= RS("Description") %>**.

6. Replace the text Placeholder in the HTML for the Cost form text box with **<%= RS("Cost") %>**.

7. Place the cursor on the blank line between the closing </BODY> and </HTML> tags and type

> **<%**
> **RS.Close**
> **Set RS = Nothing**
> **%>**

This closes the recordset and frees up the server resources it was using.

8. Save your page and then check your work so far by opening the Modify.asp page in your browser.

9. Type **S400-1** in the ProductID text box in your Modify Or Delete A Record page in your browser; then click Submit. Figure 18-16 shows the Record To Modify Or Delete page with the data for the record with the ProductID of S400-1.

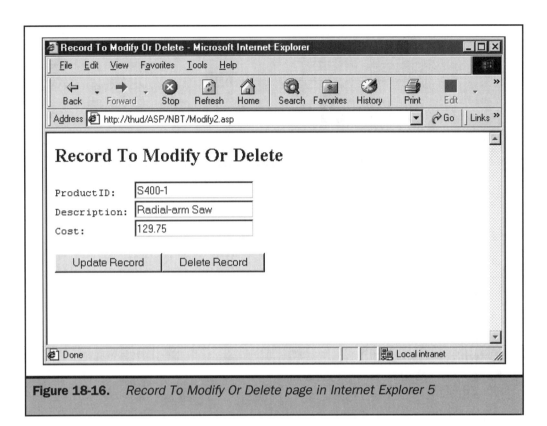

Figure 18-16. *Record To Modify Or Delete page in Internet Explorer 5*

This page will generate an ODBC driver error if you enter a ProductID that doesn't exist in the database. Figure 18-17 shows the page in Internet Explorer when this happens. You will add the code to deal with this error condition with the following steps.

10. In the Page view HTML tab, place the cursor at the end of the heading line, `<h2>Record To Modify Or Delete</h2>`, and press ENTER.

11. Type **<% If NOT RS.EOF Then %>**.

12. Move the cursor to the line after the closing form tag, `</form>`, type **<% Else %>**, and press ENTER.

13. Type **<h3>There was no matching record</h3>** and press ENTER.

14. Type **<% End If %>** and save your page.

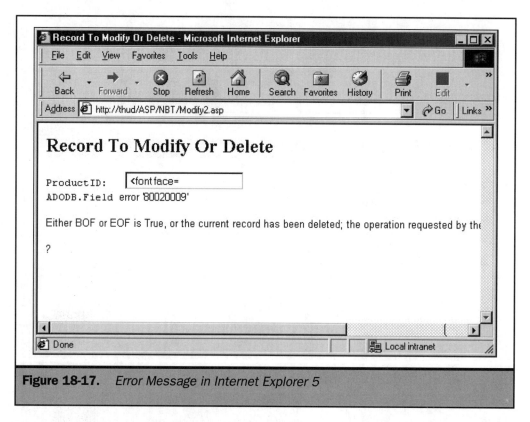

Figure 18-17. *Error Message in Internet Explorer 5*

15. Open the Modify Or Delete A Record page (Modify.asp) in your browser, and type **123** in the ProductID text box. Click Submit. Figure 18-18 shows the Record To Modify Or Delete page displaying the No Matching Record message.

The first line you entered checks for an End Of File (EOF) in the recordset. This condition exists when there are no records returned in the recordset or the last record has been read from the recordset (the database cursor is after the last record). If EOF is NOT TRUE (there is a record in the recordset), then the form is displayed. If EOF is TRUE (there are no records in the recordset), then the form code is skipped and the error message is displayed.

Next, you will create the page that will update or delete the selected record. This page will contain the SQL statements that will update or delete the record; which is executed will depend on which Submit form button was clicked on the Modify Or Delete A Record page.

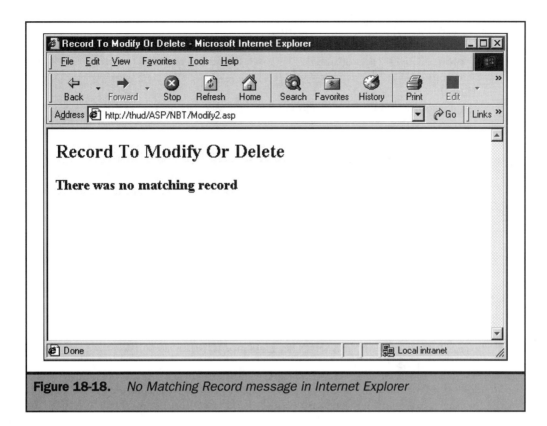

Figure 18-18. *No Matching Record message in Internet Explorer*

16. In FrontPage, create a new page and then click the HTML tab. Press CTRL+HOME then type **<!--#Include File="Adovbs.inc"-->** and press ENTER.

17. Place the cursor on the first line after the opening <BODY> tag and type

```
<%
strProductID = Request.Form("ProductID")
strDescription = Request.Form("Description")
sngCost = Request.Form("Cost")
If Request.Form("Action") = "Delete Record" Then
strAction = "D"
Else
strAction = "U"
End If
```

```
If strAction = "U" Then
SQL = "UPDATE Products SET Products.Description = '" & strDescription & "',
Products.Cost = " & sngCost & " WHERE Products.ProductID = '" &
strProductID & "'"
Else
SQL = "DELETE Products.* FROM Products WHERE Products.ProductID = '" &
strProductID & "'"
End If
Set objConnection = Server.CreateObject("ADODB.Connection")
objConnection.Open "NBT"
Set objCommand = Server.CreateObject("ADODB.Command")
Set RS = Server.CreateObject("ADODB.Recordset")
objCommand.CommandText = SQL
objCommand.CommandType = adCmdText
Set objCommand.ActiveConnection = objConnection
RS.Open objCommand, , adOpenForwardOnly, adLockReadOnly
If strAction = "U" Then
%>
<h2>Record <%= strProductID %> Updated</h2>
<% Else %>
<h2>Record <%= strProductID %> Deleted</h2>
<% End If %>
```

18. Click the Normal tab. Your page should look similar to Figure 18-19. Both
    messages are displayed because FrontPage is not interpreting the VBScript code
    that controls which will be displayed in actual use.

19. Press CTRL+END and type **NBT Home**; then select it and click Hyperlink on
    the toolbar.

20. In the Create Hyperlink dialog box, open your NBT folder and select
    Default.asp. Click OK.

21. Save your page with the Page Title **Update Or Delete Record** and the File
    Name **Modify3.asp**.

    Now it's time to test your work.

22. Open your Modify Or Delete A Record page (Modify.asp) in your browser and
    type **S400-1** in the ProductID text box. Click Submit. Your Record To Modify Or
    Delete page should open, displaying the details for the radial-arm saw with a
    price of 129.75.

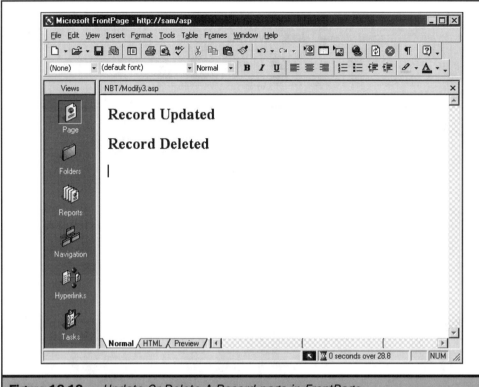

Figure 18-19. *Update Or Delete A Record page in FrontPage*

23. Change the Cost to **149.75** and click Update Record. Figure 18-20 shows the confirmation page in Internet Explorer.

    Your North Beach Tools web is almost done. All that needs to be done is to create hyperlinks from the North Beach Tools home page to the other pages in the web. When that is done, you will test your Modify Or Delete more thoroughly.

24. Open your North Beach Tools home page (Default.asp) in FrontPage.

25. Select View All Products and click Hyperlink on the toolbar. Select Allprod.asp and click OK.

26. Select Find A Product and click Hyperlink on the toolbar. Select Search.asp and click OK.

27. Select Add A Product and click Hyperlink on the toolbar. Select Addprod.asp and click OK.

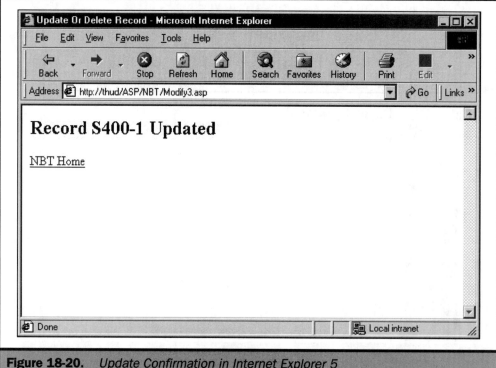

Figure 18-20. *Update Confirmation in Internet Explorer 5*

28. Select Modify Or Delete A Product and click Hyperlink on the toolbar. Select Modify.asp and click OK.

29. Save your page and then open it in your browser.

30. Click View All Products. Your browser should display the complete North Beach Tools product line.

31. Click NBT Home and then click Find A Product. Type **saw** in the Description text box and click Submit. Your Search Results page should display all the saws in the database. Click NBT Home.

32. Click Add A Product. Type **S400-2** in the Product ID text box and press TAB.

33. Type **Circular saw** in the Description text box, press TAB, type **74.95** in the Cost text box, and click Submit.

34. Click Return To The Form and then click NBT Home. Click View All Products. The circular saw should be included in your list of all North Beach Tool products. Click NBT Home.

35. Click Modify Or Delete A Product; then type **S400-2** in the ProductID text box and click Submit. The details for the circular saw should be displayed in your Record To Modify Or Delete page.

36. Change the Cost to **79.95** and click Update Record. Your Update Or Delete Record page should display the Record S400-2 Updated message.

37. Click NBT Home and then click View All Products. Your product list should display the updated price for the circular saw. Click NBT Home; then click Modify Or Delete A Product.

38. Type **S400-2** in the ProductID text box and click Submit. Click Delete Record; then click NBT Home.

39. Click View All Products. The circular saw will no longer appear in your product list.

The examples in this chapter have barely scratched the surface of what you can do with FrontPage, ASP, SQL databases, and the Web. It has been an introduction designed to give you some ideas about the possibilities of integrating databases into your webs. FrontPage streamlines the task of creating ASP database pages, but a thorough knowledge of a scripting language, SQL programming, and relational database theory are still essential. These subjects are beyond the scope of this book. For example, you haven't been introduced to the joys of inner, outer, right, and left joins, which are essential for creating SQL queries involving multiple tables, not to mention unions. If you don't have these skills yourself, consider finding a good relational database programmer who can help make your ideas a reality. More and more, the creation of world-class web sites is becoming a team effort.

Chapter 19

Activating Your Webs

The World Wide Web has come a long way since the ability to create hyperlinks between documents was a revolutionary technology. Today's web browsers support animation, video, and audio files integrated in webs, but even these advances have been overshadowed. You've seen how JavaScript, VBScript, and Active Server Pages can produce true interactivity on the Web. Java and ActiveX further expand your horizons. Java applets and ActiveX controls are computer programs that can be downloaded to and then executed on your computer by your web browser, or can be run on the server in the same manner as server-side scripting. These technologies are truly revolutionary and are the future of world-class web sites.

In this chapter, you will first learn how current web browsers support HTML features such as *marquees* (text that scrolls across a web page) that do more than statically display information, and how these are different from Java applets and ActiveX controls. Then you will learn how to use these newest web technologies in your own webs. This is the frontier of the World Wide Web.

Active Browser Features

As you've learned in the previous chapters, a web page is a text file containing HTML instructions. Your web browser loads the HTML file and creates the web page displayed in the browser by interpreting the HTML instructions. In Chapter 20, you will see how to add multimedia to your web pages by using some of the newest HTML tags. However, these features only work with web browsers that support these HTML tags. This means that there often needs to be a cycle of browser upgrades before the features are widely supported. Even after browser support is available, not everyone downloads the latest version of his or her favorite browser promptly (particularly as browser downloads have become quite large). This all means that you use these features at your own risk—only a small portion of your audience may see your webs the way you intended.

Java, ActiveX, JavaScript, and VBScript are fundamentally different. If a browser supports these programming languages, as both Netscape Navigator and Microsoft Internet Explorer do to some extent, what you can do on a web page is limited only by your imagination. This frees the web designer from waiting for browser upgrades to begin using the latest web features. The resulting stability is essential as the Web grows. One of the biggest problems in creating webs is the dependence on the user's web browser. Almost every current browser can support the standard HTML features, such as displaying tables, to one degree or another, but support of multimedia varies greatly. Since Netscape and Microsoft offer conflicting HTML tags, the situation will not resolve itself soon.

With Java and ActiveX, the problem is simply sidestepped. You can either write your own applets and controls (which requires a good knowledge of computer programming), or download them from a number of sources on the Web.

Note *Support for these technologies in current browsers is less than perfect. This situation is rapidly changing, and you can expect that most web users will soon be able to see your activated webs exactly as you intended.*

Adding a Scrolling Marquee

A good example of how an HTML tag (interpreted by a browser) differs from a Java applet (a stand-alone executable computer program) can be seen by adding a marquee to a web page. This is an HTML tag currently only supported by Microsoft's Internet Explorer. If you use this feature, it will be lost on anyone using Netscape Navigator. By creating the same effect with a Java applet, you can make it possible for more of the people visiting your web site to see your pages as you intended. To understand the differences, first create a web page with a marquee in FrontPage using the Marquee HTML tag with these instructions:

1. Open FrontPage if it's not already open, and then create a new One Page Web and name it **Active**.

2. At the top of the new page, type **Welcome To the World of Active Web Pages**, and format it as Heading 2.

3. Select the text and open the Insert menu; then choose Component | Marquee. The Marquee Properties dialog box, shown next, will be displayed. The selected text is shown in the Text text box.

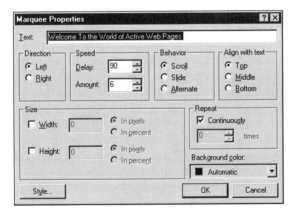

In the Marquee Properties dialog box, you specify the text to be displayed; the direction, speed, and type of movement of the text; its alignment; the number of times it repeats; the width and height of the marquee box; and the background color of the marquee.

4. Accept the defaults and click OK.

5. Click Save on the toolbar. Save your page with the Page Title of **Active Web Home Page** and the File Name **Default.htm**. Click Save. You will be prompted that this will overwrite the Default.htm page created with the web. Click Yes.

6. Open your Active Web Home Page in Microsoft Internet Explorer. The text you entered previously will scroll from the right side of the page to the left and repeat continuously.

7. Open Netscape Navigator and load the Active Web Home Page into it. The text simply sits at the top of the page, since the Marquee tag is not supported by Netscape's browser.

8. In FrontPage, right-click the marquee text and select Marquee Properties.

9. In the Marquee Properties dialog box, select the Alternate Behavior option and click OK. Save the page again.

10. In Internet Explorer, click Refresh on the toolbar. The marquee will now travel back and forth between the left and right margins of the page.

As you can see, the Marquee tag can add a little life to a web page, but only if it is supported. Since only Internet Explorer currently supports the tag, this is a feature of limited use. In the next section, you will find other ways to activate your webs that have better cross-platform support.

Java

The Java programming language was developed by Sun Microsystems, Inc., and initially released in fall 1995. Netscape was an early licenser of Java; Microsoft soon followed. With the release of Microsoft's Internet Explorer 4.0, the uneasy alignment between Sun and Microsoft came to an end. Sun has sued Microsoft for alleged violations of their licensing agreement, which Microsoft has denied. Sun claims that Microsoft changed certain core interface components in violation of the agreement. Microsoft did make the changes, but maintains that the licensing agreement allowed them to.

Note   *At the end of 1998 Sun was granted a preliminary injunction against Microsoft that has compelled Microsoft to bring its version of Java in line with Sun's. Microsoft's "improvements" are still in its own flavor of Java, but they no longer are the defaults.*

Java's proponents see it as a replacement for the Windows operating system. At the current level of development this is a bit of wishful thinking. Microsoft probably wishes Java would go away so everyone would use ActiveX. In all probability, neither side will get what it wants. Regardless of the growing pains the language is experiencing, it is and will continue to be an important language for many network and web applications.

Object-Oriented Programming

Java is an *object-oriented* programming language very similar to C++, one of today's standard programming languages. An object-oriented programming language defines an *object* as a process that accepts information, processes it, and then outputs the result of the processing. The format of the input is always clearly defined, as is the output. One object may receive its input from the output of another object. For example, an object may be a simple program that accepts a text string and then converts the text to all capitals. The input is the text string, regardless of case, and the output is the same text string converted to all uppercase. The object is the code that performs the conversion. Java applets are built by combining a number of objects, each performing a relatively simple task, into a computer program that can carry out complex operations. This concept is very powerful, as you will learn in the following sections.

> **Note**   *Programming your own Java applets is a complex subject, well beyond the scope of this book. Two excellent resources for learning more about object-oriented programming and Java are* The Java Handbook *by Patrick Naughton (Osborne/McGraw-Hill, 1996) and* Java 2: The Complete Reference *by Patrick Naughton and Herbert Schildt (Osborne/McGraw-Hill, 1999). There are many preprogrammed Java applets available on the Web, so programming your own applet is not necessary for you to add Java applets to your web. The examples in this chapter will use readily available Java applets.*

By its nature, Java offers several features besides object orientation that make it suitable for programming on the Web. It's also safe, robust, interactive, platform independent, and high performance.

Safe

Since Java applets are computer programs that are downloaded and executed on the user's computer, what's to stop the unscrupulous programmer from sending a destructive applet over the Web to wreak havoc on thousands of computers? With the rapid growth of the Internet, this has become a leading concern for many, including the creators of Java. Their solution was to strictly limit what a Java applet can do. Java applets cannot access or misuse operating system resources, which leaves little room for vandalism. It is possible, for example, to write an applet that will slow down your computer by monopolizing resources, but this does not cause permanent damage.

Robust

With millions of users around the world connected to the Internet, any program that is written to be used there must be able to function flawlessly on many different computers with unique configurations. By Java's nature, these problems are kept to a minimum. Provided the browser includes support for the Java language, applets can usually be depended on to function properly.

Interactive

Most web sites today display information passively; that is, the content is defined by the web author and displayed by a browser in much the same way as a page in a magazine is produced. In Chapter 18, you saw how databases could be integrated in webs so that information could be presented dynamically. Java and the other technologies covered in this chapter take the process a step further. As you will see in the examples in this section, Java applets, because they are computer programs running on the user's computer, can accept input from the user, process it, and display the output on a web page. All this can be done locally (on the user's computer) and so leaves the web server free to handle other tasks.

Platform Independent

On the Internet (and intranets), computers running Windows, Apple's Macintosh operating system, and UNIX (and its variants such as Linux) can coexist along with a few other minor operating systems. One of the beauties of HTML and the Web is that all these systems can access and display the same web pages. Java extends this platform independence by creating code that does not rely on a specific operating system. Each browser that supports Java applets contains a Java interpreter that handles the interaction between the applet itself and the computer operating system. In this way a single Java applet will function properly on a Windows PC, a Mac, or a UNIX computer. This is a capability with far-reaching implications. Up to this point, computer programs have been written to run only on a single operating system. With Java, it is now possible to write complex applications that can run on any operating system for which an appropriate browser is available.

> **Note**   *Though Sun's claim that Java is "write once, run anywhere" has often been rephrased to "write once, debug everywhere," it is still a quantum leap forward in platform independence.*

High Performance

All the features of Java applets mentioned so far would be of limited use if the applets were not high performance. Almost every computer user has experienced the frustration of slow response times when running some applications. Java's creators made sure that the Java code would work efficiently even on older, slower computers. Also, both Netscape and Microsoft have worked to make the Java interpreters in their web browsers as fast as possible.

The features just described combine to make Java the first of a new generation of programming languages created to work efficiently and flawlessly across the Internet or a company intranet. Now that you have some understanding of just what Java is and can do, it's time to add an applet to your web.

Banner Ad Manager Component

You need look no farther than FrontPage's Insert menu to find your first Java applet. The Banner Ad Manager is a Java applet at heart. In Chapter 17, you learned how to use the ASP Ad Rotator Component to rotate ad banners on your site. The FrontPage Banner Ad Manager performs a similar task with different options. Add your first Java applet to your Active home page by first importing the graphics to display from the included CD.

1. In the Folder List, select your Images folder in your Active web.

2. Open the File menu and choose Import. In the Import dialog box, click Add File.

3. In the Add File To Import List dialog box, select your CD drive and then open the Chap19 folder. Select Banner1.gif, press and hold SHIFT, and then select Banner2.gif. Release SHIFT and click Open and then OK.

4. In Page view place your cursor on the first line below your Marquee text; then open the Insert menu and choose Component | Banner Ad Manager. The Banner Ad Manger dialog box shown here is displayed.

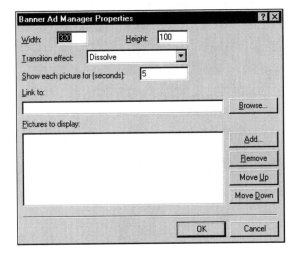

In the Banner Ad Manger dialog box, you set the size of the graphics to display, the transition effect to be used to change the graphic displayed, the length of time to display each graphic, a hyperlink for the graphics, and select the graphics to be used.

5. Type **468** in the Width text box and **60** in the Height text box.

6. Select Dissolve in the Transition Effect drop-down list, and accept the default of 5 seconds in the Show Each Picture For (Seconds) text box.

7. In the Link To text box, type **http://www.pbg.mcgraw-hill.com/computing/**. (Do not include the period.)

8. Click Add to add the graphics to display in the Pictures To Display list box.

9. In the Add Picture For Banner Ad dialog box, open your Images folder. Select **Banner1.gif** and click OK.

10. Click Add; then select **Banner2.gif** and click OK twice.

11. Save you work and then open your Active web home page in your browser. Figure 19-1 shows the page in Netscape Navigator in mid-transition.

12. In FrontPage, right-click the graphic and select Banner Ad Manager Properties.

13. Select Blinds Horizontal from the Transition Effect drop-down list and click OK.

14. Save your page and then reload it in your browser to see the effect.

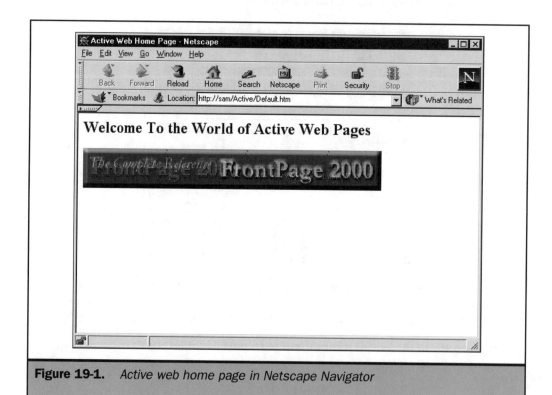

Figure 19-1. *Active web home page in Netscape Navigator*

The key difference between the ASP Ad Rotator Component and the FrontPage Banner Ad Manager Component is that the ASP component rotates banners each time the page is loaded (server-side) and the FrontPage component rotates them continuously because it is running in the browser (client-side). Another difference is that the ASP component is an ActiveX control, while the FrontPage component is a Java applet. Since only Internet Explorer supports ActiveX controls in the browser, it's necessary to use Java applets when you need cross-browser support. On an intranet, where you can control the browser in use, you could use ActiveX controls on the client. On the Web, this is impossible unless you don't care about the user experience for a large portion of your audience.

The transition effects you see are possible with both technologies, so in that respect neither offers a significant advantage over the other (though you will find programmers in both camps who will disagree with that statement). The Java applet also limits you to a single URL for the hyperlink, while the ASP component allows a separate URL for each graphic to link to. This is not an inherent limitation of the Java language, however. It is simply how the applet was written.

15. In FrontPage Page view, click the HTML tab. Here you see the HTML that displays the Banner Ad Manager applet, as shown in Figure 19-2.

WORKING BEHIND
THE SCENES

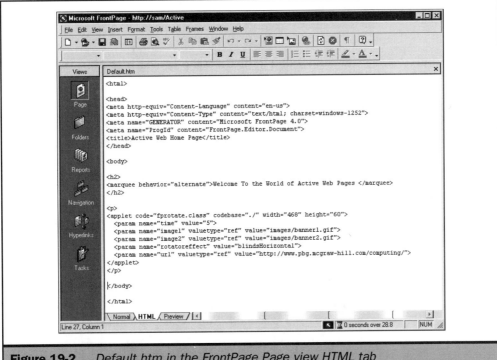

Figure 19-2.   *Default.htm in the FrontPage Page view HTML tab*

The <APPLET> tag is used to identify the Java applet using the parameters listed in Table 19-1. There will usually be a series of <PARAM> tags between the opening and closing <APPLET> tags. These are name-value pairs that contain the values passed to the applet. The correct names and the types of values are determined at the time the

Property	Description
Align	Specifies the alignment of the applet. The values are the same as for the <IMG> tag.
Alt	Is the alternative text that is displayed for that applet. This is used in the same manner as the Alt property for the <IMG> tag.
Archive	Is the location of a compressed file containing the applet and any other files it needs, such as multimedia files. This property is Netscape specific.
Class	Identifies a style sheet to use with the applet.
Code	Is the name of the applet. The location is relative to the Codebase.
Codebase	Is the URL of the directory that contains the applet.
Datafld	Is the column name from a data source that the applet is bound to.
Datascr	Is the data source that the applet is bound to.
Height and Width	Is the height and width in pixels of the applets display area.
Hspace and Vspace	Set the horizontal and vertical space around the applet in pixels.
ID	Is a unique identifier used with a style sheet or to reference it in a script.
MayScript	Is a flag that indicates if the applet can be scripted using JavaScript functions.
Name	Is a unique name for the applet that can be used by other applets on the same page to interact with the applet.
Src	Is a URL that can point to resources used by the applet.
Style	Identifies any inline styles to be applied to the applet.
Title	Is a title for the applet. This is Internet Explorer specific and is displayed as a Tool Tip when the applet is pointed to.

Table 19-1. *Applet Tag Properties*

applet is written, so there are no standard names. The values that can be passed to the applet should be explained in the documentation for it. In this case, using the FrontPage Banner Ad Manager, the parameters are exposed in the Banner Ad Manager dialog box.

FrontPage contains another Java applet accessible by selecting the Insert menu and choosing Component | Hover Button, which you will use in the next section.

Creating a Hover Button

A *hover* button is one that changes in some way or that controls an action triggered when the user moves the mouse pointer over it. The easiest way to understand how it works is to create one. Do that now with these steps:

1. Click the Page view Normal tab and place the insertion point on the third line.

2. Open the Insert menu and choose Component | Hover Button. The Hover Button Properties dialog box shown next is displayed.

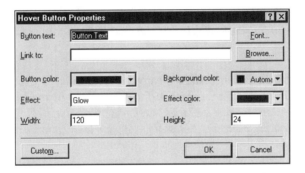

In this dialog box, you can set the text for the button, a hyperlink for it, its colors and size, and the effect. Clicking Custom displays the Custom dialog box, shown next, where you can set a sound to be played, or a custom image to be displayed when the mouse pointer moves over the button.

3. Accept the defaults in the Hover Button Properties dialog box by clicking OK.

4. Save your page, refresh it in your browser, and move your mouse pointer over the Button Text graphic to see the effect of the applet.

This example shows how easily a Java applet can be used. You can look at the HTML for the Hover button in the HTML tab to see the similarities between it and the Banner Ad Manager. The next step is understanding how Java applets are created. First, you need to download and install some Java development tools.

Finding Java Applets

Unless you're an experienced C++ programmer, your first Java applets will probably be ones that you download from the Web. There are a growing number of web sites that have applets available for downloading. The first step, then, is to get onto the Web and find some Java applets. A good place to start is Sun Microsystems' Java home page. The following steps will take you there.

Note *Web sites that offer Java applets change often as new applets are added. The descriptions of the web sites in this book reflect their status at the beginning of 1999, when this book was written.*

Tip *The current versions of both Netscape Navigator and Internet Explorer support Java, but there are differences. The current turf war between Sun and Microsoft has made it even more important to have the latest versions of Netscape's Navigator and Microsoft's Internet Explorer browsers and to test your applets with both the newest and older browser versions.*

1. Make sure your Internet connection is functioning, and open Netscape Navigator.

2. In the Location text box, type **java.sun.com/applets/** and press ENTER. In a few moments the web page shown in Figure 19-3 should be displayed in your browser.

Tip *Web sites change often, and URLs sometimes become outdated. If the URLs used in this chapter no longer work when you try them, start from the home page and follow the hyperlinks to the resources described.*

3. Scroll down the page until you see the heading "Freebie Applets." In the first paragraph under the heading, click the "free applets available for use" hyperlink.

Note *The file you download will be compressed and you will need to extract the individual files using a Zip utility such as WinZip from Nico Mak Computing, Inc.*

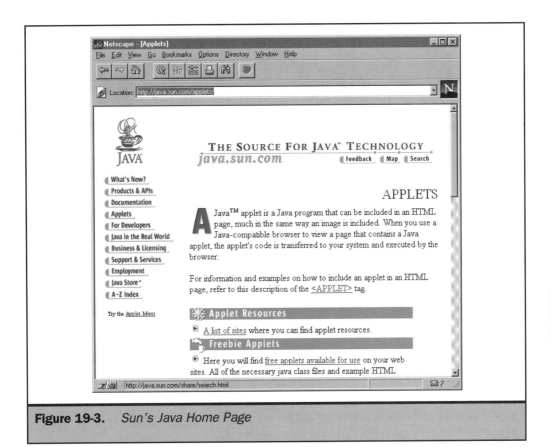

Figure 19-3.   *Sun's Java Home Page*

4. When the Freebie Applets You Can Use web page is displayed, scroll down to the Clock hyperlink and then click it. This takes you to the page (**http://java.sun.com/openstudio/applets/clock.html**) where you can download the applet's files, as shown in Figure 19-4. This page also contains sample HTML code for using the applet and lists the applet's parameters.

5. Click Download Now. If your browser prompts you to open the file or save it, choose to save it to disk. Select a work folder on your hard drive to save the file. You will have to unzip the download in this folder and then place the necessary files in your Active web. The compressed file actually contains several sample applets that you can use, but this exercise will focus exclusively on the Clock applet.

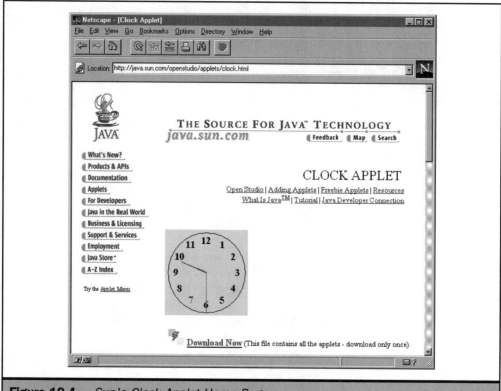

Figure 19-4. *Sun's Clock Applet Home Page*

6. When you have finished downloading the compressed applet file, you will need to unzip it. Do this in the work folder where you saved the download. When the compressed file is unzipped, it will create a folder named Demo that will contain subfolders for the Clock applet as well as the other sample applets.

7. In FrontPage, import the Clock applet to your Active web by opening the File menu and choosing Import.

8. In the Import dialog box, click Add Folder. In the Browse For Folder dialog box, locate the folder that contains the Demo folder created when you unzipped the file.

9. Open the Demo folder; then select the Clock folder and click OK twice. This will import more files than you absolutely need for this exercise, but is easier at this point than selecting the individual files. When the folder is imported, your Active web should have a folder named Clock that contains two subfolders, Classes and Src, as shown in Figure 19-5.

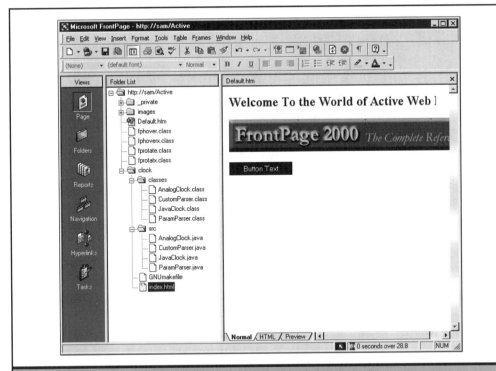

Figure 19-5.   *FrontPage Folder List with Clock applet imported*

The Classes folder contains the compiled Java applet files that have a .CLASS
file extension. These are the files you will use when you add the applet to your
page. The Src folder contains the source code for the applets, and these have a
.JAVA file extension. You will learn more about the source files and using them
in the section "Compiling Java Applets." Two other files were also imported in
the Clock folder. GNUmakefile is a batch file used to create the .CLASS files.
You will not use this file. The other file is a web page (Index.html) that displays
the Clock applet. Figure 19-6 shows this page in Netscape Navigator.

10. In your Folder List, select the file **GNUmakefile** and press DEL. In the Confirm
    Delete dialog box, click Yes.

11. In Page view place your cursor on the line below your Hover button.

12. Open the Insert menu and choose Advanced | Java Applet. The Java Applet
    Properties dialog box, shown in Figure 19-7, will be displayed.

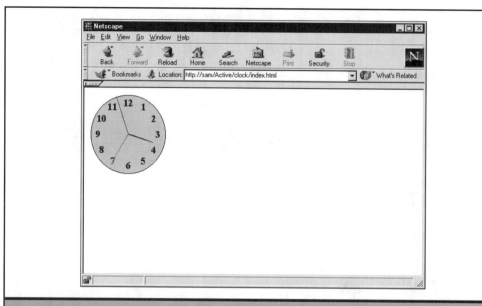

Figure 19-6. Clock applet default page in Netscape Navigator

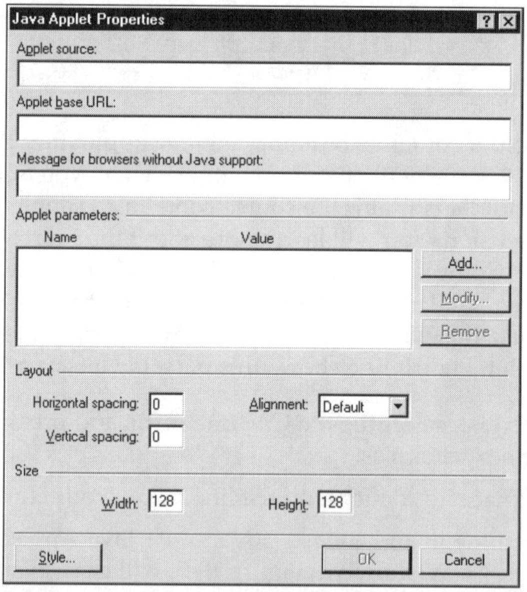

Figure 19-7. Java Applet Properties dialog box

13. Type **JavaClock.class** in the Applet Source text box; then type **Clock/Classes** in the Applet Base URL text box. Click OK. This is the minimum information FrontPage needs to properly display the Clock applet. Figure 19-8 shows the page in FrontPage Page view. FrontPage displays a graphic placeholder for the applet.

14. Save your page, and then open it in your browser. Figure 19-9 shows the page in Netscape Navigator.

    Most applets accept additional parameters that control their appearance and/or functionality. The parameters the Clock applet accepts are listed in Table 19-2. In the remainder of this exercise, you will use the Java Applet Properties dialog box to set some of these parameters. The applet will use default values for any parameters that are not specifically set.

15. In FrontPage Page view, right-click the Clock applet and choose Java Applet Properties.

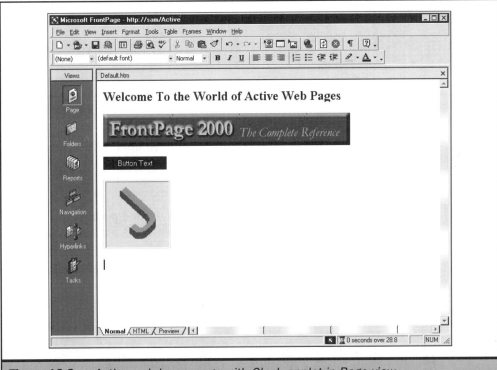

Figure 19-8. *Active web home page with Clock applet in Page view*

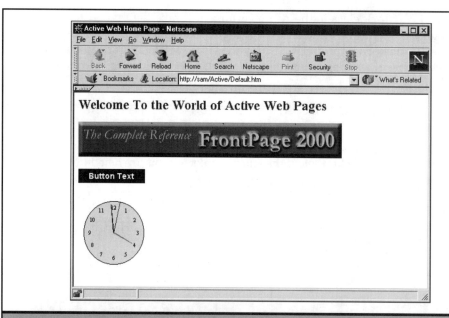

Figure 19-9. *Active web home page with Clock applet*

Parameter	Description
bgcolor	Is the RGB background color, in hexadecimal, for the applet.
border	Is the width in pixels of the space around the clock's face.
ccolor	Is the RGB color, in hexadecimal, of the clock's face.
cfont	Is a text string containing the font, style, and point size of the numbers on the clock's face. Each element is separated by the | character.
delay	Is the refresh rate in milliseconds for the applet.
hhcolor	Is the hour hand RGB color, in hexadecimal.
link	Is an optional URL if the clock is to be a hyperlink.

Table 19-2. *Clock Applet Parameters*

Parameter	Description
mhcolor	Is the minute hand RGB color, in hexadecimal.
ncolor	Is the RGB color of the numbers, in hexadecimal.
nradius	Is the radius, in pixels, where the numbers will be drawn.
shcolor	Is the second hand RGB color, in hexadecimal.

Table 19-2.   *Clock Applet Parameters* (continued)

16. In the Java Applet Properties dialog box, click Add. This displays the Set Attribute Value dialog box shown next. You will enter the name of the parameter in the Name text box and a value for the parameter in the Value text box. The Specify Value check box should be selected.

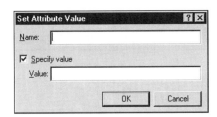

17. Type **bgcolor** in the Name text box; then type **0000FF** in the Value text box. This will give the clock a blue background. Click OK.

18. Click Add; then type **cfont** in the Name text box and **Arial | Bold | 18** (there are no spaces in this text) in the Value text box. The vertical bar (the "pipe" character) is entered by pressing SHIFT+\. Click OK.

19. Type **150** in both the Width and Height text boxes and click OK.

20. Save your work and then reload your Active web home page in your browser. Figure 19-10 shows the page in Netscape Navigator.

For any applets you have that are compiled (you have a file with a .CLASS extension), this is basically all you need to do to add a Java applet to your FrontPage webs. The next step is understanding how Java applets are created. First, you need to download and install some Java development tools.

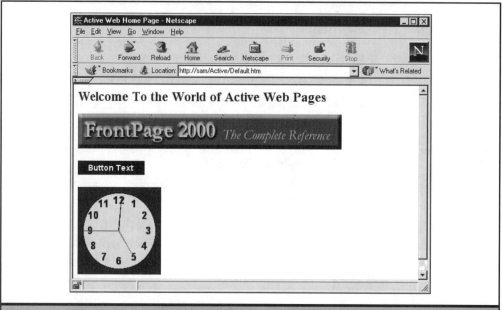

Figure 19-10.   *Active web home page with Clock applet*

The Sun Java Development Kit

Java applets are often distributed as source code that must be compiled before it can be used in your webs. This provides an additional measure of security. Rather than downloading an executable applet that may or may not perform as advertised, you download a text file that is compiled into the executable. This helps ensure that the applet will do what it's advertised to do and nothing more. There are several sources for Java toolkits. The Java Development Kit (JDK), available from Sun Microsystems' web site (**http://java.sun.com/products/OV_jdkProduct.html**), is the one you will use in the following sections. It contains the source code for a number of sample applets as well as a Java compiler for converting the Java source code into Java applets that can be included in your webs. Another useful toolkit is the Microsoft Software Development Kit (SDK) for Java (**http://www.microsoft.com/java/sdk**). If you plan on really working with Java, you should download both toolkits. They contain extensive documentation that will make working with Java much easier.

*There are also a growing number of tools, such as Microsoft's Visual J++, that simplify the process of creating Java applets. If you decide to write your own applets, you should investigate these products. Probably the best place to start looking is Sun's Java Solutions Guide at **http://java.sun.com/solutions/**.*

All the basic tools you need for working with Java code are included with Sun's Java Development Kit (JDK). The JDK includes example Java applets, both as source code and compiled applets, one of which you will use in the exercises in the following sections. The documentation files are in HTML format, and the demos also include HTML pages. Begin your exploration of Java by downloading the Java Development Kit.

Note

The JDK is a hefty download (just over 20MB for the JDK and another 16MB for the documentation), but the tools provided are necessary if you really want to work with Java. A full installation of the JDK will require about 65MB of hard drive space without the documentation.

1. In your web browser, go to Sun's Java Development Kit home page at **http://java.sun.com/products/jdk/1.2/**.

2. Scroll down the page until you see the hyperlink for downloading the JDK. At the time this was written, the link text was **JDK 1.2 Windows95/98/NT Production Release**. Click this hyperlink. This will load the first page of the download, shown in Figure 19-11, where you can choose to download the JDK as a single large file or several smaller files.

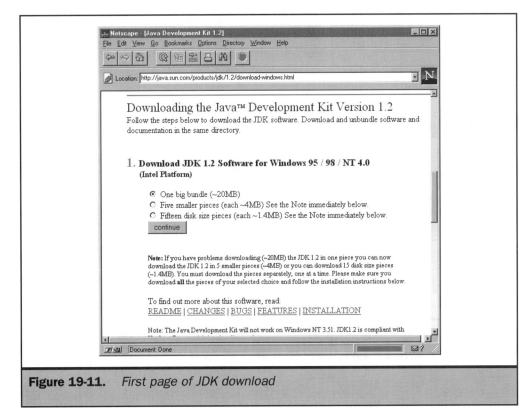

Figure 19-11. *First page of JDK download*

Note *You can choose to download the JDK as a single download or in several smaller ones. Choose whichever is easier for you. If you download the JDK as several smaller files, you will need to concatenate them into a single file after download. Instructions for concatenating the files are included on the Download page.*

3. Select how you want to download the files and then click Continue. This will load the second page for the download, which contains the Sun JDK license agreement, shown in Figure 19-12.

4. After reading the license agreement, click Accept if you accept the terms of the agreement. This will take you to the final page where you can choose to download the JDK using either the FTP or HTTP protocol. Using FTP will probably be somewhat faster, but you may have difficulties if you are behind a firewall. In that case, use the HTTP protocol. This page also contains the installation instructions for the JDK so you may want to print it for reference.

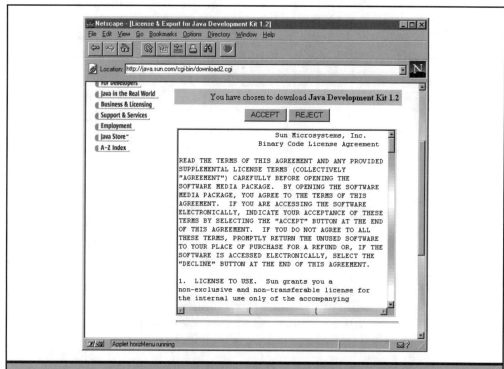

Figure 19-12. *Second page of JDK download*

5. You will be prompted for a location to save the JDK to. This should be your Temp or a work folder. Select the location to save the file(s) and click OK.

Note *At the time this was written (the beginning of 1999), the most recent release of Sun's JDK was version 1.2. By the time you read this, there may be a more recent version. If so, the filenames will have changed.*

6. Next download the documentation. The link to the documentation download page is located by scrolling down the JDK Download page in your browser until you see a series of hyperlinks under the heading "The installation procedure has the following steps:" Click number 8, *Where Do I Go From Here.*

7. You should then see a text hyperlink in the first paragraph, "JDK docs download page." Click this hyperlink. This opens the JDK 1.2 Documentation page.

8. Scroll down the page until you see a drop-down list box that displays Select A Download Package. Select *ZIP File (For Windows Or Non-Solaris) – JDK 1.2 Docs* and click Continue.

Note *You can choose to download the file as a single download or in several smaller ones. Choose whichever is easier for you. If you download the documentation as several smaller files, you will need to concatenate them into a single file after download. Instructions for concatenating the files are included on the Download page.*

9. A page similar to the JDK download page will be displayed. Click either FTP Download or HTTP Download. When prompted, select the same folder you saved the JDK to for the documentation download.

Note *The JDK file is self-extracting, but the documentation files require a compression utility, such as WinZip from Nico Mak Computing, Inc.*

10. After the files are downloaded, open the folder in Windows Explorer where you saved the JDK program file (Jdk12-win32.exe) and double-click it. A dialog box will be displayed indicating the files are being unpacked; then the installation program will start.

11. When the setup Welcome dialog box is displayed, click Next. The next dialog box will display the license agreement, as shown next.

WORKING BEHIND
THE SCENES

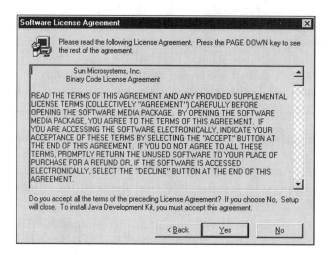

12. After reading the license agreement (use the vertical scroll bar or PAGE DOWN to see more of it), click on Yes if you agree to the terms. (If you do not agree, the software will not be installed.)

13. In the next window you can select the folder in which to install the JDK. Accept the default (C:\Jdk1.2) by clicking Next.

14. In the Select Components dialog box, shown here, select all the components and click Next. The JDK installation on your system will begin.

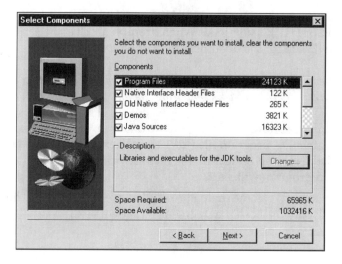

15. When the files are transferred, another Software License Agreement dialog box will be displayed. Click Yes after reading it.

16. The Choose Destination Location dialog box will be displayed. This sets the location of the Java Runtime Environment. Accept the default (C:\Program Files\JavaSoft\JRE\1.2) by clicking Next.

17. When the files are transferred, the Setup Complete dialog box will be displayed. Clear the Yes, I Want To View The Readme File check box and click Finish.

18. Open the Readme file in your browser by locating the file in Windows Explorer (C:\Jdk\1.2\Readme.html by default) and double-clicking it. The Readme file contains general information about the JDK and installation instructions. Review the file.

19. In the Windows Explorer, double-click on the documentation file (Jdk114doc.zip). If you have installed and associated an application for Zip-compressed files, the application will open.

20. Unzip the files to the Jdk1.2 folder. You must unzip the documentation files to the same folder structure as when they were originally compressed. In WinZip, you do this by selecting the Use Folder Names check box.

21. To save space on your hard drive, you can now delete the original compressed files in the temp folder you downloaded the JDK to. If you have the room, you may want to save the original compressed JDK and documentation files in case you need to reinstall them.

You now have the tools you need to compile Java applets from the source code files. In the next section you will use these tools to compile a sample applet included with the JDK.

Compiling Java Applets

While the Java Development Kit contains some precompiled applets as well as complete HTML pages that demonstrate them, knowing how to compile a Java applet from source code is a necessary skill for web designers who intend to use Java in their webs. Even if you never intend to write your own applets, you will probably still need to compile the applets you download from the Web, many of which are available only as Java source code. The process is relatively straightforward, but it does require using the MS-DOS interface included in Windows (commonly referred to as a "DOS window") and a basic knowledge of using MS-DOS command syntax. The following steps will take you through the process:

1. Create a temporary folder on your hard drive for the source code file. Name the folder **Javawork**.

2. Copy the TicTacToe.java file (C:\Jdk1.2\Demo\Applets\TicTacToe\ TicTacToe.java if you used the default folder structure) to the Javawork folder.

3. Open WordPad (Start menu, Programs, Accessories, WordPad), and then select Open from the File menu. In the Open dialog box, select All Documents (*.*) from the Files Of Type drop-down menu.

Note   *Notepad is not suitable for opening or editing the Java source code files included with the JDK. These files contain characters that do not display properly in Notepad.*

4. Open your Javawork folder from the Look In drop-down menu and then the file and folder list, and double-click TicTacToe.java. The TicTacToe.java source code file will be displayed as shown in Figure 19-13.

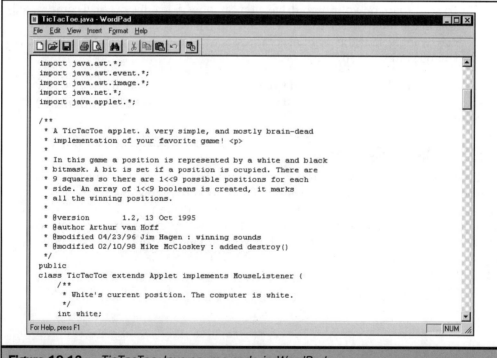

Figure 19-13.   *TicTacToe Java source code in WordPad*

The source code includes a number of comments that describe the function of each Java statement in the file. Comments are all the text between the /** and */ markers. For example, in the lines

```
/**
 * White's current position. The computer is white.
 */
int white;
```

the comment (White's current position...) explains that the Java statement int white; is an integer that represents the current grid position of white's move. The variable name, white, contains the integer value. This variable is used to pass the current position of white to other functions in the applet. It is an axiom of programming that one of the best ways to learn a new programming language is to study other people's code. This is equally true of Java. If you are familiar with programming languages such as C++, the Java code will look familiar to you.

5. Close WordPad without changing the file.

6. Open a DOS window by opening the Start menu, pointing to Programs, and then clicking MS-DOS Prompt.

7. At the C:\WINDOWS> prompt in the DOS window, type **cd C:\Javawork** (or use the path where you created the Javawork directory), as shown here, and then press ENTER. CD is the DOS command for Change Directory. This will make the Javawork directory the current directory, and the prompt will read "C:\Javawork>".

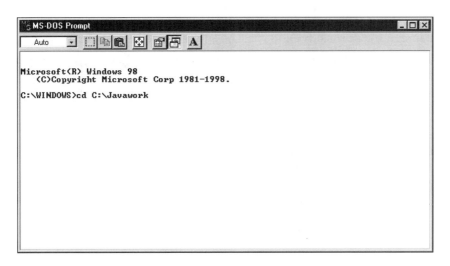

8. Type **dir** and then press ENTER. This is the command to display the contents of the current directory. Your DOS window should display a listing similar to this:

```
MS-DOS Prompt                                                    _ □ ✕
Auto        ▼  ▢ ▤ ▦  ▣  ▩▤  A

Microsoft(R) Windows 98
    (C)Copyright Microsoft Corp 1981-1998.

C:\WINDOWS>cd C:\Javawork

C:\JavaWork>dir

 Volume in drive C is SAM
 Volume Serial Number is 3A1A-12E4
 Directory of C:\JavaWork

.             <DIR>        02-02-99  8:15a .
..            <DIR>        02-02-99  8:15a ..
TICTAC~1 JAV       8,020   12-01-98  3:40p TicTacToe.java
         1 file(s)         8,020 bytes
         2 dir(s)   1,029,537,792 bytes free

C:\JavaWork>
```

Note   *The directory listing displays two names for each file. On the left is the DOS name of the file in 8.3 format, in this case TICTAC~1 JAV, and on the right, the long filename supported by Windows, TicTacToe.java.*

9. Compile the TicTacToe.java source file by typing **C:\Jdk1.2\bin\javac TicTacToe.java** at the C:\Javawork> prompt and pressing ENTER. The name of Sun's Java compiler is javac. The command you entered instructed it to convert the source file TicTacToe.java into the executable applet TicTacToe.class. Java names are case sensitive and must be entered exactly as shown.

10. When the C:\Javawork> prompt reappears in the DOS window, type **dir** and press ENTER. In the listing that is displayed you will see that there are now two files in the Javawork directory—the original source file and TicTacToe.class, the executable applet.

In the preceding steps you used the simplest form of the javac command to generate the applet. There are also a number of options you can use with javac to control the compiling or to generate messages. In the next step you will use the -verbose option to generate a list of all the steps the compiler is taking to generate the applet. This will overwrite the applet you just created.

11. At the C:\Javawork> prompt type **C:\Jdk1.2\bin\javac -verbose TicTacToe.java** and press ENTER. As each step is executed, the compile event and the time it takes to compile are displayed.

A complete listing of the options for the javac compiler can be found in the documentation web pages at *servername***/jdk1.2/ docs/tooldocs/win32/ javac.html**. You can open this page and find information about the other tools included with the JDK. You open the documentation home page (*servername***/jdk1.2/docs/index.html**) and click the Tool Docs hyperlink. This takes you to the JDK Tool Documentation index. Clicking Tool Documentation opens the JDK Tools page. Scroll down this page to the Basic Tools heading, shown in Figure 19-14, which contains a brief description of each tool and a hyperlink to the page where the tool is explained in detail.

12. Close the DOS window by typing **exit** at the C:\Javawork> prompt and pressing ENTER.

The final step in compiling a Java applet is to test it on a web page. Do that now with these instructions.

1. In FrontPage, open your Active web home page in Page view, if it isn't already open.

2. Create a new folder in your Active web with the name **TicTacToe**. Make sure the folder is selected.

3. Open the File menu and choose Import. In the Import dialog box, click Add File.

Figure 19-14.   *JDK Tools Basic Tools index in Internet Explorer*

4. In the Add File To Import List dialog box, select your Javawork folder in the Look In drop-down list. Select TicTacToe.class and click Open; then click OK.

5. With the TicTacToe folder still selected, open the File menu and choose Import. In the Import dialog box, click Add Folder.

6. In the Browse For Folder dialog box, select the folder in the JDK that contains the sound files the applet uses. The default path is C:\Jdk1.2\Demo\Applets\TicTacToe\Audio. Click OK.

7. Repeat step 6 to import the folder containing the graphic files the applet uses. The default path is C:\Jdk1.2\Demo\Applets\TicTacToe\Images. Click OK twice.

8. In Page view, place the cursor on the line below your Clock applet.

9. Open the Insert menu and choose Advanced | Java Applet.

10. In the Java Applet Properties dialog box, type **TicTacToe.class** in the Applet Source text box and **TicTacToe** in the Applet Base URL text box.

11. Type **150** in both the Width and Height text boxes, and then click OK.

12. Save your work. In Page view, your Active web home page should look similar to Figure 19-15.

Figure 19-15.   *Active web home page in Page view with TicTacToe applet added*

13. Open the page in your browser. Figure 19-16 shows the TicTacToe applet in Netscape Navigator.

14. Start the game by clicking in any empty cell. An "X" will be placed in that cell, and the applet will counter by placing an "O" in a cell that will block you, as shown here.

This has been only a brief trip through the world of Java. It is a powerful programming language that opens new doors for the web designer. Because Java is a true programming language, it also requires a comprehensive knowledge of the language and its capabilities to be used effectively. If you are a C++ programmer, the transition will be smooth. If Java is your first real programming language, you will

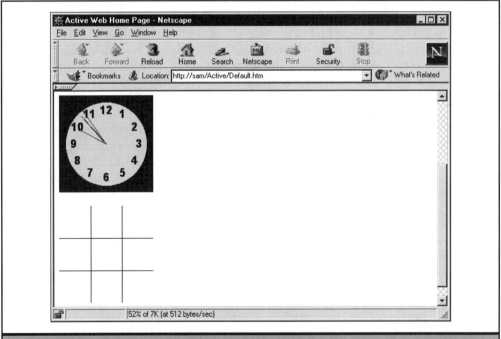

Figure 19-16.   *TicTacToe applet in Netscape Navigator*

have to devote a significant amount of time and energy to learning it. It is a language that will play an ever-increasing role in web design, so your time may be well spent. If you don't want to learn a programming language, you can find a growing number of precompiled Java applets on the Web. The information in this section has presented the basics you need to download and use applets you find on the Web.

In the next section you will learn about ActiveX, Microsoft's technology that is designed to offer even more advantages to the web designer than Java.

ActiveX

Java is a new technology. In a sense, its designers began with a clean sheet of paper. (An interesting personal history of Java is included *The Java Handbook* [Osborne/McGraw-Hill, 1996] by Patrick Naughton, one of the original team at Sun that created the language.) ActiveX is more evolutionary, having its roots in Microsoft's OLE (object linking and embedding) technology.

Note *By this point you already have experience using ActiveX controls on the Web. All the ASP components you've used in the previous chapters are ActiveX controls.*

OLE was developed as a method of sharing text and graphics, generally called objects, between applications on a computer. If an object was linked between documents, a pointer was created in the receiving document pointing to the object in the original document. When the original object was updated, the linked object was also updated. For example, you could link a spreadsheet to a word processing document. When the data in the spreadsheet changed, it would be reflected in the word processing document. When an object was linked, it actually existed only in the original document. The receiving document only contained a pointer to the original. When an object was embedded, an actual copy was placed in the receiving document.

This method, while it worked fine when both documents were on a single computer, had its shortcomings in a networked environment. This led Microsoft to develop new technologies, such as Component Object Model (COM), Distributed Component Object Model (DCOM), and OLE Control Extensions (OCX).

Essentially, ActiveX is object-oriented programming for the Web. In the section of this chapter on object-oriented programming, the concept of objects was introduced. An object was defined as a process that accepts information, processes it, and then outputs the result. ActiveX brings the same modular concept to a web page, with the addition that an object can also be a data file. This is a greatly simplified explanation of the technology, but it avoids turning this chapter into a programming handbook, rather than a guide for web designers who want to add the latest features to their FrontPage webs.

For those who do want a programming handbook for ActiveX, ActiveX from the Ground Up, by John Paul Mueller (Osborne/McGraw-Hill, 1997), is an excellent choice. It contains a thorough explanation of the evolution of ActiveX from OLE, as well as all you need to know to create your own ActiveX controls.

The ActiveX equivalent of a Java applet is an ActiveX control. Because ActiveX has evolved from OLE, ActiveX controls can be used with many different programming languages, including all the Microsoft programming and database languages. This means you can use the same control with your Access database as you do with your web page. This is also an area where ActiveX differs from Java.

ActiveX is a very useful technology, but it does have its drawbacks. In particular, it is a Windows-based technology. This leaves Mac and UNIX users out of the picture, at least for the present. If and when support is added for these platforms, the code will need to be compiled separately for each. This would lead to maintaining separate web pages for each operating system. Of course, Windows computers make up the majority of the market, and with corporate intranets, the operating system can be controlled. It also is less secure than Java, which is balanced by the fact it is potentially more powerful.

Note   *Neither Java nor ActiveX is totally secure. Creative programmers can almost always find a way to get around security safeguards. When implementing any web technology, you must use caution and pay attention to what is happening on your web site.*

These issues are not new to computing. At every stage of growth in the industry, the question of features versus compatibility has arisen. Often, as with ActiveX, compatibility has suffered in order to increase the usefulness of software. These are simply issues you need to consider before using ActiveX with your webs.

Since ActiveX controls are commonly written in Visual Basic, this section will not go into writing your own controls. Instead, you will use ActiveX controls included with FrontPage and readily available on the Web. Additional information about ActiveX and other Internet technologies can be found on the Microsoft Site Builder Network (**http://microsoft.com/sitebuilder/**).

The next section will take you right into using ActiveX with your FrontPage webs.

ActiveX and FrontPage

FrontPage comes with a number of ActiveX controls you can add to your webs, as you will see next. Your Active web home page should still be open in FrontPage.

1. In Page view, move the cursor to the line below your TicTacToe Java applet.

2. Open the Insert menu and choose Advanced | ActiveX Control. The Insert ActiveX Control dialog box, shown here, is opened.

This looks like quite a collection of ActiveX controls, but there are actually more.

3. Click Customize in the Insert ActiveX Control dialog box. The Customize ActiveX Control List dialog box shown next is opened.

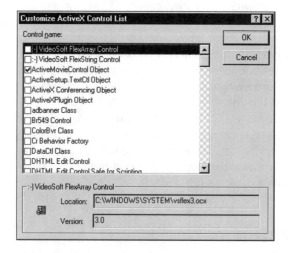

4. Click Cancel to close the Customize ActiveX Control List dialog box. In the Insert ActiveX Control dialog box, select Microsoft Office Spreadsheet 9.0 and

click OK. A functioning spreadsheet is placed on your page, as shown in Figure 19-17.

5. Save your page and then open it in Internet Explorer.

6. In Internet Explorer, scroll down until the ActiveX spreadsheet is visible. In cell A1, type **2**, and then press DOWN ARROW.

7. In cell A2, type **2** and press ENTER. Cell A3 should now be selected.

8. Click the AutoSum button on the spreadsheet's toolbar and then press ENTER. Cell A3 now contains the formula =Sum(A1:A2) and displays the total of the numbers in those cells, as shown in Figure 19-18.

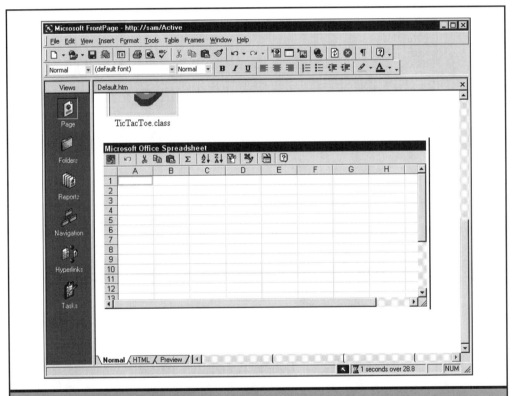

Figure 19-17.   *Microsoft Office Spreadsheet 9.0 ActiveX control in FrontPage*

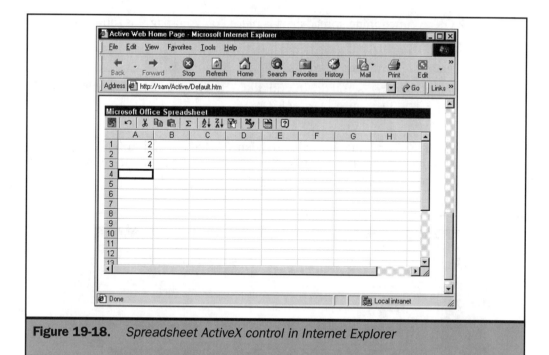

Figure 19-18. *Spreadsheet ActiveX control in Internet Explorer*

9. In FrontPage Page view, right-click the spreadsheet ActiveX control in an area outside of the cell matrix and select ActiveX Control Properties. This opens the ActiveX Control Properties dialog box, shown here.

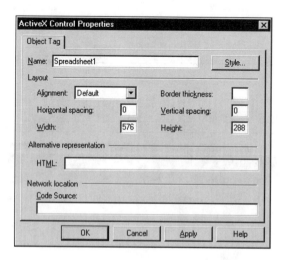

The options available in the ActiveX Control Properties dialog box will depend on the specific ActiveX control, though the choices shown here will be available for most controls.

10. In the HTML Alternative Representation text box, type **<H1>This browser doesn't support ActiveX.</H1>** and click OK.

11. Save your page and then open it in Netscape Navigator, as shown in Figure 19-19.

The preceding example illustrates one of the problems with ActiveX controls—Netscape Navigator doesn't support them without a separate plug-in. Since Netscape still holds a large share of the browser market, this currently makes using ActiveX controls in your webs a risky business. However, this situation will change as support for ActiveX grows. On an intranet, if you can control the browsers used, this limitation doesn't apply.

The Microsoft Office Spreadsheet ActiveX control is one of a number of ActiveX controls that are included with FrontPage. All the ActiveX controls installed on your system (both those included with FrontPage and those you download and install separately) are displayed in the Customize ActiveX Control List dialog box. The controls that are selected in the Customize ActiveX Control List dialog box are also available in the Insert ActiveX Control dialog box.

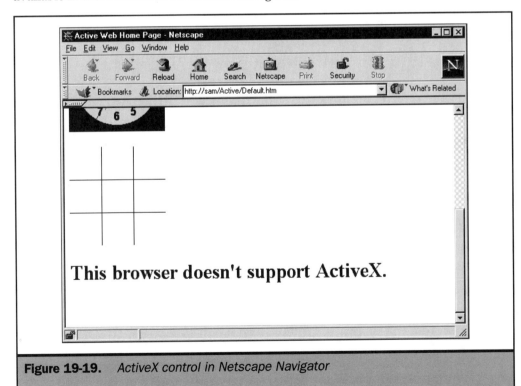

Figure 19-19.   *ActiveX control in Netscape Navigator*

WORKING BEHIND
THE SCENES

Each of the technologies covered in this chapter could easily fill a book of its own, and in fact each does. The purpose here was to give you an overview of them so that you could make an informed decision about which technologies you want to add to your own webs. Both Java applets and ActiveX controls require programming that is not for the faint of heart. If you already program in C++, the step up to these new languages will not be difficult. The Sun (**http://www.sun.com**), Netscape (**http://home.netscape.com**), and Microsoft (**http://www.microsoft.com**) web sites all have a variety of programming tools, documentation, and examples to get you started.

The coming months will see these technologies added to a growing number of web sites, as well as advances in the technologies themselves. If you want your webs to stand out in the crowd, these tools are part of your future.

The
Complete
Reference

FrontPage
2000

Part IV

Extending Your Web Site

The Complete Reference

FrontPage 2000

Chapter 20

Adding Multimedia to Your Webs

By Gordon Coale, "The WebGuy™," Producer of TestingTesting

729

The World Wide Web started off silent and motionless. Those days are over. Audio is becoming commonplace, and video and sophisticated animation are establishing a strong foothold. In webs you'll see links to WAV audio files, and AVI and QuickTime (MOV) video files. There are also links to streaming audio and video files like RealNetworks' (**http://www.real.com**) RealAudio and RealVideo and Microsoft's (**http://www.microsoft.com**) NetShow. Animation has also moved beyond the capabilities of animated GIFs with the introduction of Macromedia's (**http://www.macromedia.com**) Flash technology as well as the new dynamic HTML. The possibilities are exploding for web developers. Audio, video, and animation capabilities are changing very quickly. RealNetworks, Microsoft, and Macromedia are the major players, but there are a lot of others fighting for a piece of this pie.

Audio and video files used to have to be completely downloaded before they could be played. Because they are very large files, the download time is much longer than the playing time. This put audio and video in the category of cool but not very useful. RealNetworks changed that in 1995 when they released the first streaming audio player. With streaming audio you don't have to download the entire file to listen to it. About 10 seconds of the file downloads and then it starts playing. This broke the time barrier. Now there was no limit to the length of the file being played. Streaming audio not only allows longer pieces to be put up on the web, but it also allows live webcasting. Pretty soon radio stations began broadcasting on the web 24 hours a day with streaming audio. There are also live concerts appearing on the web. In early 1997 RealNetworks launched RealVideo, which brought streaming video to the web on a large scale. Microsoft was not far behind with streaming audio and video using their NetShow product.

Video still has its limitations on the web because of insufficient bandwidth. Streaming video over a 28.8 modem is pretty limited. The image is small and not full-motion video. Actually it is pretty amazing how good it is over slower modems, but it is still in the cool but not very useful category. The availability of larger bandwidth connections will change this. As ISDN (integrated services digital network), cable modems, and DSL (digital subscriber line) technology come online there should be an explosion of streaming video. Intranets generally are not so bandwidth limited and can make good use of this technology today.

Creating video content is not for the faint of heart or those with small pocketbooks. The equipment is more expensive than the equipment for recording sound. The software to edit video is also more expensive, and there are many more elements to consider in editing and creating video. You have all the elements of audio to deal with plus the more complex visuals. There is more than can be covered in a chapter, so this chapter will focus on audio.

Technology like Macromedia's Flash can provide some very sophisticated animations, but animation is also a very specialized field so it will not be covered in this chapter. If you want to do simple animations, look at using animated GIFs as described in Chapter 5 or dynamic HTML as described in Chapter 11.

Audio can be done with equipment that most people already have. A computer with a sound card, a CD player, a tape recorder, and/or a microphone allow you to put audio files on your web: streaming and nonstreaming, live, or on demand. Whether it is a baby's first cry or a live musical performance from your living room, you can put those sounds on the web for your friends, family, and the world to hear.

The rest of this chapter will tell you how to capture sound and use both nonstreaming and streaming files to deliver that sound in your web applications.

Capturing the Sound

The first step is to capture the sound in a digital format on your computer—to record it digitally through your sound card and create a WAV file that can be edited and saved. This includes identifying the source, connecting the source to your computer, and then actually doing the recording.

 RealAudio's new encoder, RealProducer G2, has the capability to encode a RealAudio file directly from a sound source without first producing a WAV file. Producing the WAV file first, though, allows you to edit the WAV file to delete any silent spots in the beginning and end of the selection, as well as make any other desired changes to the file.

The Sound Source

The source can be any playback device such as a CD player, tape recorder, MIDI player, or phonograph. The source could also be live from a microphone or several microphones using a mixing device. If you can get an audio signal to your sound card, you can digitally record it on your computer.

Connect the Sound Source to the Sound Card

With a sound source and a sound card, the question is, how do you connect them? There are two things to consider: the connectors and where to put them.

Connectors

Anyone who has set up a stereo has dealt with this. There are all those wires coming out of the back that go to speakers and to the tape deck or CD player. At the end of the wires are the connectors. Life would be simple if there was only one connector, but life is not simple. The wires coming out of your stereo generally do not have the connector that will fit into your sound card.

There are two types of connectors you are dealing with: the 1/8" mini-plug and the RCA plug, which are shown on the next page.

1/8" mini-plug   RCA plug

"Jacks" are female and are in the hardware being connected. "Plugs" are male and are on the ends of the cables being plugged in.

A stereo commonly has an RCA jack, which needs the corresponding RCA plug for connecting, and your sound card uses a 1/8" mini-jack, which needs a 1/8" mini-plug. If you have a source that uses an RCA jack, you will need to get an adapter. Radio Shack is an excellent place to get these adapters, or you can get a cable with a pair of RCA plugs on one end and a 1/8" stereo mini-plug on the other end.

Sometimes you may run into another type of connector. If you do, go back to Radio Shack because they have adapters and combinations that will fit most requirements.

Where to Put the Connector

Where you plug in the sound source connector is very important. You always want to connect a line-out to a line-in. Never, never, use a speaker output or the headphone output. These are amplified signals that are difficult to control and could damage your sound card. The line-out is not amplified. You connect the line-out on your sound source (tape deck, CD player, or mixer) to a line-in on your sound card.

It helps to visualize where the signal is going. Let's use the stereo receiver/amplifier connected to a tape deck as an example. When you put a tape into the tape deck and play it, the signal is going from the tape deck to the receiver/amplifier. It is going from the line-out on the tape deck to the line-in on the receiver/amplifier. When you record something, it is going from the line-out on the receiver/amplifier back to the line-in on the tape deck.

Some stereo manufacturers confuse the issue by using Play and Record designations. There you plug Play to Play and Record to Record. Here the Play on the tape deck is the line-out and the Play on the receiver/amplifier is the line-in. This gets confusing. Fortunately, if you connect them wrong, nothing will be hurt. You just won't get any sound. If this happens, just switch them around.

So, if your are recording from a tape recorder or stereo, you go from the line-out to the line-in on your sound card. This may be the most difficult part of this process because you will have to crawl behind your computer, find the jacks on your sound card, and decipher the miniscule hieroglyphics to tell where to plug it in.

Check the documentation that came with your sound card and see if you can find a schematic showing the positions of the plugs. This little bit of research may save you a lot of frustration among the dust balls behind your machine.

Record the Sound Digitally

Now that your source is attached to the sound card, you are ready to create a digital recording. There are two elements used in recording: a mixer and a digital audio editor. A mixer adjusts the incoming audio levels from several sources, and a digital audio editor edits and then creates the digital file. These elements are usually programs, which come with your sound card. How much capability they have can vary. The more expensive sound cards have programs with quite a few controls, while the less expensive cards have fewer controls. There are also some very good digital audio editors available for a reasonable price on the web. Cool Edit 96 (**http://www.syntrillium.com**) is an excellent tool for a good price. You can also get Cool Edit 96, and other audio tools, at RealNetworks' store (**http://www.realstore.com**).

Mixer

A *mixer* adjusts the level of the sound going into the sound card—the input volume. If the sound level is too high, it will be distorted. If it is too low, it will be hard to hear. A mixer lets you adjust it to the right level. A mixer can be an external hardware soundboard or a software program that comes with your sound card. Here you can see the mixer controls that come with the Sound Blaster AWE 64 Gold card:

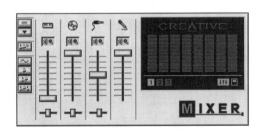

The vertical slider bars control the volume of the sound coming into the sound card. Moving the slider bar up increases the volume of the audio signal, and moving it down decreases the volume. In the illustration above, the first slider is all the way down and off. The second and fourth sliders are all the way up at full volume, and the third slider is part way down for partial volume.

Digital Audio Editor

A *digital audio editor* edits and records sound. The example used here is the digital audio editor that comes with the Sound Blaster AWE 64 Gold card. Different digital audio editors work fundamentally the same. The steps to get a finished audio (WAV) file are as follows:

1. Set the recording levels.
2. Select the recording settings.
3. Record the sound.
4. Edit the sound.
5. Save the sound.

SET THE RECORDING LEVELS   The first steps are to view the recording levels using the digital audio editor and to use the mixer to set the levels. Figure 20-1 shows the digital audio editor ready to record with the mixer also showing. Start playing what you are going to record. The left and right channel bars show the recording level. You want to check it with a loud section of what you are recording. The bars move from right to left indicating the level. When the bar is all the way to the right, you are starting to get distortion or clipping. You want it to just fill up the bar at the loudest sections of the piece you are recording. Slide the appropriate slider up and down until the levels look the way you want them. Other digital audio editors may look a little different, but they use the same principles.

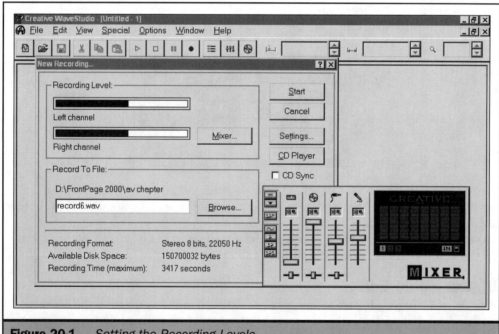

Figure 20-1.   *Setting the Recording Levels*

SELECT THE RECORDING SETTINGS AND DOING THE RECORDING   There are several recording settings that need to be set. Here are the common settings that are available:

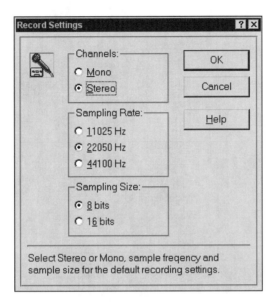

You can set to record in mono or stereo. Mono will give you smaller files, but you lose the stereo effect. You can set the sampling rate. A "sample" is a digital snapshot. When these samples are close together in time, they produce a smooth sound. CD quality is done at 44,100 HZ (hertz or cycles per second). The higher the sampling rate, the bigger the file. You also have a choice of sampling size, either 8 bit or 16 bit. Again, the bigger the sampling size, the bigger the file. It also depends on if you are doing mono or stereo. A 44,100 HZ sampling rate at 8 bits for a mono recording will give you the same quality as a 44,100 HZ sampling rate at 16 bits for stereo.

If your final product is going to be a WAV file that the user will download, then you might consider making the file as small as possible while still giving you the quality you want. If you are going to compress the file for RealAudio, or any other compression, you want the best quality file you can get.

With all the settings made, start the recording and, when the piece to be recorded is finished, stop the recording.

EDITING SOUND   Figure 20-2 shows what the recorded sound looks like in both channels. If this were mono, there would only be one channel showing. The beginning shows just a thin line. This indicates that no audio was recorded. As the line expands, there is audio. The thickness of the line indicates how loud it is. When the thickness fills the frame, there is maximum volume. Where you see the sound is at the maximum level for a while creating a flat top, that is where you are getting distortion or clipping.

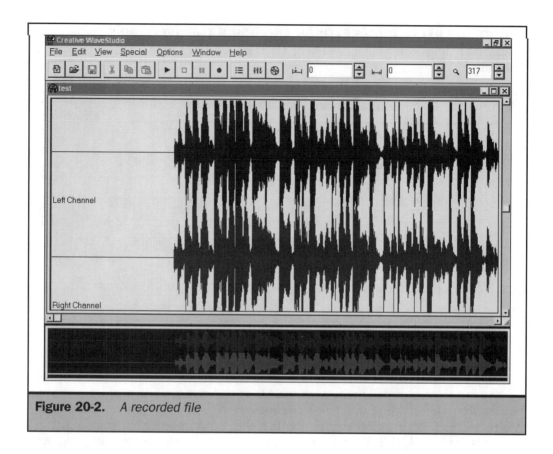

Figure 20-2.   *A recorded file*

A little bit of clipping might be all right, but listen to those sections carefully. You may have to record again with the recording levels down a little. You can play the digital recording and listen to it with the controls in the digital audio editor.

The editor provides a lot of functions for editing an audio file. Selecting a point of time or a section of time is done visually. Figure 20-3 shows a point of time selected. Just place the mouse pointer where you want and click. A vertical line appears that shows the point of time selected. This is useful if you want to insert something at that point.

To select a section of time, drag the mouse across it to indicate the selection you want. For example, you can select the beginning section for deletion. Use the Delete or Cut command to delete the section that is selected.

Copying and pasting is very similar. To copy and paste, you select the section of the audio you want to copy, press CTRL+C to copy, select a point where you want to insert it, and press CTRL-V to paste. In more elaborate digital audio editors you have a lot of control over the sound. But the above example shows the basic steps to edit your audio file.

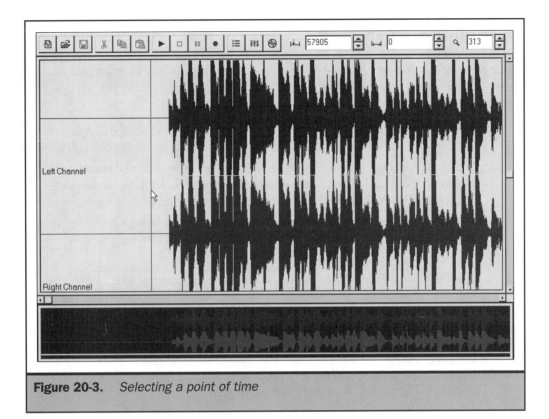

Figure 20-3. *Selecting a point of time*

SAVING THE SOUND   When you have the audio file the way you want it, give it a name and save it as a WAV file.

Using Nonstreaming Audio Files

Nonstreaming audio or WAV files should be used with caution. WAV files can be very large. A one-minute WAV file recorded at 44,100 HZ, 16-bit stereo, will be over 10MB. If you are going to put a WAV file in a web, try to keep the size down by making it very short or by using lower-quality recording settings.

Another option is using Motion Pictures Experts Group (MPEG) Layer-3 (MP3) compression. *MP3* is a new audio compression that will give you near-CD quality while compressing the WAV file to about one-tenth its original size.

Using Standard WAV Files

When you want to link to a WAV file, you need to import the file into your web and create a hyperlink to it on your web page. This is done in the same way you would create a hyperlink to any other object or page. Here are the steps to do that using a 60-second segment from "Chetzemoka Rain" by David Michael:

1. With FrontPage loaded and the page on which you want the audio file open in Page view, open the File menu and click Import. The Import dialog box will open.

2. Click Add File. Open the \Book\Chap20\ folder on the CD that comes with this book, and double-click Chetzemoka Rain.wav. Click OK in the Import dialog box. The WAV file will be imported into your web.

3. On your web page, select the word, phrase, or picture to which you want to attach a hyperlink to the WAV file, and click Hyperlink on the toolbar.

4. Double-click Chetzemoka Rain.wav and save your page.

5. View the page in FrontPage's Preview mode and select the link to the WAV file. Your default audio player will load and play the audio clip as shown in Figure 20-4.

 ("Chetzemoka Rain" is composed and copyrighted 1993 by David Michael and is played by David Michael and Randy Mead. It is taken from their CD Keystone Passage. You can reach David Michael through Purnima Productions, P.O. Box 317, Port Townsend, WA 98368, 800-646-6523, 360-379-9732, or http://www.olypen.com/bbc/Purnima/ purnimamain.htm. The piece is used with his permission).

 By importing the WAV file, it becomes part of the web and will be uploaded when you publish the web. If you use an FTP program to upload your files, remember to upload the WAV file, too.

Compressing the WAV File with MP3

While MP3 is a relatively new format, its usage is increasing rapidly because of the quality of its compression. The downside is that listening to an MP3 file requires downloading an MP3 player. This has not stopped it from becoming very popular. The web site MP3.com (**http://www.mp3.com**) has links to several MP3 players that are free. Many bands are using it for promotional purposes because they can provide a CD quality song at a reasonable size. These files are still relatively large. The Band released a three-minute and 56-second song as an MP3 file that came out to 3.61MB. While most of the bands using MP3 are unknown, some larger recording labels are starting to use the format. MP3.com is an excellent site to download copies of many of the songs that have been saved in MP3 format.

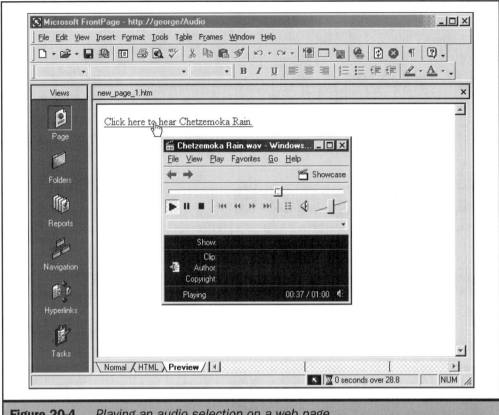

Figure 20-4.   *Playing an audio selection on a web page*

Note   *It is also easy to copy music from CDs that are copyrighted. This is illegal. Always be sure the material doesn't belong to someone else, or that you have the owner's permission to use or copy it.*

Most encoders are focused on recording from CDs and are called "rippers." When searching for an encoder, look for one that encodes WAV files. MP3.com lists a number of encoders. They are usually shareware or demoware, and you will need to eventually purchase them. One of the more interesting encoders is BladeEnc (**http://home.swipnet.se /~w-82625/).** This is not a pretty-looking program, but it is small, 221KB, and works in a very interesting way. You go into Windows Explorer, or My Computer, and then to the folder that has the BladeEnc program. Then simply drag the WAV you want to encode onto the BladeEnc program, and a DOS window appears that gives you the progress of the encoding. When it is complete, press ENTER to exit and your MP3 file is on your desktop. It is also freeware; there is no charge for it.

When you have an MP3 file you want in a web, you need to import it and create a hyperlink to it on your page as you did above with a WAV file.

If you put an MP3 audio file on your web, you are assuming that your web's users all have an MP3 player, which in most instances is not a good assumption. At the very least you need to have a link to MP3.com where users can download a player.

Using Streaming Audio Files

With streaming audio you don't need to be concerned about the length of the audio clip. The user will click on your link, the player will load, and after a short period the clip will start to play. The two major streaming audio technologies are RealNetworks RealAudio and Microsoft's NetShow. The RealAudio tools are more developed, and about 85 percent of the streaming audio on the Web is RealAudio. As a result, this chapter focuses on creating streaming audio with RealAudio.

How RealAudio Works

Before you get into the nuts and bolts of doing RealAudio, it helps to understand how the system works. Following a system description, there will be step-by-step instructions on how to implement streaming RealAudio in your own web. This section describes the primary components and how they work together.

Components of a RealAudio System

The RealAudio system is a client/server system. The RealServer provides the content, the RealAudio file, over a network (the Internet or an intranet), and it is then played by a RealPlayer.

REALPLAYER The RealPlayer G2 is the latest client that enables listening to the RealAudio files. The following illustration shows the RealPlayerG2.

There are two players: a free one with limited controls, and the RealPlayer Plus G2 that RealNetworks charges for and that has additional controls. The controls at the top, on both players, let you pause, stop, and move to any spot in the RealAudio file. Below the top controls on the Player Plus are preset buttons for RealAudio and RealVideo. The bottom area gives information about the RealAudio being played and is on both players.

You can download the players from the RealNetworks web site (**http://www.real.com**). The RealPlayer G2 is free, and the RealPlayer Plus G2 is currently $29.99.

Note   *Other players such as Microsoft's Media Player will also play RealAudio files.*

REALAUDIO ENCODER   The encoder is the program that creates the RealAudio file from a digitized audio file or a live audio signal. RealNetworks has two versions of the encoder, which they now call RealProducer G2 and RealProducer Plus G2. They are available from the RealNetworks web site (**http://www.real.com**).

RealProducer G2 is free and can be used for creating RealAudio files from recorded and real-time sources. RealProducer Plus G2 is required for creating live streams and has other advanced capabilities. The current price for the RealProducer Plus G2 is $149.95.

Both RealProducer G2 and RealProducer Plus G2 can also be used for encoding video.

REALSERVER   The RealServer G2 is the program that delivers the RealAudio files over the network. One RealServer can deliver many RealAudio files to many RealPlayers at the same time. Each file being delivered is referred to as a *stream*. RealNetworks has several RealServers with different prices and capabilities. The Basic Server is free and can serve 25 on-demand or live streams. The Basic Server Plus is $695 at this writing, includes extra tools, and can serve 40 streams. The Internet Solutions Servers are aimed at Internet service providers and currently start at around $5,000, for a 100-stream server, and go up from there. These servers are available from the RealNetworks web site (**http://www.real.com**). The prices and capabilities change regularly as the technology advances, so check the RealNetworks web site for the latest information.

While the Basic Server is free and the Basic Plus Server is reasonably priced, the limitation will be the bandwidth available to you. Even a dual ISDN line will only support around six to eight streams. If you will only need limited streaming, this may work, or you can go to an Internet service provider with a RealServer and large available bandwidth.

RealAudio Files and Metafiles

There are two file types that are commonly used in the RealAudio system: the RealAudio file (.ra) and the RealAudio metafile (.ram). With the introduction of the RealAudio G2 technology, RealAudio has added the capability to include pictures and animation with audio to create synchronized multimedia presentations. These more advanced capabilities also introduced new file types, but we will focus on the older and more common RA and RAM files.

REALAUDIO CLIP (.RA)   The RealAudio Clip is an audio file encoded in a RealAudio format. The file is created with the RealAudio encoder and delivered by the RealServer.

REALAUDIO METAFILE (.RAM)   If you linked directly to the RealAudio file, it would download like a WAV file. The RealAudio system uses a metafile that contains the location of the RealAudio file and is the file that is linked to from the web page.

How the RealAudio File Is Delivered

Figure 20-5 shows the RealAudio components and how they deliver the RealAudio file. The numbers in the figure match the following steps.

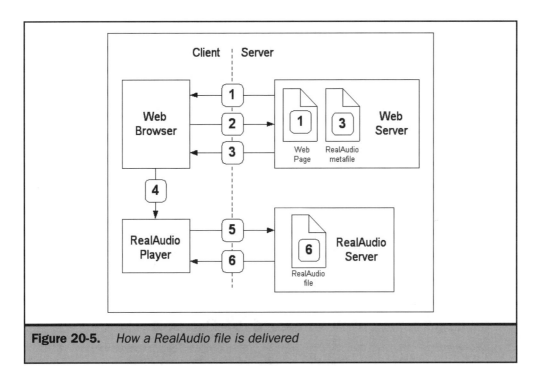

Figure 20-5.   *How a RealAudio file is delivered*

1. At the request of a web browser, the web server delivers a page to the browser that has a link to a RealAudio metafile.

2. If the user clicks the link, the web browser requests the metafile from the web server.

3. The web server delivers the metafile to the web browser. Based on the .ram file extension, the web server sets the MIME type (defined below under "Creating a RealAudio Metafile") of the file to *audio/x-pn-realaudio*.

4. Based on the MIME type, the web browser starts the RealPlayer as a helper application and passes it the metafile.

5. The RealPlayer reads the URL from the metafile and requests the RealAudio file from the RealServer.

6. The RealServer begins streaming the requested RealAudio file to the RealPlayer.

Note   *The RealPlayer does not require a web browser to function. The user can enter the URL of a .ra or .ram file directly into the RealPlayer, or use the Preset or Scan buttons on the RealPlayer Plus.*

Creating a RealAudio File

The first step in using RealAudio is to create the RealAudio file. This is for on-demand and not live streams, which will be covered shortly. RealAudio files are created with an encoder that RealAudio calls RealProducer G2, shown in Figure 20-6. The following sections will focus on the different parts of the encoder and how they are used to produce a RealAudio file for on-demand streaming.

Setting Up the RealProducer

Begin setting up the RealProducer by loading it, opening the File menu, and choosing New Session. Figure 20-7 shows the New Session dialog box that is used to define the input source and the output.

The New Session dialog box Input Source side allows you to select either Media Device or File. If you select Media Device, you can create a RealAudio file or do a live stream. If you select File, you only have the option of creating a RealMedia file. Once you have selected or entered the filename in the Input Source side of the New Session

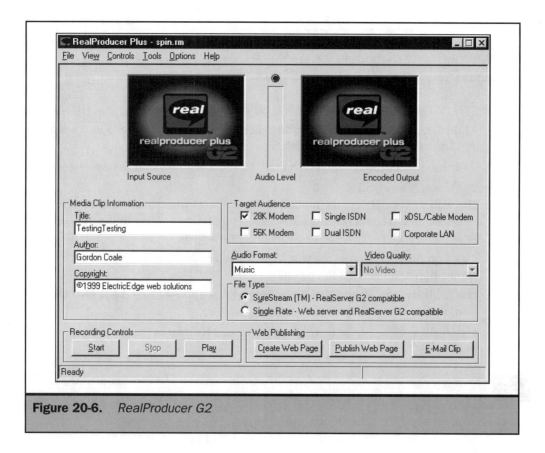

Figure 20-6.   *RealProducer G2*

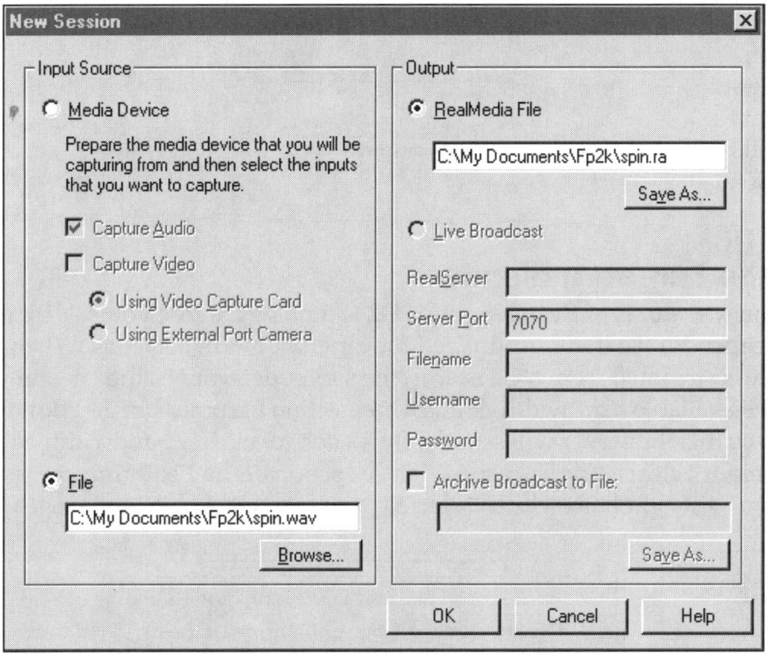

New Session ▣

┌─ Input Source ──────────────────────┐   ┌─ Output ──────────────────────┐

○ Media Device

Prepare the media device that you will be
capturing from and then select the inputs
that you want to capture.

☑ Capture Audio

☐ Capture Video

    ◉ Using Video Capture Card

    ○ Using External Port Camera

◉ File

`C:\My Documents\Fp2k\spin.wav`

Browse...

◉ RealMedia File

`C:\My Documents\Fp2k\spin.ra`

Save As...

○ Live Broadcast

RealServer [　　　　　　　　]

Server Port [7070]

Filename [　　　　　　　　]

Username [　　　　　　　　]

Password [　　　　　　　　]

☐ Archive Broadcast to File:

[　　　　　　　　]

Save As...

OK   Cancel   Help

Figure 20-7. *The New Session dialog box*

dialog box, you then enter the filename for the RealAudio file in the RealMedia section
of the Output side of the dialog box with a .ra file extension.

*The Output side of the dialog box also has the option of Live Broadcast. The Live
Broadcast section of the dialog box will be covered in the section on live RealAudio.*

You could start encoding at this point, but there are some other functions you can
set and information you can enter in RealProducer G2.

Fill Out the Media Clip Information

The Media Clip Information area of the RealProducer G2, shown in the following
illustration, allows you to enter the Title, Author, and Copyright information, which is
displayed in the RealAudio Player when the RealAudio file is played. This is how
ownership and copyright information is recorded in the RealAudio file.

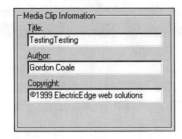

Select the Target Audience

One of the new features of RealNetwork's G2 technology is that you can create an encoded RealAudio file that is optimized for different modem speeds. When this encoded file is streamed from a G2 server, the server determines the encoding to use based on the available bandwidth. If a fast connection becomes bogged down because of network traffic, the server will seamlessly switch to a lower bandwidth encoding until the network clears. The Target Audience section of the RealProducer, as shown here, has four different bandwidths selected. You can select up to six.

Select the Audio Format

The next step is to select the type of compression or *codec* in the Audio Format area of the encoder shown here:

 Codec is short for code-decode. Each type of compression is referred to as a codec.

When you open the Audio Format drop-down box, you get the following selection:

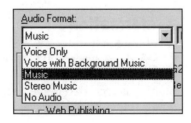

This is an indirect way to select the codecs by the type of sound being encoded. Each of these selections has codecs assigned to it. These can be changed by opening the Options menu and choosing Target Audience Settings | For Audio Clips. The Target Audience Settings-Audio Clips dialog box shown in Figure 20-8 is used to assign codecs to each selection.

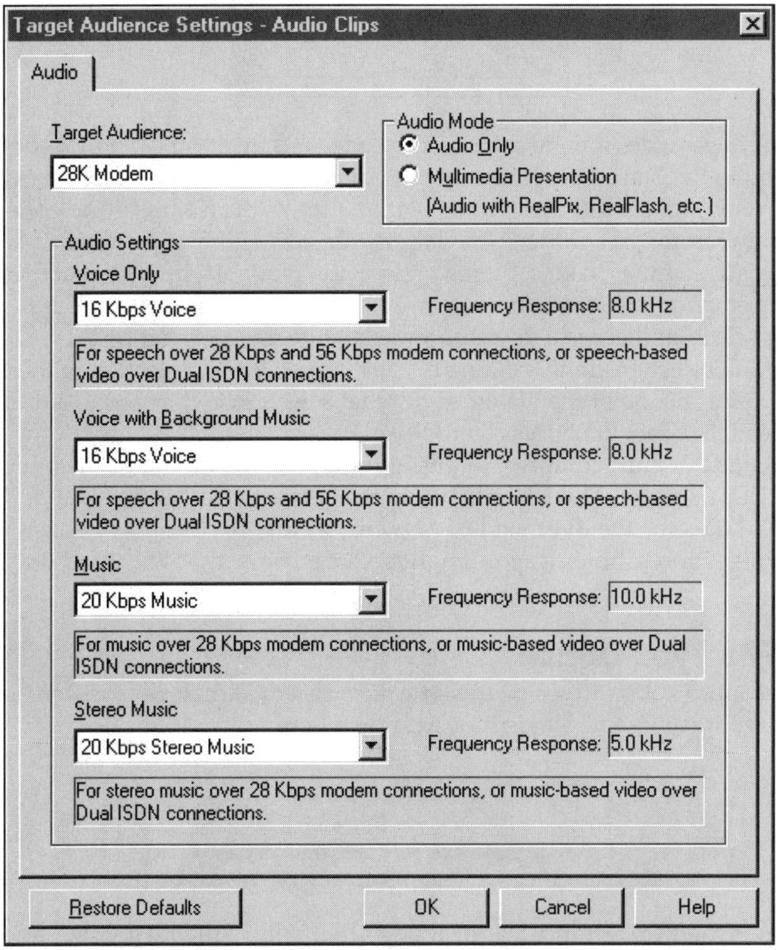

Figure 20-8.   *The Target Audience Settings-Audio Clips dialog box*

If you open one of the drop-down boxes, as shown here, you will see all the codecs available for selection.

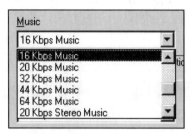

RealAudio provides a wide selection of codecs so that you can tailor the compression to the bandwidth available to your users. The largest compression, resulting in the smallest file size but lowest quality, is the 5 Kbps voice codec. The smallest compression, resulting in the largest file size and highest quality, would be the 96 Kbps stereo music codec. Stereo codecs are available, but they sacrifice audio quality, by reducing the frequency response, for the two channels of stereo. Below each codec selection there is a description for the best use of that codec

The default selections in this dialog box are driven by the selection in the Target Audience box at the top of the dialog box. If that selection is changed to a different modem speed, the default codecs change also.

The smallest default compression used for a 28 Kbps modem is a codec that gives a 20 Kbps stream. The 8 Kbps difference between the modem capability and the stream allows for the overhead of network traffic. If your users are still having network congestion problems, you might select a codec that will send out a smaller stream.

Select File Type Option

There is one more option to select in the RealProducer G2 dialog box. There is a choice between SureStream™ and Single Rate as shown here:

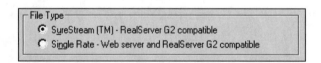

SureStream is the Real+Audio G2 technology that allows the RealServer to provide a stream that can be used by slower and faster modems. If you selected multiple modems in the Target Audience selection, and you are using a RealServer G2, then

you will need to pick the SureStream selection to enable that capability. If you have selected only one modem speed, or you are using an older RealServer, then pick the Single Rate selection.

Select Preferences

There are a few additional options to set for encoding. Open the Options menu and choose Preferences to open the Preferences dialog box, which has two tabs. The first one is the General tab shown here:

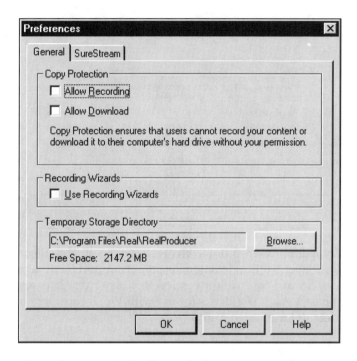

In the Copy Protection area of the General tab, you can set the streams so they can be listened to but not recorded or downloaded by the user. If you want to allow recording or downloading, pick the appropriate selection. Use Recording Wizards turns the wizards on and off. The Recording Wizards comprise many dialog boxes. One of these is the New Session dialog box shown in Figure 20-7. The temporary Storage Directory defines the location for three temporary files RealAudio uses in creating its files.

When you select the SureStream tab, the dialog box will look like this:

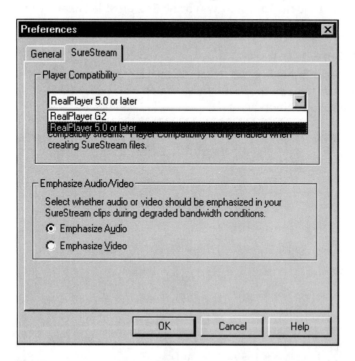

The Player Compatibility drop-down box is shown open. This allows compatibility with the older RealPlayer 5.0. Single Rate files do not support RealPlayer 5.0. If you want to have the backward compatibility, select RealPlay 5.0 or later and use SureStream. Emphasize Audio/Video is for use with Video clips. If you are not using video, keep the default Emphasize Audio.

Encode the WAV file

The final step is to start the encoding. The lower-left area of the RealProducer G2 dialog box has the recording controls shown here:

When the encoding is in progress, you can check the audio levels from the Audio Level bar in the center top of the Real Producer G2 dialog box, like this:

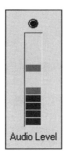

HTTP Streaming vs. Network Streaming

There are two types of streaming available for RealAudio files. Although you have seen that you need a RealServer to stream RealAudio files, you actually can stream files without the RealServer. This is called *HTTP streaming,* while streaming from a RealServer is called *network streaming.*

Many Internet service providers don't have a RealServer, so HTTP streaming is useful if you are being hosted with one that doesn't have a RealServer. The downside is that, while it will deliver multiple streams, HTTP streaming is not as robust or efficient. With network streaming you can also move ahead to any point in the file, but with HTTP streaming you cannot. You can only move backward to a point in the file that has already played. The downside of streaming using a RealServer is that, since the Internet service provider has paid for the RealServer, that cost could be passed on to you in additional fees for use of the RealServer.

If you are dealing with longer RealAudio files—15 minutes or more—or plan to have a lot of usage, it is recommended to use a RealServer. If you use shorter files that will not be streamed by a lot of users at once, use the HTTP streaming.

The RealAudio file has to be copied to a server at your Internet service provider. If you are using HTTP streaming, you will copy it to the web server. If you are using network streaming, you will copy it to the RealServer.

Creating a RealAudio Metafile

The RealAudio metafile is a one-line text file to which a web page is linked. The metafile starts the RealPlayer and then passes the location of the RealAudio file to the RealPlayer. The RealAudio metafile can be created using a text editor like Notepad. A word processor can be used, but you must save the file as a pure text file without formatting.

An HTTP Streaming Metafile

Before you can stream RealAudio files through HTTP, you need to define the following MIME type for your web server:

Audio/x-pn-realaudio (files with .ra, and .ram file extensions)

Multipurpose Internet Mail Extensions (MIME) is the standard for attaching nontext files to standard Internet mail messages. Nontext files include graphics, spreadsheets, formatted word-processor documents, sound files, and so on. Besides e-mail software, the MIME standard is also used by web servers to identify the files they are sending to the Web Clients; in this way new file formats can be accommodated simply by updating the browser's list of pairs of MIME-types and appropriate software for handling each type.

Some web servers are preconfigured with the RealAudioMIME type. There are two ways to find out if your web server is one of these. The first is to create a link to an HTTP streaming file and see if it works. If the server is not configured, it won't work. The second way is to call your Internet service provider and ask. If it isn't, request your Internet service provider to set up the RealAudio MIME type.

You should have already copied the RealAudio file to the web server because you need to use the path and the filename of the RealAudio file in the metafile. The metafile will have a single line with the following form:

```
http://hostname/path/file.ra
```

Hostname is the name of your web server. Here is a listing of a typical metafile, which you would save with a .ram file extension:

```
http://www.whidbey.net/rafiles/gcoale/testingtesting/113098.ra
```

Network Streaming Metafile

If you copied your RealAudio file to the RealServer for network streaming, you will use the path name and the filename of the RealAudio file in the metafile. The metafile will take one of two forms depending on if the RealServer is a G2, an older version of RealServer, or if you are targeting RealPlayer 3.0 to 5.0. The older RealServers and RealPlayers use the PNM protocol as shown here:

```
pnm://hostname/path/file.ra
```

Hostname is the name of your RealServer. Again the file is saved with a .ram 'tension.

The primary protocol for the RealServer G2 is RealTime Streaming Protocol (RTSP), so the metafile would appear like this:

```
rtsp://hostname/path/file.ra
```

RAM files for network streaming are identical to RAM files for HTTP streaming with the exception that they use PNM or RTSP as the protocol instead of HTTP.

Linking to the Metafile

Use FrontPage to import the RealAudio metafile to your web, and then create a hyperlink to it the same way you imported and created a hyperlink to an audio segment earlier in this chapter. When you do that, your web page will stream your RealAudio file when a user clicks the link to the metafile.

Live RealAudio

All the audio in the previous sections has been on-demand. Anyone can select the audio file at any time and listen to it from the beginning of the file. But RealAudio also can play real-time such as a radio broadcast or a live show. While a radio broadcast may be playing prerecorded material, it is still going out real-time, so if someone selected the link after the show had started, they would join it somewhere in the middle in real-time.

Doing live RealAudio requires the use of a RealServer. HTTP streaming only works with on-demand material. Otherwise it is very similar to on-demand streaming.

The big difference is that, with on-demand RealAudio, you create a WAV file from an audio signal and then encode the WAV file into a RealAudio file. With live RealAudio, you pass by the WAV file step and encode the audio signal on the fly.

Start with a Live Audio Signal

The first step is having a live audio signal. This signal is delivered to the sound card the same way you delivered a signal to record a WAV file. The signal can be prerecorded material from a CD or tape recorder, or it can be live going from a microphone to the sound card. If you are using multiple microphones, you will use a mixing device, such as a soundboard or mixer-amplifier, to combine the different microphone signals into one signal for the sound card.

Setting Up the RealAudio Encoder for Live Streaming

The RealAudio encoder is set up a little differently for live streaming. The Media Clip Information, Target Audience, Audio Format, and File Type information on the primary dialog box of the RealProducer G2 are entered as they are for an on-demand stream.

The New Session dialog box was discussed in the section for doing on-demand streams. The same dialog box is used for a live stream, but the only Input Source allowed is Media Device. Figure 20-9 shows the New Session dialog box set up for a live broadcast.

After selecting Media Device, select Live Broadcast in the Output side of the dialog box. ServerPort is the port your Internet service provider has set up for the RealServer. Port 7070 is the RealAudio default. Filename is the name of the stream and what you will use in the RealAudio metafile. Enter the Username and Password the RealServer administrator has assigned you.

Encode the Audio Signal for a Live Stream

The final step is to select Start in the Recording Controls of the primary RealProducer G2 dialog box. Keep track of the signal in the Audio Level bar the same way you would for creating on-demand RealAudio files. Use the mixer to control the sound level as you did for recording the WAV file.

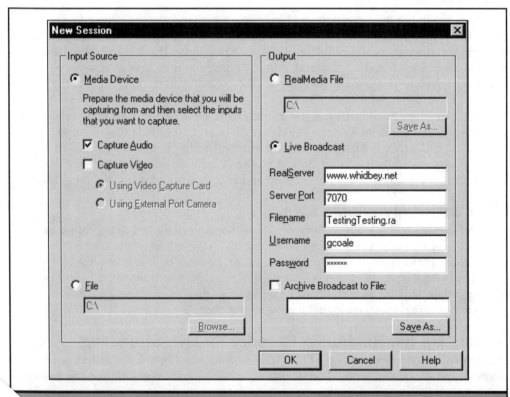

Figure 20-9. The New Session dialog box for a Live Broadcast

TestingTesting—A Live Internet Show

"Testing, testing" is a phrase commonly used in sound checks when checking microphone levels. *TestingTesting* (**http://www.electricedge.com/testingtesting**) is also a weekly live 30-minute show of interactive improvisational Internet music activity coming from the producer's living room. Open the \Book\Chap20\ folder on the CD that comes with this book and double-click TestingTesting.ra to hear a segment of one of the shows or better yet, go to the web site and listen to a live or archived show. This *TestingTesting* segment is included here with the permission of Gordon Coale of ElectricEdge Web Solutions.

Note *(Testing Testing is produced and copyrighted 1998 by Gordon Cole of ElectricEdge Web Solutions. You can contact Gordon at gcoale@electricedge.com.)*

There is a lot of streaming audio and video on the web today with concerts, sports events, and rebroadcast radio programs. One thing these all have in common is very large budgets. The *TestingTesting* crew has to work with a very small budget. The large-budget events also have another thing in common: they think broadcasting on the web is like radio or TV. The *TestingTesting* crew knows that it is something else. They don't know what else it is, but they know it is different and want to experiment with the technology and the format, hence the name TestingTesting.

In order to keep the costs down, they do the show from a living room as you can see here. The RealAudio part is happening in the upper right of the picture where the computer is.

The show has two regular musicians and a special guest musician, or musicians, each week. Because of the living room atmosphere, the performers are relaxed and it becomes much more fun than a more formal performing space. One of the differences this show has over radio and TV is that they use a guest book on their web site in which the Internet audience can enter comments during the show. Those comments are read to the performers during breaks in the music. This changes the direction of the show, making the Internet audience a part of it. The show is advertised as being 30 minutes long, but it often runs 35 to 40 minutes and sometimes longer. There are no rules. Each show is saved and is available for those who were not able to be there live. The guest book comments are saved along with digital pictures taken during the show.

Testing, Testing is put on the Internet using the procedures in this chapter. The format is being developed as the producer and performers experiment with this new medium. This is like the early days of radio or TV. The audience for a show like this isn't measured in millions; it is measured in dozens—dozens that become personally involved with those on the show.

TestingTesting uses a music format because the people involved with it are mostly musicians and there are a lot of talented players in the area where they live. But webcasting like this could use any number of formats. It could be used for some sort of talk show, or live programs like old radio, but with an interactive element from the Internet audience; or someone playing music from their record collection that others might like to hear but can't on commercial radio. This is niche webcasting on a low budget with an audience that talks back. Use your imagination in this new medium. Join the *TestingTesting* crew in figuring out what it can do.

Chapter 21

Security on the Web

There has been a lot of discussion in the media regarding security risks on the Web. You've probably heard stories about how someone has done something to compromise someone else's security on the Internet or has gotten through to a private intranet. These stories appear infrequently for two reasons: the occurrences are rare, and people don't like to report that their security has been breached. The vast majority of stories are about university or private research efforts that, with much work and a lot of computer power, have broken through the security in some obscure area of a given Internet program. A lot of hoopla is made of the weakness found, the manufacturer rushes to fix it, and few if any people ever experience a loss or misuse of their Internet information. The impact is negligible because current security measures on the Internet are very good, and because of the sheer volume of transactions on the Web. Only a tiny percentage of those transactions has value to others and therefore has any potential to be misused. However, the number of transactions that users would like to keep private is growing rapidly. If you are a regular user of the Web, chances are that you have purchased merchandise, ordered a service, or transferred some confidential information about yourself over the Internet. Fortunately, security measures are also growing in their ability to protect us.

Areas Where Security Is Needed

Look at all the activity on either the Internet or intranets now, and more importantly, consider what will be taking place in the future, and ask yourself in what areas security is an issue. The Internet, which, grossly simplified, looks something like Figure 21-1, has millions of users connected to hundreds of thousands of interconnected computers. Added to this are a growing number of intranets connected to the Internet. As information is transferred between two users on the Internet, it is routed through a large number of intermediary computers under the independent control of many different entities. There is no way to control where the information may be routed or to limit who controls the computers it is routed through. Also, for the modest price of an Internet account, anyone can get on the Internet and do what they wish. Consider what is happening on the Internet:

- E-mail is being sent, routed, and received. It can contain anything from "Hi, how are you?" to very sensitive trade secrets.

- Web sites are being accessed to read, print, or download their information. On the majority of sites access is unlimited and free, but on others access is limited (by a password or other means) for various reasons.

- In an already large and growing number of web sites, goods and services are being sold with payment by credit card or other payment forms.

- Newsgroups are being read and contributed to, again generally with unlimited access, although occasionally access is password controlled.

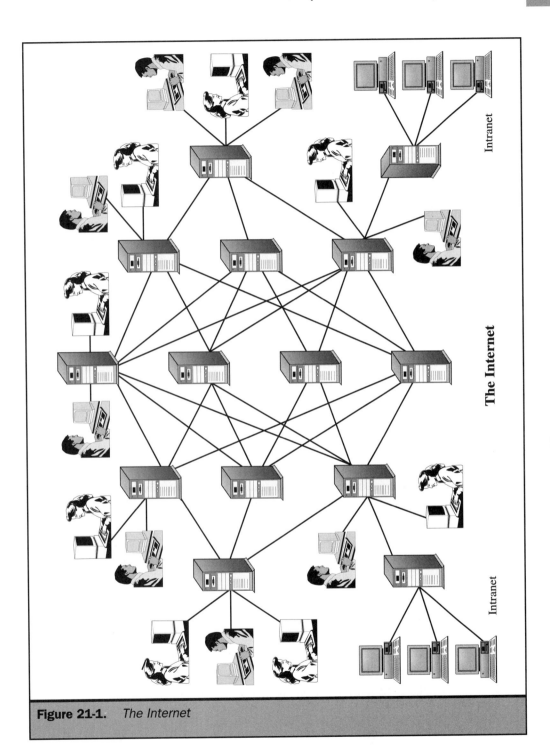

Figure 21-1.   *The Internet*

- Direct real-time audio and video communications, which today are a small part of the Internet traffic, will grow as the bandwidth of the Internet expands. For the most part the communications are not sensitive in nature, but there may be charges for its receipt.

- Telnet, Gopher, and other classical Internet services are continuing, but at a decreasing pace.

- Web servers are being maintained; web pages are being added, revised, and removed; user IDs and passwords are being changed; and scripts are being worked on.

- Increasingly, people on intranets are gaining access to the Internet.

- To a lesser and slower-growing extent, people on the Internet are gaining limited access to intranets through the use of extranets that allow businesses and corporations to conduct much of their work with off-site business partners.

Where are the risks in this Internet activity? There are, of course, many, but among them are:

- Interception and misuse or misdirection of e-mail

- Creation and sending of e-mail from someone other than who it appears to be from

- Accessing a controlled-access web site without the appropriate permission

- Interception and misuse of credit card or other financial information during an Internet business transaction

- Misrepresentation on the part of a buyer or seller in an Internet business transaction

- Gaining unauthorized access to the administrative functions of a web server to misuse the user IDs and passwords, or to otherwise upset the operation of the server

- Gaining unauthorized access to a web server and changing web pages or scripts

- Gaining unauthorized access to an intranet for whatever reason

The primary security goals, then, are just three:

- Limiting access to web pages, web servers, and intranets to only those with proper authorization

- Securing the transmission of information, whether sensitive e-mail, credit card data, or financial information

- Authenticating the sender, the receiver, and the data transferred

Controlling Access

"Controlling access" has at least two different connotations:

- Limiting access to all or part of a web site to only a certain group, such as subscribers to an electronic publication or administrators on the web site

- Securing an intranet site from being accessed via the Internet by setting up a computer called a *firewall*, which controls entry to and possibly exit from the intranet

Limiting Access to a Web Site

Limiting access to a web site means that you have a specific list of people or groups of people to whom you have granted some type of permission to access your site. When you install FrontPage on your computer, you (really your computer) are automatically given permission to access the web pages that you create. Also, a default *root web* (containing your home page) is automatically created, and The World (everyone) is given permission to access it. By default, all the web pages that you create are given the same permission as the root web, meaning that if you do nothing, everybody has permission to access all the pages you build.

If you publish your web to Microsoft's Internet Information Services (IIS) running on a Windows NT 4.0 server and then open that web in FrontPage, you can establish three levels of permissions:

| **Note** | *You cannot establish permissions in FrontPage if you are working with a web you have not published (that exists only on your hard disk), or a web that is published on the Microsoft Personal Web Server.* |

- **Browse**, which allows the user to look at, read, and navigate the web site
- **Author**, which allows the user to change as well as browse the site
- **Administer**, which allows the user to set permissions as well as to author the web site

As a default you can set the level of permission for the root web (home page), and all subwebs under it will automatically have the same level of permission. If you want, though, you can separately set the level of permission for any or all of the subwebs.

| **Note** | *To use permissions with Windows NT 4.0 and IIS, the webs must be stored in an NTFS (NT file system) partition and not a FAT (file allocation table) partition. This is because the permissions depend on access control lists (ACLs) that are implemented with NTFS. Also, your Web presence provider (WPP) must create an NT user account on the web server that you will use to access your files.* |

EXTENDING YOUR WEB SITE

To change the permissions on a web that you have published to an NT 4.0/IIS server, you must load that web into FrontPage, and then use the Security | Permissions option in the Tools menu. Do that now and see how permissions can be set.

1. Load FrontPage and then open the Exciting Travel web that you created earlier in this book. This must be the copy of the Exciting Travel web that is running on an NT Server with IIS, not the local copy using the PWS.

2. With the Exciting Travel web displayed, open the Tools menu and choose Security | Permissions. The Permissions dialog box will appear, as you can see in Figure 21-2.

   The default is Use Same Permissions As Parent Web, which means that to change the permissions, you must change them for the parent web.

3. First click the Users tab, where you should see, at a minimum, that the network administrator has Administer, Author, and Browse permissions. If you click the Groups tab, you'll see that Everyone has been granted Browse permission, the network Administrators group has full control, and other NT groups also have Browse permission, as shown in Figure 21-3.

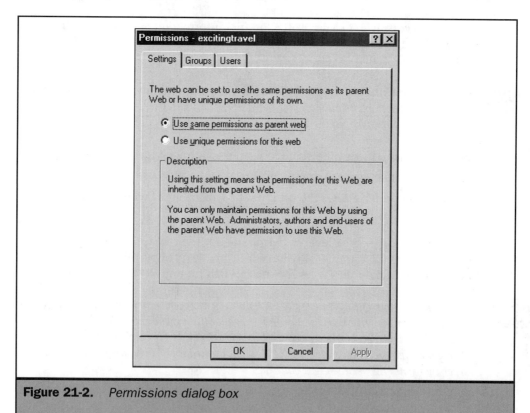

Figure 21-2. *Permissions dialog box*

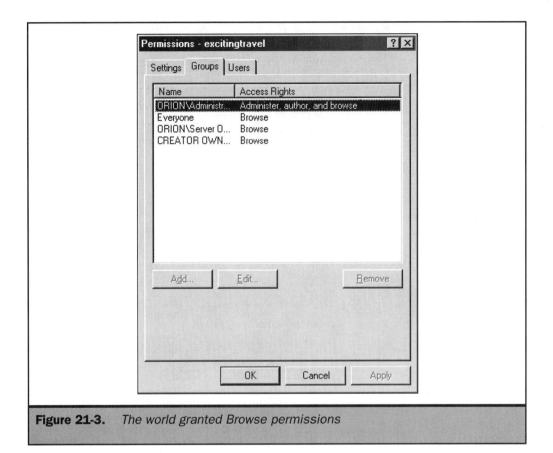

Figure 21-3. *The world granted Browse permissions*

Note

The groups you will see in the Groups tab of the Permissions dialog box will depend on how the network administrator has configured your web on their web server.

Tip

Your WPP may be reluctant to give you Administrator permission for your FrontPage web. It's very easy to misconfigure the server settings and create problems.

4. Return to the Settings tab, click Use Unique Permissions For This Web, and click Apply (if you don't click Apply, you won't be able to open the Users and Groups tabs).

5. Click the Users tab. You'll see that now only you (your NT account on the web server) have all permissions, as shown here:

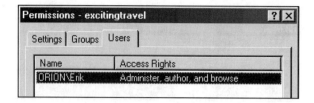

6. Click your account name in the list and then click Edit. (If Edit is dimmed, click OK to close the dialog box and then reopen it.) In the Edit Users dialog box, click Browse This Web, like this:

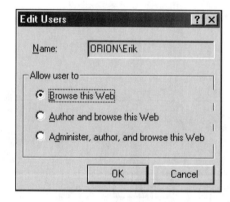

7. Click OK to return to the Users tab of the Permissions dialog box.

8. Click Add to open the Add Users dialog box. If you have a list of names on the left (this is the list of User accounts on the network of which the web server is a member), double-click one that you want to have some level of permission with this web.

9. Click the permission level you want for this person, as shown in Figure 21-4. (Given that Everyone has Browse permission, the person you're adding should have a higher-level permission.)

10. Click OK. Your User tab should now resemble this:

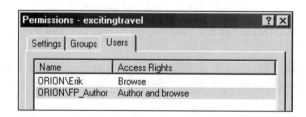

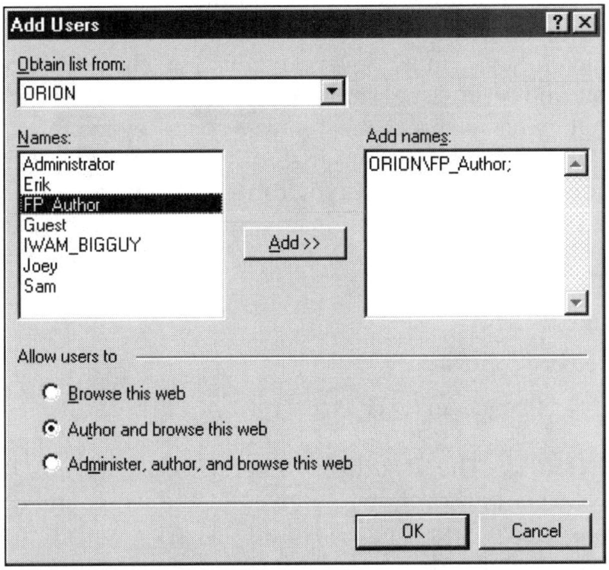

Figure 21-4.   *Adding a user*

11. Click Groups to open an empty tab. Click Add. Again, you can double-click an entry on the list on the left or type a new group on the right. Select the permission level desired, and then click OK to close the Add Group dialog box. Then click OK again to close the Permissions dialog box.

SETTING UP USERS AND GROUPS   The users, groups, and members of groups to whom you grant permission to access your web are established within the server outside of FrontPage and are maintained in *access control lists* (ACLs), which are referenced by FrontPage. The individual users are assigned IDs and passwords that they must use to gain access. The users may also be assigned to one or more groups. FrontPage can then reference the users either individually or by group. The process of setting up users and establishing groups is handled by the network or server administrator and is beyond the scope of this book.

Controlling Access to a Web Server

The permissions that you set for the web pages that you are creating are used by the web server to implement the access controls that you want. If your Internet service provider (ISP) is not using Windows NT 4.0 and IIS, then you must work with it to set up the access controls that you want by using the services that are available on the ISP's web server. Most web servers have a multiple-level permission scheme set up by user and/or group that will allow you to implement an access scheme similar to FrontPage's Browser, Author, Administrator scheme. In fact, most servers go far beyond this.

Windows NT 4.0 with IIS provides four security mechanisms, each of which can give you one or more levels of access, as you can see in Figure 21-5. These four mechanisms, which can be implemented in any combination by IIS, are

- Internet Protocol (IP) address control
- User account control
- Virtual directory control
- Windows NT File System (NTFS) control

IP ADDRESS CONTROL   The IP address control checks the *source* IP address (where the data is from) on every packet of data received by the server and compares it against a list of IP addresses that contains predefined actions to be applied to packets with that address. The packet is then handled in accordance with the predefined actions. IP address control is useful for either blocking or accepting major groups of users, like everyone from a particular company or organization within a company. This is the principal mechanism used by firewalls (discussed later in this chapter). The major limitation in IP address control is that you cannot identify particular directories that can be accessed by a given IP address.

USER ACCOUNT CONTROL   A standard part of Windows NT security is user account control, which requests a user ID and password when accessing the server or specially designated directories. Such access can be over a LAN or over the Internet, so part of the IIS security that is implemented can include the Windows NT user account control. To make user account control simpler, define an anonymous account allowing access to nonsensitive directories with limited privileges—normally read-only—for anyone who makes it through the IP address control. For additional access and privileges, users are asked to enter their user ID and password. These are checked for validity by use of either *Basic* or *Windows NT Challenge/Response* user authentication. The difference between these two authentication schemes is in the way that the ID and password are returned to the server. In the Basic scheme, the user ID and password are simply encoded in a manner that is not terribly hard to decode by someone intercepting it on the Internet. The Windows NT Challenge/Response scheme never requires that the password be transmitted, but rather uses a cryptographic challenge sequence to authenticate it. The Windows NT Challenge/Response scheme only works on Microsoft Internet Explorer 2.0 and above.

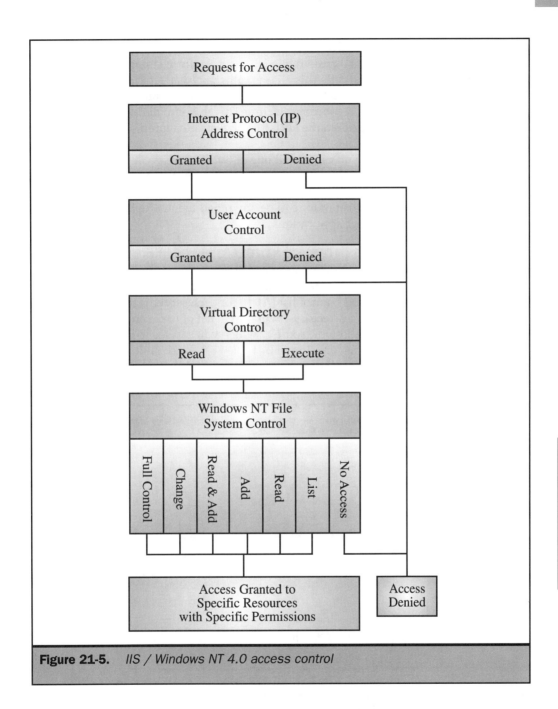

Figure 21-5.   *IIS / Windows NT 4.0 access control*

VIRTUAL DIRECTORY CONTROL   With IIS you can define an alias for a directory path on the server and then use that path in a URL (the uniform resource locator, which is an address on the Internet). This alias is called a *virtual directory*. For example, the default path for a web site called ExcitingTravel on a server named SERVER is C:\Winnt\System32\Inetsrv\Wwwroot\ ExcitingTravel. If you define the alias for this path to be /ExcitingTravel, then the URL for the web site would be **http://server/excitingtravel**.

When you define an alias, you can give it one of two access privileges, Read or Execute, used for the defined path and all files and folders within it. The Read privilege allows the user to read and download the contents. The Execute privilege only allows the user to execute the contents—not to read or download them. The Execute privilege is used for CGI scripts and other applications.

WINDOWS NT FILE SYSTEM (NTFS) CONTROL   The Windows NT File System (NTFS) control is what associates a user account (name and password) with specific directories, files, and folders, as well as other server resources. This association is accomplished through the access control list (ACL) for each server resource. The ACL for a particular resource—say, a directory—will have a list of users and groups of users and one of seven levels of permissions, some of which you can see in Figure 21-6. The permissions and their description are shown in Table 17-1. By default all users ("Everyone") have full control of all directories, files, and folders.

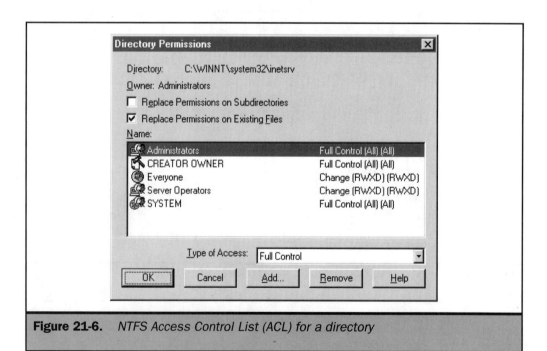

Figure 21-6.   *NTFS Access Control List (ACL) for a directory*

Permission Level	Description
No Access	Prevents any access to the directory and its files.
List	Allows the listing of filenames and subdirectory names and the changing of the subdirectories. Prevents access to file contents.
Read	Allows listing filenames and subdirectory names, changing subdirectories, viewing data files, and running applications.
Add	Allows adding files and subdirectories to directories, but does not allow viewing data files or running applications.
Add & Read	Allows listing filenames and subdirectory names, changing subdirectories, viewing data files, and running applications, as well as adding files and subdirectories to directories.
Change	Allows add and read permission, as well as changing data in files, and deleting the directory and its files.
Full Control	Allows change permission for the directory and its files, and takes ownership of the directory and its files.

Table 21-1. *Description of Permission Levels*

Limiting Access to an Intranet Site

One type of access control that is not handled by FrontPage is limiting access to an intranet web site. This is the situation in which you have an intranet that you want to connect to the Internet. It may be that you want to just allow your intranet users access to the Internet. Alternatively, you may want to allow people on the Internet—for example, your own employees who are traveling—to get onto your intranet. This is done with several schemes, but the most common is a firewall, which is a separate computer through which all traffic to and from the Internet must pass, as shown in Figure 21-7. At the simplest level, a firewall works by *packet filtering*, which checks each packet of information that is transferred, either outbound or inbound, through the firewall and makes sure that its IP address is acceptable.

To add a further level of protection and in some cases speed up this process, the firewall computer may be set up as a *proxy server*. A proxy server, which is simply software running in a computer acting as a firewall, acts as a relay station between your intranet and the Internet. It acts like an "air lock" between the two. Requests to servers on either side of the firewall are made to the proxy server, which examines them, and if they are appropriate, sends a proxy on to the addressed server to fulfill the request.

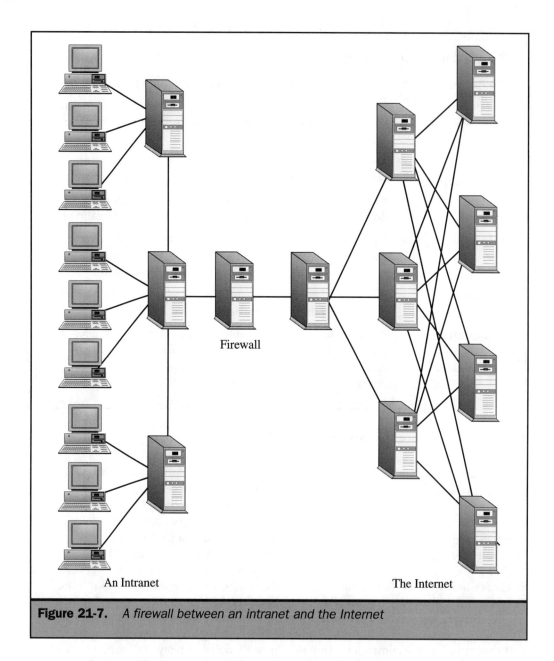

An Intranet   The Internet

Figure 21-7. *A firewall between an intranet and the Internet*

To find out more about firewalls, packet filtering, and proxy servers, see Tom Sheldon's excellent book, *The Windows NT Web Server Handbook,* Osborne/McGraw-Hill, 1996. Also see the bibliography at the end of this chapter.

Securing Transmission

Transmission security means the *encryption* or concealment of the information being transmitted so it cannot be read and misused without the ability to *decrypt* or reveal it. Encrypting of information is probably as old as the human race and has really blossomed with the advent of computers. Data encryption has become so sophisticated that the U.S. government, worried that they won't be able to decrypt the data (can you imagine that!), won't allow the technology to be exported (although this may be changing). Several encryption schemes for securing Internet transmissions are in use. They are private key encryption, public key encryption, and combinations of the two.

Private Key Encryption

Private key encryption, or *symmetric cryptography*, is relatively old and uses a single key to both encrypt and decrypt a message. This means that the key itself must be transferred from sender to receiver. If this is done over the phone, the Internet, or even a courier service, all someone needs to do is get hold of the key, and he or she can decrypt the message. Private key encryption, though, has a major benefit in that it is much faster (as much as 1,000 times faster) than the alternatives. Private key schemes are therefore valuable in situations where you do not have to transfer the key or can do so with security—for example, personal use such as encrypting the contents of a disk or sending information to someone that you first met face to face. There are several private key encryption schemes being used with the Internet, including the U.S. government's Data Encryption Standard (DES) and the private RC2 ("Rivest Cipher" or "Ron's Code" [for Ron Rivest] 2) and RC4 from RSA Laboratories.

Public Key Encryption

Public key encryption, or *asymmetric cryptography*, was developed in the mid-1970s and uses a pair of keys—a public key and a private key. The public key is publicly known and transferred, and is used to encrypt a message. The private key never leaves its creator and is used to decrypt the message. For two people to use this technique, each generates both a public and a private key, and then they openly exchange public keys, not caring who gets a copy of it. They encrypt their messages to each other using the other person's public key, and then send the message. The message can only be decrypted and read by using the private key held by the recipient. The public and private keys use a mathematical algorithm that relates them to the encrypted message. By use of other mathematical algorithms, it is fairly easy to generate key pairs, but with only the public key, it is extremely difficult to generate the private key. The process of public key encryption is relatively slow compared to private key encryption. Public key encryption is best in open environments where the sender and recipient do not know each other. Most public key encryption uses the Rivest-Shamir-Aldman (RSA) Public Key Cryptosystem, called "RSA" for short, developed and supported by RSA Laboratories.

> *You can encrypt your e-mail using the Pretty Good Privacy (PGP) software that uses RSA public key encryption and is available from NetworkAssociates (**http://www.nai.com/**) at their web store (go to **http://store.mcafee.com/** and select Encryption Products).*

Combined Public and Private Key Encryption with SSL

Most encryption on the Internet is actually a combination of public and private key encryption. The most common combination was developed by Netscape to go between HTTP and TCP/IP and is called Secure Sockets Layer (SSL). It provides a highly secure as well as fast means of both encryption and authentication (see "Authenticating People, Servers, and Data" later in this chapter).

Recall that private key encryption is very fast, but has the problem of transferring the key. And public key encryption is very secure but slow. If you were to begin a secure transmission by using a public key to encrypt and send a private key, you could then securely use the private key to quickly send any amount of data you wanted. This is how SSL works. It uses an RSA public key to send a randomly chosen private key for either a DES or RC4 encryption, and in so doing sets up a "secure socket" through which any amount of data can be quickly encrypted, sent, and decrypted. After the SSL header has transferred the private key, all information transferred in both directions during a given session—including the URL, any request for a user ID and password, all HTTP web information, and any data entered on a form—is automatically encrypted by the sender and automatically decrypted by the recipient.

There are several versions of SSL, with SSL version 3 being the one in common use as this is written (spring 1999). SSL 3 is both more secure and offers improved authentication over earlier versions. Microsoft also has its own improvement of SSL called Personal Communications Technology (PCT). Both SSL 3 and PCT have been proposed to the World Wide Web standards committee (W3C) as security standards.

> *Internet Explorer 5 has added another encryption standard called TSL 1 for "Transport Layer Security," which is an open security standard similar to SSL 3.*

Implementing SSL

You may be thinking that SSL sounds great, but it also sounds complex to use. In fact, it's easy to use. You need a web server that supports SSL, such as the Netscape Commerce Server or the Microsoft IIS, plus a supporting web browser such as Netscape Navigator 3.0 or Microsoft Internet Explorer 3.0 and their respective later releases. From the browser, you simply need to begin the URL you want with "https://" in place of "http://". SSL will then kick in, and without you even being aware that it's happening, the browser and server will decide whether to use DCS or RC4, use RSA to transfer a private key, and then use that key and the chosen private key encryption scheme to encrypt and decrypt all the rest of the data during that session. The only thing that you see is a message saying you are about to begin to use a secure connection, similar to this:

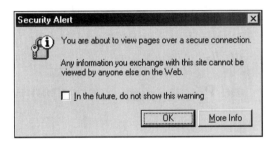

     Once you are connected using SSL, your browser will indicate that a secure connection is established. Netscape and Microsoft display an icon of a padlock in the browser's status bar.

     Even though the combination of public and private encryption is relatively fast, it is still significantly slower than no encryption. For that reason it is recommended that you only use SSL when you send sensitive information such as financial or credit card data.

FrontPage and SSL

FrontPage 2000 implements SSL in several ways. You can specify whether a new web is to use SSL by selecting Secure Connection Required (SSL) in the New web dialog box, as you can see in Figure 21-8. Also, FrontPage 2000 automatically (without you doing anything) uses SSL for all communications between the FrontPage 2000 client and the server. This provides protection when you are transferring a web page to the server and when you are doing remote web authoring. To use SSL you must create the web on a server that supports SSL, such as NT 4.0 with IIS (the Microsoft Personal Web Server does not support SSL).

Authenticating People, Servers, and Data

SSL is designed to do double duty. Not only does it provide a secure method of data transmission, but it also provides the authentication of the data and the server, and with SSL 3 it provides authentication of the user. Authentication is important for three reasons:

- To make sure that senders are who they say they are, and to prevent them from denying that they are the sender. This is authentication of the client or sender.
- To make sure that recipients are who they say they are, and to assure that they received the information. This is authentication of the server or recipient.
- To make sure that the data being sent has not been modified before it was received. This is authentication of the data.

EXTENDING
YOUR WEB SITE

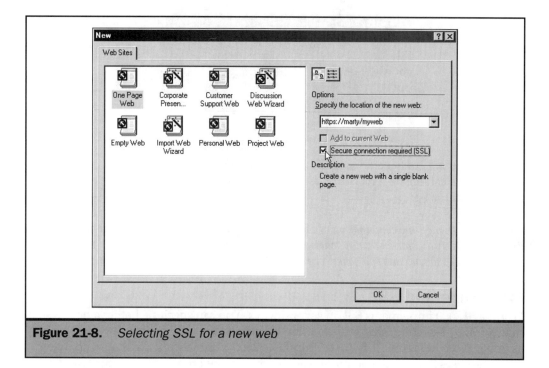

Figure 21-8. *Selecting SSL for a new web*

SSL addresses each of these areas of authentication with the following steps:

1. A *message digest* is generated for the data being sent by use of a sophisticated algorithm that is very sensitive to changes in the data. This is equivalent to computing a checksum or a cyclical redundancy check (CRC) for a large number.

2. The message digest is encrypted with the sender's private RSA key to produce a *digital signature.*

3. The recipient uses the sender's public key to decrypt the digital signature that came with the data exposing the message digest. If the public key works, then the sender is who she said she was and in fact sent the data.

4. The recipient then recomputes a new message digest using the data that was received. If the two message digests are the same, then the data has not been altered in transit.

5. The recipient next encrypts the new message digest using the recipient's private RSA key to create a new digital signature and sends it to the original sender.

6. The original sender uses the recipient's public key to decrypt the second digital signature. If the public key works, then the recipient is as claimed, and if the two message digests are the same, then the original data was received by the recipient.

This sounds complicated, but if you are using SSL, it is all done automatically, and you only know if there is a problem. There is one flaw in this security scheme—how can either the sender or the recipient be sure they have the public key of the other and not of someone masquerading as the other person? In this situation the false person would be able to use the private key that went with the false public key to decrypt and misuse the data. To counter this flaw, a public key can be enclosed in a *certificate*. A certificate uses the private key of a *certifying authority* to encrypt both a message digest of the human-readable name of the sender and the sender's public key. Then by using the public key of the certifying authority, you can get the public key along with the name of the owner. Of course, you must trust that the public key of the certifying authority is legitimate! A prominent certifying authority, where you can obtain a certificate for yourself, is VeriSign, Inc., at **http://www.verisign.com/**.

What's Coming for Internet Security

Recognizing the reluctance of the public to use the Internet as a trusted medium for transferring financial and other confidential data, Microsoft and other software leaders have developed, or are developing, several features to ease security concerns. These range from *security zones*—where you can adjust the level at which you allow active content to be run on your computer and data to be copied to your computer—to *safe houses,* where you can securely store data on your computer or removable media.

In Internet Explorer 4.0 and later you have four zones, as shown in Figure 21-9. In each of the zones you can select the level of security from among four defined levels

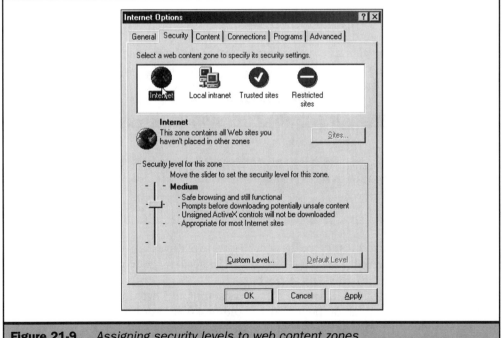

Figure 21-9.   *Assigning security levels to web content zones*

(three levels in IE 4.0) and one customizable level. You can then assign web sites to the zones. The zones and levels are as follows (note that all levels apply to all zones):

Security Zones	**Levels of Security**
Internet is a catch-all of those sites that haven't been placed in other zones.	*High* provides the most predefined security measures. It prevents damaging content from being downloaded.
Local Intranet includes fully trusted sites behind a corporate firewall.	
Trusted Sites are frequently visited web sites, such as the web site of a business partner that you trust will not adversely affect your computer.	*Medium* provides a warning message for content that may damage and won't download unsigned ActiveX controls.
	Medium-low doesn't provide warning messages, but won't download unsigned ActiveX controls (not in IE 4).
Restricted Sites are those that could adversely affect your computer.	*Low* provides no warning for content that has the potential for damage.
	Custom allows you to select specific security settings.

Note   *Due to the potential to allow damaging content in the Internet and Restricted Sites zones, you are given a warning, such as shown here, when you select a security level that may be too low.*

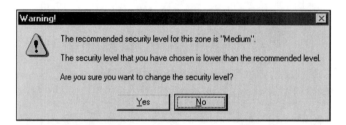

In Internet Explorer 4.0 and on, the security zone features are available from the Security tab of the Internet Options dialog box. The security zone you are currently using is displayed in the browser's status bar.

Today you can use the Microsoft Profile Assistant and Microsoft Wallet, options available in the Content tab of the Internet Explorer 4.0 or later Internet Options dialog box, to provide safe and easily retrievable access (for only those you want to have access) to personal and financial data, respectively. For example, by using Microsoft

Wallet, you can allow access to one or several of your credit card accounts to be debited by Internet merchants. On the horizon there will be support for conducting business using smart cards and Internet cash, where you electronically move "money" from one silicon repository to another.

Like it or not, much of how we conduct our daily lives in the future will be through the Internet in some capacity. As with other technologies that we may have reluctantly approached but now fully embrace, the security on the Internet will be refined and improved because too much will depend on it to do otherwise.

Bibliography

There are mountains of information on Internet and intranet security issues. Here are a sampling of documents and two books available on the subject. Most of the Internet sites mentioned had many more related documents.

Computer Security Institute, *CSI Manager's Guide to Internet Security*, 1994, **http://www.gocsi.com/mgr-guid.htm**

Library of Congress, *Computer and Internet Security, A Library of Congress Internet Resource Page*, 11/2/98, **http://lcweb.loc.gov/global/internet/security.html**

Microsoft Corporation, *Microsoft Internet Explorer 4.0 White Paper (Security Features)*, **http://www.microsoft.com/windows/ie/press/whitepaper/iwhite/white005.htm**

National Security Institute, *Connecting to the Internet: Security Considerations*, CSL Bulletin, July 1993, **http://www.nsi.org/Library/Compsec/intersec.txt**

National Security Institute, *Security Issues in WWW*, **http://www.nsi.org/Library/Internet/security.htm**

Netscape Communications Corporation, *Netscape Security Solutions*, **http://home.mcom.com/products/security/index.html**

NT Bug Traq (**http://www.ntbugtraq.com**) offers a mailing list to keep you informed of the latest security issues regarding NT Server, and a web site where you can locate the latest fixes.

Redmond, Frank III, *Making Sure Your Server's Secure*, Microsoft Interactive Developer, 11/96, **http://www.microsoft.com/mind/1196/iissecurity.htm**

RSA Laboratories, Inc., *Frequently Asked Questions about Today's Cryptography*, **http://www.rsa.com/rsalabs/faq/**

RSA Laboratories, Inc., *Public-Key Cryptography Standards (PKCS),*
http://www.rsa.com/PUBS/

Rutgers University Network Services, *World Wide Web Security,* 12/4/95,
http://www-ns.rutgers.edu/www-security/index.html

Rutgers University Network Services, *WWW Security References,* 6/2/95
http://www-ns.rutgers.edu/www-security/reference.html

Rutstein, Charles B., *Windows NT Security,* 1997, Computing McGraw-Hill

Sheldon, Tom, *The Windows NT Web Server Handbook,* 1996, Osborne/McGraw-Hill

Stein, Lincoln D., *The World Web Security FAQ,* Version 2.0, 12/20/98,
http://www.genome.wi.mit.edu/WWW/faqs/

Chapter 22

Doing E-Commerce

By Gordon Coale, "The WebGuy™," Creator of the WhidbeyStore.com and IslandArts.com

What is electronic commerce? There are many different answers to this question. E-commerce is buying a book, an airplane ticket, or a computer online. E-commerce is also an airline ordering aircraft parts for a Boeing 747 electronically, and it is a bank sending a financial transaction to another bank electronically. It can also be any aspect of buying and selling online, which could include marketing, order taking, or customer service.

E-commerce, in this chapter, is when someone offers a product for sale on the Web and someone else buys it. This sounds simple, but a lot of different things must be considered to make that sale over the Web. Many of those considerations are similar to what the traditional physical storefront deals with. You are offering products for sale and they must be marketed, sold, paid for, and delivered. The details are different for e-commerce, but, whether the store is a physical or electronic storefront, you are still running a store and your web storefront must meet many of the same requirements of a physical storefront to be successful.

The e-commerce market is also growing rapidly. There are a lot of different predictions as to how big the e-commerce market will be, but they all agree that it is growing very fast and will be very big. According to Forrester Research, a consulting firm, online shoppers spent $600 million in 1996 and $2.4 billion in 1997 (**http://www.icat.com/eguide/primer/faqs.htm**). International Data Corporation, a market research firm, predicts that the amount of commerce conducted over the Web will exceed $400 billion by 2002 (**http://www.idc.com/F/HNR/081798ahnr.htm**). International Data Corporation in the same article claims that, given the increase in Web users and the higher percentage of Web users becoming Web buyers, the number of Web buyers will expand from 18 million in 1997 to more than 128 million in 2002.

More and more companies are jumping into this market. They include Internet-only companies like Amazon.com, which currently sells books, CDs, and videos, and eBay, an online auction house. Many large companies with physical storefront and catalog sales are moving onto the Web. These include such companies as Lands End, The Gap, and Barnes and Noble. One company, Egghead Computer, has even shut down their physical storefronts and is now Internet-only as Egghead.com.

But the move to the Web is not just with large companies. In 1995 Amazon.com opened an Internet storefront selling books that was created and run with software they had to develop themselves. Today the potential web storeowner has many off-the-shelf options that can be used to create an e-commerce store. Some of these options do everything from creating the pages to handling all the ordering and payment; others rely on tools like FrontPage to create the pages while depending on software running on the server to add features for ordering and payment. The prices for various software options also vary quite a lot, but they all provide a much less expensive solution than starting from scratch like Amazon.com.

While putting a store on the Web is easier than ever, putting a successful store on the Web is not easy. It is not easy in the same way that getting a successful physical store is not easy. There is a lot of work, before the store opens, in the many details of setting up a retail store. There is a lot advice for such ventures available on the Web. Several publishing companies have web sites with information on e-commerce. ZDNet's E-business (**http://www.zdnet.com/icom/e-business**) offers a lot of news, reports, and information about e-commerce and doing business over the Web. ZDNet also has a site devoted to more general small business concerns called Small Business Advisor (**http://www.zdnet.com/smallbusiness**). Internet.com's E-commerce Guide (**http://e-comm.internet.com**) is another site devoted to e-commerce. Software companies that want to sell you e-commerce software often will have sections of their site devoted to general information of e-commerce and doing business on the Web.

Before discussing some of the options available for creating web stores, it is useful to talk about security, payment options, and ordering.

Security

In any transfer of money, security is a major issue, as it is in e-commerce. Chapter 21 discusses security on the Web. You might want to look again at the sections on encryption, private and public keys, Secure Sockets Layer (SSL), and authenticating servers. These subjects are basic to creating and maintaining a secure e-commerce site. This section will go into more detail describing how security is implemented and some options you have with digital certificates.

Sending data over the Internet is much more secure than the uninformed scare stories passed on by the popular media. But the reality of security and the perception of security by your customer are two different things. When a customer gives out personal or credit card data at a physical store, or through a mail-order catalog, that customer is basing their trust on a variety of visual clues as to the professionalism with which your data will be handled. A customer at a high-end store like Nordstrom does not question the security of their credit card data when they hand it over to a sales clerk. That same customer may think twice about handing it over to someone on the Internet he or she knows nothing about. You need to show you are taking care of the customer's data as it crosses over the Internet and that you will be handling it responsibly once you receive it.

The key to secure transactions (both actual and perceived) is the *digital certificate*. Verisign (**http://www.verisign.com**) is the leading issuer of digital certificates. Before issuing a digital certificate, Verisign reviews the applicant's credentials, such as Dun & Bradstreet number, articles of incorporation, or business license, and takes several other steps to ensure the organization is what it claims to be and not an imposter. Verisign then issues the digital certificate, which is your electronic credential. Verisign's price for this service currently starts at $349.

Not only does the digital certificate identify the owner of the web store, but it also enables Secure Sockets Layer (SSL) to establish secure communications between your server and the customer's browser. SSL provides the following components for online commerce:

- **Authentication**   By checking the Verisign digital certificate, your customer can verify that the web site belongs to you and not an imposter.

- **Message privacy**   SSL encrypts all traffic between your Web server and the customer's computer using a unique session private key. To securely transmit the session key to the customer, the server encrypts it with the customer's public key, automatically sent to the server by the customer's computer. Each session key is used only once, during a single session with a single customer.

- **Message integrity**   When a message is sent, the sending and receiving computers each generate a code based on the message content. If even a single character in the message is altered, the receiving computer will generate a different code, and alert the recipient that the message is not legitimate. If not alerted, both parties will know that what they are seeing is exactly what the other party sent.

When you open a web page that is secure, you will get a Security Alert box like this:

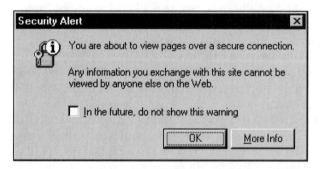

When SSL has been enabled, and the secure web page loaded, Internet Explorer shows a small, closed lock at the bottom of the browser. The lock does more than tell you that the connection is now secure. It also gives you access to information about the digital certificate. When you double-click the lock, the Certificate box appears as in Figure 22-1. The General tab has the name of the owner of the digital certificate and the time period of its validity. Selecting the Details tab gives you the details about the digital certificate, such as the serial number and dates between which it is valid, and selecting the Certification tab then tells you who issued the digital certificate and its current status.

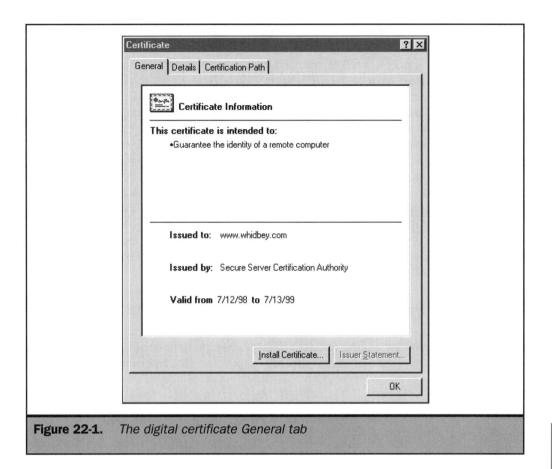

Figure 22-1.   *The digital certificate General tab*

There are a couple of options for getting digital certificates. The first is to get one from Verisign in the name of your company. The second is to use the digital certificate of the Web presence provider (WPP) who is hosting your site, if they offer that service. If you are using a simple form that is on one page, you can use the second option if your ISP has a secure server with a digital certificate. The secure page would be on a secure server, and you would access it with the HTTPS protocol.

The problem with the second option is that if the customer checks the digital certificate, a name other than the one they expect will be on the digital certificate. This will cause many to hesitate, and they may not go on. Most people know about the closed lock but not about how they can check the name of the owner of the digital certificate. You can assume that, as time goes on, more people will be checking the name on the digital certificate. The best long-term solution is to get your own digital certificate.

Many e-commerce programs process orders and then use a form-mail program to e-mail the information to you. If your WPP is also your Internet Service Provider (ISP) and handles your e-mail as well as your secure server, the information is probably going from the secure sever to the mail server to you via their network and not over the Internet. If the secure server you are using and your mail server are in different locations, and the information is being passed on via the Internet, you need to explore securing the e-mail data, too. Some e-commerce packages recognize this and provide ways to secure that data. Some e-mail programs can use SSL, and there are other encryption schemes available. Contact your WPP to see what they have to secure your e-mail data if it is going over the Internet.

When you receive sensitive data, you should also have a way to keep it secure in your offline environment. Only trusted people should have access to your customer's credit card information, so it needs to be kept locked up with password protection on your computer and you need to control access to any paper copies you might make. Leaving other people's credit card information lying around is like leaving their money lying around. It may get picked up.

Payment

Cash is not an option for paying online, but there are a number of other ways to transfer funds. Some are familiar and others are specific to the Internet. They include:

- Credit cards
- Checks
- Electronic cash
- Smart cards

Credit Cards

Credit cards are the preferred method of payment for online customers. They are easy to use, and consumers are familiar with them. Credit cards also have an advantage for the customer since they limit the customer's liability. Customers can cancel the transaction if they wish, and if credit card fraud is involved, they are only liable for $50 if they meet the card company's requirements for reporting the incident.

In any sale, you are trying to make it as easy as possible for the customer to buy. Credit cards are the easiest way for the customer. All they have to do is fill out the credit card information and submit the order. What makes it easy isn't just that credit is involved. Check cards are included here too because they act just like credit cards, but the funds are deducted from the customer's checking account. What makes it easy is the existing card company and banking infrastructure that processes the credit, or debit, card.

The Credit Card Process

The basic process for using a credit or debit card is that the customer submits the credit card number to the merchant and the merchant sends the merchandise to the customer. The merchant also sends the credit card number and amount to a *merchant processor*. The merchant processor transfers the money into the merchant's account, usually within 48 hours, and begins the process of billing the customer. The merchant's account is a bank account set up to automatically receive these funds. An easy way to sign up with a merchant processor is to go to your bank and ask for a merchant account. Not all banks offer this service, but many do. Their rates vary for this service, so shop around. Costco (**http://www.costco.com**) also sets up merchant accounts through NOVA Information Systems, a leading merchant processor, for very reasonable fees.

In the above scenario, the question is, how does the e-commerce merchant get the credit card transaction to the merchant processor? The answer is that you can either automate the process with online processing or use the historical manual processing.

Online Processing

To do online processing, you need both an e-commerce package that will submit an online order to a merchant processor and a merchant processor that will receive it. The middleman between you and the merchant processor can be CyberCash (**http://www.cybercash.com**), which offers online credit card processing for merchant processors. Many of the e-commerce software packages are set up to tie into CyberCash, and many merchant processors use CyberCash, including NOVA Information Systems. One of the things that online processing can do is quickly verify that the credit card is valid and provide authorization in real time at the time of the purchase.

Online processing with CyberCash adds another step in the process that also adds to the cost of the transaction over manual processing. If you have a small web store with a small number of transactions, it might be better to use manual processing. Manual processing has its costs also, so you will have to figure out what is best for you. But be sure to look at manual processing.

Manual Processing

Manual processing is done with the Point-of-Sale (POS) terminal. When you swipe your credit card at a store, it is at a POS terminal. Taking credit card numbers over the Internet means you can't swipe the card, but you can key in the number. This is how mail-order companies process the credit card numbers they receive. You may find that there is a higher processing charge for key-in over swiping. Terminals can be leased or purchased from the merchant processor. Leasing starts around $30 to $40 a month, and purchasing the terminal starts around $250. There are also software programs that allow you to process the numbers with your PC. NOVA charges $180 for their PC processing software. Again, shop around with different merchant processors because you need to add in the cost of the POS terminal or software along with the service charges.

Checks

Not everyone has a credit card, and even though many can get a debit card with their checking account, many people aren't able to, or choose not to. Most small businesses can't afford to turn away paying customers, so you need to decide if you want to handle check orders.

There are two ways to handle check orders. The first is to have the customer print out the order form and mail it in with the check. If the customer fills out the online form and prints it out, the entries may or may not print, so it may be easier on the check customers to create a separate snail-mail form to print out and fill in with pen or pencil. The second way is for the customer to fill out the online form and submit it electronically with Check being selected as method of payment. Then you hold the order until the check arrives, at which time you can process it. The customer has to do less this way. Always make it as easy as possible for the customer and be ready to accept as many methods of payment as you can.

Electronic Cash

Some items are too inexpensive to purchase with a credit card. Nobody uses a credit card to buy a newspaper, which is why a number of companies are working to find a way to charge customers for items costing $5 or less. These inexpensive things are not worth the service charges with credit cards. CyberCash is a player in this category too, with their Cyber Coin for transactions in the 25 cent to $10 range. These micropayment methods are not doing well. They require the customer to install and learn new software, and few merchants are participating, so acceptance has been very low. Both Compaq and IBM are working on micropayment schemes, so this bears watching.

Smart Cards

Smart cards are plastic cards into which consumers can digitally download money. They are popular in Europe, but haven't caught on in the U.S. Smart cards are efficient, secure, and easy to use in both real and virtual stores. Many banks and tech firms, including Microsoft, are working on smart card systems for the U.S. This is something whose time is yet to come.

Web Design Tips for a Web Store

Chapter 1 goes into detail on designing a web application, but there are some additional considerations with web stores.

- **Make first-time buyers comfortable**   Give them tips on shopping at your site, and possibly offer incentives for their first purchase. First-time buyers are reluctant to order online, so make sure your phone, fax, and e-mail information are listed prominently at strategic locations throughout the site. If buyers don't have a positive experience the first time, they probably won't be back.

■ **Make the process fast** Not only make it fast to load by reducing heavy graphics, but make the buying process simple from start to finish. Don't put any barriers in the way, like making them download plug-ins or filling out forms so they can shop in your web store.

■ **Make it easy to find the products** Pay attention to navigation and searching so the customer can easily find what you have to sell.

■ **Make all your products available** Provide a good selection, particularly if it is a web store that has a real-store counterpart. Customers expect to see everything online that they see in the physical store or catalog.

■ **Make it easy for the customer to give you their money** Don't hide the cash register. Make it clear how to get to the checkout stand, and make it easy to go there.

■ **Make it clear what the customer is paying** Don't hide shipping, handling, or any other extra charges. The order summary should show exactly what the customer is paying.

■ **Make communication important** Send e-mail letting your customers know their order has been received, shipped, and delivered.

■ **Make it hard for your customers to leave** Don't put links to nonshopping pages on your product pages.

Web Store Options

E-commerce sites can range from a one-page web store to major outlets like Amazon.com. These extremes use very different software packages. It doesn't take complex software to offer four or five items on a single page, but it does to offer millions of books, CDs, and videos. This section will look at the range of options available based on the size and budget of the web store.

There are two basic approaches: the simple form for web stores with just a few items, and the shopping cart site for web stores with more items than can fit on a single page. The shopping cart site uses a shopping cart metaphor to collect all the customer's choices, then adds up all the subtotals and extra charges, such as shipping and taxes, and sends the information to the merchant.

Simple Form Store

Form construction is covered in detail in Chapter 9. This section will show how a form can be used in a simple e-commerce site. This works when there are just a few items because the form limits it to one page. In that page you have to put all the items for sale as well as payment and shipping information. The page starts getting long and requires a lot of scrolling. If there are too many items to put on a single form, consider using a shopping cart site, covered later in this chapter.

EXTENDING YOUR WEB SITE

First look at a forms-based web store, and then look at how to get information from the form.

A Forms-Based Web Store

Figure 22-2 shows the home page for an e-commerce site selling items made with beach glass by Island Arts of Whidbey Island (**http://www.islandarts.com**).

All the product information is on the page you go to from the Products & How To Order link on the left navigation bar. When you go to this page, you enter a secure connection and get the security alert shown earlier in the chapter. When the page opens, note that there is a closed lock at the bottom of the browser indicating that this page is secure. If you double-click the lock, you will see the certificate shown in Figure 22-1, which is the certificate for the ISP. The page was put on a secure server, and the link to the page used the HTTPS protocol.

Part of the form page showing some of the products for sale can be seen in Figure 22-3. The pictures, product description, and the Quantity and Subtotal boxes are

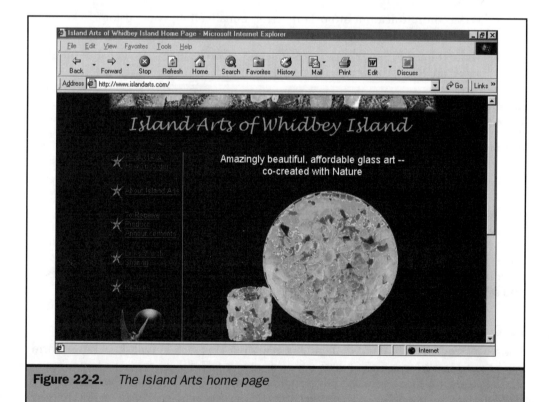

Figure 22-2. *The Island Arts home page*

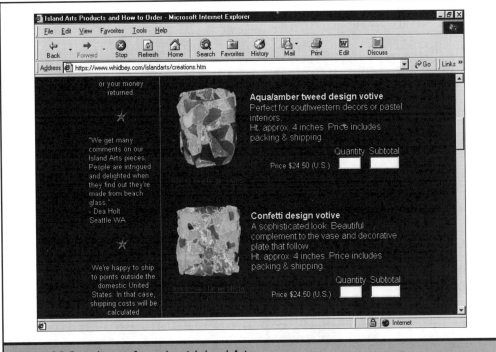

Figure 22-3. *Items for sale at Island Arts*

all inside the form. One of the disadvantages of a simple form page is that it is not intelligent. The customer has to fill in the quantity and calculate the subtotals. Although it is possible to create intelligent forms, if you want to have a site that does this, you might as well move up to a shopping cart site.

As you scroll down the page past the product descriptions, you'll come to the order subtotal, tax information, order total, and credit card information as shown in Figure 22-4. Again, all the subtotals and tax must be calculated by the customer and entered into the form. Scrolling down further brings you to the ordering information shown in Figure 22-5. This provides the necessary information for ordering and shipping. There is one more section below this for shipping information if it is different than the ordering information. It is the duplicate of the information in Figure 22-5. At the bottom of the form is the Submit button that sends the information to the web server.

This shows a way to lay out the information in a one-page form. The next step is to get the information from the form.

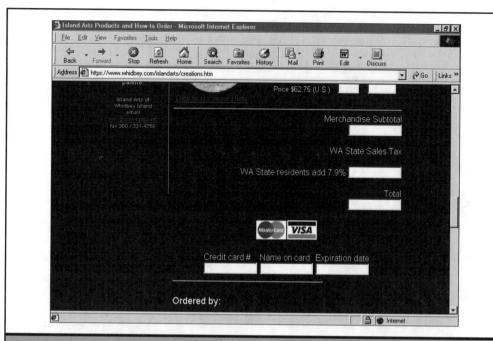

Figure 22-4. Merchandise totals and credit card information

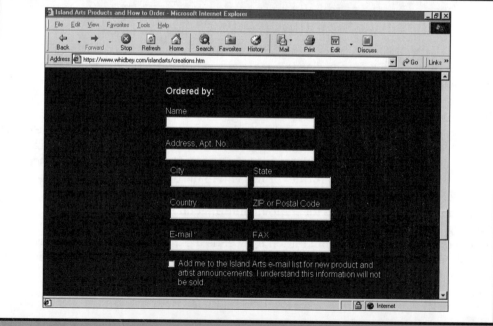

Figure 22-5. Ordering information

Getting Information from a Form

If you are using a web server with the FrontPage Server Extensions, you can get the information from a form in one of three ways: as a text or HTML file, in an e-mail message, or saved into a database, as discussed in Chapter 9. Arguably the best way to get the information from an e-commerce form is to use an e-mail message, because it is automatically sent to you and you don't have to do anything to get the information, except possibly retrieve your mail. If you or your ISP are not using the FrontPage Server Extensions, then you need to use a *form-mail program*. Most form-mail programs are CGI (Common Gateway Interface) scripts located in your ISP's web server CGI directory. A form-mail program gathers the information in the form and sends it to your e-mail box. A form-mail program has other features too. Many of the text box fields in the form need to be filled out for you to fulfill the order. You can't process a credit card without the number. A good form-mail program can be set up to check for required text box fields that you define and to ask the customer to fill out the fields they forgot. Other text box fields can be left optional. When the correctly filled-out form is submitted, an example of which is shown in Figure 22-6, a web page is returned to the customer confirming the contents of the form, as you can see in Figure 22-7. More advanced form-mail programs can enter the information into a web-accessible database and send e-mail confirmations.

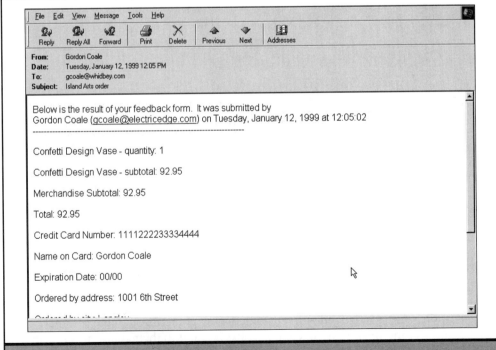

Figure 22-6.   *An order as it is e-mailed to you*

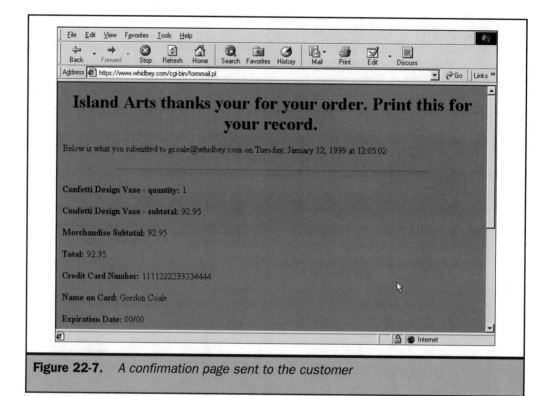

Figure 22-7. *A confirmation page sent to the customer*

Check with your ISP to see if they have a form-mail program already set up for you to use. If you have your own CGI directory, you can set up your own CGI scripts. The form-mail program used for Island Arts is a very popular one available from Matt's Script Archive (**http://www.worldwidemart.com/scripts**). A more advanced one that supports databases and e-mail is from Selena Sol at Extropia.com (**http://www.extropia.com**).

The example here has shown how Island Arts set up a form to securely take all the order information over the Internet. This is relatively simple to do if there are few items. As the number of items grows, the page starts getting very long and it becomes time to consider going to a shopping cart-based web store.

Shopping Cart Store

One hundred years ago, stores were very different than they are now. Clerks brought the merchandise from the product display to you and then added up the totals. Over the last century that all changed with customers now going through the product displays and getting their own merchandise, loading it into their shopping cart, and then going to the check-out stand for the total to be added up. The early successful e-commerce sites grabbed the shopping cart and brought it into cyberspace, using it as a metaphor. This has served e-commerce sites well in providing a way for customers to select and purchase products.

The Parts of a Shopping Cart Store

Although the shopping cart metaphor rules in the online stores, there are a number of different shopping cart programs available that all do things a little differently. All of them, though, provide the same four elements to a shopping cart store:

- Getting the shopping cart
- Viewing the product displays
- Putting the items into the shopping cart
- Buying the products at the checkout stand

This section will look at these four different elements and then explore some of the options available to you with software packages for putting that shopping cart into your web store.

The web store you will be entering, to see how this works, is WhidbeyStore.com (**http://www.whidbeystore.com**). It's a store set up to sell the products of Whidbey Island artists and craftspeople. Figure 22-8 shows the store's home page, which has links to the web sites of the artists whose products are in the store. It also asks you to enter the store to get a shopping cart and view the products. This page is the front door to the web store. The next step is to go into the store and get the shopping cart.

GETTING THE SHOPPING CART   The shopping cart is the metaphor for the parts of the e-commerce program that keep track of who you are and what you have decided to purchase. Computers are very good at keeping track of items. That is not the tricky part of the online shopping cart. The tricky part is keeping track of who you are.

Keeping track of who you are involves the concept of *state*. Maintaining state is when a constant connection is maintained, like with a telephone. Even if there is no conversation, the line is still open and the connection is maintained. That doesn't happen with the Web and HTTP. When you click a link and your browser requests a page, a connection is made with the web server. The web server passes the page back to the browser, and the connection is broken. When you click another link that asks for a page from the same web server, the web server has no clue that it has ever sent you anything in the past.

When you are in a web store, and you put something in your shopping cart, how does the web server know it is still you when you go to another page and select something else? There are a lot of ways of doing that, but one of the most common ways is the use of cookies. A *cookie* is a file the e-commerce program puts on your hard drive. When you are in the web store, it looks for the cookie to see who you are, so that it knows which shopping cart is yours. Cookies are explained in more detail in Chapter 16.

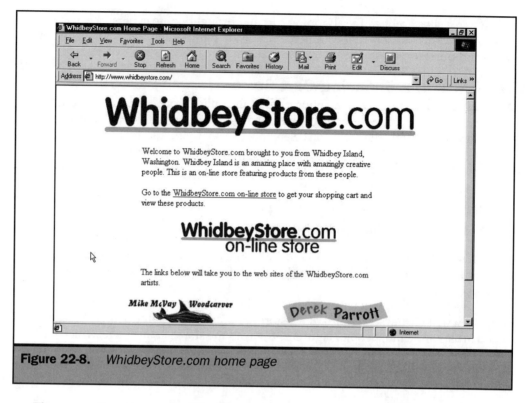

Figure 22-8. WhidbeyStore.com home page

There are other ways to do the same thing. The e-commerce program WhidbeyStore.com embeds a unique identifier into all the links and forms when it sends a page back to the browser. That way, when a page is requested from a link, or the contents of a form is sent, the identifier is returned to the e-commerce program and it knows who it came from and re-embeds that identifier into the page it sends back to the browser.

From the home page of WhidbeyStore.com, you click the link to the WhidbeyStore.com online store and you are in the online store with a shopping cart, shown in Figure 22-9. From here you can view the product displays.

VIEWING THE *STORE'S WARES* To see the products that are for sale, you need to click one of the artists' names. For example, clicking the link to Derek Parrott will take you to the product page for Derek Parrott's music, shown in Figure 22-10.

Organizing and presenting the products are web design issues discussed in Chapter 1. You might want to review Chapter 1 and make sure that all your products are easy to find and that it is easy to move around in your site. It is at this point that your customer is being sold on the product, so do your best. One thing that is done with Derek's music is that links have been set up to audio files on several pieces so potential buyers can listen and see if they like the music.

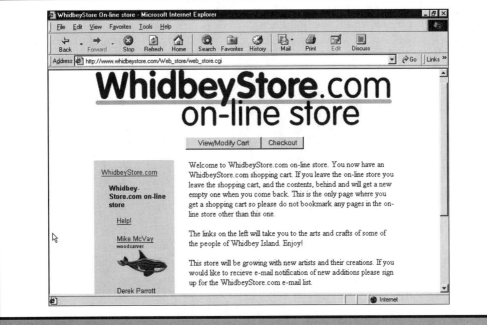

Figure 22-9. *WhidbeyStore.com online store*

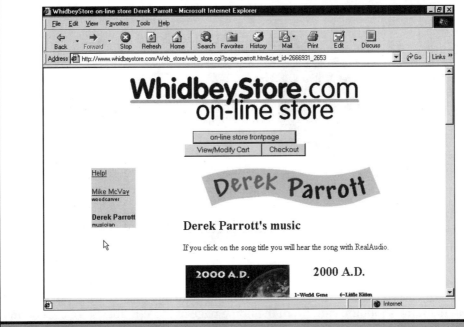

Figure 22-10. *Derek Parrott's products*

PUTTING THE PRODUCTS INTO THE SHOPPING CART   As you scroll down the page looking at items, you'll see that each item has a text box and an Add To My Shopping Cart button, as shown here. The customer simply puts a quantity in the text box and clicks "Add To My Shopping Cart" to add the items to the shopping cart.

It is also important to be able to handle options. One of Derek's albums is available as either a CD or a tape. It has a drop-down box that displays the options for the customers to choose and add to the shopping cart as here:

These items are all on the same page, like the items in the Island Arts form-based web store discussed earlier. But in this site you can go to any page in the store and add items to the same shopping cart. From the home page of the WhidbeyStore.com online store or from Derek Parrott's page, you could go to Mike McVay's pages to see his many woodcarvings and select any of his pieces like this:

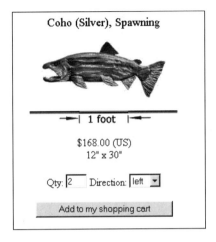

When any of the items from either of the artists are selected, they are put into the shopping cart. You also have to be able to check what is in the shopping cart. At the top of every page in the WhidbeyStore.com online store is a View/Modify Cart button that lets you look in the shopping cart as shown here:

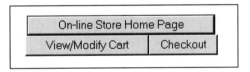

When you click View/Modify Cart, you will be shown a web page like this with all the items you have selected:

Artist	Description	Options	Price After Options	Quantity	Subtotal
Derek Parrott	2000 A.D.		15.00 $US	2	30.00 $US
Derek Parrott	My Back Yard	Tape 10.00	10.00 $US	3	30.00 $US
Mike McVay	Fish-Coho (Silver), Spawning, 12"x30" left 168.00		168.00 $US	2	336.00 $US

Pre-shipping Grand Total = 396.00 $US

Change Quantity   Delete Items   Continue Shopping   Return to Frontpage
Checkout Stand

Sometimes, in a physical store, you change your mind and take something out of the cart and put it back on the shelf. Your e-commerce program should allow you to do the same thing. Not only does the shopping cart show you what you've selected, but it also allows you to change the quantity or delete items. The Change Quantity button shows a page that allows you to change the quantity of any selection, and Delete Items shows a page that lets you delete the item completely. Other e-commerce programs may have different ways of doing this, but they should allow the same functionality.

BUYING THE PRODUCTS AT THE CHECKOUT STAND When you have selected all the items and adjusted the quantities, it is time to go onto the checkout stand. As shown earlier, at the top of every page there is a Checkout button next to the View/Modify Cart button. Selecting it opens a web page that has all the contents of the cart as well as the ordering information as shown in Figure 22-11.

As you scroll down the page, you'll have the same information for the customer to fill out as you did at the Island Arts web store shown earlier. There is a Submit button at the bottom that sends the order to the e-commerce program, which responds with a web page confirming the order and then sends an e-mail to the store owner with the order information.

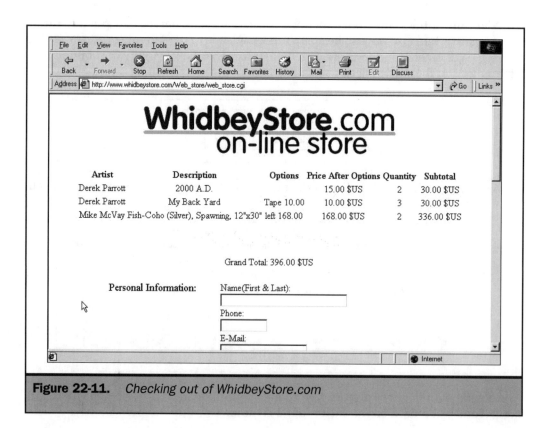

Figure 22-11. *Checking out of WhidbeyStore.com*

E-Commerce Packages

The look and feel as well as the functionality of the site are often determined by the e-commerce package you choose. Some of the packages offer a lot of flexibility in how you can build your site, while others take you down a narrower path with fewer options for laying out and organizing your site. A lot depends on your budget and how much effort you want to put into your web store.

There are a number of companies offering e-commerce solutions, and the following examples are only to illustrate what is available in each category. This is a hot topic with computer magazines, both printed and online, and they usually have associated web sites that archive their articles. The e-commerce field is changing fast, so it is important to research before committing to an e-commerce package.

Free E-Commerce Software

There is free software available to run web stores. WhidbeyStore.com online store is run with Gunther Birznieks and Selena Sol's WebStore CGI script available at Extropia.com (**http://www.extropia.com**). It is a Perl script that requires some editing of the source code. This does not mean you need to know how to program in Perl, only that you not be afraid to do a little research to learn how the program is put together. It is well documented, and they have written a book that covers the package titled *CGI for Commerce: A Complete Web-Based Selling Solution*. It is available at Amazon.com (**http://www.amazon.com**). This package allows sites that are driven by either HTML pages (as in the WhidbeyStore example) or simple flat file databases, and has support for Java and Visual Basic scripts.

All the WhidbeyStore pages were created with FrontPage, but run on a web server without the FrontPage Server Extensions. The WebStore CGI script processes these pages as they are filled out and returned by a customer, and then creates and delivers the responding summary and confirming pages. It is a simple, inexpensive solution, that is easy to install and use.

Lower-Priced E-Commerce Software

There are places on the Web that let you build your site from a browser with online-only solutions. Two of the large ones are iCat Commerce Online (**http://www.icat.com**) and Yahoo!Store (**http://store.yahoo.com**). They use predefined templates that you choose, you upload your information and pictures, which are plugged into the templates, and you are online in minutes. They both provide online malls to which you can link your store. There are no web developers or WPPsI to deal with.

Their pricing is by the month. At Yahoo!Store, a web store of up to 50 items is $100/month. A store with up to 1,000 items is $300/month. iCat's prices are comparable. Check them carefully to see just what you can get.

There are other options in this category. Mercantec's SoftCart (**http://www.mercantec.com**) is a package offered by ISPs that host web stores. You can create your site with an authoring tool like FrontPage and have the web store run with SoftCart.

Packages in this price range are usually offered by hosting companies and are charged for by the month. The costs can range from $400 to $2000 for a year. These packages offer improved order processing, site statistics, and inventory control over what is offered by the freeware option, although there is a wide range of capabilities in this price range, so look carefully at what these packages provide.

Higher-Priced E-Commerce Software

The mid-range packages run from $3500 to $8000 and can support the most demanding web store. Microsoft's Site Server 3.0 Commerce Edition (**http://www.microsoft.com**) and IBM's Net.Commerce Start 3.11 (**http://www.ibm.com**) are in this category. These provide extensive capabilities for database connection and can link to enterprise order and fulfillment systems. They require experienced programming support to use their functionality.

Marketing Your Web Store

Once your web store is up and running, you need to market it, which is discussed in Chapter 24. The types of promotion mentioned in Chapter 24 are essential for your web store, but there is an additional type that many business sites are using. It is often the case that a business going onto the Web already has a customer base and a customer snail-mail list. Take advantage of this. Do a snail-mailing using a postcard inviting your customers to check out your new web site. On the front of the card have your business logo and your web site address, as Mike McVay did for his woodcarvings as shown here. On the back of the post card you can have any additional message.

Check out your local printer to see if they do postcards. Five hundred four-color postcards should cost between $95 and $100 to print and another $100 for postage. This is an effective way to let people who already know you find out about your web store.

Keep Them Coming Back

Once customers have come to your web store, you want them to come back. A very effective way to remind customers that you are still there and let them know about sales and specials in your web store is the e-mail list. Set up a form on your web store to gather e-mail addresses. Then send periodic announcements of web store activities to keep your customers coming back.

Don't forget your e-mail manners. Let your customers how you plan to use their address. You will be more successful in getting addresses if you tell them that the addresses are to be used only for your store's communications and will not be sold. You are also asking your customer to give you something of value: their address. Offer them something in return. It could be a simple gift or a discount on future purchases.

The E-Commerce Future

The e-commerce revolution is just beginning. The large companies have staked out their claims on the Internet, and there is a lot of large corporate huffing and puffing to tell the world how great they are. But the Internet lets the small business be heard, too. The entry costs are very low to have access to a market the size of the Internet. Doing business on the Internet will benefit small businesses like Island Arts and WhidbeyStore.com. As more people turn to the Internet for their shopping, it will be the nimble who profit on the Web. Join the fun (and hopefully profit).

Chapter 23

Setting Up an Intranet Web Site

By Jessica Burdman, Aslan, Inc., San Francisco, CA

L ike the Internet with its World Wide Web, LANs and intranets are an exploding phenomenon. As this growth increases, many expect the use of intranets to exceed that of the Internet. The competitive success of a company often depends on internal communication and the ability to quickly share information—two major benefits of intranets. As with any new technology, however, there are and will be many opportunities to stumble. How a company implements an intranet may be even more important than the decision to do so.

This chapter will look at intranets—what they are, why they are needed, and how to set them up—both in terms of the hardware and software needed to make them function, and the content they should provide. You will see how intranets can help your business or organization, and how to create an intranet by using FrontPage.

What Is an Intranet?

An *intranet* site is a web site that is viewable only to those within a corporate network. Although based on the same protocols as the World Wide Web, an intranet is protected from the outside world either by not being connected to the outside or through a series of hardware and software obstacles known as a firewall.

Focusing on the World Wide Web and on connecting to the world over the Internet (a wide area network, or WAN), some people overlook the fact that the same protocols and technology can be used over a local area network (LAN). With a LAN and the Microsoft Personal Web Server, you can create your own web to link computers in an office. With the Microsoft Internet Information Server (IIS), Windows NT 4.0 server, and a LAN or private WAN, you can set up an intranet within a large office, between buildings, or even among company sites around the world.

An intranet may be as simple as two computers networked in a home office, or as complex as a network linking the offices of a global corporation. In the latter case, an intranet could link the computers within regional segments of the organization, while the Internet could be used to connect the various intranets—this is referred to as an *extranet.*

Networking computers to share information is, of course, not a new concept. Networked computers can be found in virtually every medium-to-large business and in many smaller ones. When networked, the resources on any computer can be shared by any other computer on the network. With Windows, the addition of a network interface card can turn any PC into either a network server or a workstation. For larger networks, specialized software, such Novell's NetWare or Windows NT, is required to effectively allow computers to share information.

Classical networking involves the sharing of files and some hardware devices such as printers. More recently it has included the use of e-mail. An intranet that uses the technology of the Web significantly enhances the functionality of a LAN or a corporate WAN by adding the ability to read and interact with a large set of documents that are easily created and kept up to date. Almost as important, many of these documents already exist as word processing, spreadsheet, and database files. With FrontPage they can be easily converted to interactive web pages.

Existing word processing, spreadsheet, and database files can be easily converted for use on an intranet by importing them into FrontPage. In the classic example of the company procedures manuals, the web's ready availability, search tools, and easy maintenance and updating are powerful incentives to having an intranet.

As was explained in Chapter 1, the Internet and the World Wide Web are built upon three software technologies:

- **TCP/IP** (Transfer Control Protocol/Internet Protocol), which is the underlying technology of the Internet for the exchange of information and the identification of parts of the network

- **HTTP** (HyperText Transfer Protocol), which handles the actual transmission of web documents

- **HTML** (HyperText Markup Language), which is the programming language of the Web

These same technologies are used to implement an intranet, and they must be added to the networking software that is already in place. HTTP and HTML are used only by the web server and the browser, and do not affect the classical networking software. TCP/IP, on the other hand, directly competes with classical networking protocols such as IPX/SPX or NetBEUI on Intel-based computers. TCP/IP can be used instead of or in addition to other protocols, and setting it up can be a major pitfall. The objective, of course, is to have the protocols operate in harmony to perform all of the necessary networking functions.

One of the problem areas with classical networking was linking different types of computers, such as PCs or Macintosh, Hewlett-Packard, or UNIX computers. Each operating system (or platform) requires its own specialized software, which isn't always compatible between systems. An intranet built with TCP/IP, HTTP, and HTML doesn't have the compatibility problems of other networking systems. The early support of the U.S. government ensured the widespread adoption of TCP/IP as a network protocol, and HTTP servers and HTML browsers are available for virtually every platform. For organizations that have acquired a variety of computer hardware, creating an intranet has never been easier. While a simple file-sharing network allows files to be accessed between computers, the three Internet technologies allow much greater interactivity by use of hypertext links, searches, and forms. Some of these features are available with products such as NetWare, but at greater cost and complexity. A FrontPage-created intranet presents a middle course of power and economy.

For an example of an intranet that uses Microsoft's Office family, visit the Arcadia Bay Research and Development Team intranet at **http://www.microsoft.com/office/intranet/tour/**, shown in Figure 23-1.

Why Have an Intranet?

The reasons for having an intranet are as varied as the organizations creating it, but the common purposes are to communicate among the members of the organization and to involve them in improving their effectiveness and collaboration. An intranet that is carefully planned and implemented can significantly improve overall productivity in the organization and reduce costs involved with communication, such as costs for phone calls, faxes, and paper.

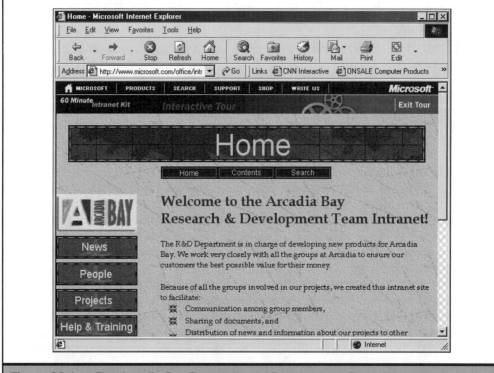

Figure 23-1. *The Arcadia Bay Research and Development Team intranet*

Communication

The intranet can replace newsletters, reports, lists of job openings, manuals, procedures, employee guidelines, meeting schedules, details of benefit plans, and lunch menus. Almost anything that is written or graphic and has an audience of more than a couple of people is a candidate for the intranet. The benefits of using the intranet are substantial:

■ An intranet document can be put up when convenient for the creator, and read when convenient for the reader.

■ Readers can keep and conveniently file an intranet document, or they can just read it and discard it, knowing the source document will be there for some time.

■ The documents can be simple text or full multimedia. By including multimedia, you can make documents more inviting to open and read.

■ The communication can be one-way, from the creator to the reader, or it can include forms and discussion groups to let the reader communicate back to the creator.

■ The documents can be easily indexed and searched, making the information they contain easier to find and use.

■ The cost of printing, distributing, and maintaining manuals, procedures, and guidelines is reduced, as are some fax and delivery expenses.

■ Information can be shared over many different computers and workstations, not just PCs. The Internet protocols and technology have been implemented on most computers, giving them the ability to attach to an intranet.

One of the biggest benefits, though, and the second major reason for using an intranet, is that it facilitates the involvement of more members of the organization in the organization's activities. The reasoning is that if you make it easier to locate, read, excerpt, file, and dispose of documents, more people will use them and acquire the knowledge they contain. If you make it easier to comment on and participate in the creation of something that can be put on an intranet, more people will. If you provide easy access and use of indexing and search capabilities, more archival information will be directly sought by end users. If you add multimedia and color graphics and thereby make a document more fun and interesting, more people will read it. If you allow many different types of computers and workstations to connect to an intranet, more people will be able to participate.

Simply stated, an intranet greatly facilitates the dissemination of information within an organization, and the communication among and the involvement of its members.

EXTENDING
YOUR WEB SITE

Productivity

An intranet can greatly increase productivity. When critical documents are located in a central place, people can find them easily. Many hours are lost in just trying to locate information within a company. Often one of the first applications built for intranets is a central repository of forms, in electronic format, so that users can find the form they need quickly, and print it at their convenience.

Cost Reduction

Several significant cost reduction studies have been performed on organizations using intranets. With intranets, you can easily track the change in copy and fax paper used per month and in telephone costs. If you communicate to users that the intranet can be used in place of the telephone (for discussion or collaborative-based communication) and in place of the printer (for on-demand information such as employee phone lists, chart of accounts information, and forms), you can begin to monitor other uses of communication within the company.

Employee Involvement

But the most important reason to have an intranet is that it enables greater employee involvement in the company. If the intranet is perceived as a team effort, and everyone is given the chance to participate in it, then they will use it and take pride in its growth.

What Do You Put on an Intranet?

The decision on what to put on an intranet is one of the most difficult; much depends on the character and philosophy of the organization. How open does your organization want to be, and how much security do you need? What does the company want to do with their intranet? Disseminating relatively simple information, such as newsletters, administrative manuals and procedures, and lunch menus, is not a problem; doing so with financial information, marketing reports, and corporate plans may well be more difficult.

Conducting a Needs Analysis

A *needs analysis* is by definition an analysis of what users need on the intranet in order to meet the intranet's objectives. If those objectives are to increase communication across the company and boost productivity, an analysis of how that might be accomplished must take place. There are many strategies you can take, depending on the overall objective of your company. First, of course, you must talk with the members of your organization who will authorize your intranet project.

Before you begin collecting information, a policy needs to be set on how open the company wants to be with its employees. This broad policy then needs to be translated into specific examples of documents in each of the major areas of the company (marketing, production, finance, and so on) that are allowed on the intranet and those that are not. It is very easy to gloss over this issue in the crush of all the other issues, but unless this is clearly thought through and then delineated, problems can occur.

Once the policy is established, specific documents and their priority have to be identified. This is best done by a committee of users and providers. A *user* is, obviously, a person or persons who will be using the intranet. The *providers* are the people who will be providing the content of the intranet. In an intranet scenario, the providers can be either a small group of users or a large independent group, depending on the kind of intranet structure you are building. There are two kinds of intranet structures: a decentralized model and a centralized model, both of which are discussed in the next section.

The users can set out their needs and desires, and the providers can respond with their ability and willingness to satisfy the requests. Either group alone is liable to create an intranet that is not as effective as it might be.

Questions to Be Answered

With the committee constituted, it should look at all the documents the company produces that fit within the policy guidelines. For each document, the following questions should be answered:

- How wide an audience does it have?
- How often is it produced, and is that schedule supportable on the intranet?
- Do the layout and graphics lend themselves to the document being easily placed on the intranet?
- Does the addition of intranet features such as searching, forms, and hyperlinks make it a particularly attractive candidate?
- Are there any pressing needs to get the document up on the intranet?
- Is the document going to be revised soon?

Based on the answers to these questions, a prioritized list of documents to go on the intranet should be drawn up, and the documents created and placed on the intranet in their designated order. The review process should be repeated periodically to confirm that the documents on the intranet should stay there and to determine what new documents should be added.

Types of Intranets

There are both decentralized and centralized intranets, and they each have pros and cons that you should consider.

Decentralized Intranets

An intranet is *decentralized* when more than one group within an organization creates and serves a web site. Very large corporations tend to have decentralized intranets, especially if the corporation does not have a department that is responsible for organizing and maintaining an intranet. There are many good reasons for having a decentralized intranet:

- It allows a "grass-roots" approach to intranet development, so departments and groups have control over what content they want to put up in their area.
- Since many groups are involved in the development of their area of the intranet, they have bought in to it and are more inclined to use the entire intranet.
- The content of the intranet tends to change more quickly because more groups are involved with its upkeep.

However, there are some cons in having a decentralized intranet—the most significant of which is that there can be many intranet servers (one per department, for example), and these servers will eventually need maintenance. This could put a heavy load on the Information Services (IS) department if they are expected to maintain these servers.

Centralized Intranets

A *centralized* intranet is an intranet that has one central group (or person) who is responsible for developing the structure (both technical and informational) and maintaining the intranet. The benefits of having a centralized intranet are

- A consistent interface design, which helps usability and navigability
- Easier maintenance from a technical perspective, because usually there is only one server

However, there are also some cons to having a centralized intranet:

- Usage levels can be low due to lack of involvement in the development process
- Site content can get out of date more easily if one group is trying to keep many different groups' content up to date
- Growth of the intranet can be slow

Whichever model you choose, it is important to consider the pros and cons of your decision and strategize ways to maximize the pros and minimize the cons. One very important task that can make or break the success of an intranet is getting buy-in from end users.

Getting Buy-In from Users

In both types of intranets, probably the most important thing you can do before you begin building or even planning your intranet is to get buy-in from your end users. *Buy-in* is the understanding from the people you want to use the intranet of how important the intranet will be for them. Depending on who your end users are, you may need to develop a campaign for the intranet, promoting its virtues in a method of communication that your community will understand and appreciate. It is very important that your end users are aware of the project, that they are asked to participate in its development, and that they are adequately trained to use it.

In a case study at the end of this chapter, you will read about how one person championed the intranet within his company. He solicited help from his colleagues in developing the intranet's information design, convinced his management team to invest in it, and then trained all users on how to use the intranet. By the time of the launch, all the users were eagerly anticipating it, and usage was very high at the end of the first week. This kind of planning is necessary to the success of your intranet project.

Building Your Infrastructure

This section broadly discusses building an intranet—covering the technical aspects of setting up your network infrastructure and providing appropriate security.

Setting Up and Configuring Your Environment

The first requirement in setting up your intranet environment is that you have a local area network (LAN) that supports the TCP/IP protocol. Two highly recommended sources of information on setting up LANs and networking are Tom Sheldon's *Encyclopedia of Networking, Electronic Edition* and *The Windows NT Web Server Handbook*, which contains an excellent section on intranets (both published by Osborne/McGraw-Hill, 1998 and 1996 respectively).

Once your LAN is functioning, you can use FrontPage as the basis for creating an intranet as small as two computers in the same office, or one that links many computers in several remote locations. The limits on growth for your intranet will be determined by the number of users and the amount of traffic on the LAN. For several computers in an office, you do not need a dedicated server. In other words, the computer running Microsoft Personal Web Server can also be used for other tasks. As the number of users and the network traffic grow, a computer will need to be dedicated to running the Microsoft Personal Web Server.

For larger intranets you should consider using a dedicated server running Windows NT and Microsoft's Internet Information Services (IIS) as your HTTP server software. IIS is more powerful than Microsoft Personal Web Server and is an integral part of Windows NT Server 4.0. FrontPage and the FrontPage IIS Server Extensions are completely compatible with Windows NT 4.0. *The Windows NT Web Server Handbook* (Osborne/McGraw-Hill, 1996), mentioned previously, is an excellent reference for creating an NT and IIS intranet or Internet web server.

Installing TCP/IP on Your Network

The first step in building an intranet on your local area network is to install the TCP/IP protocol if it is not already used. If you have a connection to the Internet, through either a dialup or network connection, TCP/IP will already be installed and configured on your computer. If you need to install TCP/IP, follow these steps:

 If you are using a dialup connection for the Internet, you may still need to install TCP/IP for your LAN, so you should go through the next set of steps just to check it out.

1. Open the Start menu and choose Settings | Control Panel.

2. When the Control Panel opens, double-click Network.

3. In the Network dialog box, select the Configuration tab if it's not already selected. Your Network dialog box should appear similar to Figure 23-2.

4. In Figure 23-2 the TCP/IP protocol is bound to both the network interface card (NIC) for my LAN connection, and to the Dial-Up Adapter (modem) for connection to the Internet. If some other protocol such as NetBEUI (NetBIOS Enhanced User Interface) or IPX/SPX (Internetwork Packet Exchange/Sequenced Packet Exchange) were bound to the NIC, then TCP/IP would have to be added. Multiple protocols can be bound to these cards, so TCP/IP can be added to the network interface card without removing any existing protocols.

5. Click Add. In the Select Network Component Type dialog box, select Protocol and click Add.

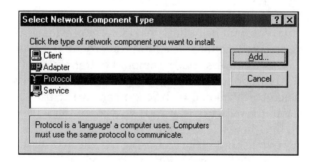

6. In the Select Network Protocol dialog box, select Microsoft from the Manufacturers list box, and then select TCP/IP from the Network Protocols list box, as shown in Figure 23-3. Click OK.

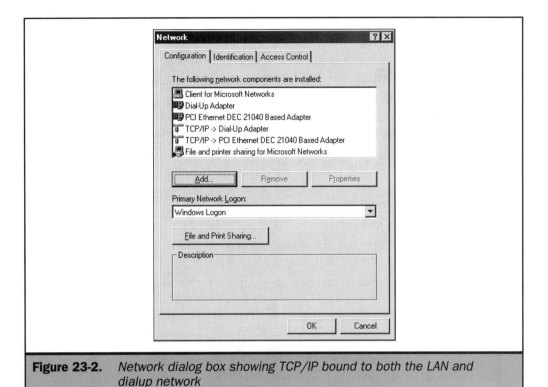

Figure 23-2. *Network dialog box showing TCP/IP bound to both the LAN and dialup network*

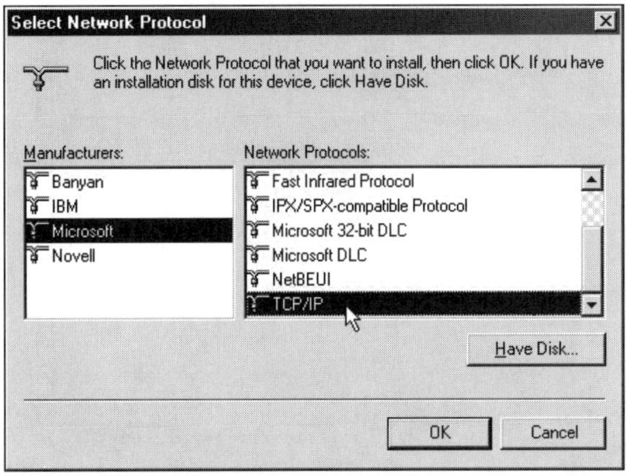

Figure 23-3. *Selecting the TCP/IP network protocol*

In a moment the Network dialog box will be redisplayed, showing that the TCP/IP protocol has been bound to your network interface card.

Configuring TCP/IP

You need to configure the TCP/IP protocol for each device it is bound to. For an intranet, the device is your network interface card. For a dialup connection to the Internet, the device is the dialup adapter. Configure your network card with these instructions:

1. In the Network dialog box, select the TCP/IP binding to your network card (in Figure 23-2 this is the line that reads "TCP/IP->PCI Ethernet DEC…" where " PCI Ethernet DEC…" represents my network card—yours will probably be different) and click Properties. Your TCP/IP Properties dialog box will open, as shown in Figure 23-4.

2. In the TCP/IP Properties dialog box, select the IP Address tab if it's not already selected.

   The IP (Internet Protocol) address is a group of four numbers that uniquely identify your computer on a TCP/IP network. For a dialup connection to the

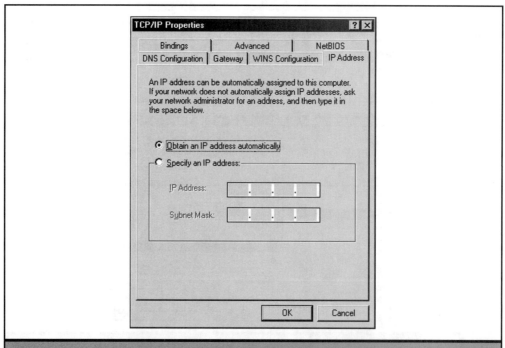

Figure 23-4. *IP Address tab of the TCP/IP Properties dialog box*

Internet, your IP address will usually be assigned automatically by the server, as might be the case with large intranets using dedicated web servers. For small intranets using the Microsoft Personal Web Server, you need to specify an IP address. You should consult your network administrator to learn what IP address you should use. However, on a small TCP/IP network, you can basically make up your own number—10.0.0.1, for example. You could then increment the number for each computer—10.0.0.2 for the next machine, and so on. As long as your computer does not try to use your IP addresses on the Internet (which it won't, if you use the dialup adapter to connect to the Internet), you will not have a problem. The IP addresses you use for your network card will not affect your settings for your dialup adapter.

An IP address is like a phone number. If you set up your own small phone system, you can use any phone numbers you want. But if you then connect your phone system to the outside world, you may have to use the phone numbers assigned by the outside authority. (Three series of numbers, though, 10.0.0.0 through 10.255.255.255, 172.16.0.0 through 172.31.255.255, and 192.168.0.1 through 192.168.255.255, have been set aside and are not currently assigned as Internet addresses. These are therefore available for you to use internally in your organization.)

Note *Do not use an IP address beginning with 127 (for example, 127.0.0.1), as this is reserved as a localhost, or loopback, address.*

3. If your server does not automatically supply an IP address, click Specify An IP Address, click the left of the IP Address text box, and type your IP address. If any number is fewer than three digits, you'll need to type a period or press RIGHT ARROW to move to the next block of numbers. If you don't have an assigned IP address, use the 10.0.0.*n* (*n* is a number between 1 and 255) set of numbers with 10.0.0.1 being the first. (Type **10**, press RIGHT ARROW, type **0**, press RIGHT ARROW, type **0**, press RIGHT ARROW, and type **1** to get the address shown below.)

4. Click the left end of the Subnet Mask text box and type **2552550.0**. This is the default subnet mask, applicable in almost all circumstances; in most instances it

is automatically entered for you. We're suggesting that you enter it here to cover the few instances where it will hang you up if it is missing.

5. Select the Bindings tab. Client For Microsoft Networks should be selected, and then File And Printer Sharing For Microsoft Networks, as you can see in Figure 23-5. Click them if they are not selected.

6. Click OK twice.

After changing your network settings, you must restart your computer for the changes to take effect. Make sure you save any open documents before restarting.

 Caution *For TCP/IP on your dialup adapter, you do not want to have File And Printer Sharing selected. This is for security. If you are connected to the Internet by use of your dialup connection, it is possible (although unlikely) for others on the Internet to access your shared resources over the TCP/IP connection. You can still share resources with others on your network by using File And Printer Sharing on your LAN adapter.*

Using Your FrontPage-Created Intranet

Once TCP/IP is configured properly on your network, accessing your FrontPage-created webs from any computer on the network is a simple process. First make sure the Microsoft Personal Web Server is running on the computer that will be the server. Then start your web browser on one of the other computers on the network. To access a web, use the URL http://*computername/webname* where *computername* is the computer's name running the Microsoft Personal Web Server, and *webname* is the name of the web you want to open.

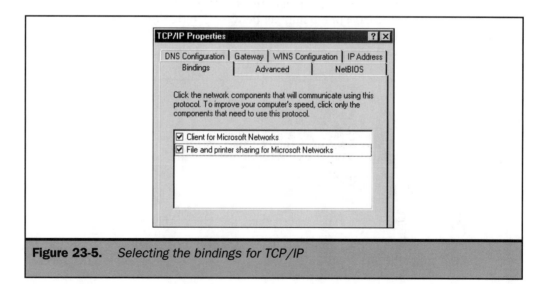

Figure 23-5.   *Selecting the bindings for TCP/IP*

For example, I have two networked computers named "Marty" and "George" using Windows and Ethernet cards. Here are the steps I went through to bring up a FrontPage intranet:

1. Set up the TCP/IP protocol bound to the LAN adapters on both computers, as described earlier.

2. Restart both computers.

3. Make sure the Microsoft Personal Web Server is running on Marty.

4. Start a browser on George, enter the address **//marty/excitingtravel/**, and press ENTER. The Exciting Travel home page that was created earlier in this book appears as shown in Figure 23-6.

If your intranet doesn't immediately come up the first time you try, take heart; mine didn't either. Here is a list of troubleshooting questions:

■ Does your network otherwise function normally between the two computers you are trying to use with an intranet? If not, you must solve your networking

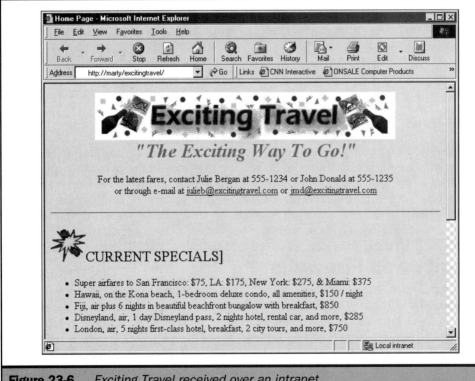

Figure 23-6.   *Exciting Travel received over an intranet*

problems before trying to use an intranet. See your network administrator or other technical network reference.

■ Has TCP/IP been successfully installed and bound to your LAN adapter (not just to your dialup adapter)? On *both* machines? Reopen your Network control panel to check this.

■ Did you restart both computers after installing TCP/IP?

■ Is the Microsoft Personal Web Server loaded on the machine where the webs are located? When you address this machine from the second machine, your hard disk light will blink.

■ Have you entered the correct server name and web name in your browser? You can determine the server name and how well your TCP/IP network is running by running the Network Test in the About Microsoft FrontPage dialog box (from FrontPage, open the Help menu, choose About Microsoft FrontPage, and click Network Test). Click Start Test, and it will respond with the "Host name," as shown next, which is the server name to use in the address. If you do not get a response similar to that shown here (obviously, your server will be named differently and your IP address may be different), then your TCP/IP network is not functioning properly.

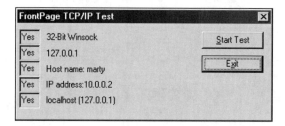

If you take a couple of minutes to make sure that each of the preceding questions is answered in the affirmative, your intranet will almost surely work. Errors we have made include forgetting to restart one of the computers and not spelling the web name correctly.

Security and Firewalls

Anytime you share resources over a network, the possibility exists that someone may access your files without your permission. The risk is greater when one or more computers on an intranet are also connected to the Internet. There are several things you can do to protect yourself and your files. One of the simplest, as mentioned previously, is to disable file and printer sharing for TCP/IP on your dialup adapter. You can still share files over your LAN, but you have closed access to everyone on the Internet coming in through TCP/IP and your dialup adapter.

Greater security can be achieved through the use of a firewall and possibly a proxy server, as was discussed in Chapter 21. A firewall is a computer that controls the flow of data between an intranet and the Internet by packet filtering.

Packet filtering passes or rejects IP packets based on the IP address that sent the packet. This allows you to configure your firewall to allow access from specific computers outside your intranet that you trust. This method isn't as secure as a proxy server because it's possible for someone to duplicate a trusted IP address.

Use of a proxy server means that every request and response must be examined by the proxy server. This can slow the response of your network, but the proxy server can also cache frequently requested information, thus speeding some responses. If the source of a request is a computer without permission to access your intranet, the proxy server will reject it.

Besides Chapter 21, check out Tom Sheldon's *Windows NT Security Handbook,* published by Osborne/McGraw-Hill (1996), on the subject of intranet security and how to implement it. If your intranet will be accessible to the outside world, you will need to take measures to protect your data. This and the books mentioned earlier in this chapter can provide a good place to start.

Building Your Intranet

Once your network environment is complete, you can begin creating content. The needs analysis that you perform in the early stages of intranet development is a critical piece of information now. This section focuses on the "front end" of your intranet: the design and the information that make up your intranet. In the first topic in this section, you will get an overview of how to quickly put up documents on your intranet. Read this first if you are raring to go. Following this overview are more in-depth discussions of how FrontPage can help you create your intranet.

Overview

In Chapter 12 you read about importing existing, or legacy, files into FrontPage to create webs both on the Internet and on your intranet with examples of word processing, spreadsheet, and presentation files being used. In Chapter 18 you saw how to access database files in a FrontPage-created web. With the techniques in these chapters, just about all corporate information can be accessed through an intranet. Once you have imported the raw material from existing files, you can add any of the interactive features that are available with FrontPage. Among these are

- **Table of Contents Component** to quickly build an index of the material that is brought in
- **Search Form Component** to add the capability to search the material
- **Shared Borders** to place headers and footers on each page with navbars, time stamps, and mailto addresses

- **Forms** to solicit responses from the reader
- **Discussion web** associated with the legacy-derived web to promote a discussion about the contents of the legacy material

Most legacy material does not contain a lot of graphics or multimedia. Consider augmenting your legacy-derived webs with additional graphics and multimedia to make them more interesting to read and/or use.

One obvious question is: Given that all the components, graphics, and multimedia are great, but I don't have time for all that, can I quickly put my legacy documents on the company intranet and have them usable? The answer is yes—most definitely yes if they have a consistently applied style in the documents. Look at the few steps it takes to put a single directory of titles on a web, and the neat results:

1. Load FrontPage, open the File menu, and choose New | Web.

2. In the New dialog box, click Import Web Wizard, name the folder **ImportTest**, and click OK. The Import Web Wizard dialog box will open.

3. Browse your hard drive or network, and select the source directory containing the files you want to import and click Next. (Make sure some Word files are in there!) Select the files in the directory that you *don't* want, and click Exclude (see next illustration). Click Next and then Finish. Your web is created!

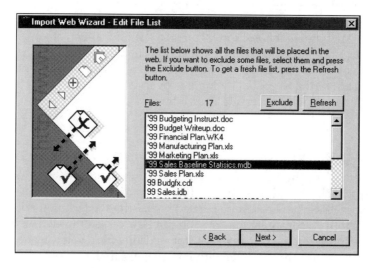

4. Without doing further work in FrontPage, open your browser, type **//servername/ImportTest/**, and you will get a list of files associated with the

web, since we didn't specify a Default.htm file ("Directory Browsing Allowed" in the WWW Administrator—Directory page of the Web Server Administrator).

5. Click a Word document and voilà! your document appears as you can see in Figure 23-7. (If your document has headings formatted as a headings style and you don't have the index on the side, open the View menu and choose Document Map if you are using Microsoft Word and Internet Explorer.)

If you have headings formatted as such, all of your headings are automatically made into a table of contents with hyperlinks to the actual headings in the document, so you have a built-in navigation system without doing anything. You can, of course, do much more to improve this document in FrontPage, but the point is that almost without doing anything, you have a web complete with navigation around a document.

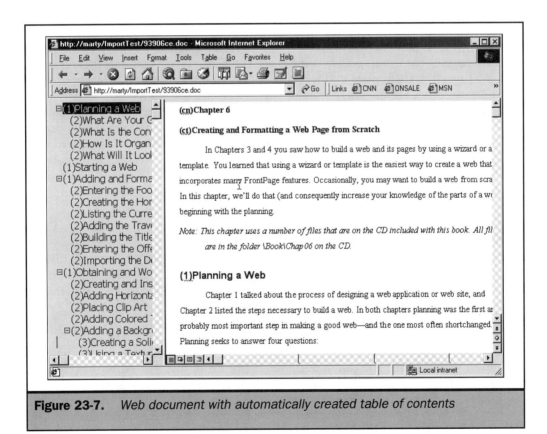

Figure 23-7. *Web document with automatically created table of contents*

Creating an Intranet from Scratch

In this section, you will be using the needs analysis and other information collected in the planning stage of your intranet project.

Organizing Information

Earlier in the chapter, you read how planning and collecting information and conducting a needs analysis was critical to the success of your intranet. If you have gone as far as assessing what the end users need to have on their intranet in order to meet the overall objective for the intranet, and you have collected documents and notes, then you are ready to begin organizing this information.

If you look at what you have assembled, you will see that certain groups need certain information, and there is some information that all groups need—such as access to Human Resources information, the cafeteria menu, and how much vacation time they have left. Look for information that you think people will want to have immediately at their fingertips. Take a large piece of poster board or butcher paper and write the word "Home" on it. This is your intranet home page, also known as the top-level page. What would people want to see at this level? Try to mimic the terms and structures that are in place and working within your organization—for example, if your Library, Office Supplies, and Imaging departments are known as Resource Services within your organization, then you will want to logically group these together under that same heading on your intranet. When you have arrived at a structure that you think will work, go back to your committee and present your ideas. Be prepared to do this at least twice before you hit upon a structure that makes sense to the majority of your end users.

Once you have a structure that is approved by your committee of users, you are ready to begin physically building your intranet.

Using Wizards to Create an Intranet

As you saw in Chapter 3, FrontPage comes with wizards that walk you through the process of creating certain kinds of web sites, as well as wizards that help you import web sites from other locations. In the next two sections you will see two wizards that are especially relevant to intranet development.

THE IMPORT WEB WIZARD   If you began to create an intranet and have its directory structure in place on a computer, you can import this set of folders by using the Import Web Wizard. You can import folders from your own hard drive, and also from any computer on your LAN. You saw the process for doing this in the "Overview" section earlier in this chapter.

THE DISCUSSION WEB WIZARD   Another wizard that can be used in an intranet is the Discussion Web Wizard. The Discussion Web Wizard creates a FrontPage web that enables bulletin-board communication among users. Users submit topics by entering text in a form, they can search previous messages using a search form, and they access articles using a table of contents. See Chapter 3 for a thorough look at the Discussion web.

Using the Microsoft Intranet Templates

Microsoft has provided two web sites exclusively for intranet building. You can visit the Microsoft TechNet Intranet site at **http://www.microsoft.com/technet/intranet/** (see Figure 23-8) and the 60 Minute Intranet Kit at **http://www.microsoft.com/office/intranet** (see Figure 23-9). The latter site showcases a kit that enables you to download, unpack, and import an intranet site into FrontPage in less than one hour. The site features 12 predesigned sites complete with complex functionality, such as discussion boards, searchable employee directories, and channels. In addition to the 12 "canned" solutions, Microsoft also gives you a Foundation Intranet template (which is also used with the full sites) and seven modules that you can use to build your own intranet.

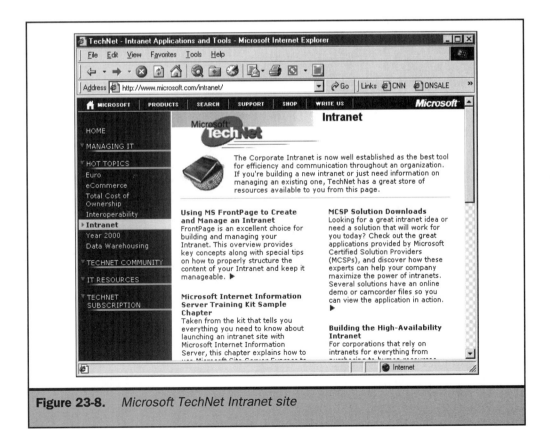

Figure 23-8. *Microsoft TechNet Intranet site*

EXTENDING YOUR WEB SITE

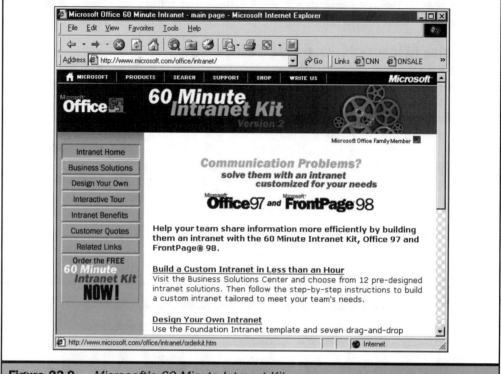

Figure 23-9.   *Microsoft's 60 Minute Intranet Kit*

> **Note**
>
> *Some of the Microsoft intranet templates require IIS 3.0 or later with Active Server Pages, as well as Internet Explorer 4.0 or later as a browser. The Foundation Intranet template, though, can run with Windows, Microsoft Personal Web Server, Internet Explorer 3.0, and FrontPage 2000. Before you download the templates, check the system and user requirements for each.*

You can choose an intranet template that's right for your needs by looking at the table of intranet objectives that Microsoft provides:

- Communicating across groups
- Communicating within a team
- Streamlining business processes
- Improving customer service

Each objective has one to four possible intranet solutions for you to download and test. As with other FrontPage wizards, it is up to you to add your look and feel, and to customize the pages that appear on the site. All the functionality, however, is in place when you finish downloading and installing the modules for each intranet.

To begin using the complete intranet sites or to have a foundation for your own custom site, you must first download their Foundation Intranet template. This template becomes part of the options in your New FrontPage Web dialog box. Once the Foundation Intranet template has been downloaded and installed, you will see "Intranet" as one of your options.

With the Foundation Intranet template in place, you can design your own intranet by downloading whichever modules you might want to use. Each module has its own set of directions for installing it, so you can try them out one at a time. You can read about each module at **http://www.microsoft.com/office/intranet/modules.htm**.

To download and install the Foundation Intranet template:

1. Connect to **http://www.microsoft.com/office/intranet/modules.htm**, and click The Foundation Intranet Template.

2. When you are prompted to Open This File or Save This File To Disk, choose Save This File To Disk. Find the C:\Program Files\Microsoft FrontPage\ folder, and click Save to download the file there.

3. When it's finished downloading, locate C:\Program Files\Microsoft FrontPage\Foundation.zip and use WinZip, which is on the CD that accompanies this book, to unzip it, extracting its contents in that same folder. This will create a new folder named Foundation Intranet.

4. Open the Foundation Intranet folder, and double-click the Foundation.exe file. You are told that you are about to place the Intranet template into \Program Files\Microsoft Office\Templates\1033\Webs folder. If not, change the destination to that. Click Unzip and then click OK and Close when told that the operation has been completed successfully.

5. In FrontPage, open the File menu and choose New | Web. Notice that the New dialog box now has a new Intranet option, as you can see in Figure 23-10.

6. Select Intranet, name the folder **Intranet**, and click OK. FrontPage will open and display a complete nine-page web, shown in Figure 23-11, which you can customize and add to as you wish.

Once you have the Foundation intranet web created, you can then choose either one of the 12 complete intranet solutions that Microsoft offers, or choose one or more of the seven modules that are available for you to use to create your own intranet web. Spend time on the **http://www.microsoft.com/office/intranet** site looking at the many options that are available there, and also look at each of the nine Foundation pages in Page view.

EXTENDING
YOUR WEB SITE

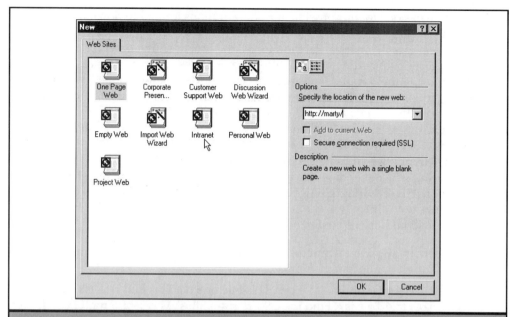

Figure 23-10. *Intranet option now available in the New dialog box*

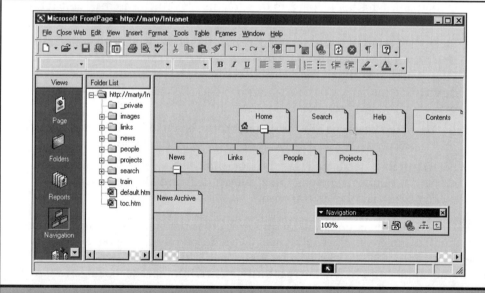

Figure 23-11. *The Foundation intranet web*

Using Themes

Themes are a feature of FrontPage 2000 that can be particularly useful when you're creating an intranet—for a number of reasons:

- Themes provide consistent graphical interfaces throughout the site.
- Themes can be easily changed, so if you use one theme and later decide you don't like it, you can easily switch to another theme.
- Themes are well designed and provide built-in hierarchy to aid in creating graphical user interfaces that work.

You can either initially create your web with a theme or add it after you have created a new web by clicking Theme on the Format menu. The Expedition theme is added by default to the Foundation intranet web site. Here is how you can change it:

1. With the Foundation Internet web loaded in FrontPage, open the Format menu and click Theme.

2. Make sure the All Pages option is selected, and choose a theme from the list. As you click a theme, it will be displayed in the right-hand pane.

3. When you have found the theme you want to use, look at the various options: Vivid Colors, Active Graphics, and Background Image. If you want to modify or customize the theme, click Modify and see Chapter 11 for the procedure. When the theme is complete, click OK to have it used throughout a web, as shown in Figure 23-12.

 The Radius theme in Figure 23-13 is one of the additional themes that are available on the Office or FrontPage CD. You can install it by clicking Install Additional Themes in the Themes dialog box.

One obvious use of themes within an intranet would be to differentiate between departments. If each individual department did not have a graphical designer to create a unique look for their department, they could use themes as a quick way to get an interface up. Remember, though, to include a link back to the home page of the intranet—ideally a graphical link that is used throughout the site—so that users begin to associate that image with the home page. You can read more about themes in Chapter 3.

Adding Content to Your Intranet

There are many ways to add content to a FrontPage web. This section discusses using page templates, dragging Office documents, and importing text into your FrontPage web.

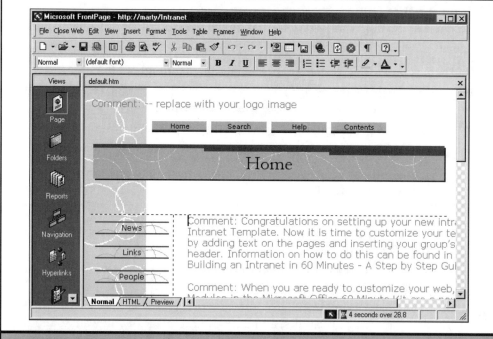

Figure 23-12.   *The Radius theme applied to the Foundation web*

Page Templates

Page templates are part of FrontPage's stock collection of content. The kinds of templates that are available to you are either content templates or formatting templates. Page templates are excellent starting points for creating web pages. *Formatting* page templates enable you to easily create pages with complex layouts. *Content* templates (such as a bibliography or meeting agenda template) help you create common types of web pages often found on a web site.

Examples of the content templates included with FrontPage are

- Bibliography
- Confirmation Form
- Feedback Form
- Frequently Asked Questions
- Guest Book
- Search Page

Some examples of formatting templates are

- Narrow left-aligned body
- One centered column
- One column with contents sidebar
- One column with two sidebars
- Three-column body
- Two columns with contents

There are many other formatting templates for you to choose from. To access these page templates, open Page view, open the File menu, and choose New Page. You will see a dialog box listing all the templates from which to choose, as shown in Figure 23-13.

To read more about page templates, see Chapter 4.

Dragging and Dropping Office Documents

Much of the content that you will want to have on your intranet site will be in the form of Office documents. Most of the critical documents produced in an organization are created in either Word or Excel, and in some cases, it's ideal to keep these documents

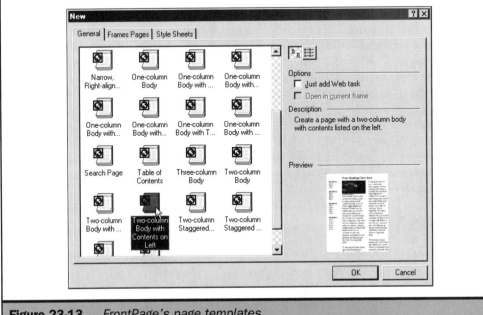

Figure 23-13. *FrontPage's page templates*

in their native form. For example, an Excel spreadsheet produced by the Finance department that includes interactive pivot tables might be of greater value in its native file format than if it was converted into HTML, because HTML is static. If you are using Internet Explorer as your intranet browser, you will want to take advantage of its ability to display Office documents over an intranet or Internet site in their native formats. Also with FrontPage 2000, you can have the best of both a static HTML document and a fully interactive Excel spreadsheet and not run the risk of having your original spreadsheet changed by using the FrontPage Spreadsheet, Pivot Table, or Chart components in an HTML page.

When you are creating your intranet, you will have many documents that you will want to get into your FrontPage web quickly, and with FrontPage you can easily drag and drop files and folders from your hard drive or network directly into your FrontPage window. See Chapter 12 for more information on importing files.

The first time you import a particular file format, whether from Word, Excel, or some other program, you will be told that the file conversion program will need to be installed. Make sure your Office 2000 or FrontPage 2000 CD is in the drive and then click Yes to install the program.

Managing Content on Your Intranet

Managing an intranet is a challenging task. To manage a large site effectively, you need to have tools that are flexible and that integrate with both your production process and your system infrastructure. This is where FrontPage really shines as a site management tool. FrontPage provides tools that check the quality of your site, allow you to perform sitewide managerial tasks, and provide flexibility in working with both large and small intranets. The tasks involved with managing an intranet site include link verification, task management, sitewide spelling, and when necessary, some level of overall site design and quality assurance.

If you have created subwebs for your departments or groups, then someone will need to become "webmaster" to each of these subwebs. These people will be responsible for managing the content of their respective webs. Web administrators can use FrontPage's management tools to perform management tasks on their web. The best place to start is in Reports view.

Using Reports View

FrontPage's Reports view, shown in Figure 23-14, provides the means to look at your web site and determine if you have problems, or if something needs attention. Reports view starts with a Site Summary, which gives you an overview of your site including the number and size of your files, the pages that may be slow in loading, broken hyperlinks, and component errors among a number of other statistics and facts.

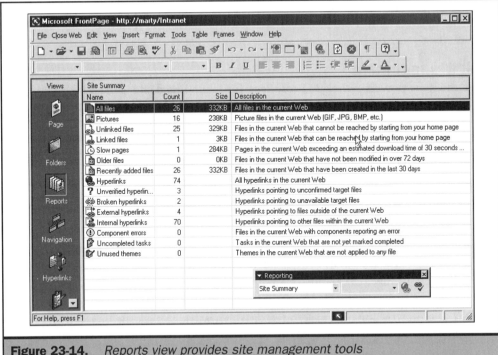

Figure 23-14.   *Reports view provides site management tools*

Note   As a default, files in hidden folders, such as the _Private folder, are not included in the files counts. You can change that by opening the Tools menu, choosing Web Settings, Advanced tab, and clicking Show Documents In Hidden Directories.

If you double-click many of the summary lines in the Site Summary, the lines will be expanded into full reports showing the individual web pages that have a certain characteristic. In some cases you can also set, in the Reporting toolbar, the criteria for determining if a page fits into a particular category. For example, for slow pages you can set the number of seconds that is the threshold of "slow," like this:

When you open a detail report, you can return to the Site Summary by selecting it in the category list on the left of the Reporting toolbar, or by opening the View menu and choosing Reports | Site Summary. Take time familiarizing yourself with the detail reports in Reports view. They can provide a lot of valuable information with which to manage a site.

Task Management

One of the most powerful tools in FrontPage for managing a site is the Task Manager. This allows you to establish tasks for creating and maintaining the site, attach those tasks to particular pages, assign the task to individuals, and then track the status of the tasks. Starting the task opens the associated page, and saving the page opens a dialog box asking if you want to change the task status. See how this is done with the following steps:

To have an associated task, you need to have a page opened when you create the task; if you create a task without a page open, you can still do it, but it won't be associated with a page.

1. To add a new task to the Tasks list, open the Edit menu and choose Task | Add Task. The New Task dialog box will open as shown in Figure 23-15. Fill out the dialog box and click OK.

2. To begin working on a task, open Tasks view, right-click the task, and choose Start Task. The associated page will be opened in Page view for you to edit.

3. When you save the page, you will be asked if you want to mark the page as completed. If you choose No, the status will be changed from "Not Started" to "In Progress." If you choose Yes, the status will be marked "Completed." You can see the three possible statuses here:

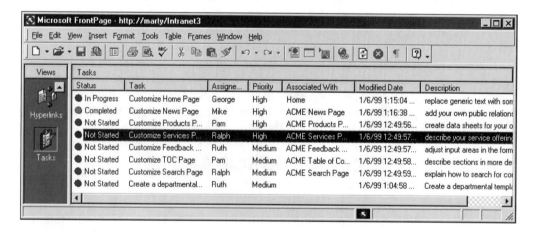

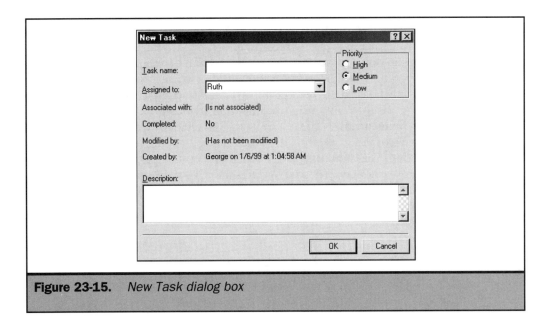

Figure 23-15.   *New Task dialog box*

While it will take some effort to create and maintain the Tasks list, it will pay significant dividends in helping you manage a dynamic site.

Facilitating Site Design and Maintaining Quality

One of the more difficult tasks of managing an intranet's content is providing consistent global navigational tools that can be used throughout the various content areas and subwebs. One common strategy is to provide a single, global navigation bar or navbar with certain visual conventions, such as Home and Search buttons or other sitewide elements. This global navbar enables the different web authors working on the site to provide a way to get to the central areas of the site from within their subweb or content area. Providing this kind of tool ensures smooth navigation, because end users become accustomed to seeing this global navbar and will quickly learn how to navigate swiftly between content areas.

Note   *Providing a global navbar may sound simply like common sense; however, in very large intranets that are decentralized and maintained by many different web authors, it is common to see almost no consistent navigational convention. These intranets are true "web" experiences in that when you click around, you are definitely entering cyberspace. In an efficient intranet, though, it is critically important that users find the information they need quickly and easily, which demands a standardized set of navigational tools.*

EXTENDING
YOUR WEB SITE

Creating Subwebs for Departmental Web Sites

It's a very good idea—in fact, it is highly recommended—that you break up your intranet into subwebs in order to manage the growing content areas. In the beginning, it might seem like overkill to assign each department its own subweb, but as the web grows, and more people take on the responsibility of creating content for it, having a separate subweb for areas that have a significant amount of content in them will end up being much more manageable.

When FrontPage webs get very large, the time it takes to open, edit, and save a page gets very irritating. This is because often when you open a page, the FrontPage Server Extensions processes every file and updates its private directories, especially if the pages are using FrontPage components such as image maps and included pages. If your web site gets to be more than about 50 pages, it's time to think about breaking sections of it into subwebs.

Using NT Permissions for Subwebs

When you partition your FrontPage intranet into subwebs that correspond to departments or groups within your organization, you can use your existing NT user/group permissions to grant access to the different subwebs. This means that any user in the Human Resources group can be granted author and browse access to the Human Resources subweb, but users outside of HR can possibly only browse or be locked out all together.

Verifying Hyperlinks Within an Intranet Site

One of the biggest maintenance problems in large, decentralized (or even centralized) intranet sites is ensuring that all of the links point to the correct files. In large web sites, this can be a full-time task without tools to help. FrontPage 2000 provides tools for verifying the hyperlinks in your web site. To verify that all your hyperlinks are valid in FrontPage, select Reports view and click Verify Hyperlinks on the Reports toolbar. The Verify Hyperlinks dialog box appears, as you can see in Figure 23-16. Click Start. The Broken Hyperlinks report lists all broken hyperlinks, both internal and external.

The hyperlink verification process can take a very long time to carry out. It is the kind of task that you want to start and then go to lunch. Hopefully, it will be done when you return. The status bar will tell you the progress.

To fix the broken hyperlinks, double-click the hyperlink entry in the Broken Hyperlink report. An Edit Hyperlink dialog box appears, as shown next, which allows

Figure 23-16. *Verifying hyperlinks in FrontPage*

you to replace the hyperlink with a new one for which you can browse, or you can edit the page containing the hyperlink and change it.

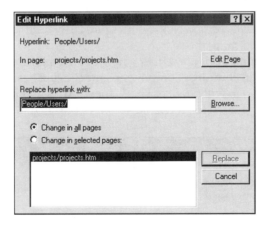

Sitewide Spelling

FrontPage has two tools to check spelling within web pages:

- In Page view the Spelling command checks the spelling within the active page.
- In all other views the Spelling command opens the Spelling dialog box, where you can choose to check the spelling in just the selected pages or throughout the entire web, as shown next.

Note *The cross-file spelling checker does not check pages open in Page view, so be sure to close all pages in Page view before using the spelling checker.*

The Spelling dialog box also allows you to have pages with misspellings automatically added to the task list.

Using FrontPage Components

Several FrontPage components are commonly used in successful intranet sites. Among these are the Search Form Component and the Table of Contents Component to make finding information easy and intuitive, and the Include Page Component and Shared Borders to place consistent elements on every page.

THE SEARCH FORM COMPONENT The Search Component provides a keyword search through all documents in a web. The Search Component creates a form in which users type the text to locate, as you can see in Figure 23-17, and then displays a list of hyperlinks to pages containing the search text.

A Search Component is added to either a new or an existing page in Page view by opening the Insert menu, choosing Component, and clicking Search Form. The Search Form Properties dialog box will open, as shown next. After making the necessary changes, click OK and a search form will be added to the current page.

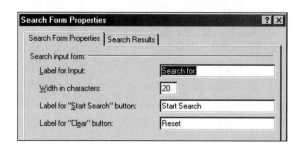

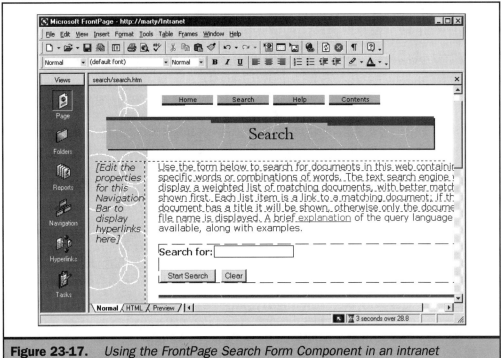

Figure 23-17. *Using the FrontPage Search Form Component in an intranet*

Tip *To protect pages from being found by users searching your web site with the Search form, move the pages into the _Private folder in the current FrontPage web. The Search form does not search in this folder.*

TABLE OF CONTENTS COMPONENT The Table of Contents Component creates a listing of all the pages on the site. You can add this component to either an existing or new page in Page view by opening the Insert menu and choosing Component | Table of Contents. This will open the Table of Contents Properties dialog box, where you can specify the starting page in the web (normally the home page) and how the table of contents should be displayed, like this:

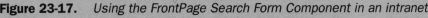

You will not be able to see the detail within a table of contents until you look at it in a browser. The table of contents is a dynamic feature that is rebuilt and displayed when someone accesses the page. When pages are added or deleted, they will automatically be added to or deleted from the table of contents when the table of contents is accessed.

The options in the Table of Contents Properties dialog box are handled as follows:

- **Page URL For Starting Point Of Table**   Supply the relative URL of the page at which to start the table of contents. For a table of contents that encompasses the entire FrontPage web, type or browse to the URL of the web's home page.

- **Heading Font Size**   Select a heading style for the first entry in the table of contents. If you do not want a heading, select None.

- **Show Each Page Only Once**   Select this check box if you want each page in your FrontPage web to appear only once in the table of contents. A page can appear more than once if it is pointed to by multiple hyperlinks in your FrontPage web.

- **Show Pages With No Incoming Hyperlinks**   Select this check box to include orphan pages in your table of contents. Orphan pages are pages that cannot be reached by following hyperlinks from the home page.

- **Recompute Table Of Contents When Any Other Page Is Edited**   Select this check box to specify that the table of contents page should be re-created whenever any page in the current FrontPage web is edited. This can be a time-consuming process if the FrontPage web is large. If you do not select this check box, you can manually regenerate the table of contents by opening and saving the page containing the table of contents.

INCLUDE PAGE COMPONENT   The Include Page Component allows you to include the contents of one web page on another web page when you load the second web page in a browser. Include pages are good to use when you have content that can change and that appears on many pages in a web site. An *include page* references another file, so when the content of the include page changes, you do not have to modify the page in which it loads. Include pages can be used to add a consistent title or banner and navbar to every page in a web, or just as easily to add the contact, update, and copyright information at the bottom of every page.

For example, to add information at the bottom of every page, you would enter the information on a new blank page, shown next, and then save that page.

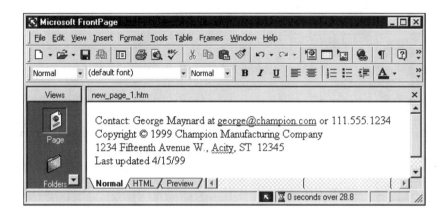

When you have the page you want included, open the page in Page view on which you want it included, open the Insert menu, and choose Component | Include Page. The Include Page Component Properties dialog box will open and ask for the URL of the page to be included. You can either enter the URL or use Browse to locate it and then click OK. The contents of the included page will appear on the current page fully formatted with whatever theme is attached to the current page, as shown in Figure 23-18. If you look at the HTML, though, all you see is a single line, like this:

```
<!-webbot bot="Include"
U-Include=http://server/intranet/contact.htm TAG="Body"->
```

SHARED BORDERS   FrontPage 2000 has a feature called Shared Borders that allows you to add common sections, such as the top heading, navigation buttons, and bottom contact/copyright information to all pages in a web, much as you can with the Include Page Component. The difference is that with Shared Borders you can work on any of the pages that share the borders, and you don't have a separate page to maintain. You choose one or more of the four page borders to share, and anything you place in those border areas appears on every page. In the top and left borders you can include a set of

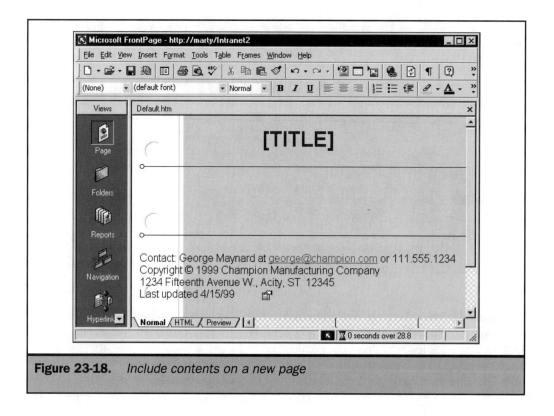

Figure 23-18. *Include contents on a new page*

navigation buttons. To add Shared Borders to a web, pick any page in the web, open the Format menu, and choose Shared Borders. The Shared Borders dialog box will open as you can see here:

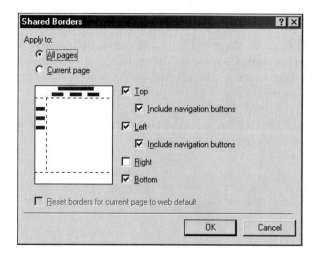

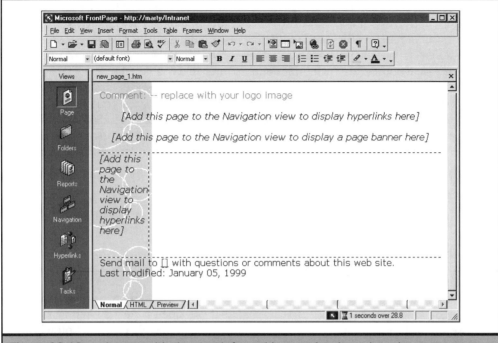

Figure 23-19.   *A page with the top, left, and bottom borders shared*

Make sure All Pages is set, choose which borders you want to share, and whether or not you want to include navigation buttons. When you click OK, all the pages in the web will have the shared borders. If you add a page to the web, it too will have the shared borders, as shown in Figure 23-19. If you want a particular page to not have one or more of the borders, open the page in Page view and then open the Shared Borders dialog box, click Current Page, and change the settings, which will only be reflected on the current page.

Web Page Version Control with Visual SourceSafe

If you have several—or especially if you have many—people working on creating material for your web site, you'll need a way to control the various versions of the many pages you'll end up with. FrontPage 2000 has provided help in this area by incorporating links between Microsoft Visual SourceSafe and the FrontPage Server Extensions running on a Windows NT server.

Microsoft Visual SourceSafe is a separate product that you must purchase. It allows you to track various versions with a project orientation, while providing tools for storing, accessing, and organizing files, and mediating among developers. The project orientation allows the system, not the people, to keep track of the relationship between files.

Use of Visual SourceSafe with FrontPage requires that Visual SourceSafe be installed on the server where the FrontPage Server Extensions and the production webs that are in use are kept. If you have Visual SourceSafe installed this way, when you place a web on the server, you'll be asked if you want to make the web a Visual SourceSafe project. If so, when you recalculate the links, the files will be checked into Visual SourceSafe. You can then use Visual SourceSafe from a client workstation using FrontPage through three commands in the context menus (opened by right-clicking the file):

- **Check Out** to edit a file
- **Check In** to return a file that has been edited and have it update Visual SourceSafe accordingly
- **Undo Check Out** to return a file that has not been changed

When you are the first or only person to check out a file, a checkmark will appear beside the filename in FrontPage. When someone else has checked out a file you are looking at, it will have a padlock beside the name. If you open Page view with a file that someone else has checked out, you'll see "(Read Only)" in the title bar, and you'll be unable to edit the file. If you open Page view with a file that you have not checked out (and no one else has either), you'll see "(Not Checked Out)" in the title bar. In this latter case you can still make changes to the file, but when you try to save the file, FrontPage will check to see if the file has changed since you opened it. If the file has not changed, FrontPage will automatically check it out and back in again in Visual SourceSafe. If the file has been modified, you will be asked if you want to overwrite the changes.

In some instances, changes you make to a page you have checked out affect pages that others have checked out. These changes fall into two categories: incidental changes and substantive changes. *Incidental* changes, for example, are like changing an included page used as a header on other pages. In this case FrontPage is not concerned about the pages on which the header is included, and the pages are not checked to see if they are being edited. *Substantive* changes, like deleting or moving a page referenced by other pages that are checked out, will not be allowed, and an error message will tell you why.

Visual SourceSafe is a powerful tool to help maintain an intranet on which multiple people are working. It does assume, though, that you are using a separate Windows NT server with the FrontPage Server Extensions and that you have published your webs to that server.

Intranet Case Study

This is a case study of creating an intranet at a medium-sized firm. The idea grew out of the Information Services (IS) application development manager thinking about how to support a major reengineering project. He knew that long before any planning could be done, he would have to begin promoting the idea of an intranet. He began talking with associates in his department and also with the management team about intranets and what other companies were doing with them.

Once the IS manager had created interest in the idea, he began collecting statistics from resources on the Internet. From these statistics, he was able to put together a presentation illustrating the trends in intranet development and making some points regarding how an intranet could improve communication within the firm, especially with remote offices.

The IS manager presented his ideas to the executive management. After a series of discussions, he was asked to put together a budget for his project. To do this, he needed to contact an outside partner to help him understand the scope of his undertaking.

Locating Resources

The IS manager contacted the Microsoft Solution Provider (MSP) network, which is an organization of firms that specialize in providing software solutions for the Microsoft product line. The company looking to build an intranet uses a number of Microsoft products, including Windows NT, Windows 95/98, Office, and FrontPage, so he knew that his choice of Internet software was going to be a Microsoft product.

The IS manager was put in touch with an MSP specializing in intranet, e-commerce, and extranet solutions. Together, the manager and the MSP scoped the project and developed a budget that met the expectations of the management and allowed for a significant Phase I intranet project.

Planning and Design

Before the MSP became involved, the manager had conducted many interviews with his coworkers to understand how they interacted with each other, so that he could determine what would be the best strategy for a Phase I effort. He determined that for Phase I, he would focus on getting out a small but relevant amount of information using the 80/20 rule. He would try to put out 20 percent of all company information that represented a usage by 80 percent of the company's population. He created the initial flowchart that the MSP would use to develop the information architecture and user interface for the site.

When the MSP became involved, they conducted more interviews with key members of departments and did a full assessment of their needs and wants. They targeted about 10 percent of the content that they collected to use for the first-phase launch, paying close attention to what kinds of software systems were in place in the Accounting, Human Resources, and other departments. These systems would need to be fully investigated to determine how they might be later implemented into the intranet.

Though a full investigation of existing systems took place, the manager and the MSP decided that for the Phase I launch to be successful, they would need to "aim low and grow." They didn't want to promise too much and then go over budget, so they focused on small wins, or "low-hanging fruit," as the manager called it. The content that would go up on launch were

- Office documents pertaining to each department
- An employee phone list
- A corporate calendar (the code can be obtained from Microsoft: **http://backoffice.microsoft.com/General/Calendar/Calendar.htm**)
- Telecom services information
- A Forms repository of all corporate forms in their native format
- A Help Desk
- A "Fun" area featuring Java puzzlers and quotes of the day (free Java shareware is available at **http://www.gamelan.com**)
- A Do-it-yourself area with downloadable templates and graphics for people who wanted to begin creating intranet documents

To support this, the MSP worked with the IS department to configure and install the Internet software and firewall. Microsoft's Internet Information Services with Active Server Pages, Visual SourceSafe, Index Server (because of its ability to provide hit highlighting for PDF files with Adobe's filter), and FrontPage as its authoring tool. The MSP and the IS manger set up a development environment and a production environment on two separate machines. The MSP provided network diagrams and documentation so that the IS department could maintain the servers themselves.

While the MSP's engineering team was working to configure the environment, their design team was creating interface composites for the IS manager to look at. The design team had to take many things into consideration, such as download time (for off-site employees) of graphics, printing capability (for forms), and usability, since many employees had never used an intranet before. They decided that not only was a simple interface with clear and obvious navigational entities important, but also that some degree of intranet training would be necessary to ensure a smooth rollout and usability on the first day.

Implementation

After the infrastructure was put into place and the design was decided on, the MSP's production and application development teams went into motion. The production team used FrontPage to create templates for each specific type of page (Department page, Forms page, Calendar page, and Fun page). They used include pages to maintain consistent header and footer information, and provided a blank include page for each department so that departments could insert changing promotional information as it came up, without having to touch each page.

The production team converted Office documents to HTML in some cases and in others, especially for financial information, they left the Office documents in native formats.

The application development team worked on setting up an employee phone list that used an Excel spreadsheet as its data source. This spreadsheet was maintained by an administrator on a weekly basis using a searchable directory on a Microsoft SQL Server. The IS manager's objective was to ensure that end users would not have to change their current modes of work unnecessarily. As a result, the MSP created a process by which the Excel spreadsheet could be used from a location that the administrator was familiar with.

Testing

A number of testing rounds were carried out. On a weekly basis for three weeks, a thorough bug report was prepared and passed on to the MSP. The MSP's production team tracked all bugs in the Excel spreadsheet, and a QA representative monitored their completion. The MSP also conducted usability tests with a controlled group of testers to assess their ability to navigate through the site. The testers were given a series of tasks to do on the site, and the production staff monitored how they achieved their tasks. Some examples of the tasks were

1. Find the Expense Report form.
2. Locate your Vacation policy information.
3. Submit a Work Order.
4. Find the company's logo template.

The MSP watched how users accomplished these tasks to make sure they could find this information within a maximum of four clicks. If they could not find the information, it was noted as a usability problem that would be fixed in the next phase.

Training

A week before the rollout of the intranet, MSP team members came on site to give training sessions to employees. During the training sessions, instructors oriented users to intranets in general and to the company's intranet specifically, explaining how to navigate, how to search, and how to get help. Instructors visited every department and content area on the site and answered any questions that arose. When users completed the training, they were eager to start using the intranet.

Both the manager and the MSP viewed these training sessions as critical to the intranet's success. These sessions motivated people to use the service, and inspired them to write and give feedback on this first phase of its development—information that could be important in revising or expanding this intranet.

Conclusion

Throughout this chapter you have seen how FrontPage can help you create an intranet site. FrontPage is a truly multifaceted tool that provides many options for creating, maintaining, and serving an intranet site. Its web-creation wizards enable you to produce fully functioning intranet sites quickly, and its page-creation templates give you a head start in creating web pages. FrontPage's ability to support Office document integration makes it possible to have access to existing documents in their native form, which is ideal for complex Word or Excel documents. With help from Microsoft's intranet templates, you have the ability to create complex database-integrated intranet sites that take advantage of emerging technologies, such as channels, dynamic HTML, and Active Server Pages, in a fraction of the time it would take if you were to undertake the project from scratch. Finally, FrontPage's site-management features and its ability to integrate with Visual SourceSafe provide the kind of control that you need in an intranet environment where multiple authors are providing content simultaneously.

The Complete Reference

Chapter 24

Publishing
and Promoting Webs
on the Internet

B y now with the help of this book, you have created your own webs with FrontPage and possibly have put them on your intranet. In this chapter, you will see how to make your efforts available to the millions of people worldwide who have access to the Internet. You'll do this by first publishing your web on a web server, a computer that is connected to the Internet. Then you'll promote your web site using web-based and traditional advertising.

Publishing Your Web Pages

Publishing a web means copying the files that contain the pages and graphics for a web to a web server connected to the Internet. Unless you have your own such server, you will need to find a web presence provider (WPP) who will rent you space on their web server for your web. Also, to get the full functionality of your web, your WPP should support the FrontPage Server Extensions.

Providing access to the Web has become a very competitive field, and you should be able to find several WPPs in your area to choose from. You can find a local WPP by asking others, by looking in your regional newspapers and other periodicals, and even by checking a recent phone book. You can also use the Internet. You can begin by using one of the many search engines available, such as AltaVista (**http://www.altavista.com**). Simply enter a search criterion such as **"Internet hosting [*your city*]"** (include the quotes). Another Internet site with a list of providers is Yahoo (**http://www.yahoo.com**). Finally, Microsoft posts a list of WPPs with FrontPage Server Extensions available by selecting "Find a Web Site Host" at **http://www.microsoft.com/frontpage/** (move your mouse pointer into the left panel under "Solutions & Resources" and "Find a Web Site Host" will appear). With a little searching, you should be able to locate several WPPs in your area. It is unnecessary that your WPP be located close to you. Most of your transactions will occur over the Internet, and there are a number of national providers, such as Netcom (**http://www.netcom.com/**) and AT&T's Easy World Wide Web Services (**http://www.att.com**), that offer the FrontPage Server Extensions as part of their service.

Generally, a WPP will provide dialup access to the Internet, as well as hard disk storage for webs. Many offer space for a personal (noncommercial) web as part of their basic Internet access package. The amount of hard disk space allowed for a personal web site varies. In many areas, this basic service costs $20 to $30 a month with unlimited Internet access. (These rates are for 14.4Kbps to 33.6Kbps modems; rates for 56.6Kbps, ISDN, DSL, and cable modems may be higher.)

Rates for commercial web sites can vary greatly—from $30 to several thousand dollars a month—depending on the WPP, the amount of hard disk storage, and the bandwidth used. *Bandwidth* is the amount of data that is transferred from your web site over the WPP's Internet connection. For example, if your web is 1 megabyte (MB) in size and it was accessed 100 times in the course of a month, you would have used 100MB of bandwidth (or transfer bandwidth) in that month.

Another point to consider is whether you want to have your own domain name. Without your own domain name, your web's URL would begin with the WPP's domain name, such as *http://www.WPPname.com/yourname.* With your own domain, your URL would be *http://www.yourname.com.* Your own domain is unnecessary for a personal web site, but should be seriously considered for a commercial web. Your WPP can help you set up a domain name for your web site. Alternatively, you can contact InterNIC Registration Services at **http://www.internic.net/**, and with some information from your WPP and $70 per year (minimum of two years), you can register your own domain name. InterNIC has complete instructions at their site. Also, at the InterNIC site you can search for existing domain names to make sure the one you want is unique.

In deciding upon a WPP, you should be more concerned about the quality of the service than the price. The Internet is a little chaotic—new technologies (particularly in data transmission) are coming into play, and finding people who truly understand and can use these technologies is not always easy. Software doesn't always work as advertised, and keeping everything flowing smoothly sometimes requires a little "spit and baling wire." When evaluating a WPP, look at the design and features of their web site, and contact others who have their webs on the WPP's server. Choosing the cheapest WPP could be an expensive decision in the long run if they don't provide the services you need, such as the FrontPage Server Extensions.

FrontPage Server Extensions

HTML used to be written by hand, using text editors such as Windows Notepad. When you wanted to include a form for the user to fill out, you had to make sure there was a script available on the server that would implement it. There were (and are) a number of scripts to do this, so you needed to know the syntax required by the particular script on your server. If your web page was transferred to another server with different scripts, your HTML would probably have to be modified.

With FrontPage those days are over. A great deal of the functionality and usefulness of FrontPage comes from the fact that it includes a standard set of server extensions that can run on virtually any HTTP server platform with any major server software. This means your FrontPage-created web can be placed on any web server running the FrontPage Server Extensions and will function correctly.

As a content creator, you simply need to know that the FrontPage Server Extensions are installed on your WPP's web server. (When you installed FrontPage on your local computer, the server extensions for the Microsoft Personal Web Server were also installed.) Then you are assured that any FrontPage Components, forms, or discussion groups you've included in your web will function on your WPP's server.

The FrontPage Server Extensions allow you to use Hypertext Transfer Protocol (HTTP) in place of the older and more complex File Transfer Protocol (FTP). Also with the FrontPage Server Extensions, FrontPage will help you maintain your web files by making sure the files on the web server are the same as those on your local hard disk and that all the hyperlinks are correct.

> *You might also want to check with your WPP to make sure their FrontPage Server Extensions is the same version or later as the version of FrontPage you used to create your web application (although many of the FrontPage 2000 components are handled by the FrontPage 98 Server Extensions).*

Installing the FrontPage Server Extensions

If you are maintaining your own web server, you need to install the FrontPage Server Extensions on it (they are automatically installed on the Microsoft Personal Web Server during FrontPage installation). Alternatively, you may have to work with your WPP to install the FrontPage Server Extensions on their server. (For a variety of reasons, including security, WPPs can be reluctant to install every piece of software a client suggests.) Therefore, the next several paragraphs provide some of the reasoning behind the FrontPage Server Extensions, and an overview of the installation process.

For the most part, the FrontPage Server Extensions use the standard common gateway interface (CGI) found on all web servers. The CGI provides a standard protocol for the transfer and processing of data between a client (a web browser, for example) and a server. With Microsoft Internet Information Services (IIS), the server extensions are implemented as dynamic link libraries (DLLs). This allows the server extensions to take up less room and to execute faster. In any case, data is transferred to the FrontPage Server Extensions from the web server software. The server extensions then process the data and hand back the output to the server software. For example, in the case of a text search, the search criteria would be passed from the HTTP server to the appropriate FrontPage Server Extension. The specified information would then be searched using the specified criteria, and the results of the search handed back to the HTTP server. It would then be formatted with HTML and sent back to the client (web browser) that initiated the search.

Adding the FrontPage Server Extensions to an existing web server is a relatively simple process. The first step is to get a copy of the FrontPage Server Extensions for your web server. These are available at no charge from Microsoft's web site (**http://www.microsoft.com/frontpage/wpp/default.htm**).

Microsoft currently provides FrontPage Server Extensions for the hardware, operating system, and web servers in the English language shown in Table 24-1. Many other languages are also available.

As you can see, the FrontPage Server Extensions are available for most web server platforms and HTTP server software. Installation of the FrontPage Server Extensions varies depending on the platform, but complete instructions are available for each platform and are relatively simple. In addition, there is a FrontPage 2000 Server Extension Resource Kit v1.4 (SERK) that is available from the **http://www.microsoft.com/frontpage/wpp/** site.

The primary issue with a WPP about installing the FrontPage Server Extensions (besides being one more thing to learn and handle) will be security. When someone

Hardware Used	Operating System Used	Web Server Used
Digital Alpha	Windows NT 4.0 Server	Microsoft Internet Information Services 2.0 through 4.0
Digital Alpha	Windows NT 4.0 Workstation	Microsoft Peer Web Services
Digital Alpha	Digital UNIX 3.2c, 4.0	Apache 1.1.3, 1.2.4, 12.5 CERN 3.0 NCSA 1.5.2 (not 1.5a or 1.5.1) Netscape Commerce Server 1.12 Netscape Communications Server 1.12 Netscape Enterprise 2.0 and 3.0 Netscape FastTrack 2.0
Intel x86	UNIX-BSD/OS 2.1, 3.0, Linux 3.0.3 (Red Hat), SCO OpenServer Release 5, SCO UnixWare 7	See Digital Alpha running Digital UNIX
Intel x86	Windows 95/98, Windows NT 4.0 Workstation	Microsoft Personal Web Server (Windows 95 or 98) Microsoft Peer Web Services (Windows NT Workstation) FrontPage Personal Web Server Netscape FastTrack 2.0 O'Reilly & Associates WebSite
Intel x86	Windows NT 4.0 Server	Microsoft Internet Information Services 2.0 through 4.0 Netscape Commerce Server 1.12 Netscape Communications Server 1.12 Netscape Enterprise 2.0 and 3.0 Netscape FastTrack 2.0 O'Reilly & Associates WebSite and Website Pro 1.x and 2.0

Table 24-1.   *FrontPage Server Extensions Availability*

Hardware Used	Operating System Used	Web Server Used
HP (PA-RISC)	HP/UX 9.03, 10.01	See Digital Alpha running Digital UNIX
Silicon Graphics	IRIX 5.3, 6.2	See Digital Alpha running Digital UNIX
Sun (SPARC)	Solaris 2.4, 2.5 or SunOS 4.1.3, 4.1.4	See Digital Alpha running Digital UNIX

Table 24-1. *FrontPage Server Extensions Availability* (continued)

accesses a web page on a server, he or she is given certain permissions. Normally these are limited to reading data on the server. The user is usually not allowed to write to the server's hard disk or to change any of the files on the server outside of the user's personal folder. The reason is obvious: if a user is allowed to place a file on a server, that file, through malicious intent or simple ignorance, could wreak havoc on the server. Network administrators protect their servers by restricting the type of access users are allowed (and some people make a hobby of beating the administrator's best efforts).

The FrontPage Server Extensions, like virtually every CGI application and script, need to allow the user to write to a file or folder on the server. The server's security is maintained by cordoning off these specific areas. Depending on the operating system and HTTP server software, the FrontPage Server Extensions generally require the same permissions as other CGI applications and do not represent an increased security risk.

The last word may simply be that FrontPage fills a tremendous gap in the quality of tools available for creating web content. If you remember the days of creating HTML in a text editor, you know how much more efficiently your time is used with FrontPage (if you don't remember, fire up Notepad and review Chapter 13).

It is possible to re-create the interactive functions of your web on a web server that is not using the FrontPage Server Extensions. Rather than the integrated set of functions that FrontPage Server Extensions provide, the web server may have a number of individual applications and scripts that provide the same functions. It may be, however, that if your WPP can't be convinced to install the FrontPage Server Extensions, you'll need to find another WPP.

Identifying Which Pages to Publish

When you create a new page, it is automatically identified to be published. If you want, though, you can change this. When you do that, the page will not be copied to the web server. You might do this if you are not finished building a page, but have other pages in the web you want published. When you are ready to publish a page, you simply have to identify the page as "Publish." It is also useful to mark certain files as "Don't Publish" if you don't want them recopied to the web server, such as pages with a hit counter or with a guest book, which would be zeroed out if they were republished. Use the following steps to identify the pages that you want published and those that you don't:

1. With FrontPage running and your local copy of the web that you want to publish open, click the View menu and choose Reports | Publish Status. The Publish Status report will appear in the FrontPage window.

2. To change the status of a particular page, click the right side of the Publish field for that page to open the drop-down list of choices, as shown in Figure 24-1.

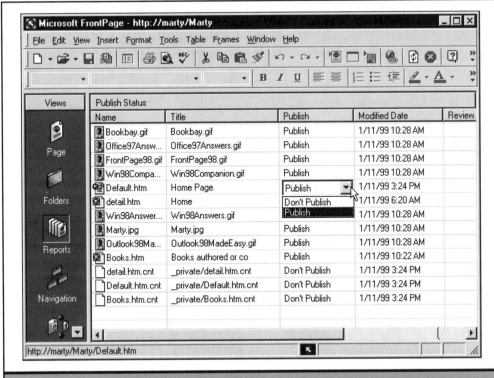

Figure 24-1. *Identifying whether an individual page is to be published or not*

EXTENDING
YOUR WEB SITE

3. Click Publish or Don't Publish as desired. Your page will be so marked, and when you publish your web, your Publish setting will be followed.

Publishing to a Server with FrontPage Server Extensions

Once your FrontPage web is completed and tested on your Microsoft Personal Web Server, it's ready for the Big Time: the World Wide Web. Hopefully, your WPP has the FrontPage Server Extensions installed and has created a folder for your web on the web server. (Publishing your web to a server without the FrontPage Server Extensions is covered in the next section.)

To publish a FrontPage web to a server with FrontPage Server Extensions, you must first have permission to write files to the server. Your webmaster or server administrator will be able to assign the proper permission to your account. Your webmaster or administrator may have you publish your web to a temporary folder as an additional security measure. Once you have the proper permissions and location on the server for your web, you would use these steps to publish your web:

Note   *If you do not have your own domain name and virtual or real server, your WPP may not let you create a new web or delete a web that is your primary folder, and FrontPage will not let you publish to a subsidiary folder. That means that you must create your web on your computer and publish it to your server. Then you can edit it, publish a new version of the web replacing the original version, add pages to it, and import other webs to it, but you cannot delete the web (you can delete individual folders and pages).*

1. Start FrontPage if necessary.

2. If you use a dialup account to access the Internet, activate your Internet connection.

3. In FrontPage, open the web you will place on the web server.

4. Open the File menu and select Publish Web. The Publish Web dialog box will be displayed like this:

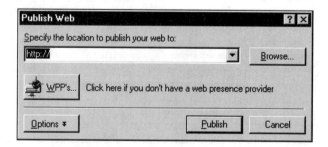

5. Select or type in the name of the destination server and the folder in which you want to place your web. Click Publish.

6. You will then be asked for your account and password. Enter them and click OK. You'll see a message telling you how the publishing is going and the percentage of the operation completed; when it is done, you'll see this message:

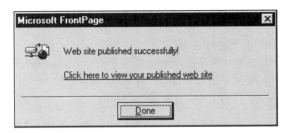

7. Test your web by clicking Click Here To View Your Published Web Site. Your web should appear, as you can see mine did in Figure 24-2. When you are done looking at your web, click Done.

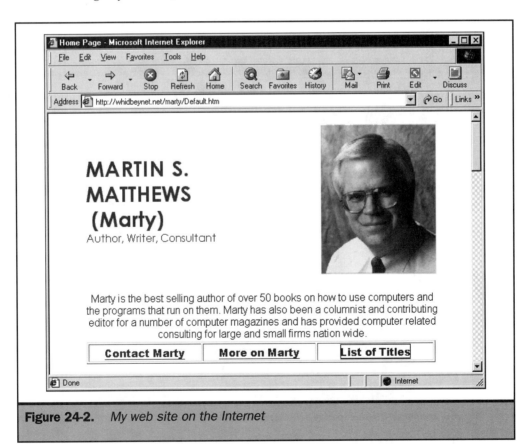

Figure 24-2.   *My web site on the Internet*

In most cases, publishing your web to a server with the FrontPage Server Extensions will be this simple. The biggest hang-up is often that in the communications with your WPP, your URL, user ID, and password have been garbled and the correct ones were not used in the above steps. If you are having problems, check this with your WPP first thing.

Editing a Web on a Server

One of the great beauties of putting your webs up on a server with the FrontPage Server Extensions is that you can directly edit your web on the server just as you would on your computer. To do this, use these steps:

1. Make sure you can connect to the server by being connected to either the Internet or an intranet.

2. Open the File menu and choose Open Web to open the dialog box of the same name, as shown in Figure 24-3. Click Web Folders, if it is not already selected, where you should see both the original local version and the one on WPP's server.

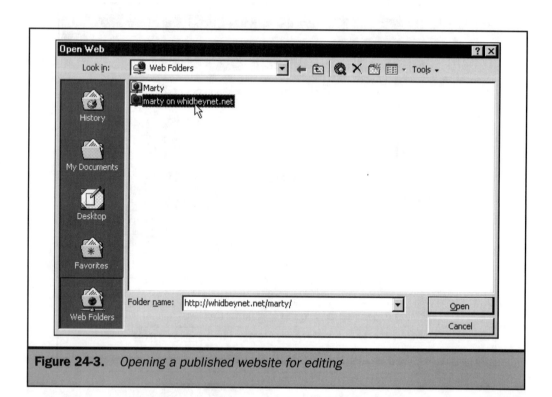

Figure 24-3. *Opening a published website for editing*

3. Double-click the web, which will open in FrontPage, as shown in Figure 24-4. Except for the fact that you are doing it long distance, this is no different than editing on your own computer.

If you can't edit online because you are using some of the new FrontPage 98/2000 features and your WPP is still using the FrontPage 97 Extensions, or for any other reason, you can still edit the web on your computer and publish it again on the server (either the entire web or just the pages that have changed).

Deleting a Web on a Server

Another approach to correcting or changing a web on a server is to delete it from the server and copy it again.

As explained earlier in this chapter, depending on how you are set up on your server, your WPP may not allow you to delete your entire web because that would be the same as deleting your primary folder on the server. You can instead delete all of the contents, and republish the web to replace the contents.

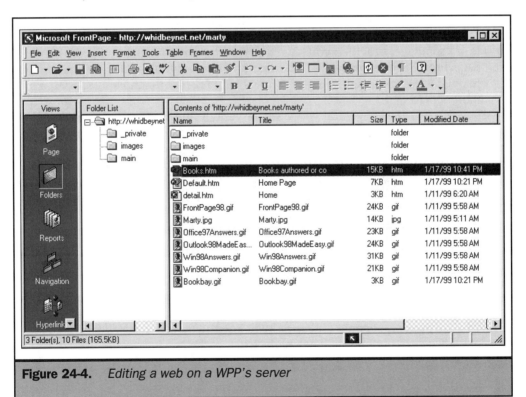

Figure 24-4.   *Editing a web on a WPP's server*

To delete your web:

1. In FrontPage, with your Internet connection active, open the web as just described to edit it.

2. When the web has opened in FrontPage, select Delete Web from the File menu. You will probably be asked for your user name and password.

Note *If you don't have Delete Web on the File menu, you can add it by opening the Tools menu and choosing Customize to open the Customize dialog box. Select the Commands tab, click File in Categories, scroll Commands until Delete Web is visible, and then drag Delete Web to the File menu in your FrontPage window, which will open allowing you to put it where you want it in the menu (I put it just below Close Web).*

Tip *To delete a single or multiple pages in a web, simply delete them on your local computer and then republish your web. FrontPage will compare your local web with the one you published and ask if you want a particular page deleted.*

Once the web is deleted, repeat the steps given previously to again copy the web to the web server. If you continue to have problems doing so, contact the webmaster or server administrator. It may be possible to delete individual files from the web server outside of FrontPage (provided you have the correct permissions), but this can confuse FrontPage. FrontPage keeps track of all the components of your web; if you change any of them outside of FrontPage, it may end up looking for files that no longer exist or are in a different place.

If you successfully copy your web to the server but find that some elements don't function correctly, first make sure that the web works correctly on your Microsoft Personal Web Server. Then contact your webmaster or server administrator and explain the problem. If other webs using the same feature work correctly on the web server, the odds are that the problem is in your web. If the problem is common to other webs on the web server, then the FrontPage Server Extensions might not be installed correctly.

Publishing to a Server Without FrontPage Server Extensions

You can also publish a web created in FrontPage to a web server that isn't running FrontPage Server Extensions. While any features relying on the server extensions (forms, FrontPage components, and so on) will not function, all the standard HTML functions, such as hyperlinks, will be unaffected.

There are several ways to publish to a web server that does not have the FrontPage Server Extensions installed. Among these are:

- FrontPage Publish Web option
- Windows 98 Web Publishing Wizard
- Classical File Transfer Protocol (FTP)

These options all use a form of the File Transfer Protocol (FTP) and are in order of increasing complexity, although there may be some increasing flexibility as well. In any case it is worthwhile to understand how each works.

Using the FrontPage Publish Web Option

Using FrontPage's Publish Web option to publish to a web server without the FrontPage Server Extensions is just like publishing with the FrontPage Server Extensions. The Publish Web option publishes your web pages to an FTP (file transfer protocol) server, rather than a web server. The FTP server usually provides access to the same directories as the WPP's web server, so a web browser can immediately open your web pages. In some cases, the webmaster or server administrator will have to activate your pages once they are uploaded to the FTP server. You will need permission to write to the destination FTP server. Your webmaster or server administrator will be able to assign the proper permission to your account.

The following instructions show you how to publish a FrontPage web to a server without the FrontPage Server Extensions using the Publish Web option. (The first several steps are exactly like those given earlier for publishing to a server with the FrontPage Server Extensions.)

1. Start FrontPage if necessary.
2. If you use dialup networking to access the Internet, activate your Internet connection.
3. In FrontPage, open the local copy of the web you will place on the web server.
4. Open the File menu and select Publish Web. The Publish Web dialog box will be displayed, as you saw earlier in this chapter. Do not enter anything here. If you were to enter the URL to your web site as you would if you used the FrontPage Server Extensions, you will get a message similar to this:

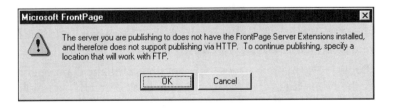

5. Click Browse. In the Look In drop-down list box, double-click Add/Modify FTP Locations to open the Add/Modify FTP Locations dialog box shown next.

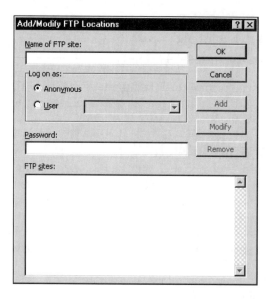

6. Enter the URL or name of the server to which you will FTP your web; for example either the URL ftp://ftp.servername.com or the name ftp.servername.com (the ftp:// will automatically be added for you) will work. Choose Anonymous or User to log on as (you probably want User); if User, enter your user ID. Enter your Password, click Add, and then click OK. The Open Web dialog box will appear.

7. Click the newly entered FTP server name. In the Folder Name drop-down list, type the complete folder path after the FTP server name. This might look like this:

```
ftp://ftp.servername.com/pub/web/yourfolder
```

where the "pub/web/yourfolder" is the path you enter here.

Note *Your folder path for an FTP transfer is probably different than the URL used in a web browser. Be sure to clearly understand from your WPP the path to use for each.*

8. Click Open. Your ID and password will be checked (you may have to enter them again) and you will be connected to the FTP server and your folder, and then returned to the Publish Web dialog box.

9. Click Publish. If you have pages that contain FrontPage components and require the FrontPage Server Extensions to work correctly, you will be given a notice like the one shown next and you can choose to Continue or Cancel.

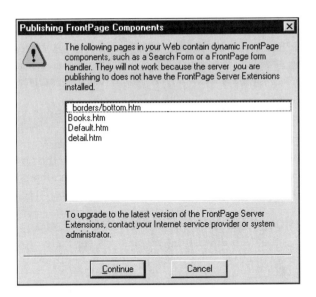

You'll then see a message of how the publishing is going and the percentage of the operation completed; when it is done, you'll see the same completion message you saw when publishing to a server with the FrontPage Server Extensions.

Note

The entry of the correct information in the above steps is crucial. If anything is wrong, it won't work. Be very clear with your WPP about the server name to which you will FTP your web (step 6); the path to your web site on that server (step 7); the user ID and password to use with FTPing (steps 6 and 8); and the URL, user ID, and password to access the Internet and view your site with a browser (step 10 below). Carefully look for typos and spurious characters. Do not assume that any of the example information used in the above steps is correct for you; it probably isn't. Keep trying. If you are using a correct server name, path and folder, and user ID and password, this will work.

10. Clicking the "Click here to view your published web site" probably won't work because it will try to open the FTP server and path and you need an HTTP URL. Therefore, to test your web, start your favorite browser and enter the URL that you have been told to use (it may not be the same server name and path that you used in steps 6 and 7). Your web should appear.

The specific information that you should enter for the FTP server name and path is unique to a WPP or network installation (for example, my WPP does not have "ftp." in front the server name, but rather use "ww2."). If after several attempts the copying is not working, you need to contact your WPP or network/server administrator.

Even if the web server that will host your web pages does not have the FrontPage Server Extensions, you may still be able to have the same functionality. For example, most servers will have an application or script for handling form input. You will need to ask your webmaster or server administrator how to access the application and then incorporate it into your web page by editing the HTML. Of course, it would be much easier if the server hosting your web were to support the FrontPage Server Extensions.

Using the Windows 98 Web Publishing Wizard

Windows 98 provides the Web Publishing Wizard as a separate program, which assists you in publishing your web to a web server that does not support the FrontPage Server Extensions. The Web Publishing Wizard is automatically installed when you install the Microsoft Personal Web Server (see Appendix A). The Web Publishing Wizard, like FrontPage in the last section, copies the web pages you select to an FTP server. Again, in some cases, the webmaster or server administrator will have to activate your pages once they are uploaded to the FTP server, and you will need permission to write to the destination FTP server.

 The Web Publishing Wizard was also available as a separate program in the FrontPage 98 package.

The following instructions can be used with the Web Publishing Wizard to publish a FrontPage web to a server without the FrontPage Server Extensions.

1. Open the Windows Explorer and locate the path to your web. This probably will be C:\Inetpub\Wwwroot*web*.

2. Open the Start menu and choose Programs | Internet Explorer | Web Publishing Wizard. The Web Publishing Wizard welcome will open. Click Next. The Select a File or Folder dialog box will open.

3. Enter the path you found in Step 1 or click Browse Folders to find the folder and click OK. If desired, click Include Subfolders (which I did, making my dialog box look like the one shown next), and then click Next.

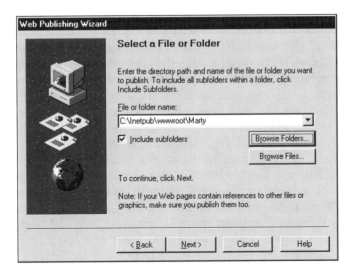

4. Enter a descriptive name for your web server. This can be any name that will refer to the settings you are about enter. Click Next. (The Advanced button allows you to choose a new WPP.)

5. Enter the URL that you will use to access the web site you are trying to publish. Then enter the path on your local computer to the web you have built and want to publish (this should be entered for you). Click Next. If needed, you will be connected to the Internet.

6. Enter the password you need to connect to your site. If you are connecting to a site that doesn't have the FrontPage Server Extensions (the whole point of this section!), you will be told that you need to specify a service provider. Click Next.

7. Accept the default service provider of FTP, and click Next. Enter the FTP server name and the subfolder path (see the discussion of these in the last section) which you have gotten from your WPP. Click Next.

8. Click Finish. A Publishing Files dialog box will open and display the progress in copying your files to the server. When the process is done, you will get a message that the Web Publishing Wizard has successfully published your files. Click OK.

9. Start your favorite browser and enter the URL that you have been told to use (it may not be the same server name and path that you used in step 7). Your web should appear.

Classical File Transfer Protocol (FTP)

File Transfer Protocol (FTP) controls how files are transferred over the web. To use FTP in the classical sense (not with FrontPage or the Web Publishing Wizard) requires an FTP program on your computer. With an FTP program you can not only transfer files to the server as you saw in the last two sections. You can also create and delete directories, delete files, rename files, transfer files back to your hard drive, and do all the things in the folder on your web server that you do in the directories on your hard drive. It therefore gives you a lot more capability and flexibility that the earlier two methods.

There are several FTP programs available. Ipswitch (**http://www.ipswitch.com**) has a very popular FTP program called WS_FTP Pro, Version 6.0, which you can download from the just mentioned site and use for 30 days free of charge. After that time you can purchase it for $37.50. If you are used to working with files on your hard drive with My Computer or Windows Explorer, you will find using WS_FTP Pro very easy since it works the same way. After downloading, which should take less than ten minutes for

the 1.4MB file at 28.8Kbps, and installing WS_FTP Pro, two icons will appear on your desktop. The first icon, labeled WS_FTP Pro, opens into the classical FTP window shown in Figure 24-5. The second icon, labeled WS_FTP Pro Explorer, opens into a window much like My Computer, as you can see in Figure 24-6. Because of its

familiarity, the WS_FTP Pro Explorer will be used here, but you are encouraged to explore classic WS_FTP Pro on your own.

The WS_FTP Pro Explorer contains icons for FTP sites you can access. When you double-click a site icon, it will connect you to the server defined in its properties. Like the icons in My Computer, it allows you to create folders to store site icons and to display the site icons as large icons, small icons, or a list, or to show details of the sites as you can do in the Windows Explorer.

CREATING A NEW SITE   Create a new site icon and folder within WS_FTP Pro Explorer for the FTP server to which you want to FTP your web pages with these steps:

1. Double-click the New icon in the WS_FTP Pro Explorer box shown in Figure 24-6. This will open the New Site/Folder dialog box shown next. This dialog box is used to start the creation of a new site icon and folder by giving it a user-friendly name.

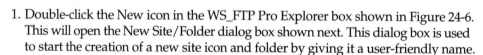

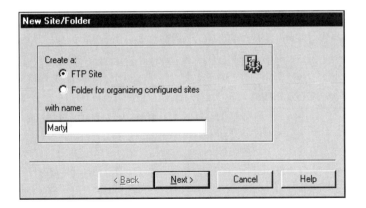

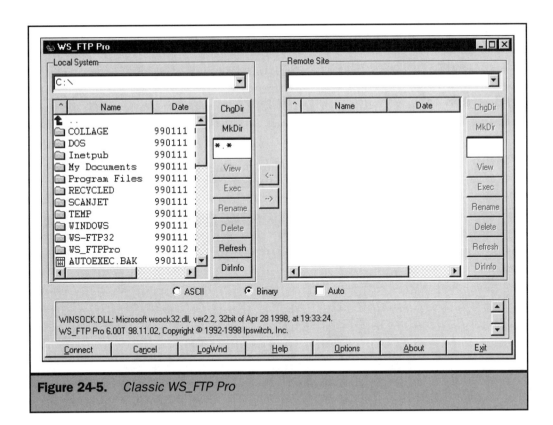

Figure 24-5.   *Classic WS_FTP Pro*

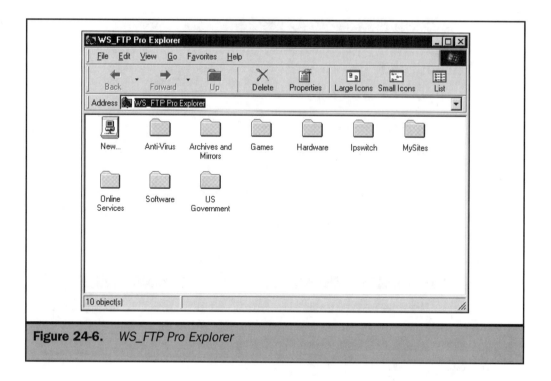

Figure 24-6. *WS_FTP Pro Explorer*

2. Enter the name of the site icon, click Next, and the Host Name dialog box opens. Here enter the address of your FTP server or its IP number, as shown next.

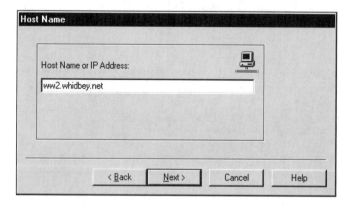

3. Click Next and the Logon Information dialog box will appear. Enter your user ID and password. Since you are going to use this to move files to your web server, you want to enter the same user ID and password you normally use to get into your web server. The Anonymous selection is for anonymous FTP sites, which are open to the public and require no special password.

4. Click Finish to complete the information for the site and create a new site icon in the WS_FTP Pro Explorer window.

   There is still additional information to enter in the properties of the new site icon. Once you log on, you want the connection to take you to the folder in your web server to which you want to transfer files.

5. Right-click the new site icon to open the context menu, and choose Site Properties. This will open the Site Properties dialog box.

6. Click the Startup tab to open the dialog box shown next. Under Remote Site Folder, enter the path on your web server to the folder you will use for your web. Under Local Folder, enter the path to the folder containing your web. These entries will allow you to go directly to the folders you want to work with in both your local machine and your web server. Click OK.

The FTP program now has everything it needs to connect directly to the folder on the web server containing your web site. Now you need to define how to transfer the files. There are two ways to do that using FTP: ASCII and binary. Your text files such as HTML files and CGI scripts can be transferred faster as ASCII files. Your JPEG and GIF image files, as well as any audio or video files, need to be transferred as binary files. Some FTP programs will give you a choice of selecting either ASCII or binary when sending the file, while others make the choice automatic. WS_FTP Pro Explorer chooses automatically, and you need to define the file extensions you want to be transferred using ASCII.

    7. Right-click the new site icon again and choose WS_FTP Pro Explorer Properties in the context menu. The WS_FTP Pro Explorer Properties box will open. Click the Extensions tab and enter the file extensions of the web pages and scripts that you want transferred as ASCII files. Normally this is .ASP, .CGI, .HTM, .HTML, .PL, and .TXT, as shown next. After entering the extensions you want to transfer this way, click OK.

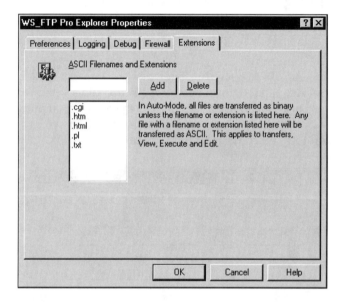

WS_FTP Pro Explorer is now set up and ready to transfer files to your web server.

TRANSFERRING FILES   To actually transfer files is very easy. Here are the steps:

    1. If you use dialup networking to access the Internet, activate your Internet connection.

    2. Open My Computer to the FrontPage web that you want to transfer to your web server.

    3. Open WS_FTP Pro Explorer and double-click the site icon. It will connect to the web server and display the folder to which you want to copy your web files. Figure 24-7 shows My Computer and WS_FTP Pro Explorer side-by-side.

The WS_FTP Pro Explorer window can be treated just as if it is a second My Computer window showing a folder on your hard drive. To transfer one or more files, you simply drag and drop them from one window to the other. When you do that, you will get a File Transfer message indicating the progress of the transfer, as shown here:

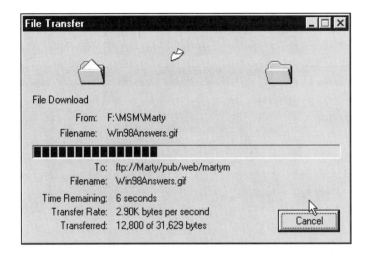

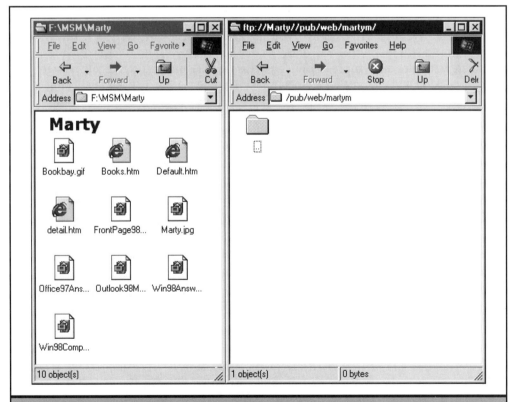

Figure 24-7.   *My Computer and WS_FTP Pro Explorer ready for a transfer*

If in transferring files you attempt to transfer a file that is already on the server you will get a message saying so, and be given a chance to replace the file or not, like this:

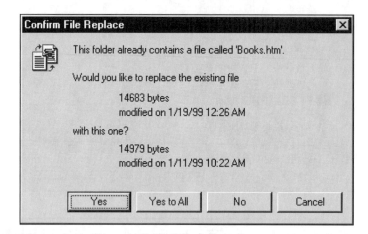

Within the WS_FTP Pro Explorer, you can also right-click the web server file icon to get a drop-down menu that will allow you to copy, delete, and rename the files. You can delete both files and empty folders by pressing DEL, and you can create new folders by right-clicking a blank area and choosing New Folder. Also, by double-clicking the folder in the upper-left corner of the WS_FTP Pro Explorer box, identified by the ellipsis (...), you can move up the folder tree in the web server. By double-clicking any other of the folders, you can move down in the folder tree.

With WS_FTP Pro Explorer you can literally do anything to a file or a folder on your web server that you can do to a file or folder on your hard drive.

Promoting Your Web Site

Once your web site has been published to a web server, you need to let people know that it is there. If your web site is business related, the first step is to tell your existing customers about it. You might include an announcement with your regular invoicing, for example. You should also include your URL in all your conventional advertising, including your business cards, invoices, statements, purchase orders, drawings, reports, and any other document you produce. It's not uncommon to see URLs on everything from television commercials to billboards.

*A good reason to get your own domain name is that normally it is a simpler address that is more easily remembered and more easily placed on other literature than if your web were hosted on another domain. For example, consider **http://www.yourserver.com/yourweb/** in comparison to **http://www.yourdomain.com**.*

Being Found on a Search Engine

You also need to make sure you can be found on the Web by anyone looking for the products and services you offer. A number of search engines for the Web have been developed. Some, like Digital's AltaVista, actively search the Web for information. Others, like Yahoo, which also searches the Web, allow web sites to suggest their information to them. Figure 24-8 shows the introduction to the pages used for suggesting web sites to Yahoo! (**http://www.yahoo.com/info/**). You can also suggest your web site to virtually all the search engines. A simple way to reach a number of search engines is to use the Submit It! web site (**http://www.submit-it.com/**), where your single entry is submitted to about 20 search engines for free, or pay a fee (currently $59 for two URLs) to be submitted to up to 400 search engines and directories that you select, as shown in Figure 24-9.

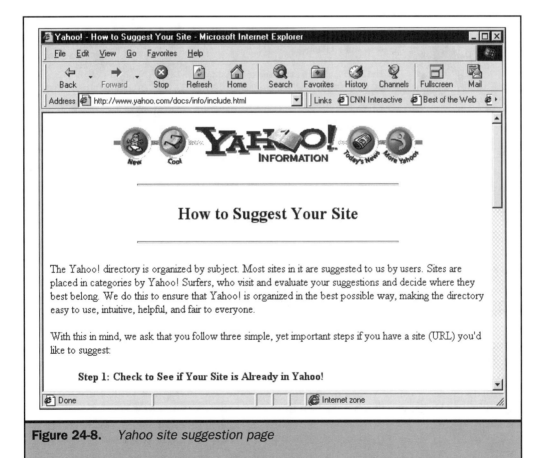

Figure 24-8.   *Yahoo site suggestion page*

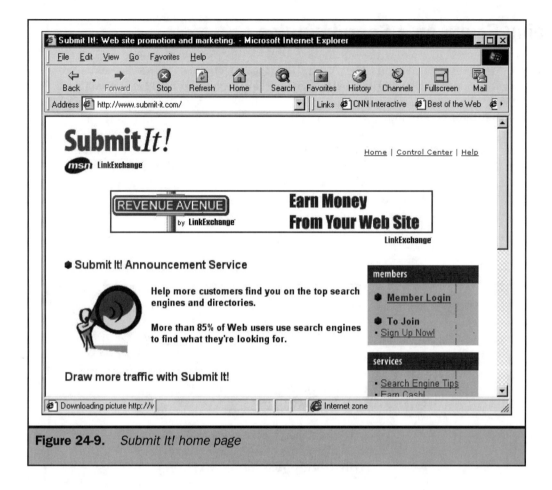

Figure 24-9. *Submit It! home page*

Table 24-2 gives names and addresses of search engines that you should make sure you are correctly listed on.

Making Your Web Search Engine Friendly

Since many search engines are actively searching the Web for sites, it helps to have an introductory paragraph on your home page that gives a concise description of your site. The introductory paragraph should include the keywords that apply to your site. Also, you can enter a page title (as distinct from the title at the top of the page) and keywords or *meta tags* on your home page and some search engines will reference your page title and index your web based on the keywords. The page title and keywords can

Search Engine	Web Address
800Go	http://www.800go.com/
AltaVista	http://www.altavista.com/
AOL NetFind	http://www.aol.com/netfind
Excite	http://www.excite.com/
GoTo	http://www.goto.com/
Hot Bot	http://www.hotbot.com/
Infoseek	http://infoseek.go.com/
Lycos	http://www.lycos.com/
MSN Web Search	http://search.msn.com/
NetGuide	http://www.netguide.com/
NorthernLight	http://www.northernlight.com/
Switchboard	http://www.switchboard.com/
Web Crawler	http://www.webcrawler.com/
Yahoo!	http://www.yahoo.com/

Table 24-2.   *Search Engines*

be entered in the Page Properties dialog box or directly in the HTML view of your page. Here are the steps to use the Page Properties dialog box:

1. With the web you want titled and indexed, open FrontPage, open the home page in Page view, open the File menu, and choose Properties (you may have to expand the menu). The Page Properties dialog box will open as shown in Figure 24-10.

Note   *The automatic page titles that get generated off pages are often not good for purposes of searching, such as "Home Page" shown in Figure 24-10. It is therefore important that you look at this and set the page title to something more appropriate.*

2. Replace the page title with one that is more descriptive of the web, and then open the Custom tab.

Page Properties dialog box:

Page Properties ? X

General | Background | Margins | Custom | Language | Workgroup |

Location: file:///C:/Inetpub/wwwroot/Marty/Default.htm

Title: Home Page

Base location:

Default target frame:

Background sound

Location: Browse...

Loop: 0 ☑ Forever

Design-time control scripting

Platform: Client (IE 4.0 DHTML)

Server: Inherit from Web

Client: Inherit from Web

Style...

OK   Cancel

Figure 24-10. *You can change the page title and the keywords in the page Properties dialog box*

3. In the User Variables section, click Add to open the User Meta Variable dialog box. In the Name text box, type **keywords**. In the Value text box, type the words you want indexed separated by commas, as shown here:

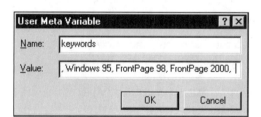

User Meta Variable ? X

Name: keywords

Value: , Windows 95, FrontPage 98, FrontPage 2000,

OK   Cancel

4. When you have entered all the keywords you can think of, click OK twice to close both the User Meta Variable dialog box and the Page Properties dialog box.

5. In FrontPage, click the HTML tab. In the Head section at the top of the listing, you should see the page title and keywords that you entered, similar to these for Marty's web:

```
<html>

<head>
<title>Martin S. Matthews, author, writer, consultant</title>
<meta http-equiv="Content-Type" content="text/html; charset=windows-1252">
<meta http-equiv="Content-Language" content="en-us">
<meta name="GENERATOR" content="Microsoft FrontPage 4.0">
<meta name="keywords" content="Martin S. Matthews, Martin Matthews, Marty Matthe
     author, writer, consultant, computer books, computer magazines, computers,
     software, Windows 98, Windows 95, FrontPage 98, FrontPage 2000, Office 97,
     Office 2000, Outlook 98, Osborne/Mcgraw-Hill, Microsoft Press">
<meta name="Microsoft Border" content="b, default">
<meta name="ProgId" content="FrontPage.Editor.Document">
</head>
```

You can see how you can also go into the HTML tab and directly enter or change a title and keywords.

Other Promotional Steps You Can Take

A useful tool for promoting your web site is *reciprocal links.* These are simply hyperlinks on your web page that point to someone who has a link to your site. Say you sell mountain climbing equipment. You could search the Web for climbing clubs and other groups with web sites relating to climbing. You then contact the owners of the sites, offering to put a link from your site to theirs if they will return the favor. This way anyone who finds any of the sites you're linked to has a direct link to your site. If you gather enough links on your site, it may become a starting point for people "surfing the Net."

You shouldn't overlook a press release, either. When your web site goes online, or you make a major addition, let the press and publications related to your business know about it. What you should *not* do is advertise your web site or business in newsgroups, unless the newsgroup is specifically run for that purpose. Say you decide to have a sale on climbing equipment. In your zeal to let the world know, you post a message on a recreational climbing newsgroup. The one result you can count on is that you will be flooded with "flames" (rather pointed e-mail messages), and frankly, you will deserve them.

A surefire way to get your web site widely known is simply to produce an outstanding web site. Today there are over 50 million sites on the World Wide Web.

Aim to be in the top 5 percent of that group. In the era of conventional marketing, that goal would have been virtually impossible for a small business, but the web is a new paradigm. Creativity and content count more than advertising budgets. Give people a reason to visit your site by providing content that is unique and useful to them. Then package it in an effective, pleasing design. Review the section entitled "Content" toward the end of Chapter 1. Take the time to explore the Web and gather ideas for your own site. (Gathering ideas is fine; gathering graphics or other actual content, no matter how easy it is, is a violation of copyright laws.)

The World Wide Web, whether you use it for business or pleasure, is having an effect on society as fundamental as the invention of the printing press. With FrontPage, you have the tools to participate in this new world.

Case Study: Promoting the BookBay

The BookBay is a small rural bookstore located on an island in Puget Sound in Washington state. Its owner, Brad Bixby, is also the innovative creator of the web site, which you can see in Figure 24-11. Since the BookBay is a small independent bookstore, the problem of trying to promote its site loomed quite large. As a result, we asked him what his secrets were. Here are his answers:

"I advertise my web site address in everything my customers see, from yellow page ads to fliers, bag stuffers, bookmarks, and business cards.

"It is important to know how each of the search engines (or directories—since they work a bit differently) operate. Do they use page titles, meta tags (company name, description, and keywords), first paragraph text, keyword frequency, or submitted site descriptions, or all of them in their search? These are the things that put your page on top of everyone else's.

Tip   *As another example of how meta tags are used, the BookBay's meta tags are shown here:*

```
<html>

<head>
<meta http-equiv="Content-Type"
content="text/html; charset=iso-8859-1">
<meta name="Description"
 content="Any book in print! The BookBay is a general interest independent
 bookstore located north of Seattle on Puget Sound's beautiful Whidbey Island.">
<meta name="keywords"
 content="Whidbey, Island, bookstore, books, BookBay, Book, Bay, Freeland,
 Oprah, Winfrey, Club, independent, general, gifts, music, mystery, fiction,
 non fiction, cooking, gay, lesbian, gardening, children, pacific, northwest,
 puget, sound, native, american, suspense, bestsellers, history, business,
 directory, chamber, commerce, owned, Bixby, Brad, Washington, Seattle">
<meta name="GENERATOR" content="Microsoft FrontPage Express 2.0">
<title>The BookBay</title>
</head>
```

Figure 24-11. *BookBay's home page*

"Also, think like someone surfing the web and tailor your keywords, titles, meta tags, etc., accordingly. What are they looking for? What keyword queries would they use in a search engine?

"Develop a 'hook' to bring people to your page. It may not be a direct income source, but the first thing you need to do is get them to your site. Not one sale has ever been made on the Internet from someone who doesn't know you exist. One 'hook' on my page is book clubs. Another is local authors. A hook not only gives people a reason to come to my page, it gives them a reason to come back. I also have Whidbey Island and Freeland history pages to attract people interested in the area. If someone is just looking for a bookstore or books, they are probably not going to find me, but if they are looking for the Oprah Winfrey Book Club, Whidbey Island, or Freeland, they are very likely to see my site in the top of the list.

"After I have submitted my site to the major search engines, I check to see how I compare to other sites that have similar information, and in the book industry, that's a lot. I use a service called Rank This! located at **http://www.rankthis.com**. You submit your site's URL address (Hint: Don't use your home page—Let Rank This! search all your pages. I use **http://www.whidbey.com/bookbay** without the index.htm extension), format a search query using keywords you think others will use, select one of the search engines, as shown in Figure 24-12, and it will tell you where you rank, if at all, in the first 200 pages listed. If I am listed 30th, chances are people are not going to get to me. My objective is to be in the top ten listings when people go searching for any of my 'hooks.' Figure 24-13 shows one search where I am listed well. (There are others where I don't come off as well.)

"Earlier, this chapter mentioned promoting your web site using reciprocal links. For a personal or informational site I think that is a good idea. The problem with using

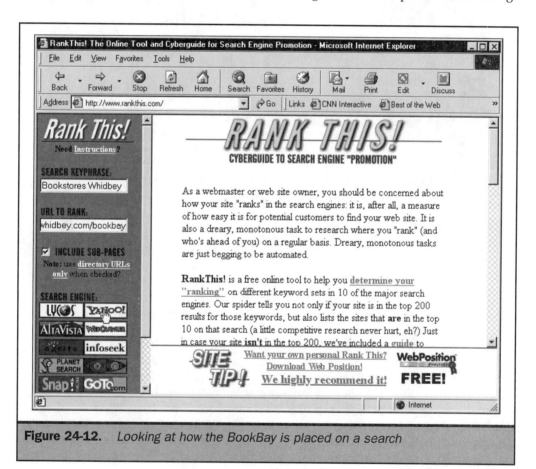

Figure 24-12.   *Looking at how the BookBay is placed on a search*

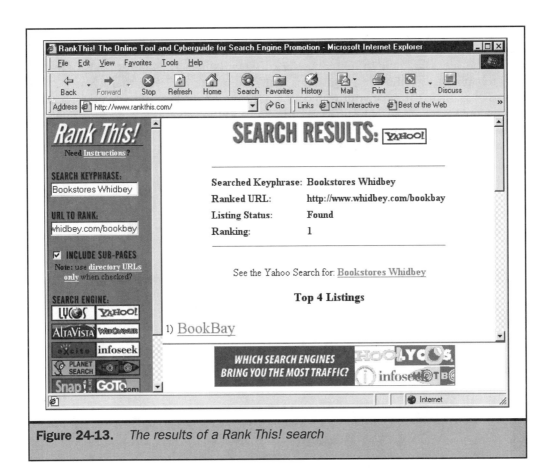

Figure 24-13. *The results of a Rank This! search*

links to other sites from a commercial site is that if someone uses the link, there is a good chance you have lost them before they have seen everything you have to offer. It's kind of like having a store that has all the popular items right next to the front door. They never get to the back to see what else you have to offer. You may get some people linking to your site from elsewhere, but is that more important than keeping the ones you have in your site? I have seen very few commercial sites that use reciprocal links.

"I do have a link in my site to my distributor's site, allowing my visitors to look at bestseller lists, and book lists by category, and even search for titles and reviews. I didn't want them to get so far from my page, however, that they wouldn't find their way back. So I set up that section of my page in frames. Visitors are able to use my distributor's services, but my logo and a link back to my site is always present."

Brad Bixby, the BookBay
http://www.whidbey.com/bookbay
(The name "BookBay" and the quotations are used with the permission of the BookBay.)

Probably the two most important tips that Brad mentioned were to use every means possible to promote your web, and to repeatedly test to see how your web is coming out on searches. By testing your ranking and then changing your title, meta tags, and keywords, you can fine-tune how people will find you. Brad has certainly done this successfully and provides a good example.

Appendix A

FrontPage 2000 Installation

Installing FrontPage 2000 is an easy task, as you'll discover in this appendix. The onscreen instructions are clear, the steps are few, and with the information in this appendix, you will soon have FrontPage ready to use.

FrontPage 2000 is available in two ways: as a component of Microsoft Office 2000 Premium Edition, and as a stand-alone product. In both cases the software comes in a CD package with several other products. In addition to FrontPage, this appendix will discuss the installation of the following products:

- **Microsoft Image Composer**   A bitmap-graphics program for creating and editing images you can put in your web pages. It is in the stand-alone package.

- **Microsoft PhotoDraw**   Both a bitmap and a vector graphics program for creating and editing images you can put in your web pages. It is in the Office 2000 Premium Edition package.

- **Microsoft Internet Explorer 5.0**   A web browser program for looking at the web pages you create with FrontPage and other pages on either the Internet or an intranet. It is in both the stand-alone and Office 2000 Premium Edition packages.

- **Microsoft Personal Web Server 4.0**   Allows web pages to be published and viewed on smaller Windows 95- or 98-based LANs. It is not in either package.

What You Need to Install FrontPage 2000

To install FrontPage 2000, you'll need the following minimum software and hardware:

- Windows 95 or 98 or Windows NT 4.0 with Service Pack 3 or Windows 2000
- A PC with a Pentium 100 or higher
- 32MB of memory
- 170MB of free disk space including 90MB for FrontPage 2000, 30 MB for the MSPWS 4, 20 MB for Internet Explorer 5, and 30MB for miscellaneous Office files
- VGA (640x480) or higher with 256 or more colors from your video adapter and monitor (Super VGA (800x600) with True Color and 2MB video memory recommended)
- Microsoft Mouse or compatible pointing device (pressure-sensitive tablet recommended with Microsoft Image Composer or Microsoft PhotoDraw)
- CD-ROM or DVD drive
- 28.8 baud modem or connection through a LAN to the Internet

To access the Internet or an intranet network in which FrontPage will be used, you also must have installed the TCP/IP network protocols (see Chapter 1 for a discussion of the protocols and Chapter 23 for the installation of TCP/IP) on a dialup network using a modem and/or on a local area network (LAN) with its adapter card. If you are using an Internet browser with Windows 95 or 98 or Windows NT, you have already installed and correctly configured TCP/IP. If you are just now coming up on the Internet or a network, you need to install TCP/IP. The easiest way to do so is to use the Internet Connection Wizard discussed in the "Connecting to the Internet" section later in this appendix.

 If you are upgrading from an earlier version of FrontPage (97 or 98), you need to have one of those versions installed on your computer, or have the floppy disk or CD available.

Installing a Personal Web Server

A personal web server allows you to publish your webs on your computer and lets others on your network view your webs. It is not necessary to have a personal web server to create FrontPage webs; you can keep your files on your computer as disk-based webs as you are creating them and then publish them to a remote server when you are ready for others to see them. Neither version (Office or stand-alone) of FrontPage 2000 comes with Microsoft Personal Web Server (MSPWS), which was packaged and used with FrontPage 98. It is available on the Windows 98 disk and downloadable from Microsoft at **http://www.microsoft.com/windows/ie/pws/main.htm**.

The Microsoft Personal Web Server is based on Microsoft's Internet Information Services (IIS) and is tightly integrated with Windows 95 or 98. IIS is included with Windows NT 4.0 or Windows 2000 Server and is the web server you need in order to run a full World Wide Web site. Consequently, MSPWS is also quite powerful. MSPWS gives you a number of options that you can use to customize it to your needs. Most importantly, MSPWS allows you to create and support a large number of webs. If you want to make your webs available to a few others on your network, and want to make extensive use of FrontPage, MSPWS will do that. This book recommends and assumes that you have installed and are using MSPWS. Here are the steps to install MSPWS from the Windows 98 CD.

(If you are installing across a network—the installation files are located on a network server instead of a CD—use the Windows Explorer to open the appropriate folder on that server instead of using the CD in the following steps.)

1. With the Windows 98 CD in your drive, open the \Add-ons\Pws folder and double-click Setup.exe, as shown in Figure A-1.

2. Click Next in the introductory dialog box, click Typical and Next in the second dialog box, and accept the default folders and click Next in the third dialog box. You will see an Overall Progress thermometer bar that tells you how the installation is going.

3. When you see the Thank You For Choosing Microsoft Software message, click Finish. At the prompt, click Yes to restart your computer.

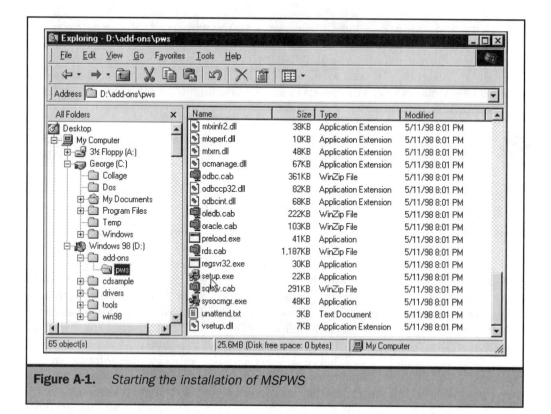

Figure A-1. *Starting the installation of MSPWS*

Publish

You should see a new icon in the tray on the right of your taskbar for the MSPWS and a new Publish icon on your desktop for the Publishing Wizard, which opens the Personal Web Manager, where you control the MSPWS and maintain your web site. The icon in the tray tells you the MSPWS is running. Use the following steps to check it out:

1. Double-click the MSPWS icon in the taskbar to open the Personal Web Manager dialog box. Click Close in the Tip Of The Day dialog box, and you will see the dialog box shown in Figure A-2.

   In the Publishing section at the upper part of the dialog box, you can see the name of your server (**http://george** in Figure A-2). To look at a web on your server, anyone on your network with the appropriate permission would just have to enter this server name followed by a slash and the web name—for example, **http://george/myweb**. Also in the Publishing section, you see a Stop button to stop the MSPWS, in which case the button changes to Start with the obvious effect. Below that you can see the default home directory that is referred to often in this book. The lower part of the Main view shows you the usage of the MSPWS.

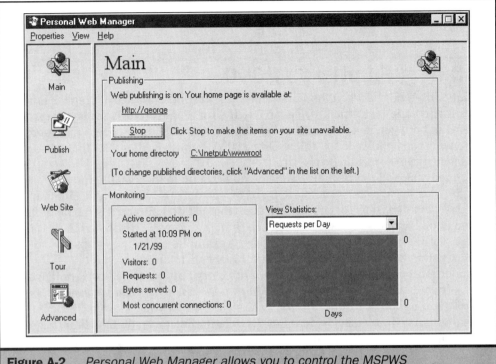

Figure A-2.   *Personal Web Manager allows you to control the MSPWS*

Tip   *The HTTP address of the MSPWS is translated by the server to the physical disk address shown for your default home directory. Use this address as the Start Page in the Internet Explorer to easily view your webs created in FrontPage, as suggested later in this appendix.*

2. Click Tour and run through a quick tour of the MSPWS. Here you will see how to use the MSPWS as an intranet host. The Publish and Web Site views allow you to add web pages to your web site and to manage those pages. The Advanced view allows you to add HTTP aliases for the directories or folders on your hard disk (for example, the alias "Home" is automatically set for C:\Inetpub\wwwroot), as well as the access permissions for those folders. The Advanced view also allows you to determine the name of your default home page—for example, Default.htm.

Note   *The name of your default home page is important because your server will automatically open it when a browser opens the web without the browser specifying a page name. Microsoft's IIS and MSPWS both require Default.htm (or Default.asp) for this, while most UNIX-based servers require Index.htm (or Index.asp).*

APPENDIXES

The MSPWS is a powerful web server and will support small- to moderate-size intranet sites very well.

Installing FrontPage 2000

The only difference between the stand-alone version and Office 2000 Premier Edition is the other components that are available with FrontPage. FrontPage itself is exactly the same in both versions. In terms of installation, the only difference is that more components can be installed with the Office 2000 Premier Edition. For that reason, that is the edition we will discuss here.

You may install FrontPage using the defaults set up in the installer for where to place the files and which files to place there, or you may use a custom installation procedure and determine what to install and where to do it. If you use the defaults, recommended for most users, all FrontPage components will be installed. This is the choice assumed in this book and reflected in its examples and illustrations. If you choose Customize, you can choose which components to install.

Under most circumstances the folder or directory path for installing FrontPage client software will be chosen for you, and *that is the assumption and recommendation of this book.* Throughout the book you'll see the statement "if you followed the default installation procedure," which identifies the default directories that the FrontPage Setup program will create for you.

It is strongly recommended that you use the default installation and let the Setup program create the default directories in which FrontPage will be installed.

Using the Default Installation

Before installing FrontPage, you should have installed a personal web server and verified it is running as described earlier. If so, follow these steps for the default installation of FrontPage:

1. Insert the Office 2000 Premier Edition's first CD into your drive. You will see several messages to the effect that the installer is being set up. Then a welcome dialog box appears and requests your name, initials, organization name, and CD key (located on the back of the CD case). Enter these and press Next.

2. Accept the license agreement and click Next. The dialog box shown in Figure A-3 appears; there you can choose between a default installation and a custom one.

3. Click Install Now. If you are upgrading from an earlier version of Office or FrontPage, Setup will tell you that it will examine your system to confirm the existence of the previous version. Click Continue. If Setup can't find a qualifying

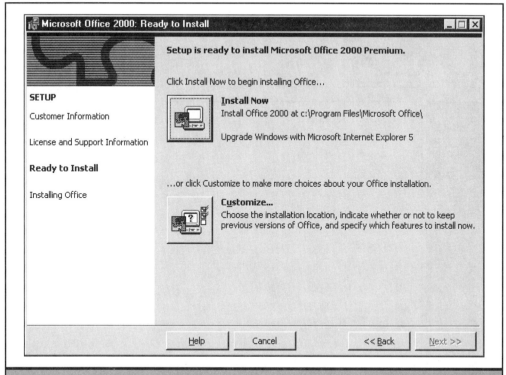

Figure A-3. *Making the choice between a default and custom installation*

product, a dialog box will appear telling you so. If you have FrontPage on another drive, or if you have already removed it but have the original disk, you need to tell Setup which drive to search. Click Locate. A Locate Directory dialog box will appear. If you want a CD or floppy searched, insert it in its drive. Select the correct drive and directory and click OK.

4. You will see an Installing Microsoft Office 2000 message box open and display the progress of the installation. When the installer is done copying files, it will tell you it needs to restart your computer. Click Yes to do that. Your computer will restart, the System Settings will be updated, and the installer will complete.

5. Start FrontPage by opening the Start menu and choosing Programs | Microsoft FrontPage. If you are asked, enter your name and initials. Then you are asked if you want to register your copy of FrontPage or Office. Click Yes or No and, if Yes, follow the instructions to do that. The FrontPage windows will open with a new page in Page view, as shown in Figure A-4.

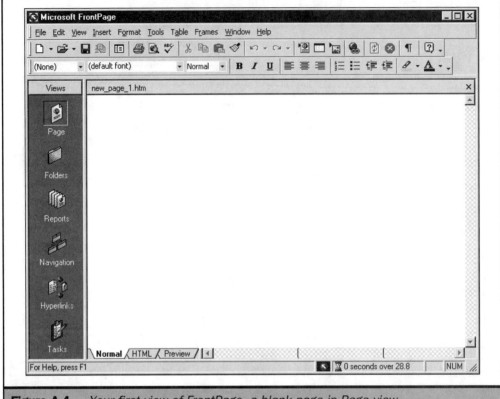

Figure A-4. *Your first view of FrontPage, a blank page in Page view*

6. Click FrontPage's Close button. You have proven that the installation was completed successfully.

If your installation did not complete successfully, look carefully at the error messages you have received. Correct any anomalies that are mentioned, like exiting from all programs that are running except Windows and MSPWS, or providing more disk space, and then rerun Setup.

Performing a Customized Installation

Use the Customize installation when you want to install only some of the Office or FrontPage component programs—for instance, if you are reinstalling FrontPage 2000. If you are installing FrontPage over a previous copy, you will want to use the same directory structure you used originally in order to preserve access to your webs. If you want to use a different directory, you will first have to uninstall the first copy and reinstall it to the desired directory.

To perform a Customize installation, follow these steps:

1. Follow the first two steps in the default installation until you have the choice between a default and custom installation. Click Customize.

2. If you want to change from the default installation location (not recommended), use Browse to select the location and then click Next.

3. You are asked if you want to install Internet Explorer 5.0 Standard version, or a Minimal version, or not install it at all. It is recommended that you install the Standard version, which is already selected. To make another choice, open the drop-down list, click the one you want, and then in any case click Next.

4. In the Select Features dialog box, shown in Figure A-5, you can choose to install the various components of FrontPage and possibly Office. Click the plus sign to open the detail choices. For each choice, click the down arrow where you have the choices shown here:

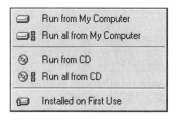

| Note | *When you select a choice, its description is shown in the lower part of the dialog box.* |

5. Go through and make the choices that are correct for you. Complete the setup by following steps 3 through 6 of the default installation discussed in the previous section.

Checking Your Network Setup

FrontPage includes the capability to test whether you are properly set up on a network with the TCP/IP protocol, and what your host name and IP address are. Run that test as follows:

1. From FrontPage, open the Help menu and click About Microsoft FrontPage. In the About FrontPage Explorer dialog box, click Network Test. The FrontPage TCP/IP Test dialog box will open.

APPENDIXES

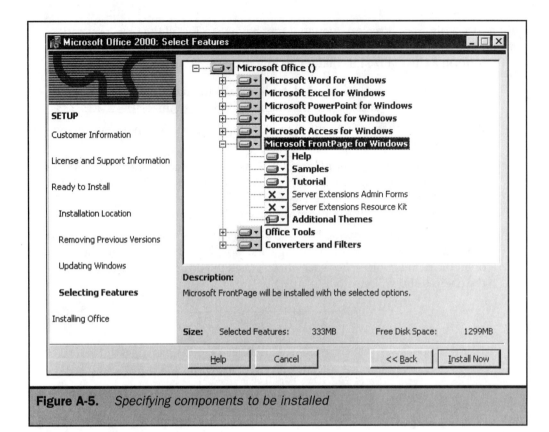

Figure A-5. *Specifying components to be installed*

2. Click Start Test. You may be asked if you want to connect to your Internet service provider (ISP). If you want to use a personal web server for the local creation of your webs, click Cancel in the Connect To dialog box. (The use of a personal web server is assumed and recommended in this book.)

3. Your test results will appear. If all is well, they will look similar to those shown here:

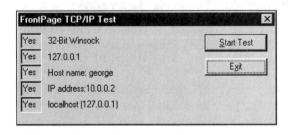

Table A-1 explains each of the boxes in the FrontPage TCP/IP Test dialog box and what a negative answer might mean.

4. Click Exit to close the FrontPage TCP/IP Test dialog box, and then click OK to close the About Microsoft FrontPage dialog box.

If any of the boxes in the TCP/IP dialog box says "No," you have a problem. Here are several ways to locate and solve these problems:

- Is a web server, personal or otherwise, running or available on your computer? If you haven't already, you should install a web server. (This is not mandatory; you

Element	Description
32-Bit Winsock	"Yes" verifies that the software connection between Windows 95/98/NT and TCP/IP networking is present. "No" means that either TCP/IP is not installed, or you have a Windows problem and probably need to reinstall it. See the list of ideas and solutions for installing TCP/IP that follows step 4.
127.0.0.1	"Yes" verifies that you have a local web server available with this standard IP address. If the result is "No" and you want a local web server, you need to install a personal web server.
Host name	"Yes" verifies the name of the web server that will be used by FrontPage. If the result is "No" and Localhost is confirmed (see last item in table), you can use "localhost." "No" may mean that a web server is not installed or not functioning.
IP address	"Yes" verifies the IP address of the web server that will be used by FrontPage. If the result is "No" and Localhost is confirmed (see next item in table), you can use "localhost." "No" may mean that a web server is not installed or not functioning.
Localhost	"Yes" verifies that the name "localhost" and its IP address can alternately be used in place of the host name. "No" means that a web server is not installed or not functioning.

Table A-1.   *Meaning of TCP/IP Test Results*

can use disk-based webs, but a web server allows you to stay on your computer while using your webs the way your clients will.) Otherwise you need to make a connection with your intranet or Internet web server.

■ Do you have two web servers assigned to port 80? If you have two servers available, only one can be assigned to port 80; the other needs to be assigned to port 8080, which can also be addressed by FrontPage.

■ Is FrontPage installed properly? Uninstall and reinstall it using nothing but defaults, and make absolutely sure nothing but Windows (and possibly MSPWS) is running during installation.

■ If you are on a network, make sure that the TCP/IP protocol has been set up. Do that by opening your Control Panel (Start menu, Settings, Control Panel) and double-clicking Network. There you should see TCP/IP as a protocol, as you can see in Figure A-6. (You may only need it on either your LAN or your dialup network, and not necessarily on both, as shown in Figure A-6.) If you don't have TCP/IP as one of your protocols, click Add in the Network control panel, double-click Protocol, click Microsoft in the left list, and then scroll the list and click TCP/IP on the right. Click OK twice and answer Yes to restarting your computer.

■ If you are using the Internet over phone lines, you need to have dialup networking installed and the TCP/IP protocol assigned to it. The Internet Connection Wizard should have installed this for you.

Connecting to the Internet

If you are not connected to the Internet and wish to be, this section will help you. It is not necessary to be connected to the Internet to use FrontPage, but if you wish to put your webs up on an Internet server and your company does not have an Internet server to which you have a LAN connection, then you need to be connected to the Internet. Use these steps to do so:

1. If you are using Windows 98 or a later version of Windows 95, you should see the Internet Connection Wizard on your desktop (its label says "Connect to the Internet"). If so, click it. Otherwise, open the Windows Explorer and the C:\Program Files\Internet Explorer\Connection Wizard folder, and double-click the Inetwiz.exe file.

2. The Internet Connection Wizard will open as shown in Figure A-7. If you wish, click Tutorial to learn more about the Internet. Then select how you want to connect to it. If you want suggestions for a new account, use the first option. If you have an account and want to set it up on your current computer, use the

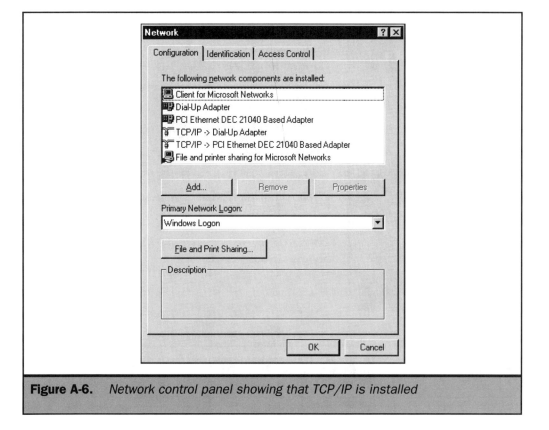

Figure A-6. *Network control panel showing that TCP/IP is installed*

second option. If you are connected to the Internet through a LAN, use the third option. After making a selection, click Next.

Note *The figures here show the dialog boxes in Windows 98. Those in Windows 95 are slightly different.*

3. You may be told that file and printer sharing is turned on for your Internet connection, and to protect you from someone on the Internet accessing your files, it will be turned off. Click OK.

4. If your modem is not set up, you are told that will be done next. Follow the instructions to do that, and finally click OK to restart your computer.

5. Depending on your choice in step 2, you will be asked a series of questions to set up your Internet access and Internet mail accounts. When you are done, you will get a congratulatory message, where you click Finish.

APPENDIXES

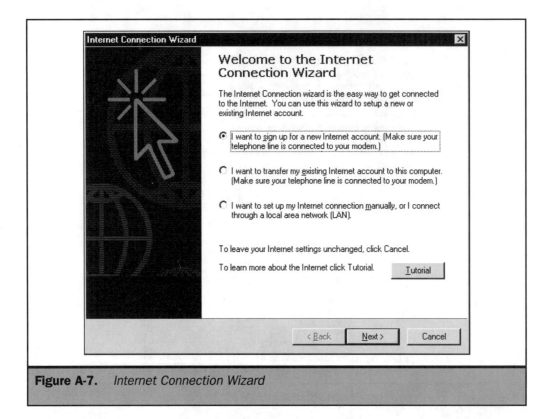

Figure A-7.   *Internet Connection Wizard*

6. To test your Internet connection, double-click the Internet Explorer icon on your desktop. When prompted, click Connect. You should hear your modem dial, and after a minute the Internet Explorer will open and display the Microsoft Home page, as shown in Figure A-8.

7. Close the Internet Explorer and click Disconnect Now to shut down your Internet connection.

If you are having trouble with your Internet connection, the problem is usually related to one of two areas: your modem; or the ID, password, or setting associated with your Internet account. To check your account, call your network administrator or Internet service provider (ISP) and go over what you are using. If that is not the problem, look into the modem by opening the Control Panel and double-clicking Modems. In the Modems control panel, click the Diagnostics tab and then click More Info. You should get a list of OKs and other responses, as shown next. If not, click Help in the Modems control panel and utilize the Modem Troubleshooter.

Installing Microsoft Image Composer or PhotoDraw

Microsoft Image Composer or Microsoft PhotoDraw is included in the stand-alone FrontPage package or the Office 2000 Premium Edition package, respectively. These are optional image creation and editing programs, which are handy for creating web graphics. They are explained and demonstrated in Chapter 5 of this book. Install the graphics program that you have. (The programs may be on different CDs from FrontPage.)

1. Look at the documentation that comes with your product and identify which CD contains your product. Insert that CD in your drive. In the case of PhotoDraw, its installer should automatically open, allowing you to simply click to install it. In the case of Image Composer, you may have to use the Windows Explorer to locate and double-click its Setup program.

2. In either case, a welcome message appears. Click Continue. Enter and confirm your name and organization, clicking OK twice.

3. Accept the default path for installing program and click OK. Select the Typical installation and the default folder. Click I Agree for the license agreement.

4. The copying will begin and a thermometer bar will appear to inform you of the progress. You will get a message when it has finished. Click OK.

APPENDIXES

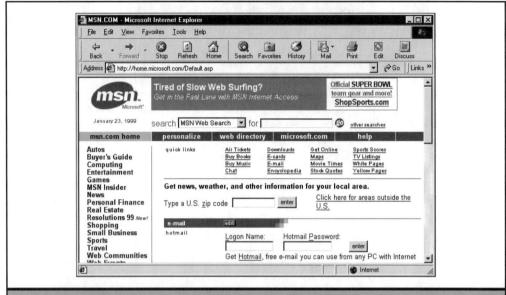

Figure A-8. *The Internet Explorer connected to the Internet*

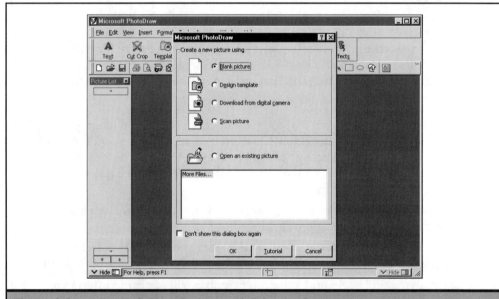

Figure A-9. *Microsoft PhotoDraw opening for the first time*

5. To make sure the program is available, open the Windows 95/98/NT/2000 Start menu, and choose Programs and your graphics program. The program should appear, shown in Figure A-9.

6. Close your graphics program.

All of your FrontPage products should now be installed and ready for you to use. Turn to Chapter 1 to begin doing so.

The Complete Reference

FrontPage 2000

Appendix B

Constructing Web Templates

In Chapter 4 you saw how to create a page template and even created a web template, although it was stored with the page templates. Here you will see how to create and properly store a full web template. A web template is just a web (simply a group of pages) stored in a special folder on your hard disk. The next exercise will show you how to create and save a web to use as a template.

1. From FrontPage, create a new web using the Empty Web template. Name the web, and the folder in which it will be stored, **Budget**.

2. In Navigation view, click New Page on the toolbar to create a page automatically named Home Page.

3. Right-click the Home Page in Navigation view, and select Rename from the context menu. Type the new name, **Annual**, and press ENTER.

4. Click New Page again to add another page to your site. Click the New Page button three more times to create a total of five pages (the Home Page plus four more).

5. Click slowly twice (don't double-click) on each of the four pages individually in the Navigation pane and rename them **Q1**, **Q2**, **Q3**, and **Q4**.

> **Tip** Click TAB to accept the first new page name change and move to the next new page.

6. Click slowly twice on the page names in the left Folder List pane one at a time. (If you do not see the files, press F5 to refresh; if your Folder List is not displayed, choose Folder List from the View menu.) Then rename them so that the page with the title "Q1" has a filename of **qtr1.htm**, "Q2" has a filename of **qtr2.htm**, and so on. The file with the title "Annual" should be named **Default.htm**. When you have renamed and retitled your pages, your Folder List and Navigation view should look like Figure B-1.

7. After you have created a web that will be used as a template, edit the content and structure of each page in the template, just the way you would to build a normal web.

> **Note** Your files and folders might not exactly match the examples, depending on the content you create.

8. When you are happy with the web, save the Annual page (Default.htm) as a template (File | Save As, change the Save As Type to FrontPage Template, click Save). In the Save As Template dialog box, change the Title to **Annual Budget**, change the Name to **Budget**, type **Create a quarterly budgeting model.** as the Description, click Save Template In Current Web, and click OK.

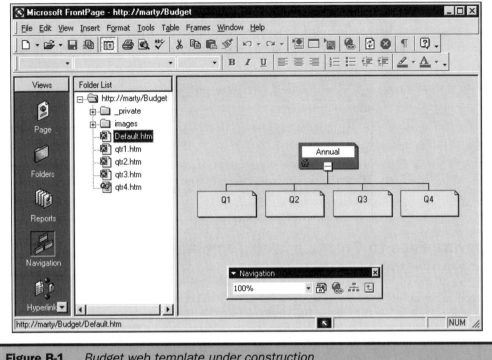

Figure B-1.   *Budget web template under construction*

If you look at the top of the FrontPage Page view pane, you will see that your template was saved in the C:\Windows\Application Data\Microsoft\FrontPage\Pages \Budget.tem folder. At this point you have a normal web (not a template) of your full (five pages) Budget web that you want to be a template, and a single *page* template with the Annual page. To complete your web template, you need to import the special template pages into the original web, copy the web to the template Webs folder, and clean up several miscellaneous files.

Importing the Template Files

The easiest way to get the template files back into the original web is to import them. Do that now.

1. From the File menu, choose Close to close the newly created template page.

2. Open the File menu again and choose Import (expand the menu if necessary). The Import dialog box will open. Click Add File. The Add File To Import List dialog box will open.

3. Click the down arrow opposite Look In, select the C:\Windows\Application
Data\Microsoft\FrontPage\Pages\Budget.tem folder, click Budget.dib, press
CTRL, click Budget.inf, click Open, and then click OK. The two template files
will be imported, and your Folders view will look like this:

Name	Title	Size	Type	Modifi
_private			folder	
images			folder	
budget.dib	budget.dib	15KB	dib	1/23/
budget.inf	budget.inf	1KB	inf	1/23/
Default.htm	Annual	1KB	htm	1/23/
qtr1.htm	Q1	1KB	htm	1/23/
qtr2.htm	Q2	1KB	htm	1/23/
qtr3.htm	Q3	1KB	htm	1/23/
qtr4.htm	Q4	1KB	htm	1/23/

Contents of 'http://marty/Budget'

Copying Files to Create a Web Template

Once you have created a web structure, you can transform that into a web template by
copying all the files from the original folder to the web template folder, and modifying
the special template files necessary for FrontPage to recognize the web as a template.
You will copy and modify these files in Windows Explorer.

1. Locate the folder that holds all the files for the Budget web you just created.
If you used the default installation for FrontPage 2000, that folder will be
C:\Inetpub\Wwwroot\Budget. When you locate and open the folder, you'll see
the five HTML files you created, as well as other folders that contain additional
files used in FrontPage webs, as you see in Figure B-2. The FrontPage folders (not
all of which are in the current web or all webs) are described in Table B-1.

Folder	Contents
_borders	Includes up to four .HTM files that are embedded in each page with the content of top, bottom, right, or left Shared Borders
_private	Pages that you don't want available to a browser or to searches; for example, Included pages
_sharedtemplates	Templates used in the web

Table B-1. *FrontPage Web Folder Structure*

Folder	Contents
_vti_bin	FrontPage-created common gateway interface (CGI) programs for controlling browse-time behavior, administrator, and author operations on the server
_vti_cnf	A configuration page for every page in the web, containing the name of the page, the created-by and modified-by names, and the creation and modification dates, among other variables
_vti_pvt	Several subfolders with both the current and historical To Do List files, meta-information for the web, and the dependency database
_vti_script	Visual Basic and Java scripts used in the web
_vti_txt	Text indexes for use by the Search boxes
Images	All images associated with a web

Table B-1.   *FrontPage Web Folder Structure* (continued)

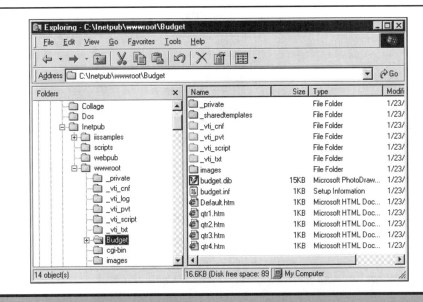

Figure B-2.   *The Budget web in Windows Explorer showing its files and folder structure*

2. Right-click the Budget web folder in the left pane of Windows Explorer, and select Copy from the context menu.

3. Click the folder where FrontPage web templates are stored to open it. If you used the default install for FrontPage 2000, this folder is C:\Windows\Application Data\Microsoft\FrontPage\Webs.

4. With the Webs folder open in the right pane of Windows Explorer, right-click the right pane and select Paste from the context menu. You have now copied most of the files required for a template.

Working with the INF and MAP Files

In addition to the files you already copied, you will need to add one file and modify another in order for FrontPage 2000 to detect and use your template web. You need to add the MAP file, which stores the navigational links that the web may contain, and modify the MAP file, which stores the information used to list your template in the New dialog box.

1. Open the folder for a web template that comes with FrontPage 2000, the Personal template. The path to the Personal folder is C:\Program Files\Microsoft Office\Templates\1033\Webs\Personal.tem

2. With the Personal.tem folder open, click Personal.map, as shown next. Press CTRL+C to copy the file.

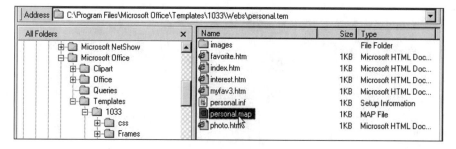

3. Open the new C:\Windows\Application Data\Microsoft\FrontPage\ Webs\Budget.tem folder you just created, right-click the right pane, and choose Paste to paste the MAP file into this folder.

4. Right-click the Personal.map file, and rename it **Budget.map**.

> **Note** *While you will have to edit your own template files by hand as described in the next several steps, to just see how it works, you can use the Budget.inf and Budget.map files in the \Book\AppenB folder on the CD that came with this book.*

5. Double-click the Budget.inf file, and edit the contents using Notepad. The new contents of the file should look like this:

The webDTM line is your current date/time stamp and doesn't have to match what is shown here.

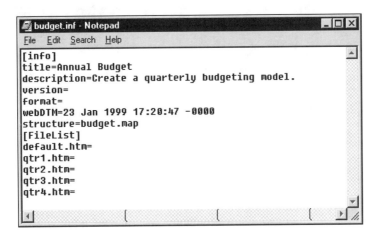

```
[info]
title=Annual Budget
description=Create a quarterly budgeting model.
version=
format=
webDTM=23 Jan 1999 17:20:47 -0000
structure=budget.map
[FileList]
default.htm=
qtr1.htm=
qtr2.htm=
qtr3.htm=
qtr4.htm=
```

6. Save and close the Budget.inf file.

7. Double-click the file Budget.map. If Windows does not recognize this file type, select Notepad as the application to open when MAP files are opened.

8. Edit the file Budget.map so it reads like this (type the first line and then copy and change it for the other three lines):

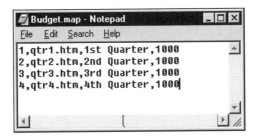

```
1,qtr1.htm,1st Quarter,1000
2,qtr2.htm,2nd Quarter,1000
3,qtr3.htm,3rd Quarter,1000
4,qtr4.htm,4th Quarter,1000
```

The MAP file changes the title of the page files from Q1, Q2, and so on to 1st Quarter, 2nd Quarter, and so on.

9. Save and close the Budget.map file. Now that you have finished the INF and MAP files in your folder, your template will be recognized by FrontPage.

10. In FrontPage, open the File menu and choose New | Web to open the New dialog box. Select Annual Budget and your description will appear, as shown here:

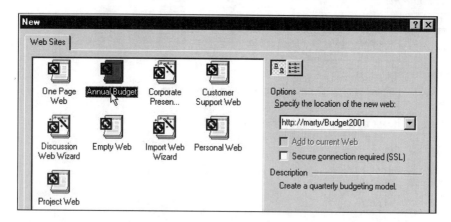

11. Enter a folder/web name of **Budget2001**, and then click OK to create a new web based on the template. The web opens with an already-designed structure and navigation links, all ready for you to customize the individual pages, as shown in Figure B-3 (your view might be different depending on the pages in your template).

12. Delete the new web you just created and close FrontPage.

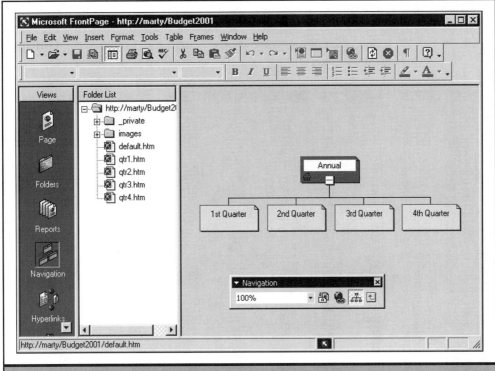

Figure B-3.   *A budget web created from the template*

If your new web does not work as you would expect, look at the files in the template. Make sure that all your files are placed where they should be and that the INF and MAP files are as shown earlier. Since you have to edit the content of those files by hand (here of course you can use the files on the CD), it's easy to make a typing mistake.

Appendix C

Using
the Companion CD

T he CD included with this book contains two contributions to the book. The first, in the Book folder, are files used within the book, organized by chapter. The second, in the Programs folder, are many fine examples of freeware, shareware, and product demos that can enhance your FrontPage and web publishing experience.

Book Material

The materials from the book include files that you are told to use in the instructions, as well as files and web pages that you can look at if you choose. The best way to handle the web pages is to import them into FrontPage into an open web or create a new web using the Import Web Wizard. Click File | New | Web, select the Import Web Wizard, provide a name for the web, and click OK. This places them in the root web on your system and properly creates all of the ancillary files. In a few places in the web pages there are image files that are included with FrontPage 2000 or one of the graphics packages and are therefore not included here. In most cases you can use any image you have available.

Note *If you don't import the webs in the \Book\ folder and try to use them directly from the CD you may get a server error telling you that it cannot open, for example, file \Book\ExcitingTravel_vti_pvt\Service.lck for writing. Importing will fix this, but you can also fix it by copying the files to your hard disk, opening the properties dialog box for \Book\ExcitingTravel_vti_pvt\Service.lck, and removing the Read-only attribute that is automatically added to the file when it is written to the CD.*

Software Programs

The software programs on this CD have been gathered for your benefit and represent three types of software:

- **Freeware** costs nothing and can be used without further consideration. However, it has limited or no documentation and no upgrade policy. If it is copyrighted, it may not be distributed without permission from the creator.

- **Shareware** costs something. It is provided free of charge to evaluate whether you want to continue using it in your own environment. If you decide you do, you must pay a modest fee to the creator. You may then receive upgrades, printed manuals, technical support, and other benefits. If you do not pay for the product, you are expected to remove the software from your computer.

- **Demos** are provided by the vendor to let you see for yourself how the product works. There is no cost for the demo, but they are usually limited in some way, such as less features, or time limits after which the product won't work.

> **Note** *Please note that the software and descriptions of the software are offered as is. Osborne/McGraw-Hill and the authors jointly and severally make no warranty, either expressly or implied, as to the usability of the software or its fitness for a particular purpose; we do not recommend any of these packages, do not guarantee that they work, and are not responsible for what they do on your computer. We assume no liability for damages, direct or consequential, that may result from using the software or reliance on the documentation.*

That said, we believe you will find many wonderful jewels among these tools. In this appendix, we have included the vendor or creator's description of each program or script. The programs and scripts are each contained in a separate folder in the Programs folder. In addition to the programs and scripts, helpful documentation may be found in the individual software folders, as a help feature, or in some cases online at a web site. If you have questions about any product, you must write or e-mail the source or vendor of the software whose name is included here and in the Readme or .TXT files in the root directory on the CD. Do not contact the authors or publisher of this book, as we will not be able to help.

EasyHelp/Web

Eon Solutions Ltd.

Jeff Hall
Eon House,
8 Bottrells Lane
Chalfont St. Giles, Buckinghamshire
United Kingdom HP8 4EX
Voice: 44 1494 581244
Fax: 44 1494 581244
E-mail: sales@easyhtmlhelp.com or support@easyhelp.com
Web: http://www.eon-solutions.com

EasyHelp/Web v3 is an easy-to-use hypertext authoring tool for use with Microsoft Word 6, 7, or 97. It supports most language versions of Word and was specially designed for nontechnical users. The same document(s) can be used for printing *and* for creating Windows Help files or World Wide Web pages. EasyHelp/Web is fully functional shareware. This version replaces all earlier versions.

EasyHelp/Web is a Word template that can either be attached to an existing document, or selected when you issue the command File | New. You select EasyHelp from the list of templates in your WinWord template directory. It gives you an additional set of editing tools that allows you to define a hypertext structure of topics and links within your Word document and then to compile it into independent hypertext files.

APPENDIXES

From the same source document, you can create either Windows Help files or HTML Web pages, suitable for uploading onto the World Wide Web.

Create a new document using the EasyHelp/Web template. Then follow these steps:

1. Create Topics

2. Create Links

3. Process as Help or Web

4. Build to see your results

A set of example documents is installed with the EasyHelp/Web software that take you through the main concepts of hypertext authoring. Installation and registration instructions are included in the .TXT file.

This version is a fully functional evaluation version that is disabled after 30 days. After that time you must order a registered version from the source or remove the program from your computer. Documentation is available online, plus there are ten tutorial example documents.

EasyHTML/Help (TM) Version 1.0a

Eon Solutions Ltd.

Jeff Hall
Eon House,
8 Bottrells Lane
Chalfont St. Giles, Buckinghamshire
United Kingdom HP8 4EX
Voice: 44 1494 581244
Fax: 44 1494 581244
E-mail: sales@easyhtmlhelp.com or support@easyhtmlhelp.com
Web: http://www.eon-solutions.com

EasyHTML/Help (WYSIWYG HTMLHelp Editor for Word 6/7/97 Copyright © 1997-1998 Eon Solutions Ltd) is a very easy-to-use HTML editor for use with Microsoft Word 6, 7, or 97. It supports most language versions of Word and was specially designed for nontechnical users. With it, you can create a complete Web site from a single document. The same document(s) can be also be used for printing. EasyHTML/Help is fully functional shareware. This version replaces all earlier versions.

EasyHTML/Help is a Word template which can either be attached to an existing document, or can be selected when you issue the command File | New. Select EasyHH from the list of templates in your WinWord template directory. You will then have an additional set of toolbars that allows you to define a hypertext structure of topics (Web pages) and links (URLs) within your Word document and then to process it to create the separate Web pages (.HTM files). It is suitable for uploading onto the World Wide Web

You can create a new document using the EasyHTML/Help template with these four easy steps:

1. Click Topic to mark separate Web pages.

2. Click Link to mark URL links.

3. Click Process to create a set of HTML files.

4. Click Results to view your compiler HTML pages.

A set of example documents is installed with the EasyHTML/Help software that take you through the main concepts of Web site authoring. Installation and registration instructions are contained on the .TXT file.

 This version is a fully functional evaluation version that is disabled after 30 days. After that time you must order a registered version from the source or remove the program from your computer. Documentation is available online plus there are ten tutorial example documents.

FileFerret

FerretSoft LLC

1209 Hill Road North, Suite 109
Pickerington, OH 43147
Voice: (614) 755-3891
Fax: (614) 575-8355
E-mail: kirk@ferretsoft.com
Web: http://www.ferretsoft.com

FileFerret is an excellent way to find files on the Internet. It's designed to query multiple search engines and Archie sites quickly and easily and can even be configured to search only particular geographic areas. It rapidly searches for the file and returns information on where it can be found. You can search for files based on name, type, or keywords and save the results of your search for later use. Best of all, once you've found the file you're looking for, you can use FileFerret to download it, without using your FTP program. FileFerret is fast, easy to use, and free!

System requirements: Windows 95, 98, or NT

APPENDIXES

GoldWave v4.02

Chris Craig

P.O. Box 51
St. John's, NF
Canada A1C 5H5
E-mail: chris3@cs.mun.ca
Web: http://www.goldwave.com/

GoldWave is a comprehensive digital audio editor for Windows. It is ideal for people who need to work with audio for CD editing, Java applications, Web pages, games, radio and TV, or just for fun. You can use it to make everything from elaborate answering machine messages to professional CD audio content.

It features real-time amplitude, spectrum and spectrogram oscilloscopes, large file editing, numerous effects, support for a wide variety of sound formats, and a CD audio extraction tool.

HTMLib 4.0

Stephen Le Hunte

8A Chichele Mansions
Chichele Road,
London,
United Kingdom NW2 3DG
Voice: 44 181 450 8970
E-mail: htmlib@htmlib.demon.co.uk
Web: http://hot.virtual-pc.com/htmlib/

The **HTMLib 4.0** is a complete HTML reference library comparing the three most popular web browsers for HTML functionality. The version on this CD contains no limitations. It covers Internet Explorer 4.01, Netscape 4.05, and Mosaic 3.0, with full cross-comparisons, examples, and screenshots. For up-to-date information on the status of the HTMLib, visit **http://hot.virtual-pc.com/htmlib/**.

HVS ColorGIF 2.0 Demo

Digital Frontiers

Cathy Cioffi
1019 Asbury Ave.
Evanston, IL 60202
Voice: (847) 328-0880
Fax: (847) 869-2053
E-mail: info@digfrontiers.com
Web: http://www.digfrontiers.com

HVS ColorGIF Demo allows you to see your own images filtered by the HVS Color GIF plug-in in a live preview window. It also shows you how big the resulting file would be and permits you to export the full product. It is full featured for 15 days, after which you may purchase online at **http://www.digfrontiers.com**.

Some of HVS ColorGIF 2.0's features are as follows:

- Filter plug-in works with most major paint programs.
- Command-F allows quick, no-intervention exports and batching.
- File Export plug-in allows seamless action-based batch processing with Photoshop 4 and 5.
- Small, highest-quality GIFs produced.
- Any combination of layers in Photoshop processed.
- Filtering from a selection allows independent reduction and GIF export of a selected portion of an image.
- Image quality and GIF size preview gives immediate feedback on reduction settings.
- HVS Dithering controls intensity and masks to a selection.
- Reduces fixed palettes with Netscape, Mac, and Windows palettes built in. Fixed palettes can be modified and saved as presets.
- Includes Java-based stand-alone HVS Animator application.
- Saves and reloads custom-designed color tables.

APPENDIXES

- Multipalette feature factors multiple images into HVS algorithm to generate high-quality global palettes for animation, multimedia use.

- Allows an unprecedented level of control over image quality using pro-quality features like gamma and thresholding.

- Color Table Optimizer uses HVS algorithms to substantially reduce color table and image size in existing GIFs.

- Sophisticated transparency controls multiple colors, extended selection, and automatic "magic wand"-style similar-color selection.

- User presets and built-ins allow various reduction/export settings.

- Includes size and download time estimate with each change of settings.

- Includes an illustrated hyperlinked manual in HTML format.

HVS JPEG 2.0 Demo

Digital Frontiers

Cathy Cioffi
1019 Asbury Ave.
Evanston, IL 60202
Voice: (847) 328-0880
Fax: (847) 869-2053
E-mail: info@digfrontiers.com
Web: http://www.digfrontiers.com

HVS JPEG 2.0 Demo allows you to see your own images in the live preview window using the HVS JPeg plug-in. It also shows you how big the resulting file is and permits export like the full product. It is full featured for 15 days, after which you may purchase on line at **http://www.digfrontiers.com**.

Some of HVS JPEG 2.0's features include:

- Filter plug-in, which works with most major paint programs

- Command-F, which allows quick, no-intervention exports and batching

- Batch processing with Photoshop 4 and 5

- Redesigned user interface to better support how artists work

- Small, high-quality JPEGs produced

- Automatic Q-Table Optimizer, which generates best Q-table for image

- User presets and built-ins for various quality settings

- Size and download time estimate with each change of settings

- Adobe Acrobat (PDF) format available

InfoFerret

FerretSoft LLC

1209 Hill Road North, Suite 109
Pickerington, OH 43147
Voice: (614) 755-3891
Fax: (614) 575-8355
E-mail: kirk@ferretsoft.com
Web: http://www.ferretsoft.com

InfoFerret is a great way to sniff out information on the Internet. It's designed to query specialized search engines for news-related items. Available categories include Current Affairs, Entertainment, Finance, Science and Technology, Sports, and more. Each category includes a list of appropriate online publications to search. You can easily launch any of the results in your default browser and save your search results to disk for later use. InfoFerret is fast, easy to use, and best of all—free!

System requirements: Windows 95, 98, or NT

Jamba

Interleaf, Inc.

62 Fourth Ave.
Waltham, MA 02451
Voice: (800) 955-5323
Fax: (781) 290-4943
E-mail: webmaster@interleaf.com
Web: http://www.jamba.com

Jamba 2.1.9 is designed for web content creators who want to take advantage of Java's ability to add functionality and interactivity to static HTML pages. Jamba offers a nonprogramming environment using a point-and-click interface that creates feature-rich Java applets that run across all major web browsers. Unlike others, which use a plug-in strategy, Jamba applets do not require the browser to first download and install plug-ins before the applet can be viewed.

Jamba is Java for the rest of us—an award-winning authoring tool that allows you to create sizzling Java applets and applications in a drag-and-drop WYSIWYG (what you see is what you get) environment, with absolutely *no programming or scripting.*

Features of Jamba 2.1.9 are as follows:

- Visual authoring environment
- No programming or plug-ins

APPENDIXES

- Based on the Java industry standard
- Complementary to HTML, not competitive
- Makes your web site come alive
- Easily creates dazzling Java animation for the Web by using graphics, text, sound, and special effects like Zoom and Fade
- Creates "path-based" animation using circles, polygons, ellipses, or freehand drawing
- Creates interactivity with events or triggers—that is, makes something happen when the user clicks the cursor on a graphic, or when the cursor passes over a certain area of the screen
- Triggers actions like playing sound, going to another web page, or interacting with another part of the animation
- Completely integrated with the Jamba environment

Jamba is complementary to other web authoring tools, such as graphic editors, HTML authoring tools, and other Java authoring tools. Creative designers will find Jamba's ease-of-use particularly attractive. It lets them put their own content on the Web, rather than passing it off to a programmer. HTML authors using tools such as Microsoft FrontPage, NetObjects Fusion, SoftQuad HoTMetaL Pro, or a text editor (like Notepad) will find Jamba to be very complementary. To run a Java applet from a web page, you can simply insert the <APPLET> tags that Jamba saves into your HTML documents. Other Java authoring tools, such as Symantec's Visual Café and Microsoft's J++, are Java programming tools designed for developers. In this environment, Jamba is a great solution for creating quick prototype applications.

MULTIPLATFORM   The Java programming language was created specifically for the Internet. By design, applets built in Java will run on all platforms that have Java support. Today, that list includes the major browsers (Netscape and Internet Explorer) on most platforms (Windows 95, Windows NT, Macintosh, UNIX, and OS/2). Therefore, you can create one applet in Jamba, and it automatically plays on multiple platforms. Plug-ins are proprietary and platform specific.

NO PLUG-INS   To make cool animations like Macromedia's Shockwave work on the Internet, users must download and install a 1.5MB plug-in from the Web. Java applets do not require a plug-in: the "run-time playback" is downloaded with each web page and is very small (Jamba's run time ranges from 15K to 134K). Once the applets are put onto a web server, they can be viewed without any special downloads or installations.

JAVA EXTENSION   Jamba's interface is designed so that even users with no programming background can create Java applets almost immediately. Using a series of drag-and-drop actions, users simply place objects on the canvas by use of a mouse.

Once in place (Jamba provides extensive functionality for aligning and layering objects), a pop-up dialog box allows authors to set the Properties, or characteristics, of the object. For example, a filename can be assigned to a Graphic object and an interval can be established for a Timer object.

Each object also has a To Do List that controls the interactivity of the Jamba applet. For example, when you move the cursor over a particular object, an audible click can be played. Since each object "knows" about all of the other objects on the canvas, objects can interact with each other, which provides a foundation for building engaging web pages.

For more advanced programmers who wish to use Jamba as a way to quickly prototype and develop Java applets, the Java Extension object allows the incorporation of native Java and JavaScript methods in Jamba applications.

WIZARDS   The new Jamba wizards are designed to ease the process of creating Jamba applets, as well as new components inside of an existing applet. The wizards are organized into five categories and allow users to create common applet components, such as banner ads, ticker-tape text, and data collection forms.

VARIABLES AND CONDITIONALS   Jamba now supports unlimited user-defined variables. It can also use variables to do mathematical computations.

CONDITIONAL PROCESSING   Jamba's To Do List supports conditional processing with If/Then clauses. For example, a Jamba applet created for a retail store can display different content depending on whether the user is male or female.

The calculator example in the Jamba Gallery is the most elementary example of variable and conditional usage.

Note   *This version of Jamba can be evaluated for 30 days. After that, you must order a registered version from Interleaf, Inc., or remove the application from your computer. A serial number, which is required to install Jamba, is found in the Important Note.doc file in the \Programs\Jamba\ folder on the CD.*

JDesigner Pro 3.0

BulletProof Corporation

15732 Los Gatos Blvd. #525
Los Gatos, CA 95032
Voice: (408) 374-2323 Fax: (408) 395-6126
E-mail: support@bulletproof.com
Web: http://www.bulletproof.com

APPENDIXES

JDesignerPro 3.0 is a 100 percent Java, visual development and deployment solution for building data-driven intranet applications. It easily meets design standards, and is used for cross-platform, interactive, professional, scalable applications. JDesignerPro 3.0 includes a scalable application server deployment and supplies JDBC data access. New in JDesignerPro 3.0 is the ability to visually develop the server-side Java with a graphical view of the code, templates, and wizards. It is available for Windows, UNIX, and NetWare 5.

J-Perk (formerly known as Java Perk)

McWeb Software

232 Kent Street
Brookline, MA 02446
Fax: (617) 277-0676
Voice: (617) 437-9393
E-mail: info@mcwebsoftware.com
Web: http://www.mcwebsoftware.com

J-Perk adds Java animations, dynamic buttons, and special effects to your web pages quickly and easily. It includes 18 pre-made applets that are easily customizable and make your web pages come alive. You simply input properties for the applets, and J-Perk creates the effect you want with just the click of a button. Put the J-Perk–generated applet code in your web page and it's ready to go! J-Perk special effects include Animations, slideshows, rotating banners/billboards, Dynamic Buttons, Status Bar Text Ticker, Typewriter Text, Swirly Text, Image Fade effect, Image Cube effect, Fading Message and Screen Color Fade in/Fade out. Now includes Microsoft FrontPage support and a new Preview Wizard!

> **Note**   *This version of Java Perk can be evaluated for 30 days. After that time, you must order a registered copy from McWeb software or remove Java Perk from your computer. Documentation for the evaluation copy is limited to online help.*

Multiquence v1.02

Chris Craig

P.O. Box 51
St. John's, NF
Canada A1C5H5
E-mail: chris3@cs.mun.ca
Web: http://www.goldwave.com/multiquence

Multiquence is a multitrack digital audio processor for Windows 95/NT. It features an incredibly fast and easy-to-use interface. All editing is performed instantly, which means you can drag and drop, trim, copy, and split files without any processing time. Several real-time effects, such as volume envelopes, flange, speed, and equalizers, can be applied to each file. Multiquence supports WAV, VOC, AIF, and AU digital audio files and can sequence CD audio, MIDI, and video files.

 Multiquence requires a Pentium 100MHz processor. This software is unregistered shareware. Updates are available from the web site.

Selena Sol's Scripts

Selena Sol's Script Archive, with Gunther Birznieks' Scripts

Extropia
3915 Clayton Ave.
Los Angeles, CA 90027
E-mail: selena@eff.org
Web: http://www.extropia.com

This collection of scripts from **Selena Sol's Script Archive** web site features various public-domain CGI scripts. This web site is was developed and is maintained by Selena Sol and Gunther Birznieks as a public service project. The scripts come with no promises or guarantees. The idea is to share ideas, not to distribute code. The creators have given up their "real jobs" to maintain this site, and so offer additional help and products for a price. But many people have also used and benefited by their free scripts. Their site also offers other scripts and links to other web sites with additional scripts. (The following 13 scripts were last modified on April 13, 1998.)

WEB STORE   Web Store is the culmination of our experience with Online Shopping Scripts. It merges both the Electronic Outlet HTML and Database versions and adds all new routines for error handling, order processing, encrypted mailing, frames, JavaScript and VBScript, and other goodies.

AUTHENTICATION SCRIPT   A natural extension of most applications is the capability to restrict or track access through the application. To do this, you need a system designed to authenticate users when they first start using the application. auth-lib.pl is a Perl authentication library that provides the three core capabilities that any security library needs. First, it allows the administrator of a Web application to maintain a registration list or password file of users who are authorized to access the application (or who have recently registered, depending on the rules that the administrator sets up). Second, it allows users to log in to the application either through the Web server's built-in HTTP

APPENDIXES

authentication or through a CGI form. Finally, once users are logged in, auth-lib.pl tracks them by using unique session files that are created when users complete a successful login. To support all these functions, the authentication library contains a great many configuration options, accommodating all sorts of security scenarios.

BULLETIN BOARD SCRIPT   There are many uses for a bulletin board system on the Web. A BBS can be used to make information continually available that would normally be shared only during infrequent meetings. Within a BBS, users can discuss topics, reading the responses to their ideas at their leisure. On the Internet, vendors can use a BBS to discuss their products or offer technical support. Additionally, users on the Internet can set up a BBS spontaneously to discuss things that interest them or just for fun. The main feature of WebBBS is that it allows a user to post messages as well as replies to existing messages. WebBBS keeps track of which messages are posts and which are replies and displays them in a hierarchical treelike fashion. Posts that start new topics are at the top of each tree, and the replies are shown indented beneath the original posts. WebBBS is also fully integrated with the user authentication library discussed above. Additionally, it allows a user to restrict the number of messages through a variety of query mechanisms. The user can conduct a keyword search and display only those messages that satisfy the search, as well as select a range of dates within which the viewed messages were posted. For example, a user could choose to see only messages posted between ?6/1/96? and ?6/10/96.? In addition, the user can select a range of posts based on age in days, and choose to see, for example, only those messages posted between two days ago and four days ago.

DATABASE MANAGER AND DATABASE SEARCH ENGINE   WebDb provides a Web interface with which to manipulate databases. Specifically, it provides the ability to add to, modify, and delete from multiple databases based on keyword recognition. No great understanding of the operating system or the database formats is necessary, because the Web provides the interface. The database administrator simply points and clicks using a Web browser. To protect the possibly sensitive information in the database, however, this application also implements the password authentication algorithms. Another useful database function you can provide through the Web is a search engine that allows users to search a shared database by keyword but doesn't give them the power of a larger database manager script. Database administrators can provide a database management interface for themselves and a corresponding database search interface for other people in the company. Users are spared the confusion of having too many options, and the sensitive database management functions are hidden behind yet another level of security.

KEYWORD SITE SEARCH   When a web site starts to grow beyond a couple of pages, it can be time-consuming for visitors to find what they are looking for. As more web pages are connected to one another via hypertext links, the resulting spaghetti-like relationship only exacerbates the complexity. Having SiteSearch installed on your web site solves these problems. First, it provides a quick way for people to find the pages they are looking for. Additionally, because the script is searching the actual pages on the web site, the results of the search are always up-to-date.

MAILING LIST MANAGER   This application provides a user interface for browsers to add their names to your mailing list as well as a web-based administrator's interface so that you can send mass mailings to those who have signed your list.

RANDOM BANNER GENERATOR   One of the basic advertising tools developed for the Web is the random banner advertisement. WebBanner is used to display a random advertisement within an HTML document to provide a link to the advertiser. This application allows site administrators to sell advertising space on their web pages and track the usage for their advertising partners.

WEB CALENDAR   Many offices have a calendar tacked to the wall in a central location. Employees add items such as scheduled vacations, reservations of conference rooms, or notices about meetings, conferences, or seminars. By using a shared calendar, employees can more efficiently coordinate their work with that of others in the organization. WebCal provides a Web interface to a similar shared calendar. Every user can read what other people have added and, if the script is configured to do it, can modify each other's entries. WebCal has two primary views: the month view and the day view. Varying levels of security are configurable. For example, WebCal can be made to be viewable by anyone or by authenticated users only. Items within the calendar database can be made to be modifiable or deletable only by the person who posts them or by everyone.

WEB CHAT   WebChat is a useful application that allows a number of people on the World Wide Web to talk to one another simultaneously. The ability to chat on the Web can be a quick way to hold a "virtual meeting."

WEB EXAM-MULTIPLE CHOICES   WebExam allows you to create your own multiple-choice exams on the Web and, if you create an answer key database, it will grade the answers submitted by a user and gather all completed exams in a database.

WEBGUESTBOOK   WebGuestbook allows users to manipulate a guestbook HTML file dynamically by adding their own entries to the document. Thus you can create a virtual guestbook that visitors can sign, leaving their contact information and perhaps comments about your pages. WebGuestbook is configurable so that you can specify what your guestbook file looks like and how the script-generated responses are displayed. Most of the configuration takes little more than a knowledge of HTML, so it is fairly easy to use. If configured to do so, WebGuestbook will e-mail the guestbook administrator the text of new entries as well as add them to the guestbook. The script will also respond to new entrants with a configurable "Thank you" message. Thus, there is no need to continually monitor the page. Finally, the application comes with

APPENDIXES

the capability of "four letter word" filtering for a child-safe guestbook. You can censor words by adding them to a list of "bad words."

WEBMESSAGE—FORTUNE COOKIE WebMessage goes through a datafile of "fortunes," chooses one of them at random, and then displays it on the Web. The application can also be configured to loop so that new fortunes are redisplayed automatically at a predefined interval. In this way, the client need not use the browser's reload option. WebMessage is a fun addition to any site, because it allows the site administrator to develop a database of short statements to be reloaded every time a client accesses the site. If you have funny or interesting fortunes, it may give the client an extra reason to visit your site a second and third time.

WEBRESPONDER—FORM PROCESSOR WebResponder allows a site administrator to process the results of web-based forms in a number of ways. The application can be used to generate dynamic e-mail or to create and build a log file or database to track usage of HTML-based forms. The processing of forms is configured by taking advantage of various hidden form tags included in the HTML form created by the administrator. So, little coding knowledge is needed to use this script. Furthermore, because the workings of the application are defined in the HTML form rather than in the application code, the HTML form author can use this one script to process all of the forms, no matter how different they are (Note: all e-mails interface with the PGP encryption library for secure communication). Examples include a form to process feedback, a form to automatically download a selected file, and a "jump box" form that allows a user to choose a URL to jump to from a list.

More at the Web Site

In addition to the individual applications listed here, which are found on the CD, you can find the following libraries at the site:

A JAVA FRONT END TO CGI/PERL Java applets can create interfaces that go beyond the capability of HTML form tags, JavaScript, and VBScript. However, Java applets are limited in their capability of doing practical things such as connecting to databases, sending e-mail, and so on. The JavaCGIBridge project leverages the strengths of using Perl to connect to databases and perform application logic, while using Java's superior GUI building facilities to provide a more user-friendly front end to CGI/Perl scripts.

WEBANIMATOR SCRIPTS These scripts use NPH technology to create basic animation examples.

MAIL TEST PACKAGE This program is used to make sure that the default mail setup for most of these scripts works on your local machine. It will help you debug mailing problems.

AUTHENTICATION LIBRARIES   These libraries help provide a CGI-based authentication system so that you can password-protect HTML files within your site without using server-based security.

MAIL LIBRARIES   These libraries help you mail with your CGI programs. There are separate libraries for UNIX and non-UNIX operating systems so that you can mail on whatever OS your web server runs on.

HTTP-LIB.PL   This library helps you create client/server CGI apps or simply apps that use sockets to communicate with other servers or CGI scripts on other servers.

SitePad Pro

Modelworks Software

Chet Murphy
4882 Old Brook Circle S.
Colorado Springs, CO 80917-1020
Voice: (719) 596-7585
Fax: (719) 596-6538
E-mail: cmurphy@modelworks.com
Web: http://www.modelworks.com

SitePad Pro is an integrated development environment (IDE) for Java, HTML, and VRML. It targets users who need to edit Java, HTML, VRML, and associated languages at the source-code level. Key features include the ability to write your own tools using JavaScript and a powerful editor supporting syntax coloring and code folding. Other features include an outline view of the content of open files, a project manager, a powerful finder toolbar, custom "first-class" file types, support for both Sun and Microsoft Java tools, and more.

Additional features include the following:

- Scripts inserted for all VRML 2.0 nodes
- Sun's JDK Java tools and Microsoft's Java SDK tools supported
- Syntax coloring for VRML, HTML, and Java files
- Syntax checking for HTML including embedded VBScript and JavaScript
- Browser with class, package, and file views
- Project and package manager with build and rebuild commands
- Symbolic debugging using Microsoft's Java SDK
- Custom templates for creating new VRML, HTML, and Java files
- Custom menus, toolbars, hotkeys, and bookmarks

- Java reformat source command
- Block indent and unindent
- Multilevel undo/redo
- Search and replace
- Multifile search
- Split windows
- Line- and column-number indicator
- Line numbers in the edit view
- Input and output options for supporting windows, UNIX, and Mac files
- Finder toolbar
- Abbreviated path name in window captions
- Support for adding new file types
- Custom scripting using JavaScript or VBScript

Note   *This evaluation version is limited to 15 days of use. Then the demo will be restricted to opening files of 2,500 bytes or less. To continue using the product, you must order a registered copy from Modelworks Software. Documentation is available in HTML pages and README files.*

WebFerret

FerretSoft LLC

1209 Hill Road North, Suite 109
Pickerington, OH 43147
Voice: (614) 755-3891
Fax: (614) 575-8355
E-mail: kirk@ferretsoft.com
Web: http://www.ferretsoft.com

WebFerret provides a handy and efficient way to use Web search engines to find information. It adds an entry to the Find option of your Windows 95/98 Start button that lets you find Web pages in addition to the standard files and folders. Enter your search terms, click on Match All Keywords or Match Any Keywords, and WebFerret will use your Internet connection to check several of the more popular search engines (Lycos, Alta Vista, Excite, Infoseek, Yahoo, Search.com, AOL Netfind, Euroseek, LookSmart). You can also do more advanced searches, limiting the number of matches in total or by engine. Once the results are returned, tooltips give you a little more information about a site. Just double-click to bring up your browser and launch the page. WebFerret is fast, easy to use, and best of all—free!

System requirements: Windows 95, 98, or NT

Key features of the WebFerret are as follows:

- **Free**   The WebFerret is free and may be shared with friends, neighbors, and visitors to your web site or web pages in its original EXE form. You may find it easier to just provide a link to our site. Please use **http://www.ferretsoft.com/netferret/** to ensure that everyone will always download the most current version.

- **Stable and dependable**   The WebFerret is over a year old with more than 601,000 users worldwide. This kind of success speaks for itself.

- **Easy to use**   Find web pages by simply entering a keyword and clicking "Find Now."

- **Unbelievably fast**   Finds results almost immediately. The whole process from launching WebFerret to receiving results takes just a few seconds.

- **Quality results**   Searches can be narrowed by choosing to match any keyword, match all keywords, or by submitting the keywords as an exact phrase.

- **Standard interface**   Uses the standard Windows 95, 98/NT 4.0 interface and design of the Find utilities that come with the operating system.

- **Integrates with browsers**   Double-click a result or use the right mouse button to open the web page using your default browser.

- **Always current**   Designed to keep up with the changing nature of the search engines by automatically updating how they are searched. If the engines change, the WebFerret changes, too, so that searches always work and are accurate.

The WebFerret is the second fastest way to search the Internet, only our WebFerretPRO is faster. See complete details at: **http://www.ferretsoft.com/netferret/webferretpro.htm**

Web Weaver 98

McWeb Software

232 Kent Street
Brookline, MA 02446
Voice: (617) 437-9393
Fax: (617) 277-0676
E-mail: info@mcwebsoftware.com
Web: http://www.mcwebsoftware.com

APPENDIXES

Create great-looking web pages quickly and easily with this feature-rich HTML editor! Here are some of the features:

- Tutorials and wizards step you through web page creation, making you an HTML expert in no time.

- It features colored HTML code for easier editing; wizards for creating advanced HTML such as Imagemaps, Frames, Tables, and Forms; toolbars at your fingertips; context-sensitive help and an HTML glossary; spell checking, web site/hyperlink checking tools, web page traffic analysis tools, and more.

- Preview your web page with the click of a button.

- Web Weaver Gold supports all HTML 2 and 3.2 tags as well as Netscape and Internet Explorer HTML extensions.

- It includes free images, animated images, JavaScripts, and a Form processing script.

- Ideal for beginners as well as advanced users.

> **Note**   *This version of Web Weaver can be evaluated for 30 days. After that, you must order a registered copy from McWeb Software or remove the program from your computer. Documentation is limited to online help for the shareware version.*

WebWorks Publisher

Quadralay Corporation

9101 Burnet Road, Suite 105
Austin, TX 78758
Voice: (512) 719-3399
Fax: (512) 719-3606
E-mail: sales@quadralay.com
Web: http://www.quadralay.com

WebWorks Publisher is the most powerful and cost-effective solution available for retargeting FrameMaker documentation to the rapidly growing and fast changing world of online formats. Using WebWorks Publisher, you can easily transform all of your FrameMaker documents and books into suitable online representations for the Web, online help, and CD-ROM with the click of a button. Finally, a single-source publishing solution that really works!

Here are some of the key features that WebWorks Publisher applies to FrameMaker:

- **Multiple online formats**   Produces documents formatted for HTML, HTML Help, WinHelp, JavaHelp, and Oracle Help for Java—all from a single source document or book. Even emerging online formats, like XML, are supported through WebWorks® Publisher's extensible templates and macro language.

- **Precise image control**   Precisely controls all aspects of conversion of individual graphics. Users can specify all output parameters, including output file format, scaling, DPI, transparency, and rotation.

- **Enterprise integration**   Processes documents in batch mode for easy integration into your enterprise publication process. Ideal for large publication operations that require offline processing and automated delivery.

- **Multiple FrameMaker book support**   Preserves the full integrity of multiple cross-referenced FrameMaker books, all with a one-step conversion process.

- **Customizable character set support**   Character-by-character configurable support for nonstandard fonts. WebWorks Publisher is shipped with a library of GIF-sized characters to provide direct support for FrameMaker's Symbol font.

- **Easily extensible user macros**   Easily modifies or creates macros for maintaining commonly used items such as running headers and footers. WebWorks Publisher includes many easy-to-customize prebuilt user macros that can be used as building blocks to suit a variety of needs.

- **Easy and configurable online navigation**   Quickly creates easy-to-navigate online documents. WebWorks Publisher's built-in navigation macros are automatically applied to the document sequence in projects of any size. In addition, the end-user interface can be configured to take advantage of the latest HTML advances, such as frames or multiple windows.

Note   *To activate WebWorks Publisher for evaluation, please visit* ***http://www.quadralay.com/publisher/try.asp***, *or e-mail sales@quadralay.com to receive a 30-day key.*

WinZip

Nico Mak Computing

P.O. Box 540
Mansfield, CT 06268
E-mail: support@winzip.com
Web: http://www.winzip.com

WinZip brings the convenience of Windows to the use of Zip files and other compression formats.

WinZip features include:

- **Windows 95/98/NT integration**   WinZip includes long filename support and tight integration with the Windows 95/98/NT shell. Drag and drop to or from Explorer, or zip and unzip without leaving Explorer.

- **Internet support** WinZip features built-in support for popular Internet file formats: TAR, gzip, UUEncode, XXencode, BinHex, and MIME. ARJ, LZH, and ARC files are supported via external programs. You can use WinZip to access almost all the files you download from the Internet. In addition, the freely downloadable WinZip Internet Browser Support Add-On lets you download and open archives with one click using Microsoft Internet Explorer or Netscape Navigator.

- **Automatic installation of most software distributed in Zip files** If a Zip file contains a setup or install program, WinZip's Install feature will unzip the files, run the installation program, and clean up temporary files.

- **The WinZip wizard** This optional feature uses the standard and familiar "wizard" interface to simplify the process of unzipping and installing software distributed in Zip files. The WinZip wizard is not targeted at experienced users, but is ideal for the rapidly growing number of PC users getting started with Zip files. When these users gain confidence or want to use more advanced zipping features, the full WinZip Classic interface is just a click away.

- **Favorite Zip folders** WinZip lets you organize Zip files into one convenient list that is sorted by date, making it easier to locate all Zip files regardless of where they came from or where they are stored. Unlike the standard File->Open Archive dialog box, the Favorite Zip Folders dialog box treats the contents of multiple folders as though they were one folder. A Search facility will find any Zip files lost on your hard disk.

- **Create files that unzip themselves** WinZip Self-Extractor Personal Edition is now included with WinZip. Self-extracting files are ideal for sending compressed files to others who may not own or know how to use file compression software.

- **Virus scanner support** WinZip can be configured to work with most virus scanners.

| Note | *This version of WinZip is a shareware evaluation version, not the registered version of the current release of WinZip 7.0. To order the registered version, refer to the web site, http://www.winzip.com.* |

Index